Software Engineering

Chandramouli Subramanian
Senior Manager
Cognizant Technology Solutions
Chennai

Saikat Dutt
Director
Cognizant Technology Solutions
Kolkata

Chandramouli Seetharaman
Director
Catalysts
Chennai

B. G. Geetha
Professor and Head
Department of Computer Science
K. S. Rangasamy College of Technology
Tiruchengode

Pearson

Editor—Acquisitions: S. Shankari
Editor—Production: C. Purushothaman

ISBN 978-93-325-3729-3

First Impression, 2015
Eighth Impression, 2019
Ninth Impression, 2020

Published by Pearson India Education Services Pvt. Ltd, CIN: U72200TN2005PTC057128,

Head Office: 15th Floor, Tower-B, World Trade Tower, Plot No. 1, Block-C, Sector 16, Noida 201301, Uttar Pradesh, India.

Registered Office: The HIVE, 3rd Floor, Metro zone, No 44, Pilliayar Koil Street, Jawaharlal Nehru Road, Anna Nagar, Chennai, Tamil Nadu 600040, Fax: 080-30461003, Phone: 080-30461060
Website: in.pearson.com, Email: companysecretary.india@pearson.com

Compositor: Map Systems, Bengaluru.
Printed in India by Saurabh Printers Pvt. Ltd.

Contents

Foreword *xi*

Preface *xiii*

Acknowledgements *xv*

About the Authors *xvii*

Section 1 – Introduction to Software Engineering

1 Software Engineering – Introduction **1**

1.1 Introduction to Software Engineering 1
1.2 Software Process 12
1.3 Software Process Models 20
1.4 Software Product 28

Section 2 – Requirement Engineering

2 Requirements Engineering Principles **41**

2.1 Introduction 41
2.2 What is Requirements Engineering? 41
2.3 Importance of Requirements 42
2.4 Types of Requirements 43
2.5 Steps Involved in Requirements Engineering 45

3 Requirement Analysis Modeling **83**

3.1 Analysis Modeling Approaches 83
3.2 Structured Analysis 85
3.3 Object-Oriented Analysis 102

Section 3 – Design and Architectural Engineering

4 Design and Architectural Engineering **107**

4.1 Design Process and Concepts 107
4.2 Basic Issues in Software Design 108
4.3 Characteristics of a Good Design 108
4.4 Software Design and Software Engineering 108

4.5 Function-Oriented System vs Object-Oriented System 108
4.6 Modularity, Cohesion, Coupling, Layering 109
4.7 Real-Time Software Design (RTS Design) 113
4.8 Design Models 114
4.9 Design Documentation 122

5 Object-oriented Concepts 129

5.1 Introduction 129
5.2 Fundamental Parts of Object-oriented Approach 130
5.3 Data Hiding and Class Hierarchy Creation 134
5.4 Relationships 139
5.5 Role of Unified Modeling Language (UML) in OO Design 141
5.6 Design Patterns 141
5.7 Frameworks 143

6 Object-oriented Analysis and Design 149

6.1 Introduction 149
6.2 Object-oriented Analysis 150
6.3 Object-oriented Design 152

7 User Interface Design 175

7.1 Introduction 175
7.2 Concepts of User Interface 176
7.3 Elements of the User Interface 177
7.4 Designing the User Interface 182
7.5 User Interface Evaluation (User Interface Design Evaluation) 185
7.6 Golden Rules of User Interface Design 185
7.7 User Interface Models (User Interface Design Models) 194
7.8 Usability 194

Section 4 – Software Coding

8 Software Coding 199

8.1 Introduction 199
8.2 Programming Principles 200
8.3 Programming Guidelines 201
8.4 Coding Conventions (Programming Practices) 202
8.5 Key Concepts in Software Coding 210

Section 5 – Software Metrics and Estimation

9 **Introduction to Software Measurement and Metrics** **235**
9.1 Introduction 235
9.2 Measurement 235
9.3 Metrics 240
9.4 Other Concepts 249

10 **LOC, Function Point, and Object-oriented Metrics** **257**
10.1 Introduction 257
10.2 Lines of Code 257
10.3 Function Point Count (Fp Estimation) 260
10.4 Extended Function Point Metrics 269
10.5 Object-oriented Metrics 274
10.6 DeMarco's System BANG 279

11 **Software Estimation Tools, Techniques and Models** **291**
11.1 Introduction 291
11.2 Definition of Estimation 291
11.3 Importance of Accurate Estimation 292
11.4 Efforts and Duration 292
11.5 Estimation Process 292
11.6 Basic Estimation Principles 294
11.7 Estimation Techniques 294
11.8 Estimating Styles 299
11.9 Precision versus Accuracy 300
11.10 Tools for Analyzing Metrics and Estimations 300
11.11 Project Cost Estimation 304
11.12 Earned Value Management 314
11.13 Other Concepts in Costing 316

Section 6 – Software Configuration

12 **Software Configuration Management** **331**
12.1 Introduction 331
12.2 Basic Concepts of Configuration Management 331
12.3 Software Configuration Management Process 332
12.4 Configuration Identification 332
12.5 Configuration Control 333

12.6 Configuration Status Accounting 333
12.7 Configuration Authentication 333
12.8 Tools Used in Software Configuration Management 333
12.9 SCM and SEI Capability Maturity Model 334
12.10 Configuration Management Activities 334
12.11 Software Configuration Management Plan (SCMP) 334

Section 7 – Software Project Management

13 Project Management Introduction **341**
13.1 Introduction 341
13.2 Process 341
13.3 Project 343
13.4 Environmental Factors that Mandate Projects in Organizations 349
13.5 Project Management 350
13.6 Program Management 352
13.7 Portfolio Management 352
13.8 Project Management Office 353
13.9 Project Planning and Monitoring 354
13.10 Project Scope Management 354
13.11 Project Quality Management 357

14 Risk Analysis and Management **365**
14.1 Introduction 365
14.2 Software Risk 366
14.3 Types of Risk 366
14.4 Plan Risk Management 367

15 Communication and Team Management **385**
15.1 Introduction 385
15.2 Dimensions of Communication 385
15.3 Forms of Communication 386
15.4 Process of Communication 387
15.5 Handling Communication in a Software Project 388
15.6 Project Performance Reports 391
15.7 Managing the Project Team 392

16 Project Time and Cost Management **399**
16.1 Introduction 399
16.2 Time Management 399
16.3 Cost Management 416

17 Project Stakeholder Management 429
17.1 Introduction 429
17.2 Stakeholders and their Characteristics 429
17.3 Identifying the Stakeholders 430
17.4 Managing the Stakeholder Engagement 433
17.5 Procurement Process and Suppliers 434

18 Computer-aided Software Engineering 443
18.1 Introduction 443
18.2 Case Tool 443
18.3 Case-Building Blocks 444
18.4 Components of Case Tools 444
18.5 Quality of Case Tools 445
18.6 Productivity of Case Tools 445
18.7 Functions of A Case Tool 446
18.8 List of White Box Testing Commercial Tools and Their Purpose 449
18.9 Workbenches 450

Section 8 – Software Testing

19 Introduction to Software Testing 455
19.1 Introduction 455
19.2 Psychology of Testing 456
19.3 Software Testing Scope 457
19.4 Software Testing Objectives 457
19.5 Strategic Approach to Software Testing 461
19.6 Types of Software Testing 463

20 Software Testing Plan and Test Case Preparation 485
20.1 Introduction 485
20.2 Test Plan 485
20.3 Introduction to Test Case 492

21 Test Automation 513
21.1 Introduction 513
21.2 Expectations from Test Automation 513
21.3 Limitations of Automation 515
21.4 Automation Strategy 516
21.5 Automation Frameworks 520
21.6 Automation Metrics 524

Section 9 – Software Maintenance

22 Software Maintenance **529**

22.1 Introduction 529
22.2 Maintenance Activities 530
22.3 Maintenance Process 532
22.4 Maintenance Cost 533
22.5 Software Evolution 534
22.6 Reverse Engineering 534
22.7 Re-engineering 535
22.8 Re-structuring 537
22.9 Maintenance Strategies 537
22.10 Maintenance Mind Set 537
22.11 Service Perspective to Software Maintenance 537
22.12 Gap Model - Service 538
22.13 Software Maintenance Tools 539
22.14 Issues in Software Maintenance 540
22.15 Difference between Software Maintenance and Support 541
22.16 Common Metrics in Software Maintenance and Support 541

Section 10 – Web Engineering

23 Web Engineering **553**

23.1 Introduction 553
23.2 Introduction to Web 553
23.3 General Web Characteristics 554
23.4 Web Applications Categories 556
23.5 How Web Application Work? 556
23.6 Advantages of Web Applications 557
23.7 Drawbacks of Web Applications 557
23.8 Web Engineering 557

Section 11 – Emerging Trends in Software Engineering

24 Emerging Trends in Software Engineering **569**

24.1 Introduction 569
24.2 Web 2.0 569
24.3 Rapid Delivery 571
24.4 Open Source Software Development 571
24.5 Security Engineering 572
24.6 Service-oriented Software Engineering 573

24.7 Web Service 573
24.8 Software as a Service 574
24.9 Service-oriented Architecture 575
24.10 Cloud Computing 575
24.11 Aspect-oriented Software Development (AOSD) 576
24.12 Test-driven Development (TDD) 576
24.13 Social Computing 576

Section 12 – Introduction to Agile Software Development

25 Introduction to Agile Software Development 579

25.1 Introduction 579
25.2 What is Agile? 579
25.3 Various Characteristics of Agile Projects 581
25.4 Agile manifesto 583
25.5 Generic Agile Project Life Cycle 586
25.6 Agile-related Concepts 588
25.7 Epics, Features, User Stories 589
25.8 Communication in Agile Projects 590
25.9 Different Agile Methodologies 592

26 Case Studies on Software Engineering Practices 609

Case Study 1: Software Project Management Lifecycle – A Product Development Case study 609
Case Study 2: Maintenance Project Case Study – Lifecycle and How it is Managed 618
Case Study 3: Agile Project Case Study – How it is Structured and Executed 621
Case Study 4: Testing Case Study – How the Testing Methodologies are Used in a Project 625
Case Study 5: Software SDLC Case Study 629

Model Question Paper *633*

Model Solved Question Paper *635*

Index *647*

Foreword

Software plays a vital role in every field of human activity and we are literally relying on them to do anything in our lives today. It has become an integral part of life for banking, shopping, communicating, and even in commuting as software is part of automobile functioning today. Currently, they are simply embedded in everything we have in our car, in our office, and in our home. With the day-to-day advancement of the internet, we will find them taking over our life in everything we have and everything we do and the controls to come even from what we wear as they become wearable devices.

With this accelerated growth of software, one thing is certain. The complexity of the software development has become multi-fold and with the ever-changing spectrum of new methodologies, new languages, and new paradigms, it is very difficult to keep track of everything to stay on top in this field. Especially, the new trends are not taught very formally in the current educational system and with the shortage of man power to do all the development work when we add more and more people to this field of software engineering, the issues related to software engineering are exploding. We keep hearing every day from the software development houses the issues they have on low efficiency, low quality, unhappy customers, poor communication, changing requirements, ineffective testing, poor management, and so on.

There is clearly need of a book which will give clear-cut, explicit, and definite answers to software reengineering, especially in the application development areas. It is an excellent attempt by the authors, who are the practitioners of software engineering to take up this challenge and have accomplished a superb job in keeping the software engineering Practices in focus while also covering the aspects of Project Management, agile development, etc. They have organized the material in a logical fashion that will aid the readers to understand all aspects of software engineering easily. The readers will find all the important software engineering concepts and some of their implementations within the covers of a single book which should really make this book a valuable asset for every software professional.

The readers can keep this book as a reference book on software engineering and refer to it whenever they need even after becoming qualified software engineers. I wish the readers of this book a great success in not only becoming expert software engineers but also in managing software engineering projects more efficiently.

Raj Bala
Chief Technology Officer
Cognizant Technology Solutions

Software engineering has evolved steadily over the last 70 years since its inception in the 1940s. Software is not only a part and parcel of our life now, but without it many complex and mission critical system would not have worked at all. In many cases, the importance and complexity of the software part are almost the same as the hardware part. For example, the size and complexity of the software programs that control a satellite are no less substantial and complex than the intricate hardware parts building the satellite. So there is a growing demand for software professionals well equipped with the concepts, the technologies, and the new innovations in this field. A software engineering text book thus needs to explain the complex concepts in a lucid manner, cover all the technological aspects, and should delve into the new developments happening in the software engineering domain.

Although there are many learning tools and published materials available for software engineering, some great features make the present book unique. The team of four authors of this book has provided a distinctively comprehensive and complete coverage of the subject. The flow of this book matches exactly with the flow of software development such as Requirement, Design, Coding, Testing, and Maintenance. Special emphasis is given on the key items such as testing, metrics, estimation techniques, and project management. I feel that this book will help undergraduate students to learn the logical structure as well as finer points of software development, while aiding other students and practitioners to hone their software engineering skill and clearly understand its associated concepts covering the entire Software Engineering syllabus.

The authors' great collective expertise and vast experience in teaching, research, and industry are reflected through the pages of this well-written book. This presents concepts with great clarity and provides valuable insights making it a ready reckoner at any point. A few of the innovative ideas incorporated in the book are the Watch Snippets highlighting the important topics, an impressive database of 1000 Practical Solved Questions, and exclusive access to web content, which will help students to prepare for the university exams. Software development methodologies are undergoing tremendous changes, and it is important to understand advanced concepts such as automation, agile, and cloud computing. This book has exclusive chapters about new trends in software engineering and various agile methodologies to make the student industry-ready in all aspects. Real-life case studies at the end of the book demonstrate all the essential software engineering principles practiced in the software industry.

I am sure that this book, by a team of excellent authors, will help the readers understand the concepts better and enhance their self-confidence in the practice of Software Engineering. I strongly recommend this book for improved performance and results.

Sipra DasBit
Professor and Head
Department of Computer Science and Technology
IIEST, Shibpur
(Formerly Bengal Engineering and Science University)

Preface

Repeated requests from software engineers who are the readers of our previous books encouraged us to write this book on software engineering. The trend of number of software project failures is still disturbing and even though there is some improvement made over past few years, it still needs further improvement. Hence, we thought of writing this book specifically for techies, college students, and junior managers so that they understand the software engineering concepts easily and execute their projects successfully. The term "software engineering" and the related concepts may be 45 years old, but the pace at which it is growing, it makes sense to update and accommodate new concepts to keep it fresh and energetic.

This book addresses software engineering concepts and is intended as a text book for an undergraduate-level engineering course. Due care has been taken to present the concepts in a simple and easy way. In addition to covering the concepts of software engineering, this book also addresses the perspective of decreasing the overall efforts of writing software requirements and increasing the understanding of how to write quality software. Although, it is primarily designed for using as a textbook for a course in software engineering, it can also serve as a good point of reference for software practitioners.

We have tried to provide the blend of practical as well as theoretical concepts of software engineering in this book. It explains the agile concepts also for the benefits of modern software engineers which will enable them to excel in executing agile projects. Software engineering is not a single person's job and is a team work which consists of business analysts, developers, architects, user interface designers, testers, system engineers, and project managers. Thus, this book covers all software engineering aspects taken into consideration for all those stakeholders and special attention is given to Software Testing, Software Project management and Agile concepts.

This book covers the entire gamut of software engineering life cycle starting from the requirement until the implementation and maintenance of the project.

Why This Book?

There are many concepts in software engineering which requires critical reading and in-depth understanding. It was our endeavor to present the concepts in a simple language. All the complex topics are decomposed into sub-topics so that the readers can understand the concepts easily. Explanations and examples were given based on the real-time experience and pictorial representations facilitate the easy assimilation.

Whom Is This Book For?

Readers of this book will gain a thorough understanding of principles of software engineering. Not only students but also developers, including testing professionals, will find a variety of techniques with sufficient discussions that caters to the needs of the professional environments. Technical managers will get an insight into how to weave software project management into the overall software engineering process. Students, developers, and technical managers with a basic background in computer science will find the material in this book easily readable.

How Is This Book Organized?

Each chapter starts with an introductory paragraph which gives overview of the chapter along with a chapter coverage table listing out the topics covered in the chapter. Sample questions at the end of the chapter helps the students to prepare for the exam. Discussion points and Point to Ponder given inside the chapters help to clarify and understand the chapters easily and also explores the thinking ability of the students and professionals.

A recap summary is given at the end of each chapter for quick review of the topics. Throughout this book you will see many exercises and discussion questions and please do not skip these as they are important in order to understand the software engineering concepts fully.

No matter whether a project is large or small, the project management is an integral part of the project for successful delivery. Software Engineering Implementation is not just about writing codes but is also for ensuring that the proper project management processes are in place along with proper testing of the implemented code. Effective Project management is only possible with the proper implementation of metrics management. Testing includes unit testing, system testing, integration testing, and the activities such as writing test cases, test plan, and executing those. This book covers all the topics discussed above. The exercises and discussion points are a key benefit of this book.

Notes for Instructors

This book can be used in an introductory course in software engineering or as a supplementary text in an undergraduate software engineering course. An introductory graduate-level or an undergraduate-level course in software engineering can be covered by using this book. This book has a complimentary web extension **www.pearsoned.co.in/chandramoulisubramanian**, where you can find solutions/answers to all the questions at the end of each chapter.

S. Chandramouli

Saikat Dutt

Chandramouli Seetharaman

Dr B. G. Geetha

Acknowledgements

The journey through our professional career has been very enriching so far. Along the way, several individuals have been instrumental in providing us with guidance, opportunities, and insights to excel in our fields. We are grateful to Pearson India Education Services Pvt. Ltd, who came forward to publish this book. Sojan Jose, S. Shankari Sekar, and C. Purushothaman of Pearson India Education Services Pvt. Ltd, who were always kind and understanding and reviewed this book with abundant patience and added value to this book with their professional touch. Their patience and guidance were invaluable.

All Authors

We would like to express our sincere gratitude to Mr Chandra Sekaran, Executive Vice Chairman, Cognizant Technology Solutions, Mr Raj Bala, Chief Technology Officer, Cognizant Technology Solutions, Mr Pradeep Shilige, Senior Vice President, Cognizant Technology Solutions, and Mr Subhayu Paul, Director, Cognizant Technology Solutions for their constant encouragement and support. With their vast experience and knowledge they not only helped us in enriching professionally but also guided us in taking this project to a successful completion.

S. Chandramouli
Saikat Dutt

I would like to thank Mr Chandrasekhar, CIO at Standard Chartered Bank, a wonderful and cheerful person who inspired me to write and also encouraged me when he launched my first book "Virtual Project Management Office." I also thank Mr Natarajan, a good human being, a good family friend of mine, who encouraged me to work on the subject, and helped me to understand complex topics through easy mind mapping in a logical way. He gave me the first writing assignment in 1999, on a technical subject. I am grateful to Mr Balu Mohan Rao, Senior Vice President, Scope International, Mr Govindaswamy Abbupillai, Senior Vice President, Mahindra Satyam, Mr Sriram K, Senior Vice President, Mahindra Satyam, and Mr Narayana Murthy K, Vice President, Mahindra Satyam. I would like to express my gratitude to all those who provided support, discussed subject, and offered comments. Above all, I thank my father (M. Subramanian), mother (S. Lalitha), wife (R. Ramya), and two kids (Shrikrishna and Shrisivaranjani) who were unfailingly supportive and encouraging during the long months I spent glued to my computer while writing this book. My sincerest apologies to all those who have been with me over the course of the years whose names I have failed to mention. Last but not the least, I thank all authors for devoting their time and efforts toward this book.

S. Chandramouli

This book would have not been possible without constant inspiration and support of my lovely wife Adity. My parents have always been enthusiastic about this project and provided me continuous guidance at every necessary step. The unconditional love and affection my sons, Deepro and Devarko ushered on me constantly provided me the motivation to work hard on this crucial project. This book is the culmination of all the learning that I gained from many highly reputed professionals in the industry. I was fortunate to work with them and gain knowledge from them which helped me to mold my professional career. Mr Kollol Hazra, Managing Director, CSG Systems International, India, and Dr Rathi Dasgupta, former Managing Director, Intec India guided me enormously in different aspects of life and career. I would also like to thank few highly intellectual people who helped me in gaining knowledge: Saikat Biswas, Head, Customer Engineering and Delivery at Sixth Sense Media, Kushal Ghosh, Director, Ericsson India Global Services, and Indrajit Sanyal, Director and Head System Integration and package Solution, Ericsson. My heartfelt thanks to all the wonderful people who contributed in many ways in conceptualizing this book and wished success of this project.

Saikat Dutt

I would like to thank my co-author and former colleague Chandramouli Subramanian for providing the opportunity to work on this book. I would not have been a part of this book if not for his guidance and efforts in putting up a good team together along with other co-authors, Saikat and Dr B. G. Geetha, Since my college days Mr Jeppiar (Chancellor, Sathyabama Deemed University) has been a great pillar of strength, encouragement, and support to me in all my endeavors. The sheer enthusiasm, energy, and vision of Mr Jeppiar has inspired many to achieve higher goals whatever may be the given situation one may be in. I am proud to be one of the many he has inspired. My friend Boopathy Rajendran, Director, Cognizant has been a great well-wisher who always has words of encouragement and helps others without any expectations which is really wonderful and refreshing in the corporate world. Personally, I would like thank my wife Gayathri for her patience and the extra hard work to take care of my little daughters, Meenakshi and Padmakshe. My parents Seetharaman and Kalyani have always put my requirements as their highest priority and have always been there whenever possible. This is just a small token of my appreciation and thanks to them. Finally, I would like to thank Venkatram Vasi, Project Management Consultant, Catalysts for assisting with creative diagrams to present some concepts in the book in a simple understandable manner.

Chandramouli Seetharaman

I am very grateful to my coordinators for their discussion and consideration of the subject and their knowledge sharing with great enthusiasm. I thank P. Kanmani, AP/CSE, KSRCT enormously for helping me in writing this book. Thanks to all my family members for their patience with me for having taken yet another challenge which took away family time.

Dr B. G. Geetha

About the Authors

S. Chandramouli, PMP, PMI ACP, is a recognized industry thought leader in Project and Program Management and has authored two books "PMP Certification Excel with Ease" and "PMI Agile Certified Practitioner Excel with Ease" published by Pearson. He is an alumnus of the Indian Institute of Management, Kozhikode (IIM-K), and a prolific writer of business management articles dealing with delivery management, competitiveness, IT, organizational culture, and leadership. His vast experience includes corporate and project governance, customer relationship management, and organization strategy.

He was an active member in PMI OPM3, and PMCDF project works. He is a certified "Green Belt" in six sigma methodology and is also ITIL (F) Certified. He is actively associated with academia and various research professional bodies in India.

A continuous learner and conference enthusiast, he has authored a paper on "Strategy based Service Model" which won the first runner up award at the International IT Service Management Conference 2013 (ITSM 2013). His another paper titled "SCRUM TEA Model – Best Practices of Agile Program Management" was awarded second runner up by QAI at the International Program and Portfolio Conference 2013.

Saikat Dutt is a Project Management Professional (PMP) and PMI Agile Certified Professional certified by Project Management Institute (PMI) USA, and a Certified Scrum Master. He has more than 16 years of IT industry experience and has expertise in managing large-scale multilocation and mission critical projects. Saikat is working as Director in Cognizant Technology Solutions. He is an active speaker on Agile Best Practices and Project management methodologies in several forums and is involved in regular training sessions on Project management and Agile topics.

Saikat has been passionate about grooming new talents in the areas of project management and Agile project execution and handling. His book on PMI ACP certification "PMI Agile Certified Practitioner – Excel with Ease" is one of the most recognized books for the PMI ACP certification. Saikat has worked with big multinationals in the software industry such as Cognizant Technology Solutions, Ushacomm, CSGi and has been instrumental in percolating the Project and Program management knowledge and coaching Agile methodologies in these organizations.

Chandramouli Seetharaman is currently the Founder-Director of CATALYSTS responsible for the project management consulting, training, and mobile application testing practices. He has over 20 years of experience in the IT industry. He worked with Syntel for over 13 years consulting for several top companies in the US such as AMEX, Xerox, Mattel, CNA, and Allstate holding various responsible positions. He also worked in Europe as a successful delivery manager for GMAC, Birmingham and for Deutsche Bank, Frankfurt. The design and development of a highly successful test data generator was a highlight of his tenure at Syntel. He joined Cognizant in 2011 and headed the Customer Solutions Practice Testing in Chennai. He worked with multiple clients in testing applications in BPM, CRM, and MDM areas. As part of the innovation team at Cognizant, with a bunch of enthusiastic fresher's he designed and developed a tool for automatic generation of test scenarios for java-based BPM applications.

Dr B. G. Geetha holds a Ph.D. degree in Computer Science Engineering and has around 21 years of experience in Engineering teaching. Her specialized areas include software engineering, software testing, cloud computing, information storage management, and object-oriented programming. She has guided 122 projects for UG and PG students and is guiding 13 research scholars of Anna University.

Section 1:
Introduction to Software Engineering

1

Software Engineering – Introduction

CHAPTER COVERAGE

1. *Introduction to Software Engineering*
2. *Software Process*
3. *Software Process Models*
4. *Software Product*

1.1 INTRODUCTION TO SOFTWARE ENGINEERING

The success of mankind in performing a process with perfection and accuracy commenced with the origin of computers. The digitalized computing machines, initialized in 1940s, merely carried out arithmetic operations marking the first step toward today's innovative computers. The development attained today in the field of computing was never predicted. Speaking of computers, we cannot miss the components that make it up as a whole device. Man developed many individual components to aid him in day-to-day life. Every device invented simplified the efforts to a larger extent. Starting from the pulley, the wheel and eventually the computer, relieved the stress and strain and proved to be a masterpiece.

Initially, the computer performed simple tasks and produced results. However, the device has so rapidly progressed today to perform analysis, comparison of details and make decisions that its functions require only minimum human intervention. Applications of this incredible device can be seen everywhere. Extended functionalities of the computer have, to a great extent, reduced the need for investing human effort in nearly all fields. The primary components of the computer included a memory space to store the variables, a procedure to perform the operations and a display to show the results to the user. Instructions to the first-generation computer were provided by wired components, which were too messy. Gradually, the idea of storing the programmed instructions internally into the device without further need to input every single instruction was developed. This required a programming language to create a procedure for every task. A programming language has certain formats to guide the user for easier and faster designing of the program. Programs of individual functions grouped together form software. Software is a collection of similar tasks that provides a single interface to the user to obtain the results for a variety of requests. Software is the controlling unit of a hardware component. Both the components complete the computer structure; software or hardware alone is useless. A memory device, a power unit, capacitors, resistors, processor, monitor, and cables to connect are the hardware components used in a computer. The software defines the functions of data transfer, path of control messages and transfer of input and output between the hardware.

This chapter explores the concepts of software, its development stages and explains its importance in the evolution of computers. The application of software involves many tiring tasks that have evolved to the present stage. Different methods have been proposed for the development of software and its deployment in a suitable environment. The deployment of software does not end the life cycle of a software, but it continues until the next version is developed. The development team continues to have its relationship with the software as they release periodic updates of the software to meet the ever demanding needs of the clients and the end users. Software engineering deals with the terminologies of designing and delivering software to the client's satisfaction. The origin of software, its phases, the level of applicability and the role it plays in the functioning of the computer are discussed in the following sections.

1.1.1 What Is Software?

Software is defined as the tool with designated order of instructions, performing tasks to provide the desired results after obtaining the requirements of the users. The methodology of how to perform the operations in an optimal path to obtain accurate results quickly states the functions of computer software.

Software also consists of procedures, rules, software-related documents and the associated basic data required to run the software (Refer Figure 1.1).

Software = Computer Programs (Instructions) + Procedures + Rules + Associated documents + Data

Procedures and rules include step-by-step instructions of how to install (deploy) and use the software. Documents include requirement documents, design documents and testing-related documents. To run the software basic data needs to be fed in.

Computer software resides in the memory space of the computer, commanding it in every situation. The process of the software begins with the booting of the computer until it is shut down.

POINTS TO PONDER

Software = Computer Programs (Instructions) + Procedures + Rules + Associated documents + Data

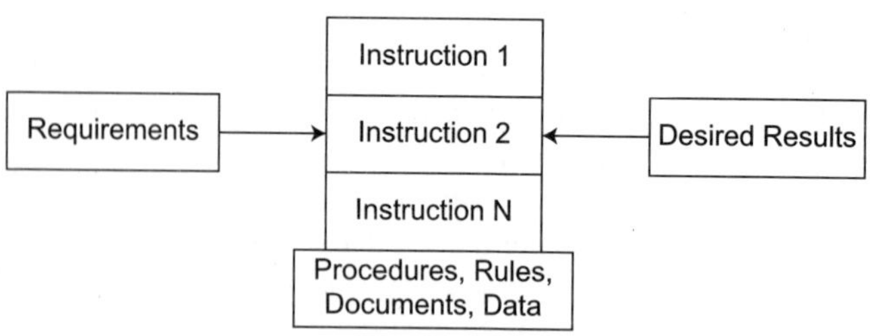

Figure 1.1 Components of Software

Examples of Software:

1. Microsoft Word
2. Microsoft Excel
3. Microsoft Power Point
4. Linux
5. MySQL
6. Adobe Photoshop

1.1.2 Evolving Role of Software

Software has evolved from a single instruction provided to the machine to the present stage of decision-making software (refer Figure 1.2). Initially, the devices were operated by inputting single real-time instructions; later a programming language framed a structure to combine programs into software. The software was then divided into categories based on their implementation areas.

Individual programs perform an operation; collectively they form software and perform a function for the user (refer Figure 1.3). Software is classified into two types based on the areas they command, namely application software and system software.

System Software comprises programs that control the operations of the hardware components (refer Figure 1.3). The technical functioning of the computer is dependent on the operating system, built in with a number of adequate system software. System software controls the transfer of messages handling the internal processes, which are mostly abstracted from the external users of the computer.

Examples:

1. Operating systems like Dos, Windows and Linux.
2. Device drivers (hardware controllers) such as video device driver software.

Application Software consists of programs purely for the tasks of the users, obtaining the inputs and processing them in the instructions already defined (refer Figure 1.3). They have no access to the hardware and the prerecorded system software of the device. As they are intended for interfacing and processing with the user, they have been adorned with the unifying taste of the users.

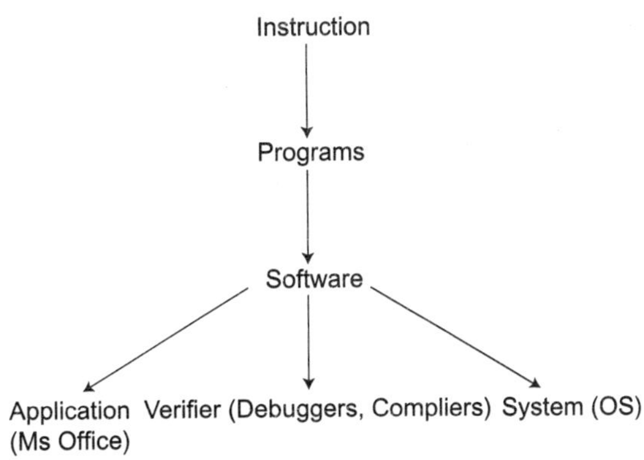

Figure 1.2 Evolution of Software

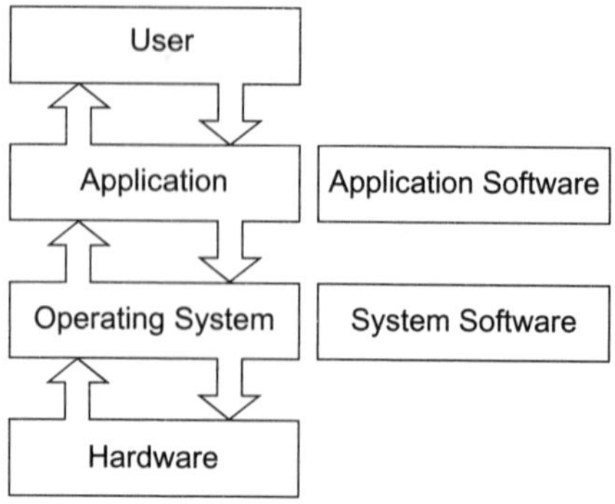

Figure 1.3 Interrelationship of Software

Examples: MS Office suite, Microsoft Calculator, Notepad, etc.

There are other types of software which are dedicated to the verification of the programs in terms of coding, formats, flow of control and order of execution. These verifying software are not involved in any other part of the operation. They are used to detect and report the syntax errors in the designed program. Without the report of verifiers and stated rectifications the program is not allowed to execute.

Examples: Compilers and Debuggers.

1.1.3 Phases in Software Development

The phases in software development define the steps of organizing the development of the software. Each step is called a phase. Each phase will have at least one deliverable (output).

The general software development phases are described as follows:

1. Requirements Analysis Phase
2. Designing Phase
3. Coding and Testing Phase
4. Implementation Phase
5. Maintenance Phase

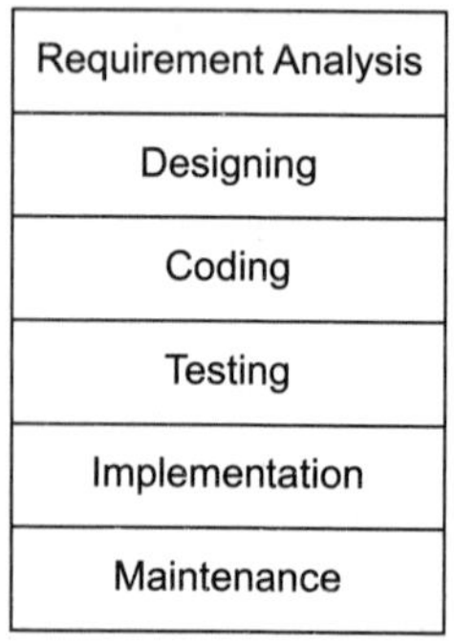

1.1.3.1 Requirements Analysis

The requirements analysis is the first phase of software development wherein the customer and the business analysts (usually developer) interact with each other and document the requirements of the outcome of the software. The customers would state their requirements how and what the end product should perform. Requirements form the stepping stone of any project or product. The requirements include the appearances (Interface requirements), the functionalities (Functional requirements) and the software output expectations (Nonfunctional requirements). The requirement gathering team discusses the noted requirements with the experts for their implementation into the product, which is called as analysis part of the phase. The expert team analyzes the possibilities and impact of implementing the stated requirements. The analysis of the requirements includes the budget and the time span required for completing the product. The complete analysis of the requirements is documented for future reference.

It is easy to fix a problem in the requirements at the requirements analysis stage. However if that faulty requirement percolates through later stages of design and coding, then it would cost 10–100 times more to fix the same. Capturing the requirements fully and correctly at the early stage of the project is essential to make the project profitable.

Types of requirements include:

- Functional Requirements
- Nonfunctional Requirements
- Interface Requirements

The steps in Requirement Engineering phase include:

- Feasibility Study
- Eliciting Requirements
- Requirements Analysis
- Specify and Validate Requirements
- Requirements Management

Requirement Analysis Models (Approach) include:

- Structured Analysis Model
- Object Oriented Analysis Model

Requirement Engineering Principles and Requirement Analysis Modeling are discussed in Chapters 2 and 3, respectively.

1.1.3.2 Designing

During the design phase, the software requirement is converted into design models. Each design outcome is verified and validated before moving to the next phase.

The design of the software depends on the complexity level of the product, the graphical interfaces required and ease of use requirements of the end users. The design should not leave out any of the agreed requirements of the user. The Design Phase acts as a bridge between the Requirement Analysis phase and the Coding Phase. The Design Phase converts the business requirements into technical requirements. The design has no functionality but only the structure of the product.

The design of the software product should

1. Be precise and specific
2. Conform to budget and requirements
3. Provide a direct solution to the problem

Modularity, cohesion, coupling and layering are the factors to be considered while designing the software. UML is a modeling language used to model software and nonsoftware systems. UML and the above factors are discussed in detail in the later chapters.

Software design includes Data Design, Architectural Design, User Interface Design, Procedural Design and Deployment Level Design.

Software Design Concepts discussed in Chapter 4 includes design models, architectural engineering, etc.; Object Oriented Concepts in Chapter 5 include Class, Objects, Inheritance, Polymorphism, Design Patterns, etc.; Object Oriented Analysis and Design in Chapter 6 includes Use Case Modeling, UML notations, etc. and User Interface Design is discussed in Chapter 7.

1.1.3.3 Coding and Testing

Coding is defined as the phase where the documented design is transformed into lines of codes in programming language. In a typical waterfall model, coding is done after the requirement analysis (requirement clarification) and design. Writing standardized codes for software helps not only to maintain it properly once it is built, but also to enhance the code easily at a later point of time; it also helps to identify and fix the bugs quickly and easily. Therefore just writing a proper working code is not enough, but the focus should be on writing a standard code. So codes are instructions that execute the program in the environment where it is supposed to be. The designs in high level language are converted into machine level language for implementation in the real-world environment. Coding conventions and coding standards are discussed in detail in the later chapters.

After coding phase is completed, the code have to be tested for ensuring its right functionality in the platform. Testing is carried out by a separate team of experts (software testers) specialized in generating sample cases and subjecting the product to various tests. Only after the product has been proved to be reliable by the tests, it enters into the implementation phase. The process of testing and its procedures are discussed in detail in the later chapters.

Chapters that are related to coding and testing aspects are:

Chapter 8 Software Coding

Chapter 9 Introduction to Software Measurement and Metrics

Chapter 10 LOC Function Point and Object Oriented Metrics

Chapter 19 Software Testing Plan and Test Case Preparation

Chapter 20 Software Test Automation

1.1.3.4 Implementation

This phase involves the release of the developed software into the market and to the end users. This phase is also called as Deployment Phase. The tested software product is then implemented in the customer's domain. The software developed is installed in the platform for its prescribed function. The success of the implemented product depends on how much the end users like the product and prefer to use it regularly. There will be similar products satisfying the same functionalities from competing organizations in the market, racing for people's attraction. Hence, the implemented product should be simple to use (user interface intensive organizations) and accurate (in the case of financial and trading organizations).

1.1.3.5 Maintenance

Software maintenance is the core aspect of software engineering. After the system development, the system gets deployed into the production environment. The process of modifying the production system after the delivery to correct the faults, improve the performance and adapt to the changing environment is called as software maintenance. The responsibility of the team of developers does not end after the product is implemented, but continues for a considerable long time. Training has to be provided to the clients and users on handling the product. Without proper training and knowledge on how the product works, there are chances of errors and failures. Every user will not be skilled in the technical aspects of the software other than the developers themselves. The software is maintained and upgraded with ever increasing demands and requirements of the clients and end users. All the changes during the maintenance stage are clearly documented for further reference. When a new product of similar characteristics needs to be developed, these documents are referred for analyzing the components which could be reused. The reusable component shortens the time and effort of the development team by facilitating them to skip the design and coding process for that particular portion of the code. The maintenance and its corresponding process are discussed in Chapter 9 Introduction to Software Measurement and Metrics.

1.1.4 Software Characteristics

A software has the following characteristics (refer Figure 1.4):

1. **It should be complete:** The software product being developed should meet all the requirements of the customers no matter how complex the product is, and the requirements agreed upon should be present in the product. The final product should not miss out any of the required functions.
2. **It should be exclusive and reliable:** Unique software delivers its ensured performance to a particular problem, and should concentrate on the given problem or requirements. The solution obtained after using the software should be distinct. The software needs to be stable for a considerable time and usage, providing an unfailing service.
3. **It should be precise:** Unwanted steps and operations should be eliminated and shorter operations with the right solution should be preferred. Unwanted steps lead to wastage of resources, manpower and hence the cost. These extra operations would have no effect on the final solution of the software. Selective and adequate processes should be enough and thus the structure needs to be clear-cut.
4. **It should be efficient:** A well organized software produces an optimal result at every moment of usage. The structure of the software needs to obey a strict and predefined order

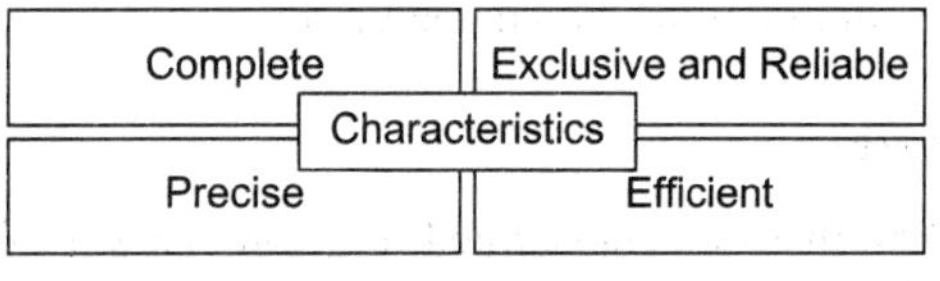

Figure 1.4 Characteristics of Software

to be efficient. It should also be flexible in nature so that it can be extended at a later point of time.

1.1.5 Changing Nature of Software

In the beginning, binary instructions were fed into the computer machine. Today the software has evolved to a matured level and has sophisticated tools to develop the software and no longer requires to type the binary instructions. Now-a-days Object-based software development is in use. The urge of increasing features and demands of the business users lead to necessary changes in the software development. The source code was earlier visible only to the development team but is now available to the customers as well. Open source software is a big hit in the market and anybody can change the code while using and customizing it as per the need. Tools are now developed to facilitate the users to design a software product themselves by dragging and dropping the components (contents) at their intended positions. Proper knowledge of coding and testing is not required to design and code the software. Software development tools simplified the design and implementation phases drastically. The process of developing software becomes simple.

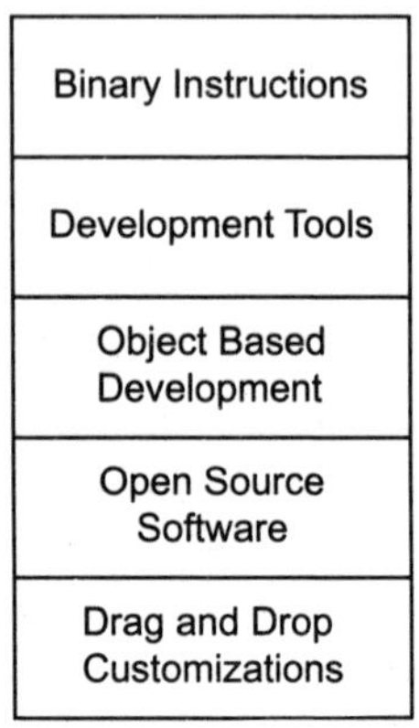

1.1.5.1 In-built Software

Various mechanisms of automobiles, planes and robots employed for various operations in the fields of military and research involve dedicated software with complex operations and decision-making skills. These devices need embedded software as they involve serious analysis and take appropriate actions at the right time. The in-built software are deeply sensitive and efficient, prescribing the intelligence functions of the devices. The intelligence includes decision-making skill sets because no human can be practically involved to command the robot, which reports on the atmospheric conditions of the planet Mars. Engineering and scientific research use this type of software mostly, reducing the participation of the mankind in in-human conditions.

1.1.5.2 System-based Software

The system-based software has also some prescribed function, but they are limited to simpler devices. Home computers or computers of any kind necessitate an operating system and additional driver softwares for the functioning of the entire system. The system-based software is related to programs, which define the functionality of the hardware components of a particular computer. The operation of a computer as a whole is facilitated by the system software containing the basic and advanced modes of operations at different instances of the end user. Without this software, the hardware is merely a machine. Compliers, linkers and debuggers are also some of the important system software for testing the programs.

1.1.5.3 Application-based software

These kinds of software delivers functionality or service to the requesting users. They obtain an input condition or a query from the end user, analyze it and display the results on the monitor. They are not as complex as the above-mentioned type. The structure and the language used for the applications vary by a large extent, such as for a web-based application the HTML and XML languages are used while for a database application, an ORACLE program is used. Different applications possess distinguishable styles and frameworks. Every field has its very own requirements, area of interests, functional aspects and thus different application softwares belong to different category and need not be the same.

1.1.6 Software Myths

The software development brackets many myths. The myths have created an incomplete and false image of the software development processes. Some of the myths are listed below.

1.1.6.1 Software Is Better than Implementing Devices

Devices have been limited to the wear and tear prone to usage. They include the definitions of being used. Software programs are theoretically known to change indefinitely with alterations in the code and reusability factor. Software does not come with an expiry date, but practically there is a limit to its usage. Although the changes are easier to be updated in the software than devices, they need to be verified.

1.1.6.2 Reusability Ensures Better Solution

The conceptual model of reusing a component is an incredible strategy to improve the performance reduce the time in designing and implementing the software. But there is a major factor of adaptability of the existing component into the newer component. Certain modifications may be needed in the component to be reused. Testing identifies errors and reports these kind of compatibility issues. Further remedial actions are taken for a component to be the best fit into the product.

1.1.6.3 Additional Features Add Efficiency

As already mentioned, the product being developed needs to have a direct and dedicated solution to the present problem. More straightforward software is preferred over the software with additional and unwanted features. One has to keep in mind that the product may not run accurately at the very first time, and testing alone cannot identify all the problems.

1.1.6.4 More Designers–more Delay

This is absolutely not true because the development team comprises of engineers with great knowledge on the strategies of rapid development. Expertise and experience of supplementary engineers will surely help in deploying the product at a faster rate. But there should be balance between how much work is pending and how many resources we deploy to get that done.

1.1.7 What is Software Engineering?

Software engineering comprises strict disciplines that need to be followed to develop a programmable solution to solve customer's problems.

Strategies are defined to obtain a viable, efficient and maintainable software solution, which takes care of the costs, quality, resources and other expenditures. These strategies have been proposed by various engineers after implementing and analyzing the merits and demerits of each strategy.

1.1.8 Why Study Software Engineering?

Software engineering encompasses every concepts and standards of the disciplines in relation to design, coding and developing maintainable software complying with the available resources and budget constraints. Without a minimal intellect on software engineering and its disciplines, the developer would find it difficult to cope and control a vast area of designing, converting the design into a code, and finally implementing and upgrading the product with the changing market and conditions. Every developer cannot just jump into the ocean of creativity and in-depth programming skills without an assessment of software engineering terminologies.

1. It is the basic of any software development
2. It helps to produce reliable, reusable and quality software
3. Software engineering understands the customer needs and develop the software
4. It helps the developers to understand the disciplines of software life cycle
5. It helps to develop software in efficient way
6. Software engineering teaches the best practices of software development
7. Software engineering helps to write software, which can be integrated easily with other software

1.1.9 Generic View of Software Engineering

The sequential steps that describe the stages of a product being developed are the generic view of software engineering. Every action required for the development is categorized into three generic stages (phases) as follows (Refer Figure 1.5):

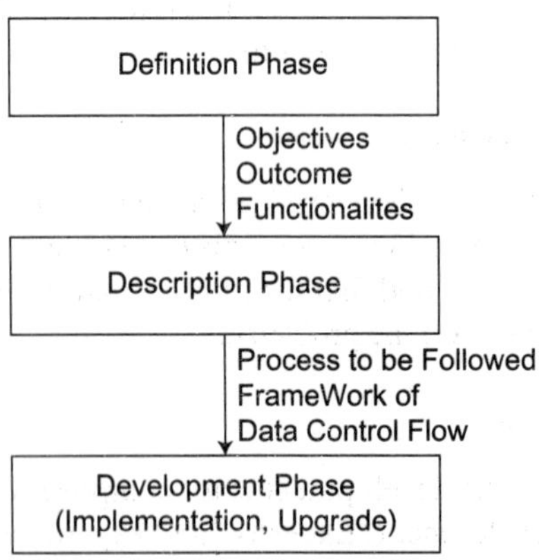

Figure 1.5 Generic view of Software Engineering

1. **Definition Phase:** The desired outcomes, functionalities and objectives are obtained from the customers and documented. These objectives are the driving force for a product to be developed. The team of developers and customers agree upon the final and feasible list of goals to be implemented into the product.
2. **Description Phase:** The next generic phase takes the necessary steps for further development; the desired outcomes are framed with optimal preceding and succeeding processes. The framework of data and control flow in a product, how the processes are ordered and how the functionalities are defined are described in this phase.
3. **Deployment Phase:** After the processes are described, they have to be transformed into the corresponding codes and implemented in the real-world environments. Implementation of the software product also includes the training provided to the customers and end users, maintenance and upgrade at regular intervals.

1.1.10 Role of Management in Software Engineering

Management of the software products depends on the following factors (refer Figure 1.6).

1.1.10.1 Participants

Members with various skill sets, from the team member to the team leader and manager, are responsible for every process of software development. The customers are the initial participants of a product. They put forward their problem and request a solution. A team of skilled personnel will discuss different solutions obeying the technical and administrative constraints. This participating team of developers is assigned by the top-level management based on the acquired and proficiency level of each member. Staffing requires the analysis of how proficient a member is in a particular field.

Managers play a crucial role in the development of the software. They are not only responsible for the final outcome of the project, but also responsible for the execution of the project from the beginning to the end. The manager prepares a plan and tries to execute the project as per the plan to create the deliverables. Manger is also responsible for managing scope, time, cost and quality of the overall project.

1.1.10.2 Procedure

Procedure describes the way in which the product is being developed. The order and types of procedures are devised by the team members and the final plan to be implemented is approved by the team

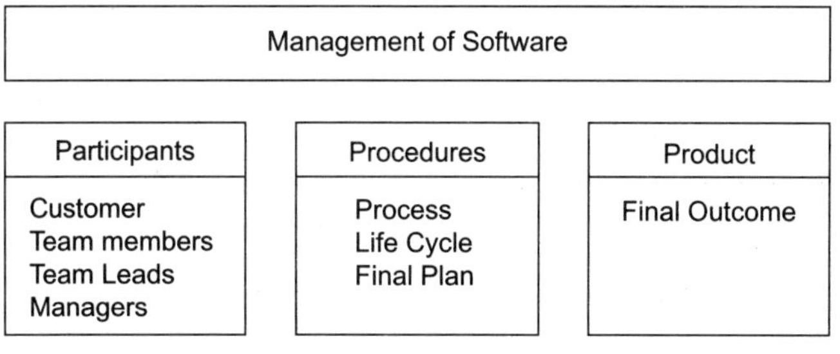

Figure 1.6 Participants, Procedures and Product

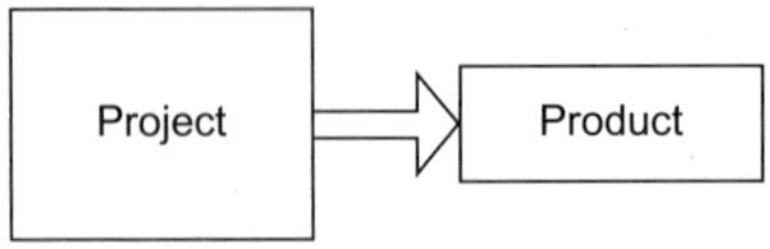

Figure 1.7 Project vs Product

manager. Managers also determine the life cycle that has to be followed among the various models. The best option would help to conserve the resources and money invested by the management. A slight deviation from the proposed procedure would disturb the efficiency of the entire process.

1.1.10.3 Product

The selection of best plans and procedures, and assigning the right and efficient staff to the project ensure the success of the project thereby ensuring the final outcome of the project called as product (refer Figure 1.7). Product is the outcome of the project.

There are many models of developing a product, evolved from the very beginning era of software development. Different models proposed increased the efficiency of the team of developers by altering and speeding up the actions of normal methods.

1.2 SOFTWARE PROCESS

A set of interrelated actions and activities to achieve a predefined result is called as process. Process has its own set of inputs and produces the output(s). Tools and techniques acts on the process to achieve the desired outcome. The processes have to be planned with great care and the knowledge about the effects of each implementation and activity on the product should be understood clearly by all the stakeholders. Groups of individual processes constitute whole software.

For example: Preparing a dosa (an Indian dish) as a process. If we call five different people (chefs) and give them the same ingredients and tools required to make the dosa, will the output be the same? The size and taste of the dosa is bound to vary. Why is it so? This is not only because of the difference in skills possessed by the chefs, but also because of the techniques they have learnt over a period. Thus, we need to understand and learn the techniques of a process to produce a better output.

In the following few sections an overview of different software development processes are given.

1.2.1 The Linear Sequential Model

A sequence of actions describes the order in which the execution of activities are planned and followed. Linear sequential model was the initial step in developing a software product, otherwise known to be the lifecycle model (refer Figure 1.8).

The process of development is divided into sequence of actions (steps) from requirements analysis, designing, coding and testing, implementation and finally maintenance. Each activity is carried out in a linear order (in sequential fashion) and no other order of execution is followed other than the flow mentioned. The result of the first activity is forwarded to the next stage and thus to the final stage. Without the completion of the previous step and forwarding the result, the next activity cannot be executed. It follows a strict sequence and it is strongly believed that no step can be overlapped.

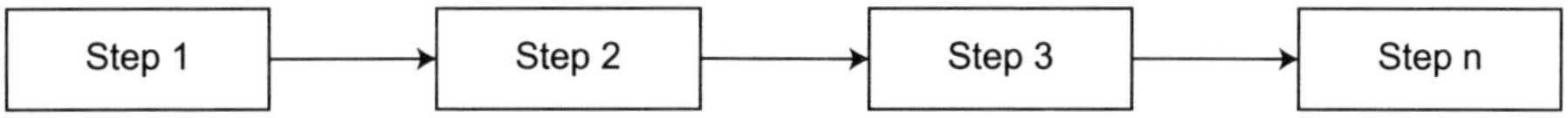

Figure 1.8 Linear Sequential Model

This model is a straightforward approach. Linear Sequential model is also called Predictive Life Cycle Model and Classical Life Cycle Model. Prototyping Model and Rapid Application Development Models can be the best examples of this model.

Examples for Linear Sequential Model include developing a portal that follows the steps of Requirement Analysis, Design, Coding, Testing and Implementation.

Some of the advantages of Linear Sequential Model are:

1. Easy to understand
2. Easy for implementation
3. Widely used and known; hence all stakeholders understand this
4. Identifies deliverables and milestones upfront.

Some of the disadvantages of Linear Sequential Model are:

1. This model assumes that requirements can be frozen before starting the Design Phase, which is not true in most of the situations.
2. Requirements are elaborated over a period of time.
3. Strictly following this model takes longer time to finish the project as each step takes its own time.
4. Specialists are required to run each step, which is difficult in long-term projects.

1.2.2 A Layered Technology

Similar to the linear sequential model, the layered technology (refer Figure 1.9) introduced the concepts to use the software technologies and terminologies even better than the previous strategies. A layered approach ensures a much stronger product. The layered model of software engineering divides the activities into four broad categories:

1. Quality Process: For the successful engineering process there should be a strong base of quality processes.

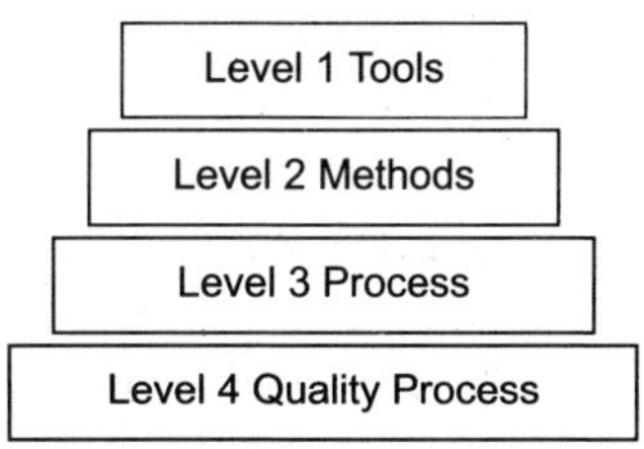

Figure 1.9 Layered Technology

2. Process: The software engineering processes ensure that all the technology layers work together and enable the timely development of the software system.
3. Methods: The methods in software engineering provide the technical capabilities to the system. The requirement analysis, design, modeling, development, testing, etc. are the tasks related to the methods.
4. Tools: The tools provide the support to the process and methods by making the tasks automated or semi-automated.

For example: the roads are layered with four or five layers (refer Figure 1.10). The bottom layer is a combination of clay and large stones, followed by another layer of smaller stones and tar. The next layer combines tar and even smaller stones for providing a neat finish. The quality of the roads depends on the tar used, the number of times run over by a roller machine and the time given for the settlement of those combinations. The layered technology is compared with many construction techniques for ensuring a well-built structure.

Layers are responsible for defining the activities in the order of execution. The layers begin with the requisition of input conditions and storing them at a location, and the next layers are dedicated to describing the most advantageous processes and methodologies to produce the preferred outcome. The last layer concentrates on submission of the designed product with the best quality beyond every difficulty. Developing a quality product includes important approaches, such as selecting and engaging valued resources and staff.

1.2.3 Prototyping Model

The product once developed using layered approach cannot be reversed easily. But in the real-life situations, the requirements are subject to numerous changes until they are implemented into the product. Thus with the ever-changing requirements, the product cannot proceed with mere predictions and prove to be right.

Hence the prototyping model (refer Figure 1.11) was proposed with a completely different strategy. Every product to be developed initially receives the requirements from the customers. With the given requirements, a sample or test model called the prototype is developed and displayed to the customer. The customer would respond by giving their opinion and rectifications needed over the current prototype. The prototype is altered until the customer is satisfied on the style, design and execution of the processes. Otherwise the development team continues to consider different options for creating the prototype. The final list of requirements reported will lead the development team to the next phase of design.

There are two types of prototypes (refer Figure 1.12) developed in this model, namely evolutionary and throwaway prototypes.

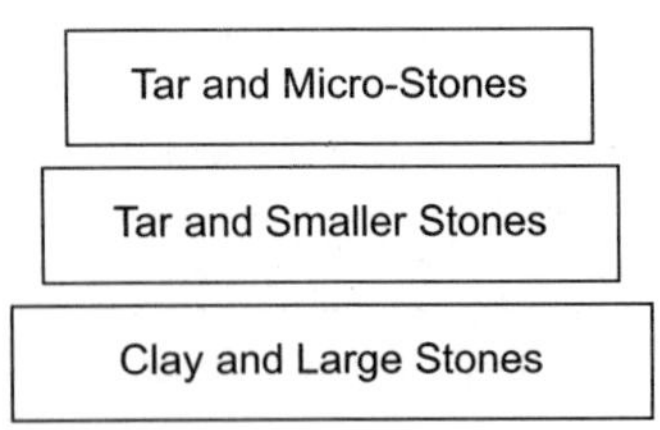

Figure 1.10 Example of Layered Technology

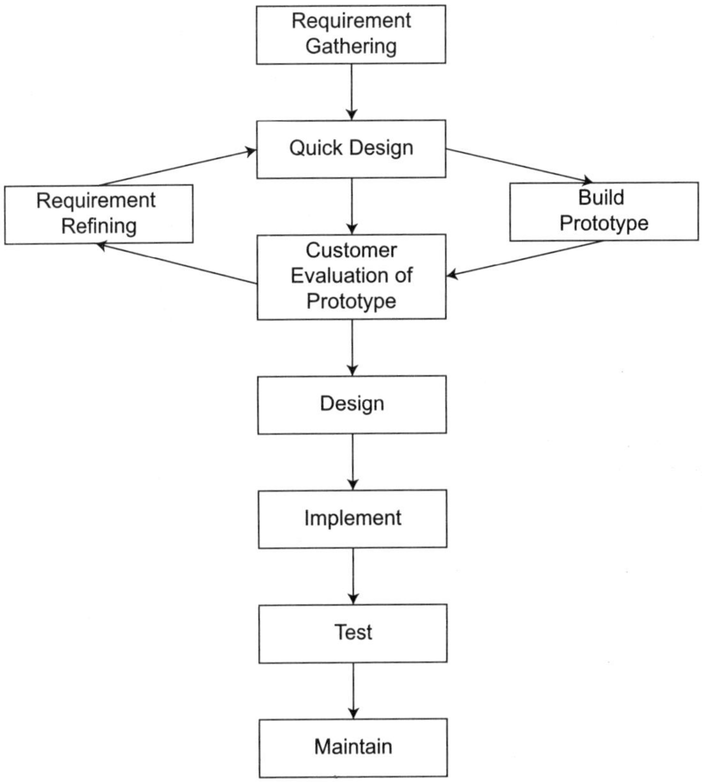

Figure 1.11 Prototyping Model

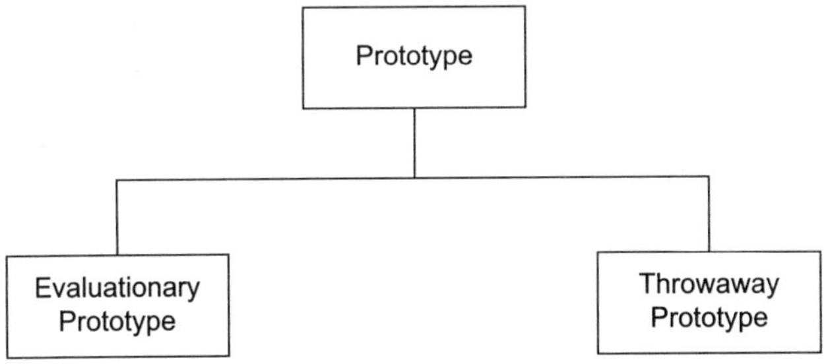

Figure 1.12 Prototyping Model

In the former type wrong prototype will be reused and the changes are implemented in that particular prototype. The new changes and corrections are updated in the existing prototype until the final list of requirements is obtained, without wasting the used resources. The other type, as the name suggests, destroys the wrong prototypes. Throwaway prototypes are proved to be wrong and thus the new prototypes are developed in the next stages. The resources used in the previous prototypes are either freed or rejected.

POINTS TO PONDER

Two types of prototypes are Evolutionary Prototype and Throwaway Prototype.

1.2.4 RAD Model

Rapid Application Development (RAD) model is the methodology proposed for quicker design and deployment of a product (refer Figure 1.13). This model includes the technologies and concepts of prototyping and iterative designs. RAD model requires a very short time span of 60–90 days for completing the software and delivering it to the customer. Unlike the traditional approaches, many innovative and simpler strategies of less time consuming activities are executed by the team of developers. RAD model proves to be the most preferable solution to quick needs and implementation of web-based applications. An organization needs to promote itself through World Wide Web by deploying a web application. This application should be simple to use and produce the desired results. Already present with numerous applications in web-based concepts, the customer may have to just refer the available applications and select from the same. Reuse of existing prototypes in the referred application facilitates faster deployment of the new application.

RAD model includes the following five phases for development:

1. Business modeling
2. Data modeling
3. Process modeling
4. Application generation
5. Testing and turnover

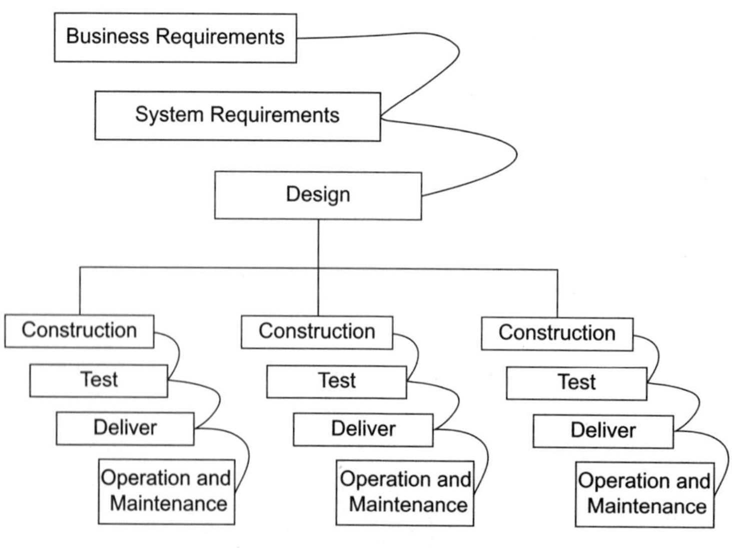

Figure 1.13 RAD Model

1.2.4 1 Business Modeling

Business modeling is the stage in which the types of information that are prime factors of the application are defined. The category of information involved in the processes, the procedures that use the information for various computations, initiators of the information and transfer of data between the processes are defined in the business modeling phase. With the details on the information being processed, the area of functionality of the application can be determined.

1.2.4.2 Data Modeling

The obtained information from the previous phase is filtered into useful and meaningful sets of data. They are refined into entities of high importance. The characteristics of the entities and their relationships are also defined in this data modeling phase. Attributes and entities enable a better understanding on the chief factors around which the entire processes are framed.

1.2.4.3 Process Modeling

Process modeling defines the activities needed to process the entities. Every instruction is framed in this phase. The instructions concern the processing of the data from the initial to the final stages of the application. Processes are defined for the storage and retrieval of the objects, their attributes and their associated metrics. Without proper design of these processes, the desired outcome cannot be achieved.

1.2.4.4 Application Generation

Application generation is a phase that uses automated tools to generate the working model of the designed application. The automated tools are used for faster analysis of similar components for reuse and save the time for new designs. Software tools have provided a wide range of amenities for faster deployment of an application with the same accuracy.

1.2.4.5 Testing and Turnover

The final phase is to test the correctness and consistency of the developed application. With such a short time and implementation of many reusable components, the accuracy of the application has to be tested with greater care. Reusing a component involves increased risk factors because the interfacing modules need to relate to the different modules of varying applications.

POINTS TO PONDER

The business modeling is the stage in which the types of information that are prime factors of the application are defined. Application generation is a phase that uses automated tools to generate the working model of the designed application.

1.2.5 Process Framework

Framework activities are processes of basic functionalities and are common to almost all software products. These actions can be applied to every product without any further modifications. For example, a user login form always commences further session of every user. The login form consists of only two requirements: username and password. The new application with the same requirement need not create a new design but can reuse the whole module. The login form also requires a database for storing the usernames and the corresponding passwords.

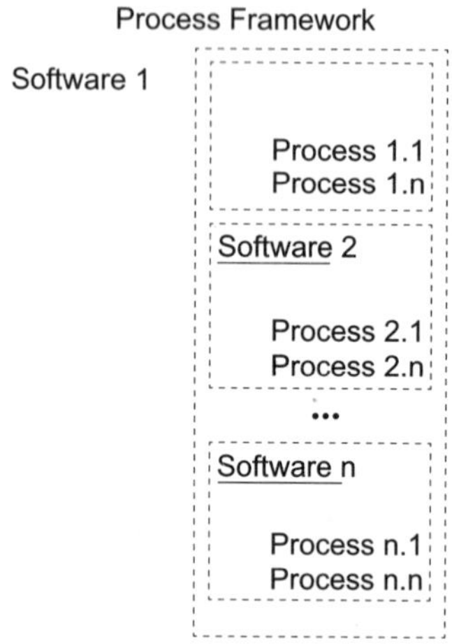

1.2.5.1 Analysis on the Process Framework Activities

1. **Gathering the requirements:** The customary process framework activities begin with the analysis and observations made on the requirements. This process called as communication phase involves intended customers and the team of developers. Concluding the communication process produces a list of gathered and approved requirements.
2. **Scheduling and staff allocation:** Based on the gathered information and the plans the model is selected for development, processes are framed and the analysis on the feasible risks are made. In addition, the schedule for the development is also agreed. Appropriate members are assigned depending on the knowledge possessed for every task.
3. **Design and Deployment:** The team members start designing and developing the coding for their assigned task. The design process may be eliminated by reusing a module. Efficient modeling and processes ease the risks at the later stages of a product.
4. **Supplementary Framework Activities:** The product being developed has to be checked at regular intervals to ensure that it is proceeding in the right path. Slight deviations from the intended path would result in starting over the whole process again. Risk analysis is also another major course of action to prevent disastrous outcomes at the end. Detection and mitigation of risks at the earlier stages would shorten the final stages.

POINTS TO PONDER

Framework activities are processes of basic functionalities and are common to almost all software products. These actions can be applied to every product without any further modifications

1.2.6 Capability Maturity Model Integration

Capability Maturity Model Integration (CMMI) is an approach for improving the process level operations (refer Figure 1.14). The CMMI is a compilation of many best approaches to enhance a product's efficiency, quality and endurance. It collects the strategies for improving the processes at many levels of functionality, on teams, tasks, subtasks, and the whole project. As the name denotes, many actively superior methodologies are combined and incorporated into a single process for betterment in many ways. Individual products have their own processes perfectly designed and implemented. Identifying such best processes and integrating them into the new products of other organizations is the ultimate goal of CMMI. The levels of CMMI are depicted as follows.

CMMI heeds about three areas:

1. Product and Service Development
2. Service Establishment and Management
3. Product and Service Acquisition

The products are the functional units to be designed and the services are functionalities of such products. Integrating numerous individual services into a product is the prime accomplishment of CMMI. The services are analyzed for resemblance, the level of matching and how well they suit themselves into the new product.

CMMI Levels

The CMMI model was evolved from the software CMM for integrating many different and well-organized models into new models. There are five levels of model that are evolutionary.

1. Initial
2. Repeatable
3. Defined
4. Managed
5. Optimizing

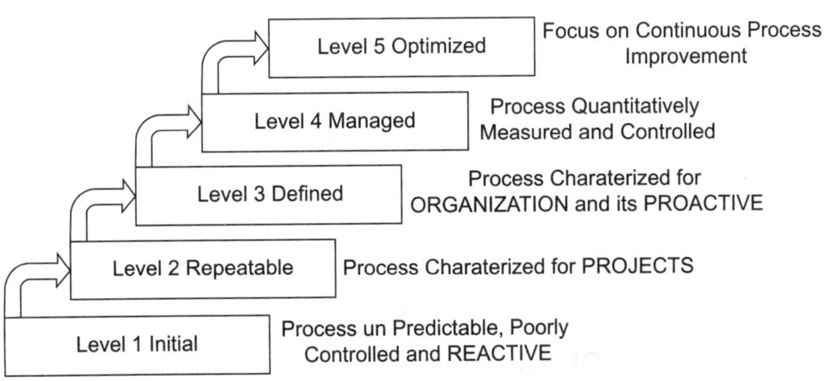

Figure 1.14 CMMI Levels

The 'initial' level is a poorly controlled phase with no proper designation of the schedule and the resources needed for the development. The primary requirements are analyzed, selected and advanced to the next level of the model. In the succeeding level, certain processes are chosen to produce the desired outcomes after organizing the schedule and resources needed. Yet those processes are in urge of additional consistency in the 'repeatable' level. The control processes are ordered and in position.

The third level 'defined' requires stringent measures to be followed. The processes are regulated, well understood and thus properly ordered. The consistency of all the processes is achieved in this stage. 'Manage' is the fourth level in which adequate steps are taken to determine the actions to update and upgrade the processes in the product. The level defines measures to widen the functionality of every process. This level forwards its outcome to the 'optimizing' level which concentrates on smoothening of approaches for better, faster and risk-free execution of the processes.

All these levels are proposed to achieve a process incremental model helping the development team to nominate an efficient product with minimal effort.

People Capability Maturity Model (PCMM) is another model of capability maturity model released in 1995 (book form in 2001) and it deals with the improvement of human resources (assets) of the organization. The people management process areas addressed in PCMM contain the common features and key practices.

1.2.7 Process Pattern

There has been a standard order of activities for completing a task. The order may not be altered, as the pattern has been proven as the most optimal solution. There will not be another alternative with an equal strength as an existing pattern. Patterns compile a set of activities or tasks or actions, following a prescribed sequence of execution. These patterns are considered in software lifecycles, customer communication, coding, reviews and test patterns.

1.2.8 Process Assessments

Every process has its own strength, weakness and associated risks. These factors have to be discovered to determine the level of applicability. With high risks and weaknesses a process cannot be applied to a product. The strength of all possible affirmative solutions has to be resolved to decide on the applicable solution and on the first alternative. Evaluation of the strengths, weaknesses and risks of every process against a process model is called as Process Assessment.

Process assessment describes the results of evaluation as

- Incomplete-Still needs revision and modifications
- Performed-Complete definition and satisfies the customer
- Managed-Controlled and maintained
- Established-Standard procedure applied
- Predictable-Defined with limits of execution
- Optimizing-Slight alterations required

1.3 SOFTWARE PROCESS MODELS

Software process models are systematic methods for controlling and coordinating the development of a software product achieving all the stated objectives. Methodical processes are followed from the initial requirements analysis process to maintenance phase. The systematic processes provide guidelines and prevent the development team deviating from the intended path leading to a failure.

Software process models help the developer team to recognize the following:

1. Set of tasks, subtasks and interfaces
2. Resources needed for every process
3. Adequate time span

1.3.1 Traditional Software Process Models

Traditional approaches of software process do not include the improved and simplified procedures attained today. Linear sequential model is already discussed in Section 1.2.1. Some of the traditional approaches are explained below.

1.3.1.1 Waterfall Model

Waterfall model (refer Figure 1.15) is the first and foremost methodology of Software Development Life Cycle (SDLC). The original methodology consisted of the following activities: Requirements Specification (phase 1), Design (phase 2), Construction (phase 3), Integration (phase 4), Testing (phase 5), Debugging (phase 6), Installation (phase 7) and Maintenance (phase 8). These activities proceed one after the other (like a waterfall). This conceptual model is based on the construction and infrastructure domain. The process model of construction activity is to design a blueprint, collect all the raw materials for construction, organize the workers and determine the time needed for the project to be completed.

The waterfall model was devised by Royce in 1970, and many organizations implemented this process model in earlier days. The requirements and conditions are obtained from the customer in the first step. This specification and analysis is obviously the first process that leads the development team. The development team will start designing a framework for achieving the objectives. The design of a software product is like a blueprint of a construction site. Following the efficient design, the coding begins. This resembles a construction with walls. Testing is the phase that ensures correctness of the product being developed. Without testing, no product will be allowed to be implemented in the real-world environments. The maintenance process cannot be predicted and assumed. The software needs additional features after deployment based on the demand from users and customers.

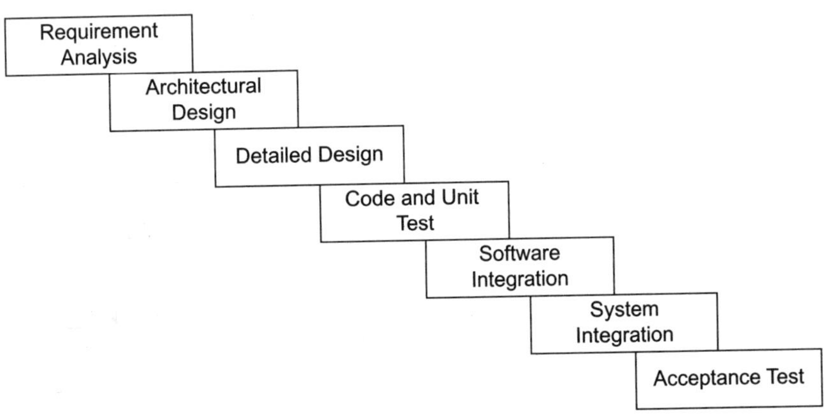

Figure 1.15 Waterfall Model

All the processes of the waterfall model ensue in sequential order. These processes are documented, and the confirmed information are printed and stored for future references. This model is also called as document-driven approach.

Advantages of Waterfall Model

1. Easy to understand
2. Easy for implementation
3. Widely used and known; hence, all stakeholders understand this
4. Identifies deliverables and milestones upfront

Disadvantages of Waterfall Model

1. Does not match well with reality
2. It is unrealistic to freeze the requirement upfront
3. Software is delivered only at the last phase
4. Difficult and expensive to make changes (CRs always)

1.3.1.2 Incremental Process Model

The incremental model is one of the evolutionary models, which overcame the drawback of the linear execution style of the waterfall model (refer Figure 1.16). Incremental model has the capability of multiple streams being progressed independently and simultaneously. Once the requirements are gathered, separate teams can work individually to produce a product assigned. The whole product is achieved by integrating all the individual components developed.

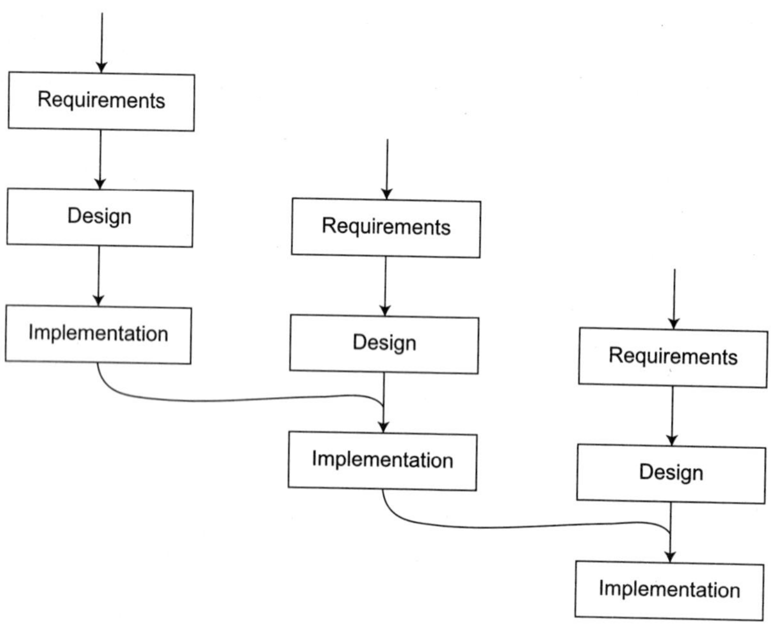

Figure 1.16 Incremental Model

The major advantage of the incremental model is that the consecutive steps do not have to wait until the preceding function completes its activity. This assists the team of developers to complete the design process much faster. The large and complex problem can be divided into a number of smaller and unique tasks, providing an easier chance to solve. Incremental model is suitable for applications that need additions and alterations in its contents after certain time period. For example, the shopping mall application needs to introduce new offers and concessions on the price list of all items for festive moments. They cannot be stable at all times and the waterfall model is not the right method to develop the product. The constraints on time and expenses justified the need of the incremental model at once. The already existing product can be combined with a new requirement by means of the integrator. Incremental model also facilitates the isolation of errors and faulty components at a faster rate, the modules being independent and capable of running without the support of other modules. Faulty modules remain intact until rectified.

Versions and higher configurations of an existing product can be developed with incremental process model. Links would have been established to permit the linkage of additional features in a next version. The links are the functional spots of the integrator component, which builds up a communication link between the versions.

Advantages of the Model

1. Quick feedback loop from business stakeholders
2. Focus on customer feedback
3. Customer feels the product early

Disadvantages of the Model

1. Scheduling of development is difficult with incremental model
2. Although the final product is given in pieces, tracking and monitoring is difficult
3. Testing needs to be exhaustive for each part

1.3.2 Evolutionary Process Models

The Evolutionary process models smoothen the progress of a software development in a number of ways. These strategies are like - creating prototypes and making steps overlapping and autonomous. The demerits of linear sequential models are eliminated and these models stand among the best process models in software development. Some of the evolutionary process models are described as follows:

- Spiral Model
- Components-based Development Model
- Formal Methods Model

1.3.2.1 Spiral Model

The spiral model was proposed by Boehm as an evolutionary model; it introduced the concept of risk analysis in the earlier stages of development process. Spiral model is also called Risk Spiral Model. This model combines the software development life cycle with Risk Management principles to control the risks at early stage of the project.

The previously mentioned methodologies did care about the detection of risks, but only at the near end of the project that increased their burden of rework. If a risk was found to be too disastrous, then the product had to be designed anew. Taking the importance of a risk management process and testing process into account, the spiral model defined new strategies.

A spiral model encompasses the iterative steps in a spiral representation as shown in Figure 1.17. Each circle in the model denotes a succeeding level of the previous state. These are divided task regions, which represent the selective process. The task regions may vary from the complexity level of different products.

The planning part includes the tasks for designing an efficient framework as a solution to the objectives. Planning also happens in steps: Life Cycle Plan is prepared first; Development Plan is prepared in the next level; and Integration Plan is in the last level.

In the Risk Analysis Phase the prototype is being developed. The risk analysis would report the identification and effects of the present risks in the prototype. Assessments of risks at every rotation of the spiral evolution reduce the problems and the time required for solving at the final stage. The risk analysis strategies have to be stringent enough such that even small errors are not left out. Prototyping, incremental and premature risks detection proves this to be an efficient method over the other process models. Elimination of risks occurs in next iteration. The feedback from the customers is noted for updating the next prototype. The final prototype is developed after stated suggestions are subjected to risk analysis process.

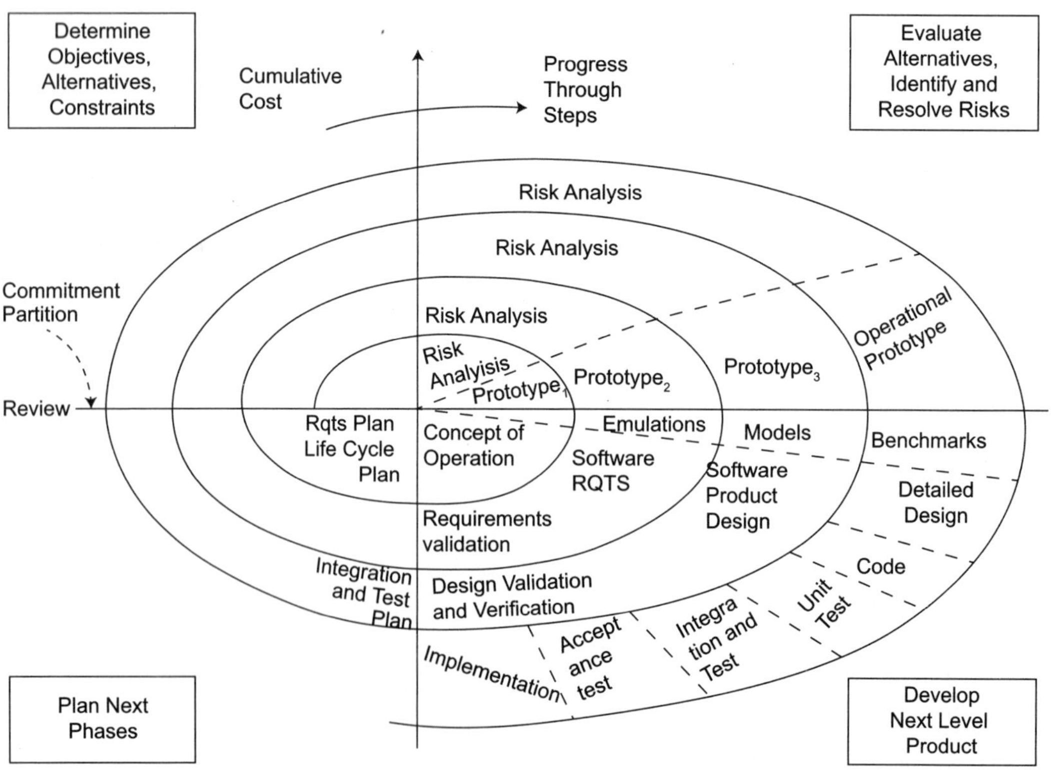

Figure 1.17 Spiral Model

Construction and release also happens in iterative fashion based on the base prototype developed. At every level it is also being strengthened and the final level is the final code to be delivered to the customer.

The number of iterations is determined by the team manager depending upon the rectifications made and completion of the product. The cost and schedule cannot be assumed right at the beginning phase as the prototypes are altered at every rotation. The team manager adjusts cost and time metrics after every circle. The spiral model is selected for software of higher level organizations.

POINTS TO PONDER

A spiral model encompasses the iterative steps in a spiral representation. Each circle in the model denotes a succeeding level of the previous state. There are divided task regions, which represent the selective process.

WIN–WIN Spiral Model

The results are based on the negotiations made by the customers. WIN–WIN result is decided for best negotiations. The customers have their own requirements and needs about the system or product. The customer wins by getting the system or product that satisfies the majority of the customer's needs. The developer has some criteria and budgets given by their organization and the developer wins by working to realistic and achievable budgets and deadlines. Boehm's WIN–WIN spiral model defines a set of negotiation activities at the beginning of each pass around the spiral.

The activities of the system are decided by identifying the key stakeholders and the win condition for the system. Negotiation of the stakeholders' wins conditions are reconciled into a set of winwin conditions for all concerned.

The WIN–WIN spiral model introduces three process milestones, called anchor points. These points help to establish the completion of one cycle around the spiral and provide decisions before the software project initiates its forthcoming cycle.

The anchor points represent three different views of progress

1. Life Cycle Objectives (LCO): It defines a set of objectives for each major software engineering activity.
2. Life Cycle Architecture (LCA): It establishes goal that must be met as the system and software architecture is defined.
3. Initial Operational Capability (IOC): It represents a set of objectives associated with the preparation of the software for installation/distribution, site preparation prior to installation and assistance required by all parties that will use or support the software.

1.3.3 Component-based Development Model

This development model is one of the evolutionary practices for developing a software product. Component-based development (refer Figure 1.18) introduced the concept of reusability to the full extreme. After analysis of the requirements, instead of entering into the design phase, components or modules of the existing similar products are checked for their match. Software reuse is the main motto of this evolutionary model. This model becomes the best in faster and cheaper deployment of the desired product.

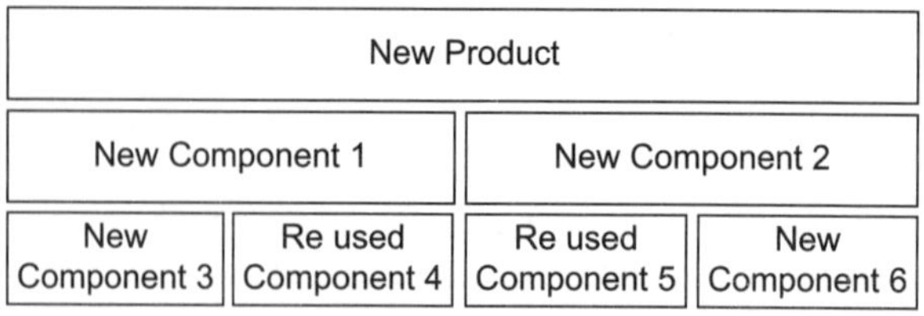

Figure 1.18 Component-based Model

1.3.3.1 Requirements Comparison

The requirements needed for a new product are compared with the recorded list of requirements from the existing products. The percentage of match between the new and existing requirements is evaluated. The matching level should be considerably high enough to be a perfect match.

1.3.3.2 Modification and Implementation

After a suitable match or a near-matching component is perceived, they are implemented in its place. But the question is whether a 100% match can be obtained or not. The result is a NO in most cases. No component can be directly implemented into a new product. The near-matching product needs some modifications to meet the stated requirements. Interfacing needs to be perfect to make the reusable component adapt to a new environment. Modifications and design of interfaces are comparatively easier than designing a whole new component.

1.3.3.3 Risk Analysis

Integration of existing modules has a greater level of risk than the newly developed components. The outcome of the product may be similar but the preceding and succeeding activities may disturb the new component. Hence, a more sincere risk analysis methodology is required for eradication of the risks.

The cost, manpower and time can be reduced to a great extent by using this evolutionary process model. Prototyping and spiral model enhanced the speed of developing a product by its means, and thus component-based software engineering.

1.3.4 The Formal Methods Model

There are some methodologies with strong technical and mathematical background for eliminating most of the errors missed out by other paradigms. Applying mathematical constants improves the rate of detecting errors relating to ambiguity, inconsistency and irregularity. The errors are quantified with notations and standards of mathematical expressions. Although this approach ensures an error-free software product, many other reasons prevent the usage of Formal Methods Model.

This model is

- Time consuming
- Training is needed for proper usage of mathematical expressions
- Customers and end users are mostly unfamiliar with the strategy

Knowledge on the mathematical implications is absolute in this case for detecting an error-free software product, whereas most products do not need such efficient methodologies considering the extra cost and time factors.

1.3.5 Software Engineering Process

Engineering process defines a dedicated and disciplined order of activities with a clear-cut view on how to reach the destination. A software product of high significance needs a pertinent roadmap leading to the objectives. Deriving such an efficient path toward the destination can be achieved only if the order is obeyed completely. The engineering process has gained expertise in many of today's applications and products. The engineering process, unlike other problem-solving strategies and design approaches, orders activities with respect to profound technical information of the product statement.

Software engineering process differs from the ordinary process models in the following means. Normal problem-solving strategies define and solve the problem by verification of the proposed solution, whereas in the engineering processes, the software requirements are analyzed and specified followed by designing and implementating a suitable product and, finally, verifying the designed product with respect to the specified requirements. Efficiency is promoted as the prime factors are narrowed down and the knowledge on the processes is imparted to all employees and participants. This knowledge is acquired by working on the previous successful projects and exposure to the technical background.

1.3.5.1 Primary Steps of Software Engineering Process

As mentioned, the initial step is to 'Analyze' and 'Specify'; the requirements are analyzed for general aspects, such as identifying the main objectives of the entire product and then the associated objectives of next importance and other indirect activities that support the objectives are analyzed, ensuring problem identification and determination of the functional and nonfunctional requirements. These functional and nonfunctional requirements are the resources, which have a direct or indirect impact on the outcome of the product. These analyses produce a list of specifications on the requirements and the identified problem.

'Designing and Implementation' of a well-organized technical plan would deduce the number of designs to meet the goals of the product. Once the design has been proved as an efficient solution, it can be developed as a prototype for examination by the customer for any changes. The prototype eliminates the chances of later delays if properly verified. A prototype is extended with full functionalities and implemented in the final product.

'Verifying' the deployed product involves the cross-checking of how well the whole product works in the real-time environment. Usually, the product is developed and enhanced by introducing additional features when the demands increase. The data design and the flow design are separately verified to ensure maximum efficiency. Functional design verifies the relationships among the existing processes and transfer of data in between the available functions without any conflicts.

1.3.6 Business Process Engineering

Software products are employed in almost every field, mostly in business applications. They are implemented in business areas and are never constant in backdrop as the customers and end users need features of global influence. Distributed environments of a same business process cannot be the same. Operational responsiveness is the ability of a software product to respond to different queries from the customers. The serviceable business processes are intended to respond, provide solutions regarding the business outsources and purpose. The detailed information on the available services to the customers is promised to every requester with 100% satisfaction.

Operational responsiveness advocates the principles, intentions and functional aspects of a particular organization. The organization develops a software product with its business processes employed. The software developed concentrates on the devoted business processes unlike other software solutions.

1.3.7 Fourth-generation Techniques

The Fourth-Generation Techniques (4GT) combines distinguished directory of software tools with assisting amenities for a software developer. Nonprocedural languages for databases maintenance and data manipulation operations, high end graphics interfacing, spreadsheet operations, drag and drop creations of web-based applications are some of the high-level 4G technologies. Imagine a whole system implementing all of these separate techniques into a single procedure. 4GT is designed to generate the source code by themselves with minimal specification from the designer. The developer does not put any extra effort other than inputting the complete requirements and other conditions. Positioning the preconditions, post conditions and the flow conditions at the correct location would be enough; the rest of the coding is taken care automatically by the procedure itself. After mentioning such conditions a nonoperational prototype is developed as a sample output. The foremost point is that the customer should be able to understand every functionality and error-prone zones in the prototype. This procedure aids in faster development and deployment of a software product with greater interactive sessions and participation of a customer. As all the processes eliminate the abstract terminologies, the entire process becomes completely visible from architecture to coding. The major drawback is that a customer himself may lack the optimal way of describing the requirements, and unwanted processes may be wasting the efficiency of the 4GT.

This technique includes the following processes:

- Requirements Specification
- Prototype Design
- Implementation
- Constructing the Original Framework

1.4 SOFTWARE PRODUCT

1.4.1 Characteristics of A Good Software Product

A good software product should possess the following characteristics:

Completeness–The developed software products should cover all the stated and agreed requirements without missing out any.

Consistency–Operations of the product should be stable and capable of handling the problems in implementation.

Durability–Customers may vary in technology requirement or geographical aspects, and the product should respond to a diversity of environments.

Efficiency–The product should not waste the resources, execution and waiting time of operations and the memory spaces allocated for the processes.

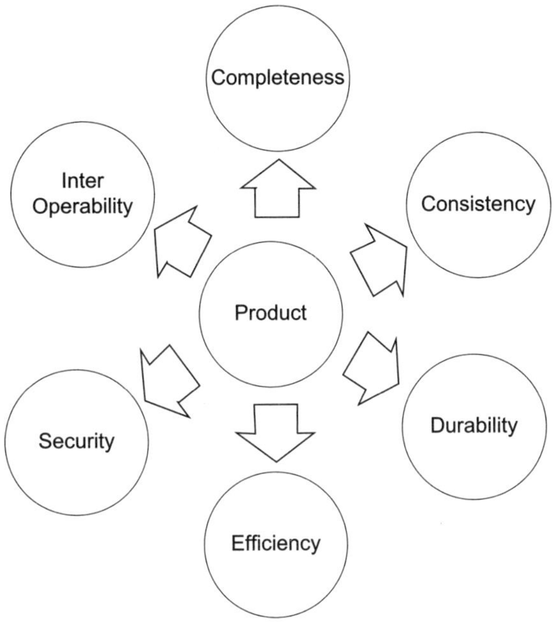

Figure 1.19 Product Characteristics

Security–The stored contents and the input statements of the software should be confidential and conserved if they possess a high significance.

Interoperability–Communication between other processes and environments should be enabled to apply a product universally.

1.4.2 Engineering Aspects of Software Product

A software product has different views of understanding. For technical and engineering aspects of software product, the customers see an abstract image of the product. Engineering aspects contemplate the description of a product in terms of its practical implications and has an impact over the platform. The technical aspects include the following:

1.4.2.1 Purpose

The aim of a software product needs a strong justification and thus represents the urge of being developed. The areas the product is supposed to cover, the necessary conditions for the product to work and the dependability on other processes are the primary aspects considered.

1.4.2.2 Process

Definition of the operations needs engineering skills for the right placement and interrelationships. The experience of the developers in previous projects aids them for better design approaches. Unlike normal methodologies, engineering process needs strong background on the construction ideologies.

1.4.3 Role of Management in Software Products

Management plays an important role in driving the processes of development in the right path benefitting the customer and the organization. The ultimate goal is to limit the budget and achieve a reasonable profit satisfying the quality standards. Managing the development process includes the following steps.

1.4.3.1 Defining the Vision

The goal of the organization is different from that of the objectives of the product. The vision is the force that motivates the development team. This defines the standards and principles of the organization apart from the desired outcomes of the product. The vision keeps the team on track to maintain the standards under any condition.

1.4.3.2 Defining the Plan

The plans are the operations derived with inputs and desires on the outputs. Plan is the blueprint, which has to be followed for achieving the outcomes. The plan encompasses many individual processes, structured in an ordered sequence. This structure defined is an optimal solution for perfect execution of operations. Without a proper plan, the solution cannot be obtained as promised. There are also additional plans designed as a backup in case of failures. The alternative plans are also numbered as the first alternative and so on. Secondary options are initiated only if the optimal plan fails to succeed.

1.4.3.3 Defining the Designation

Every participating member in a development process is assigned with a role and jobs to perform. The leader of the team has supplementary duties to ensure that every activity is performed as scheduled and planned. Every member follows the vision and principles of the organization besides their prescribed role. The members are categorized according to their authority level and decision-making capability. But all members have the liberty to express their views and ideas over the tasks.

1.4.3.4 Testing the Pathway

Testing is an important process in managing the defined plans. Testing includes the verification of the correctness and consistency of the product, checking on whether the resources are properly used, and whether budget and time constraints are met. Thus testing process ensures that the development team proceeds in the destined path as defined. This reports the deviation from the defined pathway, if the results are different from the sample outputs.

1.4.3.5 Supportive Activities

There are many associated processes beyond the normal procedures. Licensing the product as the registered outcome of a particular organization and marketing the product among the competitive organizations are some of the additional and adequate activities, which support the delivery of the software product. End user training has to be provided after delivery to ensure efficient utilization. Not every user can readily use the software product as many may lack the basic knowledge to understand the functionality.

The project management concepts are discussed in the following chapters:

Chapter 13–Project Management Introduction
Chapter 14–Risk Analysis and Management
Chapter 15–Communication and Team Management
Chapter 16–Project Time and Cost Management
Chapter 17–Project Stakeholder Management

1.4.4 Role of Metrics and Measurements

The terms representing the quality and quantity of a particular process are metrics and measures. They are used in determining the level of any means in the form of numbers or units. Understanding these terms needs the definition of data points. These are units that denote the condition of a process, the variables involved and the errors in a particular spot.

A 'Measure' is when the data point values are noted. A 'Measurement' is the representation of data points after review of a whole module or processes collectively. Measurements are of two types, either direct or indirect. Direct measurements denote the values after quantifying the errors in lines of code, resources misuse and memory misuses. Indirect measurements estimate the errors in functionality, complexity, reliability and maintainability.

'Metrics' are quantitative details obtained by monitoring and controlling the budget and time span of the product. Any deviations from the scheduled path would be reported by the metric values observed at regular intervals.

Software measurement and metrics are discussed in Chapter 9 Introduction to Software Measurement and Metrics and LOC Function Point and Object Oriented Metrics in Chapter 10.

1.4.5 Product Engineering Overview

Global implementation of software products has forced the introduction of many innovative techniques for delivering a high-quality product within a short duration and with low expenses. This urge had driven the methodologies toward simpler and faster completion motives. Agile methodology, Pair Programming, Extreme Programming and Reusability are some of the concepts that enabled today's goals. Product engineering methodology groups all these strategies and the resultant method has overcome all the drawbacks of traditional methodologies. This engineering model is purely dedicated to the development of products, differentiating it from software or process engineering concepts.

Summary

This chapter explains the definition of software. Software is defined as the tool with designated order of instructions, performing tasks to provide the desired results after obtaining the requirements of the users. Software has evolved from a single instruction provided to the machine to the present stage of decision-making software.

- The general software development phases are described as follows:
  1. Requirements Analysis Phase
  2. Designing Phase
  3. Coding and Testing Phase
  4. Implementation Phase
  5. Maintenance Phase
- General software characteristics are as follows:
  1. It should be complete
  2. It should be exclusive and reliable
  3. It should be precise
  4. It should be efficient
- Software Myths:
  1. Software products are better than implementing devices
  2. Reusability ensures better solution
  3. Additional features adds efficiency
  4. More designers means more delay
- Software engineering comprises strict disciplines that need to be followed to develop a programmable solution to solve the problems of the customers.
- Why study Software Engineering?
  1. It is the basic of any software development.
  2. Software engineering understands customer's needs and develops software.
  3. It helps the developers to understand the disciplines of software life cycle.
  4. It helps to develop software in efficient way.
  5. Software engineering teaches us the best practices of software development.
  6. Software engineering helps to write software that can be integrated easily with other software.
- Generic view of software engineering:
  1. Definition Phase
  2. Description Phase
  3. Deployment Phase
- Management of the software products depends on the following factors: Participants (people), Procedure and Product. Product is the outcome of the Project.

- Linear Sequential Model was the initial step in developing a software product, otherwise known to be the lifecycle model. Each activity is carried out in a linear order and no other order of execution is followed other than the flow mentioned.
- A layered approach ensures a much stronger product. Basic level is being ensured strongly before going to the next level.
- Prototype Model: With the given requirements, a sample or test model, called the prototype, is developed and displayed to the customer. There are two types of prototypes, namely evolutionary and throwaway prototypes.
- Rapid Application Development (RAD) model is the methodology proposed for quicker design and deployment of a product.
- Framework activities are processes of basic functionalities and are common to almost all software products. These actions can be applied to every product without any further modifications.
- Capability Maturity Model Integration is an approach for improving the process level operations. There are five levels of the model that are evolutionary.
    1. Initial
    2. Repeatable
    3. Defined
    4. Managed
    5. Optimizing
- The waterfall model was devised by Royce in 1970, and many organizations implemented this process model in earlier days. Incremental model has the capability of being progressed independently and simultaneously. A spiral model encompasses the iterative steps in a spiral representation. Each circle in the model denotes a succeeding level of the previous state. In component-based model, after analysis of the requirements, instead of entering into the design phase, components or modules of existing similar products are checked for their match.
- The Fourth Generation Techniques (4GT) combines distinguished directory of software tools with assisting amenities for a software developer.
- Characteristics of Good Software Product are as follows:
    1. Completeness
    2. Consistency
    3. Durability
    4. Efficiency
    5. Security
    6. Interoperability

Discussion Questions

1. Provide three examples of software projects that can follow waterfall model. Give specific examples.
2. Is it possible to combine various process models? If so, provide at least few examples.
3. List down the merits and demerits of the waterfall model.
4. Is it important to understand the customer's problem before developing a software solution? Justify.
5. Apply Spiral Model or Waterfall Model for the development of the Railway (Train) Reservation System.
6. Suppose that you have to build a product to determine the inverse of 2.656885 to four decimal places. Once the product has been implemented and tested, it will be thrown away. Which life-cycle model will be used? Elaborate reasons for the answer.
7. Consider an automated ticket-issuing system used by the passengers while reserving a seat in a government bus. Design an architecture based on the model.

Model Questions
PART A (Objective type)

1. All of the following are the components of software, except:

A. Instructions B. Rules C. Data D. Compact Disk

Answer: D

2. Which part of software packages explains about how to install (deploy) the software?

A. Computer Programs B. Procedures C. Data D. Documents

Answer: B

3. Which of the following is not an example of Operating System?

A. DOS B. Windows C. Linux D. PowerPoint

Answer: D

4. This type of software comprises programs that concern the operations for the hardware components of the computer.

A. System Software B. Application Software
C. User Interface Software D. Hardware Interface Software

Answer: A

5. Which of the following is not a part of General Software Development Phase?

A. Requirement Analysis Phase B. Customer Acceptance Phase
C. Coding and Testing Phase D. Implementation Phase

Answer: B

6. In which phase of the software development the customer and the business analysts interact with each other?

   A. Requirement Analysis Phase B. Design Phase
   C. Coding Phase D. Implementation Phase

Answer: A

7. All of the following are the types of requirements, except:

   A. Functional Requirements B. Nonfunctional Requirements
   C. Interface Requirements D. Feasibility Requirements

Answer: D

8. Which of the following is not a step in the Engineering Phase of the project?

   A. Feasibility Study B. Eliciting Requirements
   C. Requirement Analysis D. Design

Answer: D

9. Which of the following phase acts as a bridge between the requirement analysis phase and coding phase?

   A. Feasibility Study Phase B. Design Phase
   C. Testing Phase D. Eliciting Requirement Phase

Answer: B

10. All of the following are the types of Software Design, except:

    A. Architectural Design B. User Interface Design
    C. Deployment Level Design D. Database Design

Answer: D

11. Implementation Phase can also be called as Deployment Phase.

    A. True B. False

Answer: A

12. The software product being developed should meet all the requirements of the customer, no matter how complex the product is. This is referred to as:

    A. Software should be complete B. It should be reliable
    C. It should be precise D. It should be efficient

Answer: A

13. Unique software delivers its ensured performance to a particular problem (or) should concentrate on the given problem or requirements. This is referred to as:

    A. Software should be complete B. It should be reliable
    C. It should be precise D. It should be efficient

Answer: B

14. Unwanted steps and operations should be eliminated and shorter operations with the right solution are preferred. This is referred to as:

A. Software should be complete
B. It should be reliable
C. It should be precise
D. It should be efficient

Answer: C

15. The software being well organized indeed produces an optimal result at every moment of usage. This is referred to as:

A. Software should be complete
B. It should be reliable
C. It should be precise
D. It should be efficient

Answer: D

16. A software development process in which sequence of actions describes the order in which the execution of activities are planned and followed is called:

A. V-Model
B. Linear Sequential Model
C. Simple Model
D. Design Model

Answer: B

17. Which of the following is one of the disadvantages of Linear Sequential Model?

A. This is a very complex model
B. This model is not understood by most software professionals
C. This model assumes that requirements can be frozen before starting the Design Phase which is not true in most of the situations
D. This model needs more resources than other models

Answer: C

18. Which of the below is the lowest layer (categories) of the Layered Technology?

A. Quality process
B. Methods
C. Tools
D. People

Answer: A

19. Which software development model is used as the most preferable model for web-based application development?

A. CAD
B. RAD
C. TAD
D. Layered Model

Answer: B

20. Which of the below is not one of the phases of RAD Model?

A. Business Modeling
B. Data Modeling
C. Testing and Turnover
D. Program Writing

Answer: D

21. The Capability Maturity Model, released in 1995, which deals with the improvement of human resources (assets) of the organization is called

A. PCMM
B. ICMM
C. CMMI
D. CMM level 5

Answer: A

22. Which of the following is not a product characteristic?

A. Completeness B. Consistency C. Profitability D. Efficiency

Answer: C

23. Operations of the product should be stable and capable of handling the problems in implementation. This is referred to as

A. Completeness B. Consistency C. Efficiency D. Interoperability

Answer: B

24. The product should not waste the resources, execution and waiting time of operations and the memory spaces allocated for the processes. This is referred to as

A. Completeness B. Consistency C. Efficiency D. Interoperability

Answer: C

25. Communication between other processes and environments should be enabled to apply a product universally. This is referred to as

A. Completeness B. Consistency C. Efficiency D. Interoperability

Answer: D

26. Third Level of CMMI model is called as

A. Repeatable B. Defined C. Managed D. Optimizing

Answer: B

27. Name the level of CMMI in which adequate steps are taken to determine the actions to update and upgrade the processes in the product. The level defines measures for widening the functionality of every process:

A. Repeatable B. Defined C. Managed D. Optimizing

Answer: C

28. This level of CMMI concentrates on smoothening of approaches for better, faster and risk-free execution of the processes:

A. Repeatable B. Defined C. Managed D. Optimizing

Answer: D

29. This software development model was devised by Royce in 1970:

A. Waterfall Model B. Incremental Model

C. Iterative Model D. RAD Model

Answer: A

30. Which of the below is one of the characteristics of software

A. It should be exclusive and reliable B. It should be profitable

C. It should have some cost D. It is developed by some people

Answer: A

31. Which of the following is one of the disadvantages of linear sequential model?
A. This is a very complex model
B. This model is not understood by most software professionals
C. This model assumes that requirements can be frozen before starting the Design Phase, which is not true in most of the situations
D. This model needs more resources than other models

Answer: C

PART B (Answer in one or two lines)

1. Define the term Software?
2. What are the components of software?
3. Give any three examples of software.
4. List down the generic software development phases.
5. Define System Software?
6. Define Application Software?
7. What are the types of Requirements?
8. Name two Requirement Analysis Models?
9. Write notes on Software Maintenance.
10. Write any three characteristics of software?
11. What is Software Engineering?
12. Write any three reasons why we study Software Engineering?
13. What is process? Write notes on it.
14. Write notes on Linear Sequential Model.
15. List down few advantages of Linear Sequential Model.
16. List down the disadvantages of Linear Sequential Model.
17. Write notes on Layered technology.
18. What are all the categories used in the Layer Model of Software Engineering?
19. Write notes on prototyping model.
20. Name the types of prototypes.
21. What is evolutionary prototype mode?
22. What is Throwaway Prototype?
23. Write short notes on RAD Model.
24. Write short notes on CMMI?
25. What are all the levels of CMMI model?

26. What is process pattern?
27. What is Waterfall Model?
28. What are the advantages of Waterfall Model?
29. What are all the disadvantages of Waterfall Model?
30. What is incremental model?
31. What are the advantages of the incremental Model?
32. What are the disadvantages of the model?
33. What is Evolutionary process model?
34. Give examples of Evolutionary process models.
35. Write notes on Spiral Model.
36. What is WIN–WIN Spiral Model?
37. Write notes on Component-based Development model.
38. What are the characteristics of a product?

PART C (Descriptive type)

1. What are the phases of Software Development? Explain in detail.
2. Discuss the characteristics of software in detail.
3. Explain Generic View of Software Engineering in detail.
4. Explain the role of management in software engineering in detail.
5. Explain the linear sequential model in detail along with advantages and disadvantages.
6. Explain Layered Technology Model in detail.
7. Discuss the prototype model of software development in detail.
8. Discuss RAD model of software development in detail with its phases.
9. Explain Process Framework in detail.
10. Discuss CMMI Model in detail.
11. Explain Waterfall model in detail.
12. Explain Incremental Process Model in detail.
13. Discuss Spiral Model in detail.
14. Explain WIN–WIN Spiral Model in Detail.
15. Explain component-based model in detail.
16. Discuss the formal methods model of software development in detail.
17. Discuss fourth generation technique in detail.

Section 2:
Requirement Engineering

2

Requirements Engineering Principles

CHAPTER COVERAGE

1. *Introduction*
2. *What is Requirements Engineering?*
3. *Importance of Requirements*
4. *Types of Requirements*
5. *Steps Involved in Requirements Engineering*

2.1 INTRODUCTION

As discussed in the previous chapter, in software development, the software project life cycle starts with capturing the requirements of the project. Developing a product or executing a project is nothing but catering and taking the requirements to the next level. Gathering, documenting, disseminating and managing the requirements is the key to success of any project. Although it sounds easy, gathering the requirements effectively and managing them efficiently is a complex task and needs to be handled in a systematic manner. Requirements engineering principles help to do this task in a better way.

According to industry average, more than 90% of the software projects fail due to faulty or incomplete requirements capturing. This certainly gives an idea of how important this step is for the success of any software project. In this chapter, we will cover the different aspects of requirements engineering with steps and guidelines.

2.2 WHAT IS REQUIREMENTS ENGINEERING?

Before getting into the details of requirements engineering, let us understand what "requirement" is.

According to IEEE Standard 610.12-1990, requirement is defined as "a condition or capability needed by a user to solve a problem or achieve an objective" or "a condition or capability that must be met or processed by a system or system component to satisfy a contract, standard, specification, or other formally imposed documents."

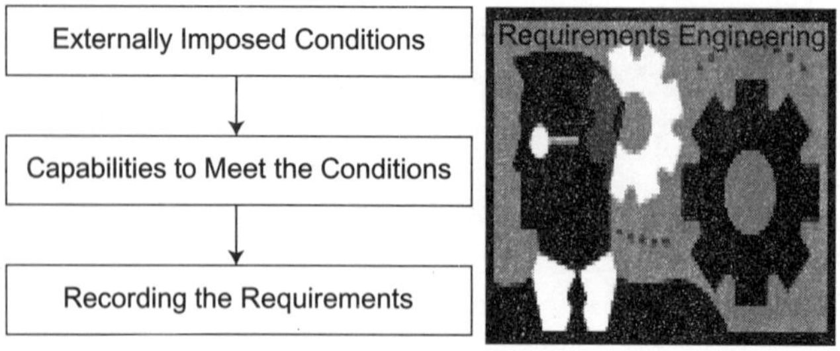

Figure 2.1 Requirements Engineering

This means that the requirements originate from the user's needs and are then captured and tracked to satisfy a contract or a specification.

Now, let us look into the definition of "requirements engineering."

"Requirements engineering is the discipline that explores the externally imposed conditions on a proposed computer system and tries to identify the capabilities that will meet those imposed conditions and recording the same in the form of documentation called the requirement document of the computer system."

The whole gamut of activities related to requirements from inception to understanding, tracking and maintaining the requirements is termed requirements engineering (Figure 2.1).

2.3 IMPORTANCE OF REQUIREMENTS

Requirements are the stepping stones to the success of any project. If software projects get started without properly understanding the user's needs or without exploring the multiple dimensions of the requirements, there will be misalignment at the end between the final result delivered and the user's expectations of the project resulting in a lot of rework.

In software development, primary focus is usually given to the construction phase, which leads to a lot of problems at the end.

A software project has to be completed within a specified time frame and budget. However, in some cases, rework has to be done due to incomplete requirements understanding, which is the primary cause of schedule and budget overruns.

Figure 2.2 shows the relative cost of repairing a defect at each stage of the software project life cycle. It is evident that the earlier the error is detected, the easier and cheaper it is to fix the error.

For example, if a defect in the requirements is found at the requirements review stage, then it will cost less (e.g., $x) to fix the issue, but as this faulty requirement percolates through the later stages it would cost more to fix the same issue: 3 times the cost to fix it during the design stage, 5 to 10 times the cost to fix it during the construction stage, 10 times the cost to fix it during the system testing stage of the project and 10 to 100 times the cost to fix it during the postrelease phase. Therefore, identifying and fixing errors at an early stage will cost less to the organization.

This signifies that capturing the requirements completely and correctly at the early stages of the project life cycle is essential to keep the project within the budget so that it is profitable. The only way to ensure this is to follow a disciplined requirements engineering process.

Cost correct an Error		Stage detected				
		Requirements	Design	Construction	System Test	Post release
Stage introduced	Requirements	1X	3X	5-10X	10X	10-100X
	Design	-	1X	10X	15X	25-100X
	Construction	-	-	1X	10X	10-25X

Figure 2.2 Cost of Fixing Errors at Different Stages

POINTS TO PONDER

The cost of fixing an error in the system increases exponentially with the stage of the project.

2.4 TYPES OF REQUIREMENTS

Requirements can be categorized into three main types: functional requirements, nonfunctional requirements, and interface specification.

Types of Requirements

- Functional Requirements
- Non Functional Requirements
- Interface Specification

2.4.1 Functional (User) Requirements

The set of requirements (Figure 2.3) that defines what the system will do or accomplish is called functional requirements. These requirements determine how the software will behave to meet users' needs.

Figure 2.3 Functional Requirements Characteristics

The requirements may be for performing calculations, data manipulation, processing, logical decision-making, etc., which form the basis of business rules. Functional requirements are often captured in use cases. Functional requirements are the main drivers of the application architecture of a system. An example of functional requirement is a retail shop billing software having the functionalities of capturing commodity prices, calculating discounts, generating bills, printing invoices, etc.

2.4.2 Nonfunctional (System) Requirements

Functional requirements are supported by nonfunctional requirements (see Figure 2.4). The quality attributes and the design and architecture constraints that the system must have are called nonfunctional requirements (NFRs).

Some of the quality attributes of the system from an end user's perspective include performance, availability, usability and security and from a developer's perspective include reusability, testability, maintainability and portability.

NFRs as shown in Figure 2.4 are critical in most of the software projects than functional requirements. NFRs cater to the architectural needs of the overall system, whereas functional requirements cater to the design needs of the overall system.

Some examples of NFRs are:

"The system should be available 24 × 7" (Availability)

"The system should save or fetch 1000 records in 1 second" (Performance)

NFRs may be related to the product or the organization or to the external requirements of the system. Product-related NFRs include performance, availability, maintainability, portability, reliability, security, scalability, testability and usability, whereas organization-related NFRs include standards requirements and implementation requirements. External NFRs include legal requirements and ethical requirements.

Measuring NFRs We need to first define measurable criteria for each NFR and then realize the metrics by measuring it. For example, Availability can be first defined in terms of percentage and then define the duration within which we are going to measure it. To measure the availability, we can assume the availability of the system in the past 1 week to be 100% as the system was running continuously without any downtime (another related metrics). A Service Level Agreement is established with the customer for setting an agreed level of availability depending on the stability of the system. If the system is more stable without any downtime, we can fix the agreed limit of availability as 100%. If the system is not stable, then there will be frequent system shut downs and the target availability needs to be reduced accordingly (e.g., 95% or 90%).

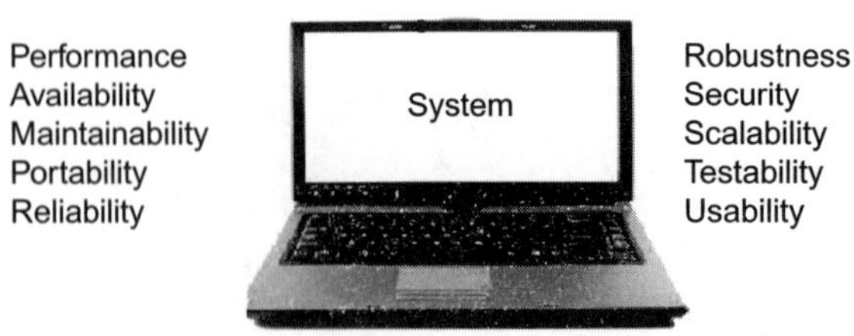

Figure 2.4 Nonfunctional Requirements Characteristics

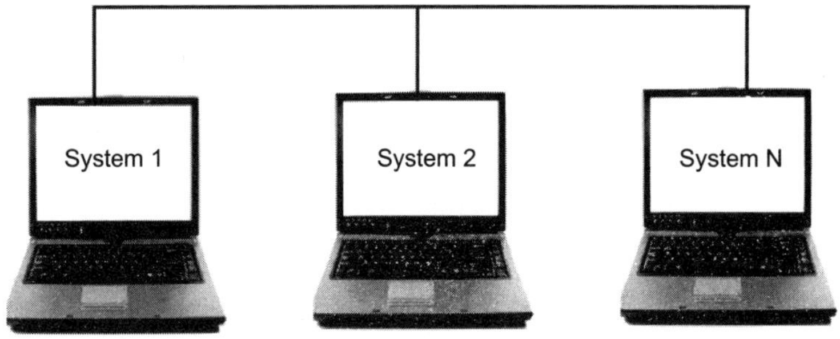

Figure 2.5 Interface Specification Characteristics

Approaches to NFRs NFRs can be approached in two ways- product-oriented and process-oriented approaches. As the names suggest, the product-oriented approach concentrates on the product and its associated NFR aspects, while the process-oriented approach concentrates on the process and its associated NFR aspects. Second, the NFRs can be approached qualitatively and quantitatively. The qualitative approach concentrates on non-numeric-related NFRs, whereas the quantitative approach focuses on the numeric aspects of the NFRs.

2.4.3 Interface Specification

Most of the software systems do not work alone and need to interact with other systems in order to work (Figure 2.5). They interact with many other systems to receive and send data, get help in processing logic, store information in other systems, etc. The interaction requirement of one system with another is defined in the interface specification.

Interface specification helps in building different systems in such a fashion that they can seamlessly interact with each other to produce the desired outcome. Let us consider our previous example of the retail shop billing system. It may interact with another system – an inventory system – to ensure that the warehouse keeps track of the stock of the material at hand. The protocol of how these two systems interact with each other are captured in the interface specification document.

POINTS TO PONDER

Functional requirements define what the system must do to fulfill the user's needs, nonfunctional requirements put forth the constraints on design and architecture, whereas interface requirements define how the system will interact with other external systems.

2.5 STEPS INVOLVED IN REQUIREMENTS ENGINEERING

Although the requirements engineering process may vary based on the application domain, a few generic steps are common across all types of software projects.

Requirements engineering includes requirements development and requirements management (Figures 2.6 and 2.7). The basic aims of the requirements engineering process are to provide a

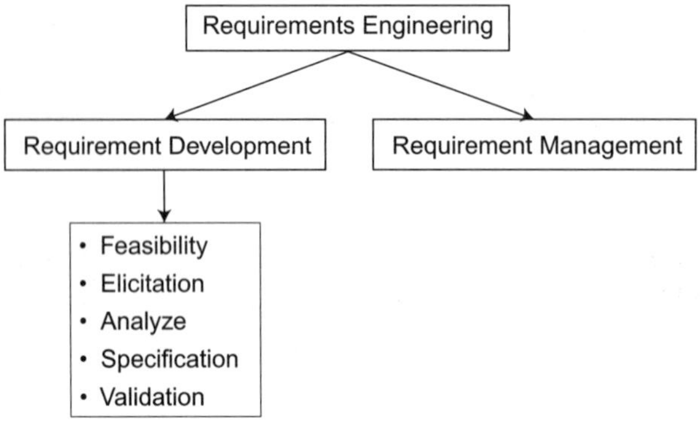

Figure 2.6 Requirements Engineering Steps

mechanism to understand the user's needs, analyze the need, assess the feasibility, specify and validate the requirements and proposed solution, and manage the requirements over the whole life cycle of the project, which are discussed in the following sections:

- Feasibility study
- Requirements elicitation
- Requirements analysis
- Specifying and validating requirements
- Requirements management

Figure 2.7 shows how each step of requirements engineering is related to each other.

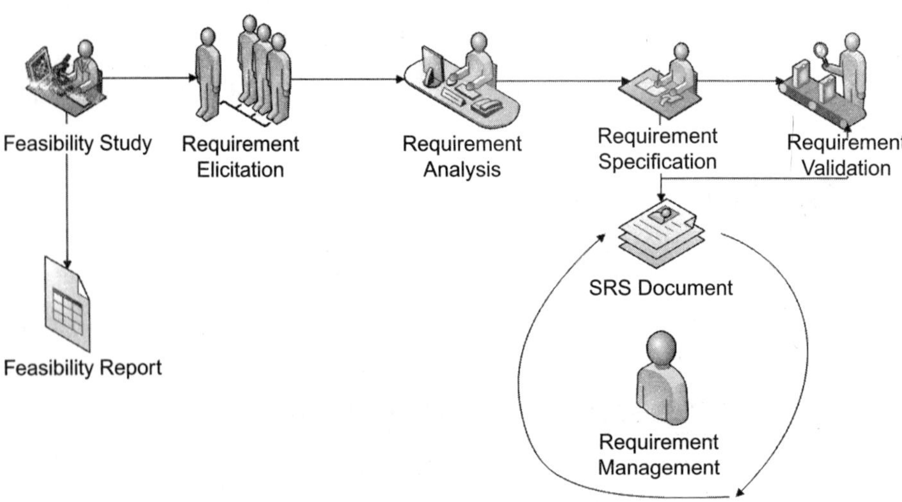

Figure 2.7 Requirements Engineering Process

2.5.1 Feasibility Study

Feasibility study is the first step of the requirements engineering process. The worthiness of the proposed software system should be determined before spending efforts on building the system.

A feasibility study (Figure 2.8) helps in deciding whether the proposed system is worthwhile and has the following characteristics:

- Whether the system contributes to organizational objectives
- Whether the system can be developed using the current available technology and within the specified time and budget
- Whether the system can easily be integrated with other surrounding systems as required by the overall architecture

Thus, feasibility can be classified into three broad categories (Figure 2.9): operational feasibility, technical feasibility and economic feasibility.

Operational feasibility: This checks the usability of the proposed software. If the operational scope is high, then the proposed system will be used more ensuring the acceptance from the sponsors of the project.

Technical feasibility: This checks whether the level of technology required for the development of the system is available with the software firm, including hardware resources, software development platforms and other software tools.

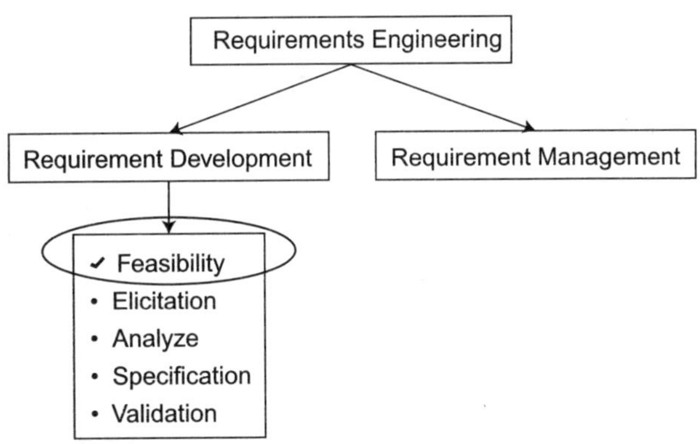

Figure 2.8 Requirements Feasibility

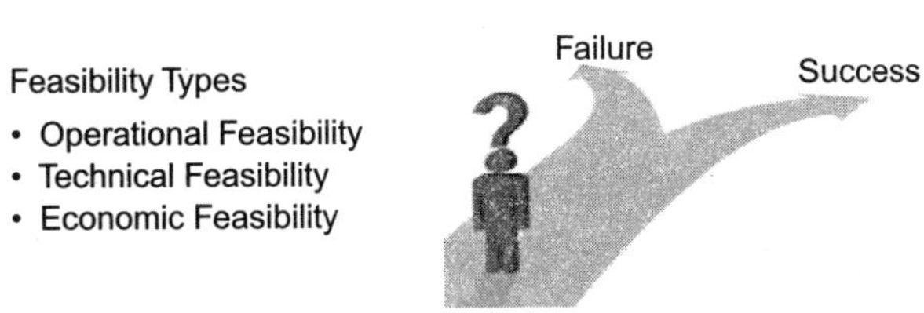

Figure 2.9 Feasibility Types

Economic feasibility: This checks whether there is scope for enough return by investing in this software system. All the costs involved in developing the system, including software licenses, hardware procurement and manpower cost, needs to be considered while doing this analysis. The cost–benefit ratio is derived as a result and based on the justification the stakeholders make a decision of going ahead with the proposed project.

POINTS TO PONDER

Before investing in any project, the sponsors will be keen to know whether the investment is worth and the project can succeed technically as well as economically. Thus, a feasibility study step provides an insight to all stakeholders at the very beginning.

2.5.2 Requirements Elicitation

Requirements elicitation is the second step of the requirements engineering process (Figure 2.10).

In this phase, the source for all the requirements are identified and then by using these sources, the user's needs and all the possible problem statements are identified. Although it looks simple, this phase is often iterative and at the end of each iteration the customer needs may become clearer and new needs may emerge. The stakeholders involved during this phase include end users, managers, development and test engineers, domain experts and business analysts.

2.5.2.1 Identifying Stakeholders

Before the requirements are gathered for a system, it is important to know the people who can contribute and help gather the requirements. If key stakeholders are not identified during the requirements elicitation phase, it can lead to nonidentification of important requirements causing rework at a later stage. Thus, stakeholder identification is the first step in starting the requirements elicitation.

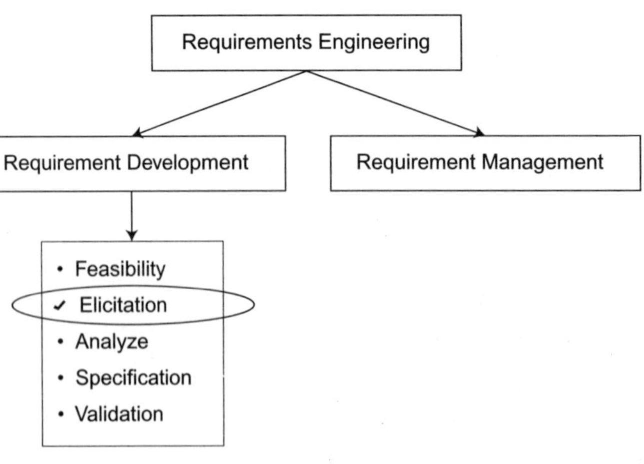

Figure 2.10 Requirements Elicitation

Stakeholders are people or entities (organizations) actively involved in the projects. They are affected by outcomes of the defined project.

Discussion Questions

Can you think of the important stakeholders for a medical insurance claim processing software development project?

1. ________________________
2. ________________________
3. ________________________
4. ________________________

2.5.2.2 Characteristics of Stakeholders

Stakeholder interests may be either positively or negatively impacted by the performance of the project. Stakeholders may have an influence on the project and its results. Thus, it is important for the project manager to identify all the stakeholders and their requirements (sometimes requirements may be implicit and not explicitly stated – the project manager should also try to understand such requirements). Stakeholders may have conflicting interests and objectives; therefore, managing them may not be easy. Involving stakeholders in the project phases improves the probability of success of the project.

Stakeholder involvement is always situation-specific; what works in one situation may not be appropriate in another. Ask a few simple questions to identify appropriate and required stakeholders. Although it is not intended to provide an exhaustive list of questions here, this will give you a fare idea of the type of questions appropriate for this purpose:

1. Who are the people likely to be affected/benefited?
2. Who is responsible for what we intend to do?
3. Who is likely to move for or against what is intended?
4. Who can make what is intended better?
5. Who can contribute to financial and technical resources?

POINTS TO PONDER

Properly identifying stakeholders and managing the stakeholder's expectation hold the key to success of any project. Maintaining a prioritized list of stakeholders according to their say in the project helps in avoiding the bottlenecks created by them at the later stages of the project.

2.5.2.3 Problems in Eliciting Requirements

There are several problems which can surface while eliciting requirements, which are discussed below (Figure 2.11).

- **Users not sure about the requirements:** This situation arises very often when the system to be developed is a completely new system and there is no corresponding manual system or any

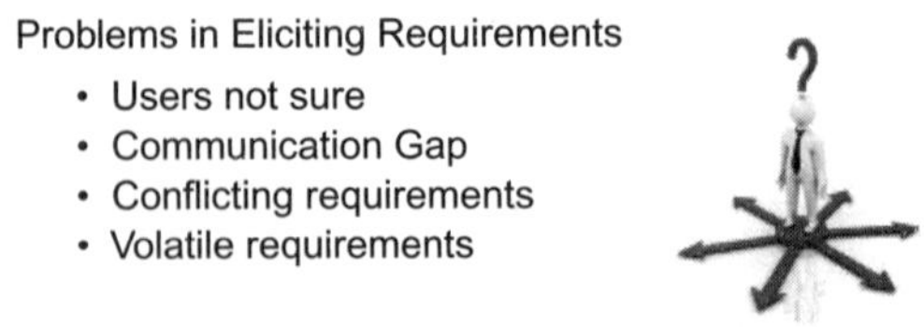

Figure 2.11 Problems in Eliciting Requirements

previous software system that can be analyzed to get the requirement. In this situation, the users will be looking for either similar systems developed elsewhere or mock-up screens, workflows, prototypes, etc. during the requirements gathering stage, which will aid their imagination in coming up with the requirements for the new system.

- **Communication gap:** Even if the end users and stakeholders are clear about the need for developing the new system, they may find it difficult to express it in a concrete manner due to their less exposure to the computing systems. They may state the requirements in an ambiguous or nontestable fashion. Sometimes the obvious basic requirements may be omitted and they concentrate on explaining the peripheral requirements. The system engineer needs to drive the stakeholders in the right direction throughout the requirements gathering stage so that they focus only on the most important requirements.
- **Conflicting requirements:** This problem increases with the number of stakeholders involved in the project. There may be conflicting needs and priorities for each stakeholder based on the business areas they are covering. For example, a stakeholder from the marketing team will try to provide requirements that will expedite the creation of new products, while the end users of the system will look for efficient screens that help easy data capture. During the analysis phase, the requirements analyst and the client should collaboratively discuss and resolve any conflicting requirements from multiple stakeholders.
- **Volatile requirements:** Requirements may get changed during the elicitation stage due to the entry of new stakeholders who have different perspectives of the system. Although this is helpful in clarifying the requirements better, it sometimes creates friction between the requirements engineer and the stakeholders due to continuous change in the scope.

Discussion Questions

Suppose you are the end user of a mainframe-based banking software that is going to be replaced by a new Java-based software. The requirements engineers from this new company have approached you to understand the requirements for the new system? How you will ensure that they have noted down all your requirements correctly?

1. ______________________________
2. ______________________________
3. ______________________________
4. ______________________________

2.5.2.4 Requirements Elicitation Techniques

Several techniques (Figure 2.12) can be employed for eliciting the requirements as listed below. Based on the project scope, domain, customer preparedness, etc., one or a combination of techniques needs to be used for gathering the requirements in an organized manner.

- Interviewing
- Focus groups
- Facilitated workshops
- Prototyping
- Questionnaires
- Brainstorming
- Direct observation
- Apprenticing

Interviewing Begin the interviews with the stakeholders who are believed to have complete understanding of the requirements. Face-to-face interactions with users through individual interviewing is the primary source of requirements (Figure 2.13).

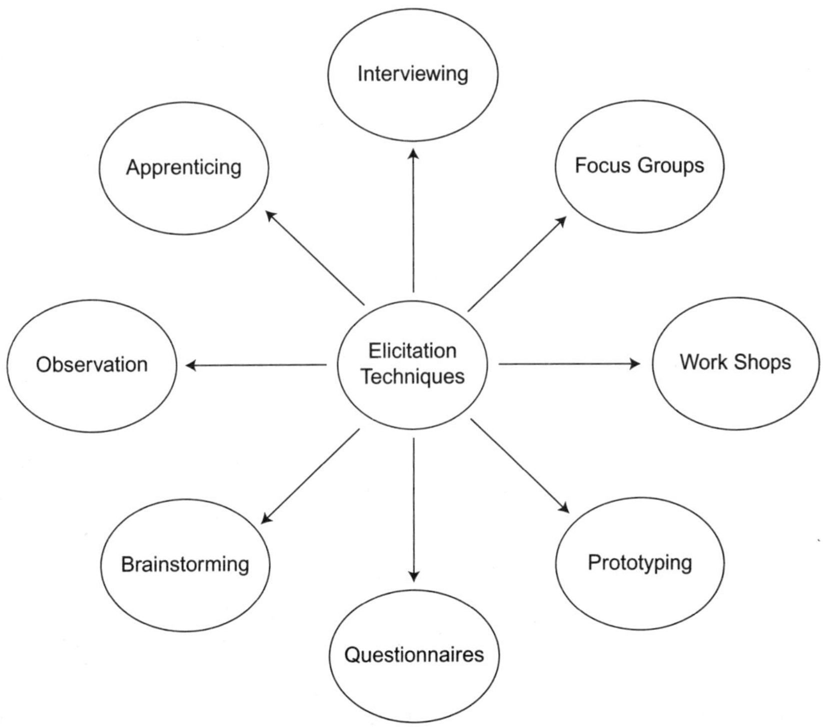

Figure 2.12 Requirements Elicitation Techniques

Figure 2.13 Interviewing Technique

Interviewing is an important and effective way to gather and validate the requirements. Interviewing is used when the requirements are detailed and differing opinions are likely or are sought. In distributed agile projects, interviewing is the main technique used to gather requirements. Even if the team and the customer are collocated, we can use interviewing to clarify doubts. During the execution of the project, at any point in time, interviews may happen with the product owner to clarify doubts.

Focus Groups A focus group is similar to the interviewing technique, but has a group of 6 to 10 people at a time. We can get a lot of information during a focus group session because of the enhanced level of discussion among the group members.

Types of Focus Groups There are several types of focus groups that facilitate group discussions, which are discussed below.

Two-way focus group: As the name suggests, two focus groups are used. One focus group will continuously watch the other focus group so that the interaction happens as per the predefined rules and proper discipline is followed.

Dual moderator focus group Model 1: Instead of two different focus groups as in the above model, two moderators do the job. One looks into the discipline and the other looks into the content flow. This will ensure the smooth progress of the session as well as the entire topic of discussion is covered.

Dual moderator focus group Model 2: In this model also two moderators are present but they take completely opposite stands, that is, if one says that something is possible, the other says why it is not possible. This is more helpful in finding the pros and cons of both views and will be helpful to make a final decision.

Respondent moderator focus group: Respondents are asked to act as the moderator temporarily and because of this they take ownership of the session. Hence, we can collect the requirements successfully and the outcome will be helpful (Figure 2.14).

Client participant focus group: Client representatives participate in the discussion and will ensure ownership from the client on the decision taken. Most of the projects fail at the last stage of the project life cycle, particularly in the User Acceptance Testing phase. The reason being the client may not take ownership as the end users have more ownership at that stage. However, client participant focus groups help overcome these kinds of problems.

Mini focus group: Groups are restricted to four or five members rather than 8 to 12 and is helpful to avoid confusion and manage and gather the requirements quickly.

Teleconference focus group: Telephone network is used to facilitate the discussion sessions.

Online focus group: Computers connected via the internet are used to facilitate the discussion sessions.

Facilitated Workshops Workshops (Figure 2.15) can be used for rapidly pulling together a good set of requirements. A workshop is a very quick and best way to gather requirements compared with all other techniques. A workshop is expensive because it involves many people, but it saves a large amount of time. Requirements are discussed at a high level. Workshops are useful in situations where

Figure 2.14 Focus Group Technique

Figure 2.15 Facilitated Workshop Technique

the requirements are focused on one area of business in which the participants have knowledge and consensus is being sought. In workshops, different alternatives are given to the customers so that they choose the appropriate options.

Prototyping The word "prototype" is derived from the Greek word "prototypon." Prototypes and models are the best ways of presenting ideas to users. They give users a glimpse of what they might get. More requirements are likely to emerge when users are able to see what they will get as an outcome of their suggestion. This technique aims to get users to express their requirements. Prototyping is used to get feedback from users. Business logic may not be coded in prototyping and experimental systems are developed using prototyping. It is actually the initial version of the system.

POINTS TO PONDER

During the requirements phase, the prototype is generally document-based, where the user interface design, use cases, overall look and feel, navigation, etc. are discussed with the end users. The scope of a working prototype normally comes at the construction phase.

Types of Prototypes As discussed in Chapter 1, prototypes are classified into two broad categories, namely, evolutionary prototype and throw away prototype. The former type is reused and the changes are implemented in that particular prototype. The new changes and corrections are updated in the existing prototype until the final list of requirements is obtained, without wasting the used resources. The latter type, as the name suggests, destroys the wrong prototypes. Throw away prototypes are proven to be wrong and thus the new prototypes are developed in the subsequent stages. The resources used in the previous prototypes are either freed or rejected.

Figure 2.16 shows the different types of prototypes, which are discussed below.

Proof-of-principle prototype (bread board): Only the intended design is tested and visual appearance is not in the scope of this prototype. For understanding purposes, a few working codes are part of this prototype.

Form study prototype: Only visual appearance is considered and the functionalities are not considered.

Visual prototype: It simulates the appearance, color, fonts and surface textures of the intended product, but it does not represent of the final function(s) of the final product.

Functional prototype: It is also called a working prototype, which means it simulates the actual functionality of the intended work.

Questionnaires Questionnaires can be used to collect input from multiple stakeholders quickly, which can be consolidated to create a list of requirements. As the stakeholders targeted for the questionnaire need not be physically present with the requirements elicitation team, this process can be run with a large number of participants in quite an inexpensive fashion.

However, the questionnaires have their own limitations such as designing an exhaustive questionnaire becomes difficult especially if the complexity of the system is high. As the stakeholders are not in direct contact with the elicitation team, there may be ambiguity in questions that lead to erroneous responses. Moreover, the response rate may be low and may need a lot of follow-up for getting sufficient input through this technique.

Brainstorming Brainstorming is a powerful technique using which a large number of requirements or ideas can be generated in a short period of time.

- In these sessions, members meet face-to-face and rely on both verbal and nonverbal interactions to communicate with each other.
- The main purpose of the brainstorming technique is to get as many ideas as possible to obtain different views of the requirements, thereby helping to capture better requirements.

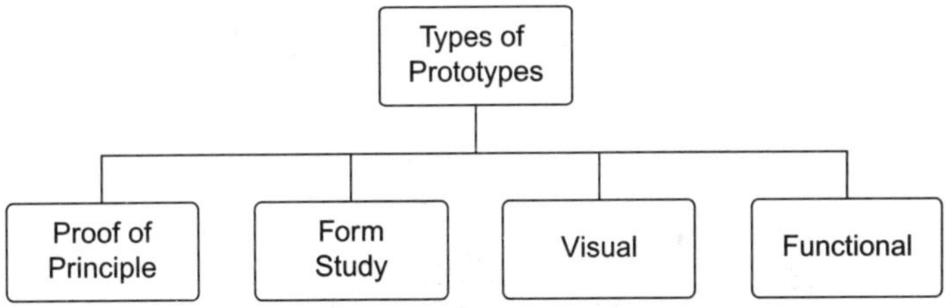

Figure 2.16 Types of Prototypes

In a typical brainstorming session, about six people are involved and the group leader states the problem in a clear and understandable manner so that it is understood by all the participants involved. Members are allowed to suggest as many alternatives as they can in a given period of time. No criticism is allowed. Alternative ideas generated are also recorded and are used for later analyses and discussions. Brainstorming, however, is merely a process used to generate ideas and may not be effective for decision-making purposes.

Discussion Questions

Do you think the brainstorming sessions can help in a situation where the end users do not have a clear idea of the features they want from the software to be developed?

1. ______________________
2. ______________________
3. ______________________
4. ______________________

Direct Observation and Apprenticing In many cases a new system is developed to replace an existing system, in which either a lot of manual intervention is involved or it is not efficient and suitable for doing the job. In such scenarios, it is very useful to gather knowledge of the requirements by observing (Figure 2.17) what is actually done by the user of the system. This is far more powerful than going through the documents of the capability of the existing system as it provides an opportunity to capture the real objective behind creating the new system.

A better technique will be the apprenticing model where the requirements engineer performs the tasks that the user of the system carries out. Although this requires the understanding of the business

Figure 2.17 Observation Technique

process carried out by the user, this has a huge benefit of getting an in-depth insight into what tasks the users perform with the current system and the areas they need improvement or automation in the new system.

2.5.3 Requirements Analysis

Requirements analysis is the third step of the requirements engineering process.

The aim of the elicitation phase is to gather the requirements, whereas in the analysis phase the requirements are understood in detail. This is the phase that bridges the gap between requirements engineering and design (Figure 2.18). Thus, the requirements analyst refines the data and functional and behavioral constraints of the software, which acts as the input to the design. Various modeling techniques are used during the analysis phase, which helps in problem evaluation and solution synthesis during this stage.

The focus areas for the analyst during this stage are

a. Externally observable data objects
b. Flow and content of information
c. Software functionality elaboration
d. Behavior of the software on an external input
e. Interface requirements
f. Design constraints

After analyzing each of these areas, the analyst starts working on the solution part. The system architecture, database requirements, etc. are discussed with the customer to ensure that the system design is based on the customer's need. For example, the data flow analysis may reveal that a real-time interface is not required in the system, which will reduce the complexity and cost of the proposed solution. The analyst creates models of the system to capture the data requirement and flow, functional processing, operational behavior and information content. These models become the stepping stones for the software design phase.

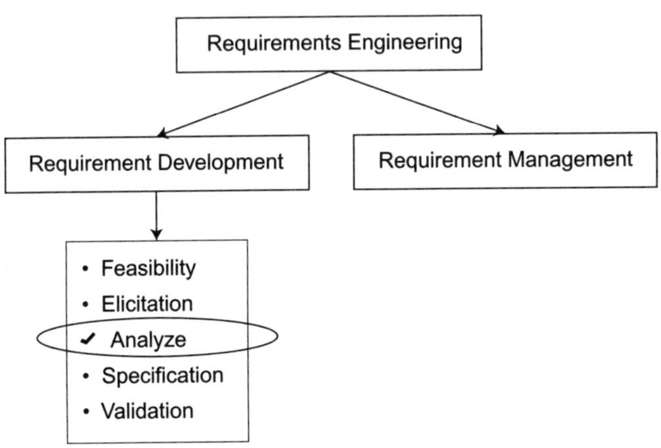

Figure 2.18 Analysis Phase of Requirements Engineering

The following modeling techniques are widely used in requirements analysis and are discussed in Chapter 3.

- Use case models
- System models (context, behavioral, data, object, structure methods)
- Data modeling
    - Data flow diagram
    - Data dictionary
    - Entity relationship model
    - Control flow model
    - Decision tables
- Information modeling
- Object-oriented analysis
- Scenario-based modeling
- Flow-oriented modeling
- Class diagram

2.5.4 Specifying Requirements

After the successful completion of requirements elicitation and analysis, the next step is to put all the knowledge gathered during these steps in a clear, concise and unambiguous manner so that the design and development teams can use it going forward. This is called the requirements specification phase (Figure 2.19).

While specifying the requirements, it is also important that it is validated with the customers and users to confirm if all the requirements are captured at this stage. Software Requirement Specification (SRS) is the outcome of this requirements specification and validation stage.

2.5.4.1 Specifying Requirements in the SRS Document

Once created, the SRS document becomes the main source for any requirements clarification and dissemination to all stakeholders. The SRS document can be used for several purposes:

- It may form the basis for the contractual agreement between the customer and the suppliers. The suppliers in an unambiguous fashion describe what will be developed as part of the project, thus any change in this agreed understanding will be renegotiated between the customer and the suppliers.
- This is the foundation document for the test engineers to develop their strategy on how to test the proposed system fully.

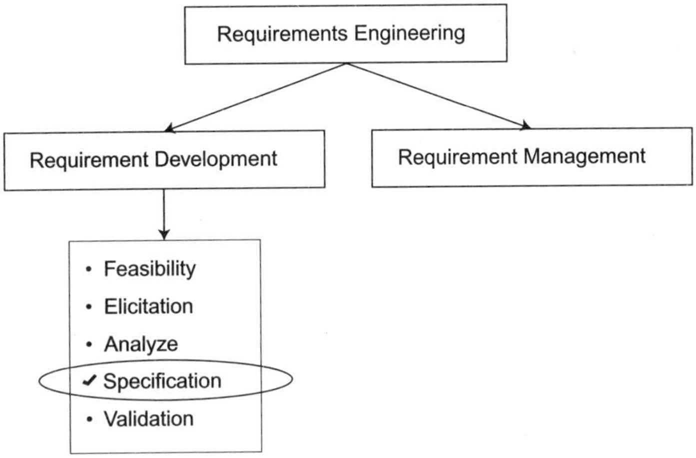

Figure 2.19 Specification Phase of Requirements Engineering

- The design and development team start their work based on this document. As all the stakeholders think through what they need from the system and get it documented in the SRS. The chance of redesign or reconstruction is minimized if the SRS is developed well.
- The resourcing, budgeting, scheduling and pricing for the project are based on the volume and complexity of the requirements captured in this document. The modern estimation techniques take direct input from the use cases and models developed in the SRS.
- A good SRS ensures future maintainability of the project and enables the customer to switch to a different supplier during the maintenance phase of the project. The new supplier's team will use the SRS document as the primary artifact to understand the capabilities required by the stakeholders from the system and can validate this against the developed capabilities.

Discussion Questions

List down the qualities of an SRS document that will help it to become the primary reference document for all the requirements?

1. ______________________
2. ______________________
3. ______________________
4. ______________________

2.5.4.2 IEEE Standard SRS Template

The aim of the SRS document is to provide an understanding of what the stakeholders want from the system and how the system should behave to cater to these needs. As discussed above, this document forms the foundation for downstream processes such as design, construction and testing, and thus it is very important to take proper care while creating this document. The IEEE Standard "*IEEE Recommended Practice for Software Requirements Specifications*" (IEEE Std 830-1993) provides a template for creating the SRS document as shown in Figure 2.20.

Based on the application domain, complexity and involvement of third-party systems, the sections may get added or removed from the above template.

IEEE standard SRS Template

1. Introduction
- 1.1. Purpose
- 1.2. Scope
- 1.3. Definition, acronyms & abbrevations
- 1.4. References
- 1.5. Overview

2. Overall description
- 2.1. Product perspective
  - 2.1.1. System interfaces
  - 2.1.2. User interfaces
  - 2.1.4. Software interfaces
  - 2.1.5. Communictions interfaces
  - 2.1.6. Memory constraints
  - 2.1.7. Operations
  - 2.1.8. Site adaptation requirement
- 2.2. Product functions
- 2.3. User characteristics
- 2.4. Constraints
- 2.5. Assumptions and dependencies
- 2.6. Apportioning of requirements

3. Specific Requirements
- 3.1 External interface requirments
  - 3.1.1 User interfaces
  - 3.1.2 Hardware interface
  - 3.1.3 Software interfaces
  - 3.1.4 Communication interface
- 3.2 Specific requirments
  - 3.2.1 Sequence diagrams
  - 3.2.2 Classes for classification of specific requirments
- 3.3 Performance equirments
- 3.4 Design constraints
- 3.5 Software system attributes
  - 3.5.1 Reliability
  - 3.5.2 Avilability
  - 3.5.3 Security
  - 3.5.4 Maintainability
- 3.6 Other requirments

4. Supporting information
- 4.1 Table of contents and index
- 4.2 Appendixes

Figure 2.20 IEEE Standard SRS Template

2.5.4.3 Checklist for Writing a Good SRS Document

The consumers of the SRS document are all the stakeholders of the project – the customer, end users, project engineers, interface developers, managers, etc. Thus, ensuring correctness and completeness of this document is crucial for the success of each stage of the project. The checkpoints listed in Figure 2.21 provide a guideline on how to create an SRS document that serves its purpose.

1. **Correctness**
   a) Will the requirements meet the customer's need?
   b) Do the requirements capture how the system should transform, produce and provide the exact outcome expected from the system?
   c) The correctness of requirements typically refers to the accuracy of the requirements and whether everything agreed is delivered.
2. **Completeness**
   a) Are all the requirements captured which will form a system that fully provides a solution to the customer's problem?
   b) Are each requirement detailed enough and supported by necessary diagrams, figures, data and use cases so that all the stakeholders get their necessary input from the requirement?
   c) Are all functional, nonfunctional and interface requirements captured for the system?
3. **Consistency**
   a) Are there requirements that conflict with each other? This may happen when multiple stakeholders have different views of the proposed system and provide requirements that create conflicts while grouped together.
   b) Are the terminology, diagrams, tables and figures consistent and provide a consistent view of the proposed system?
4. **Verifiability**
   a) Are the requirements verifiable – that is, will the test engineers be able to check whether the requirement fulfills the customer's need in entirety before the product is shipped to the customer.

Figure 2.21 Checklist for Writing a Good SRS Document

b) Are the requirements validated and verified by all the stakeholders before they are baselined for consumption of downstream processes?

5. **Clarity**

   a) Is the requirements statement explicit enough and can be interpreted only in one way? Along with unambiguous language, it is important to take help of pictorial representations such as diagrams, figures and use cases to eliminate ambiguity in requirements.

   b) Will the design and construction engineer be able to determine the single way of implementation from the requirements document? In case there are multiple interpretations of a requirement possible, then there is a possibility that it is implemented in a way not desired by the customer and thus causes rework.

6. **Priority**

   a) Is the relative priority of the requirements vis-a-vis the others captured? Prioritization of the requirements is important as it drives the plan for implementing these. In the case when the project is under time or budget constraint, the priority of the requirements becomes important as it will provide a clear guideline of which requirements should be tackled first, and which requirements are less important.

7. **Modifiability**

   a) How much dependency does the requirement have on other requirements? This will depict how easily the requirements can be modified. A requirement that has dependency on several other requirements should be structured in a fashion so that the impact of any modification to this requirement across other requirements can be easily traceable. There are several requirements management tools such as Doors and RequisitePro that are available which help in this regard.

POINTS TO PONDER

Note the seven points to be taken care of in a good SRS document – correctness, completeness, consistency, verifiability, clarity, priority and modifiability.

2.5.5 Validating Requirements

Validating requirements (Figure 2.22) is an important step as invalid requirements may cost more to rectify at later stages of the project life cycle. The main aim of requirements validation is to ensure that the customer needs are captured completely, clearly and consistently.

The validation step should provide enough confidence to all the stakeholders that the proposed system will provide all the features required and will be completed within the time and budget allocated for the project. The different stakeholders who should be involved in the validation process are:

1. Customer
2. End user
3. Domain expert
4. Architect
5. Construction and test engineer
6. Third-party systems interacting with the proposed system

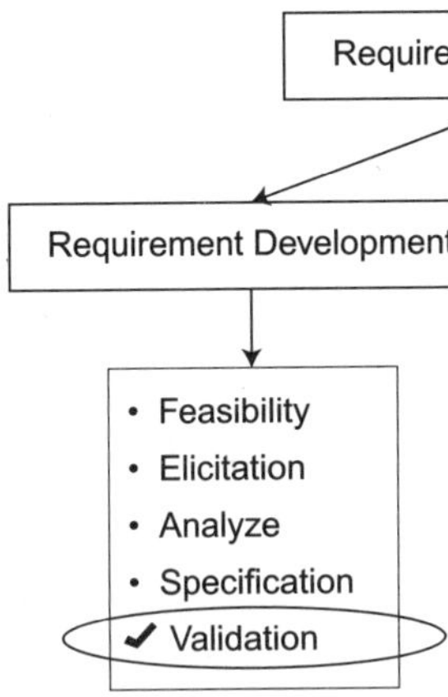

Figure 2.22 Validation Phase of Requirements Engineering

There are different approaches taken for validating the requirements, which are discussed below.

Walkthrough, Review and Inspection

There is some subtle difference between the validation processes – walkthrough, review and inspection (Figure 2.23).

Walkthrough: This is an informal process where the author of the document presents the document to a group of people, and the observations or issues found by the group are reported and corrected after the walkthrough session. Generally, minutes of the meeting are not maintained for the walkthrough sessions.

Figure 2.23 Walkthrough, Review and Inspection

Review: This may be either a formal or an informal process where the group of stakeholders will critically go through the SRS document and check that the following:

a) The standards and guidelines available in the organization are followed in the document.
b) The completeness, consistency and other points mentioned in the Checklist for Writing a Good SRS Document are followed.
c) All the requirements could be traced back to their origin. This will ensure that only the valid requirements are captured and implemented and not just any wish list from the user groups.

In this process, the minutes of the review sessions are captured and all the findings are tracked until satisfactory closure.

Inspection: This is a more structured way of review where the nonconformances found in the SRS document based on the points discussed above are listed as defects and tracked until the defects are closed satisfactorily.

Modeling and Prototyping

The other approaches for validating the requirements include creating models and prototypes.

Models: Use case modeling using the Unified Modeling Language (UML) is the most frequently used technique for capturing and validating the business case, interactions and flows in the proposed system.

Prototypes: As discussed in the Requirements Elicitation section, the prototyping method is a very effective way to validate the technical feasibility and the user's need because a smaller version of the actual system is developed and showcased to the stakeholders. Therefore, prototypes can be considered as the *executable* models used for requirements validation.

2.5.6 Requirements Management

The requirements management (Figures 2.24 and 2.25) discipline deals with how the existing requirements can be stored and tracked and how the changes to these requirements and also the introduction of new requirements can be handled during the requirements phase as well as throughout the life cycle of the project.

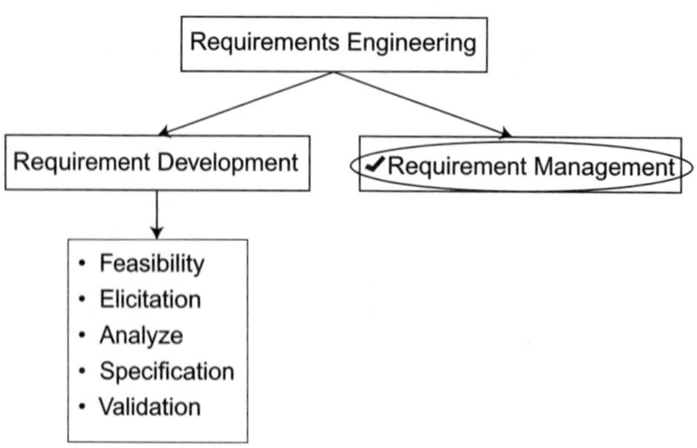

Figure 2.24 Requirement Engineering-Management

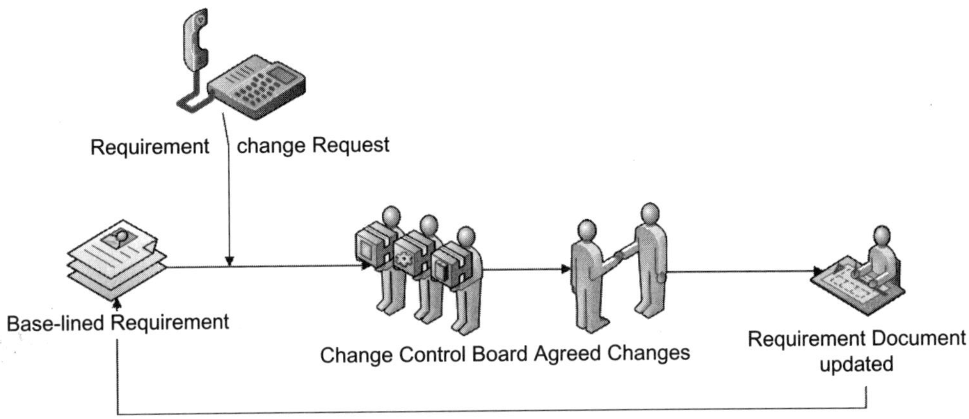

Figure 2.25 Requirements Management

Discussion Questions

If there is no requirements management process defined for a project what will be the problems faced by the team?

1. ______________________
2. ______________________
3. ______________________
4. ______________________

2.5.6.1 Requirements Management Plan

During requirements engineering, the plan for managing the requirements should mention how to manage the following:

- Requirements identification
- Requirements change
- Requirements status tracking
- Requirements traceability

2.5.6.2 Requirements Identification

Requirements identification is the first step in requirements management, which is discussed in detail in the first few sections of this chapter. This creates the baseline set of requirements on which the implementation team starts working.

2.5.6.3 Requirements Change

Requirements are bound to change during the course of time. There can be several reasons for the change in requirements:

1. The customer and the users of the system get more insight into the system as they see a few working prototypes of the system. This leads to change in existing requirements and emergence of new requirements. This is a very common phenomenon as no human being can foresee a future system fully just by thinking about it. Let us consider a simple example of designing the interior of your house. While providing the specification, you have to imagine how the different furniture will be oriented, the colors of the walls, electrical fittings, etc. However, when you see the first model design created by the designer you get a more concrete idea on how things will look and you make modifications to the design more confidently. The changes may occur until the different pieces of the interior are built and fixed. In the similar way, as more insight comes out of the system as we progress on the project, there may be changes or clarifications to the existing requirements.
2. The market and the business needs are ever changing. To cope with the changing market needs, the specification of the product to be developed may have to be changed.
3. The priority of the requirements may change due to change in market scenario, business priority change and change in viewpoint of the different stakeholders of the system.

A strong change management process is essential in tracking the changes in requirements. This will ensure that all the changes are incorporated during the project and minimize the chance of missing out on the new requirements or changes that have been found after the requirements phase of the project. The stages of requirements change management are mentioned below.

Change Control Process Once the initial requirements are agreed upon with different stakeholders, it is important that any change in these requirements are controlled well. Changes in requirements are almost always related to change in project effort, timeline and cost. By introducing a *Change Control Board*, all the stakeholders try to ensure that everyone gets good transparency on the changes agreed upon. A change control board is a group of people comprising members from each stakeholder group who are directly linked with the project outcome. This group sets forth the steps to be followed whenever a change or a new requirement crops up after the initial set of requirements are signed off by everyone.

2.5.6.4 Requirements Status Tracking

After the requirements gathering phase, the set of requirements get baselined, which can be modified after the change control board approves a requirement for implementation. It is important to track the status of all these requirements throughout the life cycle of the project, that is, until the requirements are available to the customer. This is to ensure that at any point in time the stakeholders should be able to find out the progress on these requirements. Figure 2.26 shows a sample of the change request tracker.

2.5.6.5 Requirements Traceability

The most commonly used artifact to track the requirements in each stage of the project life cycle such as design, construction, unit testing and system testing is a traceability matrix that maintains the tracing information as shown in Figure 2.27.

Note that each column of this table can be used to capture and maintain the traceability in the downstream phases for particular business and system requirements. Forward traceability provides

Change Request Details													Change Request Implementaion Details					
CR Id	Requested By	Requested Date	Priority	Change Description	Impact				CR Ap-proved By	CR Ap-proved date	CR status	Reason (if Rejected / Deferred/ Cancelled)	Planned Start Date	Planned End Date	Actual Start Date	Actual End Date	Actual Effort (in PH)	CR Imple-mentation Status
					Sl. No.	CI Id	Name	Existing Version (in PH)										
					1													
					2													
					3													
					4													
					5													

Figure 2.26 Change Request Tracker

Require-ment Clarifi-cation	Business Require-ments	System Re-quirements		NFR Re-quire-ments	Related Require-ments	User Interface Proto-type	System Testing		Performance Testing		Design				Coding		Unit Testing		Integration Tesing	
Clarifi-cation ID	Business Requir-ment ID	System Requir-ment ID	System Use Case ID	NFR Requir-ment ID	Related Requir-ment ID	Screen /Wire-frame ID	Docu-ment Name (SCI ID)	Test Case ID	Docu-ment Name (SCI ID)	Test Case ID	Com-ponent/ Class Diagram ID	Se-quence Diagrm	Use Interface Specifica-tionScreen ID/Name	Data-base Table	Program/ Source Code File Name(s)	Method/ (Proce-dures)	Docu-ment Name (SCI ID)	Test Case ID	Docu-ment Name (SCI ID)	Test Case ID

Figure 2.27 Requirements Traceability Matrix

the ability to track a requirement up to the system test case and through backward traceability the source for each of the system test or code or design can be traced back up to the requirements. This ensures that ALL and ONLY the agreed upon requirements are delivered to the customer.

POINTS TO PONDER

Due to the complexities involved in handling the changes, there is a general tendency to try to avoid requirement changes. But for a long-duration and complex project requirement change is inevitable, and thus rather than pushing back the customer to resist the requirement change it more advisable to plan for a well-structured change management process.

Summary

- The requirements engineering phase creates the foundation for any software development project. Thus, it is important to follow a systematic approach in this phase to avoid issues with the software at later stages.
- Feasibility study is conducted at the beginning to ensure that all the expectations of the stakeholders are analyzed and a consensus is reached on how much of that can be created with the current time and cost constraints of the project.
- Requirements elicitation techniques are used to ensure that all the needs from the system are captured. The different and conflicting viewpoints of the different stakeholders and user groups of the system need to be merged and agreed upon before proceeding to the next step.
- Modeling techniques are used to analyze the requirements and synthesize a solution, which becomes the input to the design phase. System analysts will critically analyze the information flow and content, functional behavior, data flow behavior and external system interfacing requirements to create a model with which both the customer and the engineers are comfortable.
- Specifying the requirements in a correct, complete, clear, verifiable and prioritized fashion is critical to ensure that the outcome of the requirements engineering phase is useful for the subsequent stages of the software development life cycle. Review and inspection methodologies are used to ensure the quality of the SRS document.
- Throughout the project life cycle, tracking the requirements for proper implementation and any change is crucial. The requirement traceability matrix provides a standard way of tracking the requirements throughout the project life cycle. Apart from this, a sound change management process and change tracker is recommended to track the changes to the initial requirements and avoid requirements creep.

Case Study

An SRS review checklist is a critical item in the requirements phase of the project. A sample checklist that covers the aspects discussed in the SRS creation and validation sections is provided below.

Software Requirements Specification Review Checklist				
		Yes	No	Not Applicable
Completeness				
	Is there a table of contents?			
	Are all figures, tables and diagrams labeled?			
	Are all figures, tables and diagrams cross-referenced?			
	Are all terms defined?			
	Are all terms indexed?			
	Are all units of measure defined?			
	Are areas where information is incomplete because development has not started been specified?			
	Is the missing information defined in the requirement?			
	Should any requirement be specified in more detail?			
	Should any requirement be specified in less detail?			
	Are all of the requirements defined?			
	Are all of the requirements related to functionality included?			
	Are there any requirements that make you feel uneasy?			
	Are all of the requirements related to performance included?			
	Are all of the requirements related to design constraints included?			
	Are all of the requirements related to attributes included?			
	Are all of the requirements related to external interfaces included?			
	Are all of the requirements related to databases included?			
	Are all of the requirements related to software included?			
	Are all of the requirements related to communications included?			
	Are all of the requirements related to hardware included?			
	Are all of the requirements related to inputs included?			
	Are all of the requirements related to outputs included?			
	Are all of the requirements related to reporting included?			
	Are all of the requirements related to security included?			
	Are all of the requirements related to maintainability included?			
	Are all of the requirements related to installation included?			
	Are all of the requirements related to criticality included?			
	Are all of the requirements related to the permanency limitations included?			
	Are possible changes to the requirements specified?			
	Is the likelihood of change specified for each requirement?			

Consistency				
	Are there any requirements describing the same object that conflict with other requirements with respect to terminology?			
	Are there any requirements describing the same object that conflict with respect to characteristics?			
	Are there any requirements that describe two or more actions that conflict logically?			
	Are there any requirements that describe two or more actions that conflict temporally?			
Clarity				
	Are the requirements described in a nontechnical understandable language?			
	Are there any requirements that could have more than one interpretation?			
	Is each characteristic of the final product described with a unique terminology?			
	Is there a glossary in which the specific meaning(s) of each term is(are) defined?			
	Could the requirements be understood and implemented by an independent group?			
Traceability				
	Are all requirements traceable back to a specific user need?			
	Are all requirements traceable back to a specific source document or person?			
	Are all requirements traceable forward to a specific design document?			
	Are all requirements traceable forward to a specific software module?			
Verifiability				
	Are any requirements included that are impossible to implement?			
	For each requirement is there a process that can be executed by either a human or a machine to verify the requirement?			
	Are there any requirements that will be expressed in verifiable terms at a later time?			
Modifiability				
	Is the requirements document clearly and logically organized?			
	Does the organization adhere to an accepted standard?			
	Is there any redundancy in the requirements?			

Content				
General				
	Is each requirement relevant to the problem and its solution?			
	Are any of the defined requirements really design details?			
	Are any of the defined requirements really verification details?			
	Are any of the defined requirements really project management details?			
	Is there an introduction section?			
	Is there a general description section?			
	Is there a scope section?			
	Is there a definitions, acronyms and abbreviations section?			
	Is there a specific requirements section?			
	Is there a product perspective section?			
	Is there a product functions section?			
	Is there a user characteristics section?			
	Is there a general constraints section?			
	Is there an assumptions and dependencies section?			
	Is there a specific requirements section?			
	Are all of the necessary appendixes present?			
	Are all of the necessary figures present?			
	Are all of the necessary tables present?			
	Are all of the necessary diagrams present?			
Specific				
Inputs				
	Are all input sources specified?			
	Are all input accuracy requirements specified?			
	Are all input range values specified?			
	Are all input frequencies specified?			
	Are all input formats specified?			
Outputs				
	Are all output destinations specified?			
	Are all output accuracy requirements specified?			
	Are all output range values specified?			

	Are all output frequencies specified?			
	Are all output formats specified?			
Reports				
	Are all report formats specified?			
	Are all calculations/formulas used in reports specified?			
	Are all report data filter requirements specified?			
	Are all report sorting requirements specified?			
	Are all report totaling requirements specified?			
	Are all report formatting requirements specified?			
Functions				
	Are all software functions specified?			
	Are all inputs specified for each function?			
	Are all aspects of the processing specified for each function?			
	Are all outputs specified for each function?			
	Are all performance requirements specified for each function?			
	Are all design constrains specified for each function?			
	Are all attributes specified for each function?			
	All security requirements specified for each function?			
	Are all maintainability requirements specified for each function?			
	Are all database requirements specified for each function?			
	Are all operational requirements specified for each function?			
	Are all installation requirements specified for each function?			
External Interfaces				
	Are all user interfaces specified?			
	Are all batch interfaces specified?			
	Are all hardware interfaces specified?			
	Are all software interfaces specified?			
	Are all communications interfaces specified?			
	Are all interface design constraints specified?			
	Are all interface security requirements specified?			
	Are all interface maintainability requirements specified?			
	Are all human-computer interactions specified for user interfaces?			

Internal Interfaces				
	Have all internal interfaces been identified?			
	Have all internal interfaces characteristics been specified?			
Timing				
	Are all expected processing times specified?			
	Are all data transfer rates specified?			
	Are all system throughput rates specified?			
Reliability				
	Are the consequences of software failure specified for each requirement?			
	Is the information to protect from failure specified?			
	Is a strategy for error detection specified?			
	Is a strategy for correction specified?			
Tradeoffs				
	Are all acceptable trade-offs specified for competing attributes?			
Hardware				
	Is the minimum memory specified?			
	Is the minimum storage specified?			
	Is the maximum memory specified?			
	Is the maximum storage specified?			
Software				
	Are the required software environments/OSs specified?			
	Are all of the required software utilities specified?			
	Are all purchased software products that are to be used with the system specified?			
Communications				
	Is the target network specified?			
	Are the required network protocols specified?			
	Is the required network capacity specified?			
	Is the required/estimated network throughput rate specified?			
	Is the estimated number of network connections specified?			
	Are minimum network performance requirements specified?			
	Are the maximum network performance requirements specified?			
	Are the optimal network performance requirements specified?			

Model Questions
PART A (Objective type)

1. What is the whole gamut of activities related to requirements from inception to understanding, tracking and maintaining the requirements termed as?

   A. Requirements engineering B. Requirements analysis
   C. Requirements management D. Requirements elicitation

Answer: A

2. What is the discipline that explores the externally imposed conditions on a proposed computer system and tries to identify the capabilities that will meet those imposed conditions and recording the same in the form of documentation called?

   A. Requirements engineering
   B. Requirements analysis
   C. Requirements management
   D. Requirements elicitation

Answer: A

3. The primary cause of schedule and budget overruns is rework due to incomplete understanding of:

   A. Customer B. Coding
   C. Requirements D. Design

Answer: C

4. The cost of fixing an error in the system increases exponentially with the stage of the project.

   A. True B. False

Answer: A

5. Which of the following is not a category of requirement?

   A. Functional requirements B. Nonfunctional requirements
   C. Interface specification requirements D. Customer requirements

Answer: D

6. What is the set of requirements that defines what the system will do or accomplish called?

   A. Functional requirements B. Nonfunctional requirements
   C. Interface specification requirements D. Customer requirements

Answer: A

7. What are functional requirements are often captured in?

   A. Use cases B. Video tapes
   C. Function points D. Test cases

Answer: A

8. What are the main drivers of the application architecture of a system?

A. Functional requirements
B. Nonfunctional requirements
C. Database design
D. Interface specification

Answer: A

9. What are the quality attributes and the design and architecture constraints that the system must have called?

A. Functional requirements
B. Nonfunctional requirements
C. Database design
D. Interface specification

Answer: B

10. All of the following are quality attributes of the system from an end user's perspective except:

A. Availability
B. Usability
C. Security
D. Reusability

Answer: D

11. All of the following are the quality attributes of the system from a developer's perspective except:

A. Reusability
B. Maintainability
C. Availability
D. Portability

Answer: C

12. NFRs are critical in most of the software projects than functional requirements.

A. True
B. False

Answer: A

13. Which of the following is an examples of organization-related NFR?

A. Standards requirements
B. Legal requirements
C. Ethical requirements
D. External requirements

Answer: A

14. All of the following are examples of product-related NFRs except:

A. Performance
B. Scalability
C. Testability
D. External requirements

Answer: D

15. Which of the following is not a category of feasibility?

A. Operational feasibility
B. Technical feasibility
C. Economic feasibility
D. Resource feasibility

Answer: D

16. Which of the following categories of feasibility checks the usability of the proposed software?

A. Operational feasibility
B. Technical feasibility
C. Economic feasibility
D. Resource feasibility

Answer: A

17. Which of the following categories of feasibility checks whether the level of technology required for development of the system is available with the software firm, including hardware resources, software development platforms and other software tools.

A. Operational feasibility
B. Technical feasibility
C. Economic feasibility
D. Resource feasibility

Answer: B

18. Stakeholder interests may be either positively or negatively impacted by the performance of the project.

A. True
B. False

Answer: A

19. Which technique is used when the requirements are detailed and differing opinions are likely or are sought?

A. Interview
B. Focus group
C. Prototype
D. Direct observation

Answer: A

20. Which of the following techniques is used as main technique to gather the requirements in distributed agile projects?

A. Interviewing
B. Focus group
C. Prototype
D. Direct observation

Answer: A

21. Which technique is similar to interviewing, but has a group of 6 to 10 people at a time?

A. Interviewing
B. Focus group
C. Prototype
D. Direct observation

Answer: B

22. Which requirements gathering technique can be used for rapidly pulling together a good set of requirements?

A. Interviewing
B. Focus group
C. Workshop
D. Direct observation

Answer: C

23. In which requirement gathering technique, different alternatives are given to the customers to choose the appropriate options?

A. Interviewing
B. Focus group
C. Workshop
D. Direct observation

Answer: C

24. Which requirement technique is the best way of presenting ideas to users?

A. Interviewing
B. Focus group
C. Workshop
D. Prototype

Answer: D

25. Which of the following is called a working prototype?

A. Proof-of-principle prototype
B. Visual prototype
C. Functional prototype
D. Form study prototype

Answer: C

26. By using which technique can a large number of ideas be gathered in a short period of time?

A. Prototype
B. Brainstorming
C. Direct observation
D. Questionnaire

Answer: B

27. Which of the following is an informal process where the author of the document presents the document to a group of people, and the observations or issues found by the group are reported and corrected after the session?

A. Walkthrough
B. Review
C. Inspection
D. Audit

Answer: A

28. Which of the following is either a formal or an informal process where the group of stakeholders critically goes through the SRS document?

A. Walkthrough
B. Review
C. Inspection
D. Audit

Answer: B

29. Which process follows a more structured way of review where the nonconformances found in the SRS document are listed as defects and tracked until the defects are closed satisfactorily?

A. Walkthrough
B. Review
C. Inspection
D. Audit

Answer: C

30. By introducing a change control board, all the stakeholders try to ensure that everyone gets good transparency on the changes agreed upon. In which stage of the change management process does the change control board become functional?

A. Requirements identification
B. Requirements change
C. Requirements status tracking
D. Requirements traceability

Answer: B

31. Which of the following stakeholders is not required during the requirements validation process?

A. Customer
B. End user
C. Domain expert
D. Third-party systems that are not interacting with the proposed system

Answer: D

32. During the requirements analysis stage, the analyst focuses on all the following areas except:

A. Software test cases
B. Software functionality elaboration
C. Behavior of the software on an external input
D. Interface requirements

Answer: A

33. What are the seven points that need to be taken care of while writing a good SRS document?

A. Correctness, completeness, consistency, criticality, clarity, priority and modifiability
B. Correctness, individuality, consistency, verifiability, clarity, priority and modifiability
C. Correctness, completeness, consistency, verifiability, clarity, priority and modifiability
D. Correctness, completeness, consistency, verifiability, clarity, traceability and modifiability

Answer: C

34. How many members are normally there in a mini focus group?

A. 8 to 9
B. 4 to 5
C. 1 to 2
D. No limit

Answer: B

35. All of the following are possible issues that the team may face while eliciting requirements except:

A. Users not sure about the requirements
B. Conflicting requirements
C. Volatile requirements
D. Project is not approved

Answer: D

36. Which of the following is not an example of NFRs?

A. Performance
B. Maintainability
C. Data logic
D. Security

Answer: C

37. At which of the following stages is it least expensive to fix a requirement understanding error?

A. Post release
B. Requirement review
C. Design
D. Testing

Answer: B

38. If a software project gets started without proper requirements understanding, then which of the following is the outcome?

A. Lack of understanding of the user's needs or without exploring the multiple dimensions of the requirements
B. Misalignment at the end between the final result delivered and the user's expectations of the project
C. Lot of rework
D. All of the above

Answer: D

PART B (Answer in one or two Lines)

1. Define "requirement" as per the IEEE standard.
2. Why are requirements important?
3. What are functional requirements?
4. What are NFRs?
5. List a few NFRs from an end user's perspective.
6. List a few NFRs from a developer's perspective.
7. What are product- and process-oriented approaches to NFRs?
8. Write short notes on interface specification.
9. What is feasibility study? What are its characteristics?
10. What are the types of feasibility studies?
11. What is operational feasibility?
12. What is technical feasibility?
13. What is economic feasibility?
14. List the problems in eliciting requirements.
15. List any three requirements elicitation techniques that you are aware of.
16. List the various types of focus groups.
17. What are facilitated workshops?
18. What are the types of prototypes?
19. How can questionnaires be used to gather requirements?
20. What are the disadvantages of questionnaires while collecting requirements?
21. How is brainstorming used to gather requirements?
22. What is requirements analysis?
23. List any three models of requirement analysis.
24. List any three check points for writing a good SRS document.
25. What is clarity checkpoint of an SRS document?
26. Who are the stakeholders involved in the requirements validation process?
27. List the approaches of validating requirements.
28. Write notes on walkthroughs.
29. What is inspection?
30. List any three reasons for requirements change in any project?

PART C (Descriptive type)

1. Discuss the various categories of requirements in detail.
2. Describe feasibility study in detail.
3. What are the problems in eliciting requirements?
4. Describe the focus group technique of eliciting requirements in detail.
5. Describe the prototyping model of eliciting requirements in detail.
6. Describe the requirement analysis phase of a project in detail.
7. Discuss the various checklist points for writing a good SRS (System Requirement Specification) document.
8. Explain the concept of validating requirements in detail.
9. Discuss the contents of the requirements management plan in detail.

Section 2:
Requirement Engineering

3

Requirement Analysis Modeling

CHAPTER COVERAGE

1. *Analysis Modeling Approaches*
2. *Structured Analysis*
3. *Object-Oriented Analysis*

3.1 ANALYSIS MODELING APPROACHES

As discussed in Chapter 2, the analysis stage acts as the bridge between design and requirement and it happens after the requirement phase. The analyst critically explores the requirements and ensures that the system's operational characteristics are understood clearly, interfacing requirements with other systems are brought out and the constraints that the proposed system should meet are established in detail. Figure 3.1 helps to understand the requirements in a better way.

During the Requirement Analysis stage, the analyst aims to fulfill the following objectives (Figure 3.2).

1. Clearly illustrate the user scenarios
2. Explain the functional activities in detail

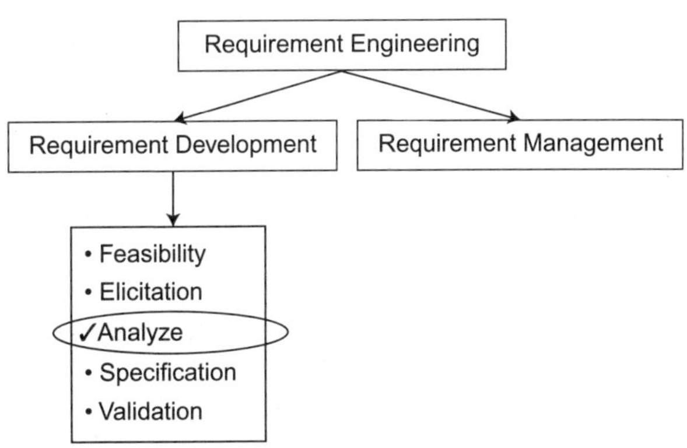

Figure 3.1 Requirement Analysis

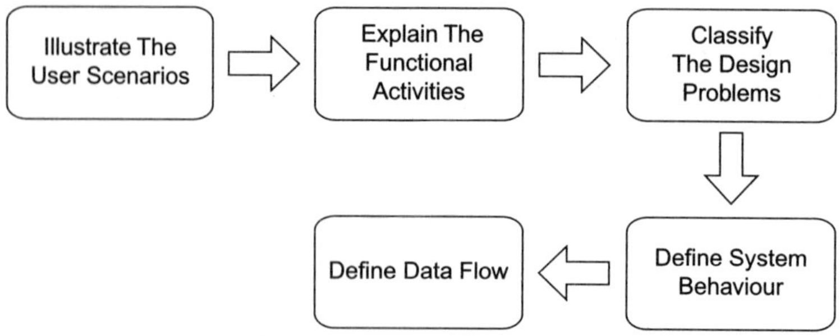

Figure 3.2 Requirement Analysis Objectives

3. Classify the design problems and their relationships
4. Define system behavior and class structure
5. Define data flow as it is transformed

Discussion Questions

Discuss the importance of the above objects in detail. List down at least 4 important points.

1. ______________________________
2. ______________________________
3. ______________________________
4. ______________________________

Providing a graphical representation of the system behavior (Figure 3.3), which is depicted as a combination of functional flow and data flow to create the input for the design phase is called the analysis modeling.

The below-mentioned guidelines (Figure 3.4) are followed while creating a model.

During the early days of software development in 1960s–1970s, most of the systems were written in languages available in those days (for example, COBOL and FORTRAN). There were not much focus on documenting the requirements and transforming the user needs into a system design. When the systems gradually started becoming bigger and complex, the structured analysis became popular. The two most popular approaches to software analysis, which have developed and got fine-tuned over years, are *structured analysis* and *object-oriented analysis* (Figure 3.5).

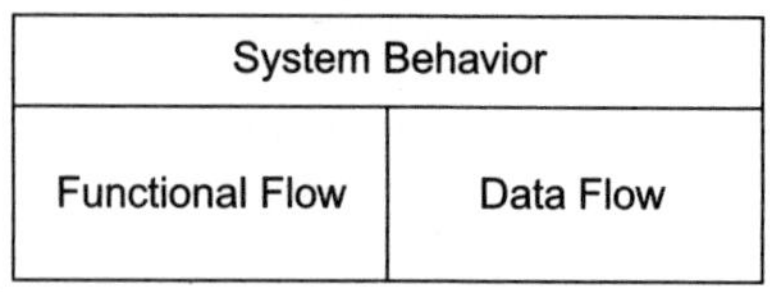

Figure 3.3 System Behavior

- Are the elements of the model improving the understanding of the requirements and addressing each of the area - domain, functional and behavioral requirements?
- Is the model focusing on the requirements that are captures during the requirements gathering phase?
- Is the model keeping analysis at relatively high level so that the architectural decisions can be made during the design?
- Is the graphical representation providing good insight of the system to all stakeholders?
- Is the model kept simple and as modularized as possible to avoid interdependencies?
- Can all the inputs required for starting the design be derived from this madel?

Figure 3.4 Requirement Analysis Guidelines

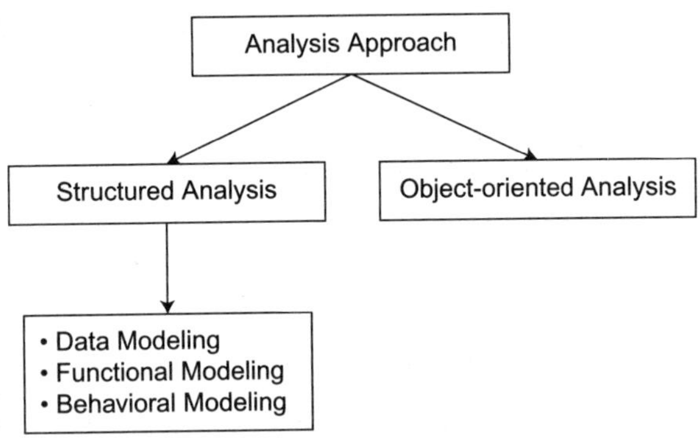

Figure 3.5 Analysis Approach

3.2 STRUCTURED ANALYSIS

The term structured analysis was first used by Douglas Ross and then popularized by DeMarco. The graphical notations and models suggested by DeMarco created the basis for structured analysis, which then got enriched by the works of Page–Jones and Gane and Sarson. In mid-1980s, the work of Ward and Mellor followed by Hatley and Pirbhai added notations to capture the control and behavioral aspects of the real-time engineering problems along with the information systems applications also called as function-oriented analysis.

The domain of structured analysis comprises three modeling approaches, which collectively describe the requirement and intended behavior of the proposed system

- Data modeling
- Functional or flow-oriented modeling and
- Behavioral modeling

As we go through elements of each of the modeling approaches it becomes clear that these techniques need to be used in conjunction with each other to get the full view of the system. By breaking the system into these three models, the analyst tries to make the designer's job easy who can elaborate each part of data, flow and the system's reaction to the data flow separately to create a modular design.

POINTS TO PONDER

The domain of structured analysis comprises of three modeling approaches

- Data modeling
- Functional or flow oriented modeling and
- Behavioral modeling

3.2.1 Data Modeling

Data modeling is an analysis technique (Figure 3.6) that deals with the data processing part of an application. It deals with identifying the data elements in a system, the structure and composition of data, relationships and different processes that causes transformation to these data.

The objective of data modeling is not to capture the details of the processes that cause data transformation or to reveal how data is transformed. Rather, this modeling technique focuses on independently analyzing the data elements and their relationship in the overall system. This visual representation, which is called the Entity Relationship Diagram (Table 3.1), helps the engineers understand and design data elements and finally the data dictionary of the system.

Some of the notations that help to draw the diagram are explained in the following section.

3.2.1.1 Data Objects, Attributes and Relationships

Data object or an entity (Figure 3.7) in a system is the identity which has multiple attributes and is related to other entities in the system. Identifying all entities in the system is a crucial task as these form the basis of all the relationships and flows inside the system that the engineers create.

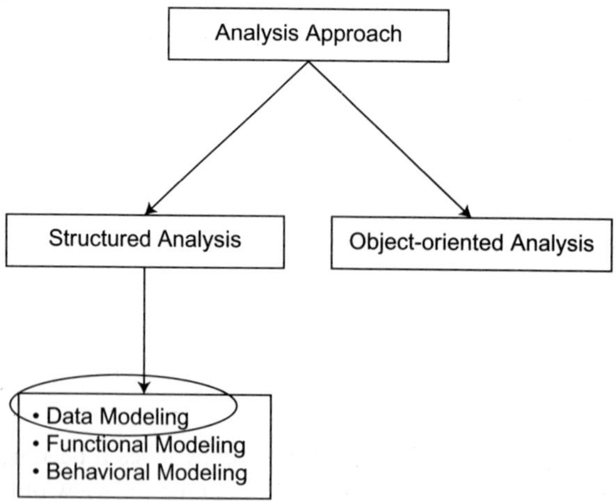

Figure 3.6 Data Modeling

Table 3.1 Structured Analysis – ER Diagram

Structured Analysis	
Type	**Corresponding Diagram**
Data Modeling	ER Diagram
Functional Modeling	Data Flow Diagram
	Control Flow Diagram
Behavioral Modeling	State Transition Diagram

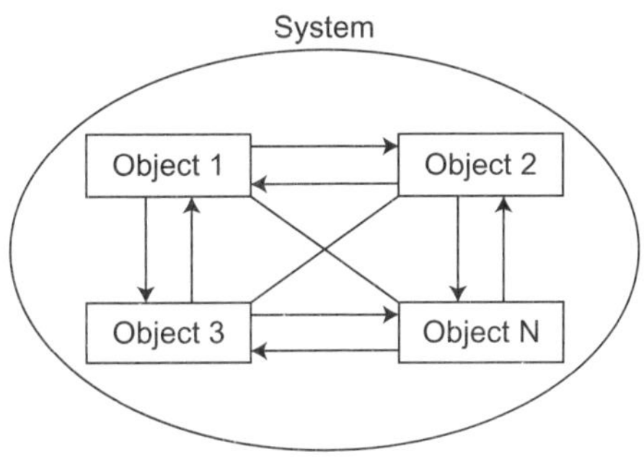

Figure 3.7 System versus Data Objects

POINTS TO PONDER

A System consists of multiple objects. The data flow occurs between objects which are inside the same or with the objects insider other system.

For example, in a health insurance system the entities will be

1. The insurer
2. The insurance service provider
3. The policy
4. The claims, etc.

Each of these entities possesses a set of attributes and also holds relationship with other entities. An insurer has attributes such as ID number, name, address, age, whereas a policy comprises attributes such as policy number, policy tenure, nominee, policy value, etc. (Figure 3.8).

The properties that describe the entity and are common across all the instances of the entity are called the *attributes*.

Entities are related to each other. For example, an insurer can hold one or multiple policies whereas an insurance provider may have several insurers attached to it. This leads to the concept of

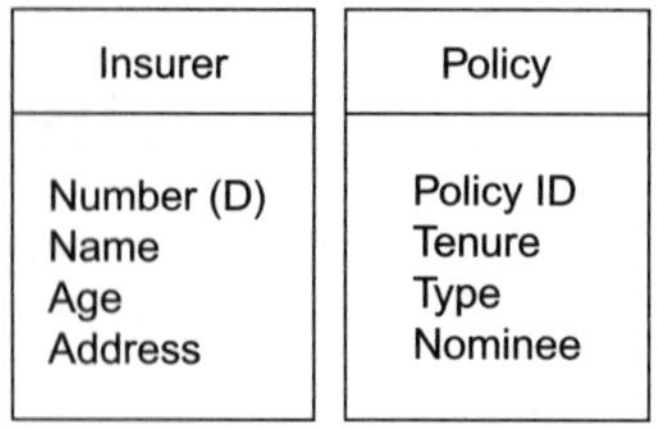

Figure 3.8 Insurer and Policy Objects

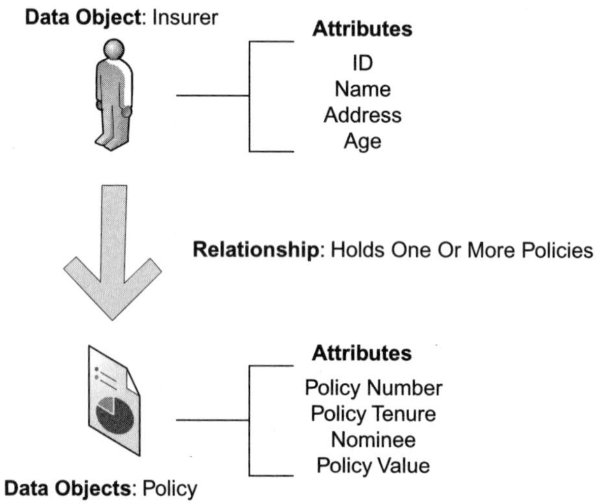

Figure 3.9 Data Object, Attributes, Relationship

relationship where the entities can be linked to each other in a system. Figure 3.9 shows the entity, attributes and relationships in a health insurance system.

Data objects hold only the data components and there should be no intent to hold the processes that deal with the data inside data objects. If the process, which a claim approval of a policy undergoes, needs to be captured then the data flow diagram needs to be initiated and it should not be captured inside the ERD. Here, the structure of the database or the system that holds the data for the system logically comes out from this analysis.

3.2.1.2 Cardinality and Modality

Along with the relationship information of different objects, it is also important to capture how many types of each object can be attached with other objects, which is called *cardinality* and whether it is mandatory to attach an object with the another object type which is called *modality*.

In the example of the health insurance system, an insurer can have one or many insurance policies which will give rise to one-to-many relationship, whereas a policy can be attached to one insurer only giving rise to one-to-one relationship. Thus, the cardinality provides the information on the maximum number of relationships an object can hold with another object and can be classified as:

1. One-to-one relationship (1:1)
2. One-to-many relationship (1:M)
3. Many-to-many relationship (M:N)

However, the modality holds the information on whether two objects must enter into a relationship or not. In case it is mandatory to enter into a relationship, then the modality is 1. But in case the relationship is optional and the objects may not carry any relationship, then the modality is 0.

POINTS TO PONDER

Along with the relationship information of diffrent objects it is also important to capture how many of each object types can be attached with other objects, which is called Cardinality and wether it is mandatory to attach an object with the another object type which is called Modality.

There are several types of notations used for creating an ERD. The "information engineering" notations for different cardinality and modality representation are shown in Figure 3.10.

Refer to Figure 3.10 for examples of the modality depiction.

The cardinality and modality information are combined (Figure 3.11) to represent the relationship among the objects completely.

According to Figure 3.11, the mandatory (Modality) options are as follows.

It is clear 0 means there is no relationship and 1 means there is a relationship.

Insurance provider should have at least one insurance policy to be called as an insurance provider. An insurance policy may not be provided by all the insurance providers. It is optional for the insurance provider to provide a particular policy.

Now cardinality determines whether the relationship is

1. One-to-one relationship (1:1)
2. One-to-many relationship (1:M)
3. Many-to-many relationship (M:N)

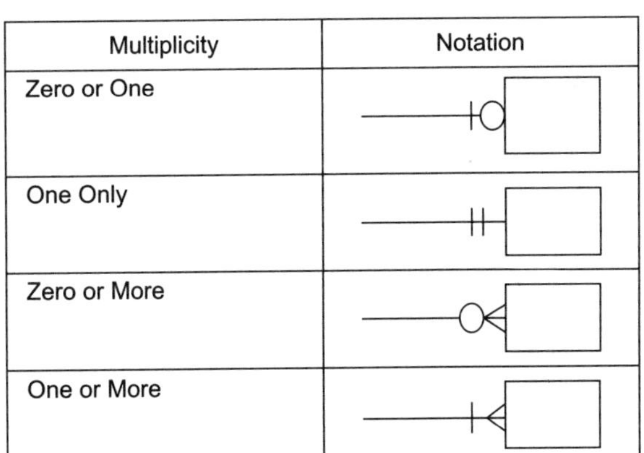

Figure 3.10 Relationship Notations

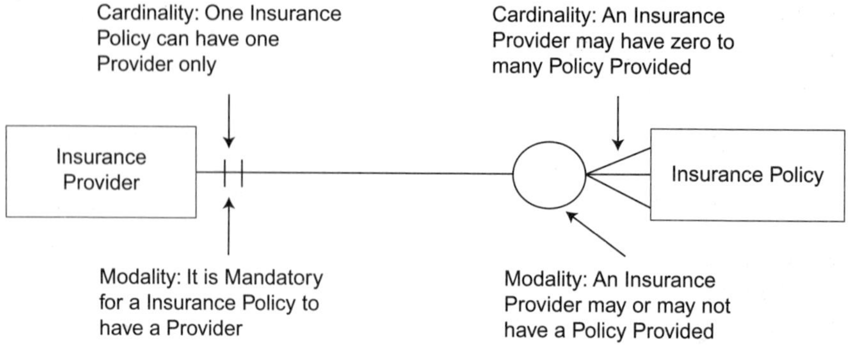

Figure 3.11 Cardinality and Modality Combined

3.2.1.3 Entity Relationship Diagrams

The relationships of the objects present in a system are represented graphically through the ERDs. The *entities* are represented as a rectangle. The relationships are represented with lines with the ends representing the cardinality and modality as shown in Figure 3.11. Thus the various components of an ERD are

- Data objects or entities
- Attributes
- Relationships and
- Various indicators describing the relationships

The ERD for a simplified insurance policy management system is depicted in Figure 3.12.

Here insurer, insurance provider, policy and claim are the objects.

An insurer should have at least one policy. An insurer can have more than one policy.

An insurance provider should issue at least one policy. A particular policy may be with zero or multiple insurance provider.

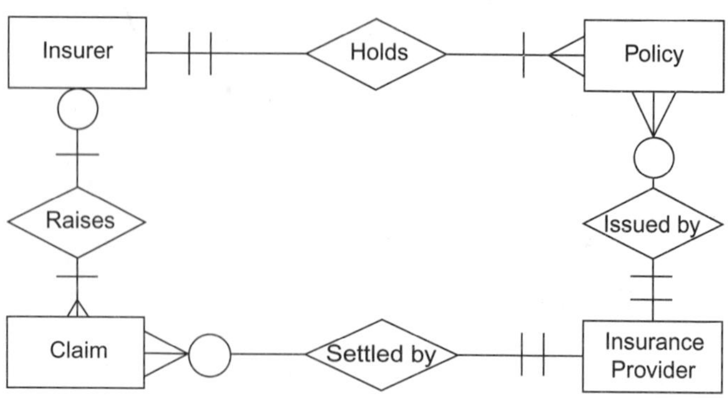

Figure 3.12 Requirement Management

3.2.1.4 Data Dictionary

Data dictionary is the place where the description and information about all data objects produced and consumed by the software system is maintained. Some of the attributes that normally gets stored inside a data dictionary are such as

Name	Each data, data store and external entity is identified with this primary name.
Alias	Each data object can have alternate names.
Where-used/how-used	Processes that use the data/control item and how it is used are represented. The use may be • as a store • input to process • output from process • as an external entity
Content description	This notation is used for representing content.
Supplementary information	Other information such as the preset values, restrictions, limitations, etc. is captured.

Few common notations used for describing data objects in a data dictionary are

=	is composed of
+	and
()	optional
{}	iteration
[|]	either - or
..text...	comment
{ }n	n repetitions of
(...)	delimits a comment

An example of data dictionary maintained for the customer of a banking system is as follows:

Customer Name = Title + First Name + (Middle Name) + Last Name
Title = [Mr.| Ms.| Mrs.]
Address = {Address Text}^{2} *... Home and Office Address..*

Along with the basic information that normally becomes part of the data dictionary, other information may optionally be stored inside it.

Below is a list of properties that can be stored inside a data dictionary item if these help in clarifying the data structure in the system.

- Name
- Aliases or synonyms
- Default label

- Description
- Source (s)
- Date of origin
- Users
- Programs in which used
- Change authorizations
- Access authorization
- Data type
- Length
- Units (cm., °C, etc.)
- Range of values
- Frequency of use
- Input/output/local
- Conditional values
- Parent structure
- Subsidiary structures
- Repetitive structures

3.2.2 Functional Modeling or Flow-oriented Modeling

Functional modeling or flow-oriented modeling (Figure 3.13) is the second model of structural analysis. In data modeling, ER diagram was discussed, and in functional modeling, data flow diagram (DFD) is discussed.

Functionality flow is also known as the data flow.

3.2.2.1 Data Flow Diagrams

DFD (Table 3.2) is a diagram of functional modeling. Entire system is shown as a process and data are interlinked to each other. Data flows between one object to the other.

These data get transformed (takes different form) as they flow through the software (Processes) (refer Figure 3.14).

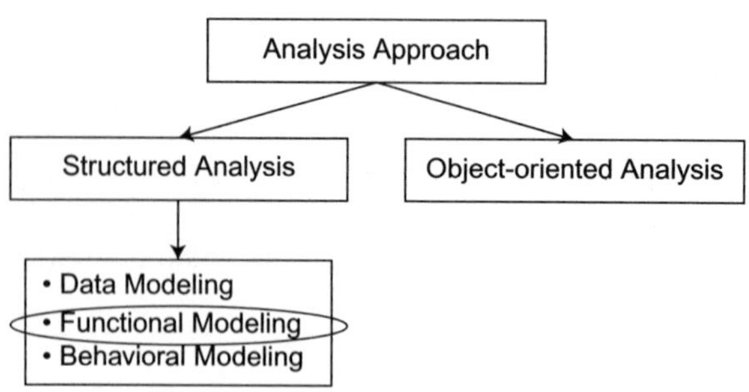

Figure 3.13 Structured Analysis, Functional Modeling

Table 3.2 Structured Analysis, Data Flow Diagram

Structured Analysis	
Type	**Corresponding Diagram**
Data Modeling	ER Diagram
Functional Modeling	Data Flow Diagram
	Control Flow Diagram
Behavioral Modeling	State Transition Diagram

Any portion of the system can be depicted as a sub process that processes the input data, make some change to it or takes some decision based on it and produces the output data.

To clarify the concept of the data flow, think about a software program which calculates the insurance premium based on the information of the insurer. Figure 3.15 shows how the input data is processed by the software system to produce the desired output – the premium amount (called as premium information) and it is also stored (recorded) in "insurance policy record" for further analysis.

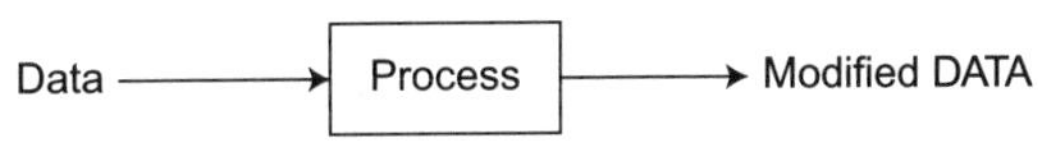

Figure 3.14 Data versus Process

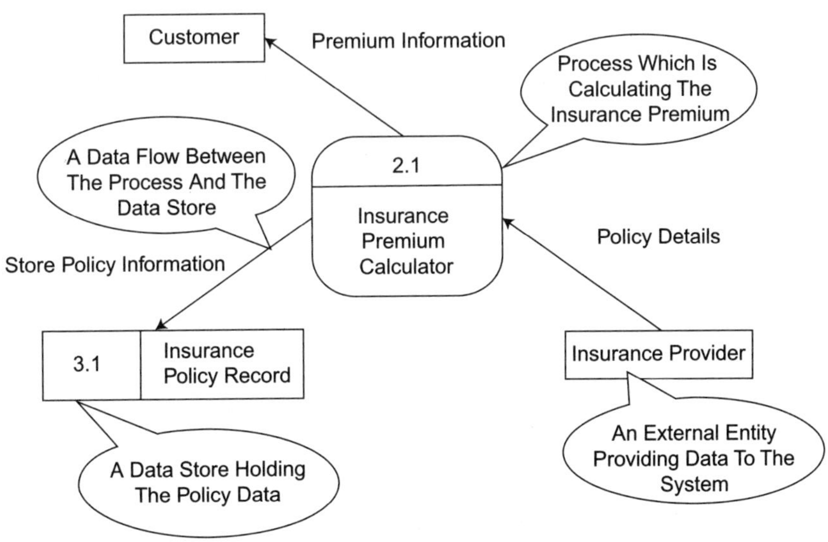

Figure 3.15 Level 1 DFD

DFDs demonstrate the relationships between the various components in a program or system. This modeling technique reveals the high-level details of a system by showing how input data is transformed to output results after processing through the functional modules.

The four main components (Figure 3.16) of a DFD modeling are

- Entities
- Processes
- Data stores and
- Data flows

Entities

The external systems which either provide data to the system or receive from it are called entities. An entity which provides data to the system is called a source and an entity which receives data from the system is called a sink (Figure 3.17).

Entities are represented as rectangles (Figure 3.18) with a name that clearly represents its kind. The entities are closely related to the identification of the system boundary.

Process

A process is the manipulation or work that transforms data while it flows through the system. A system can have one or multiple processes (Figure 3.19) that are interlinked and cause the data transformation through computations, logical decisions, or workflow branching based on business rules. A process receives some input and generates some output.

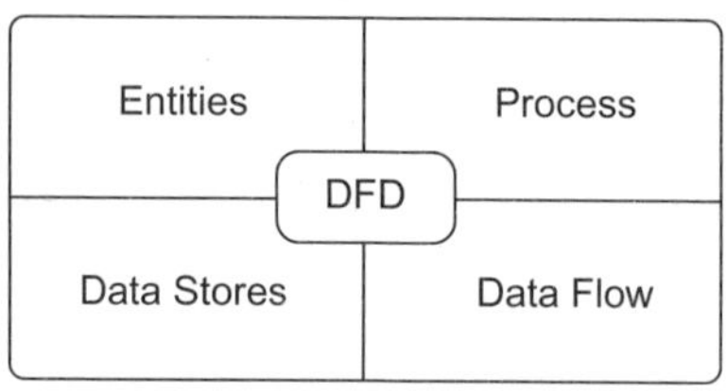

Figure 3.16 Components of DFD

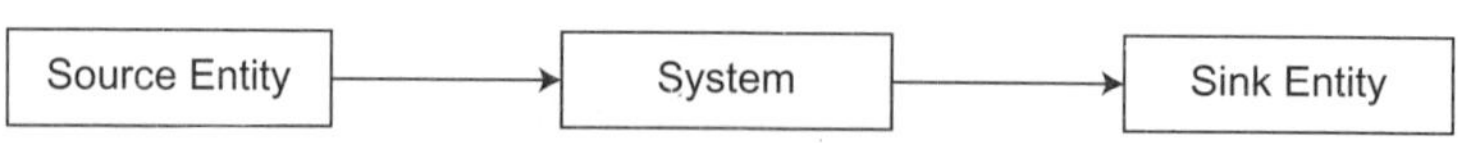

Figure 3.17 Source and Sink Entity

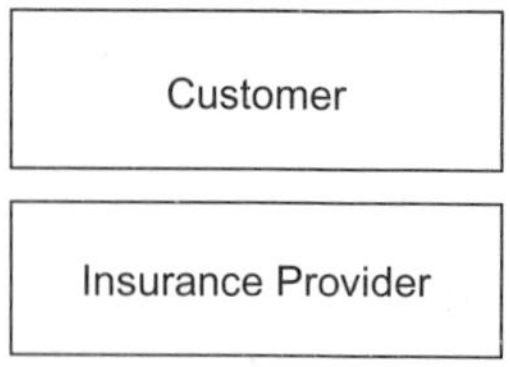

Figure 3.18 Entity Notations – Example

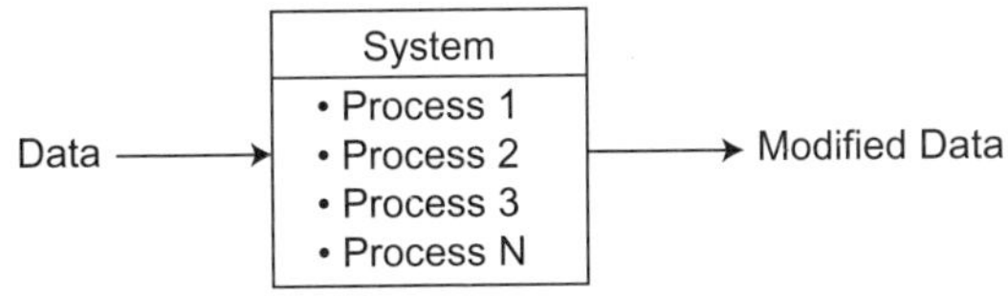

Figure 3.19 System versus Process

There are two kinds of notations being used in DFD (Figure 3.20).

1. DeMarco–Yourdon symbols
2. Gane–Sarson symbols

Their notations of process, data store, source/sink, dataflow are represented in Figure 3.20.

Processes (Figure 3.21) include a process name and process number. Mentioning the process names in a descriptive fashion, such as "calculate premium," "store in database," help conveying the purpose of the process to the DFD users.

Data Store

At the time of data processing the processes may store the data intermittently for future use. These stored data can be retrieved and used by the same process at later point of time or by a separate process. Files and tables are examples of types of data stores (Figure 3.22). Data stores are usually represented as shown in Figure 3.22.

Discussion Questions

1. Discuss and list down various data sources used in the college to run the college.

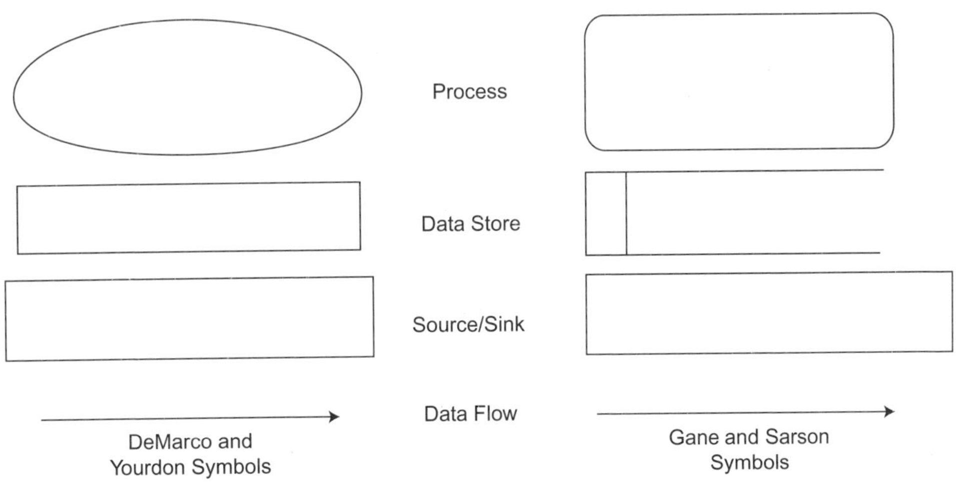

Figure 3.20 Data Flow Notations

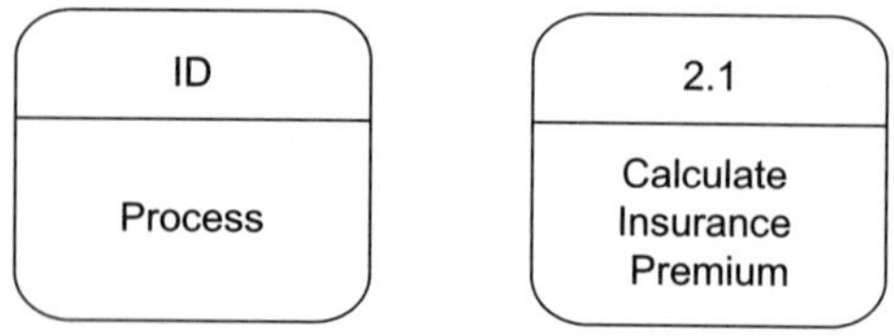

Figure 3.21 Process Notations

Figure 3.22 Data Source Notation

Data Flow

All the above three parts are connected to a DFD using data flow. Data flow (Figure 3.23) demonstrates the movement of data between the entity, the process and the data store revealing how the components of the DFD interface with each other. Arrow is used to represent data flow and the data name is written on top of it and should be unique within a specific DFD.

Difference between Flow Diagram and DFD

The arrows in DFD show that the data is being flown from one component to the other, and it does not specify whether the data is being pushed by the component. Components in DFD do not describe whether data will be executed by the components. Data in DFD can go through multiple components via multiple connections.

How to create a DFD

The DFD for a system may get progressively elaborated with multiple levels of DFDs. It starts with a context diagram (Figure 3.24) where the entire system is represented as a single process and associated with external entities.

Then the Level 0 diagram is created which shows general processes and the data stores. Then in subsequent level of DFDs each of the processes depicted in the Level 0 diagram gets elaborated. The highest level of DFD is generally called as context diagram as it depicts the context of the entire system.

Developing the Level 0 DFD

The main purpose of the Level 0 DFD (Figure 3.25) is to represent the system boundary. All components inside the system boundary are included in a single process box in the DFD. External entities

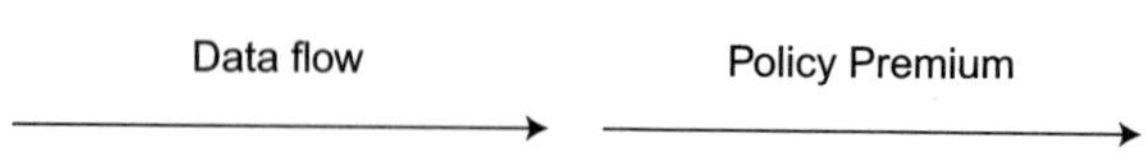

Figure 3.23 Data Flow Notations

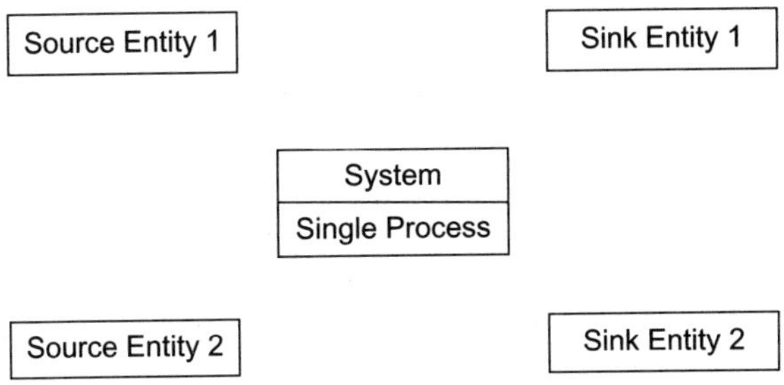

Figure 3.24 Context Diagram

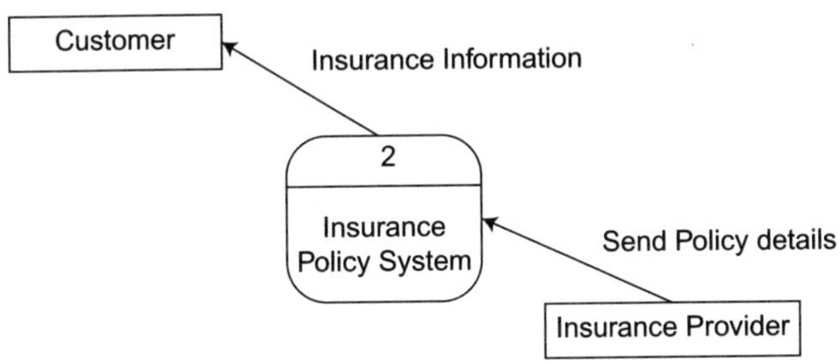

Figure 3.25 Level 0 DFD

are shown and the arrows to and from the external entities show the system's relationship with its environment. It is not required to show the data flow happening between the external entities, but if depicting such a data flow helps in adding clarity to the overall DFD then such interactions can be shown using hashed lines.

Level 0 DFS shows the data stores of the system clearly.

Child (Level 1+) Diagrams

Each of the sub-processes is then elaborated in subsequent Child DFDs. Refer Figure 3.26 where the insurance premium calculator is elaborated as one of the Child DFD. The symbol and notations are same as Level 0 diagram, but more information is added about the process in this level.

Some Good Practices While Creating the DFD

DFDs act as the principle source of information for the design team and thus, the volume of information and correctness are very importantly to be ensured. There is no right or wrong way to create a DFD, but definitely there are efficient and inefficient DFDs. Some guidelines for creating efficient DFDs and some caveats to avoid the inefficient ones are as follows:

1. Discover all the data items: This is the first and the most important step for creating a DFD. These data items may come out from the requirement document or get unearthed during the later stages while analyzing the requirement. Each and every data item has some origin (from where they come) and a target (where they go). Create a table to document this information in the below-mentioned format.

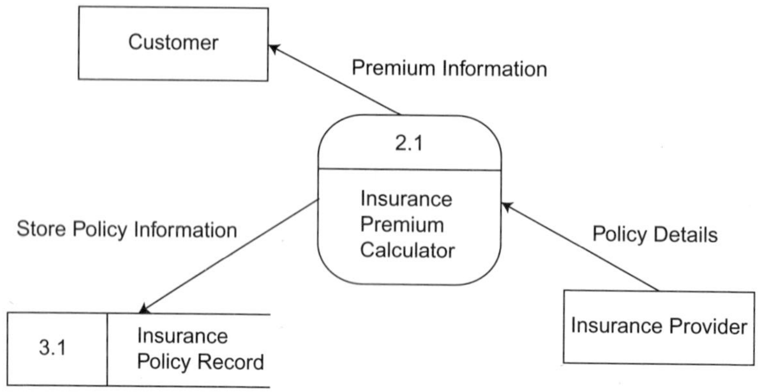

Figure 3.26 Level 1 DFD

Data Item	Origin	Target

2. Determine the system boundaries: Analyze the table created in the above step for each of the data items and find out whether it belongs to internal system or outside the system. This defines the system boundary.
3. Develop Level 0 DFD: At this stage, all the data items inside the system boundary should be contained in one DFD and connected with others. The interaction of data items external to the system with those inside the system needs to be shown as well this defines how the system interacts with its environment. All the interactions crossing the system boundaries should be captured in Level 0 DFD before moving to the lower level blow ups. There should not be any new data flow crossing the system boundary in child level figures.
4. Develop child (Level 1+) level DFD: The aim of the first level DFD is to provide a high-level view of the system which has all the major processes and data stores identified. List down all the incoming and outgoing data flows so that the corresponding sources and destinations can be found. There may be some data stores shared by multiple processes. Understand that creating of the DFD is an iterative process – each level of DFD can be refined till all the desired information is part of it. Hence, more granular level DFDs may be elaborated based on the complexity of the system.

Some of the best practices that can be taken into consideration while creating the DFDs are mentioned below. This also provides guidelines on what a valid and non-valid DFD is based on.

1. There should not be any data flow directly from one data source to another. This is because the data stores are simply the storage area and cannot initiate a communication. In between there should mandatorily be one or more processes which initiate the process flow.
2. Entities are people or systems outside the system boundary. The data from the entities may not be matching the syntax of the data stored in the data stores inside the system boundaries. Thus, it is important to avoid the direct data flow between the entity and the data store.
3. If the DFD contains the data flow between the entities then it will be difficult for the system to validate the same as the entities are outside the system boundary. Model only the flows which the system is expected to now or react to.

4. If there are two processes in the system which are not running simultaneously, then it is not valid to show a data flow between them. This is because the processes have no memory and cannot store any intermediate results.
5. There are 3 types of valid data flows:
   (a) Between a process and an entity
   (b) Between a process and a data store
   (c) Between two processes that run simultaneously
6. If there is a process which has only input data flow then it is an invalid process and is called a Black Hole
7. Similarly a process which has only output flow is not valid and is called a Miracle
8. Validate whether there is sufficient input data flow to produce the intended output data flow. A process with insufficient data input for the predicted output is called a Grey Hole.

3.2.2.2 Control Flow Model

Data flow diagram which is used to show the data flow in a system is already discussed. There are systems where the flow is controlled by events rather than by data. A control flow diagram (Table 3.3) is used to represent such systems.

These diagrams are generally time dependent. The flow of controls activates some processes. Here the model contains same processes as the DFD, but instead of showing the data flow here, the control flow is shown.

The concept of Control Specification (CSPEC) is introduced which is like a window that controls the processes represented in the DFD based on the event that is passed through the window. Below is an example where the control flow and the CSPEC are shown (Figure 3.27).

The inflow of water is stopped once the water level in the tank reaches the safety mark. Note that the control flow is represented with dotted lines. And the CSPEC is represented with a solid bar (Figure 3.28).

A control model and a process model are connected through data condition. Data condition occurs when data input to a process causes a control output. The simple guideline for creating a CFD is discussed below.

1. Draw the data flow diagram and then get rid of all the data flow arrows.
2. Add control items and windows into CSPEC wherever applicable.
3. Create the CFD from the Level 0 and elaborate into more granular child CFDs.

Table 3.3 Structured Analysis, Control Flow Diagram

Structured Analysis	
Type	**Corresponding Diagram**
Data Modeling	ER Diagram
Functional Modeling	Data Flow Diagram
	Control Flow Diagram
Behavioral Modeling	State Transition Diagram

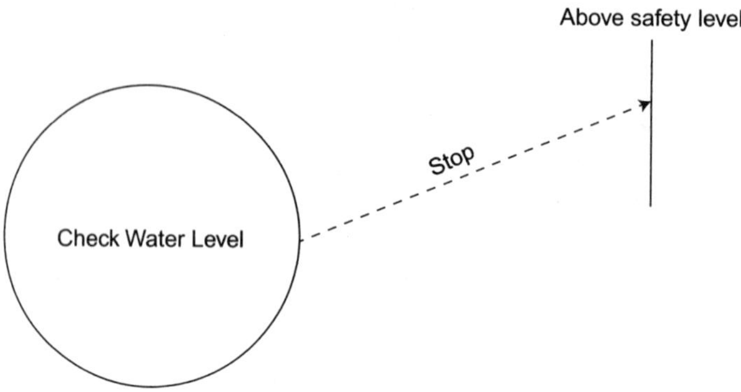

Figure 3.27 Control Flow Example

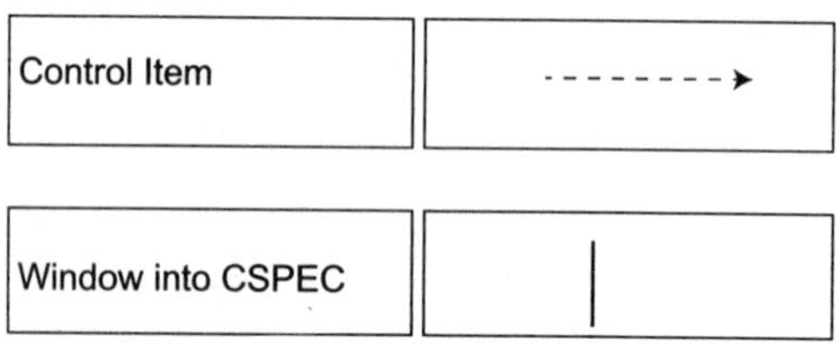

Figure 3.28 Control Flow Notations

Discussion Questions

1. Discuss the control flow of a road traffic signal system.

3.2.3 Behavioral Modeling

Behavioral modeling (Figure 3.29) is the third type of structured analysis approach.

The type of analysis models which try to capture the change in behavior of the system as an effect of some event or trigger are grouped as the behavioral models. State transition diagram (STD) is one example of behavioral modeling.

3.2.3.1 State Transition Diagram (STD)

STDs (Table 3.4) represent the system states and events that trigger state transitions or state change.

The actions (e.g., activation of some process) as a result of triggers in the system are captured in this model. A state can be an observable mode of behavior. STDs are created for objects which have significant dynamic behavior. For example, the customer entry form of the banking system may add a new customer where the customer's status is "open". If the customer fails to maintain the minimum balance for a considerable time then the account status may change to "suspended." See Figure 3.30 where the state transition for the banking system is elaborated.

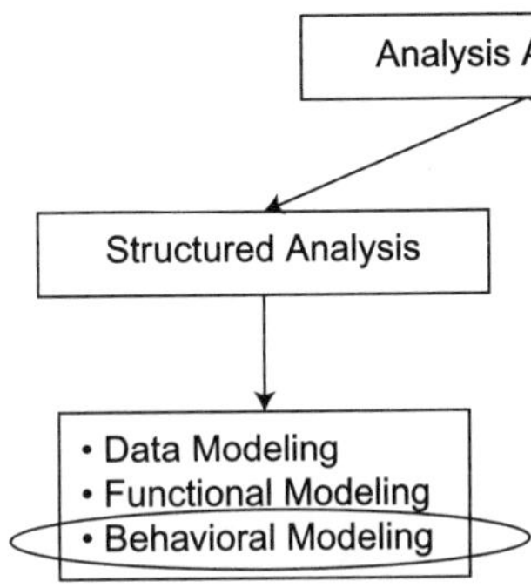

Figure 3.29 Structured Analysis, Behavioral Modeling

Table 3.4 Structured Analysis, State Transition Diagram

Structured Analysis	
Type	**Corresponding Diagram**
Data Modeling	ER Diagram
Functional Modeling	Data Flow Diagram
	Control Flow Diagram
Behavioral Modeling	State Transition Diagram

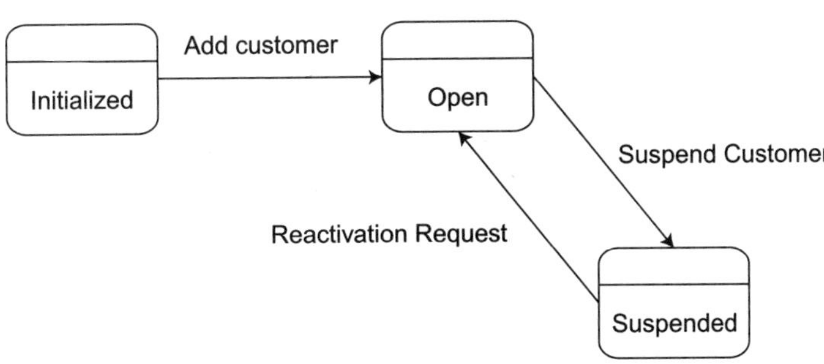

Figure 3.30 State Transition Diagram

Discussion Questions

List down various state transition status in a college student life from morning till evening.

1. ________________________________
2. ________________________________
3. ________________________________
4. ________________________________

3.3 OBJECT-ORIENTED ANALYSIS

In an object-oriented analysis the system is depicted as a group of interacting objects. The attributes of the objects are represented by its class, the state and the behavior. With modern tools and techniques which support creation of object-oriented analysis, these analysis techniques have become very popular. The details of the Object-oriented analysis and design models are discussed in detail in the subsequent chapters.

Summary

The domain of structured analysis comprises three modeling approaches:

- Data modeling
- Functional or flow-oriented modeling and
- Behavioral modeling

Structured Analysis	
Type	**Corresponding Diagram**
Data Modeling	ER Diagram
Functional Modeling	Data Flow Diagram
	Control Flow Diagram
Behavioral Modeling	State Transition Diagram

- Entity relation diagram is a form of data modeling technique. It diagrammatically shows the relationship between different objects inside a system.
- Data flow diagram is a highly effective model which is used for showing the flow of information through a system. DFDs can be used in the early stages of systems analysis to help understand the current system and to represent a required system. The DFDs represent external entities sending and receiving information (called entities), the processes that change information (called processes), the information flows (called data flows), and the place where the information is stored (called data stores). Level 0 or the context diagram is the top level diagram which can be decomposed into lower level diagrams (Level 1, Level 2...Level N) to represent different areas of the system.
- STD is an example of the behavioral modeling technique. It shows the system states and events that trigger state transitions or state change.

Model Questions
PART A (Objective type)

1. Providing a graphical representation of the system behavior which is depicted as a combination of functional flow and data flow to create the input for the design phase is called

A. Analysis modeling B. Data modeling

C. Functional modeling D. Behavioral modeling

Answer: A

2. The two most popular approaches to software analysis, which have developed and got fine-tuned over the years, are structured analysis and object-oriented analysis.

A. True B. False

Answer: A

3. What are the notations to capture the control and behavioral aspects of the real time engineering problems along with the information systems applications?

A. Analysis modeling B. Data modeling

C. Functional-oriented analysis D. Behavioral modeling

Answer: C

4. All of the following are examples of structured analysis except?

A. Data modeling B. Functional or flow-oriented modeling

C. Behavioral modeling D. Design analysis

Answer: D

5. Which is an analysis technique that deals with the data processing part of an application?

A. Analysis modeling B. Data modeling

C. Functional modeling D. Behavioral modeling

Answer: B

6. This is the identity which has multiple attributes and is related to other entities in the system.

A. Flow object B. Attributes object

C. Data object D. Information object

Answer: C

7. Along with the relationship information of different objects, it is also important to capture how many types of each object can be attached with other objects. This is called

A. Modality B. Cardinality

C. Modularity D. Attach ability

Answer: B

8. Along with the relationship information of different objects, it is also important to know whether it is mandatory to attach an object with another object. This is called

A. Modality B. Cardinality

C. Modularity D. Attachability

Answer: A

9. All of the following relationship is possible between objects as per cardinality, except:

A. One-to-one relationship (1:1)

B. One-to-many relationship (1:M)

C. Many-to-many relationship (M:N)

D. Many-to-one relationship (M:1)

Answer: D

10. Modality value is possible between objects as per modality 0, 1, N.

A. True B. False

Answer : B

11. All of the following are the components of ER diagram, except:

A. Attributes B. Data objects C. Data flow D. Relationship

Answer: C

12. The place where the description and information about all the data objects produced and consumed by the software system is maintained.

A. System consumption B. Data object storage C. Data memory D. Data dictionary

Answer: D

13. Which of the following is an example of data modeling?

A. ER diagram B. Data flow diagram

C. State transition diagram (STD) D. Control flow diagram

Answer: A

14. Modeling deals with DFD and modeling deals with ER diagram

A. Data modeling, functional modeling B. Functional modeling, data modeling

C. Analysis modeling, behavioral modeling D. Behavioral modeling, data modeling

Answer: B

15. Data flow diagram is an example of?

A. Data modeling B. Functional or flow-oriented modeling

C. Behavioral modeling D. Design analysis

Answer: B

16. The external systems which either provide data to the system or receive from it are called

A. Entities B. Attributes C. Data feeds D. Information flow

Answer : A

17. Entities are usually represented as

A. Square B. Triangle C. Rectangle D. Dotted line

Answer: C

18. Files and tables are examples of

A. Data objects B. Data stores C. Data dictionary D. Data

Answer :B

19. There are systems where the flow is controlled by events rather than by data. Choose the correct option which is used to represent such systems.

A. Control flow diagram B. System flow diagram

C. Data flow diagram D. Event flow diagram

Answer: A

20. The concept which is like a window that controls the processes represented in the DFD based on the event that is passed through the window.

A. SCPEC B. CSPEC C. CSEPC D. SCEPC

Answer: B

21. State transition diagram (STD) is a best example of

A. Data modeling B. Functional modeling

C. Behavioral modeling D. Design analysis

Answer: C

PART B (Answer in one or two lines)

1. List down the objectives to be fulfilled by the requirements analysis during the requirement analysis stage.
2. What is Analysis Modeling?
3. List down the names of popular approaches to software analysis.
4. What is function-oriented analysis?
5. List down the three modeling approaches of structured analysis.
6. What is data modeling?
7. Write notes on data objects.
8. What is cardinality and modality?
9. What are all the relationships possible between objects as per cardinality?
10. What are all the relationships possible between objects as per modality?
11. What is ER diagram?
12. What are all the components of ER diagram?
13. List down the relationships and notations used in ER diagram.
14. What is data dictionary?
15. List down examples of data dictionary contents?
16. What is functional modeling?
17. What is data flow diagram?
18. List down the four main components of DFD modeling.
19. Write notes on source entity and sink entity of data flow diagram.

20. Represent source entity and sink entity in the form of a diagram.
21. Name two kinds of notations being used in DFD.
22. Write notes on data stores.
23. What is control flow model?
24. What is CSPEC?
25. What is behavioral modeling?
26. What is state transition diagram (STD)?
27. What is object-oriented analysis?
28. What is the difference between flow diagram and DFD?
29. Write three simple guidelines for creating CFD?

PART C (Descriptive type)

1. List down the guidelines while creating analysis model.
2. Discuss data modeling in detail with ER diagram as example.
3. Discuss cardinality and modality in detail with example.
4. Discuss data dictionary in detail.
5. Discuss functional modeling in detail with example.
6. What is Data flow diagram (DFD)? Discuss various components of DFD in detail.
7. List down the data flow notations used by Demarco–Yourdon and Gane–Sarson.
8. Discuss 3 steps of creating a data flow diagram.
9. Explain control flow diagram in detail.
10. What is behavioral modeling? Explain it with examples of state transition diagram (STD).

Section 3:
Design and Architectural Engineering

4

Design and Architectural Engineering

CHAPTER COVERAGE

1. *Design Process and Concepts*
2. *Basic Issues in Software Design*
3. *Characteristics of a Good Design*
4. *Software Design and Software Engineering*
5. *Function-Oriented System vs Object-Oriented System*
6. *Modularity, Cohesion, Coupling, Layering*
7. *Real-Time Software Design (RTS Design)*
8. *Design Models*
9. *Design Documentation*

4.1 DESIGN PROCESS AND CONCEPTS

During the design process, the software requirements model (discussed in the previous chapters), which was prepared for the requirements is converted into suitable and appropriate design models (Figure 4.1) that describe the architecture and other design components.

Each design product is verified and validated before moving to the next phase of software development.

In the requirements analysis stage, the decision about implementation is consciously avoided. In the design stage, the decision about implementation is consciously made and a step-by-step procedure is followed.

The design process encompasses a sequence of activities that slowly reduces the level of abstraction with which the software is represented.

Design activities are subdivided into high-level design activities and low-level (or detailed) design activities. Architecture is the outcome of high-level design activities, whereas the data structure and the corresponding algorithms are the outcomes of low-level design activities.

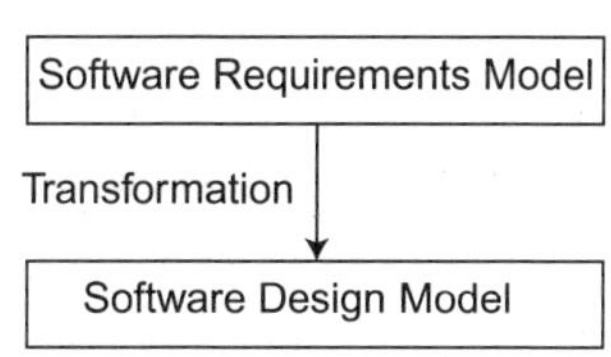

Figure 4.1 Software Design Model

4.2 BASIC ISSUES IN SOFTWARE DESIGN

The following are the basic issues in software design:

1. If the requirements model is wrongly represented then the design model also will go wrong.
2. Mapping each functional requirement into design representation is difficult.
3. Mapping all the requirements into a single design model is a tedious job.
4. Modeling a design that enables easy coding as well as catering to all the requirements is difficult.
5. Requirements keep changing and evolve over a period of time, but changing the design accordingly is difficult.
6. Balancing simplicity and efficiency is difficult.
7. Balancing clarity and code safety is difficult.
8. Balancing the robust design and the system response time is difficult.
9. Following standards in design and simultaneously catering to and matching the requirements is difficult.
10. Error function handling is also a difficult part of design.

4.3 CHARACTERISTICS OF A GOOD DESIGN

1. Should be able to convert all the requirements into design
2. Should be easily understandable and maintainable
3. Should be easy to change the design
4. Should be easily scalable

4.4 SOFTWARE DESIGN AND SOFTWARE ENGINEERING

A software design is an appropriate engineering representation of a software product under study and is the process of problem solving by converting the requirements of the product into a software solution (Figure 4.1). Traceability between the requirements and design is important so that it is possible to independently assess the design for requirements mapping. Software design should also be assessed for its own quality parameters such as robustness, flexibility, security, and design clarity. Software design can be considered as a plan for coding.

Software engineering comprises strict disciplines that need to be followed to develop a programmable solution to solve the problems of customers. Strategies are defined to obtain a runable, efficient, and maintainable software solution that takes care of the costs, quality, resources, and other expenditure. These strategies have been proposed by various engineers after implementing and analyzing the merits and demerits. It includes disciplines related to requirements collection, requirements analysis, designing, coding (development), testing the developed code, operation, and maintenance of the complete software.

4.5 FUNCTION-ORIENTED SYSTEM VS OBJECT-ORIENTED SYSTEM

The design of function-oriented system is called function-oriented design and the design of object-oriented system is called object-oriented design (Figure 4.2).

Since the function-oriented system is made up of functions, the function oriented design and the corresponding design structure is also based on functions. Data are stored outside the system in a

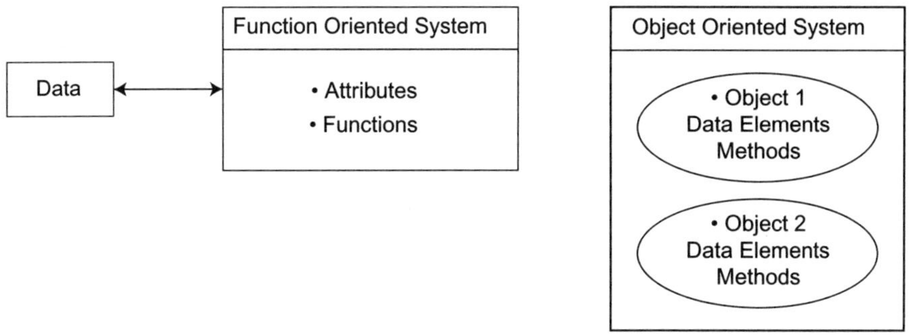

Figure 4.2 Function-Oriented System vs Object-Oriented System

function-oriented system. Functions are used to access, process, modify the data and store it back into the data storage system. The system state is maintained in the data. Functions are easily mapped to modules (subsystems).

Object-oriented design is the design concept of an object-oriented system, which is completely made up of objects. Objects have data and functions inside them. In this system also, functions (inside objects) are used to access the data (inside objects). We will be discussing the object-oriented concepts in detail in Chapter 5.

4.6 MODULARITY, COHESION, COUPLING, LAYERING

The possibility of dividing a single project into smaller units called modules is termed modularity (Figure 4.3) of the project. Modularity helps in designing the system in a better way and ensures that each module communicates and does the specific task assigned to it. It also helps in reusability and maintainability.

The two main characteristics that need to be considered while designing the modularity of projects are cohesion and coupling.

Cohesion refers to "how strongly" one module is related to the other, which helps to group similar items together. Cohesion measures the semantic strength (high and low cohesion) of relationships between modules within a functional unit. Internal cohesion of a module is the strength of the elements within the modules, whereas external cohesion of a module is the strength of relationships between modules (Figure 4.4).

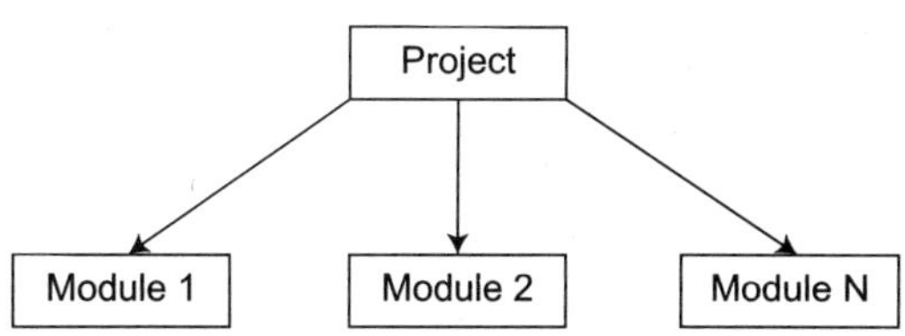

Figure 4.3 Modularity

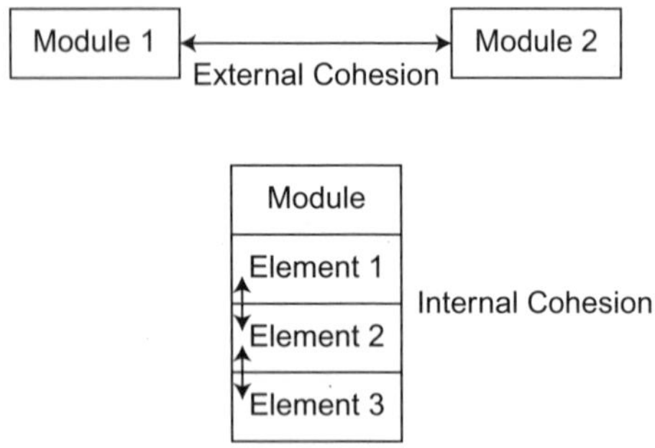

Figure 4.4 External vs Internal Cohesion

POINTS TO PONDER

Cohesion refers to "how strongly" one module is related to the other, which helps to group similar items together. Cohesion measures the semantic strength (high and low cohesion) of relationships between modules within a functional unit.

In a highly cohesive system code readability and reusability increases, and complexity is kept at a manageable level.

There are several types of cohesion, which are discussed below (Figure 4.5):

- Coincidental cohesion
- Logical cohesion
- Temporal cohesion
- Procedural cohesion
- Communicational cohesion
- Sequential cohesion
- Functional cohesion

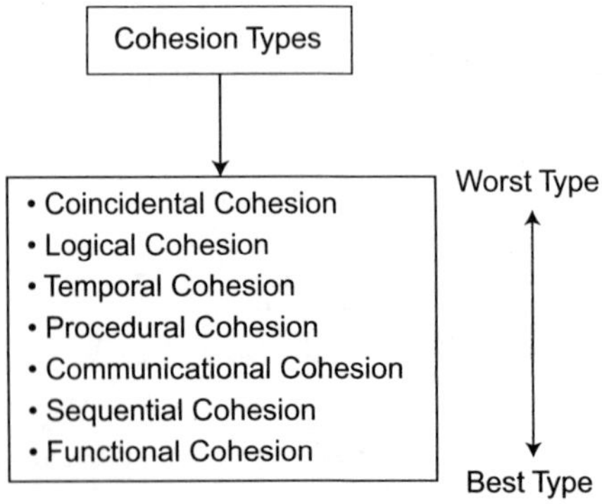

Figure 4.5 Cohesion Types

Coincidental cohesion: As the name indicates, in this type the cohesion (grouping) occurs coincidently. Elements or modules are grouped together for different purposes and there is no common reason for grouping. The only common thing is that they are grouped together.

Logical cohesion: In this type, as the name indicates, cohesion (grouping) occurs logically based on similarity and not based on functionality. Elements or modules are grouped together based on common logic. Logical grouping may be based on the functionality, nature, and behavior of the elements/modules.

Temporal cohesion: In this type, cohesion (grouping) occurs during run time at a particular time of program execution. Modules that are being called during the exception handling procedure can be grouped together. Modules that are being executed at time T, T + X, or T + 2X can be grouped together.

Procedural cohesion: In this type, cohesion (grouping) is used to execute a certain procedure. Modules that are used for a procedure can be grouped together. Note that the same module can be grouped together with another module for executing another procedure.

Communicational cohesion: In this type, cohesion (grouping) occurs because part of the module shares same data (acts on same data) for communication purposes. For example, functions A, B, and C access common data (same database). Modules A, B, and C access a common database.

Sequential cohesion: In this type, cohesion (grouping) occurs as the output of one module is an input of another module. This will look like an assembly line sequence.

Functional cohesion: In this type, cohesion (grouping) occurs as all the functions contribute to a single task of the module. In order to execute a single task, all modules contribute. Within a function, each part is executed in order.

Coupling is a measure of "how tightly" two entities or modules are related to each other. Coupling measures the strength of the relationships between entities or modules. It is very easy to measure coupling both quantitatively and qualitatively.

Figure 4.6 shows the difference between loosely coupled and highly coupled modules.

POINTS TO PONDER

Coupling is a measure of "how tightly" two entities or modules are related to each other. Coupling measures the strength of the relationships between entities or modules. Coupling is very easy to measure quantitatively and qualitatively.

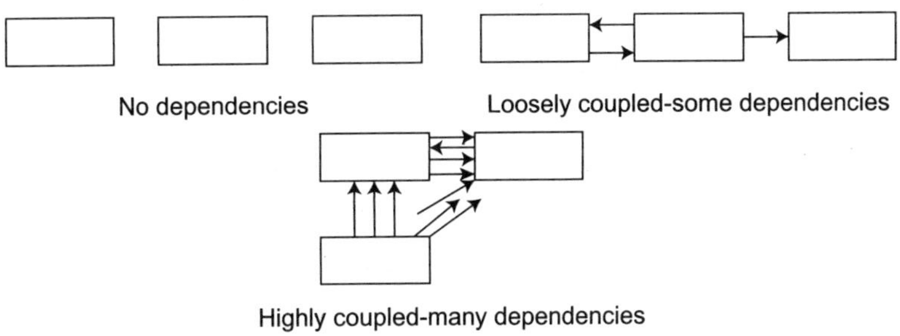

Figure 4.6 Coupling

Minimize coupling and maximize cohesion is the principle of design. This means that a module should be as independent as possible.

There are different types of coupling, which are discussed below (Figure 4.7):

- Content coupling
- Common coupling
- Control coupling
- Stamp coupling
- Data coupling
- Uncoupled

In content coupling, one component refers the content of another component and here the coupling is considered to be higher. For example, Module 1 accesses the data of Module 2 and changes it (Figure 4.8).

In common coupling, one or more modules share the same data which is common. This is an example of bad design and should be avoided (Figure 4.9).

In control coupling, a module passes its control component to another module. Depending on the control being passed, it is considered as good or bad. Module 1 calls Module 2 and Module 2 passes the flag that indicates a status (Figure 4.10).

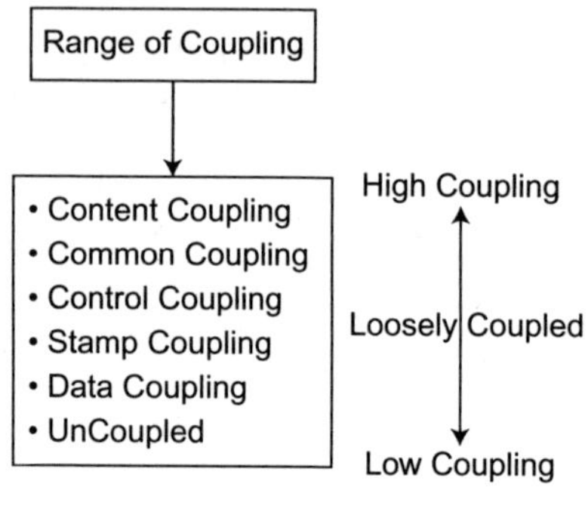

Figure 4.7 Types of Coupling

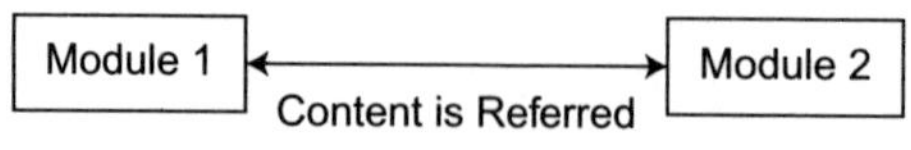

Figure 4.8 Content Coupling

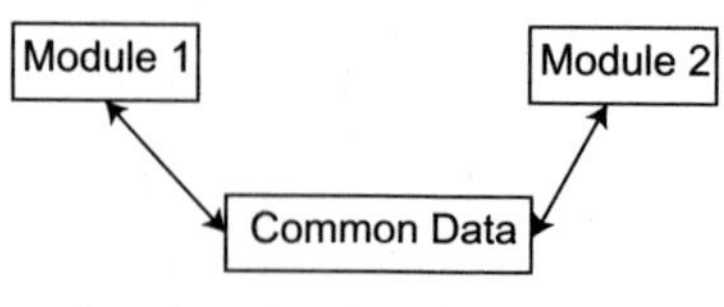

Figure 4.9 Common Coupling

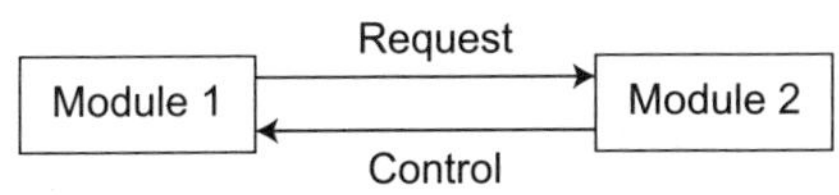

Figure 4.10 Control Coupling

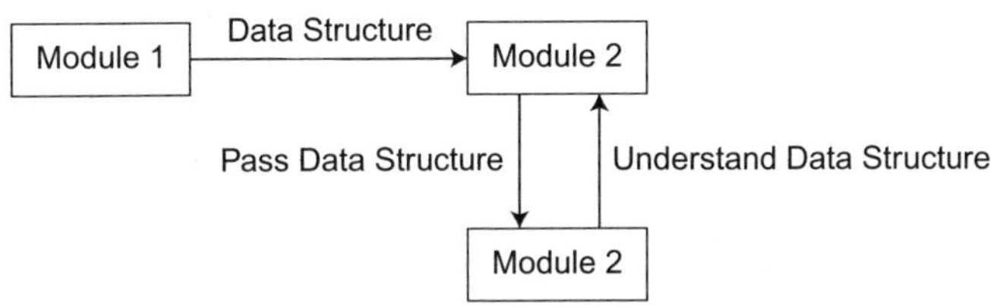

Figure 4.11 Stamp Coupling

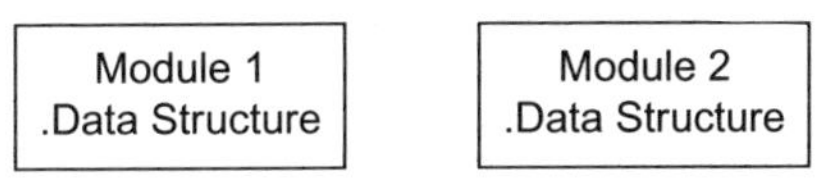

Figure 4.12 Data Coupling

In stamp coupling, a module passes a data structure to a module, which does not have access to the entire data structure. The module sends the data structure to another module to understand it. The module does not have any power and just acts as a stamp and is therefore called stamp coupling (Figure 4.11).

Two modules are data coupled, if there are homogeneous data items or structures (Figure 4.12).

POINTS TO PONDER

Scope of Effect and Scope of Control: The scope of effect of a module refers to the other modules that are affected by a decision made by a particular module. Note: The module can be at any level, that is, it can be at the same level, higher level, or lower level.

The scope of control of a module refers to that module and all of its subordinate modules belonging to that particular module.

4.7 REAL-TIME SOFTWARE DESIGN (RTS DESIGN)

Real time refers to designing the software systems whose behavior is subject to timing constraints and is embedded in a large hardware system. This kind of software monitors and controls the system and its environment by gathering different sets of data using sensors. Actuators act in the opposite way and they change the environment of the system.

A microwave oven has a functionality to stop the cooking after a specified time period. In this case, the sensor continuously monitors the time and the actuator stops the control of the microwave oven after a specified time period. Burglar alarm is another classic example of real-time software.

> **POINTS TO PONDER**
>
> Real time refers to designing the software systems whose behavior is subject to timing constraints and is embedded in a large hardware system. This kind of software monitors and controls the system and its environment by gathering different sets of data using sensors. Actuators acts in the opposite way and they change the environment of the system.

4.8 DESIGN MODELS

The software engineer creates a design model, the end user develops a mental image that is often called the user's model, and the implementers of the system create a system image. These models differ drastically. The role of an interface designer is to reconcile these differences and derive a consistent representation of the interface.

Figure 4.13 shows the design models of an entire system.

4.8.1 Data Design

In data design, a high-level model is depicted (drawn) based on the user's view of the data or information. Data design is actually derived from the ER diagram (refer to Structural Analysis – Data Modeling in Chapter 3). Designing to correctly fit the data structure is essential for creating a high-quality application. Transforming this data model into a database structure is critical for implementing the business requirements. The data warehouse structure, if any, is also designed in this step.

Database is the center of this design. Analysis that is applicable to a function, is also to be applied on the data. Data dictionary (information about data) is also established here.

4.8.2 Architectural Design

The objective of software design is to derive an architectural design (diagrammatic representation) of a system and this representation provides a framework from which more detailed design activities are conducted. Architectural design is derived from requirements analysis and is also based on already available architectural patterns and styles. It defines the physical and logical relationships between the major structural elements of a system and also between the corresponding components at a high level.

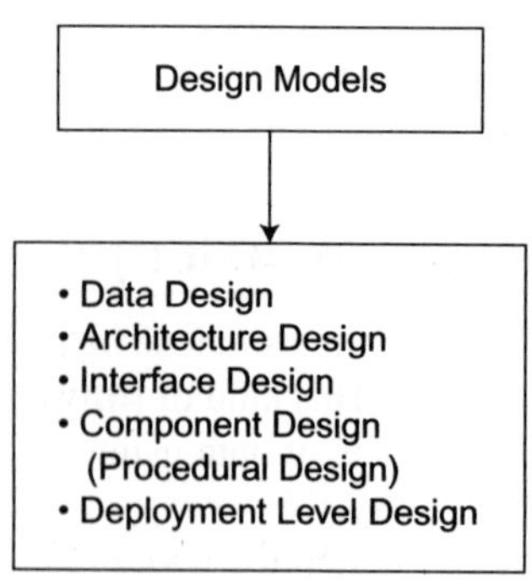

Figure 4.13 Design Models

4.8.2.1 What Is Software Architecture?

Software architecture defines the logical relationships between the major structural elements of a system and also the relationship between the corresponding components at a high level to execute the functionalities of the overall system.

4.8.2.2 Software Architecture vs System Architecture

The representation of software architecture in physical components of machines is called system architecture.

4.8.2.3 Architectural Notations

To represent the architectural design, different notations are used to represent the flow of control hierarchy. Depth indicates the number of levels of control and width represents the overall span of control (Figure 4.14).

Fan-in indicates the number of modules that directly control a given module. In Figure 4.15, Module 1 is controlled by three other modules and therefore fan-in of Module 1 is 3.

Fan-out is a measure of the number of modules that are directly controlled by another module. In Figure 4.16, Module 1 controls three different modules and therefore fan-out of Module 1 is 3.

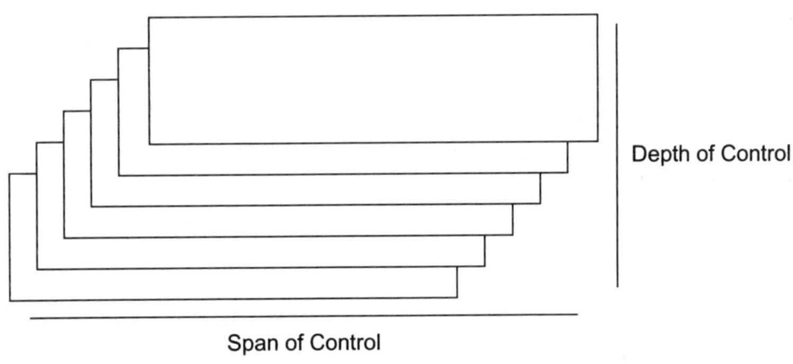

Figure 4.14 Level and Span of Control

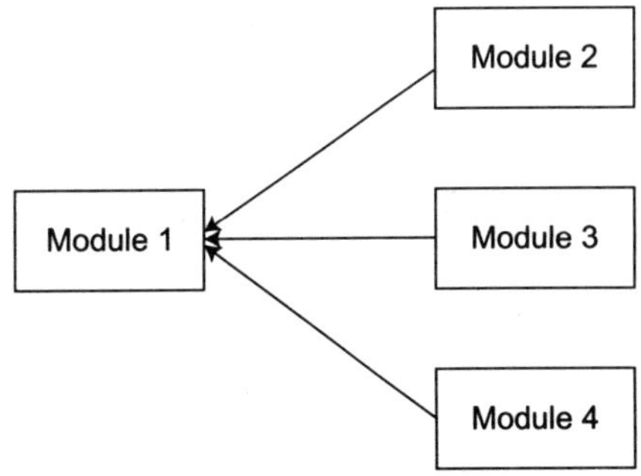

Figure 4.15 Fan-in Notation

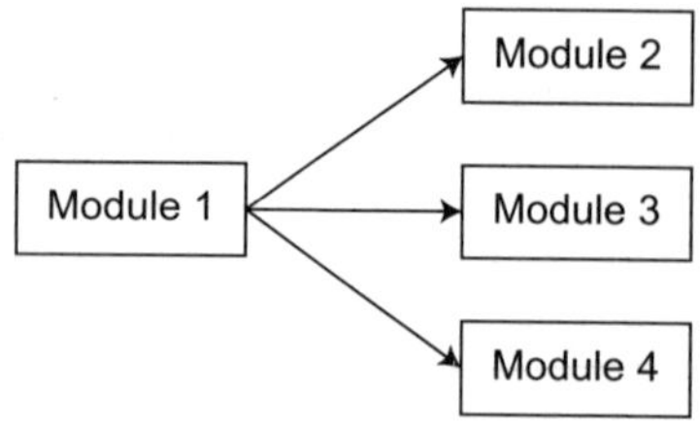

Figure 4.16 Fan-out Notation

A pipe-and-filter pattern (Figure 4.17) has a set of components called filters and they are connected by pipes, which transmit data from one component to the next.

A data store (Figure 4.18) resides at the center of this architecture and is accessed frequently by other components.

POINTS TO PONDER

Fan-out is a measure of the number of modules that are directly controlled by another module.

4.8.2.4 Mapping Requirements into Architecture

Requirements (data flow and control flow) are transformed into design using the architectural diagram. This diagram establishes the information flow between various components. There are two types of information flow (or data flow), namely, transform flow and transaction flow. In the transform flow, the data flow occurs sequentially and in straight line paths, whereas one data triggers the flow of data in one or various paths in the transaction flow.

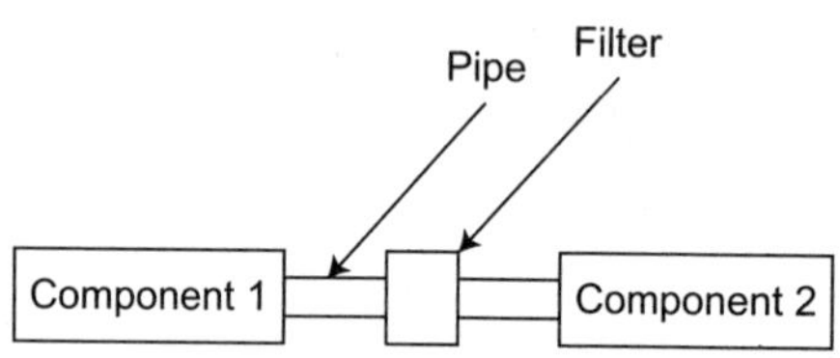

Figure 4.17 Pipe and Filter

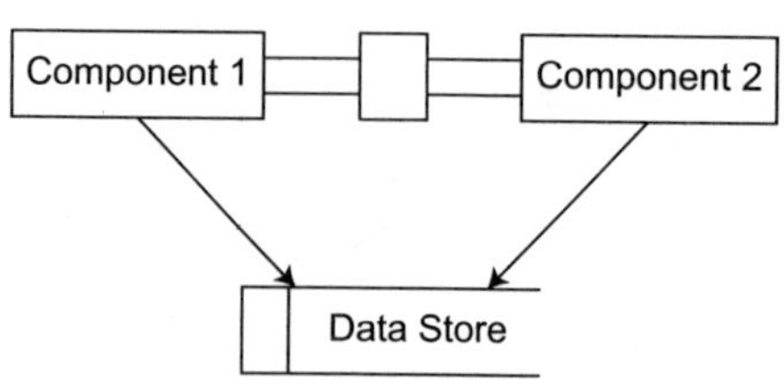

Figure 4.18 Data Store Representation

Design Heuristics Design heuristics are used in both transform and transaction mapping. First, let us look into design heuristics before getting into the details of transform and transaction mapping.

Heuristic is a Greek word that means "to find or to discover," indicating that it is an experience-based technique and is simply a thumb rule or an intuitive judgment. Design heuristic is a heuristic for the design – which is purely based on previous experience.

The following are the simple and basic design heuristics:

- Evaluate the design first using the principle "minimize coupling and maximize cohesion"
- Minimize a high fan-out structure (refer to Fan-in and Fan-out structures given in this chapter)
- Move to a fan-in structure as depth increases (refer to Fan-in and Fan-out structures given in this chapter)
- Scope of effect of a module should be within the scope of control of that particular module (refer to Scope of Effect and Scope of Control given in this chapter)

Transform Mapping Transform mapping has several steps, which are as follows (Figure 4.19):

Step 1: Analyze and refine the existing DFD (DFD is a functional model structure which was discussed in Chapter 3 in detail)

Step 2: Find out the transform and transaction characteristics of DFD

Step 3: Try to isolate the transform center by providing input, output, and boundary conditions

Step 4: After factoring (minimum of two levels), use design heuristics to improve the mapping

Transaction Mapping The steps in transaction mapping are similar to transform mapping, except that in Step 3, we try to isolate the transaction center instead of the transform center which are as follows (Figure 4.20):

Step 1: Analyze and refine the existing DFD

Step 2: Find out the transform and transaction characteristics of the DFD

Step 3: Try to isolate the transaction center

Step 4: After factoring (minimum of two levels), use design heuristics to improve the mapping

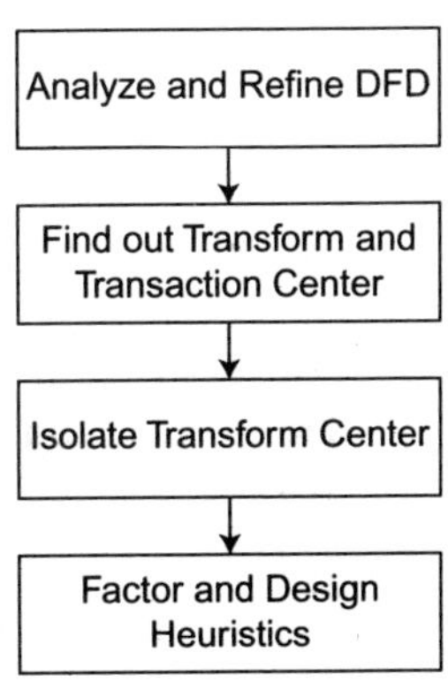

Figure 4.19 Transform Mapping

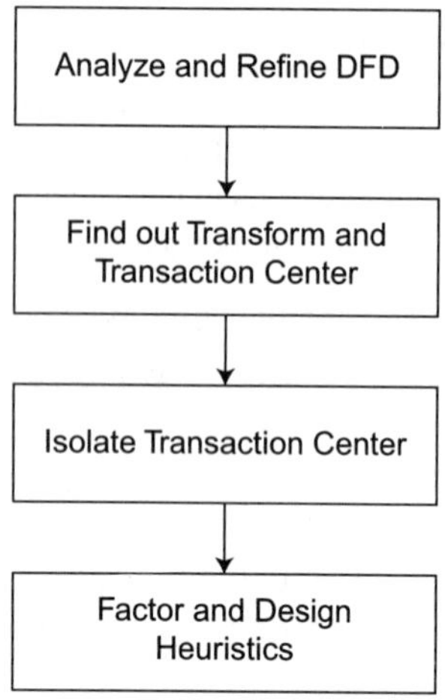

Figure 4.20 Transaction Mapping

Refining Architectural Design After carrying out transform and transaction mapping, the architecture can be further refined using the following steps (not inclusive):

- Define a processing account for every component of the architecture
- Develop an interface description for every component of the architecture
- Define design limitations and boundaries clearly
- Conduct a set of design reviews
- Make further refinement if needed

Refinement of software architecture during the early stages of design is encouraged. Alternative architectural styles may be derived, refined, and evaluated to obtain the "best" approach. This approach to optimization is one of the true benefits derived by developing a representation of software architecture. It is important to note that structural simplicity often reflects both elegance and efficiency. Design refinement should strive for the smallest number of modules that is consistent with effective modularity and the least complex data structure that adequately serves information requirements.

Assessing Alternative Architectural Design Each decision has two outputs. While representing the project in architectural design at one position, the design changes and an alternative design is needed.

4.8.2.5 Distributed System Architecture

Distributed System A distributed system has three main components, namely, data, process, and interface. If these components are distributed across locations, it is called a distributed system. A computer network connects the components which are at different locations.

Centralized Structure In a centralized structure, the server (data and process components) resides in a centralized place. The interface component (called client) is distributed across locations. When the number of clients increases, the load of the server also increases (Figure 4.21).

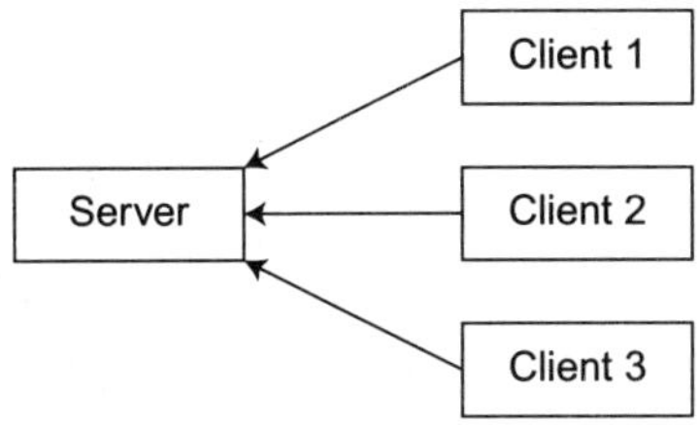

Figure 4.21 Centralized Structure

Decentralized Structure In a decentralized structure, both the client and the server reside in the same machine and they also communicate with another machine to share the resources (server and client components), which is also called peer-to-peer communication. Both the computers (system) perform the same functionality, which is called symmetric functionality (Figure 4.22). The connection between one computer (system) and another computer (system) is unstructured.

Hybrid Structure A combination of the centralized structure and the decentralized structure is called a hybrid structure (Figure 4.23).

POINTS TO PONDER

A distributed system has three main components, namely, data, process, and interface. If these components are distributed across locations, it is called a distributed system. The three types of systems are centralized, decentralized, and hybrid.

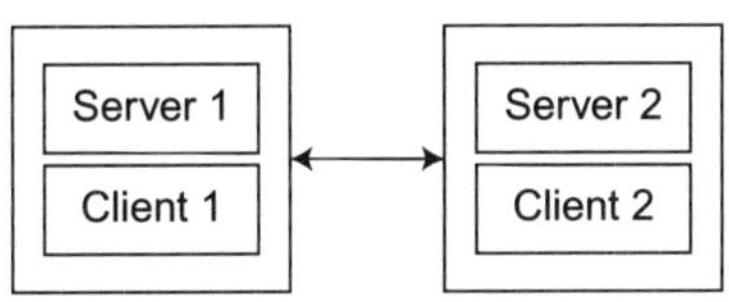

Figure 4.22 Decentralized Structure

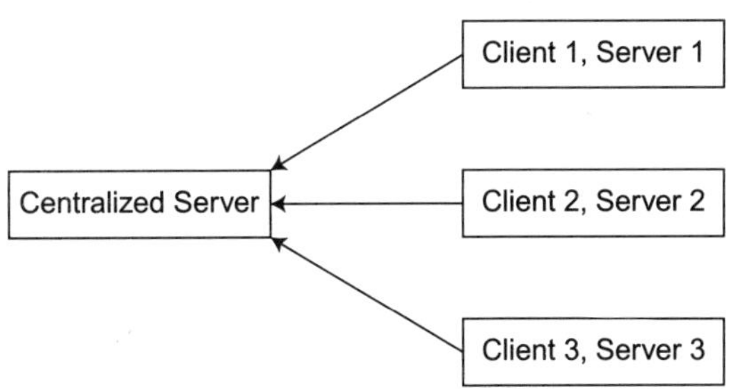

Figure 4.23 Hybrid Structure

4.8.2.6 Top-Down Approach and Bottom-Up Approach of Design

The top-down approach is represented by the hierarchical structure. It starts from the highest level to the lowest level in the hierarchy structure. This approach identifies the major components of the system and divides the components into lower level components. The root module is called the main module and the lower level components are called the subordinate modules. The top-down approach describes the organization and interaction of software components (Figure 4.24).

The bottom-up approach is just the opposite of the top-down approach and it starts with the basic lower level components of the system and proceeds to the higher level components (Figure 4.25).

4.8.2.7 Modular Design Approach

In this approach, the overall system is divided into modules (subsystems), which can be tested separately and can be combined (integrated) to form the overall system at a later point in time (Figure 4.26). We discussed this approach while discussing coupling and cohesion.

A modular system has the following characteristics:

- Each module will act as a separate system
- Each module is scalable and reusable
- Modules (subsystems) can be integrated easily to form the overall system
- Industry standards will be used in all modules
- Interface is consistent across the modules

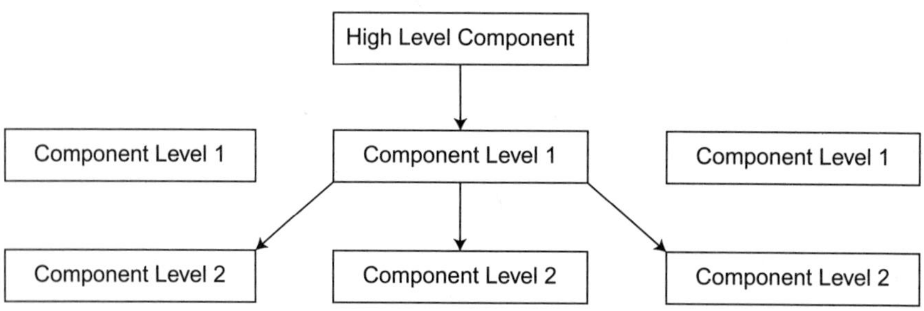

Figure 4.24 Top-Down Approach

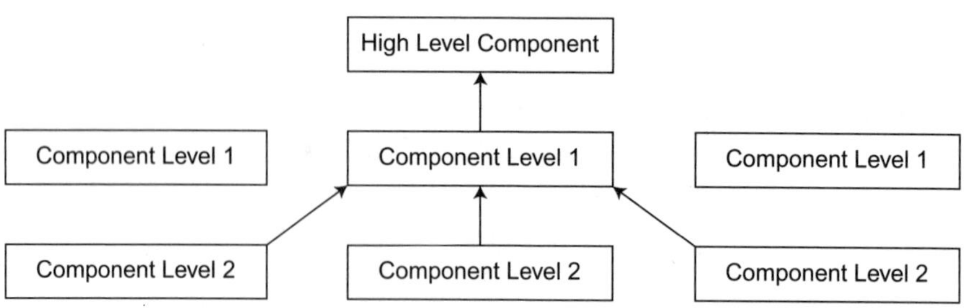

Figure 4.25 Bottom-Up Approach

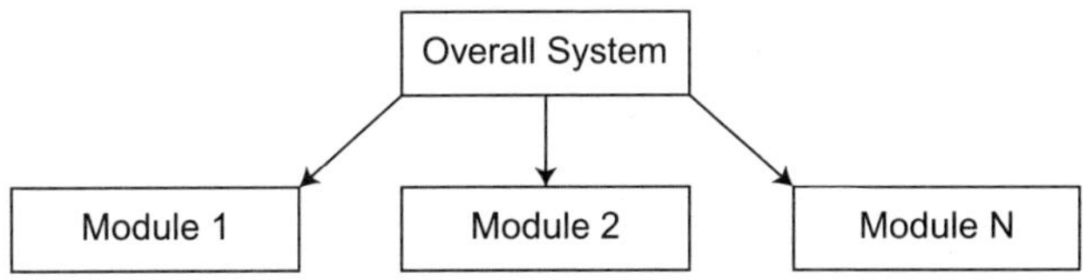

Figure 4.26 Modular Approach

4.8.3 User Interface Design

The data flow diagram (requirements analysis model) helps both architectural design and user interface design.

The user interface design creates an effective communication medium between a human (user of the system) and a computer. It proposes a set of interface design principles such that it identifies the objects and methods involved and then creates a screen layout that forms the basis for a user interface.

The user interface design focuses on three basic areas:

1. Interface between components of the system
2. Interface between the system and humans (users)
3. Interface between the system and other systems (nonhumans)

According to Theo Mandel, the three "golden rules" of interface design are:

1. Place the user in control
2. Reduce the user's memory load
3. Make the interface consistent

These three golden rules are discussed in detail in Chapter 7.

4.8.4 Procedural Design

Procedural design is also called component design. It is completely based on process specification (PSPEC) and control specification (CSPEC). The "state transition diagram" of the requirements analysis model is also used in component design.

Component design is usually done after user interface design. During user interface design, we discuss the components and details of their interface. At the component design stage, these interfaces get fine tuned. Component-level architecture and data designs are fine tuned and lower level algorithms are defined in detail for each component.

Component-level design depicts the software at a level of abstraction that is very close to the code. At the component level, the software engineer must represent data structures, interfaces, and algorithms in sufficient detail to guide in the generation of programming language source code. To accomplish this, the designer uses one of a number of design notations that represent component-level detail (text, graphical, or tabular formats).

Structured programming is a procedural design philosophy that constrains the number and type of logical constructs used to represent algorithmic detail. The intent of structured programming is to assist the designer in defining algorithms that are less complex and therefore easier to read, code, test, and maintain.

4.8.5 Deployment-Level Design

Deployment-level design takes care of the procedure of implementing the actual systems and their components within a physical environment. The Unified Modelling Language (UML) deployment diagram is used for this purpose and we will be discussing UML in detail in Chapter 6.

4.9 DESIGN DOCUMENTATION

There are two types of design documents, namely, high-level design document and low-level design document. A high-level design document contains architectural details.

System architecture document (SAD) is the design document where all the design and architectural elements are captured. An SAD along with a low-level design document is used as an input to the coders (developers). A low-level design document contains the data structure and its associated components along with interaction details.

Summary

A software design is an appropriate engineering representation of a software product under study and is the process of problem solving by converting the requirements of the product into a software solution. Software Engineering comprises strict disciplines that need to be followed to develop a programmable solution to solve the problems of customers. Strategies are defined to obtain a runable, efficient, and maintainable software solution that takes care of the costs, quality, resources, and other expenditure.

- The design of function-oriented system is called function-oriented design and the design of object-oriented system is called object-oriented design
- The possibility of dividing a single project into smaller units called modules is termed **modularity**.
- **Cohesion** refers to "how strong" one module is related to the other, which helps to group similar items together. Cohesion measures the semantic strength (high and low cohesion) of relationships between modules within a functional unit.

  The various types of cohesion are:
  - Coincidental cohesion
  - Logical cohesion
  - Temporal cohesion
  - Procedural cohesion
  - Communicational cohesion
  - Sequential cohesion
  - Functional cohesion
- **Coupling** is a measure of "how tightly" two entities or modules are related to each other. Coupling measures the strength of the relationships between entities or modules.

  The different types of coupling are:
  - Content coupling
  - Common coupling
  - Control coupling
  - Stamp coupling
  - Data coupling
  - Uncoupled

- The **scope of effect** of a module refers to the modules that are affected by a decision made by a particular module.
- The **scope of control** of a module refers to that module and all of its subordinate modules belonging to that particular module.
- A distributed system has three main components, namely, data, process, and interface. If these components are distributed across locations, it is called a distributed system. A computer network connects the components which are at different locations. In a centralized structure, the server (data and process components) resides in a centralized place. The interface component (called client) is distributed across locations. In a decentralized structure, both the client and the server reside in the same machine and they also communicate with another machine to share the resources (server and client components), which is also called peer-to-peer communication.
- **Procedural/component design** is completely based on process specification (PSPEC) and control specification (CSPEC). The "state transition diagram" of the requirements analysis model is also used in component design.
- **Deployment-level design** takes care of the procedure of implementing the actual systems and their components within a physical environment. The UML deployment diagram is used for this purpose.

Model Questions
PART A (Objective type)

1. What is an appropriate engineering representation of a software product under study and is the process of problem solving by converting the requirements of the product into a software solution referred to as?

   A. Software design   B. Software engineering
   C. Software coding   D. Software validation

Answer: A

2. What is the study that comprises strict disciplines that need to be followed to develop a programmable solution to solve the problems of customers?

   A. Software design   B. Software engineering
   C. Software coding   D. Software validation

Answer: B

3. What is the possibility of dividing a single project into smaller units called modules termed as?

   A. Modularity   B. Cohesion   C. Coupling   D. Encapsulation

Answer: A

4. Which of the following terms refer to "how strongly" one module is related to the other, which helps to group similar items together?

   A. Modularity   B. Cohesion   C. Coupling   D. Encapsulation

Answer: B

5. All of the following are types of cohesion except:

   A. Logical cohesion   B. Physical cohesion
   C. Functional cohesion   D. Communicational cohesion

Answer: B

6. What is the type of cohesion in which elements or modules are grouped together for different purposes and there is no common reason for grouping?

   A. Coincidental cohesion B. Logical cohesion

   C. Temporal cohesion D. Communicational cohesion

Answer: A

7. What is the type of cohesion in which elements or modules are grouped together based on similarity and not based on functionality?

   A. Coincidental cohesion B. Logical cohesion

   C. Temporal cohesion D. Communicational cohesion

Answer: B

8. In which of the following cohesion types does cohesion occur during run time at a particular time of program execution?

   A. Coincidental cohesion B. Logical cohesion

   C. Temporal cohesion D. Sequential cohesion

Answer: C

9. What is the type of cohesion in which cohesion occurs as the output of one module is an input of another module?

   A. Functional cohesion B. Logical cohesion

   C. Temporal cohesion D. Sequential cohesion

Answer: D

10. In which of the following cohesion types does cohesion occur as all the functions contribute to a single task of the module?

   A. Functional cohesion B. Logical cohesion

   C. Temporal cohesion D. Sequential cohesion

Answer: A

11. Which of the following is a measure of "how tightly" two entities or modules are related to each other?

   A. Modularity B. Cohesion C. Coupling D. Encapsulation

Answer: C

12. All of the following are types of coupling except:

   A. Content coupling B. Logical coupling C. Common coupling D. Data coupling

Answer: B

13. In which of the following types of coupling one component refers the content of another component?

   A. Content coupling B. Logical coupling C. Common coupling D. Stamp coupling

Answer: A

14. In which type of coupling does a module pass a data structure to a module, which does not have access to the entire data structure?

A. Content coupling B. Logical coupling C. Common coupling D. Stamp coupling

Answer: *D*

15. What indicates the number of modules that directly control a given module?

A. Fan-in B. Fan-out C. Fan-deep D. Fan-control

Answer: *A*

16. All of the following are the components of a distributed system except:

A. Data B. Process C. Interface D. Infrastructure

Answer: *D*

17. Which of the following approaches is represented by the hierarchical structure?

A. Top-down approach B. Bottom-up approach
C. Modular design approach D. User interface design approach

Answer: *A*

18. In which of the following approaches is the overall system is divided into subsystems, which can be tested separately?

A. Top-down approach B. Bottom-up approach
C. Modular design approach D. User interface design approach

Answer: *C*

19. Which of the following types of approaches creates an effective communication medium between a human and a computer?

A. Top-down approach B. Bottom-up approach
C. Modular design approach D. User interface design approach

Answer: *D*

20. Which of the following is not part of three "golden rules" of interface design?

A. Place the user in control B. Reduce the user's memory load
C. Make the interface consistent D. Make the interface colorful

Answer: *D*

PART B (Answers in one or two lines)

1. List any three issues in software design.
2. List the characteristics of a good design.
3. What is software design?
4. What is software engineering?

5. Write notes on function-oriented design.
6. Write notes on object-oriented design.
7. What is modularity?
8. What are the main characteristics to be considered while designing the modularity of projects?
9. What is cohesion?
10. What are the types of cohesion?
11. What is coincidental cohesion?
12. What is logical cohesion?
13. What is temporal cohesion?
14. What is procedural cohesion?
15. What is communicational cohesion?
16. What is sequential cohesion?
17. What is functional cohesion?
18. What is coupling?
19. What are the types of coupling?
20. What is content coupling?
21. What is common coupling?
22. What is control coupling?
23. What is stamp coupling?
24. What is data coupling?
25. Write notes on real-time software design.
26. Write notes on data design.
27. What is architectural design?
28. What is software architecture?
29. What is fan-in and fan-out?
30. Write notes on design heuristics.
31. List a few basic design heuristics.
32. List the steps in transform mapping.
33. List the steps in transaction mapping.
34. What is a distributed system?
35. Write notes on a centralized distributed system.

36. Write notes on a decentralized distributed system.
37. What is a hybrid system?
38. What is top-down approach of design?
39. What is bottom-up approach of design?
40. What is modular design approach?
41. What are the characteristics of a modular system?
42. Write notes on user interface design.
43. What are the three "golden rules" of interface design?
44. What is procedural design?
45. What is structured programming?
46. What is deployment-level design?
47. Write notes on high-level and low-level design documents.

PART C (Descriptive type)

1. List the 10 basic issues in software design.
2. Describe briefly about mapping requirements into architecture.
3. Describe the different types of cohesion.
4. What is coupling? Discuss the different types of coupling.
5. What is a distributed system? Discuss the different types of distributed systems.
6. Explain the various architectural notations.
7. Explain the difference between software design and software engineering.

Section 3:
Design and Architectural Engineering

5

Object-oriented Concepts

CHAPTER COVERAGE

1. *Introduction*
2. *Fundamental Parts of OO Approach*
3. *Data Hiding and Class Hierarchy Creation*
4. *Relationships*
5 *Role of Unified Modeling Language (UML) in OO Design*
6 *Design Patterns*
7 *Frameworks*

5.1 INTRODUCTION

In the previous chapter, it was noted that design principles can be categorized in function-oriented design and object-oriented (OO) design. The concept of function-oriented design was discussed in detail in previous chapter. In this chapter we will discuss the OO design concepts. The object-oriented approach has made a rapid progress since the 1980s. After its introduction, most of the software developments are done through this approach. The primary reason for wide acceptance of OO concept is its close resemblance with the real world system. If we think about the very basic building block of an OO model – it is an object. In a real world system everything around are actually objects and thus using a model which is based on the objects can depict the real system more efficiently (Figure 5.1).

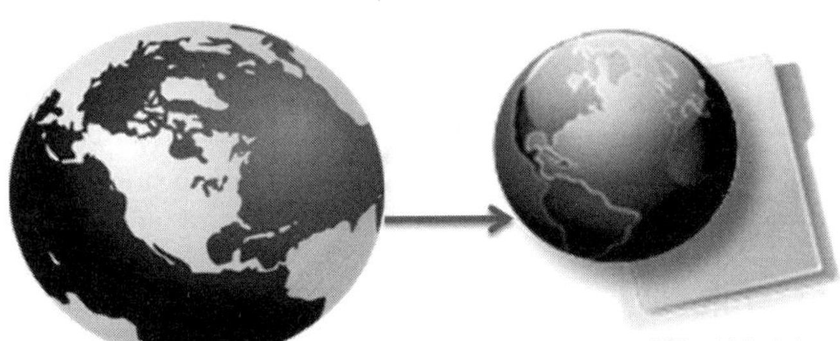

Figure 5.1 Real versus Model

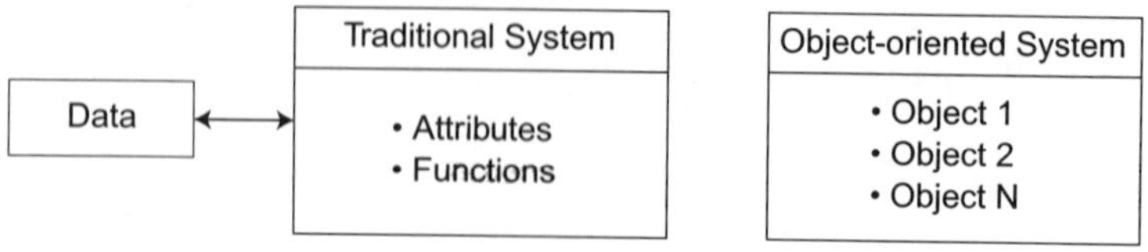

Figure 5.2 Traditional vs Object-oriented System

In the traditional structured models of analysis and design, systems are described with attributes and functions. Also, the data is considered to be outside the system. This makes the reusability and maintainability difficult. With an object concept, the OO methodologies tried to encapsulate the data within the object and the functions and capabilities of these objects are made generic (Figure 5.2) so that there is chance of reuse—making the software development much faster.

Table 5.1 shows the differences between the traditional procedure-oriented concepts and object-oriented concepts.

Table 5.1 Procedure-oriented Concepts vs Object-oriented Concepts

Procedure-oriented concepts	Object-oriented concepts
Algorithm centric.	Object centric.
Data and functions are separate.	No separation between data and methods that operate on the data.
Programs are broken into tasks independently as functions or subroutines.	In OOP the concept of subroutines or functions is associated with data structure called "class."
Basic unit of testing is a subroutine or function.	In OOP it is a class. A class has characteristics such as polymorphism, inheritance and encapsulation. Testing these properties is necessary in OOP.

5.2 FUNDAMENTAL PARTS OF OBJECT-ORIENTED APPROACH

For understanding the OO concept, the first stepping stone is to understand what is an *object* followed by *class* and then the content of the class—the attributes and the methods.

5.2.1 Object

Objects are the physical and theoretical things we find in the universe. Everything in this universe can be considered as an object. An object can be defined as an instance of a class. An object in software engineering refers to the representation of object in the real world entity. Each object has some data or attributes associated with it. These attributes (data) can maintain the state and behavior of the object.

For example, a fruit – mango. Mango is a member of the larger group of objects called fruit. Fruit is a class and mango is an object of that class.

All the members of this larger group have some common characteristics, such as they have some shape, size, weight, seed, smell, etc. But each individual fruit have some specific characteristic also, such as some fruits may be poisonous. These lead to some basic concepts of OO methodologies, such as the object *mango* is *inherited* from the bigger class *fruit* (Figure 5.3).

There are several *attributes* of fruit like shape, size and weight, and there will be some methods (not represented in Figure 5.3) through which these attribute can be accessed or modified. For example, "cut" may be a method through which the shape and size attributes can be altered (see Figure 5.3).

An important point to note is that the data elements are stored (*encapsulated*) within the class and can be accessed only through predefined methods. This makes the attributes more safe and controlled. The collection of common features in the classes makes it easier for reuse by using the inheritance. So, if we have to create a new fruit, say "yummy", we simply have to inherit it from the class fruit and add only the specific attributes, say for example it has a "thorn around it" and the methods to access and manipulate this new attribute. This provides all attributes and methods already present in the fruit along with some specific attributes that make the "yummy" different from other fruits. The concept is depicted in Figure 5.4.

5.2.2 Class

Collection of objects that form a common name and behavior is called the class. The class contains the data (attributes) and the processes (methods, services, functions) that are capable of manipulating the data. Class used to explain the state and behavior of the objects. All objects within a class inherit the attributes and services of the class.

A collection of classes is called a superclass and the specialized instance of a class is called a subclass. For example, the class mango can be inherited from the bigger class fruit, which means the fruit is the superclass of class mango. Alfanso mango (a type of mango) is a subclass of mango. This is called the class hierarchy depicted in Figure 5.5.

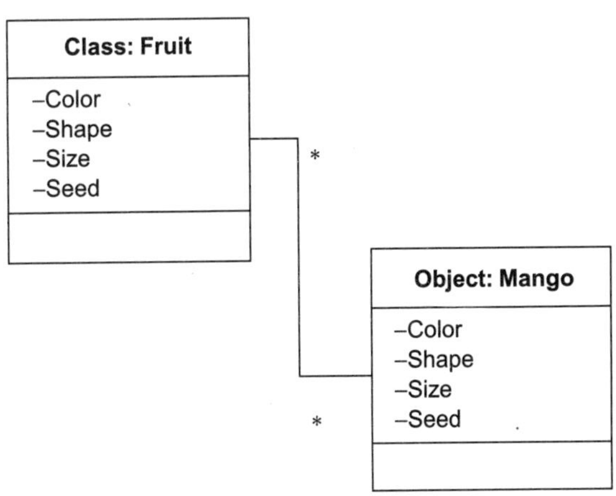

Figure 5.3 Class vs Object

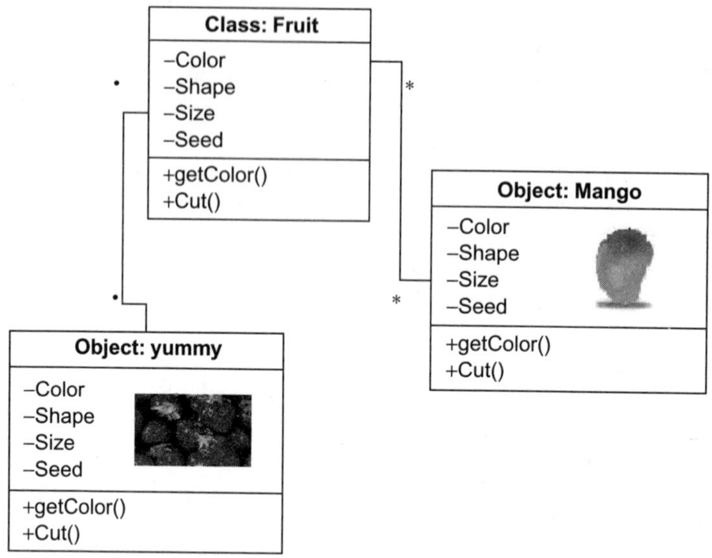

Figure 5.4 Creating New Objects from the Class

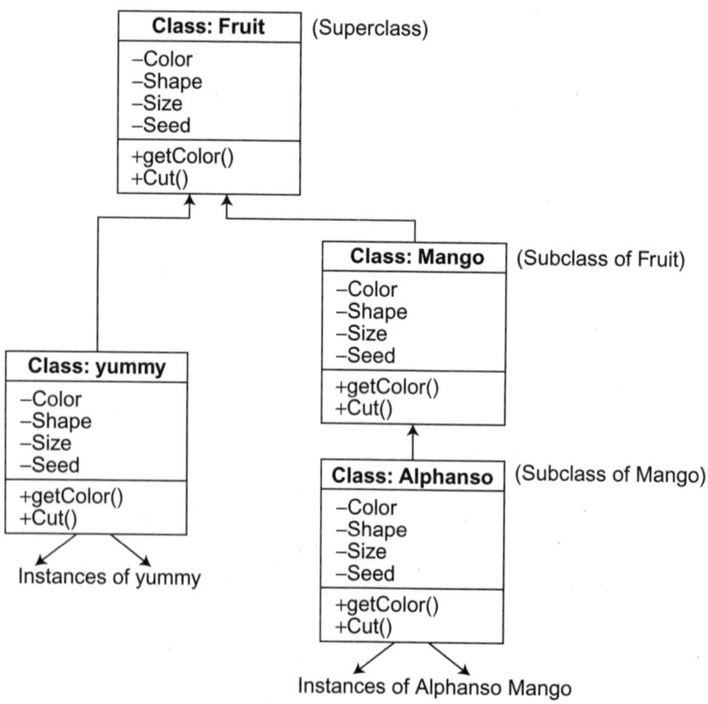

Figure 5.5 Class Hierarchy

5.2.3 Attributes

Properties or characteristics that represent the state of an object are called attributes. The attribute may be of simple data type such as numeric, text, and binary to complex types such as list of values (for cases where the attribute can have only a set of value) to even another class.

Below is the example of the class car which shows different types of attributes it can possibly have.

```
Class Car
{
   Make (simple data type),
   Model (simple data type),
   Color (list of values: white, red and black)
   Transmission system (this is another class with many other attributes)
}
```

Make, model, color, transmission system are the attributes that describes the state of a car.

Make (of a car) can have possible values of Maruthi, Tata, Chevrolet, Chrysler, Ford, Toyota, etc. Model can have values such as Tata Indica, Tata Vista, Tata Safari, etc.

> **POINTS TO PONDER**
>
> Objects are the physical and theoretical things found in the universe. Everything in this universe can be considered as an object. An object can be defined as an example of a class.

5.2.4 Methods

The method implements the behavior of an object. The collection of method that exhibits what the object is going to function is called the behavior. These methods wrap the behavior the objects and maintain the internal structure of the objects. Objects take the responsibility of its own behavior. The data encapsulated within the object can be processes with these methods and that initiates the behavior. For example, the method gets color () will send the message to the mango class to send back the color of the mango (Figure 5.6).

5.2.5 Messages

The objects interact with each other through messages. The messages act as the stimulus to invoke the methods within a class. Different objects can respond to the same messages passed. With the

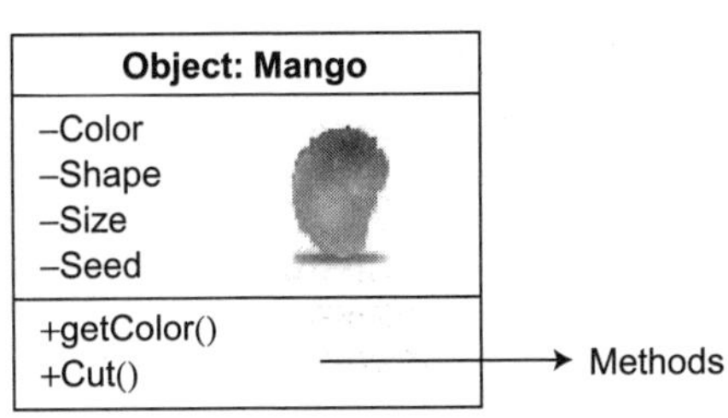

Figure 5.6 Methods

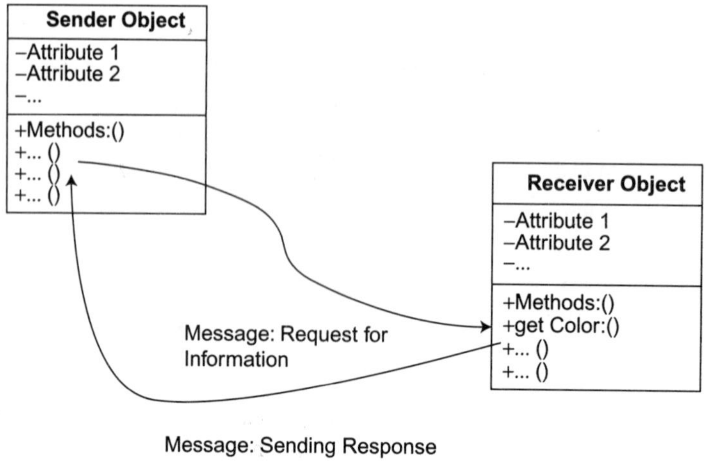

Figure 5.7 Messages

messages the OO system works as a whole. Figure 5.7 shows how objects interact with each other using the messaging.

5.3 DATA HIDING AND CLASS HIERARCHY CREATION

As discussed in the previous section, the basic differentiator for OO concept over the traditional design approach is the ability to do data hiding and class hierarchy creation. The concept of data hiding and class hierarchy creation leads to three major characteristics of the OO concept that differentiates it from the traditional design concepts: encapsulation, inheritance, and polymorphism (Figure 5.8).

5.3.1 Encapsulation

Encapsulation refers to protecting of data from the users. It is otherwise known as the information hiding. No object can access the other object's data directly; instead data is accessed only by sending the messages to the other object requesting for the information. This means the user need not know what is happening inside the object, but can only use the object by calling the object's methods. This will provide insulation for the data inside the object from accidental manipulation by another object or user (see Figure 5.9).

In a good OO design the object should reveal its data only through the interfaces or methods, and the other objects should use the interface or methods to interact with it. The attributes that are only

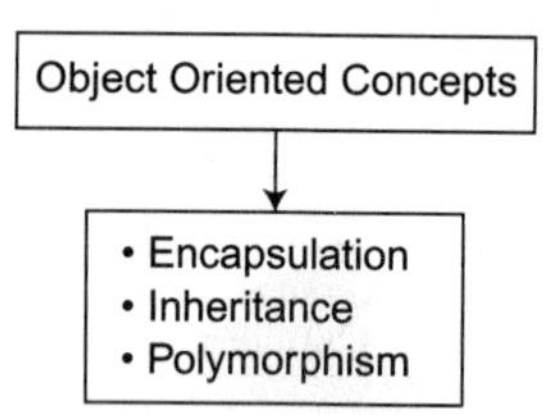

Figure 5.8 Object-oriented Concepts

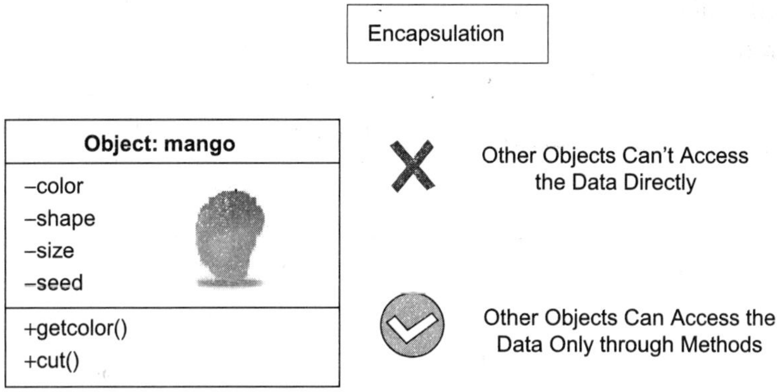

Figure 5.9 Encapsulation

for the internal use of the object and not to be revealed are completely hidden from other objects. In those cases the attributes are declared as "private." This also protects the object attributes getting changed erroneously, while some other attributes are getting changed.

For example, in the class car engine there are many parts (attributes) inside it. Every one applies a common technique in accessing the engine functionalities no matter how the engine is made of. The detail and design of the engine are hidden from the knowledge of the driver.

5.3.2 Inheritance

This is the most powerful feature of the OO methodology which makes it easy for the code reuse and faster development. The concept of inheritance relies on finding out the commonality of the related objects and grouping them together to build a base class and then reusing the capability of this base class as many times as needed in the inherited (child) classes (Figure 5.10).

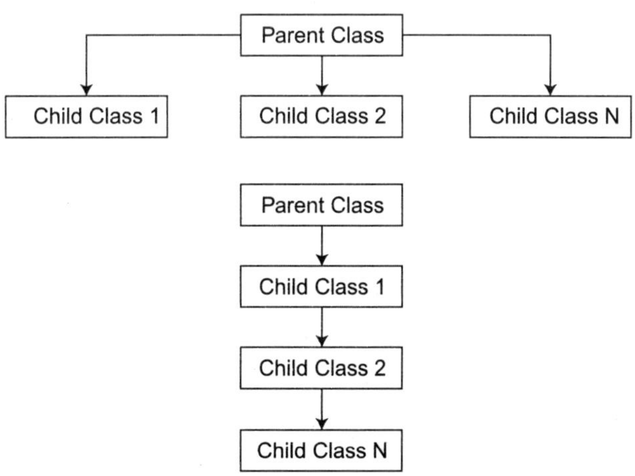

Figure 5.10 Inheritance Concepts

As shown in the previous examples, all fruits such as apple, mango, pear, etc. have common set of attributes like color, size, weight, etc., and there is common way of getting information about the data and manipulating them. So it makes sense to create a base class fruit where all these attributes are kept and the methods for accessing and manipulating these attributes are maintained.

Apple, mango and pear when inherited from fruit by default will get all the attributes and they do not have to build those capabilities separately. While creating a new class, the very specific class attributes and methods only need to be built saving lot of time in development.

Figure 5.11 shows how the inheritances refer objects built from other object. Only the delta part is added in the inherited classes and the capability of the base class gets automatically propagated to the child classes.

The concept of inheritance has popularized the creation of reusable components in the software industry. A library of the classes providing generic attributes and functionalities is created. While creating a new object, instead of creating everything from the scratch, the existing class hierarchy is

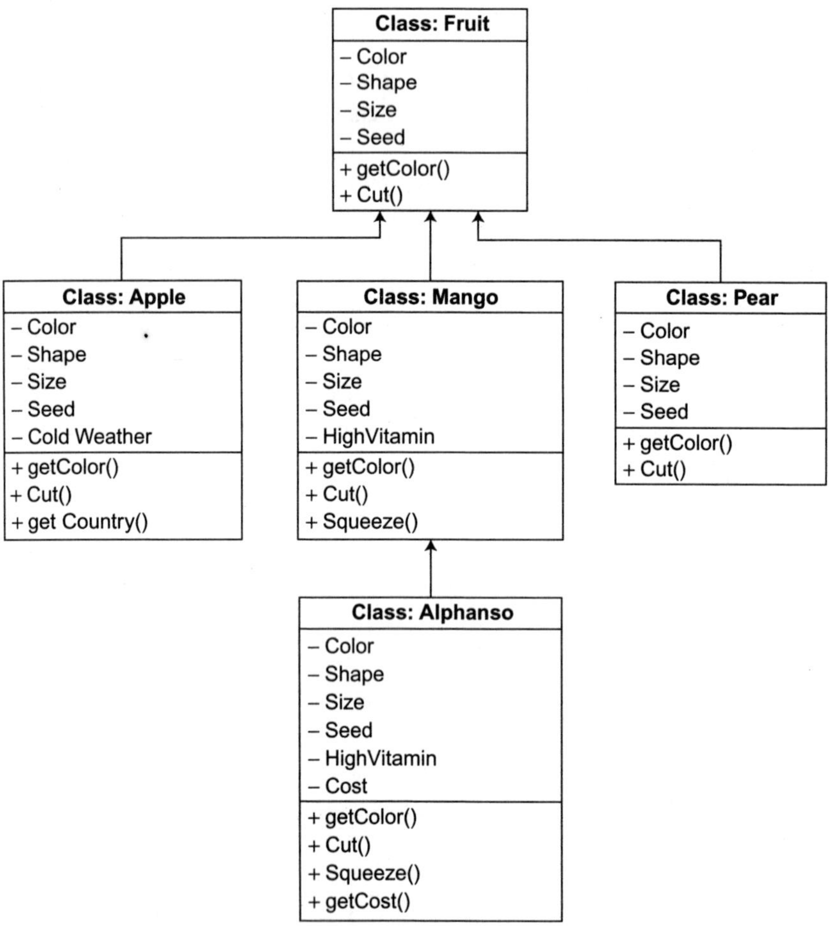

Figure 5.11 Inheritances of Attributes and Methods

searched for the closest match of the desired functionality. The class showing the best fit for the desired attribute and functionality is inherited and to this, specific functionalities are added to make the new class behave as desired.

Advantages of Inheritance

1. It encourages code reusability
2. It helps to understand the problem clearly
3. Step-by-step program and testing is possible

There are three types of inheritance based on how it is inherited from other class (Figure 5.12) namely, simple, multi-level and multiple.

First type of inheritance is called as simple or single inheritance where only one class getting inherited from another.

In multi-level inheritance a class be can derived from already derived class. In Figure 5.12 (2), class B is inherited from class A. Class C is inherited from class B.

In the multiple type of structure, one class is inherited from more than one class. In Figure 5.12 (3), class C has two parents namely class A and class B. Class C is inherited both from class A and class B.

Hybrid type of inheritance is the combination of two or more types of the above inheritance.

The OO design provides a great flexibility by allowing the child classes to override any functionality of the base class. This helps in achieving the polymorphism.

POINTS TO PONDER

Encapsulation refers to protecting of data from the users. It is otherwise known as the information hiding.

5.3.3 Polymorphism

Object that can take different forms is termed as polymorphism. "Poly" refers to many and "morp" refers to forms and so polymorphism means may forms. It means same operation or function may

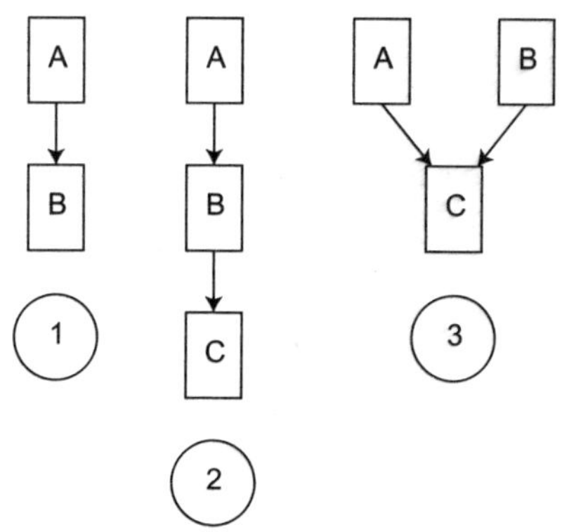

Figure 5.12 Types of Inheritance

behave differently on different classes. This leads to a powerful advantage of OO class model as the external interface sending the message for accessing the class attributes need not know the class hierarchy of the system. Even more important is the fact that if there is a new class introduced, the external interface need not change its message.

There are two types of polymorphism namely run time polymorphism and compile time polymorphism (Figure 5.13).

Assume there are three separate classes namely apple, mango and pear. Each one of them has a method called as getColor() that responds to a message and sends back the color of the object. To get the color of 3 objects in traditional model, three different types of function need to be written and called.

```
If Fruit = Apple
        Then Apple.getColor
If Fruit = Mango
        Then Mango.getColor
If Fruit = Pear
        Then Pear.getColor
```

If there is a new class created called "yummy" fruit and the external caller now wants to get the color of that, the external interface need to change its call to add another line and understand how it will get the color of this new fruit.

OO methodology through the use of the base class standardized the propagation of the messages so that the class structure is transparent to the calling party. In OO concept, there will be a base class fruit which implements the generic functionality of the getColor(). The subclasses—mango, apple and pear will be inherited from fruit. Each one of these classes can either use the base functionality or modify functionality of the getcolor to add any specific need.

The external interface will send the message as follows:

Fruit.getColor()

Based on the instance of the class (whether apple or mango or pear), the corresponding getColor() will be invoked and will return the specific response. Tomorrow if there is a new subclass "yummy" introduced, which is inherited from the fruit class, then the caller will send the same message Fruit.getColor(), and if the instance is of type yummy then its specific color will be returned.

The above example is called as run time polymorphism (Figure 5.12).

In compile time polymorphism same method with different parameters are written inside the class. For example, a method called add (int x, int y) and also another method called add (int x, int y, int z) is written inside the same class. When the method add () is called by passing 2 parameters, the first method is being invoked. If the method add () is called by passing 3 parameters, the second method will get invoked.

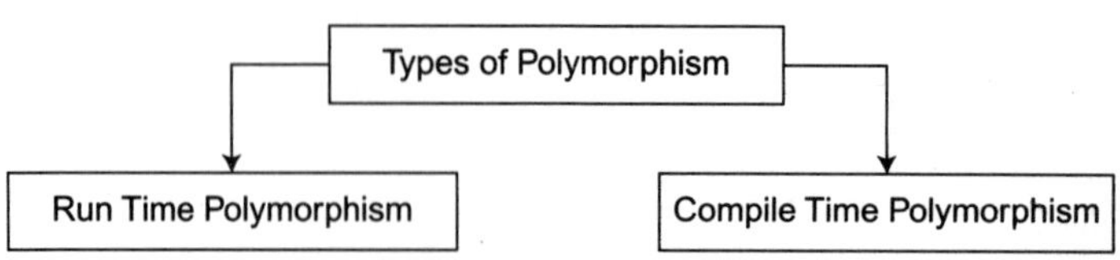

Figure 5.13 Types of Polymorphism

POINTS TO PONDER

Object that can take different forms is termed as polymorphism. "Poly" refers to many and "morp" refers to forms and so polymorphism means may forms. It means same operation or function may behave differently on different classes.

5.3.4 Abstraction

Abstraction ensures that only necessary information is exposed to other objects. Abstraction principles support inheritance and polymorphism. Data are abstracted by methods. Only the allowed methods can access the data portion of object.

POINTS TO PONDER

Abstraction ensures only necessary information is shown out to other objects. Abstraction principles support inheritance and polymorphism. Data are abstracted by methods. Only the allowed methods can access the data portion of object.

For describing the system behavior it is important to depict how the classes are interconnected. There are several relationships that can be depicted in the OO model.

5.4 RELATIONSHIPS

Relationships between objects can be denoted in three forms namely

1. Is–a relationship
2. Has–a relationship
3. Uses–a relationship

5.4.1 Is–A Relationship

It describes the inheritance relationship between the classes. When an object A is a specialized version of another object B the objects are said to be in a relationship. Inheritance is used to create an "is–a" relationship among classes. This type of relationship help the classes to extend its functionalities by creating another class that is the specialized version of it. Subclass is the extended version of the superclass. Generalization is also called as the "is–a" relationship (see Figure 5.14).

Example 1: A car is a vehicle.

Here the specialized object car has all the characteristics of the general object (vehicle). Car also has some added characteristics that make it special.

Example 2: A cycle is a vehicle.

Here the specialized object cycle has all the characteristics of the general object (vehicle). Cycle also has some added characteristics that make it special.

5.4.2 Has–A Relationship

Aggregation is also called as the "has–a" relationship. When a class has another object as the data member or attribute then it is said to be of "has–a" relation (Figure 5.15).

Example: A car has a wheel.

Figure 5.14 Is–A Relationship

Figure 5.15 Has–A Relationship

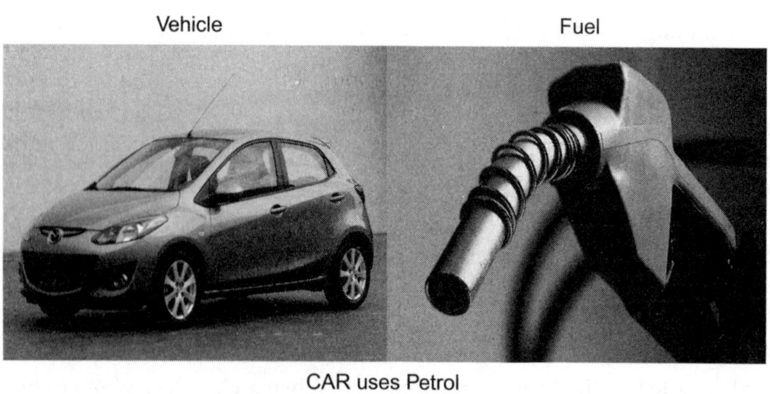

Figure 5.16 Uses–A Relationship

5.4.3 Uses–A Relationship

The method of one class may use the object of another class. This is called a uses–a relationship (see Figure 5.16).

Example: A car uses petrol for functioning, but petrol is an object of the class fuel.

5.5 ROLE OF UNIFIED MODELING LANGUAGE (UML) IN OO DESIGN

Unified modeling language (UML) is a modeling language used to model software and non-software system and gives more emphasis on modeling OO software applications. The objects are real-world entities that exist around us and the object-oriented basic concepts such as abstraction, encapsulation, inheritance – polymorphism all can be represented easily using UML. So, the relation between OO design and UML is very important. The OO design is converted into UML diagrams using appropriate notations.

UML is powerful enough to represent all existing concepts in OO notations. UML diagrams are representations of OO concepts only. UML is discussed in detail in Chapter 6.

POINTS TO PONDER

Points to Ponder: UML is powerful enough to represent all the concepts exist in object-oriented notations. UML diagrams are representation of object-oriented concepts only. UML is discussed in detail in other chapter.

5.6 DESIGN PATTERNS

The key focuses of the OO design are to find out the objects within a system, translate them into classes, find out the class interfaces, build the class hierarchy and the relationship among the classes and maintain the right granularity while defining the classes. Although this sounds simple, it is a difficult task to define and model the class which is flexible as well as reusable. Because of highly reusable nature of the OO framework the library of design models can be created, which can solve general design problems; thereby time taken to create a design reduces drastically.

General reusable solution to more frequently/commonly occurring software design problems is called as design pattern.

Design patterns has 4 essential parts namely

1. Pattern name
2. Problem
3. Solution
4. Consequences

Pattern name: Each design pattern should have a meaningful name which describes in a word or two the problem domain it addresses and the solution.

Problem: This explains the problem and the context so that the designer is able to understand when to apply this design pattern.

Solution: This is the high-level abstraction of the class structure and their relationship that solves the design problem. As the patterns are like the templates for resolving many design problems and the actual implementation depends on the specific situation, it contains a description of how a general arrangement of classes solves the design issues.

Consequences: Any trade-offs made for applying the pattern that is important for the cost benefit analysis is mentioned here.

The design patterns are categorized in three (Figure 5.17) broad sections/types based on what the pattern does.

1. Creational patterns
2. Structural patterns
3. Behavioral patterns

5.6.1 Creational Patterns

This group of patterns helps in abstracting the object instantiation process. Unless the system is made independent of how the objects are created and composed, then there will be more chance of hard-coding the class behavior and create specific objects. Some of the examples of this type of pattern are singleton, builder and prototype. These patterns use inheritance to group the small repeatable behavior of objects to create logically related classes.

5.6.2 Structural Patterns

As the name suggests, these patterns describe how to compose the classes and object to build larger structures. The basis for composition in these patterns is inheritance. Multiple inheritances help missing the capabilities of different classes and create a larger class structure. The examples of this type of pattern are – bridge, composite, decorator, proxy, etc.

5.6.3 Behavioral Patterns

This group of patterns abstracts the communication between the objects. In case complex control flow among the objects, this pattern is useful as the designer can focus mostly on how the objects are connected and the communication part is taken care by the template. The examples of this type of pattern are chain of responsibility, mediator, observer, visitor, etc. The object composition is used to build these patterns and describes the cooperation of a group of objects to perform a task which each individual will not be able to perform alone.

OO design is a vast area. Thus, it is difficult for the novice programmers to design a system utilizing all the flexibilities offered by the OO framework. By providing some standardized templates for efficient and proven designs, the design patterns reduce the chance of creating inefficient and low-performing designs. A pattern involves number of objects which collaborate in some way. Instead of

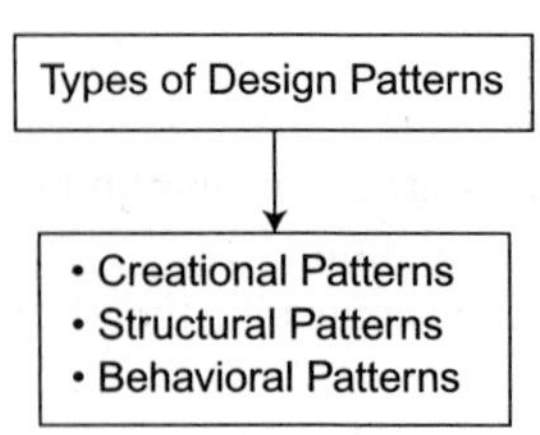

Figure 5.17 Types of Design Patterns

giving any concrete implementation details, it tries to document the problem addressed by the pattern, and the abstract, graphical, OO specification of how that problem may be solved along with the consequences of using that pattern.

A complete catalog of design patterns is provided below.

Purpose	Pattern Names
Creational	Abstract factory Builder Prototype Singleton
Structural	Adapter Bridge Composite Decorator Façade Flyweight Proxy
Behavioral	Chain of responsibility Command Iterator Mediator Memento Observer State Strategy Visitor

5.7 FRAMEWORKS

A more specific solution description for design problems is found in the form of framework. A single framework may consist of multiple design patterns which depicts the implementation of a whole system. This means the object creation pattern, structural pattern and behavioral pattern are combined together to form the whole system design and presented as a framework which will work specifically for that particular type of system.

5.7.1 Differences between Design Patterns and Frameworks

- Design patterns are at more abstract level than frameworks. Frameworks will be applicable only for specific system for which it is designed, but the design patterns are more generic and will be applicable to all situations for a particular design problem.
- Design patterns are smaller design elements than frameworks.
- Design patterns are more generalized than frameworks.

Summary

- The OO approach has made a rapid progress since the 1980s. After its introduction, most of the software developments are done through this approach.
- For understanding the)) concept the first stepping stone is to understand what an object is. Objects are the physical and theoretical things found in the universe. Everything in this universe can be considered as an object.
- Collection of objects that form a common name and behavior is called the class. The class contains the data (attributes) and the processes (methods, services, functions) that are capable of manipulating the data. Class used to explain the state and behavior of the objects. All objects within a class inherit the attributes and services of the class.
- Properties or characteristics that represent the state of an object are called attributes. The attribute may be of simple data type such as numeric, text and binary to complex types such as list of values (for the cases where the attribute can have only a set of value) to even another class.
- The method implements the behavior of an object. The collection of method that exhibits what the object is going to function is called the behavior. These methods wrap the behavior the objects and maintain the internal structure of the objects. Objects take the responsibility of its own behavior.
- The objects interact with each other through messages. The messages act as the stimulus to invoke the methods within a class. Different objects can respond to the same messages passed. With the messages the OO system works as a whole.
- Encapsulation refers to protecting of data from the users. It is otherwise known as the information hiding. No object can access the other object's data directly; instead data is accessed only by sending the messages to the other object requesting for the information.
- The concept of inheritance relies on finding out the commonality of the related objects and grouping them together to build a base class and then reusing the capability of this base class as many times as needed in the inherited (child) classes

Advantages of inheritance:

1. It encourages code reusability
2. It helps to understand the problem clearly
3. Step-by-step program and testing is possible

- Object that can take different forms is termed as polymorphism. "Poly" refers to many and "morp" refers to forms and so polymorphism means may forms. It means same operation or function may behave differently on different classes.
- Abstraction ensures only necessary information is shown out to other objects. Abstraction principles support inheritance as well as polymorphism. Only the allowed methods can access the data portion of object.

- Inheritance is used to create an "is–a" relationship among classes. This type of relationship help the classes to extend its functionalities by creating another class that is the specialized version of it.
- Aggregation is also called as the "has–a" relationship. When a class has another object as the data member or attribute then it is said to be of "has–a" relation.
- General reusable solution to more frequently/commonly occurring software design problems is called as design pattern.

PART A (Objective type)

1. The primary reason for wide acceptance of object-oriented concepts is

   A. Its close resemblance with the real world system

   B. Easy to write code using OO concepts

   C. Easy to test code using OO concepts

   D. Easy to integrate codes written using OO concepts

Answer: A

2. Reusability and maintainability is difficult with function-oriented language.

   A. True   B. False

Answer: A

3. Basic unit of testing in object-oriented programming is

   A. Class   B. Methods

   C. Objects   D. Attributes

Answer: A

4. An instance of a class is called as

   A. Subclass   B. Methods

   C. Objects   D. Attributes

Answer: C

5. If fruit is a class, then mango is a(n)

   A. Subclass   B. Methods

   C. Objects   D. Attributes

Answer: C

6. Collection of objects that form a common name and behavior is

   A. Class   B. Superclass

   C. Group objects   D. Super objects

Answer: A

7. A collection of classes is called as

A. Class B. Superclass
C. Group objects D. Attributes

Answer: B

7. Characteristics that represent the state of an object are called as

A. Behavior B. Superclass
C. Group objects D. Attributes

Answer: D

8. The collection of method that exhibits what the object is going to function is called as

A. Behavior B. Messages
C. Group objects D. Attributes

Answer: A

9. The objects interact with each other through

A. Behavior B. Messages
C. Group objects D. Attributes

Answer: B

10. This refers to protecting of data from the users in OO concepts

A. Encapsulation B. Inheritance
C. Polymorphism D. Security

Answer: A

11. In OO concepts, this aspects helps to build a base class and then reusing the capability of this base class as many times:

A. Encapsulation B. Inheritance
C. Polymorphism D. Security

Answer: B

12. Which of the following is not a type of inheritance in OO concept?

A. Simple inheritance B. Multi-level inheritance
C. Multiple inheritance D. Complex inheritance

Answer: D

13. Only one class getting inherited from another class is called as

A. Simple inheritance B. Easy inheritance
C. Multiple inheritance D. Complex inheritance

Answer: A

14. This means same operation or function may behave differently on different classes.

A. Encapsulation B. Inheritance
C. Polymorphism D. Security

Answer: C

15. Two types of polymorphism in OO concepts are

A. Run time polymorphism and compile time polymorphism

B. Code time polymorphism and testing time polymorphism

C. Inheritance polymorphism and class polymorphism

D. Easy polymorphism and difficult polymorphism

Answer: A

16. This ensures only necessary information is shown out to other objects

A. Abstraction B. Methods

C. Behavior D. Relationship

Answer: A

17. Which of the following is not a form of object relationship?

A. Is–a relationship B. Has–a relationship

C. Uses–a relationship D. Calls–a relationship

Answer: D

18. UML stands for

A. Unified modeling language B. Uniform modeling language

C. Unified method language D. Uniform method language

Answer: A

19. General reusable solution to more frequently/commonly occurring software design problems is called as

A. Design patterns B. Design framework

C. UML D. Design heuristics

Answer: A

20. Which of the following is not an essential part of design patterns?

A. Pattern name B. Pattern problem

C. Pattern solution D. Pattern author(s)

Answer: D

21. Which of the following is not one of the main category of design pattern?

A. Creational patterns B. Structural patterns

C. Behavioral patterns D. Relational patterns

Answer: D

PART B (Answer in one or two lines)

1. List out the differences between the traditional procedure-oriented concepts and object-oriented concepts.
2. Define Object?

3. Define Class?
4. Define Attributes?
5. Give example of the class car which shows different types of attributes it can possibly have.
6. Define Methods?
7. Define Messages?
8. Define Inheritance?
9. Define Abstraction?
10. Define Encapsulation?

PART C (Descriptive type)

1. Explain the concept of fundamental parts of OO approach?
2. Explain in detail about data hiding and class hierarchy creation?
3. Explain in detail about various types of relationships between Objects?
4. Explain Role of UML in OO Design?
5. Explain in detail about Design Patterns?
6. Explain in Detail about Design Frameworks?

Section 3:
Design and Architectural Engineering

6

Object-oriented Analysis and Design

CHAPTER COVERAGE

1. *Introduction*
2. *Object-oriented Analysis*
3. *Object-oriented Design*

6.1 INTRODUCTION

After the basic concepts of Object-Oriented (OO) Philosophy have been discussed in the previous chapter, let us now deep dive into the area of Analysis and Design where these OO concepts are used. In this chapter, we will discuss the purview of Object-Oriented Analysis and Design (OOAD).

Object-oriented analysis (OOA) can be defined as a structured process of investigation; to be more specific, it involves investigation of objects. Design involves collaboration of identified objects. It is important to understand OOAD concepts because of the wide applicability of these concepts in software design and development. Most important function of OO analysis is to identify the objects of a system that needs to be designed. This analysis can also be used for an existing system. An efficient analysis can only be performed if the objects are identified correctly. After identifying the objects, their relationships with each other should be identified and then finally designed.

The purpose of OOAD is to

- Identify the objects of a system
- Identify their relationships
- Create the design, which can be converted to executable format using OO languages

There are three basic steps of applying and implementing OO concepts, as shown in Figure 6.1.

The steps mentioned in Figure 6.1 are explained further as follows:

- The aim of OOA is to identify the objects in the system and describe the state and behavior of the objects. Design, the

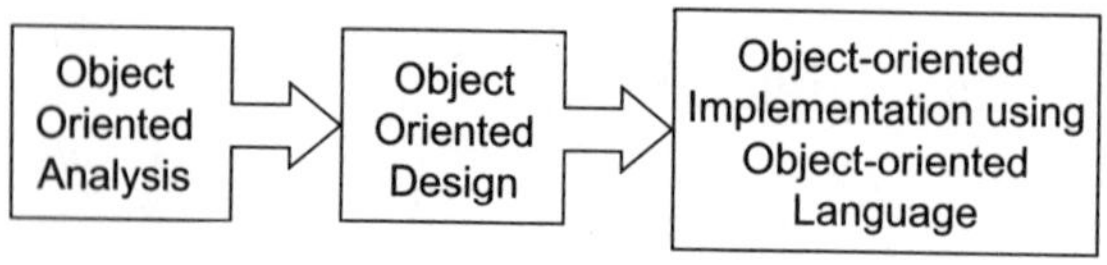

Figure 6.1 Object-oriented Concept

next step in the process, can be successful only if the objects are identified efficiently during the analysis phase. Functionality of each object within a system is referred to as the capability of the object. In order to maintain the capability of the system, the individual functionalities of the objects in a system should be collaborated with the communication among the objects.

- In the second phase of the OO design, the requirements should be realized. The establishment of association among the objects is important to complete the design.
- With the input from the previous steps, in the third phase of the OO implementation, the design gets converted to a running software. The OO languages such as Java, C++, etc. are used for this implementation, as these languages have matching capability for implementing OO design.

6.2 OBJECT-ORIENTED ANALYSIS

During structured analysis, the requirements have to be analyzed and elaborated for designers to understand the system capabilities correctly. Development of the OO concepts has modified the requirement analysis approach to resemble the real-world systems. Objectives of OOA are:

1. To identify the classes
2. To identify the attributes of the classes
3. To identify the methods required for each class
4. To find out the class hierarchy
5. To find out the relationship and communication among the classes to represent the whole system

The approach starts with domain analysis followed by modeling, which is based on the use of case-modeling technique. But, before getting into the details of the OOA, it is important to understand the difference between the structured analysis (also known as Conventional Analysis Technique) and OOA.

6.2.1 Structured Analysis versus OOA

Structured analysis relies completely on the input→process→output aspects of the requirement. Data and functions that process these data are considered as separate entities. The system view is secondary and the primary focus is on the individual components of the system. On the other hand, the OOA recognizes the fact that the data are an integral part of the system. Thus, the class (the combination of data and function) is considered as the building block. The system behavior becomes important for the analysis model, as it is the interaction among the classes that controls the behavior of the whole system.

Another difference between these two approaches is that structured analysis decomposes the system top down to find out the granular-level entities in the system. Whereas, the wholesome approach of the OOA does not use the top down decomposition technique to find out the classes present in the system.

6.2.2 Domain Analysis

The OOA starts with domain analysis step, whose objective is to identify and understand the domain to which the proposed system belongs to and also to find out the reusable components already present in the domain. Purposes of finding out the reusable component are multifold:

1. It reduces the development effort drastically if the number of reusable components already present in the problem domain is high.
2. It reduces the total implementation time as well.
3. The standardization of the developed system is enhanced because it follows the principles of already developed components.

So, the domain analysis first focuses on identifying, analyzing and specifying the domain in which the proposed system should operate, and then to analyze and specify the common reusable capabilities that can be used by multiple projects within the common domain.

Following steps outline the domain analysis process:

- **Define the domain:** This involves identifying the business or technical area to which the proposed system is related. The already created reusable components may be identified and used based on the domain.
- **Group the items in the domain:** During the domain analysis, analyzing the system becomes easier if the components are grouped based on criteria such as implementation similarity, language used for implementation, functionalities provided.
- **Create the analysis model:** The collection of well-defined packages of components that are ready for reuse forms the basis of the analysis model.
- **Identify the reusability prospect:** After grouping the items in the domain and creating the analysis model, it becomes clear how much of the system can be made generic so that it can be reused by other systems. For example, in banking domain, a generic component that validates the credit cards can be made as a reusable component; and any software developer who generates a banking system can reuse that component for easy and quick development.

The use case modeling is the most accepted modeling technique for requirement analysis phase. In this approach, each business case or requirement is captured as individual use case. The use cases can be gradually elaborated starting from the system-level view to the individual business requirements.

6.2.3 Use Case Modeling

The use cases are pictorial representation of the scenarios in order to capture the system requirements clearly. A use case is an interaction between the users and a system, refer Figure 6.2 for Object-oriented Analysis flow. The use case model captures the goal of the user and the responsibility of the system toward its users.

The use case description must contain following constraints:

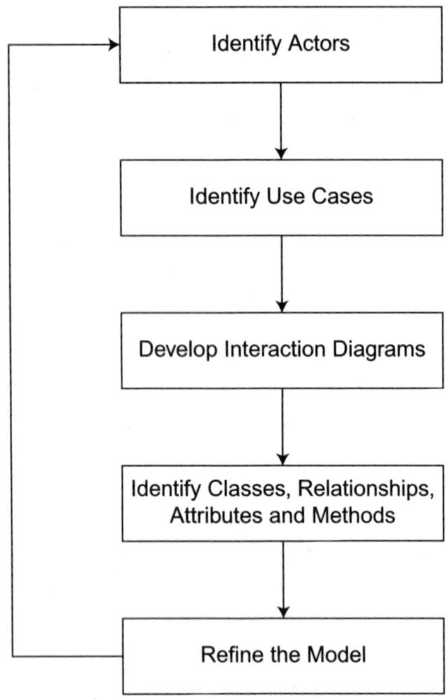

Figure 6.2 Object-oriented Analysis Flow

- How and when the use case begins and ends?
- The interaction between the use case and its actors, including when the interaction occurs and what is exchanged?
- How and when the use case needs the data stored in the system or will store data in the system?
- Exceptions to the flow of events and how and when the concepts of the problem domain are handled.

A use case describes the main flow of events; and an exceptional or additional flow of events could also be added. The exceptional use case extends another use case to include the additional one. The use case model employs "extends" and "uses" relationships. The "extends" relationship is used when there is one use case that is similar to another use case, but does a bit more, which means it extends the functionality of the original use case. Whereas, the "uses" relationship reuses the common behavior in different use cases.

Use cases could be viewed as concrete or abstract. An abstract use case is not complete and has no actors to initiate, but it is used by another use case. This inheritance could be used in several levels. Abstract use cases are also the ones that have uses or extend relationships.

6.3 OBJECT-ORIENTED DESIGN

After completing the analysis of the requirement, the next step is to translate it to the design of the proposed system. After the introduction of OO design concepts, the consideration for reusability has been highly focused on. With the popularity of the OO languages such as C++ and Java, the ease with which the design and the code can be mapped with each other has increased manifold, creating the way for the automatic code generation from the design itself.

6.3.1 Conventional versus OO Approach

The concept of the object differentiates the OO framework from the procedural design framework. In procedural model, the system behavior or capability is fragmented into multiple methods or functions, with which the data is divided into separate structures. The functions access these data and manipulate those. In order to provide access to multiple functions, many times the data are kept in global structures, making them vulnerable to outside disturbances. But in an OO model, the data (attributes) and the behavior (methods) are contained in a single object. This is the most powerful feature of the object, as the data are accessed and manipulated by the selected methods within the object, where in the data are protected from the global view. As discussed in the previous chapter, this is called data hiding (encapsulation). This ensures data integrity in the system in huge amount. Figure 6.3 shows the differentiation between the conventional and OO designs in the system flow.

For the OO design to be successful, it is important to

- Identify the objects and classes
- Identify the relationships between classes
- Build the optimum class hierarchy for maximum reusability
- Identify the communication (messages) among the classes

6.3.2 OOD Modeling Techniques

Modeling techniques provide a set of tools and guidelines which help the analysts and designers in performing robust requirement analysis and design. The aim of these techniques is to help in modeling the business problem and implement that in the OO technique. Several important models available for OO modeling are discussed further.

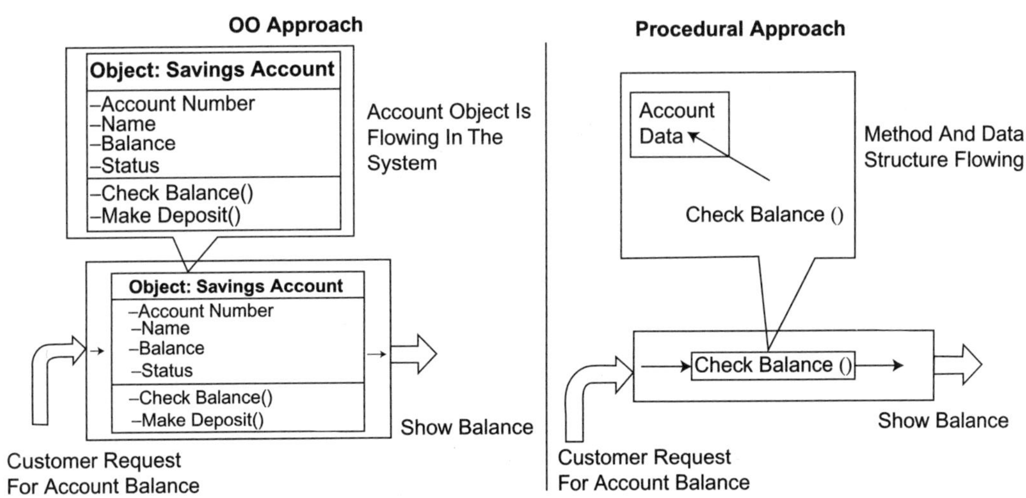

Figure 6.3 OO versus Conventional Design Approach

Some of the powerful modeling methodologies and notations are:

- Rumbaugh et al. Methodology
- Booch Methodology
- Jacobson Methodology
- Unified Modeling Language (UML)

Each method has its own merits; for example, Rumbaugh et al. method is capable of describing the object model, while the Jacobson et al. method is suitable for producing user-driven analysis model. The Booch method helps in producing detailed OO design models.

6.3.2.1 Rumbaugh et al.'s Object Modeling Technique

The Object Modeling Technique (OMT) involves the analysis, design and implementation of a system using an OO technique. OMT aims at identifying and modeling all the objects that build up a system. The dynamic behavior of objects within a system can be described using the OMT dynamic model. This model helps specify detailed state transitions and their descriptions within a system. Finally, description of a process and consumer–producer relationships can be expressed using OMT's functional model.

Four phases of OMT have to be carried out repeatedly to develop a useful object model for a system:

Phase 1: Analysis
Phase 2: System design
Phase 3: Object design
Phase 4: Implementation

Analysis phase helps identify the objects and functional models; system design phase gives the blue print of the system; object design phase helps generate detailed description of the objects (static and dynamic) and functional models; and implementation phase helps generate reusable and robust code. Figure 6.4 represents the basic structure of the OMT models.

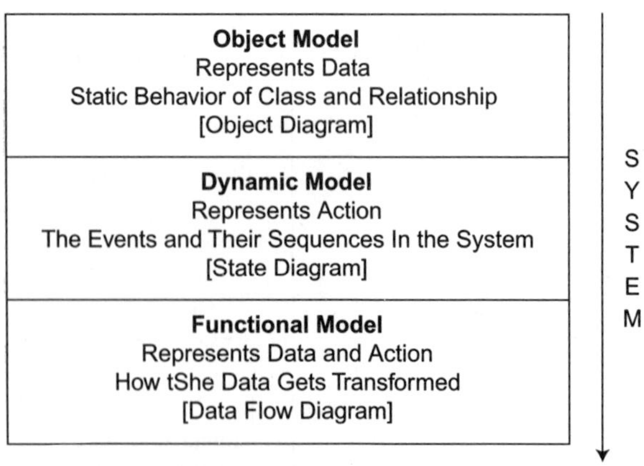

Figure 6.4 OMT Modeling

Object model: The object model describes the structure of objects in a system, including their identity, relationships to other objects, attributes and operations. It is represented by an object diagram, which contains classes interconnected by association lines. Each association line represents a set of links from the objects of one class to the objects of another class. These association lines establish relationships among the classes, where each class represents a set of individual objects.

OMT Dynamic Model: Dynamic state represents the states that keep changing, such as state of objects, transitions, events and actions. OMT helps develop a detailed and comprehensive dynamic model. The OMT state transition diagram is a network of states and events, where each state receives one or more events, during which it makes the transition to the next state. The next state depends on the current state as well as the events.

OMT Functional Model: The OMT data flow diagram (DFD) represents the flow of data among different processes in a system. An OMT DFD involves a simple and intuitive method for describing business processes without focusing on the details of computer systems.

DFDs perform four primary tasks:

1. A process is any function being performed; for example, verifying user authentication in the Library Management.
2. The data flow shows data that flow throughout the system; for example, authentication.
3. The data store is a repository, where the data is being stored; for example, Book Details are stored in the data store of the Library Management System.
4. An external entity is a source or destination of a data element; for example, the ID card reader.

6.3.2.2 Booch Methodology

The Booch methodology helps design the system using the object model. It concentrates on the analysis and design phases of an OOA. The disadvantage of Booch method is that it uses large set of symbols.

It starts with class and object diagram in the analysis phase, and it introduces notations that interconnect classes and objects with each other to enable the code for the system. This method consists of following diagrams:

- Class diagrams
- Object diagrams
- State diagrams
- Module diagrams
- Process diagrams
- Sequence diagrams

The Booch methodology demands an iterative and evolving modeling technique. The micro- and macro development processes together describe the whole system with required level of granularity.

Macro Development Process The function of the macro process is to identify the primary task of the system, that is, outer sketch, irrespective of what is going on inside the system. The macro (large) process serves as a controlling framework for the micro process. Tasks are not performed based on the actual design, instead on the extent to which the project corresponds to the requirements set for it. The requirement phase functions to know whether the project is produced on given time period.

The macro development involves following processes:

Conceptualization: This process finds initial requirements of the system, and it also helps set goals and develop a prototype to prove the concept.

Analysis and development of the model: Roles and responsibilities of the objects are carried out by using class diagram, and the behavior of the system is also identified.

Designing the system: In the design phase, the class diagram is used to decide on classes that should exist and to know how they should be related to each other. Object diagram is used to decide how to collaborate the objects. Module diagram helps map out where each class and object should be declared. At the end, the process diagram helps determine the system to which a task must be allocated.

Implementation: In this process, reusable code, which involves number of iterations, is generated.

Maintenance: This process involves making localized changes to the system to add new requirements and update the system for versioning.

Micro Development Process As micro refers to small, the micro process involves description of the day-to-day activities by a single or a small group of software developers because the analysis and design phases are not clearly defined.

The micro development process involves following steps:

- Identifying classes and objects
- Identifying class and object semantics
- Identifying class and object relationships
- Identifying class and object interfaces and implementation

POINTS TO PONDER

Every method has its strengths. Rumbaugh et al.'s method is used for creating object models. Jacobson et al.'s method is used for creating user-driven requirement and OOA models. The detailed object-oriented design models have been created by using Booch method.

6.3.2.3 Jacobson's Model

Jacobson et al.'s model comprises methodologies such as Object-oriented Business Engineering (OOBE), Object-oriented Software Engineering (OOSE) and Object factory for software development (Objectory). These methodologies together cover the entire life cycle of a software system and also emphasize the traceability among the different phases such as Analysis, Design, Implementation and Test (Figure 6.5).

The model is based on the use case model which captures the business requirement and then evolves into an object factory that encourages the reuse.

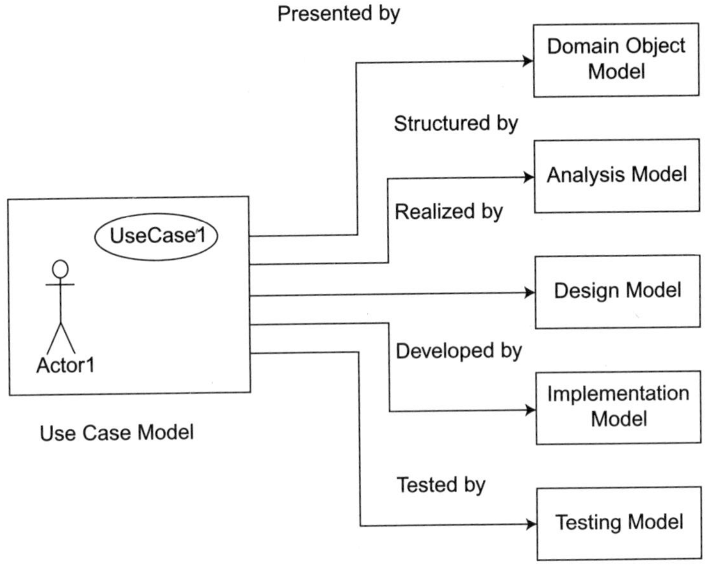

Figure 6.5 Jacobson Methodologies

6.3.3 Unified Modeling Language

As discussed in the sections above, Gary Booch, James Rambaugh and Ivar Jacobson had suggested three different models for depicting the OO design, and each of these models used its own notations, tools and guidelines. Finally, in January 1997, three of them together formed the Object Management Group and combined the best practices of these three methodologies to propose the single standard model called UML. Although, the name suggests that this is a programming language, but it is actually not. This is a standard set of notations for specifying, visualizing, constructing and communicating the OO design. Applications of UML include software as well as non-software industries such as aviation, manufacturing, infrastructure, etc. for depicting the process flow.

UML uses a set of static and dynamic visual models to capture the structure as well as behavior of the system. The primary goal of UML is to develop a generic modeling language that can be used to model all possible systems in a simple way so that it can be easily understood by those who are interested to understand the system.

6.3.3.1 UML Basic Notations

As UML describes the real-time systems, it is very important to generate a conceptual model and then proceed gradually. Conceptual model of UML can be mastered by knowing following three major elements:

- UML building blocks
- Rules to connect the building blocks
- Common mechanisms of UML

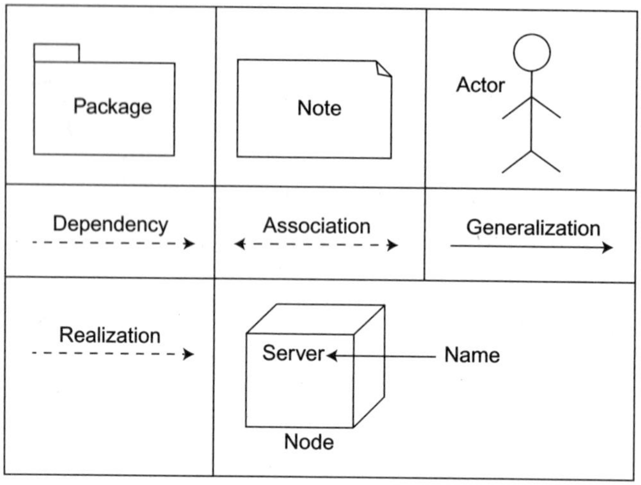

Figure 6.6 Common UML Notations

UML is popular for its diagrammatic notations (Figure 6.6), and it is used for visualizing, specifying, constructing and documenting the components of software and non-software systems. Among these, the visualization is the most important part which needs to be understood and remembered.

UML notations are the most important elements in modeling. Efficient and appropriate use of these notations is very important for making a complete and meaningful model. The model is useless unless its purpose is defined properly.

Hence, learning notations should be emphasized from the very beginning. Notations are different for things and relationships; and the UML diagrams are developed using the notations of things and relationships. Extensibility is another important feature that makes UML more powerful and flexible.

Relationships A model is not complete unless the relationship among elements is described properly because the relationship describes an UML model correctly. Following are different types of relationships available in UML.

- Dependency
- Association
- Generalization
- Extensibility

Dependency Notation Dependency is an important aspect in UML elements, as it describes the dependent elements and the direction of dependency. Dependency is represented by a dotted arrow as shown in Figure 6.7. The arrow head represents the independent element, and other end represents dependent elements.

Dependency is used to represent dependency between two elements of a system.

Association Notation Association describes how the elements in an UML diagram are associated, which means it describes number of elements taking part in an interaction.

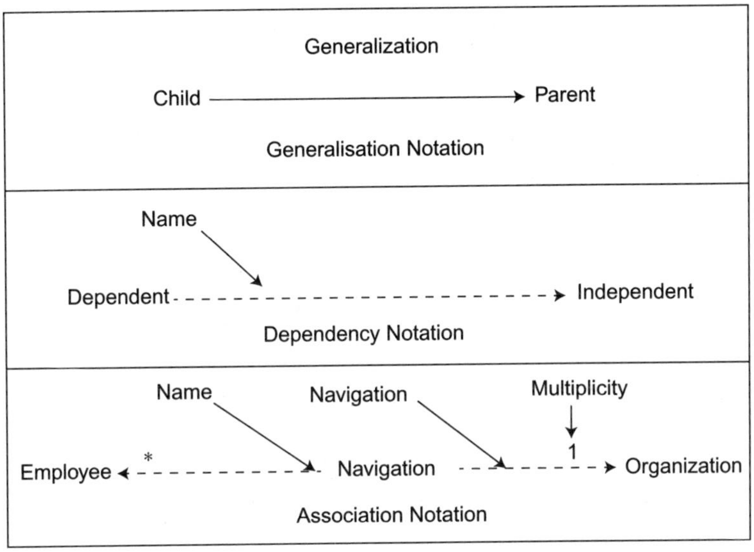

Figure 6.7 Common UML Notations

Association is represented by a dotted line with (without) arrows on both the sides. The two ends represent two associated elements, as shown in Figure 6.7. Multiplicity is also mentioned at the end (1, *, etc.) to show the number of objects associated.

Association is used to represent the relationship between the two elements of a system.

Generalization Notation Generalization describes the inherited relationship of the OO world, which is parent and child relationship.

Generalization is represented by an arrow with hollow arrow head in Figure 6.7. One end represents the parent element and the other end represents child element.

Generalization is used to describe parent–child relationship of two elements of a system.

6.3.3.2 UML Architecture

A real-world system is used by different users. The users can be developers, testers, business people, analysts, etc. Hence, before designing a system, the architecture of the system is built keeping in mind different perspectives of the system. The most important part is to visualize the system from different viewers' perspective. Better understanding leads to development of a better system.

UML plays an important role in defining different perspectives of a system, which are as follows:

- Design
- Implementation
- Process
- Deployment

These perspectives are connected through Use Case view, which is the center and represents the functionality of the system.

Design of a system consists of classes, interfaces and collaboration, and UML provides class diagram and object diagram to support this.

- Implementation defines the components assembled together to make a complete physical system, and UML component diagram is used to support implementation perspective.
- Process defines the flow of the system. The elements used in Design are also used to support this perspective.
- Deployment represents the physical nodes of the system that form the hardware, and UML deployment diagram is used to support this perspective.

6.3.3.3 UML Modeling Types

As discussed, the purpose of UML is to define and describe a real system completely; but, it is not possible to capture all the aspects of a system fully in a single diagram. For example, a system may exhibit both static behavior and dynamic behavior. Separate UML diagrams are needed to capture these static and dynamic natures efficiently. UML diagrams can be broadly classified into four categories based on the type of information they depict:

1. Structural Diagrams (Static)
    - i) Class diagrams
    - ii) Object diagrams
2. Behavioral Diagrams (Dynamic)
    - i) Activity diagrams
    - ii) Interaction diagrams
        - Sequence diagrams
        - Collaboration diagrams
    - iii) Use case diagrams
    - iv) State chart diagrams
3. Implementation Diagrams
    - i) Component diagrams
    - ii) Deployment diagrams
4. Architectural Diagrams
    - i) Package diagrams

It is important to understand the difference between each of diagram categories and the types in order to create and use the diagrams correctly.

Structural Diagrams The structural diagrams describe different components of a system that interact with each other to generate the system's behavior. For OO purview, these components are the classes. It is important to note that the structural model shows only the components, but the dynamic nature of the components is not depicted by these types of diagrams. Class diagram is the most important in this category.

Class Diagram This is the most frequently used diagram in an OO system, the purpose of which is to help analyze the structure of the classes present in a system and different interactions among them. Hence, the associations, collaborations and interfaces are part of the class diagram.

The class diagrams can be easily mapped with the OO languages such as C++, Java, due to which the class diagrams are widely used during the design and construction phases of the projects. Many tools which can generate executable codes from the class diagrams are available, if the diagrams are created properly.

The class diagram works as the base diagram for most of the other UML diagrams such as sequence diagram, component diagram, deployment diagram.

Basic components of the class diagrams are:

- Collection of classes (with attributes and processes)
- Interfaces
- Associations
- Collaborations
- Constraints

Guidelines to Draw Class Diagram It is important to draw the class diagram correctly, as this acts as building block for the subsequent diagrams of the system. Class structures of the system that are developed after the analysis phase and the relationships established among different classes act as necessary inputs for drawing the class diagram.

Many properties have to be considered for creating class diagram from the UML standard and real-life system development perspectives. But, only high-level considerations or guidelines have been discussed in this book, which are as follows:

- Identify the classes and their interactions before beginning drawing the class diagram, which will save a lot of rework later.
- Identify the most important attributes and functionalities of the classes in advance, which helps create the class hierarchy during the diagram preparation.
- The name of the class diagram should be meaningful so that it describes the aspect of the system.
- It helps put the design considerations, assumptions, constraints, etc. as a Note for each class as well as the diagram, which helps the user of the diagram (developers/coders) to understand the diagram better.
- The relationships have to be used judiciously. Many possible relationships that can be depicted through UML have been discussed in the previous section. It is important to make sure that the correct relationship is shown in the diagram, so that the code following this design is correct.

Figure 6.8 shows the simplified class diagram of a banking system.

- It is important to note that the common attributes and functionalities of three different types of accounts (i.e., Savings, Current and Deposit) are collated into a super class, that is, Bank Account. Each of these three types of accounts should be inherited from this super class so that all these attributes and functionalities are automatically brought in them.

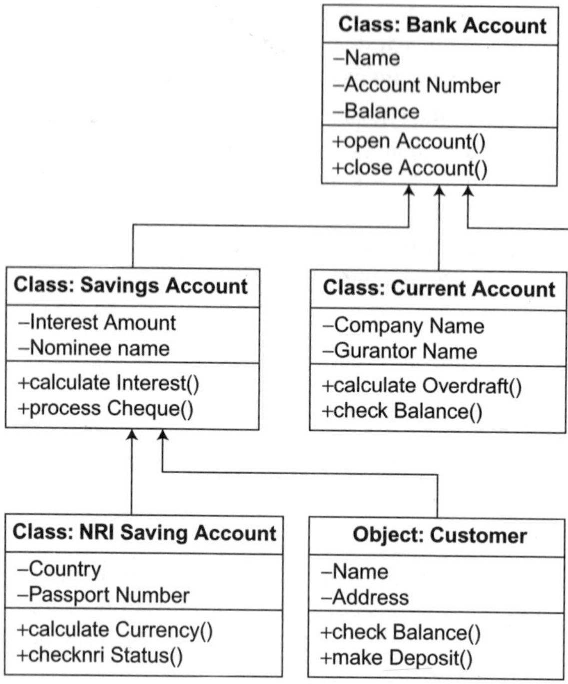

Figure 6.8 Class Diagram of a Banking System

- Specific attributes and functionalities for each subclass are then added so that each account type can behave differently.
- According to the diagram, the Customer object uses the Saving Account class because a customer can have one or more savings account.
- When this diagram is translated into an OO coding language, then the coder creates a Bank Account class, writes the generic behavior of opening and closing an account and then creates three specific classes Saving Account, Current Account and Deposit Account by inheriting from the Bank Account class.

Object Diagram Object Diagrams are closely related to Class Diagrams. An object diagram can be interpreted as the instance of a class diagram. Hence, the snapshot of the system at a specific point of time is captured in an object diagram. Uses of the object diagram are as follows:

1. Before creating the class diagram, we have to create a few object diagrams to analyze the interaction among the classes in the system.
2. After creating the class diagram, a few corresponding object diagrams may be created for validating the class diagram as test cases.

Figure 6.9 explores the object diagram corresponding to the class diagram explained in the previous section.

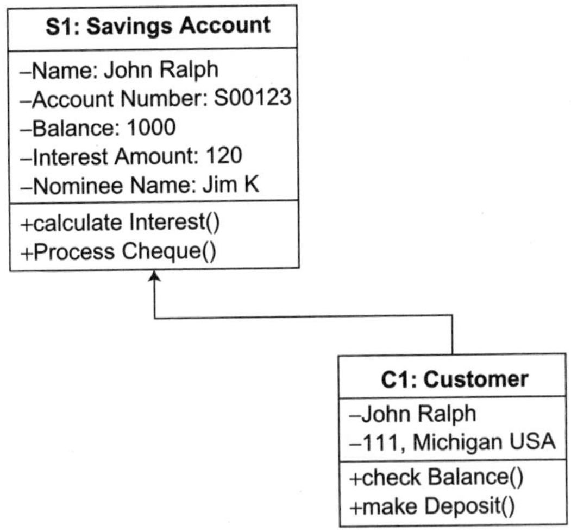

Figure 6.9 Object Diagram of a Banking System

Behavioral Diagrams The interaction among the structural models is represented in Behavioral model. Different behavioral models such as Activity Diagrams, Interaction Diagrams, Use Case Diagrams represent the dynamic sequence of flow in a system.

Activity Diagram One of the important behaviors of the system to be captured is the flow of activities and control within the system. In this instance, activities mean the functionalities of the system. A system can have different functionalities, which need to be understood, and for performing each functionality, a series of activities have to be performed in a particular sequence. It is important to note that the control flow from one activity to another can be sequential, branched or concurrent.

As the activity diagram shows the dynamic behavior of the system, there can be many activity diagrams for a particular system based on different flows and functionalities performed by it.

Guidelines to Draw Activity Diagram Activity list is one the main elements in any activity diagram. Among various functionalities of the system, identify different activities performed and the interrelationship among them. It is also important to understand different conditions and constraints associated with the activities; for example, a constraint for opening a new account is that the account type should be either Savings or Current, which means that in the activity diagram, this has to be entered as a conditional check.

The activity diagram depicts the business process. Thus, it is useful to get the view of the business functionalities of the system from the business users before creating the activity diagram of the system.

Figure 6.10 represents the activity diagram of the account opening system. For simplicity, we have created a constraint that the account type should be mentioned as either Savings or Current, without which the system would not allow to open an account.

Four main activities represented in this diagram are:

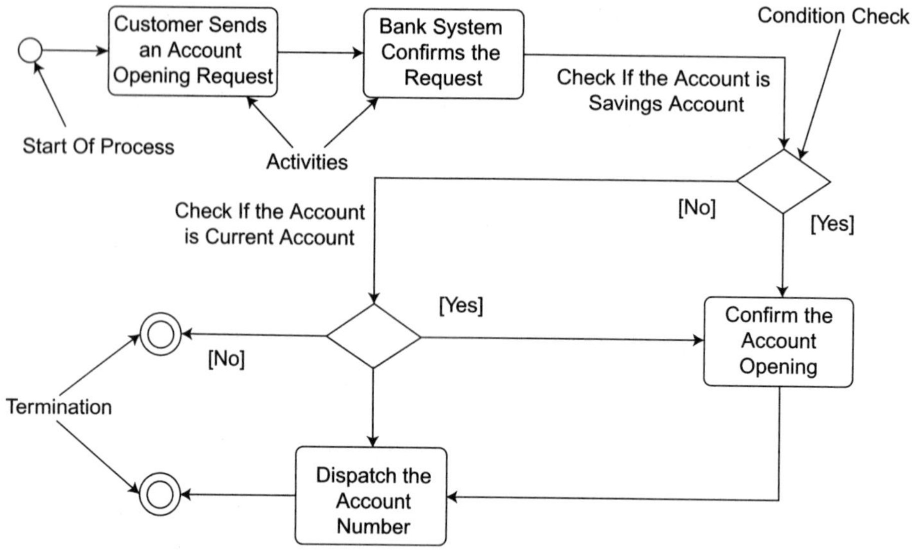

Figure 6.10 Activity Diagram of Account Opening System

- Account opening request by the customer
- Confirmation for receiving the request
- Confirmation for account opening
- Dispatch account number

After the receipt of the request, it is checked whether the account type requested matches the valid account types available. The business users will be able to understand the flow of the system from the activity diagram. If other external systems such as Database, file system are involved, then the activity diagram represents the flow from these systems as well.

Sequence Diagram A sequence diagram is one of the interaction diagrams and this shows the interaction among the objects in a system in a time sequence. While performing a particular functionality of the system, the objects in the system need to exchange a sequence of messages, which is captured in a sequence diagram. Requirements captured in a use case diagram are analyzed in the logical view of the sequence diagrams. Sometimes, these sequence diagrams are also called event diagrams, event scenarios and timing diagrams.

This diagram is useful for both the business users and the developers. The requirement of the system can be very well refined by showing the sequence of interactions among different objects in the system. Similarly, the developers get a clear idea of the different messages flowing between the objects and their sequence to code the application fulfilling the system need.

A sequence diagram represents different processes and objects as parallel vertical lines called lifelines and the messages exchanged between them as horizontal lines. The basic building blocks of the sequence diagram are discussed as follows.

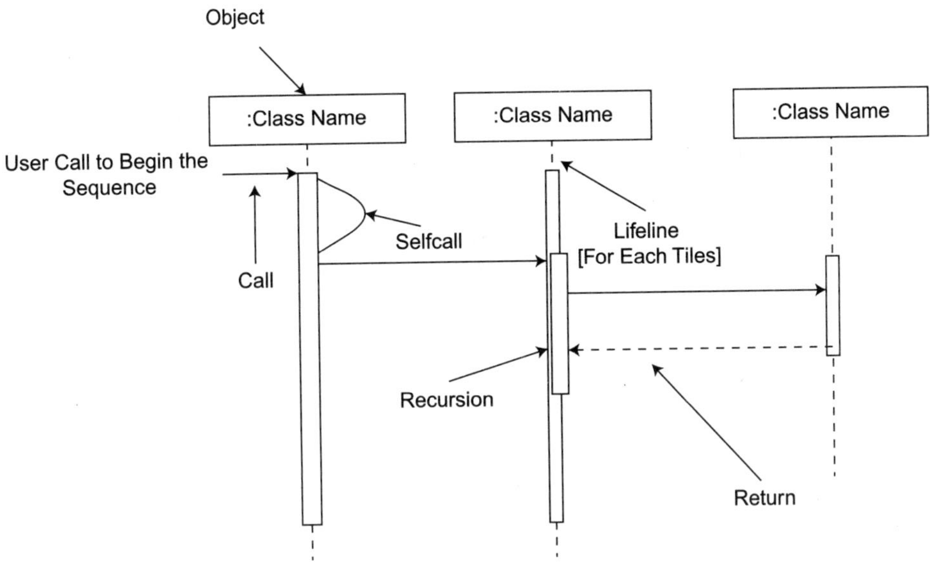

Figure 6.11 Sequence Diagram Notations

Guidelines for Drawing the Sequence Diagram Figure 6.11 shows the basic notations of a Sequence Diagram.

The vertical dimension of the sequence diagram indicates the message sequencing from top to bottom in the order and the horizontal dimension shows the object instances involved in the message exchange. There are three basic building blocks, Lifelines, Messages and Guards.

Lifelines Lifeline notations are indicated by the parallel vertical dashed lines with a box at the top, which represents the object instance that participates in the sequence diagram. The name of the lifeline is placed within the box. The messages enter and terminate into these lifelines.

Messages The first message of a sequence diagram that represents the beginning of the message flow is shown at the top left hand side. Subsequent messages then add below in the order of their flow. The message flow is shown as a line from the sending object to the receiving object and these lines have arrowheads. The name of the message is written above the message line. It is important to note that the receiving object should implement the message it receives.

Guards Guards represent the conditional statements for the message flow. The message flows from the sender to the receiver object only if the conditions are met.

Figure 6.12 represents the simplified sequence diagram for the account opening system. The first message flows from the customer object to the Bank Account class requesting the opening of the account, and then the request is processed by the Savings Account object. This diagram represents the actual scenario of flow of messages when the system is running.

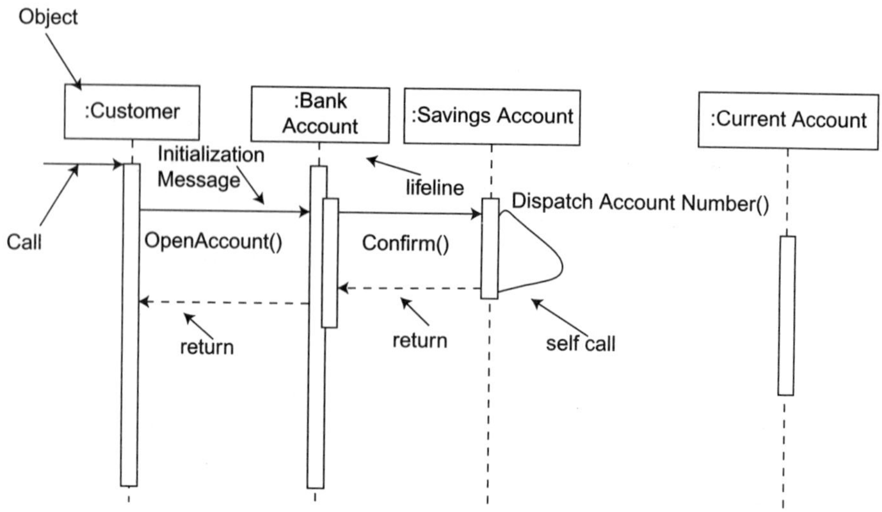

Figure 6.12 Sequence Diagram of the Account Opening System

Collaboration Diagram Collaboration diagram is another form of Interaction Diagram, which represents the structure of the object interaction along with the flow of messages and their sequence. Although, the Sequence Diagram and Collaboration Diagram may seem to convey the same information, such as messaging between participating classes, the sequence of message flow, the main difference is that the collaboration diagram focuses more on showing the structure of the interactions rather than the sequence of interactions.

Figure 6.13 represents Account Opening Functionality in the collaboration diagram. Propagation of information is indicated by the sequence numbers against the flow of messages.

Use Case Diagram As discussed in Section 6.2.3, the use case diagrams are used to represent the interaction of the system components with the users and the external systems. This is the simplest form of the pictorial representation of the functionalities to be performed by the system and how different users of the system will be using it. For example, for a banking system the users can be the customer, the accountant, the bank manager, the auditors, etc. Each of these users wants different functionalities from the same banking system. Thus, the use case for each of these users will be different.

The users, internal and external agents (either human users or the other interfacing systems), are called Actors. The interactions of the Actor and the system are called the use cases. Hence, "Deposit Money" and "Check Balance" can be the use cases for a bank account system.

The main use of the use cases is capturing and elaborating the requirements. It acts as the bridge between the requirement and the high-level design; and some of the design details can be added into the detailed use cases as progressed through the design of the system. It is also possible to show the relationship of different components (classes) with the system such as association, generalization, delegation.

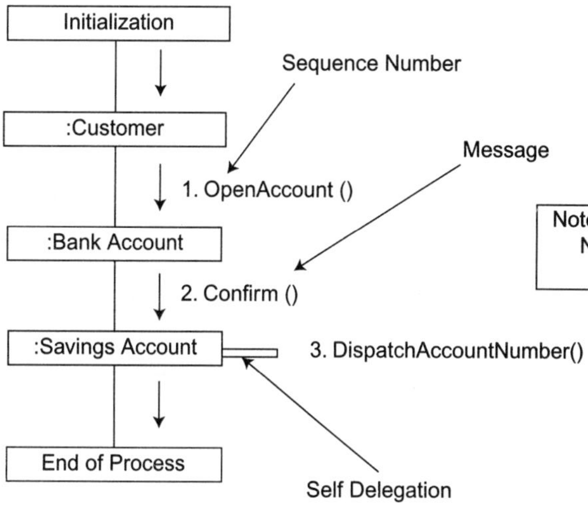

Figure 6.13 Collaboration Diagram of Account Opening System

Guidelines for Drawing the Use Case Diagram First step in creating the use case diagram is to identify the different Actors in the system. Then, the activities performed by these actors on the system and the relationship between the functionalities need to be identified. So, on a high level, the first three steps for creating the use cases are:

1. Identify the Actors
2. Identify the use cases performed by the actors on the system
3. Identify the interactions and relationships between the use cases

As the use case diagram can be used as the main mode of communication of the capability of the proposed system to all stakeholders, it is important that the details maintained in this diagram follow some basic guidelines, such as

1. The use case should be named in such a way that it conveys the functionality that is expected by the user from the system. For example, a use case name such as "Check Account" may not depict the exact functionality, but if it is named as "Check Account Balance," then it is clear what is expected from the system.
2. For the same reason, the Actors should also be identified accordingly.
3. Only the important relationships among the use cases should be showed. All possible relationships included among the use cases should not be captured, but only relationships required from the system should be captured.
4. "Note" should be used to mention any important points regarding the use cases. This helps the designer and all other stakeholders who look at the use case diagram.

Figure 6.14 represents the use case of the Account Opening System. The Customer requests for Opening an account as an Actor, which is a use case for the system. Request is considered based on the type of account to be opened, either the savings account or the current account. So, the Open

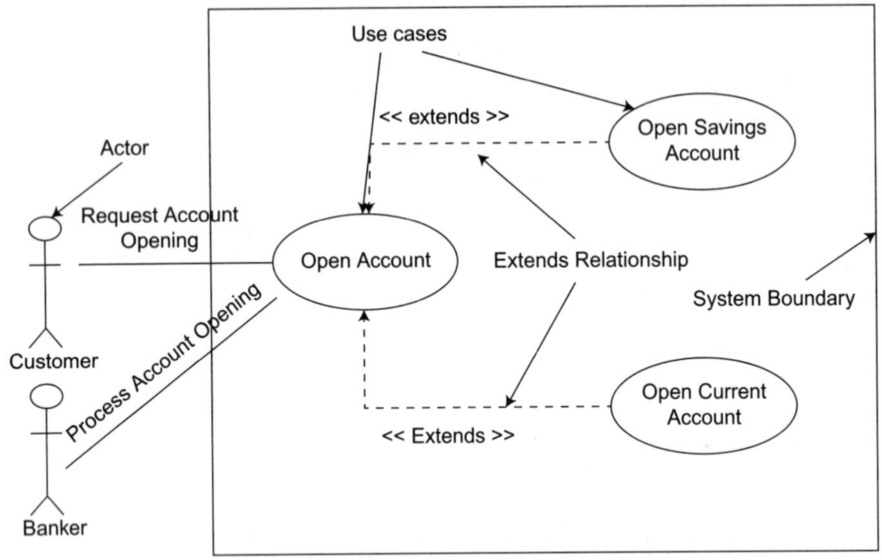

Figure 6.14 Use Case Diagram of an Account Opening System

Savings Account use case extends the account opening functionalities of the bank account. Similarly, the banker can send process account opening request to the open account use case. Based on all these requirements, the design of the open account has the capability of handling both the customer request and the Banker's request.

State Chart Diugram The dynamic behavior of a system and effect of external and internal stimuli can be effectively represented using the State Chart Diagram. It is also called as the state machine because the states of the objects or interfaces inside the system are shown in this diagram. Important components of the state chart diagram are the objects and the events, and changing states of the objects has also been represented. In a particular workflow, the state chart shows the lifetime of an object from creation till the termination.

This diagram is useful in explaining the system behavior during the execution. The state chart diagram represents changes that occur in different events in the state of the components of the system and possible exceptions encountered by components.

Guidelines for Drawing the State Chart Diagram The following points have to be clarified before starting to draw the state chart diagram:

1. The important objects to be identified
2. The states of those objects that are to be identified
3. The events that cause the state change to be identified

Figure 6.15 represents changes that occur in Bank Account object as the account-opening event is triggered into the system. It is important to note the exceptional flow which marks the final state of the object as failed and the successful execution of the processes and event flows which complete the transaction.

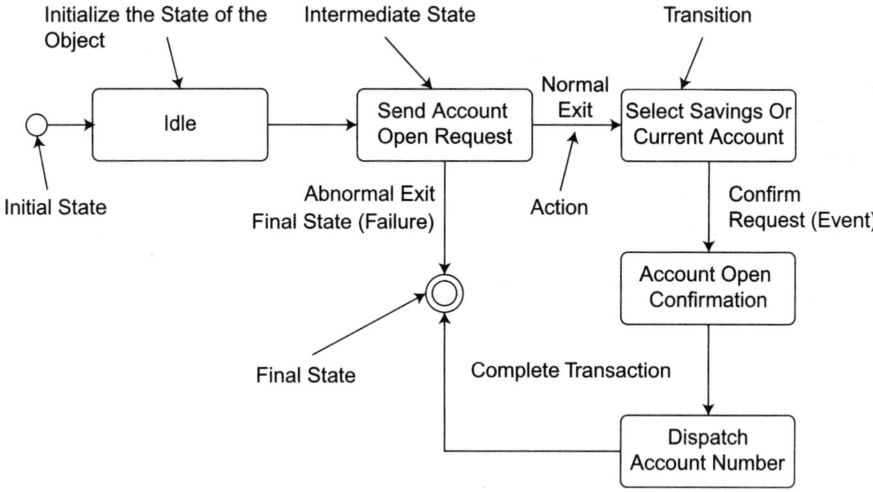

Figure 6.15 State Chart Diagram of Account Opening System

Implementation diagrams Implementation diagrams give details of the system that need to be considered while deploying the system. Component diagram and deployment diagram belong to this category.

Architectural Diagrams A Package Diagram represents the packaging of the components and interaction among different object packages.

The OO design model has evolved to a great extent over the years. It is evident from the discussion of the popular models used in OOD that the focus now is to reduce the effort of coding by accommodating as much information in design as possible. This has also made creating codes and test cases possible automatically from the design diagrams saving a lot of time during the development stage.

Summary

- The OOA is a structured process of investigation and, to be more specific, it is the investigation of objects. Design means collaboration of identified objects.
- Use cases are scenarios for understanding system requirements. A use case is an interaction between the users and a system. The use case model captures the goal of the user and the responsibility of the system towards its users.
- Modeling techniques provide a set of tools and guidelines which help analysts and designers to analyze the robust requirement and design.
- Class diagram shows the structure of the classes present in a system and interactions among them. So, the associations, collaborations and interfaces are part of the class diagram.

Model Questions
PART A (Objective type)

1. Which of the following statements is true?

   A. In the structured analysis, the data and the functions that process the data are considered as part of same entities

   B. The Object-Oriented Analysis recognizes the fact that the data are an integral part of the same system

   C. Structured analysis decomposes the system bottom up

   D. The Object Oriented Analysis recognizes the fact that the data are not considered as part of same entities

Answer: B

2. Which of the following is considered as a pictorial representation of the scenarios for clearly capturing the system requirements?

   A. Use Cases B. Test Cases

   C. Object Cases D. Class diagram

Answer: A

3. A use case describes one main flow of events. An exceptional or additional flow of events could also be added.

   A. True B. False

Answer: A

4. Use case model employs following two types of relationships:

   A. "extends" and "uses" relationships B. "extends" and "inherits" relationships

   C. "support" and "oppose" relationships D. "contributes" and "uses" relationships

Answer: A

5. Abstract use cases also have uses or extend relationships.

   A. True B. False

Answer: A

6. Rumbaugh et al.'s method of OOD Modeling Technique is capable of:

   A. Object Model

   B. Attributes Model

   C. User-Driven Analysis Model

   D. producing detailed Object-Oriented Design Models

Answer: A

7. Jacobson et al.'s method of OOD Modeling Technique is capable of:

   A. Object Model

   B. Attributes Model

C. User-driven analysis model

D. producing detailed Object-Oriented Design Models

Answer: C

8. The Booch method of OOD Modeling Technique is capable of:

   A. Object Model

   B. Attributes Model

   C. User-driven analysis model

   D. producing detailed Object-Oriented Design Models

Answer: D

9. Object Modeling Technique (OMT) has been developed by:

   A. Rumbaugh et al. B. Jacobson et al.

   C. The Booch D. Newton

Answer: A

10. Which of the following is not a phase of OMT?

    A. System Design B. Object Design

    C. Implementation D. Testing

Answer: D

11. Which phase of OMT gives the blue print of the system?

    A. System Design B. Object Design

    C. Implementation D. Analysis Phase

Answer: A

12. Which phase of OMT produces reusable and robust code?

    A. System Design B. Object Design

    C. Implementation D. Analysis Phase

Answer: C

13. The main disadvantage of Booch methodology is its usage of large set of symbols.

    A. True B. False

Answer: A

14. Two types of development processes of Booch methodology are:

    A. Macro development process and micro development process

    B. Easy development process and difficult development process

    C. Minor development process and major development process

    D. Class development process and object development process

Answer: A

15. Object-Oriented Business Engineering (OOBE) belongs to:

A. Rumbaugh et al. B. Jacobson et al.

C. The Booch D. Newton

Answer: B

16. Phases of Jacobson et al.'s methodologies comprise:

A. OOBE, OOSE, Objectory B. OOCE, OODE, Objectory

C. OOAE, OOBE, OOCE D. OOCE, OOSE, OOTE

Answer: A

17. Four categories of UML diagrams are

A. Structural Diagrams, Behavioral Diagrams, Implementation Diagrams, Architectural Diagrams

B. Class Diagram, Object Diagrams, Component Diagrams, Architectural Diagrams

C. Interaction Diagrams, Sequence Diagrams, Activity Diagrams, Deployment Diagrams

D. Package Diagrams, Deployment Diagram, Class Diagram, Object Diagram

Answer: A

18. These diagrams describe different components of a system that interact with each other to generate the system's behavior.

A. Structural Diagrams B. Behavioral Diagrams

C. Implementation Diagrams D. Architectural Diagrams

Answer: A

19. Two types of Structural Diagrams are:

A. Activity Diagrams and Interaction Diagrams

B. Class Diagrams and Object Diagrams

C. Component Diagrams and Deployment Diagrams

D. Activity Diagrams and Architectural Diagrams

Answer: A

20. Most frequently used diagram in an object-oriented system is:

A. Object Diagrams B. Behavioral Diagrams

C. Class Diagrams D. Package Diagrams

Answer: C

21. Two types of Implementation Diagrams are

A. Class Diagrams and Object Diagrams

B. Activity Diagrams and Interaction Diagrams

C. Component Diagrams and Deployment Diagrams

D. Component Diagrams and Collaboration Diagrams

Answer: C

22. There can be many activity diagrams of a particular system.

A. True

B. False

Answer: A

23. The dynamic behavior of a system and effect of external and internal stimuli can be effectively represented using

A. State Chart Diagram

B. Architectural Diagrams

C. Implementation Diagrams

D. Deployment Diagrams

Answer: A

24. The diagram useful in explaining the system behavior during the execution is

A. State Chart Diagram

B. Architectural Diagrams

C. Implementation Diagrams

D. Deployment Diagrams

Answer: A

PART B (Answer in one or two lines)

1. Describe the concepts of object-oriented analysis and design.
2. What are the three main purposes of OO analysis and design?
3. What are the three basic steps of applying and implementing OO concepts?
4. What are the objectives of Object-Oriented Analysis?
5. Give overview of the domain analysis process.
6. What is use case modeling?
7. Draw the Class Diagram of a Banking System.
8. What are the basic components of the class diagrams?
9. Define different perspectives of a system.
10. Write the conceptual model of UML learning.

PART C (Descriptive type)

1. Briefly describe the object model for a system.
2. Briefly describe the Booch methodology, the macro development process and the micro development process.
3. Describe in detail Jacobson's Model.
4. Write short notes on **unified modeling language (UML)**.
5. Describe in detail about **Class Diagram**.

6. Describe in detail about **Object Diagram**.
7. Describe in detail about **Activity Diagram**.
8. Explain in detail about **Sequence Diagram**.
9. Explain in detail about **Collaboration Diagram**.
10. Explain in details about **use case diagram**?
11. Write in detail about **State Chart Diagram, Implementation Diagram and Architectural Diagram**.

7

User Interface Design

CHAPTER COVERAGE

1. *Introduction*
2. *Concepts of User Interface*
3. *Elements of the User Interface*
4. *Designing the User Interface*
5. *User Interface Evaluation (User Interface Design Evaluation)*
6. *Golden Rules of User Interface Design*
7. *User Interface Models (User Interface Design Models)*
8. *Usability*

7.1 INTRODUCTION

One important part of the design process is the user interface design. User interface plays a crucial role in the success of software projects. First impression is the best impression and hence first look into the user interface (UI) should impress the end users. User interface is not only the reflection of the functionalities of the system, but also the reflection of the culture of the end users. For example, white color is the symbol of purity in Western cultures, whereas the same color is the symbol of bad luck in India, Japan and China. Pink color is being appreciated in Japan but not in India. If the portal/website is intended for particular demographics then we need to choose the colors appreciated by that region.

Additionally, each color has its own meaning (refer Figure 7.1) and this also needs to be considered while choosing the color. Below mentioned are few colors and their common meanings.

- Black: mystery, secrecy.
- Blue: coolness, peace.
- Brown: strength, stability.
- Gray: maturity, reliability.
- Green: life, naturalness, health.
- Orange: warmth, courage.
- Red: danger, energy, power, aggression.
- White: purity, freshness, peace.
- Yellow: happiness, brightness, joy.

Usability measurement plays a crucial role in the success of any product and it is applicable for the software systems and the portals also. This chapter discusses the important usability concepts and procedures of applying the same.

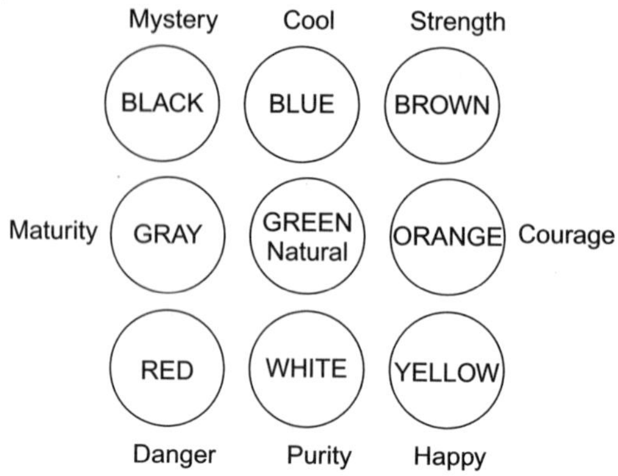

Figure 7.1 Colors and Characteristics

7.2 CONCEPTS OF USER INTERFACE

A user interface has 3 basic components namely (refer Figure 7.2)

- End users
- User interface
- System (machine)

A UI helps the people (users) to interact with a machine (system). User interface includes its own software and hardware components which helps the users to interact with the machine (system).

UI input allows the users to manipulate the system. User interface output helps the users to understand the system behavior. In general, user interface helps human machine interaction.

For Example, while driving a car the driver (user) uses the accelerator, break, clutch and gearing system to interact with the engine of the car (machine). They all are acting as UI input. Speedometer, fuel level meters helps the driver to understand the engine. They act as UI output (refer Figure 7.3).

The goal of the UI is to effectively control the machine (system) at the user's end and pass the feedback from the machine (system) back to the user in efficient manner which helps the user to make decisions. This means the user needs to provide minimal input to achieve the desired output and stopping machine to provide undesired output.

The design of the UI is directly linked to the disciplines of ergonomics and psychology.

The following is the definition of ergonomic by International Ergonomics Association (IEA) (Source: www.iea.cc).

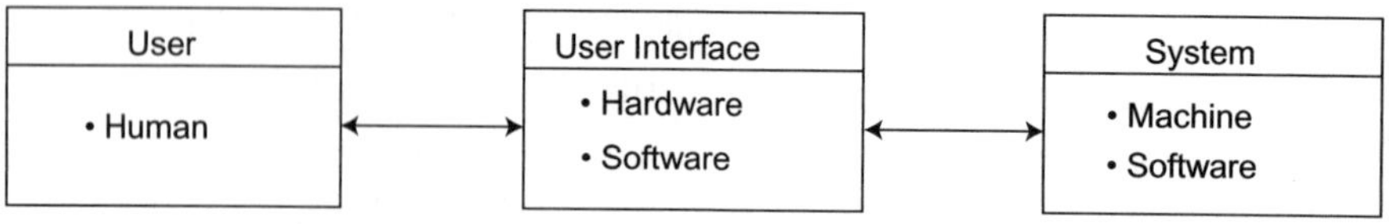

Figure 7.2 Components of User Interface

Figure 7.3 User Interface Example

Ergonomics (or human factors) is the scientific discipline concerned with the understanding of the interactions among humans and other elements of a system, which helps to optimize human well-being and overall system performance.

User interface is also called as human–computer interface (HCI) and man–machine interface (MMI).

7.3 ELEMENTS OF THE USER INTERFACE

User interface has four elements (Figure 7.4) namely

1. Users
2. Tasks
3. Contents
4. Environment

Users interact with the system through the user interface. Tasks are the activities performed by the users to interact with the system. Contents are the output of the system that is displayed to the users through the user interface. The environments in which these tasks are executed are also part of the user interface.

Based on the four elements the analysis is also classified into four types

1. User analysis
2. Tasks analysis
3. Contents analysis
4. Environment analysis

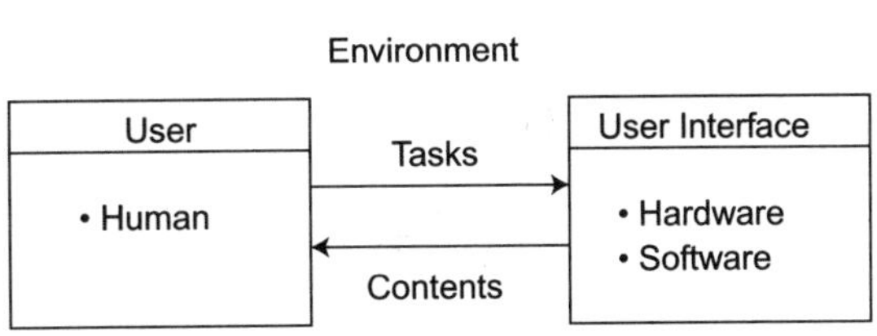

Figure 7.4 User Interface Elements

7.3.1 User Analysis

User analysis (refer Figure 7.5) helps to understand the end users as well as how the end users use the system which will help them to design the UI in a better way. Information about the end users can be obtained directly from the end users in the form of interview and also getting input from others who are interacting with the end users like sales, marketing and support people. Basic set of questions is prepared that can be used to gather the basic information from all the above set of people.

- User interviews conducted directly with the end users to understand the basic information about them, their likings, mental models, etc.
- Sales input (interviews) conducted with the sales people who interact with end users on a regular basis to understand more about the end users.
- Marketing input (interviews) conducted based on a market analysis to understand the likings of the segmentations.
- Support input (interview) happens with the support to understand the likings of the users and what will work and what will not work out.

User Analysis Questions

Following questions are sample user analysis questions which help to understand the end users.

1. What level of formal education does the user have?
2. Age of the user
3. Home country of the user
4. Gender of the end user
5. Primary spoken language of the user
6. Office hours of the user
7. Is the system integral part of the user's work?
8. Can the user learn the system by looking into user manuals?

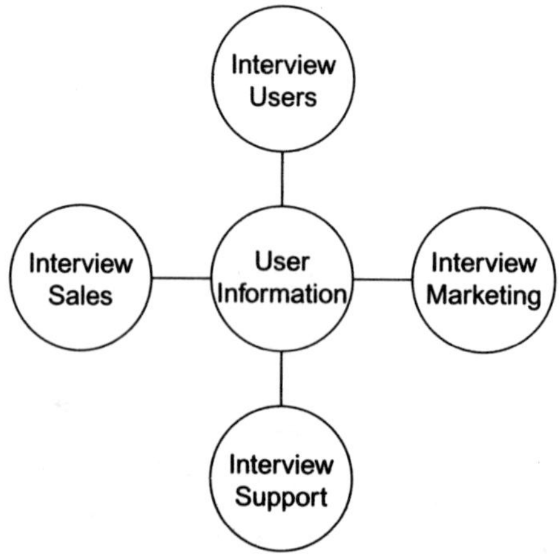

Figure 7.5 User Analysis

9. Is the user trained to use the system?
10. Do the user knows the technology behind the system or want to know the technology?
11. Is the user subject matter expert of the system?
12. What are the consequences if the user makes a mistake in the system?

7.3.2 Task Analysis

Task analysis (refer Figure 7.6) helps to understand the tasks done by the end users under a specific circumstance. It helps to understand the sub tasks done by the end users, its sequence levels, hierarchical levels and problems faced by the end users while executing the tasks. As an output of tasks analysis use case diagram is drawn which helps to understand how the end users performs the tasks along with the workflow of the interaction. It helps to understand the overall flow of the users as well as the tasks performed by the users.

Task Analysis Questions

Following questions are sample task analysis questions which help to understand the tasks performed by the end users.

1. List of tasks performed by the particular end user.
2. What are the sub tasks of the tasks describe above?
3. What are the sequencing levels of the sub tasks defined above?
4. What are the hierarchical levels of the sub tasks?
5. How work flow moves from one user to the other?
6. Who is the next user acting on the task(s) performed by this user?
7. What is the duration of the tasks performed?

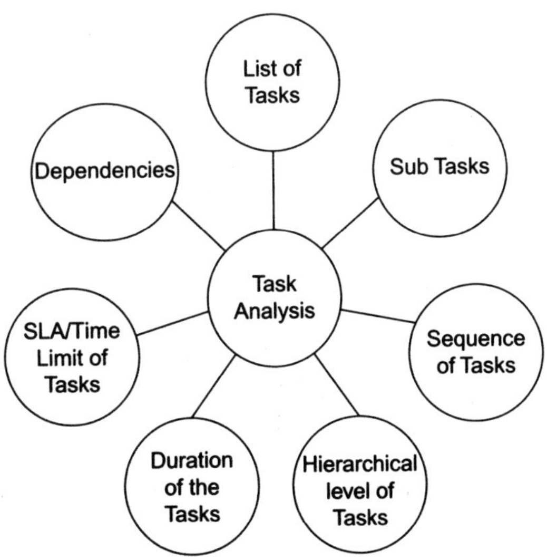

Figure 7.6 Task Analysis

8. Is the task performed manual or automated?
9. Is there any email communication to other users about the tasks?
10. Is there any service level agreement set for the tasks with the customer?
11. Is there any time limit for the tasks to be performed?
12. Do tasks depend on the external parties (inside and outside the organization)?

7.3.3 Content Analysis

Content analysis (refer Figure 7.7) is an important element of the overall user interface as it directly satisfies the end users. Content analysis helps the end users to understand the machine language. Content may be in the form of single word, graphical representation or in the form of sound files. For example, reverse guider fitted into the car gives a deep beep sound if there is any object nearby the car prompting the driver to apply the break. In few cars the reverse guider system also has visual display in the front that can be used by the driver of the car. Content analysis helps to understand the content requirement of the users. Display content may be acquired from already stored database of the system as well as data transmitted from external system to the application. For example, radio system being used in a car. The format of the content is the main component of the study along with the data/information to be displayed.

Content Analysis Questions

Following questions are sample content analysis questions which help to understand the contents.

1. What information is required by the end user?
2. What is the form of contents (graphical, tables, text)?
3. What is the frequency of updating the content? Is it LIVE update?
4. How long the content needs to be displayed? Is it permanent display?
5. Can the user customize the place holder of the information (Content)?
6. How to use the color to enhance the understanding (RED/GREEN, etc.)?
7. Can the user navigate through the information?

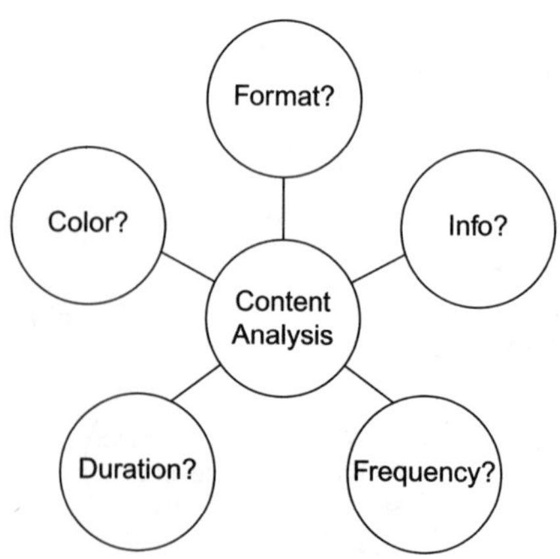

Figure 7.7 Content Analysis

7.3.4 Work Environment Analysis

Work environment analysis (refer Figure 7.8) plays a crucial role as the designed product is fitting into the environment. For example, the intensity level of the head light in a car will always be higher than the intensity of the light used inside the car. Both are bulbs but the light intensity levels varies and it depends on the environment in which it operates. Same logic is applicable to the software products. For example, surrounding noise level plays a crucial role while designing an audio/video system.

Environmental Factors to be Analyzed

1. Surrounding temperature
2. Surrounding noise level
3. Surrounding light level
4. Time restrictions if any
5. Weather condition
6. Space (place size) limitation
7. Product size, height
8. Input device to be used
9. Size of the input device
10. Output device to be used
11. Size of the output device
12. Alternatives input and output device

POINTS TO PONDER

Based on the four elements the analysis is also classified into four types: user analysis, tasks analysis, contents analysis, environment analysis.

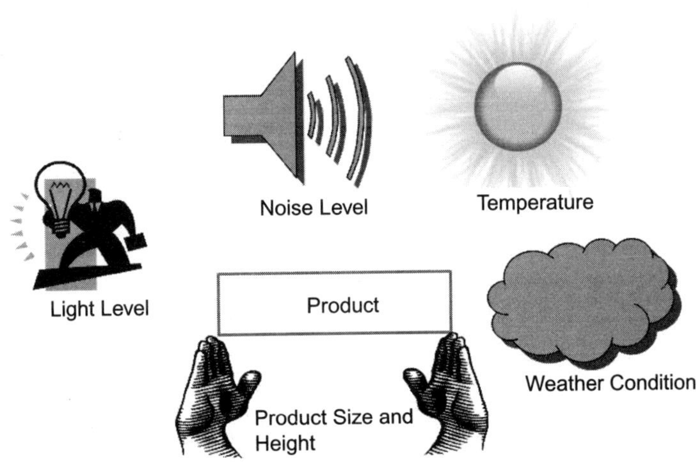

Figure 7.8 Environment Analysis

7.4 DESIGNING THE USER INTERFACE

UID or user interface design is an iterative process (refer Figure 7.9) – the fine tuning happens at every stage of the design. Three golden rule of the user interface (three golden rules of Mandel) to be kept in mind while designing the UI are

- Place users in control
- Reduce users' memory load
- Make the interface consistent

UID – User Interface Design Steps:

1. Do user interface analysis (user analysis, tasks analysis, content analysis, environment analysis)?
2. Define the events changing the user interface state.
3. Depict the user interface state.
4. How user interprets the states of the system from the information provided?

User interface design starts with the analysis of the user interface which is already discussed. The questionnaires prepared will help the designer to understand the users, tasks, contents and the environment better.

Events consists of series of actions (tasks) performed by the end users. Events are performed on the interface objects through clicks, reading, writing, etc. So Interface Objects and the corresponding actions of the users need to be defined. Interface objects are classified into source objects, target object and application object. Source objects are placed over the target object. Application objects represent the applications and are specific to the application. For example, "list" data displayed on the screen. After identifying the objects, the designer needs to identify the actions performed by the objects (refer Figure 7.10). Interface designer creates the layout of the screen (screen layout) after identifying all the objects and its actions.

Screen layout design generally involves the following steps:

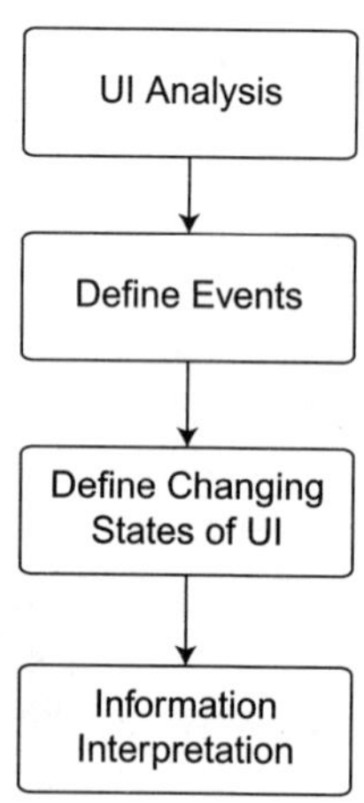

Figure 7.9 User Interface Design

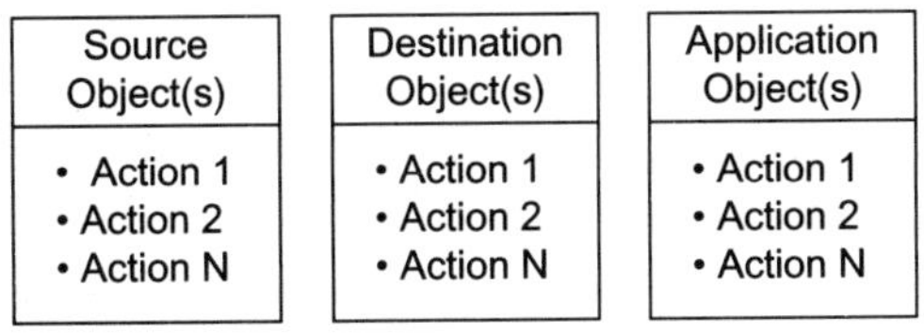

Figure 7.10 Source, Destination and Application Objects

1. Graphical design of the overall screen
2. Placement of icons and place holders
3. Proper titling to the screen and place holders
4. Definition of menu items and its actions
5. Placement of objects on the place holders and its actions
6. User help facilities (help menu)
7. Appropriate error message

Designing dialog:
Sequence in which the information is displayed (output) and obtained (input) from the end users is called as dialog. In other words, dialog is the sequence in which the information is exchanged between the end users and the system.

Three major steps in designing the dialog are

1. Designing the sequence of information (dialog)
2. Building a prototype for the dialog
3. Assessing usability of the dialog using prototype

Guidelines for designing the dialogs are

1. Simple and easy
2. Maintain consistency
3. Maintain the sequence
4. Focus on control

7.4.1 Common User Interface Design Issues

1. Improper error messages to the users (Figure 7.11)
2. No proper menu labeling
3. Improper help facilities to the users
4. Response time of the system

User interface should convert the system errors, which are technical in nature, into a user specific error message which is understandable by the users in their business language. Basically, the technical message needs to be converted into a business message which is plain so that it is easy for the business users to interpret and act accordingly.

Following are the characteristics of the error messages:

Figure 7.11 User Interface Issues

1. It is easily understandable and non-judgmental
2. The message should not blame the end users under any circumstance
3. The message should also use visual cue so that the end users understand it easily
4. The message should indicate the reason for the error (e.g., input file format is not correct, etc.).
5. The message should indicate the advice to overcome the current situation (e.g., Input file format is not correct. Please correct the format and try this option again).
6. Even successful transaction to be shown to the customer in the form of message (e.g., Application successfully submitted. Please check the email for the next step).

Menu labeling is to be designed in such a way so that it is easy and consistent across all the screens. It should have the internationalization facility if required. It should also display consistently across all the environments.

Menu labeling should address the following (refer Figure 7.12)

1. All menu labels are self explanatory
2. Short cut options available for menu actions (example, [CTRL] O, etc.)
3. Can menus be customized by the users
4. Sub menus are consistent with the main menu

Help manuals should describe all the scenarios of the system and it should be written in easy language so that any novice users can understand and use the system. Response time of the system is very important and it needs to be taken care even while designing the user interface.

Figure 7.12 Menu

7.5 USER INTERFACE EVALUATION (USER INTERFACE DESIGN EVALUATION)

While evaluating the UI, the evaluator needs to act as a pseudo user experiencing the system thereby come out with the difficulties the evaluator is facing which in turn lead to the improvement action plan.

Factors to be considered while evaluating/reviewing the user interface

1. Time spent by the users to perform tasks
2. Response time of the system (each screen and actions)
3. Amount of learning the users should undergo
4. Memory load on the users
5. How easy the help and error messages are
6. The complexity of the user interface look and feel (how easily the users are able to understand what needs to perform)
7. Check UI rules being followed in the design

7.6 GOLDEN RULES OF USER INTERFACE DESIGN

Three famous golden rules of Mandel are

- Place users in control (10)
- Reduce users' memory load (9)
- Make the interface consistent (5)

Source: http://theomandel.com/resources/golden-rules-of-user-interface-design/

Each rule has its own sub rules as depicted above with the numbers within braces.

The first main rule is placing the users in control which includes providing customizable screen based on the user profile, proper help, proper navigation of the system, different options to the customers for interacting with the system, interactive display system, etc. By providing the control to the users the users feel as if he owns the system and will start liking it.

The second main rule is to reduce users' memory load – which includes providing visual cues, promoting visual clarity, providing interface short cuts, etc. By reducing the users' memory load, it becomes easy for the customer to use the system.

The third main rule is making the interface consistent. This is not only to ensure keeping the look and feel of the users consistent across the pages, but also includes continuity from one screen to the other in terms of experience, expectations and predictability.

POINTS TO PONDER

Three famous golden rules of Mandel are

- Place users in control
- Reduce users' memory load
- Make the interface consistent

Section 7.6.1 lists the sub rules of the above main rules in detail.

7.6.1 Sub rules of Place Users in Control

There are 10 sub rules for the first main rule (place users in control).

Allow users to customize the interface (preferences): I have recently visited a website in which they allowed the end users (logged in users) a facility preference to change the font size of the website and also back ground color of the website. It was fantastic. They have also allowed the end users to change the position of the objects. End user feels as if they got the full control of the website. In the below example (Figure 7.13) the user is given preferences to choose either Exam Mode or Learning Mode selection of the PMP Quiz Portal.

Display descriptive messages and text (helpful). In the following website (Figure 7.14) the descriptive messages are used which helps the end users to do their actions.

Allow users to use either the keyboard or mouse (flexible). In the following website the users were given an option to use their mouse or key board to enter the password. Virtual key (refer Figure 7.15) board option uses the mouse to enter the data.

Allow users to change focus (interruptible). In the same website the users were given an option to use change the focus to any menu even during login. It allows the users to change focus while login (refer Figure 7.16).

Make the UI transparent (facilitative). In the same website the users were given highlighted message "New" against all the new options added facilitating the end users to know the new futures added recently (refer Figure 7.17).

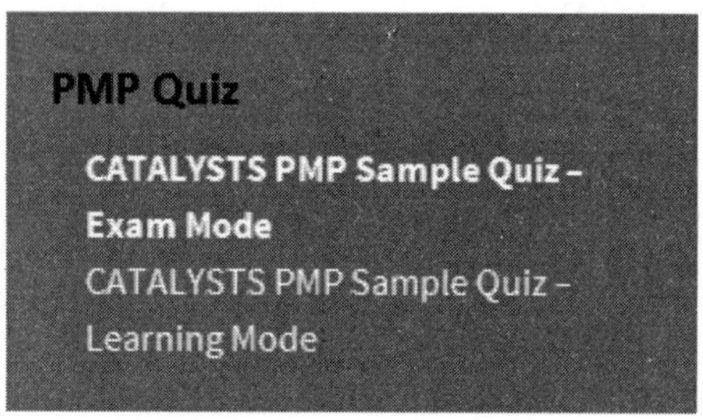

Figure 7.13 User Preference

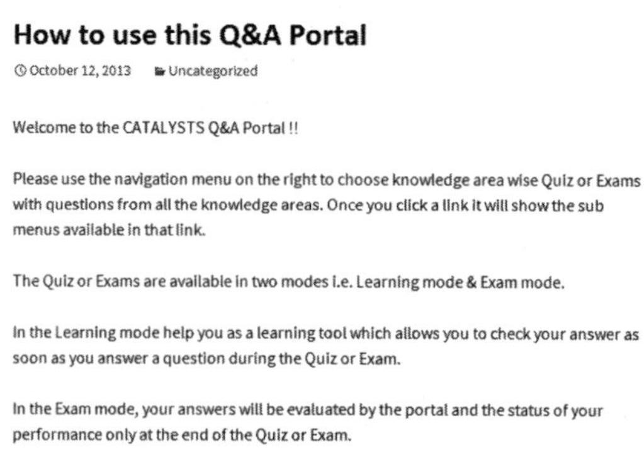

How to use this Q&A Portal

October 12, 2013 Uncategorized

Welcome to the CATALYSTS Q&A Portal !!

Please use the navigation menu on the right to choose knowledge area wise Quiz or Exams with questions from all the knowledge areas. Once you click a link it will show the sub menus available in that link.

The Quiz or Exams are available in two modes i.e. Learning mode & Exam mode.

In the Learning mode help you as a learning tool which allows you to check your answer as soon as you answer a question during the Quiz or Exam.

In the Exam mode, your answers will be evaluated by the portal and the status of your performance only at the end of the Quiz or Exam.

Figure 7.14 End User Help – Descriptive Messages

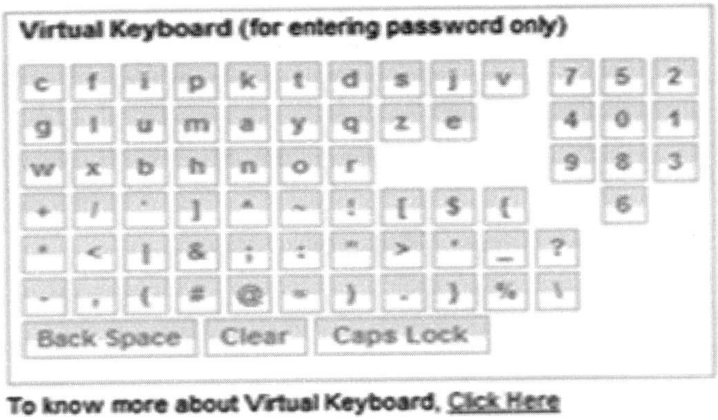

Figure 7.15 Key Board or Mouse Option to Enter Data

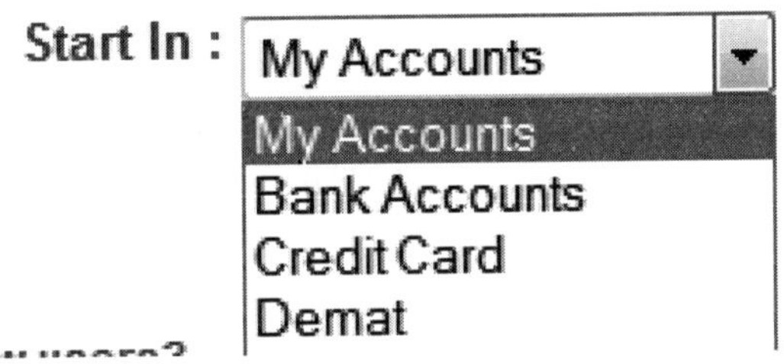

Figure 7.16 Start-in Choices

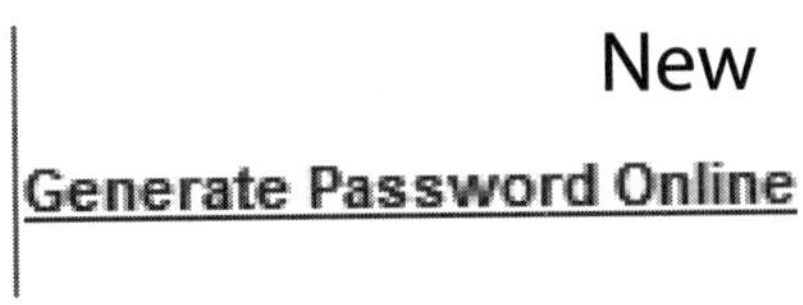

Figure 7.17 New Options

Provide immediate and reversible actions and feedback (forgiving). Most of the website displays the message such as below, double confirming the actions of the users and also gives the option to reverse the actions of the users (refer Figure 7.18).

Provide meaningful paths and exits (navigable). In the below website (refer Figure 7.19) the users were given meaningful paths of where they are and also given an option to exits (log out) from that page. User can also navigate to other sub menus.

Figure 7.20 is also an example of navigability, which indicates present screen and sub menu user are in.

Accommodate users with different skill levels (accessible): The above website is accessible by anybody and no education or experience generally required using the website. It is accessible by all.

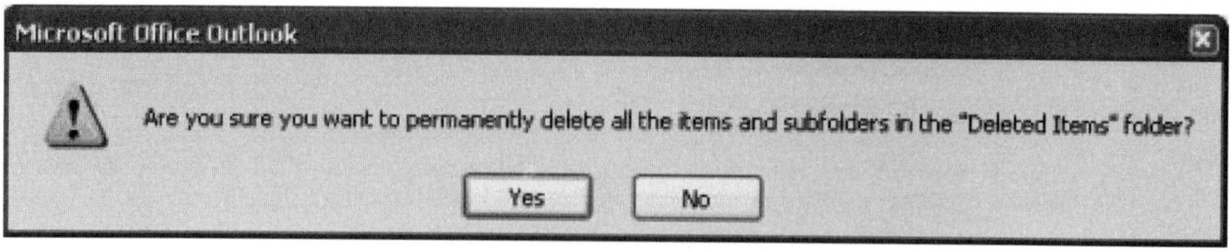

Figure 7.18 Reversible Action

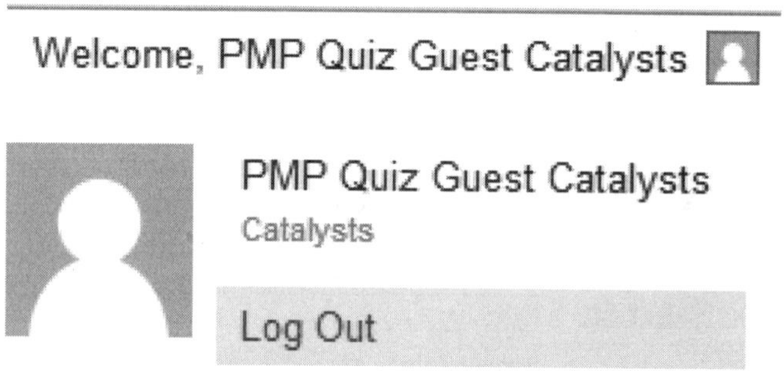

Figure 7.19 Meaningful Paths and Exits

Figure 7.20 Navigability

Allow users to directly manipulate interface objects (interactive). For example, while using text box (refer Figure 7.21) user will be using the vertical and horizontal scroll bars which will be used to navigate through the text box and it helps to manipulate the text box which is the interface object.

Use modes judiciously (modeless). Judicious means cautious. User modes are to be used cautiously. For example, "Session time out" mode needs to be used cautiously depending on the situation. If session time out happens every now and then, users may not like using the system. User mode also includes "You have logged in as Administrators," "You have logged in as Users," etc.

7.6.2 Sub Rule to Reduce Users' Memory Load

There are nine sub rules for the second main rule (reduce users' memory load).

Provide visual cues (inform). Visual cues are given on informing the purpose of the link thereby clarifying clear purpose of the links (refer Figure 7.22).

Rely on recognition, not recall (recognition only). In one of the website (refer Figure 7.23) while booking the class, as soon as we type the first character of the "Course", it displays the options

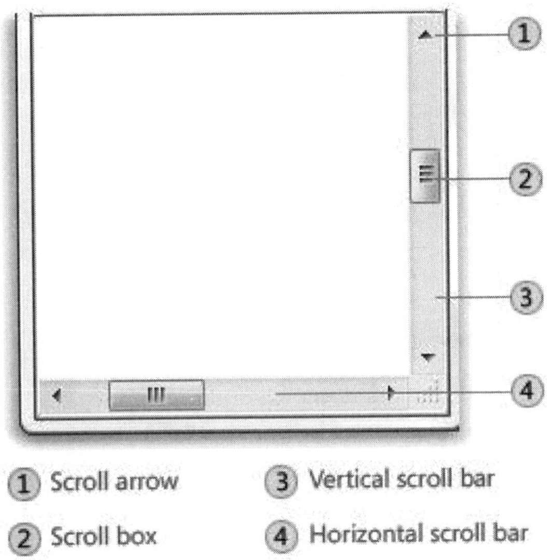

Figure 7.21 Horizontal and Vertical Scroll Bars

(Figure 7.23) helping the users to choose the right option, instead of users recognizing the code "PMP" "CAPM" etc.

Relieve short-term memory (remember). In Indian Railway ticket booking website while booking the return tickets, the system will remember the names used in the previous transaction and it will display the same names for return ticket booking, which helps the users to book the return ticket for all the members (which relieve short-term memory).

Provide interface shortcuts (frequency). In few of the websites the short cut options are given as mentioned in Figure 7.24 which helps to do the actions quickly.

Provide visual clarity (organize). In Figure 7.25 it is clear that "f" stands for Facebook, "t" stands for Twitter, "in" stands for LinkedIn giving more visual clarity.

Figure 7.22 Visual Cues

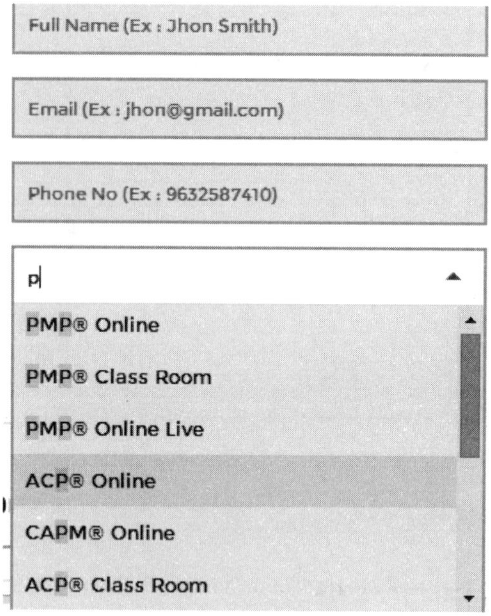

Figure 7.23 Recognition

Promote an object-action syntax (intuitive). In Figure 7.26 "BUY NOW" option is an object – action syntax and users will click it only when he decided to buy the course under discussion.

The "Silver" picture depicted also pictures the subject under discussion clearly.

Use real-world metaphors (transfer). Metaphors are the words used to represent an action or word which is not related to its own literary meaning. For example, in Figure 7.27, Hit the button does not mean the real literary meaning of "Hit" rather it means press the button.

Figure 7.24 Menu with Short Cuts

Figure 7.25 Visual Clarify

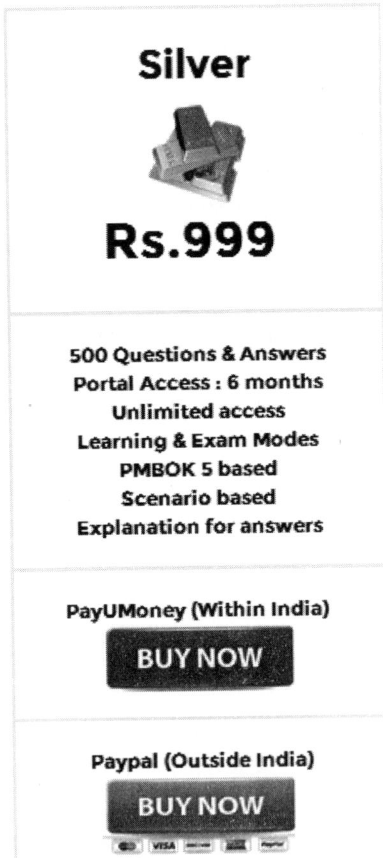

Figure 7.26 Intuitive – Know More

Figure 7.27 Metaphor – Hit the Play Button

In Figure 7.28 “Find Train” does not mean that it will find the train rather it will only display the details of the train. This is also another example of metaphor.

Provide defaults, undo and redo (forgiving). In Figure 7.29 default values are given in the place of “Courses”.

User can also redo and undo until selecting the final value.

User progressive disclosure (context). Progressive disclosure means providing/displaying information on a need basis (display only what is required at a particular point of time). In Figure 7.30 the

Figure 7.28 Metaphor – Find Trains

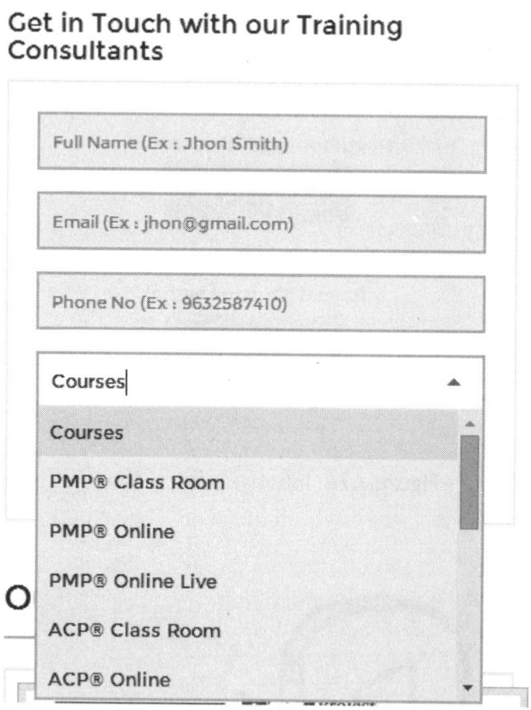

Figure 7.29 Default Value

Figure 7.30 Progressive Disclosure

user need to click "Down arrow" button to know other details. Service section only displays service related details.

7.6.3 Sub Rules to Make the Interface Consistent

There are five sub rules for the third main rule (make the interface consistent).

Provide aesthetic appeal and integrity (attitude). Aesthetic feel means initial feeling by looking into something; it actually deals with nature of beauty and taste. Color plays a crucial role here. Website Designers need to choose the color and pictures likeable by the audience. This is the reason most of the company has region specific websites. Culture also plays a crucial role in this factor.

Encourage exploration (predictable). In Figure 7.31 "START LOGGING" button encourage the users to explore further. The action of the button is clearly predictable. It explores a sample test available at the site.

Sustain the context of users' tasks (continuity). In ecommerce website after adding products to the baskets, the site will display the number of items in the basket, value of items in the basket and as well as allow the user to continue the shopping or another option to check out the basket items taking them to payment gateway. This is an example of continuity.

Maintain consistency within and across products (experience). In all popular website the consistency is maintained in terms of back ground color, fonts and other place holders across the products to give same experience to the users within and across the products.

Keep interaction results the same (expectations). The error message display and pop up message display are maintained same across the products making the interaction results the same way across the product.

Figure 7.31 Encourage Exploration

7.7 USER INTERFACE MODELS (USER INTERFACE DESIGN MODELS)

7.7.1 User Profile Model

In this model the entire UID is based on the user profile of the system like his age, gender, general experience, education level, culture, personality, frequency of usage (novice user, intermittent user, frequent users) and knowledge (syntactic and semantic).

Steps for user profile model

1. Establish the profile of the users and capture all the profile information above
2. Capture the knowledge of the users (syntactic knowledge, semantic knowledge)
3. Identify the frequency of usage (novice, intermittent, frequent user)
4. Design the UI based on the user profile defined

7.7.2 Design Model

In this model the UI is derived (designed) based on the requirement of the system. Entire designed is constrained by the information depicted in the requirements. Requirements include the interface requirement, data requirement and architectural requirements.

7.7.3 Implementation Model

This model looks into the requirement and sees the best possible way of implementing the requirements. It takes care of the look and feel of the interface as well as the requirements of the system. This model is also in alignment with user's mental model, thereby users feel comfortable using it. It links the user profile model with user's mental model.

7.7.4 User's Mental Model

This takes care of the user's perception of using the system. User's mental model is considered before designing the user interface. Accuracy here depends on the user's profile because user profile and user mental model are related to each other.

7.8 USABILITY

Usability is the degree of user interface design consideration which takes care of making the system effective, efficient and satisfying for the users by taking into account the human psychology and physiology of the users. Usability is linked to the human psychology and physiology of the users of the system. Users expends time to provide input to the system as well as understand the output of the system, and usability helps the end users do this effectively.

7.8.1 Measuring Usability

Effectiveness: a user's ability to successfully use a website to find information and/or accomplish tasks.

Efficiency: a user's ability to quickly accomplish tasks with ease and without frustration.

Satisfaction: how satisfied the user is with site.

Error frequency and severity: how often users make errors while using the system, how serious the errors are and how users recover from the errors.

Memorability: a user's ability to remember enough to use the site effectively after his or her first visit.

(Source: http://www.usability.gov)

Summary

- UI is not only the reflection of the functionalities of the system, but also the reflection of the culture of the end users.
- Usability measurement plays a crucial role in the success of any product and it is applicable for the software systems and the portals also. This chapter discusses the important usability concepts and procedures of applying the same.
- A user interface has three basic components namely
  - End users
  - User interface
  - System (machine).
- User interface has four elements namely
  1. Users
  2. Tasks
  3. Contents
  4. Environment
- Based on the four elements the analysis is also classified into four types
  1. User analysis
  2. Tasks analysis
  3. Contents analysis
  4. Environment analysis
- User analysis help to understand the end users as well as how the end users use the system which will help them to design the UI in a better way. Information about the end users can be obtained directly from the end users in the form of interview and also getting input from others who are interacting with the end users like sales, marketing and support people.
- Task analysis help to understand the tasks done by the end users under a specific circumstance. It helps to understand the sub tasks done by the end users, its sequence levels, hierarchical levels, problems faced by the end users while executing the tasks, As an output of tasks analysis use case diagram is drawn which helps to understand how the end users performs the tasks along with the workflow of the interaction.
- Content analysis is an important element of the overall user interface as it directly satisfies the end users. Content analysis helps the end users to understand the machine language. Content may be in the form of single word, graphical representation or in the form of sound files.

- Work environment analysis plays a crucial role as the designed product is fitting into the environment. For example: The intensity level of the head light in a car will always be higher than the intensity of the light used inside the car.
- UID is an iterative process – the fine tuning happens at every stage of the design. Three golden rule of the UI (three golden rules of Mandel) to be kept in mind while designing the UI are
    - Place users in control
    - Reduce users' memory load
    - Make the interface consistent
- Designing dialog: Sequence in which the information is displayed (output) and obtained (input) from the end users is called as dialog. In other words, dialog is the sequence in which the information is exchanged between the end users and the system.
- Common user interface design issues:
    1. Improper error messages to the users
    2. No proper menu labeling
    3. Improper help facilities to the users
    4. Response time of the system
- User interface evaluation (user interface design evaluation). While evaluating the UI we need to act as a pseudo user experiencing the system thereby come out with the difficulties we are facing which in turn lead to the improvement action plan.
- User profile model. In this model the entire UID is based on the user profile of the system like his age, gender, general experience, education level, culture, personality, frequency of usage (novice user, intermittent user, frequent users) and knowledge (syntactic and semantic).
- Design Model. In this model the UI is derived (designed) based on the requirement of the system. Entire designed is constrained by the information depicted in the requirements. Requirements include the interface requirement data requirement, and architectural requirements.
- Implementation Model. This model looks into the requirement and sees the best possible way of implementing the requirements. It takes care of the look and feel of the interface as well as the requirements of the system. This model is also in alignment with user's mental model, thereby users feel comfortable using it. It links the user profile model with user's mental model.
- User's Mental Model. This takes care of the user's perception of using the system. User's mental model is considered before designing the user interface. Accuracy here depends on the user's profile because user profile and user mental model are related to each other.
- Usability. Usability is the degree of user interface design consideration which takes care of making the system effective, efficient and satisfying for the users by taking into account the human psychology and physiology of the users. Usability is linked to the human psychology and physiology of the users of the system. Users expends time to provide input to the system as well as understand the output of the system, and usability helps the end users do this effectively.

Model Questions
PART A (Objective type)

1. User Interface is not only the reflection of the functionalities of the system, but also the reflection of the culture of the end users.

   A. True B. False

Answer: A

2. Each color has its own meaning

   A. True B. False

Answer: A

3. Blue color indicates

   A. Mystery, secrecy B. Strength, stability
   C. Purity, freshness, peace D. Coolness, peace

Answer: D

4. Which of the following is not an element of user interface?

   A. Users B. Contents
   C. Environment D. Business logic

Answer: D

5. Sequence in which the information is displayed (output) and obtained (input) from the end users is called as

   A. Dialog B. Output
   C. Environment D. Interface

Answer: A

6. Which of the following is not part of common user interface design issues?

   A. Improper error messages to the users B. Improper help facilities to the users
   C. Response time of the system D. Improper calculations

Answer: D

7. This model takes care of the user's perception of using the system.

   A. Design model B. User's mental model
   C. Implementation model D. Usability model

Answer: B

8. The degree of user interface design consideration which takes care of making the system effective, efficient and satisfying for the users by taking into account the human psychology and physiology of the users is called as

   A. Usability B. User satisfaction
   C. User ability D. User comfort level

Answer: A

PART B (Answer in one or two lines)

1. List any three color with its characteristics.
2. Name three basic components of user interface.
3. List down three famous golden rules of Mandel.
4. What is design model?
5. What is user's mental model?
6. What is implementation model?
7. Define usability?
8. What is task effectiveness?
9. What is measures of learning?
10. What is productive period of the user?

PART C (Descriptive type)

1. Discuss color and culture relationship with user interface design.
2. Discuss three basic components of user interface in detail.
3. Name four elements of user interface.
4. Discuss four user interface elements in detail.
5. Write notes on user analysis.
6. Write notes on task analysis.
7. Write notes on content analysis.
8. Write notes on work environment analysis.
9. Discuss user interface design steps in detail.
10. Notes on user interface design evaluation.
11. Discuss "Place users in Control" the first golden rule of Mandel in detail.
12. Discuss "Reduce User's Memory Load" the second rule of Mandel in detail.
13. Discuss "make the interface consistent" the third golden rule of Mandel in detail.
14. Discuss three golden rule of Mandel in detail with examples.
15. Discuss user profile model in detail.

Section 4:
Software Coding

8

Software Coding

CHAPTER COVERAGE

1. *Introduction*
2. *Programming Principles*
3. *Programming Guidelines*
4. *Coding Conventions (Programming Practices)*
5. *Key Concepts in Software Coding*

8.1 INTRODUCTION

Software coding is the core aspect of software engineering that acts as a catalyst for creating the software product. In a typical waterfall model, coding is done after the requirement clarification and design.

1. Conversion of detailed design specification into the actual software code is called as coding.
2. It converts functional aspects into technical aspects using design.
3. It is performed by people called as coders or programmers.
4. The coding phase usually takes lesser time than the design phase.
5. Lots of sophisticated tools are available to write the code easily.

Writing standardized code for software not only helps to maintain it properly once it is completely deployed into production but also helps to enhance the code easily at a later point of time. It also helps to identify and fix the bugs quickly and easily. So writing the proper working code alone is not enough, but focus should also be on writing a standard code (refer Figure 8.1). Writing a standard code also reduces the cost of development over a period of time. Standard code helps to reuse the same code for some other similar purposes, thereby reducing the cost of development.

This chapter focuses on guidelines of writing standard codes along with various best practices associated with it.

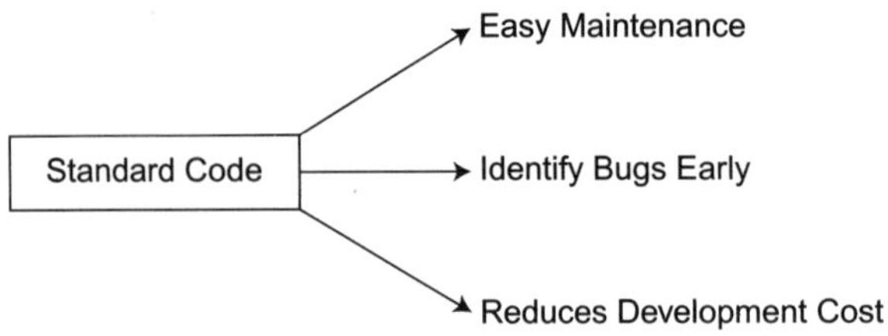

Figure 8.1 Standard Code Advantages

8.2 PROGRAMMING PRINCIPLES

Computer programming is directly associated with writing a standard code. Computer programming means writing a standard code, testing the written code, and debugging and maintaining the code (Figure 8.2).

Programming can be considered as both art and science (refer Figure 8.3). Programming is a science as it needs to follow a set of engineering principles and guidelines. It is also being classified as art as there are lots of possibilities of using creative and innovative minds.

POINTS TO PONDER

Programming can be considered as both art and science. Programming is a science as it needs to follow set of engineering principles and guidelines. It is also being classified as art because there are lots of possibilities of using creative and innovative minds.

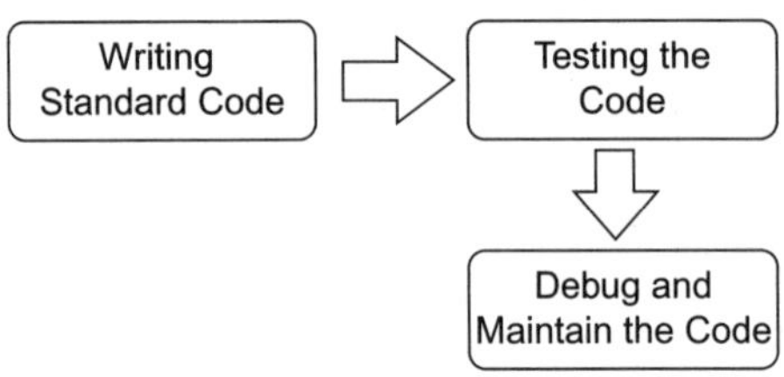

Figure 8.2 Programming Steps

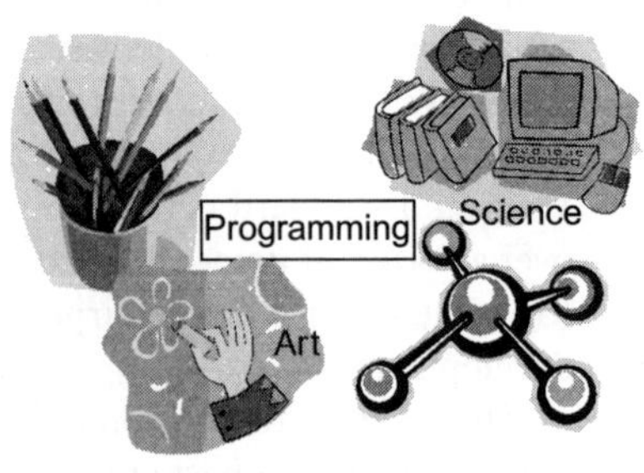

Figure 8.3 Art and Science

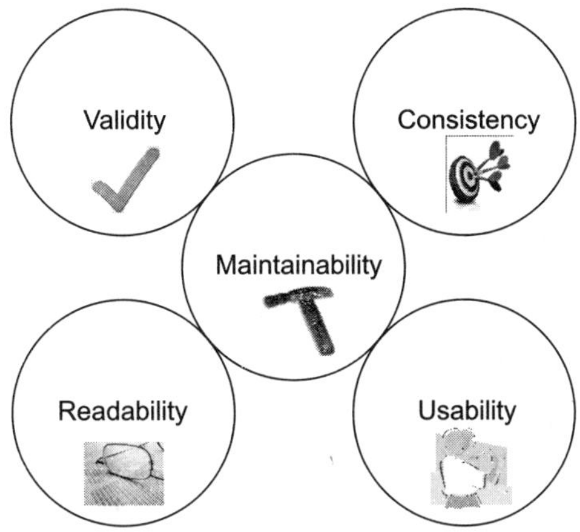

Figure 8.4 General Programming Principles

Following are the five general programming principles (refer Figure 8.4):

1. Validity: The program must give the correct result which is valid. For example, let us consider a program intended to add two numbers say add (x, y). When we pass the value (4, 5), it should give the value 9 as output and when we pass the value (–4, 5), it should give the value 1 as output.
2. Consistency: The program must do repeatedly what it intends to do. The program should give the output consistently. For example, if add (4.2, 5.4) gives the output as 10, add (5.4, 4.2) also should give the output as 10.
3. Maintainability: The program must be easily changeable (addition and modification) and should have proper documentations.
4. Readability: The program must be easily readable so that it is easily maintainable.
5. Usability: The program must be usable for the specific purpose without any trouble.

8.3 PROGRAMMING GUIDELINES

Guideline means best practices. Programming best practices (guidelines) includes programming practices (coding conventions), naming conventions, comments, and programming principles rule of thumb.

POINTS TO PONDER

Guideline means best practices. Programming best practices (guidelines) includes programming practices (coding conventions), naming conventions, comments, and programming principles rule of thumb.

Programming guidelines will vary across programming languages, but still there are general guidelines that can be followed across the languages. Writing a standardized code for software not only helps to maintain it properly once it is completely deployed into production but also helps to enhance the code easily at later point of time. Standard coding also helps to identify and fix the bugs quickly and easily and so writing the proper working code alone is not enough. Focus should also be on writing a standard code. Coding conventions can be documented in a central place so that the team can follow it; it can also be informal. Not following some or all of the rules (guidelines) will not impact the output (functionality) of the code.

8.4 CODING CONVENTIONS (PROGRAMMING PRACTICES)

Coding conventions (refer Figure 8.5) are a set of best practices that helps to write the software code in an efficient manner. Coding conventions cover the aspects of programming style, programming practices, and methods. This will vary from one programming language to another. For example, Java programming language has a set of programming practices and Visual basic has its own set of programming practices and guidelines.

POINTS TO PONDER

Coding conventions are a set of best practices that helps to write the software code in an efficient manner. Coding conventions cover the aspects of programming style, programming practices, and methods.

Advantages of coding convention:

1. Code becomes reusable saving money for all.
2. It is easy to maintain.
3. Enhancing the code becomes easy.
4. It saves cost for the company.
5. It helps to identify coding problems quickly.
6. Knowledge transfer becomes easy.

In general, coding conventions cover the following:

1. Naming convention
2. Programming principles and rule of thumb

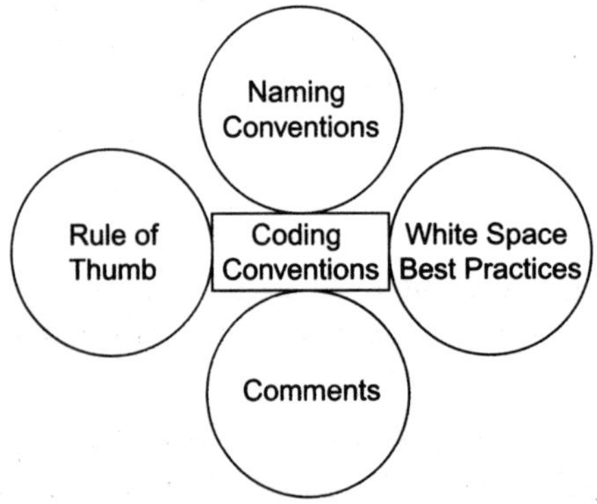

Figure 8.5 Coding Conventions

3. Comment writing within the code
4. Declarations and statements best practices
5. White space best practices
6. Bad practices to be avoided

Coding conventions may be formal or informal. Not following coding convention has no impact on the executable programs created by the source code.

8.4.1 Naming Convention

Naming convention (refer Figure 8.6) is a set of rules for choosing the character sequence to be used for identifiers (names).

Naming convention can be applied to:

1. File name
2. Folder name
3. Variable name
4. Function (method) name
5. Length of the identifiers
6. Letter case and numerals
7. Multiple word identifiers
8. Hybrid conventions

Many companies nowadays define their own coding conventions to be used across all projects.
$A = B \times C$ is syntactically correct, but the purpose of this code snippet is not known.
We can write the same code as below, which has more meaning and conveys the purpose.
Work = Duration × Number of resources

Length of the Identifiers

A fundamental element of naming conventions is the rule related to the length of the identifier and the combination of characters allowed in the identifier (Figure 8.7).

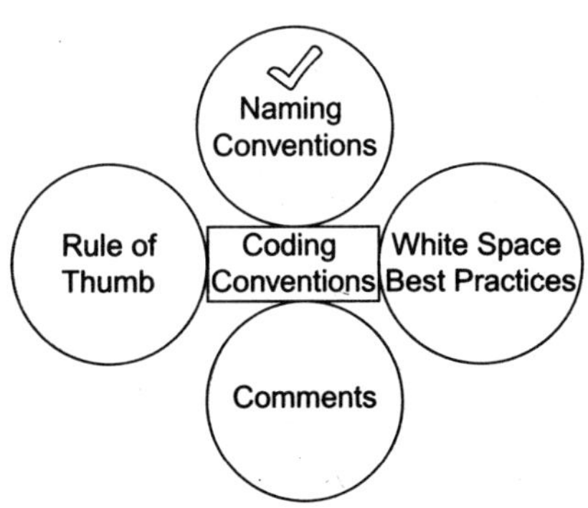

Figure 8.6 Coding Conventions–Naming Conventions

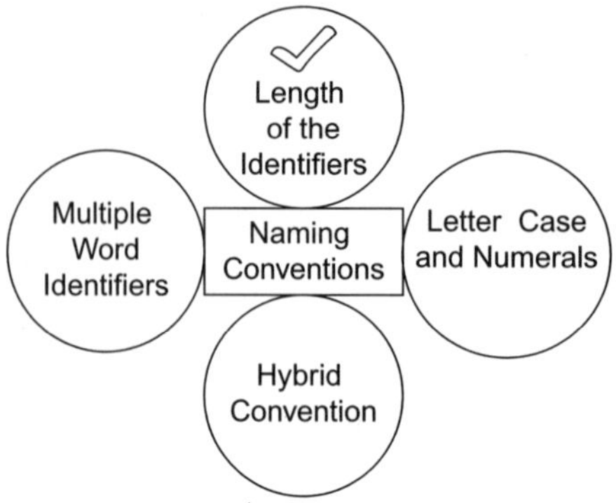

Figure 8.7 Coding Conventions–Length of the Identifiers

Some considerations in deciding the length of the identifiers are as follows:

- Shorter identifiers are preferred over lengthy ones (difficult to identify and remember).
- Longer identifiers are preferred because it is easy to encode them.
- Extremely short identifiers (example: *a*, *b*, *c*) are very difficult to distinguish each other.
- Longer identifiers may not be preferred because of visual clutter.

Letter Case and Numerals

- Some naming conventions limit the letter case (Figure 8.8) of the variable to be only in uppercase or lowercase (WEIGHT or weight).
- Some naming conventions do not limit the letter case of the variable but attach a defined meaning with the letter case (Chair Weight).
- Some naming conventions specify that the variable name should start with an upper case and should use at least one numeric within (password characters have this kind of restrictions).

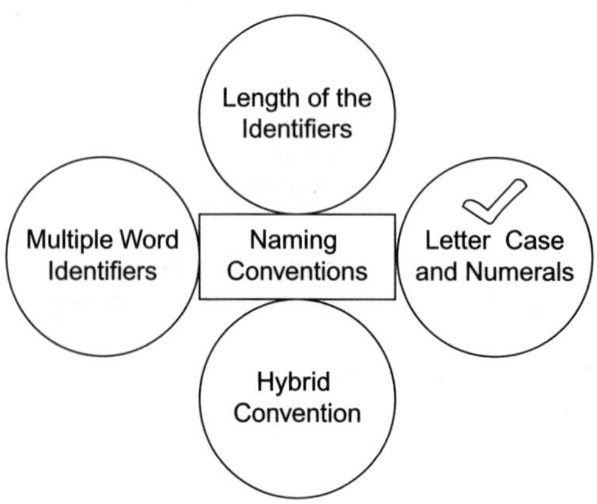

Figure 8.8 Coding Conventions – Letter Case and Numerals

Multiple Word Identifiers

A single word may not be enough to specify the clear purpose and meaning of an identifier, and we may need to use a combination of identifiers to make it meaningful (e.g., Chair Weight).

When we use a combination of words for a single identifier, it is called as "compound identifier" (which contains more than one word). Most programming languages do not allow white spaces in the identifiers and so we need a delimiter in between for that purpose (refer Figure 8.9).

Delimiter-separated Words

Using delimiters in between to separate the words (in an identifier) helps to understand the meaning easier. Underscore ("_") and Hyphen ("-") are most commonly used delimiters (e.g.,: Chair_Weight or Chair-Weight)

Letter-case-separated Words

Without using delimiters in between (in an identifier), we can use uppercase characters for words that help to understand the meaning easier.

It is also called as CamalCase (e.g.,: Chair Weight). Sometimes, instead of using big names, we can also use acronyms such as "XML".

Hybrid Convention

Some naming conventions in addition to its name also represent a set of principles defined by the architecture, underlying programming language, or any cross-project methodology. Composite word scheme (OF Language), Hungarian notation, and positional notation are the types of hybrid conventions (refer Figure 8.10).

Composite word scheme (OF Language) One of the earliest published convention systems was IBM's "OF Language" documented in 1980s. It recommends using names such as "CUST-ACT-NO" to indicate "customer account number". It also used names such as PRIME (meaning major entities), CLASS (meaning data type), TXT (meaning text), QTY (meaning quantity), No (meaning number),

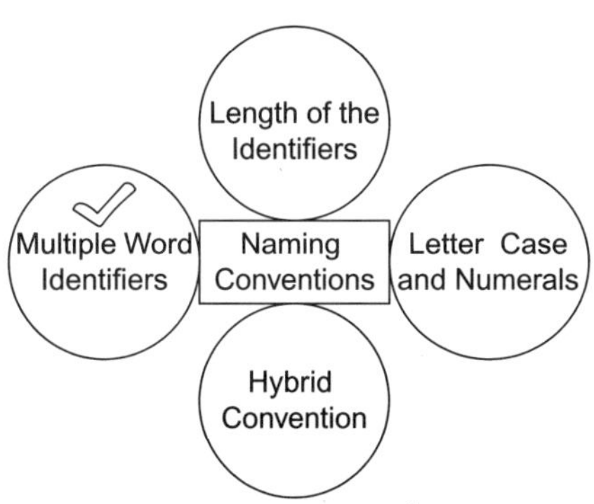

Figure 8.9 Coding Conventions – Multiple Word Identifiers

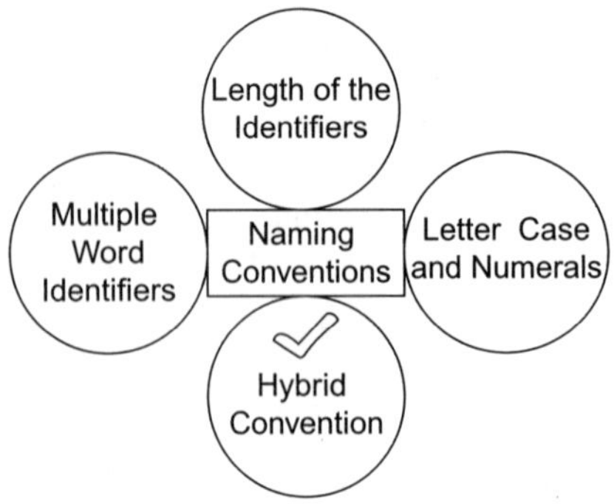

Figure 8.10 Naming Conventions–Hybrid Convention

and AMT (meaning amount). FL (meaning flag) is represented using two possible values "TRUE" or "FALSE".

Hungarian notation It either encodes the purpose or the type of the variable. There are two types of Hungarian notation namely Apps Hungarian and Systems Hungarian.

Apps Hungarian: When it encodes for a "purpose" inside the application, it is called "Apps Hungarian". For example, in FORTRAN language, variables whose names start with letters I through N are denoted as integers by default.

Systems Hungarian: When it encodes the "type," it is called "Systems Hungarian". Here, the prefix encodes the actual data type of the variable.

Arru8 Number List is a name (variable) and represents an array of unsigned 8-bit integers ("arru8").

POINTS TO PONDER

Hungarian notation: It either encodes the purpose or the type of the variable. There are two types of Hungarian notation namely Apps Hungarian and Systems Hungarian.

Positional notation Positional notation is still used in mainframes dependent on JCL. A style used for very short (eight characters and less) could be LCCIIL01, where LC would be the application (letters of credit), C denotes COBOL, IIL denotes particular subset of a process, and the 01 indicates a sequence number.

Benefits of Naming Convention

Following are some of the benefits of naming convention (Figure 8.11):

- It provides additional information (i.e., metadata) about the use.
- It promotes consistency within a development team.
- It enhances clarity during ambiguity.
- It gives professional appearance to the work product developed.

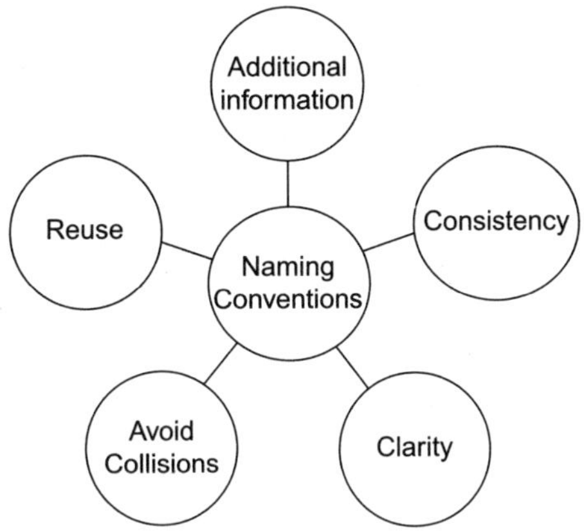

Figure 8.11 Naming Conventions – Advantages

- It helps to avoid naming collisions (two or more people using the same name for different purposes).
- It provides a better understanding in case of code reuse.

Challenges of Naming Convention

Defining the naming convention is not enough for the success, and the success depends on the execution part, that is how meticulously we follow the naming convention. Naming convention should be easy to apply and easy to remember, otherwise it will be perceived as more burden rather than beneficial.

8.4.2 Programming Principles and Rule of Thumb

Senior software engineers in various IT organizations do follow various programming principles and rules of thumb (refer Figure 8.12) which are derived based on their experience and skills. Few of the best practices are listed below. Due care is to be taken before implementing those in the project as they are context specific.

- Choose appropriate and sufficient data type for a variable ensuring the size is not large (use integer data type, short data type and float data type appropriately).
- Try to avoid declaring all variables as global variable.
- Keep specific name for variables and methods rather than using generalized name.
- Use and keep variables and methods for one and only purpose and try to avoid multipurpose variable and methods.
- Avoid writing "public class" for security purpose.
- While using database connection, create the connection object as late as possible and release it as early as possible.
- Avoid using database connection using specific user's credentials. We cannot reuse those connections.

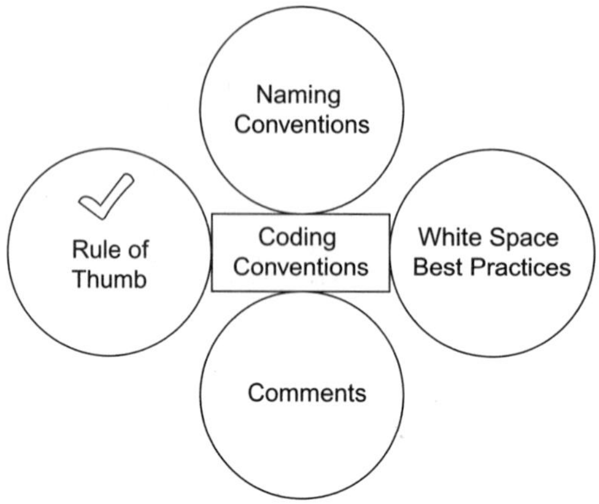

Figure 8.12 Coding Conventions –Rule of Thumb

- Avoid using session variable in ASP. Session variables are stored in local machines. Store the session in database instead.
- Avoid using forced data conversion (converting integer to long or float to be avoided).
- Release object references wherever not being used to release memory usage for some other object.

8.4.3 Comments

Properly commented code serves no purpose for the compilation as well as executing the code, but it improves the readability of the code. It also helps to understand the purpose and business logic behind the code. All software engineers write the comments on the first version of the code, but it is really a challenge to keep these comments up to date with further changes in the code (Figure 8.13).

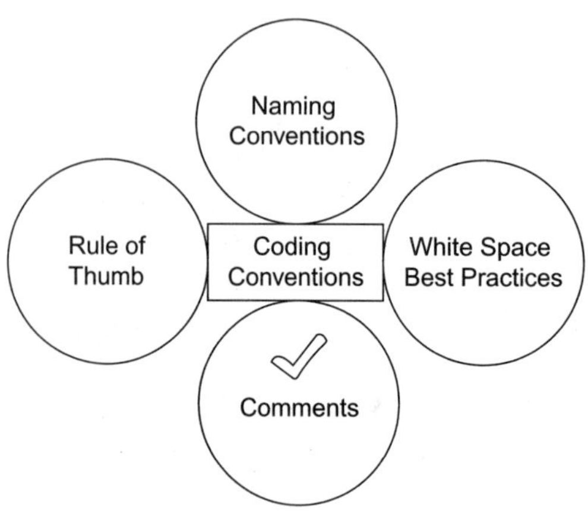

Figure 8.13 Coding Conventions – Comments

POINTS TO PONDER

Properly commented code serves no purpose for the compilation as well as executing the code, but it improves the readability of the code.

Following are some of the recommendations of commenting techniques:

- Keep the comment always up to date while modifying the code.
- Write the comments first before changing the actual code.
- Write the comments in the beginning of every method, indicating the purpose of the method, assumptions, and limitations.
- Try to avoid end-of-line comments.
- Prior to deployment, remove all unnecessary and temporary comments to avoid confusion.
- Before variable declarations, write the purpose of the variable in comments which will enhance the readability and understanding of the code.
- Avoid writing series of asterisks in the comments that may look good, but maintaining it is difficult.
- Use complete sentences while writing comments.
- Comments should help to understand the code, not add confusion.
- Use uniform style throughout the code for comments, with consistent punctuation and structure.

8.4.4 White Space Best Practices

Blank lines and white spaces (refer Figure 8.14) improve the readability of the code. It logically subdivides the codes.

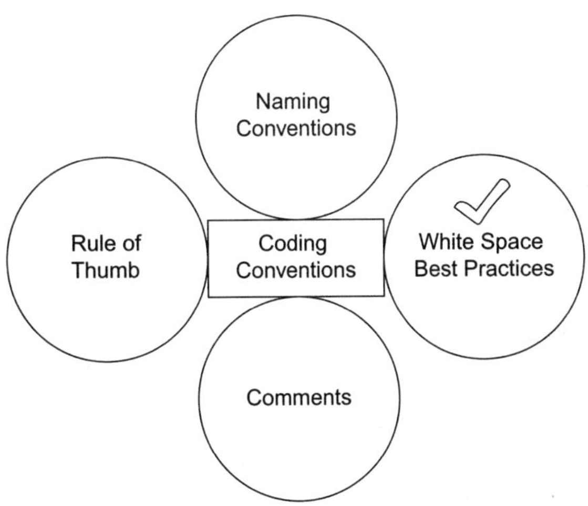

Figure 8.14 Coding Conventions – White Space

Blank Lines

1. Two blank lines can be used between sections within the source code
2. Two blank lines can be used between class definitions within the source Code
3. Two blank lines can be used between interface definitions within the source code
4. One blank line can be used between methods before a block within the soruce Code

Blank Spaces

A blank space should always be placed after comma in any argument list. Any keyword followed by a parenthesis must be separated by a space. Binary operators should be separated by blank spaces for readability.

8.5 KEY CONCEPTS IN SOFTWARE CODING

In the world of software development, coding is considered as the most critical part because at this stage the real software gets written. Unless proper focus is maintained for keeping the standard of this stage high, the software will break at the later stages, causing huge effort in fixing the defects called bugs. There are few key concepts in software coding which needs to be understood properly to create an efficient software.

8.5.1 Structured Programming

It is the subset of procedural programming. It is also called as modular programming (refer Figure 8.15). It represents the usage of a logical structure on the program being written to make it more readable, efficient, reliable, and easily maintained. In a typical structured programming language, the overall program is divided into logical structure for meaningful implementation. Common functions across the structures are taken out and coded in a separate module (or separate program) itself so that the functions can be reused and memory usage also minimized. Modules are tested separately before fitting into the overall programming structure. Unstructured programming (BASIC, FORTRAN) relies upon the discipline of the software developer to avoid structural problems. Certain

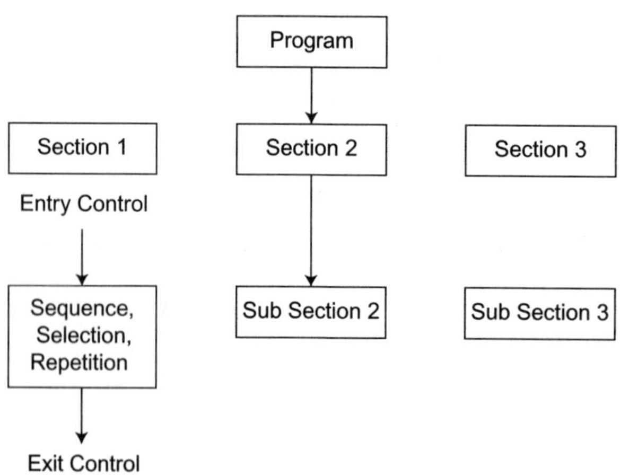

Figure 8.15 Structured Programming

programming languages such as Pascal, COBOL, C, C++, Java, and dBASE are designed with features that enforce a logical program structure.

Object-oriented programming structure (OOPS) is a type of structured programming that uses structured programming techniques for program flow and adds more structure for class, object, and data to the model.

Structured programming was first suggested by Corrado Bohm and Guiseppe Jacopini, who demonstrated that any computer program can be written with just three structures namely decisions (to decide the course of action), sequences (order), and loops (iterative execution).

The most common methodology employed was developed by Dijkstra. He suggests avoiding "GO TO" statement. In this model, programs are divided into sections and then subsections. Each subsection has only one entry point and one exit point and in which control is passed downward through the structure from the top without unconditional branches to higher levels of the structure.

POINTS TO PONDER

Structured programming was first suggested by Corrado Bohm and Guiseppe Jacopini, who demonstrated that any computer program can be written with just three structures namely decisions (to decide the course of action), sequences (order), and loops (iterative execution).

There are three types of control namely sequence, selection, and repetition. Sequence refers to the orderly execution of statements one by one. Selection refers to the selection of statements based on some conditions. This is usually expressed with keywords such as if..then..else..endif, switch, or case. Repetition refers to the same statement executed repeatedly depending on a condition such as for loop, while loop, and do loop.

8.5.2 Information Hiding

Users will be exposed to only the required details. For example, while we use any software (say Microsoft Word), we (users) know only how to use that software not how it was built and its related software. Encapsulation (refer Figure 8.16) uses the principle of information hiding. No object can access the other object's data directly; instead, data are accessed only by sending the messages to the other object requesting for the information. This means the user need not know what is happening

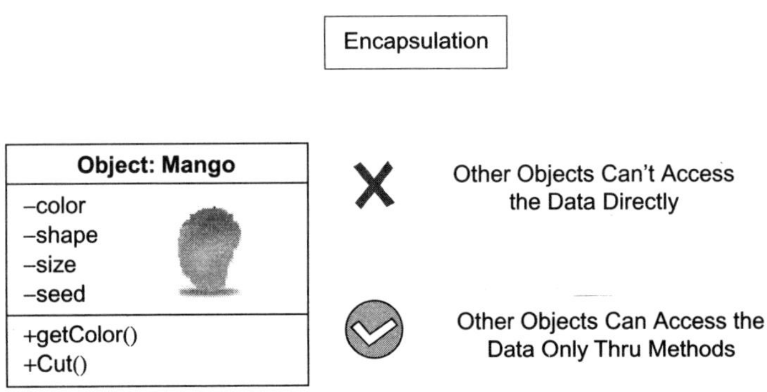

Figure 8.16 Encapsulation – Information Hiding

inside the object but can only use the object by calling the object's methods. This will provide insulation for the data inside the object from accidental manipulation by another object or user.

In a good OO design/code, the object should reveal its data only through the specified interfaces or methods, and the other objects can only use this interface or methods to interact with the object. The attributes which are only for the internal use of the object and not to be revealed are completely hidden from other objects. In those cases, the attributes are declared as "private". This also protects the object attributes getting changed erroneously while some other attributes are getting changed.

For example, in the class Car engine, there are many parts (attributes) inside it. Everyone applies a common technique in accessing the engine functionalities no matter how the engine is made of. The detail and design of the engine are hidden from the knowledge of the driver.

Information hiding technique reduces complexity and increases usability and maintainability. Information hiding principle is used to prevent other programmers or other program to change this program – intentionally or unintentionally.

8.5.3 Coding Standards and Guidelines

Good developers always follow the coding standards and guidelines while writing the code. Code written using the standards and guidelines are easy to review/understand/debug. It is also easy to maintain and enhance the code if it follows the standards and guidelines.

Advantages of coding standards:

Refer Figure 8.17 for the advantages of coding standards.

- Reusability (easy to reuse parts of code as it is written in standard code)
- Maintainability (easy to identify bugs, easy to add new features)
- Readability (coding standard increases easy reading)
- Understand ability (easy to understand – this is not the same as readability, e.g., repetitive code may be is readable, but not understandable)
- Robustness (code that can handle unexpected inputs and conditions)
- Reliability (code i.e., unlikely to produce wrong results)

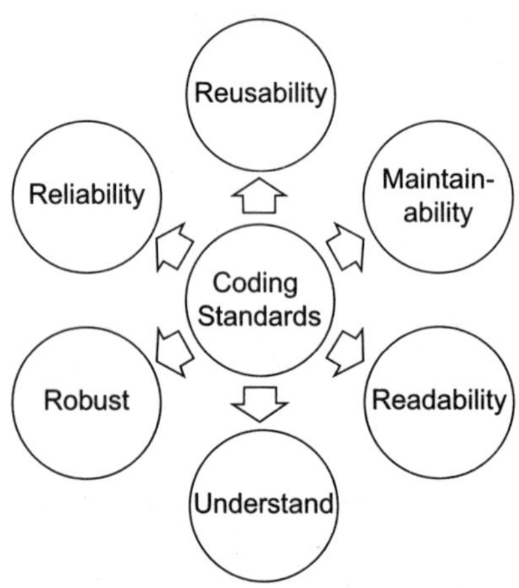

Figure 8.17 Coding Standards – Advantages

The sample coding standards and guidelines are as follows:

- Write comments before writing the code
- Use meaningful names for varibles and functions. (Try to avoid single character varible names and function names)
- Avoid extremely long names
- Format the code properly using the standards specific to the programming language
- Use tools to improve coding standards if possible
- Prefix "is" for Boolean variable - For Example: is Open+ True
- Comment should explain "Why" instead of "How" (Why a particular aldorithm was chosen)
- Comments should be blended into the code
- Avoid deeply nested code
- Never use "Go To" Statement
- Don't duplicate the code
- Avoid using multiple inheritance

8.5.4 Top-Down and Bottom-Up Coding

Top-down coding: Here the implementation starts with the top of the hierarchy. The top main module is written first before writing the bottom submodules.

Testing top-down coding: Top main module is written first and hence the test cases are written completely for it. A stub is written in place of bottom submodules.

Bottom-up coding: It is the reverse of top-down coding, and here the implementation starts with the bottom submodules. The top main module is written after that until it reaches the top of the hierarchy.

Testing bottom-up coding: Bottom submodules are written first, and hence the test cases are written completely for it. A driver module is written to involve those modules under testing.

8.5.5 Incremental Development of Code

Project delivery is divided into parts – analyze, design, code, test, and deliver product (release). The delivery of product is also divided into parts. Initially, a part of the product is released and then, additional developments are made based on feedback. These developments are linked and the overall solution is finally completed. The solution from each part is reviewed and tested. Results from the testing are assessed, and any required changes are incorporated into the next stage (next part) of solution development.

Unified process model (RUP) is an example of incremental model, and there are four phases associated with it, namely inception, elaboration, construction, and transition.

- Inception: Requirements and scope identified at high level.
- Elaboration: Working architecture delivered that fulfils the non-functional requirements.
- Construction: Production ready code is developed incrementally.
- Transition: Deployment of the code into production happens here.

The spiral model is also a type of incremental model (refer Figure 8.18).

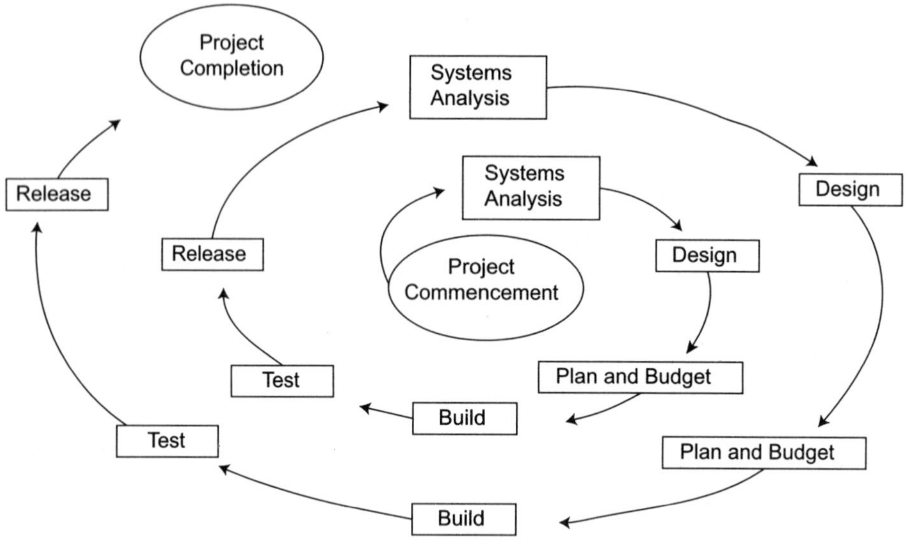

Figure 8.18 Incremental Life Cycles

Advantages of incremental life cycle model:

1. Quick feedback loop from business stakeholders
2. Focus on customer feedback
3. Customer feels the product early.

Disadvantages of incremental life cycle model:

1. Even though the final product is given in pieces, tracking and monitoring is difficult.
2. Testing needs to be exhaustive in each part.

Iterative Life Cycle Model

Professor Barry Boehm's paper describes this model as "Analyze a little, design a little, test a little, and loop back". Development happens in iterations that encompass the activities of requirements analysis, design, coding, and testing.

The early iterations produce a small system, which gradually expands over a series of iterations to become the overall complete system. Feedback is implemented from one iteration to the next iteration. During iteration, activities from all Project Management Process Groups will be performed. At the end of each iteration, a set of deliverables will be completed (refer Figure 8.19).

Advantages of iterative life cycle model:

1. Quick feedback loop from business stakeholders.
2. Focus on customer feedback.
3. Focus on getting the highest priority features first.
4. Ability to validate pieces of deliverables incrementally.

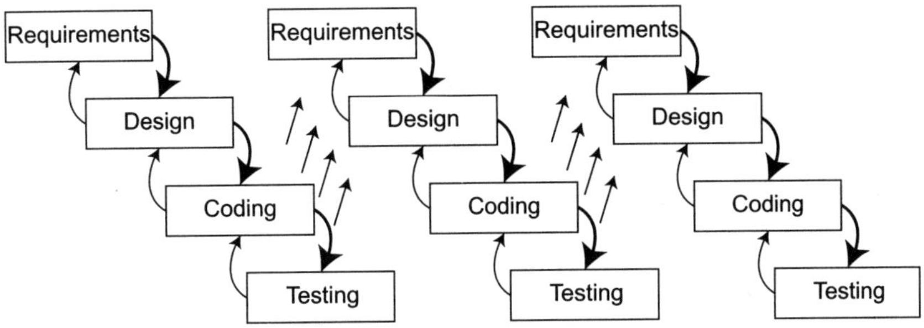

Figure 8.19 Iterative Life Cycles

Disadvantages of iterative life cycle model:

1. Getting feedback from customer on time is difficult.
2. Even though deliverables are given in pieces, tracking and monitoring is difficult.
3. Project may not proceed further if customer is not cooperating.
4. The fully developed solution requires the partial developments to be implemented, and this is often complicated and costly.

8.5.6 Programming Style

Set of rules and guidelines followed while writing a computer program is called as programming style. This programming style varies across the programming languages because the styling used in BASIC is different from C, styling used in C++ is different from C. Following a particular style improves readability of the code and also helps to avoid errors. Programming styles are based on organization standards and guidelines. But most of the authors (coders) create their own programming styles. Creating a common coding standard will help formulating a programming style across the team and the organization.

8.5.7 Code Sharing

Code share concept (refer Figure 8.20) is famous in aviation business arrangement where one flight is shared by different airline operators. Tickets are sold by different operators (marketing carriers), and the flight will be operated by another operator (operating carrier).

In software engineering also, third-party codes are being used (integrated) while writing the code. For example, credit card payment gateway is a commonly used code share. PayPal integration is also another example of code share.

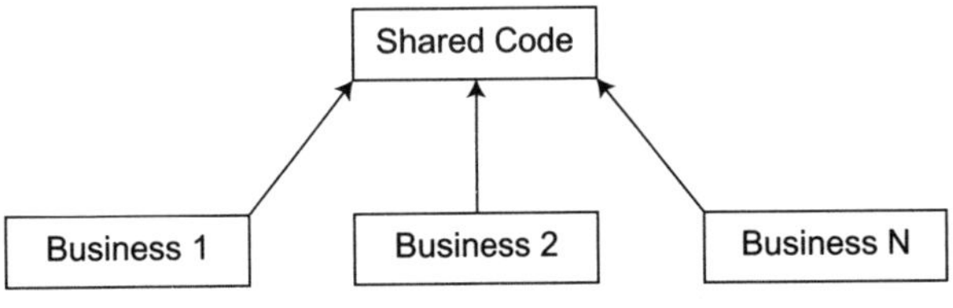

Figure 8.20 Code Sharing

Bookmytickets.com and meraevents.com are also examples of code share providers. As software engineers, we can make use of those code shares which save lot of time and money; the service from the code share providers is also professional in nature.

8.5.8 Code Review

Code review is a systematic process, which is also called as peer review which is used to find and fix the mistakes in the early phase of the coding, and it helps to improve the code quality and improve the coding skills of the developers.

POINTS TO PONDER

Code review is a systematic process which is also called as peer review which is used to find and fix the mistakes in the early phase of the coding.

Code reviews (refer Figure 8.21) happens in the form of:

1. Formal inspection
2. Lightweight code review
3. Pair programming
4. Automatic code reviewing software

In the case of formal inspection, a review checklist is being used to review the code along with proper plan such as scheduled time, duration of review, scope of review, coding standards, etc. Multiple stakeholders take part in formal inspection process and the entire code set is being reviewed line by line. Most of the time, the review happens in multiple iterations as it takes longer time to go through line by line. Formal inspection processes is thorough in nature and have been effective.

Fagan inspection is an example for formal code review process. According to Fagan, “A defect is an instance in which a requirement is not satisfied”. Fagan inspection refers to a structured process of finding defects in all the artifacts related to the coding such as the programming code, software specifications, designs, and other documents during various phases of the software development process. Fagan inspection is a group review process. It defines prespecified entry and exit criteria. Michael Fagan is the inventor of formal software inspections.

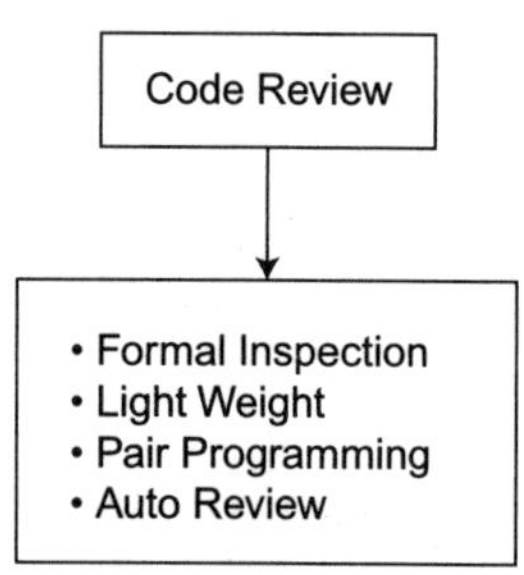

Figure 8.21 Code Review Forms

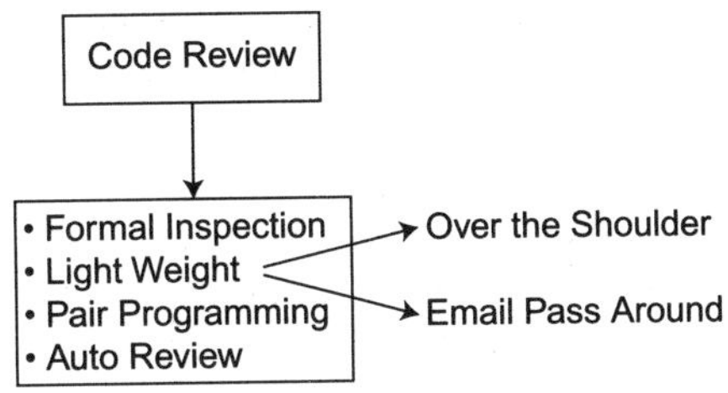

Figure 8.22 Code Review Forms–Lightweight

Lightweight walkthrough (refer Figure 8.22) happens at any point of time in convenience to both the parties, and no checklist is being used here and the review happens in an ad hoc manner. It required less overhead than the formal code review method. It is equally effective with formal review process if conducted properly. Lightweight processes are usually conducted as part of the development process.

Following are the examples of lightweight process:

- Over the shoulder: The reviewer (another developers) looks over the shoulder of the developer while writing the code.
- E-mail pass-around: Source code management system automatically emails the code to the reviewers after check in.

In pair programming, the review happens simultaneously while the code is getting developed. We have sophisticated monitors that help to do the code review. Pair programming overall saves a lot of time and reduces rework; the mistakes are identified in the beginning stage itself.

Automatic code review software helps to do the code review in a more efficient manner with just one time setting.

8.5.9 Static Program Analysis

Static program analysis (refer Figure 8.23) is the analysis of computer software that is performed without actually executing programs. Static program analysis tool is being used by the developers. The term is usually applied to the analysis performed by an automated tool. Static program analysis is an extension of compiler technology. It can find possible faults such as unreachable code, undeclared variables, unused variables, parameter type mismatches, uncalled functions and procedures, possible array bound violations, etc.

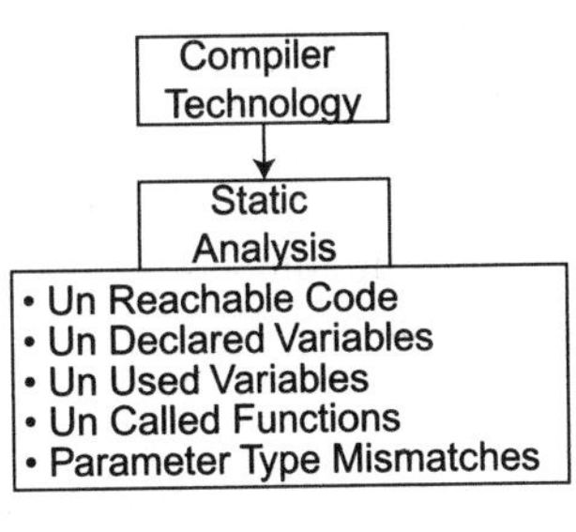

Figure 8.23 Static Analysis

Reverse engineering can be described as a form of static analysis. Static program analysis is being used frequently in medical, nuclear software, and embedded software.

8.5.10 Symbolic Execution

Symbolic execution refers to the analysis of programs by tracking symbolic value rather than actual values. A program that is executed using actual data results in the output of a series of values. In symbolic execution, the data are replaced by symbolic values. A set of expressions, one expression per output variable, is produced. Symbolic execution has a variety of potential uses. It may be used in path domain checking, test data generation, program proving, program reduction, and symbolic debugging. There are few limitations to symbolic execution such as it cannot be used for path exploration and is also program dependent.

POINTS TO PONDER

Symbolic execution refers to the analysis of programs by tracking symbolic rather than actual values.

8.5.11 Proving Correctness

Algorithm is the pseudo code written before writing the actual code.

A problem is a collection of problem instances. An algorithm is correct for a problem if it is correct for all instances of the problem.

Hoare Logic of Correctness

The central feature of Hoare logic is the Hoare triple which has the following format:

$$\{P\}\ C\ \{Q\}$$

where P is the precondition, Q is the postcondition and C is a command.

It actually means that when the precondition is met, the command establishes the post condition. There are rules for concurrency, procedures, jumps, and pointers.

Functional correctness refers to the input–output behavior of the algorithm (i.e., for each and every input the algorithm produces the correct output as per the functional specification).

Partial correctness refers to the algorithm that returns an answer.

Total correctness refers to the algorithm that terminates (exit for every input) in addition to the functional correctness. A termination proof (mathematical proof) plays a critical role in formal verification as total correctness of an algorithm depends on termination. A termination proof would have to be a mathematical proof, assuming both the given algorithm and functional specifications are given formally. Hoare logic is a specific formal system for reasoning rigorously about the correctness of computer programs.

An initial assertion characterizes conditions expected to be true upon entry to the program and a final assertion characterizes conditions expected to be true upon exit from the program.

In program with no branches, symbolic execution technique can be used. In order to prove the correctness of programs that are going in an infinite loop, a more general assertion structure must be provided and it is called as inductive assertion.

8.5.12 Code Inspections

Code inspection process was first developed by Michael Fagan.

Inspection process has entry criteria and exit criteria. Entry criteria are the conditions that must be met before starting the inspection of the code. The condition includes checking whether we have

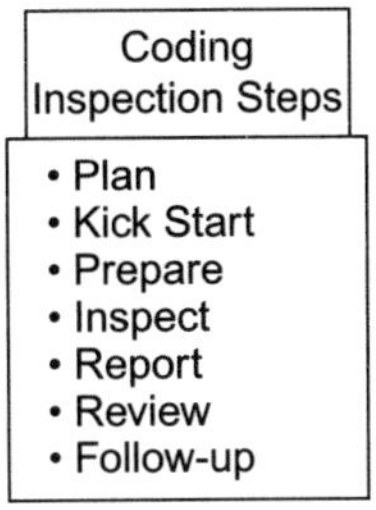

Figure 8.24 Code Inspection Steps

completed work product (code) and gathering necessary data and information to inspect the code. Once all the entry conditions are met, it gives the green signal that the code inspection process can begin.

Exit criteria of a code inspection process include preparing a report usually in an excel sheet format indicating the outcome of the process.

Steps followed in coding inspection are (refer Figure 8.24):

1. Planning the code inspection
2. Kickstart code inspection
3. Prepare for code inspection
4. Code inspection
5. Code inspection report
6. Review and rework
7. Follow-up

Steps 3, 4, and 5 happen in multiple steps (iterative fashion).

Planning the code inspection: Here the decision to inspect the code is taken along with the details of: (1) What code will be inspected? (2) When the code inspection will happen? (3) Who are all the people to be involved for the inspection? (4) Define the various roles involved.

Kickstart code inspection: Here the reviewer describes his plan to all the stakeholders. This helps to get the buy-in all stakeholders' for the inspection along with clear timelines and responsibilities.

Prepare for code inspection: Here, the reviewer gathers all the possible data along with the work product to be inspected.

Code inspection: Actual inspection happens here and the work product is subject to inspection to find out possible defects.

Code inspection report: Here, the inspectors explain the identified defects to the team.

Review and rework: Changes to the work product happens as per the agreed outcome.

Follow-up: Changes to the work product are verified to ensure everything is fine.

During an inspection, the following three roles are predominantly used:

- Coder: The person who coded the work product being inspected.
- Inspector: The person who will do the inspection.
- Moderator: The person who monitors the entire process.

8.5.13 Programming Productivity

Productivity of programming can be measured in writing a code with less number of errors, writing cost-effective code, and writing easily maintainable code. Programmer productivity can be measured using the errors per line of code by a programmer, cost per line of code, source lines of code maintained by the programmer per day, learning curve of the programmer, knowledge of emerging trends of technologies, and speed of code generation.

8.5.14 Rapid Prototyping

In Rapid prototyping (RP), the prototype is being created automatically (rapidly) using three dimensional computer-aided design (CAD). It required just 3 to 72 hours building an object which saves a lot of time (without CAD, it takes months to build the same object). Computer-aided machine (CAM) is used to convert the prototype into real product using layered material deposition.

POINTS TO PONDER

In RP, the prototype is being created automatically (rapidly) using three-dimensional CAD.

Steps in RP:

1. Create the design of the product using CAD.
2. Convert CAD model into STL format (stereo lithography).
3. Slice STL format file into cross-sectional layers.
4. Covert each layer into a model.
5. Finish and fine tune the model (fabrication).
6. Postprocessing (cleaning).

8.5.15 Intelligent Software Agent

Software acting as agent (refer Figure 8.25) of a user which monitors and reports set of activities can decide the course of action to be taken on behalf of users based on set of predefined set of rules.

Software agent also helps to automate complex as well as repetitive tasks as per the predefine set of rules.

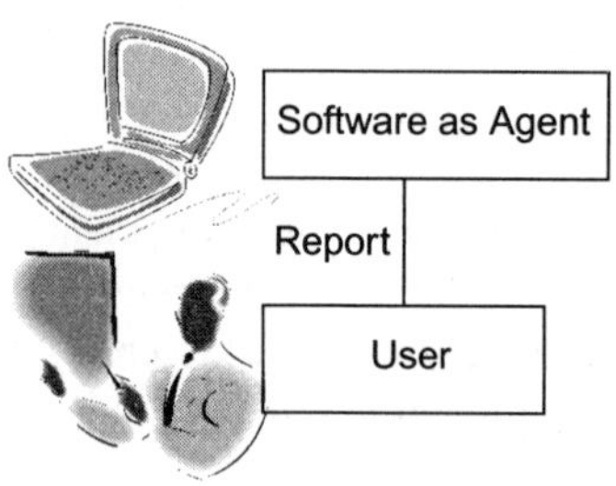

Figure 8.25 Intelligent Software Agent

Example:

1. Virus scanning software
2. Data warehousing agents (for data mining)
3. Automatic share trader

8.5.16 Software Reuse

Reusability (refer Figure 8.26) is the ability to reuse parts of code to create new code. Reusable part includes entire code, functions, classes, and data structures (database). Writing a standard code helps to reuse the same code for some other similar purposes, thereby reducing the cost of overall software development.

There are three types of stakeholders in reusing area:

1. Consumer
2. Contributor
3. Facilitator

A consumer uses the already existing code whereas a contributor creates and contributes a reusable code to the reusable repository. Note: A consumer can also be a contributor of another code and vice versa. A facilitator helps the consumer and the contributor in order to utilize the reusable repository in better way. Facilitator also should be technically capable in order to help the stakeholders.

There are two reusability types: internal reuse and external reuse

In internal reuse, the team uses the repository internally for its own purpose, whereas in the external reuse the team licenses the code to outsiders also.

Contributor-reusability process steps:

1. Register-reusable component
2. Classify reusable component
3. Review reusable component
4. Quantify value
5. Approve registration

Register-reusable component: In this step, a contributor needs to fill in a registration form which has the basic details of the reusable component submitted to the repository. Registration form contains the basic details such as name of the component submitted, description of the component, domain involved, technology involved, name of the contributor, how to use the component, etc.

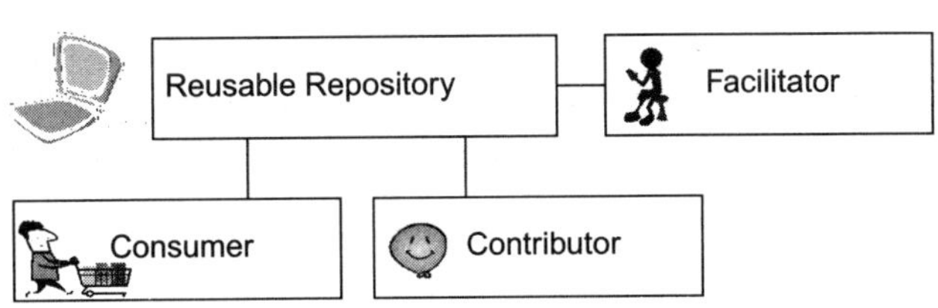

Figure 8.26 Software Reusability

Classify reusable component: In this step, the facilitator tries to classify the reusable component based on its usage, domain, and technology. In this step, the facilitator also indentifies suitable reviewer of the component who will check, validate, and certify this component.

Review reusable component: In this step, the reviewer of the component (who got identified in the previous step) will check, validate, and certify this component based on a standard set of guidelines.

Quantify value: The reviewer may also ask the contributor to do some minor changes in the submitted component before it is completely accepted and which will also ensure that a quantified value is attached to the component.

Approve registration: The reviewer will once again check the component for completeness before approving the registration after which the component will get entry into the reusable repository and will also become searchable. The component may get rejected if it is not meeting the basic criteria.

Consumer-reusability process steps:

1. Search reusable component
2. Look for fitment
3. Register and procure

Search reusable component: The consumer will search the repository to identify a needed component. Reusable component search page will have the basic searching functionality to search by name, type, domain, etc. in addition to advanced search facilities such as "Search within search" etc.

Look for fitment: Searched components may not be fitting into the real requirement, and proper fitment is required by analyzing various related components. This step will ensure choosing the best available component that can be reused.

Register and procure: Proper registration needs to be done on the system so that facilitator can provide the required components and other files to the consumer. Depending on the situation and policy, the component will be deployed for use.

Reuse-oriented development: The reuse-oriented model (ROD) is also called as ROD. It is a method of software development in which a program code is refined by producing a sequence of various prototypes. Each prototype is derived from the preceding one according to a sequence of defined rules. ROD reduces the overall development cost as we use prototype instead of various types of documents. It also saves time as it reduces lot of rework. It also reduces the overall number of bugs in the system as we keep on refining the prototypes continuously.

Summary

- Software coding is the core aspects of software engineering which acts as a catalyst for creating the software product. In a typical waterfall model, coding is done after the requirement clarification and design.
- Computer programming means writing a standard code, testing the written code, and debugging and maintaining the code.

- Programming can be considered as both art and science. Programming is a science as it needs to follow a set of engineering principles and guidelines. It is also being classified as art as there are lots of possibilities of using creative and innovative minds.
- Guideline means best practices. Programming best practices (guidelines) includes programming practices (coding conventions), naming conventions, comments, and programming principles rule of thumb.
- Coding conventions are a set of best practices that helps to write the software code in an efficient manner. Coding conventions cover the aspects of programming style, programming practices, and methods.
- Naming convention is a set of rules for choosing the character sequence to be used for identifiers (names).
- Hungarian notation: It either encodes the purpose or the type of the variable. There are two types of Hungarian notation namely Apps Hungarian and Systems Hungarian.
- Apps Hungarian: When it encodes for a "purpose" inside the application, it is called "Apps Hungarian". For example, in FORTRAN language, variables whose names start with letters I through N are denoted as integers by default.
- Systems Hungarian: When it encodes the "type," it is called "Systems Hungarian". Here the prefix encodes the actual data type of the variable. Arru8NumberList is a name (variable) and represents an array of unsigned 8-bit integers ("arru8").
- Senior software engineers in various IT organizations do follow various programming principles and rules of thumb which are derived based on their experience and skills. Few of the best practices are listed below. Due care is to be taken before implementing those in the project as they are context specific.
- Properly commented code serves no purpose for the compilation as well as executing the code, but it improves the readability of the code. It also helps to understand the purpose and business logic behind the code. All the software engineers write the comments on the first version of the code, but it is really a challenge to keep these comments up to date with further changes in the code.
- Blank lines and white spaces improve the readability of the code. It logically subdivides the codes.
- Structured programming: It is the subset of procedural programming. It is also called as modular programming. It represents the usage of a logical structure on the program being written to make it more readable, efficient, reliable, and easily maintained. In a typical structured programming language, the overall program is divided into logical structure for meaningful implementation.
- Information hiding: Users will be exposed to only the required details. For example, while we use any software (say Microsoft Word), we (users) know only how to use that software not how it was built and its related software.
- Good developers always follow the coding standards and guidelines while writing the code. Codes written using the standards and guidelines are easy to review/understand/debug. It is also easy to maintain and enhance the code if it follows the standards and guidelines.

- Top-down coding: Here, the implementation starts with the top of the hierarchy. Top main module is written first before writing the bottom submodules.
- Testing top-down coding: The top main module is written first, and hence the test cases are written completely for it. A stub is written in place of bottom submodules.
- Bottom-up coding is the reverse of top-down coding, and here the implementation starts with the bottom submodules. Top main module is written after that until it reaches the top of the hierarchy.
- Testing bottom-up coding: Bottom submodules are written first, and hence the test cases are written completely for it. A driver module is written to involve those modules under testing.
- Programming style: A set of rules and guidelines followed while writing a computer program is called as programming style. This programming style varies across the programming languages.
- Code share concept is famous in aviation business arrangement where one flight is shared by different airline operators. Tickets are sold by different operators (marketing carriers), and the flight will be operated by another operator (operating carrier).
- Code review is a systematic process which is also called as peer review which is used to find and fix the mistakes in the early phase of the coding, and it helps to improve the code quality and improve the coding skills of the developers.
- Static program analysis is the analysis of computer software that is performed without actually executing programs.
- Symbolic execution refers to the analysis of programs by tracking symbolic rather than actual values. A program which is executed using actual data results in the output of a series of values. In symbolic execution, the data are replaced by symbolic values.
- Coding inspection process was first developed by Michael Fagan. Inspection process has entry criteria and exit criteria. Entry criteria are the conditions that must be met before starting the inspection of the code. The condition includes checking whether we have only completed work product (code), gathering necessary data and information to inspect the code. Once all the entry conditions are met, it gives the green signal that the coding inspection process can begin.
- In RP, the prototype is being created automatically (rapidly) using three-dimensional CAD. It required just 3 to 72 hours building an object which saves a lot of time (without CAD, it takes months to build the same object).
- Software acting as agent of a user which monitors and reports set of activities can decide the course of action to be taken on behalf of users based on a set of predefined set of rules.
- Reusability is the ability to reuse parts of code to create new code. Reusable part includes entire code, functions, classes, and data structures (database). Writing a standard code helps to reuse the same code for some other similar purposes, thereby reducing the cost of overall software development.

Model Questions
PART A (Objective type)

1. Which of the following is not true about coding?
   A. Conversion of detailed design specification into the actual software code is called as coding
   B. It coverts functional aspects into technical aspects using design
   C. It is performed by people called as coders or programmers
   D. Coding phase usually takes more time than the design phase

Answer: D

2. All of the following are true about standardized code, except:
   A. It helps to enhance the code easily at later point of time.
   B. Standard coding also helps to identify and fix the bugs quickly.
   C. It reduces the cost of development over a period of time.
   D. It increases the cost of maintenance.

Answer: D

3. Programming is considered as both art and science.
   A. True B. False

Answer: A

4. Computer programming means writing a standard code, testing the written code, and debugging and maintaining the code.
   A. True B. False

Answer: A

5. The program must do repeatedly what it intends to do. This is called as
   A. Validity B. Consistency C. Maintainability D. Readability

Answer: B

6. Which of the following is the definition of maintainability?
   A. The program must be usable for the specific purpose without any trouble
   B. The program must be easily readable
   C. The program must be easily changeable and should have proper documentations
   D. The program must do repeatedly what it intends to do

Answer: C

7. Which of the following is the definition of consistency?
   A. The program must be usable for the specific purpose without any trouble
   B. The program must be easily readable
   C. The program must be easily changeable and should have proper documentations
   D. The program must do repeatedly what it intends to do

Answer: D

8. Programming guideline will not vary across programming languages.
   A. True B. False

Answer: B

9. Set of best practices that helps to write the software code in an efficient manner is called as
   A. Coding conventions B. Naming conventions
   C. Rule of thumb D. Comments

Answer: A

10. All of the following are advantages of coding convention, except:
    A. Enhancing the code becomes easy B. It saves cost for the company
    C. It helps to identify coding problems quickly D. Helps fixing problems quickly

Answer: D

11. Naming convention is a set of rules for choosing the character sequence to be used for identifiers:
    A. True B. False

Answer: A

12. All of the following are true about length of identifiers, except:
    A. Shorter identifiers are preferred over lengthy one (difficult to identify and remember).
    B. Longer identifiers are preferred because it is easy to encode them.
    C. Extremely short identifiers are very difficult to distinguish each other.
    D. Shorter identifiers may not be preferred because of visual clutter.

Answer: D

13. When we use combination of words for a single identifier, it is called as
    A. Compound identifier B. Combo identifier
    C. multiple identifier D. Pseudo identifier

Answer: A

14. All of the following are examples of hybrid naming convention, except
    A. Positional notation B. Hungarian notation
    C. Composite word scheme D. Compound identifier

Answer: D

15. Hungarian notation either encodes the purpose or the type of the variable.
    A. True B. False

Answer: A

16. Hungarian notation which encodes for a "purpose" inside the application is called as:
    A. Systems Hungarian B. Apps Hungarian
    C. Purpose Hungarian D. Encoded Hungarian

Answer: B

17. In FORTRAN language, variables whose names start with letters I through N are denoted as integers by default. This is an example of

A. Systems Hungarian B. Apps Hungarian
C. Purpose Hungarian D. Encoded Hungarian

Answer: B

18. Hungarian notation which encodes for a "Type" inside the application is called as:

A. Systems Hungarian B. Apps Hungarian
C. Purpose Hungarian D. Encoded Hungarian

Answer: A

19. All of the following are advantages of naming conventions, except:

A. It enhances clarity during ambiguity
B. It gives professional appearance to the work product developed
C. It helps to avoid naming collisions (two or more people using the same name for different purpose)
D. It helps to identify problems quickly

Answer: D

20. Senior software engineers in various IT organizations do follow various programming principles which are derived based on their experience and skill. This is called as

A. Coding conventions B. Naming conventions
C. Rule of thumb D. Comments

Answer: D

21. Which of the following is an example of coding convention rule of thumb?

A. While using database connection, create the connection object as earlier as possible and release it as late as possible.
B. While using database connection, create the connection object as late as possible and release it as early as possible.
C. Write lots of "public class" for security purpose.
D. Do not release object references until the program gets over as it can be used anywhere.

Answer: B

22. Properly commented code helps to compile the code quickly and it also improves the readability of the code.

A. True B. False

Answer: B

23. Which of the following are not programming principles of coding comments?

A. Write the code first before writing the comments
B. Write the comments in the beginning of every method, indicating the purpose of the method

C. Try to avoid end-of-line comments

D. Keep the comment always up to date while modifying the code

Answer: A

24. All of the following are true about blank space in a code, except:

A. A blank space should always be placed after comma in any argument list

B. Any keyword followed by a parenthesis must be separated by a space

C. Binary operators should be separated by blank spaces for readability

D. One blank space should be used between methods, before a block

Answer: D

25. One blank line should be used to between sections within the source code, between class and between interface definitions within the source code.

A. True B. False

Answer: B

26. Which of the following is not true about structured programming?

A. It is also called as modular programming.

B. It is the subset of procedural programming.

C. It makes the program more readable, efficient, and reliable.

D. BASIC and FORTRAN are examples of structured programming.

Answer: D

27. Which of the following is not a type of control in a program?

A. Sequence B. Structure C. Selection D. Repetition

Answer: B

28. if..then..else..endif is an example of

A. Sequence B. Structure C. Selection D. Repetition

Answer: C

29. Which of the following is false about information hiding?

A. It reduces complexity B. It increases usability

C. It reduces usability D. It prevents others to change the program

Answer: C

30. Main module is written first before writing the submodules is an example of:

A. Top-down coding B. Bottom-up coding

C. Incremental development of code D. Iterative development of code

Answer: A

31. Find out the correct sequence of rational unified process.

A. Inception, elaboration, construction, transition

B. Elaboration, inception, construction, transition

C. Transition, inception, elaboration, construction

D. Elaboration, construction, transition, inception

Answer: A

32. Spiral model Is a type of:

A. Iterative model B. incremental model C. RUP model D. Waterfall model

Answer: B

33. All of the following are advantages of incremental life cycle model, except:

A. Quick feedback loop from business stakeholders.

B. Focus on customer feedback.

C. Customer feels the product early.

D. Tracking and monitoring is easy.

Answer: D

34. "Analyze a little, design a little, test a little, and loop back" is an example of:

A. Iterative model B. Incremental model

C. RUP model D. Waterfall model

Answer: A

35. Which of the following is not true about iterative life cycle model?

A. Getting feedback from customer on time is difficult.

B. Even though deliverables are given in pieces, tracking and monitoring is difficult.

C. Project may not proceed further if customer is not cooperating.

D. The fully developed solution has no relation with the partial developments.

Answer: D

36. Code review happens not in the form of:

A. Formal inspection B. Lightweight code review

C. Pair programming D. Heavy-weight code review

Answer: D

37. A review checklist is being used in this type of review which uses proper plan such as scheduled time, duration of review, scope of review, coding standards, etc.

A. Formal inspection B. Lightweight code review

C. Pair programming D. Heavy-weight code review

Answer: A

38. "A defect is an instance in which a requirement is not satisfied".

A. True B. False

Answer: A

39. This happens at any point of time in convenience and no checklist is being used and the review happens in ad hoc manner.

A. Formal inspection B. Lightweight code review

C. Pair programming D. Heavy-weight code review

Answer: B

40. Over the shoulder is an example of:
A. Formal inspection B. Lightweight code review
C. Pair programming D. Heavy-weight code review

Answer: B

41. The review happens simultaneously while the code is getting developed is an example of:
A. Formal inspection B. Lightweight code review
C. Pair programming D. Heavy-weight code review

Answer: C

42. The analysis of computer software that is performed without actually executing programs is called as
A. Static analysis B. Symbolic analysis C. Stop analysis D. Code analysis

Answer: A

43. Pseudo code written before writing the actual code is called as:
A. Test B. Design C. Algorithm D. Logic

Answer: C

44. As per Hoare logic of correctness, letter "P" denotes
A. Postcondition B. Precondition
C. Pastcondition D. Preliminary value

Answer: B

45. As per Hoare logic of correctness, letter "Q" denotes
A. Postcondition B. Quality
C. Past condition D. Quantitative value

Answer: A

46. Total correctness refers to the algorithm that terminates (exit for every input) in addition to the functional correctness.
A. True B. False

Answer: A

47. Which of the following role is not used in code inspection process?
A. Coder B. Inspector C. Moderator D. Manager

Answer: D

48. Programming productivity can be measured using all of the following parameters, except:
A. Errors per line of code by a programmer
B. Learning curve of the programmer
C. Speed of code generation
D. Hours spent by the programmer inside the office

Answer: D

49. Which of the following is not an example of intelligent software agent?

A. Virus scanning software B. Data ware housing agents

C. Automatic share trader D. Operating system

Answer: D

50. Which of the following is not a type of stakeholder in reusing area?

A. Consumer B. Contributor

C. Facilitator D. Business analyst

Answer: D

51. It is a method of software development in which a program code is refined by producing a sequence of various prototypes:

A. ROD B. RAD C. JIT D. PRD

Answer: A

PART B (Answer in one or two lines)

1. Write notes on software coding.
2. Why we need to write a standard code?
3. What is computer programming?
4. Why programming is considered as both art and science?
5. What is programming guidelines?
6. Write notes on coding conventions.
7. List down any three advantages of coding convention?
8. What is naming convention? List down any three applicabilities in software coding.
9. What is the length of identifiers in naming conventions?
10. What are all the considerations while deciding the length of identifiers in naming convention?
11. How letter case and numerals are used for naming convention?
12. What are multiple word identifiers?
13. What is hybrid naming convention?
14. Write notes on composite word scheme of languages?
15. What is Hungarian notation of naming convention?
16. What is positional notation of naming convention?
17. Write any three benefits of naming convention.
18. What are all the challenges of naming convention?
19. Write notes on programming principles and rule of thumb.

20. List any three coding conventions in rule of thumb.
21. Write notes on programming principles of coding comments.
22. List down any three programming principles of coding comments.
23. Write notes on programming principles of blank lines and white space (blank space).
24. What is structured programming?
25. Give examples for unstructured and structured programming languages.
26. What is OOPS?
27. List down three structures of computer programming as suggested by Corrado Bohm and Guiseppe Jacopini
28. Write notes on structure programming principles as suggested by Dijkstra.
29. Write notes on sequence, selection, and repetition.
30. What is information hiding?
31. Give examples for information hiding.
32. What are all the advantages of information hiding?
33. List down any three advantages of following coding standards?
34. List down some of the sample coding standards and guidelines you are aware of.
35. What is top-down coding and testing?
36. What is bottom-up coding and testing?
37. What is incremental development of code?
38. Write notes on rational unified process (RUP).
39. What are all the advantages of incremental life cycle model?
40. What are all the disadvantages of incremental life cycle model?
41. What is iterative life cycle model?
42. What are the advantages of iterative life cycle model?
43. What are all the disadvantages of iterative life cycle model?
44. Write notes on programming style.
45. What is code sharing?
46. What is code review? What are all its forms?
47. What are all the forms of code review?
48. Write short notes on formal inspection of code review.
49. Write notes on lightweight code review.
50. Give two types of lightweight process of code review.
51. Write notes on pair programming of code review and automatic code review.

52. Write notes on static program analysis used by automatic code review software.
53. Write notes on symbolic execution concepts used by automatic code review software.
54. How will you prove correctness using algorithm?
55. Write notes on Hoare logic of correctness.
56. What is functional correctness, partial correctness, and total correctness?
57. What is code inspections?
58. List down various roles used in code inspection process.
59. What is programming productivity?
60. What is RP?
61. What is intelligent software agent?
62. Give three examples of intelligent software agent.
63. Write notes on software reuse and list down stakeholders involved in it.
64. Distinguish consumer, contributor, and facilitator in a software reuse process.
65. What are all the types of reusability?
66. Write notes on reuse-oriented model (ROD) in detail.

PART C (Descriptive type)

1. Write five general programming principles.
2. What are all the advantages of coding convention?
3. List down the aspects covered in coding convention.
4. Discuss naming convention in detail.
5. List some of coding conventions rule of thumb.
6. Discuss coding comments in detail.
7. What are all the advantages of coding standards?
8. Discuss rational unified process (RUP).
9. Discuss iterative life cycle model in detail.
10. Discuss formal inspection of code review in detail.
11. What is code inspections? Explain the steps followed in coding inspection?
12. What is RP? List down the steps in creating it.
13. What is software reusability? Discuss various stakeholders involved with process in detail.
14. Discuss static program analysis in detail.

Section 5:
Software Metrics and Estimation

9

Introduction to Software Measurement and Metrics

CHAPTER COVERAGE

1. *Introduction*
2. *Measurement*
3. *Metrics*
4. *Other Concepts*

9.1 INTRODUCTION

Nothing can be more true than the saying "which can't be measured can't be controlled." Metrics and measurement are crucial part for executing the software projects successfully. The topic of software measures and metrics has created a lot of interest over the last two decades. In 1960s and 1970s the main focus of IT was on the product evaluation. Then in 1980s and 1990s the focus shifted toward process evaluation, as it was understood that only an efficient process can create an effective product. In late 1990s, the integration of measurement process with the software lifecycle started to happen because it was evident that to create an efficient process the measurement of how the process is performing is very important. Thus, this chapter discusses the details of the measurement and metrics in software domain.

9.2 MEASUREMENT

Measurement is a process or the result by which numbers or symbols are assigned to attributes of entities in the real world in such a way as to describe them in order to clearly defined rules. Example: length, time, and temperature; each measurement describes some attributes of the objects in the real world.

Software measurement is a quantified attribute of a characteristic of a software product or the software process. The content of software measurement is defined and governed by ISO Standard ISO 15939 (software measurement process).

Examples: Number of lines of code (LOC), number of classes and interfaces provide us some idea about volume of code and also about complexity of the developed software.

A *unit of measurement (as per standard definition)* is a definite magnitude of a physical quantity, defined and adopted by convention and/or by law, which is used as a standard for measurement of the same physical quantity.

Example: Length of a single brick = 40 cm

In the above example, length is a physical quantity. Centimeter is a unit of length that represents a definite predetermined length.

> *When you can measure what you are speaking about and express it in numbers, you know something about it; but when you cannot measure, when you cannot express it in numbers, your knowledge is of a meager and unsatisfactory kind: it may be the beginning of knowledge, but you have scarcely, in your thoughts, advanced to the stage of science.*
>
> — Lord Kelvin

9.2.1 Why and Where Measurement is Important in Life

Measurement is not only important for software, but also in our day-to-day life also (refer Figure 9.1). Think about the very common scenarios on how measurement plays a crucial role in our day-to-day life.

1. To take proper medicine (1 spoon, 2 spoon)
2. To cook correctly (correctly measured ingredients)
3. To fill sufficient fuel in a car (how many liters?)
4. To fill sufficient water in overhead tank
5. To pay correct money at shop/hotels
6. To decide winning side in sports (high goal, score)
7. To measure performance of the students (higher marks)
8. Performance appraisal at office
9. To come office on time (time measurement)
10. To fix office temperature (AC cool measurement)

Figure 9.1 Measurements in Life

11. Proper use of capacity (Room/Office)
12. Proper use of goods (inventory measurement)
13. Measuring investments (ROI)
14. Measuring cash outflow/inflow

All the above indicates the importance of measurement in day-to-day life.

9.2.2 Why to Measure Software?

You cannot control what you cannot measure — De Marco, 1982.

What is not measurable, make miserable — Galileo

Measurement is important in software development for the following reasons (not limited).

To Understand What we do: It helps to understand the past by measuring the product and the process already executed and thereby helps to compare different process and product. It also helps to understand the process and the product on hand.

For Realistic Planning (Future Prediction): To plan and predict the future based on the past measurements.

For Control: To compare the actual parameter values against the planned values and take necessary actions if there is deviation.

To Improve the Process and Product: Measurement provides baseline measures for making improvements in the process and the product.

Benchmarking: Software metrics help to create benchmarks with similar kind of organizations.

Cost Reduction: Cost reduction is possible only after measurement of the current cost.

To Define Quality Level: We need measurement on software so that we can understand and agree on product quality.

9.2.3 Characteristics of Effective Measurement Program

Proper focus on measurement at the organization level will yield the intended benefit.

The following basic characteristics are necessary to keep the measurement program effective (refer Figure 9.2).

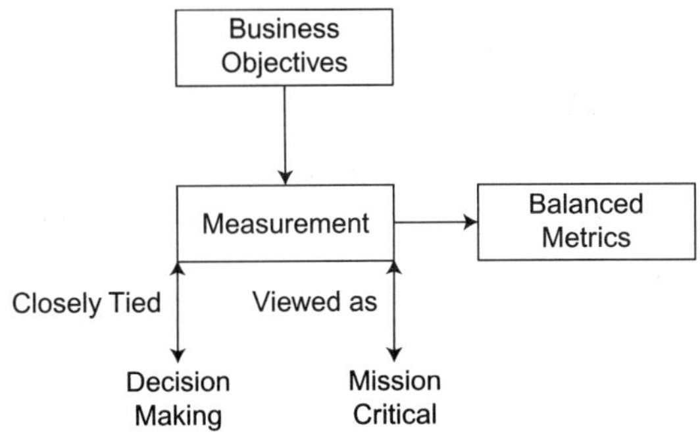

Figure 9.2 Effective Measurement

1. Aligned with the organization business objectives,
2. Tied to decision making at lowest level possible,
3. Balanced metrics at all levels,
4. Focused on measuring processes, and
5. Viewed as mission critical.

Discussion Questions

1. Discuss characteristics of effective measurement program in detail with known examples (in a student life at college).
2. Discuss characteristics of effective measurement program in detail with known examples (in a student life for society).

9.2.4 Types of Measure

Direct Measures: It is measured directly in terms of the observed attribute (usually by counting). Examples: length of source-code written, time taken for a process execution, and number of defects discovered in a particular phase of the project.

Indirect Measures: It is calculated from other direct and indirect measures.

Example 1: Module defect density = Number of defects discovered/length of source.
Example 2: Temperature (usually derived from the length of a liquid column).

True Performance Measures: Customers – use "true" performance measures. True performance measures are used by the customer to measure the performance of the product they use, in their own language as per their own view.

Example 1: A true measure of a book may be "easy to read."
Example 2: A true measure of software may be "fast response."

True performance measures typically vary from customer to customer. The parameter and the calculation logic also changes form the customer to customer.

Substitute Performance Measures: Producers – use "substitute" performance measures. Substitute measures are quantifiable units.

Example: A substitute measure of a book may have "less grammatical mistakes," "less number of pages," and "covering full syllabus."

A true measure of software may be "average response time."

9.2.5 Activities of a Measurement Process

A measurement process aims for continuous improvement through regular checking of the current performance. Figure 9.3 shows cyclic execution of the steps in measurement.

Plan: First decide what needs to be measured and the unit of measurement. Identify the mechanism to collect the data. Identify tools if any to collect the metrics and analyze the metrics.

Collect: Accumulate the data required to derive the formulated metrics using the tool if any.

Analyze: The computation of the metrics and also the application of tools to analyze the metrics happen here. This step combines various metrics data and also use the filtration of metrics based on the plan. It is better to automate the data collection and analyze process.

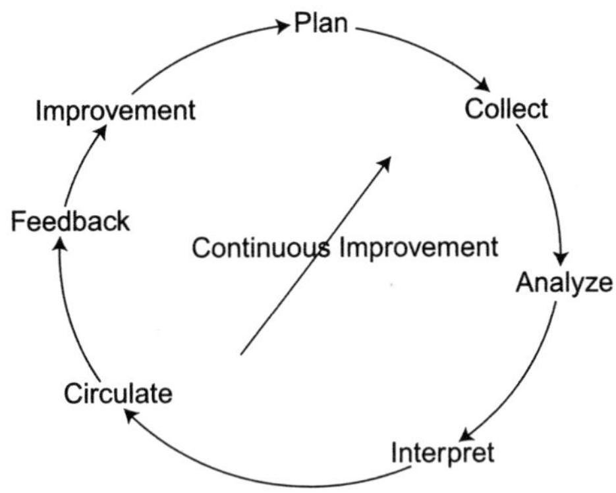

Figure 9.3 Activities of a Measurement Process

Interpret: Actual interpretation of the metrics to give a meaningful thought and also steps/actions to be taken based on the analyzed metrics happen here. Interpretative guidelines and recommendations should be established well before for each metrics so that interpretation happens in a methodological way. Target dates should be defined against each action points.

Circulate: Interpretation along with the steps/actions is passed on to the software development team for taking necessary actions as defined.

Feedback: Get feedback from the team to gain insight into the effectiveness of the measurement/metrics along with the effectiveness of the action taken to produce the desired results.

Improvement: Continuous improvement of the measurement process based on the feedback received incorporating changes in the process and the metrics if required.

9.2.6 Halstead Measure

Maurice Halstead of Purdue University attempted to tie physical, syntactical objects, and psychological measurements together with a set of definitions:

$n1$ = total number of unique operators in a program (software)
$n2$ = total number of unique operands in a program (software)
$N1$ = total number of occurrences of the operators
$N2$ = total number of occurrences of the operands

Volume (V) = mental comparison needed to write the program

$$V = N * (\log 2\ n)$$

Where $N = N1 + N2$ and

$$n = n1 + n2$$

Volume of a function should be >20 and <1000

Volume of a function without parameter and with one line code is about 20;
Volume > 1000 tells that the function probably does too many things;
The volume of a file is usually >100 & < 8000;
Level (L) = Level of program (software)

$L = V^*/V$ where V is volume and V^* is minimum volume needed to write the program.

Difficulty of a program = $1/L = V/V^*$

Faults of program = $V/3000$; based on psychological assumption that a person can make 3000 decisions before making an error.

The problem with Halstead measure is that the psychological assumptions along with the projections of numbers have been subject to dispute.

9.2.7 Cyclomatic Measure

This measure was introduced by McCabe to look at the number of unique paths for testing. Initially it was based on graph theory, but can also be attained by

$$M = \text{number of binary decisions} + 1$$

There have been numerous studies that looked for correlations between cyclomatic complexity and defect rate. Results have been much more positive than the Halstead measure.

9.3 METRICS

Metric is a standard of measurement. A metric indicates the nature and/or strength of an attribute, usually by means of a number, often in conjunction with a unit. For example, 40 cm actually mean 40 times the definite predetermined length called "1 cm". Software metric relates individual measures in a meaningful way.

In Figure 9.4, a person is mapped to height. For example, 182 cm actually mean 182 times the definite predetermined length called "1 cm".

Software metric relates individual measures of software(s) in a meaningful way like what we discussed about metrics in day-to-day life.

Software metrics are quantifiable measures that could be used to measure characteristics of a software system (product) or the software development process through which the software is getting developed. Figure 9.5 shows how metrics and measurement are related.

It (measurement and metrics) is required for effective management. Managers need quantifiable information (metrics) to take appropriate action.

"A quantitative measure of the degree to which a system, component, or process possesses a given attribute" – IEEE Standard Glossary.

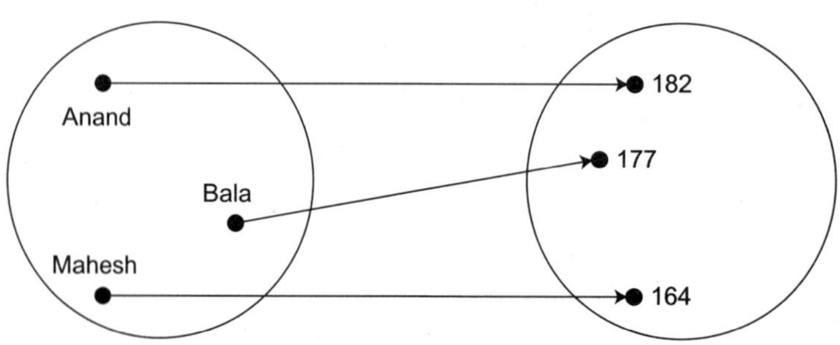

Figure 9.4 Example: Measure Mapping Height Attribute of Person on a Number Representing Height in Centimeter

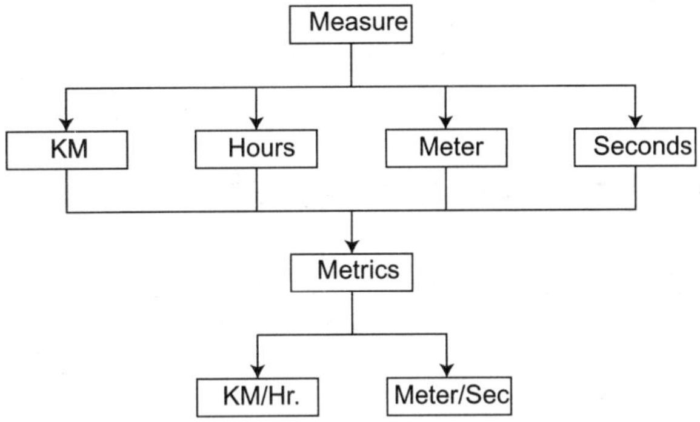

Figure 9.5 Relationships between Measure and Metrics

9.3.1 GQM Paradigm of Metrics (Goal/Question/Metric)

It identified meaningful metrics of a product just by following three important steps (Figure 9.6).

1. Establish the measurement goal that is specific to the process or product under study.
2. Define a set of questions that are appropriate and are necessary in order to achieve the specified goal identified in Step 1.
3. Identify metrics that help to answer the questions identified in Step 2.

Example for GQM paradigm.

1. Goal: Increase the customer satisfaction level.
2. Questions: What is the current customer satisfaction level? What are all the factors important to customers? What is the priority level of the factors?
3. Start with possible metrics (based on factors) to achieve the desired level. If the factors are First Time Right (FTR) and On Time Delivery (OTD), try to achieve FTR in the beginning before attempting to OTD because OTD without FTR will create more problems.

9.3.2 Black Box and White Box Metrics

Metrics are also classified as Black Box Metrics and White Box Metrics.

If the inside and outside logic of a metrics (how the metric is calculated) is not known then it is called as Black Box Metric. Example for Black Box Metric is Function Point (FP) Metrics (where the inside logic is not known).

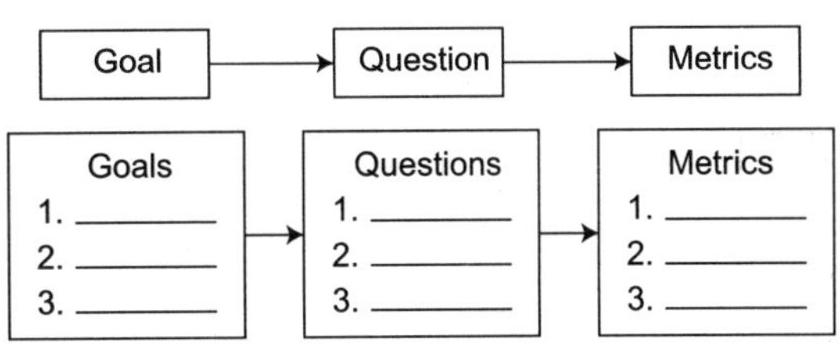

Figure 9.6 GQM Paradigm

If the inside and outside logic of a metrics (how the metric is calculated) is clearly known then it is called as White Box Metric. Example for White Box Metric is LOC (where the inside and outside logic is clearly known)

9.3.3 Types of Software Metrics (Classification of Metrics)

Figure 9.7 depicts the classification of metrics.

Product Metrics: Metrics that are related to the product (LOC).

Process Metrics: Metrics that are related to the process of development (length of the iteration).

Resources Metrics: Metrics that are related to the usage of personnel and resources and their properties (developer productivity).

External Metrics: Measured with respect to environment/context (productivity, usability).

Internal Metrics: Not dependent on the environment/context (LOC).

Direct Metrics: Directly measurable (LOC, FP).

Indirect Metrics: Not measurable directly (code quality, defect density, temperature).

9.3.3.1 Product Metrics

Metrics that are related to the software product developed is called Product Metrics (refer Figure 9.8). They quantify the characteristics of the product being developed.

Examples: Size of the product LOC, complexity of the product, test metrics (product related) and quality metrics of the product. It focuses on the quality of the deliverables.

McCall's Quality Factors McCall, Richards, and Walters group the quality factors of a product into three categories which are focused on three aspects of a software product (product operation, product orientation, and product transition) – refer Figure 9.8.

1. Product operation: This focus on operational characteristics of the product (correctness, reliability, usability, integrity, and efficiency).

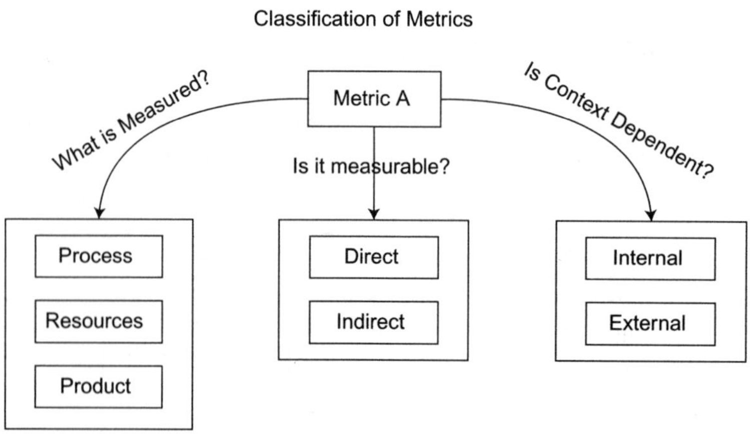

Figure 9.7 Classifications of Metrics

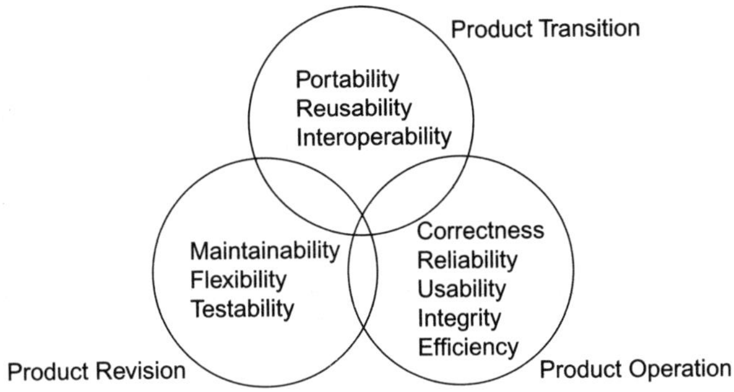

Figure 9.8 McCall's Quality Factors

2. Product revision: This focus on the revision characteristics of a product when it undergoes change (maintainability, flexibility, and testability).
3. Product transition: This focus on the product adaptability to new environments (portability, reusability, and interoperability).

Product Operation

Correctness: The extent to which software (product) meets its specifications (requirement documentation) is called as correctness. If the correctness is 100% then it exactly meets the requirement.

Reliability: The extent to which software (product) perform its intended function is called as reliability. If the reliability is 100% then it exactly does its intended function.

Usability: Usability is the ease of use and learn-ability of software (product).

Integrity: Integrity indicates how software (product) is protected from unauthorized usage (unauthorized user accessing the product, user accessing unauthorized data).

Efficiency: Effort, time, cost are required to produce the desired output in a product. Efficiency is the ability to produce specific outcome effectively with a minimum input.

Product Revision:

When a product undergoes change the main focus is on the revision characteristics such as maintainability, flexibility, and testability.

Maintainability: The effort required to find out and correct mistakes in a product.

Flexibility: The effort required to modify a part of software (product).

Testability: The effort required to test software (product) to ensure that it works properly and fulfils the intended purpose.

Product Transition:

This focuses on the product's adaptability to new environments and the characteristics that are measured are portability, reusability, and interoperability.

Portability: The effort required to transfer the software (product) from one environment (hardware) to another.

Reusability: The extent to which part of the product or the full product can be used in making new software (product).

Interoperability: The extent to which product can be coupled with another product.

9.3.3.2 Process Metrics

Metrics that are related to the software development process is called Process Metrics. Set of process creates a product. Flaw in the process will affect the product, and hence it is required to watch the process metrics continuously and take appropriate action at appropriate time.

It is commonly used by management to check the budget and office procedures for efficiency. This is also used by the project managers to check and control the project in efficient manner.

Examples: Length of the iteration, schedule variance, cost variance, and effort variance

In the above example length of the iteration is a direct measure. Schedule variance, cost variance, effort variance are indirect measure.

Process stability is also another example of indirect measure (Different formulas are used to derive it).

Process metrics are used for making strategic decisions. Attributes (properties of a process) for improvement are decided first before making the metrics for the attributes, then the metrics are used to provide the indicators for strategic improvement (refer Figure 9.9).

Process effectiveness is measured based on the outcome of the process such as, work products delivered, human effort expended, calendar time expended, conformance to the schedule, and time and effort to complete each generic activity.

9.3.3.3 Resource Metrics

Metrics that are related to the resources (including human resources) are called as Resource Metrics.

Example:

- Effort per FP per resource
- Cost per FP per resource
- Defects per FP per resource

All the examples given above are indirect measure. Cost of a human resource is a direct measure.

Resource metrics are usually used for

1. Project management purpose
2. Financial purpose
3. HR management purpose

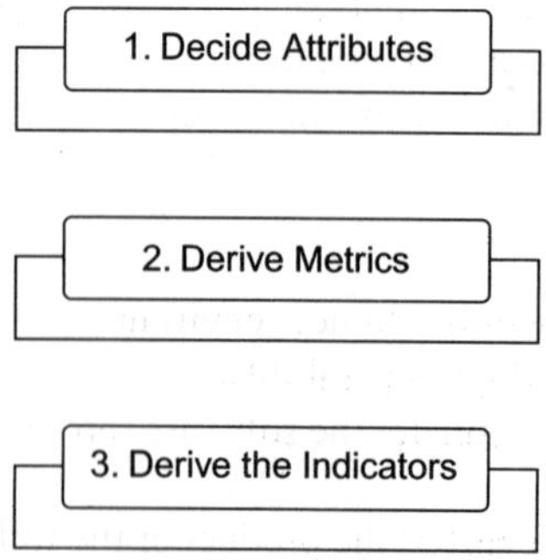

Figure 9.9 Process Metrics Steps

Project manager – Kumar needs to spend 2 hours per day extra in order to finish his work on time.

Finance – Putting Kumar into the new project will cost 5 USD per FP.

HR management – On an average Kumar produce 10 defects per day.

9.3.4 Metrics for the Analysis Model

Requirement analysis phase (refer Figure 9.10) happens after collecting the requirments from the customer and hence requirement-related metrics are part of this phase of the project. Following are the observations based on the requirement

1. How many functionalities the system will deliver? – Functionality delivered.
2. What is the size of the system to be developed? – Size of the system to be developed.
3. What is the quality level of the requirement? – Quality of the requirement (level of completeness).

9.3.5 Metrics for the Design Model

Design phase (refer Figure 9.10) happens after requirement analysis phase.

Architectural metrics: Provide an indication of the quality of the architectural design.

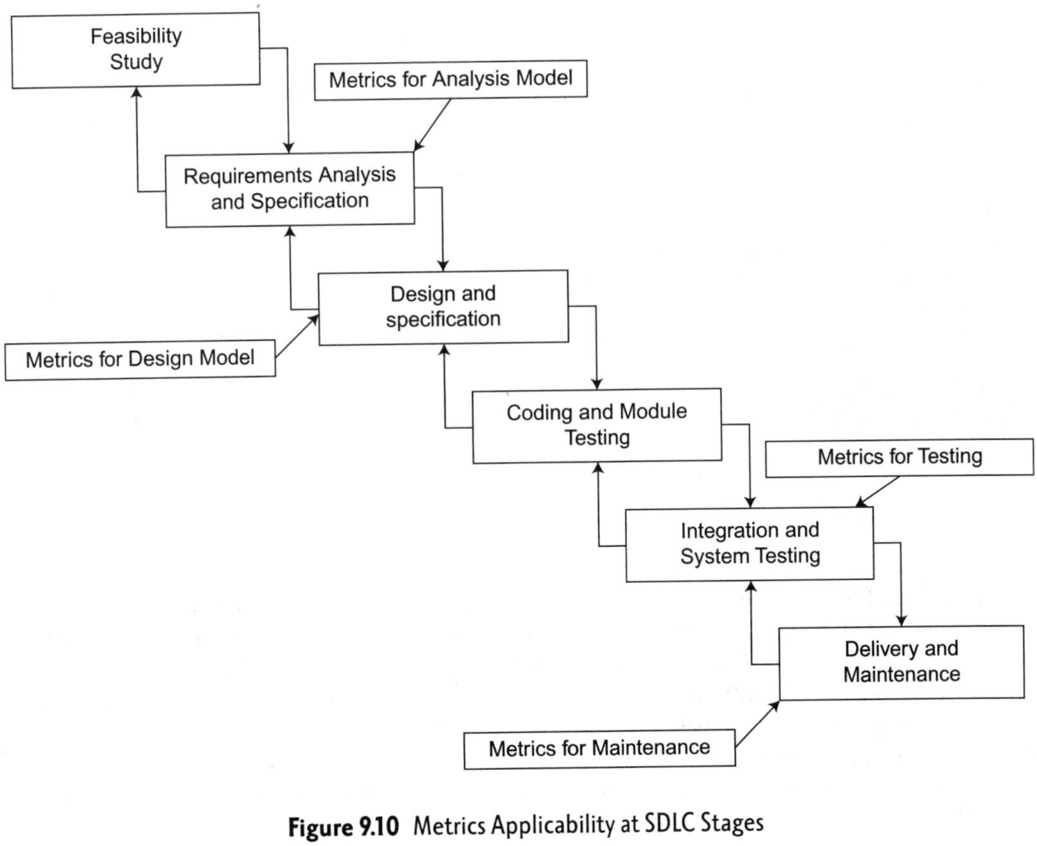

Figure 9.10 Metrics Applicability at SDLC Stages

Component-level metrics: Measure the complexity of software components and other characteristics that have a bearing on quality.

Interface design metrics: Focus primarily on usability.

Specialized object-oriented design metrics: Measure characteristics of classes and their communication and collaboration characteristics (refer Chapter 10 on Object-Oriented Design Metrics).

9.3.6 Metrics for Testing

Testing phase (refer Figure 9.10) happens after coding phase.

Defect-related metrics: focus on defects (i.e., bugs) found rather than on the tests themselves.

Testing effectiveness metrics: provide a real-time indication of the effectiveness of tests that have been conducted.

In-process metrics: process-related metrics that can be determined as testing is conducted.

Statement and branch coverage metrics: lead to the design of test cases that provide program coverage.

Metrics for Testing (Process Related)

Examples of testing-related metrics are

1. Defect removal effectiveness
2. Response time for fixing
3. Productivity metrics

Defect Removal Effectiveness: The metric can be calculated for the entire development process, for each phase, or before code integration.

DRE = Metrics for design model/metrics for analysis model

The higher the value, the more effective the development process and fewer defects escaping to next phase or the field for example, calculated for specific phases = *phase effectiveness*.

Phase defect removal effectiveness and related metrics are useful for quality management and planning. Measurements that indicate clearly which phase of the process needs improvement and should be focused on. Using the right tools, analyzes can be done for the entire project as well as for local areas.

POINTS TO PONDER

Software = Every organization set some benchmark for the important metrics and DRE is one of them. The project team tries to make sure that the DRE value is at least minimum the benchmark value or better than it.

Response Time for Fixing (Metrics for Testing): Most organizations have established guidelines on the time limit within which the fixes should be available for the reported defects. Severe problems are usually fixed as soon as possible, less severe problems has more relaxed time for fixing. Fix response time metric is calculated as follows: Mean time of all problems from open to closed. Sometimes there are less severe problems that customers just ignore, so the problem remains open for a long time when the mean time is not available then we can use median time in the formula.

Short time in fix process leads to customer satisfaction and determines how good the process is in this field.

9.3.7 Metrics for Maintenance

Software maturity index (SMI): It provides an indication of the stability of a software product based on changes that occur for each release.

SMI = (Total Modules – Changed Modules)/Total Modules

SMI will go down if the changes occur in higher number of modules.

Changed modules include number of added module + number of changed module + number of deleted modules.

Product is stable when SMI is nearby 1. The average time to produce a release can be proportional to SMI. When SMI is near 0, it will take more time to deliver the changes.

Figure 9.10 shows what metrics is applicable in which SDLC stage of the software development.

9.3.8 Productivity Metrics

Software productivity is a complex subject as it considers lots of factors (including number of resources, resource usage, quality, time, etc..).

Sample Productivity Metrics include:

1. Line of Code (LOC)/hours used to write the Code
2. Function Point (FP)/person-month used to write the Code
3. Average Person- days/Number of Classes (in object metrics)

Usually number of units of output per unit of effort is considered as productivity.

Law of Diminishing Returns: Just by adding more resources project cannot finish early, addition of more resources may increase overall output in the beginning, but will eventually decrease individual productivity. Adding thrice as many people to the same task may not cause the task to be finished thrice as fast.

9.3.9 Characteristics of a Good Metrics

We need to follow correct metrics as per the situation. Characteristics of good metrics can be remembered using "Consistent Reliable LIER".

Consistent – required
Reliable – required
Linear – nice, but not necessary
Independent – required
Easy to use – nice, but not necessary
Repeatable – required

Consistent metrics means it is comparable across systems indicating the meaning and the logics of measurement is consistent across various systems. If it is inconsistent it is impossible to compare across systems.

Reliability of a metrics is the ability to perform and maintain its functions in routine as well as unexpected circumstances.

Linear performance of metrics is the ability to maintain its linear level. For example, if metrics increases two times, then the performance also increases two times.

Independency of a metrics indicates that it is not dependent on external pressure or influence of other metrics. For example, pressure to change the meaning of a metric/pressure to change the definition of a metric/pressure to influence the definition of a metric.

Easy to use character of a metric indicates that the metric should be easy to use always. No one will use if it is hard.

Repeatability is the important characteristics of metrics. Same value is measured each time an experiment is performed.

9.3.10 Measurement and Metrics Indicators

Indicators are the metrics or combination of metrics that provides insight into the software process, project, or product itself which helps to take a decision. Earned value metrics is an example.

Earned Value Management: It is a method of measuring project performance and any professional project manager/scrum master should know how to calculate this for the project to have better control on the project. It is calculated by comparing planned amount of work with the actually accomplished work, in order to determine if cost and schedule performance are going as per the plan. We will be discussing more about Earned Value in Chapter 11.

POINTS TO PONDER

It is important for the project team to look out for indicators though out the project lifecycle. These provide insight into the problem and improvement areas.

9.3.11 Kaner and Bond's Evaluation Framework for Metrics

The researchers (Kaner and Bond) developed a general framework for evaluating a metric. They laid out 10 points to check for, based on the IEEE software metric criteria. See Figure 9.11 for the explanation of this framework.

1. What is the purpose of the measure? Helps you understand the stakes in making the measurement so that you know how much to invest in ensuring its validity.
2. What is the scope of the measure? Does it impact one team or developer or multiple parts of a large project. The authors point out that as the scope broadens so does the number of confounding variables to the system.

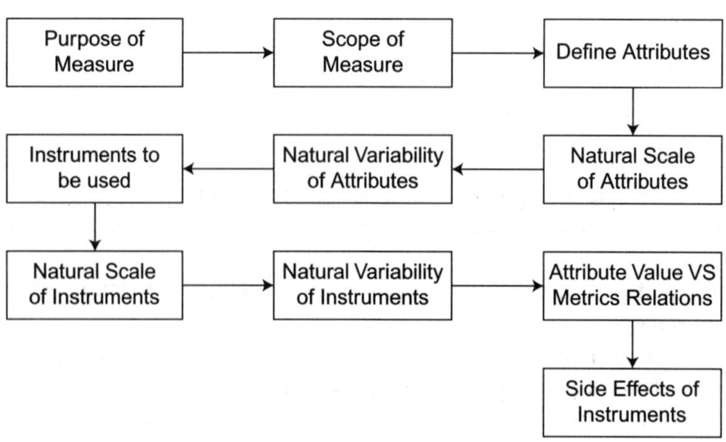

Figure 9.11 Kaner and Bond's Evaluation Framework for Metrics

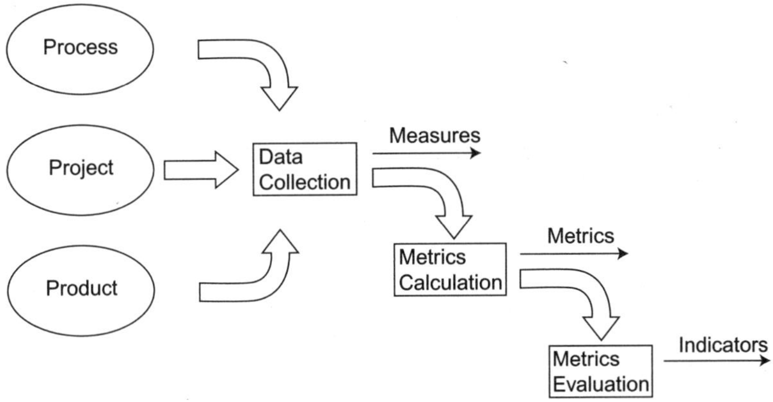

Figure 9.12 Software Metrics Baseline Steps

3. What attribute of the software is being measured?
4. What is the natural scale of the attribute to be measure?
5. What is the natural variability of the attribute? What numbers is expected to see?
6. What measuring instrument is used to perform the measurement?
7. What is the natural scale for this metric?
8. What is the natural variability of readings from this instrument? Are small differences to be expected? Or does even the slightest change mean that a huge improvement has been reached.
9. What is the relationship of the attribute to the metric value? Make sure you are measuring the right thing.
10. What are the natural and foreseeable side effects of using this instrument? If a metric is used will the effects of writing code that makes the metric better be as per choice? The authors point out too that an improvement in the metric should mean an equal increase in code quality, or else there may be something the metric is not showing,

9.3.12 Software Metrics Baseline Steps

In order to baseline the metrics, the data (measures, metrics, and indicators) from various similar kinds of process/project and product is analyzed. It can be filleted out/modified before the metrics is baseline for the current project. The data is to be collected from as many similar projects as possible with consistent measures. After the data collection the metrics are computed and baseline is established (see Figure 9.12).

9.4 OTHER CONCEPTS

9.4.1 S-Curve

A simple technique for tracking project costs is to develop a periodical cumulative budget spend plan and then track actual costs against the plan. The slope of the graph indicates the project expenditure rate, sometimes called the "burn rate". (Cost Burn up Graph)

By plotting actual costs against the budget planned, the differences can be seen between actual spending and the plan (Figure 9.13).

9.4.2 Learning Curve

Learning curve theory indicates that because of learning, people will start doing the work efficiently and thereby overall cost will reduce. As time moves on the total costs will increase; but the cost per unit will drop because repetition increases efficiency of the work involved in producing the output.

$$Y_x = Kx^{\log_2 b}$$

where

K is the number of direct work hours to produce the first unit
Y_x is the number of direct work hours to produce the Xth unit
X is the number of unit produced
b is the learning percentage

The above is also applicable for agile projects and hence, the customer expects the team to improve the productivity thereby delivering more velocity as the iteration cycle progresses.

Discussion Questions

Discuss how learning curve affects the estimations?
Discuss various metrics associated with a college student?

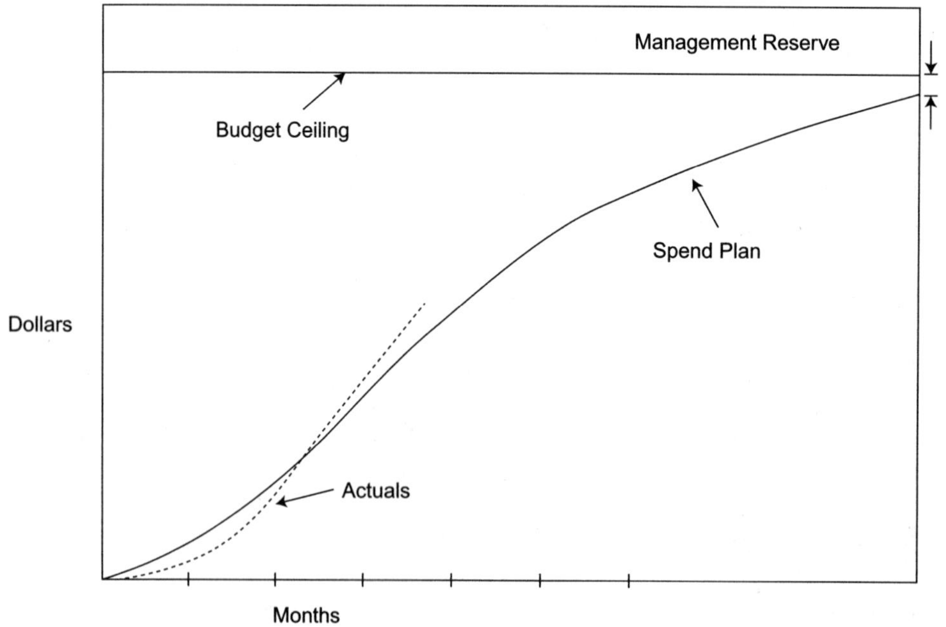

Figure 9.13 S-Curve

Summary

This chapter gives the introduction to various terms related to measurement, metrics, and estimations. Once the estimation and planning part is complete for a project, the metrics come handy in tracking the execution and progress of the project. This chapter discusses the concepts of measurement, metrics, types of software metrics, Halstead metrics, Kaner and Bond's evaluation framework for metrics, and cyclomatic measure.

- Measurement is the process or the result by which numbers or symbols are assigned to attributes of entities in the real world in such a way as to describe them according to clearly defined rules. Example: length, time, and temperature. Measurement is not only important for a software, it is important in our day-to-day life also. Maurice Halstead of Purdue University attempted to tie physical, syntactical objects, and psychological measurements together with a set of definitions. Cyclomatic measure was introduced by McCabe to look at the number of unique paths for testing.
- Metric is a standard of measurement. A metric indicates the nature and/or strength of an attribute, usually by means of a number, often in conjunction with a unit. GQM paradigm of metrics stands for (Goal/Question/Metric).
- Various types of software metrics is discussed in this chapter. If correct metrics is not followed then it will be the consistent reliable LIER what need to be remember as the characteristics of the metrics.
- Kaner and Bond's evaluation framework for metrics discussed in detail.

Model Questions
PART A (Objective type)

1. This is defined as the process or the result by which numbers or symbols are assigned to attributes of entities in the real world in such a way as to describe them in order to clearly defined rules

A. Measurement | B. Metrics
C. Software | D. Rule book

Answer: A

2. This is defined as a standard of measurement.

A. Measurement unit | B. Metrics
C. Measurement standard | D. Rule book

Answer: B

3. This is define as quantifiable measures that could be used to measure characteristics of a software system (product) or the software development process through which the software is getting developed.

A. Software measurement unit | B. Software metrics
C. Software measurement standard | D. Rule book

Answer: B

4. This is a quantified attribute of a characteristic of a software product or the software process.

A. Software measurement | B. Software metrics
C. Software measurement standard | D. Rule book

Answer: A

5. All of the following are the reasons to measure software except
   A. To understand what to do inside the software product
   B. For realistic planning of the development of the software (future prediction)
   C. It helps to control the development of software
   D. It gives the customer satisfaction

Answer: D

6. All of the following are the reasons to measure software except
   A. It helps for benchmarking with other software
   B. It helps to reduce cost
   C. It helps to define quality level
   D. It gives the customer Satisfaction

Answer: D

7. Following are the characteristics of effective measurement program except
   A. It is to be aligned with the organization business objectives,
   B. Tied to decision making at lowest level possible,
   C. Balanced metrics at all levels available, and
   D. It should be easy and simple to measure.

Answer: D

8. Following are the types of measure except
   A. Personal measure
   B. True performance measures
   C. Substitute performance measures
   D. Indirect measures

Answer: A

9. Module defect density = Number of defects discovered /length of source is an example of which type of measure?
   A. Direct measure
   B. True performance measures
   C. Substitute performance measures
   D. Indirect measures

Answer: D

10. Who uses true performance measures?
    A. Software engineers
    B. Producers
    C. Customers
    D. Testers

Answer: C

11. A measure of "fast response" of software is an example of ?
    A. Direct measure
    B. True performance measures
    C. Substitute performance measures
    D. Indirect measures

Answer: B

12. Who uses substitute performance measures?
    A. Software engineers B. Producers C. Customers D. Testers

Answer: B

13. If the inside and outside logic of a metrics (how the metric is calculated) is not known then it is called as
    A. Black Box Metrics
    B. White Box Metrics
    C. Brown Box Metrics
    D. Gray Box Metrics

Answer: A

14. If the inside and outside logic of a metrics (how the metric is calculated) is clearly known then it is called as
    A. Black Box Metrics
    B. White Box Metrics
    C. Brown Box Metrics
    D. Gray Box Metrics

Answer: B

15. This measure was introduced by McCabe to look at the number of unique paths for testing.
    A. Cyclone measure
    B. Cyclomatic measure
    C. McCabe measure
    D. McCabe unique path measure

Answer: B

16. All the following are examples of product revision metrics, except
    A. Maintainability
    B. Portability
    C. Flexibility
    D. Testability

Answer: B

17. The effort required to modify a part of software is called as
    A. Maintainability
    B. Portability
    C. Flexibility
    D. Testability

Answer: C

18. The effort required to find out and correct mistakes in a product is called as
    A. Maintainability
    B. Portability
    C. Flexibility
    D. Testability

Answer: A

19. All of the following are examples of product transition metrics, except
    A. Maintainability
    B. Portability
    C. Reusability
    D. Interoperability

Answer: A

20. The effort required to transfer the software product from one environment to another is referred as
    A. Maintainability
    B. Portability
    C. Reusability
    D. Interoperability

Answer: B

21. The extend is to which a product can be couple with another product is referred as
    A. Maintainability
    B. Portability
    C. Reusability
    D. Interoperability

Answer: D

22. Which of the following activities of a measurement process are in order?

A. Plan, Collect, Analyze, Interpret, Circulate, Feedback, Improvement

B. Collect, Plan, Analyze, Interpret, Circulate, Feedback, Improvement

C. Plan, Collect, Analyze, Circulate, Interpret, Feedback, Improvement

D. Plan, Collect, Analyze, Interpret, Circulate, Improvement, Feedback

Answer: A

23. Which of the following measure attempted to tie physical, syntactical objects, and psychological measurements together with a set of definitions?

A. Halstead measure
B. Cyclomatic measure
C. McCabe measure
D. McCabe unique path measure

Answer: A

24. In GQM paradigm, Q stands for?

A. Quantitative
B. Qualitative
C. Quality
D. Question

Answer: D

25. In GQM paradigm, M stands for?

A. Metrics
B. Measures
C. Maintainability
D. Mute

Answer: A

26. In GQM paradigm, G stands for?

A. Goat
B. Get
C. Goal
D. Government

Answer: C

27. McCall's quality factors concentrate on the following aspects of a product except

A. Product operation
B. Product orientation
C. Product transition
D. Product support

Answer: D

28. All the following are examples of operational aspects of a product, except

A. Correctness
B. Reliability
C. Portability
D. Usability

Answer: C

29. All the following are examples of revisional characteristics of a product, except

A. Correctness
B. Testability
C. Maintainability
D. Flexibility

Answer: A

30. All of the following are examples of adaptability characteristics of a product, except

A. Portability
B. Reusability
C. Maintainability
D. Interoperability

Answer: C

31. The extent to which software product perform its intended function is called as

A. Integrity
B. reusability
C. Maintainability
D. Reliability

Answer: D

32. Which of the following indicates how software product is protected from unauthorized usage?

A. Integrity
B. Reusability
C. Maintainability
D. Reliability

Answer: A

PART B (Answer in one or two lines)

1. Define the term measurement.
2. Define the term software measurement.
3. Define the term unit of measurement.
4. Why do we measure software?
5. List down the characteristics of effective measurement program?
6. List down various types of measure.
7. What are direct measures?
8. What are indirect measures?
9. What are true performance measures?
10. What are substitute performance measures?
11. List down the various activities of a measurement process.
12. Define the term metrics?
13. Define software metrics.
14. Draw a simple diagram depicting the relationship between measure and metrics.
15. What is Black Box Metrics?
16. What is White Box Metrics?
17. Define cyclomatic measure.
18. Write notes on Productivity Metrics.

19. Write notes on product revision and its metrics.
20. Write notes on product transition and its metrics.
21. Name the metrics that are applicable to analysis phase of a project?

PART C (Descriptive type)

1. Give some examples in our life scenario where we use various measurements?
2. Why to measure software?
3. Discuss types of measurement in detail.
4. Characteristics of effective measurement program in detail.
5. Discuss the measurement and metrics indicators.
6. Discuss various activities of a measurement process.
7. Discuss Halstead measure in detail.
8. Discuss GQM paradigm of metrics in detail with an example.
9. Discuss the details of Process Metrics.
10. Discuss McCall's quality factors in detail with example.
11. Write notes on metrics of a design phase.
12. Discuss resource metrics in detail.
13. What are all the characteristics of a Good Metrics? Discuss in detail.
14. Discuss Kaner and Bond's evaluation framework for metrics.
15. Discuss metrics related with maintenance activities of a project.
16. Discuss the metrics of testing phase of a project.

Section 5:
Software Metrics and Estimation

10

LOC, Function Point, and Object-oriented Metrics

CHAPTER COVERAGE

1. *Introduction*
2. *Lines of Code*
3. *Function Point Count (FP Estimation)*
4. *Extended Function Point Metrics*
5. *Object-oriented Metrics*
6. *Demarco's System Bang*

10.1 INTRODUCTION

The metrics and measures used in software domain are quite different from that in traditional industries. The ways how the bigness or complexity of a software system is depicted are quite different from how it is done in other industries like civil or manufacturing etc. In this chapter, we will discuss the various measurement and metrics in the software along with a special focus on the object oriented metrics.

10.2 LINES OF CODE

Lines of code (LOC) specifically include all lines containing program headers, declarations, and executable and non-executable codes in a software program. Source LOC (SLOC) are software metrics that are used to measure the size of a software program by just counting the number of lines in the source code of the program. SLOC are used to predict (approximate) the efforts required to write the code and are also used to estimate the maintainability hours after the code is written.

10.2.1 Types of SLOC Measures

Refer Figure 10.1 that depicts the following SLOC types:

1. Physical SLOC (PLOC)
2. Logical SLOC (LLOC)
3. Comment SLOC (CLOC)
4. Reused SLOC (RLOC)

PLOC is a count of lines in the text of the physical source code including comment lines, declarations, and blank lines.

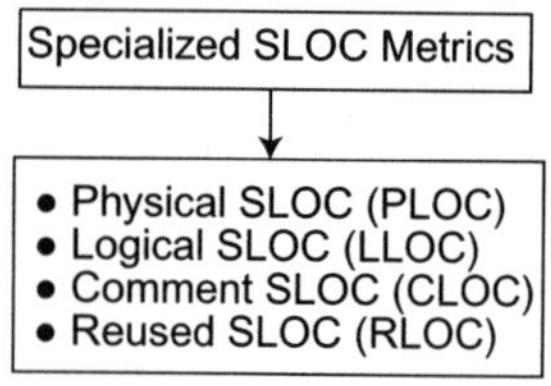

Figure 10.1 Specialized SLOC Metrics

LLOC is a count of lines of only the executable "statements." Lines of the comments, declarations, and blank lines are not counted for this purpose. This definition varies with computer language because the meaning of the "executable statements" varies across computer language. LLOC is a widely used concept for various LOC estimations.

CLOC is a count of lines consisting of only the comments in the source code. Codes written without any comments are considered as poor code. Good codes tend to have appropriate comments.

RLOC is the count of lines reused in the particular code, which will not be counted for calculating the efforts. People encouraged writing and using the reusable code, which saves lot of efforts during the development process.

POINTS TO PONDER

PLOC is a count of lines in the text of the physical source code including comment lines, declarations, and blank lines. LLOC is a count of lines of the only executable "statements". Lines of the comments, declarations, and blank lines are not counted for this purpose.

Let us see an example (C program):

```
1. /* Beginning of the for loop */
2. for (i = 50; i < 0; i -= 1)
3. {
4. printf("Hai Students");
5. }
6. /* End of the for loop */
```

Physical SLOC is represented by PLOC.

LLOC is represented by LLOC.

Comment SLOC is represented by CLOC.

How many total LOC are there in the above program?

How many executable LOC are there in the above program?

How many comments LOC are there in the above program?

PLOC = 6 (totally there are six lines – Lines 1–6)

LLOC = 2 (totally there are two executable lines – Lines 2 and 4)

CLOC = 2 (totally there are two comments line – Lines 1 and 6)

FORTRAN and Assembler are line-oriented languages in which the LOC concepts are used effectively.

Various widely used LOC measurements along with meaning are given in Table 10.1.

Table 10.1 LOC Measurement and Meanings

Measurement	Meaning
KLOC	1000 lines of code
KDLOC	1000 delivered lines of code
KSLOC	1000 source lines of code
MLOC	1,000,000 lines of code
GLOC	1,000,000,000 lines of code

10.2.2 Advantages of the Line of Code Measure

1. Easy to learn
2. Easy to measure (scope of automated counting)
3. Easy to report and check
4. Complex formulas not used
5. Repeatability is possible
6. Measurement easily automatable

Since it is easy to calculate, easy to measure and easy to report (refer Figure 10.2), even junior people can use LOC for estimation purposes.

10.2.3 Drawbacks of the Line of Code Measure

1. There is no standard definition of what is LOC – There are different versions of measurement.
2. Functionality of the code not taken into consideration for the calculation. This is the big drawback of LOC.

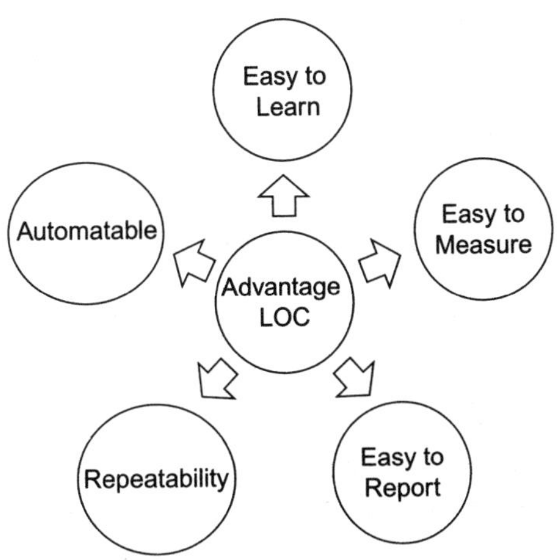

Figure 10.2 Advantages of LOC

3. Skilled coders can develop the same code with less lines (as per LOC, they are considered as less productive, which is not correct).
4. Developer who produce more lines does not mean productive.
5. Complexity of the code is not taken into the consideration (complex code may be written in few lines but may take longer time to code).
6. LOC is non-comparable across languages (Java program LOC is not comparable with C language LOC).
7. Estimates based on LOC can adversely go wrong because LOC is not a direct measure of functionality or productivity.
8. If LOC is used for measurements, people may add junk code *j* to increase LOC which may not add any value to anybody.
9. Low utility as sizing measure.

Constructive cost model (COCOMO) and other series of models by Barry Boehm et al. use SLOC as an input parameter. We will be discussing this model (COCOMO) in detail in the later part of this chapter.

LOC should not be used to measure the software productivity.

> *"Measuring software productivity by lines of code is like measuring progress on an airplane by how much it weights."*
>
> — Bill Gates

10.3 FUNCTION POINT COUNT (FP ESTIMATION)

Introduction: Function points (FPs) measure software size by quantifying the functionality provided to the user based solely on logical design and functional specifications. Note: LOC does not consider the functionality of the code. FPs are often preferred over SLOC. It has gained acceptance in terms of productivity (e.g., FP/year) and quality (defects/FP). The International Function Point Users Group (IFPUG) counting practices committee (http://www.ifpug.org) is the de facto standard for counting methods. Function point analysis (FPA) has been around since the late 1970s and is still used by many organizations.

POINTS TO PONDER

Function points (FPs) measure software size by quantifying the functionality provided to the user based solely on logical design and functional specifications.

10.3.1 Function Point Analysis

FPA is a method of quantifying the size and complexity of a software system in terms of the functions that the system delivers to the user. FPA is independent of the computer language, development methodology, technology, or capability of the project team used to develop the application.

10.3.2 Function Point History

1. It was developed by Allan Albrecht in the late 1970s while working at IBM.
2. The FP counting manual was produced by IBM's GUIDE organization in the early 1980s.
3. The IFPUG was founded in the late 1980s and produced its own Counting Practices Manual.
4. In 1994, IFPUG produced Release 4.0 of its Counting Practices Manual.
5. The Function Point Counting Practices Manual 4.1 was released in 1999.

10.3.3 Objectives of Function Point Counting

1. Measure functionality that the user requests and receives (which is not part of LOC).
2. Simple enough to minimize the overhead of the measurement process.
3. A consistent measure among various projects and organizations.

10.3.4 The Function Point Estimation Process Steps

In FP, only logical files are internal (because it is internal to the system). Input is called as external input (EI) (since the input is coming external to the system). Output is called as external output (EO). Inquiries are called as external queries. Interface files are called as external interface file (EIF) (refer Figure 10.3).

Internal logical files (ILFs) and EIFs are called as data functions. Others (EIs, EOs, and external inquiries) are called as transactional functions.

- Data functions
  - ILFs
  - EIFs
- Transactional functions
  - EIs
  - EOs
  - External inquiries

Process steps (refer Figure 10.4):

Stage 1: Compute the unadjusted function points (UFPs).
Stage 2: Compute the total degree of influence (TDI) for the project (TDI varies between 0 and 70)
Stage 3: Compute the number of FPs:

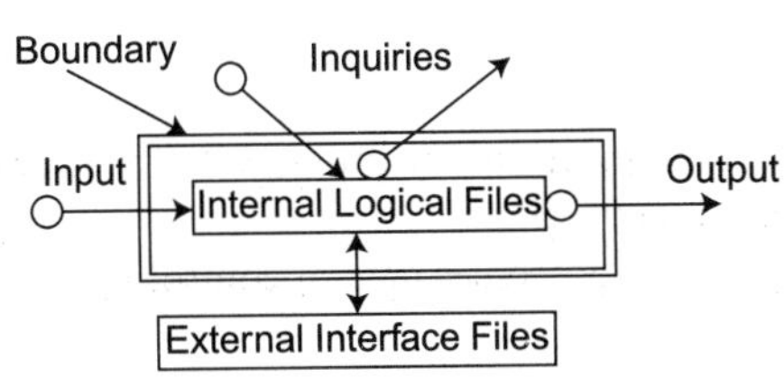

Figure 10.3 Function Point (FP) Analysis

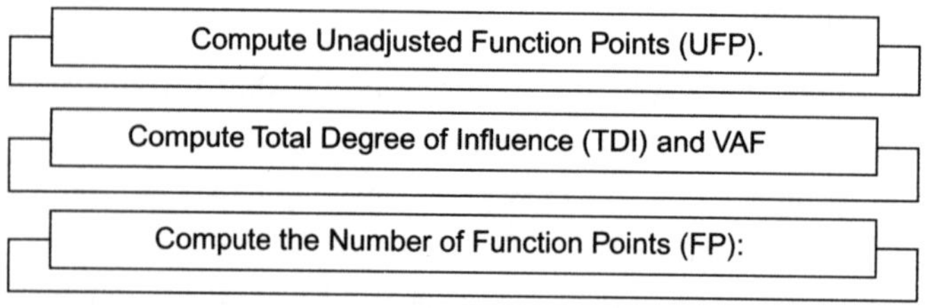

Figure 10.4 Function Point Process Steps

10.3.4.1 Step 1: Compute the unadjusted function point (UFP) count

The UFP count reflects the specific countable functionality provided to the user by the project or the application. The UFP calculation is broken into two categories with five sub-categories:

- Data functions
  - ILFs
  - EIFs
- Transactional functions
  - EIs
  - EOs
  - External inquiries

Count Data Functions:

Data functions (the functionality provided to the user) are either ILFs or external logical files (ELFs).

An ILF is a user identifiable group of logically related data or control information maintained within the boundary of the application.

An EIF is a user identifiable group of logically related data or control information referenced by the application, but maintained within the boundary of another application. It resides entirely outside the application. It is maintained by another application. It is an ILF for another application.

Assign each identified ILF and EIF a functional complexity based on the number of data element types (DETs) and record element types (RETs) associated with the ILF or EIF.

DET is a unique user recognizable field from a business perspective which participates in a transaction or is stored on a logical data file. RET is a user recognizable subgroup of data elements within an ILF or EIF (orders types).

Count Transactional Functions:

Transactional functions represent the functionality provided to the user to process data. Transactional functions are EIs, EOs, or external inquiries.

An EI is an elementary process that processes data or control information that comes from outside the application's boundary.

Examples for EI:

1. Data input screen
2. Another application
3. Business data: does update ILF
4. Control data: does not update ILF

An EO is an elementary process that sends data or control information outside the application's boundary.

Examples for EO:

1. Creates reports
2. Creates output files sent to other applications
3. Created from ILF and ELF

An external inquiry (EQ) is an elementary process that sends data or control information outside the application boundary. It is an elementary process with both input and output components that result in data retrieval from one or more ILF and ELF

1. EQ is sent outside the application boundary
2. It is an input process that does not update ILF
3. The output side does not contain derived data

Assign each identified EI, EO, and EQ a functional complexity based on the number of file types referenced (FTRs) and DETs.

Example:
In a particular development program, we have five data functions (two ILFs and one EIFs), 13 transaction functions (three EI, four EO, six external queries).

Table 10.2 represents its complexity split up.

Table 10.2 Components Versus Complexity

	Number of Components		
Components Vs Complexity	Simple	Average	Complex
External Input (EI)	2	0	1
External Output (EO)	0	2	2
External Query (EQ)	2	1	3
Internal Logical files (ILF)	2	0	2
External interface Files (EIF)	0	0	0

Table 10.3 represents the Table 10.2 along with the weighting factor of complexity calculating UFP.

Table 10.3 Complexity Weighing Factor

Software System Components	Complexity level									Total UFP
	Simple			Average			Complex			
	Count	Weight Factor	Points	Count	Weight Points	Points	Count	Weight Factor	Points	
	A	B	C= AxB	D	E	F= DxE	G	H	I= GxH	
External Input (EI)	2	3	6	---	4	---	1	6	6	12
External Output (EO)	---	4	---	2	5	10	2	7	14	24
External Query (EQ)	2	3	6	1	4	4	3	6	18	28
Internal Logical files (ILF)	2	7	14	---	10	---	2	15	30	44
External interface Files (EIF)	---	5	---	---	7	7	1	10	10	10
Total UFP										118

10.3.4.2 Step 2: Compute total degree of influence and value adjustment factor

The VAF indicates the general functionality provided to the user of the application. The VAF is comprised of 14 general system characteristics (GSCs) that assess the general functionality of the application. Each characteristic has associated descriptions that help determine the degree of influence (DI) of the characteristic. The degrees of influence range on a scale from 0 to 5, from no influence to strong influence.

Evaluate each of the 14 GSCs on a scale from 0 to 5 (refer Table 10.4) to determine the DI. Add the degrees of influence for all 14 GSCs to produce the TDI.

Insert the TDI in the following equation to produce the VAF.

$$VAF = (TDI \times 0.01) + 0.65$$

Table 10.4 Value Adjustment Factor and Degree of Influence

		0 – No influence, 5 – Strong Influence
S.No.	**Value Adjustment Factors**	**Degree of Influence**
1	Data communication	0 1 2 3 4 5
2	Distributed data processing	0 1 2 3 4 5
3	Performance	0 1 2 3 4 5
4	Heavily used configurations	0 1 2 3 4 5
5	Transaction rate	0 1 2 3 4 5
6	Online data entry	0 1 2 3 4 5
7	End-user efficiency	0 1 2 3 4 5
8	Online update	0 1 2 3 4 5
9	Complex processing	0 1 2 3 4 5
10	Reusability	0 1 2 3 4 5
11	Installation ease	0 1 2 3 4 5
12	Operational ease	0 1 2 3 4 5
13	Multiple sites	0 1 2 3 4 5
14	Facilitate change	0 1 2 3 4 5

In our previous example, the following VAF is calculated if there are two degrees of influence for each of the 14 GSC descriptions (2×14).

$$\text{VAF} = (28 \times 0.01) + 0.65$$
$$\text{VAF} = 0.93$$

10.3.4.3 Step 3: Calculate the function point

The FP count is calculated using a specific formula for a development project, enhancement project, or application (system baseline) FP count.

$$\text{FP} = (\text{UFP} + \text{CFP}) \times (0.65 + 0.01 \times \text{TDI})$$
$$\text{FP} = (\text{UFP} + \text{CFP}) \times \text{VAF}$$

CFP is the UFPs added by the conversion UFP count.

The development project FP calculation consists of three components of functionality: application functionality included in the user requirements for the project, conversion functionality included in the user requirements for the project, and application VAF.

Development project FP formula:

DFP = (UFP + CFP) × VAF
DFP is the development project FP count.
UFP is the UFP count for the functions that will be available after installation.
CFP is the UFPs added by the conversion UFP count.
VAF is the value adjustment factor.

10.3.5 Uses of Function Points

FPs are used to measure productivity (e.g., number of FPs achieved per work hour expended), to measure quality (e.g., rate of change, completeness), financial measurement (e.g., cost per FP), maintenance measurement (e.g., maintainability).

10.3.5.1 Function point for productivity

Hours per function point It measures the number of hours required to develop one FP.

Total number of project hours/ number of FP delivered.

Information technology productivity It is the overall productivity of the IT department.

Total FPs/total IT work effort

Delivered functionality and Development functionality Indicate how much functionality was actually delivered to the end user in relation to the rate of productivity of the developed functionality.

Total cost/total functionality delivered.
Total development effort hours/total functionality developed in-house.

10.3.5.2 Function point for quality measurement

Functional requirement size It measures the total number of functions requested by end user expressed in terms of FPs. The calculation derives the FPs required by a requesting user organization.

Completeness It measures the functionality delivered versus the functionality originally requested.

Rate of change It measures the calendar time to deliver the required software solution to the end user (number of FP/elapsed calendar time).

Defect removal efficiency Formula for defect removal efficiency = (total number of defects found prior to delivery/ total number of defects).

Defect density It measures the number of defects identified across one or more phases of the development project life cycle and compares that value with the total size of application. Formula for defect density = (total number of defects/total number of FPs).

Test case coverage It measures the number of test cases that are necessary to adequately support thorough testing of a development project. The formula for test case coverage = (number of test cases/total number of FPs).

Volume of documentation It measures or estimates the number of pages produced or anticipated in support of the development effort. The formula for volume of documentation = (number of pages/total number of FPs).

10.3.5.3 Function point for Financial Measurement

Cost per function point It identifies the cost for each FP developed. The formula for cost per FP = (total cost/total FPs).

Repair cost ratio It is used to track the costs to repair applications that are operational. It is commonly used as a monitoring metric for newly installed applications. The formula for repair cost ratio = ((total hours to repair × cost per hours)/release FP).

10.3.5.4 Function point for maintenance measurement

Maintainability It measures the cost required to maintain an application. The formula for maintainability = (maintenance cost/application FPs).

Reliability It measures the number of failures an application experience relative to its function size. The formula for reliability = Number of production failures/total application FP.

Assignment scope It measures the number of FTE resources required to support an application. The formula for assignment scope = total application FPs/number of full-time resources required to support the application.

Rate of growth It measures the growth of an application's functionality over the specific period of time. The formula for rate of growth = (current number of FPs/original number of FP).

Backfire value It is the number of LOC factored by a language complexity multiplier to derive the number of FPs.

Stability ratio It is used to monitor how effectively an application or enhancement has met the expectations of the user (base on the number of changes that were required during the first 60 to 90 days of production). The formula for stability ratio = (number of changes/number of application FPs).

Discussion Questions

1. How can we use maintenance measurement in a project?
2. How can we use FP for financial measurement?

POINTS TO PONDER

FPs are used to measure productivity (e.g., number of FPs achieved per work hour expended), to measure quality (e.g., rate of change, completeness), financial measurement (e.g., cost per FP), maintenance measurement (e.g., maintainability).

Exercise 10.1

PIMS is a basic Project Invoice Management system that is planned to serve a business employing 5000 people

The system is planned to have interfaces to the company's other software packages: attendance system, which tracks attendance of all the people allocated to the project and project system, which tracks all the projects executed by the business (company). Report-MASTER is planned to produce several reports and online queries.

Table 10.5 reveals the analysis of various systems and complexity.

Table 10.5 Components Vs Complexity

	Number of Components		
Components Vs Complexity	**Simple**	**Average**	**Complex**
External Input (EI)	2	0	1
External Output (EO)	1	2	2
External Query (EQ)	2	1	2
Internal Logical files (ILF)	2	1	0
External interface Files (EIF)	0	1	1

Calculate FP of the system using the same complexity factor defined above for the components considering the value adjusted factor as 1.3.

10.3.6 Benefits of FPA

1. Improves return on IT investments
2. Improves the estimating process
3. Communication of workload happens clearly
4. Improves the understanding of business functions
5. Improves traceability of requirements through implementation
6. Improves the allocation of resources and reduces overtime

10.3.7 Drawback of FPA

1. The calculation of function counts tends to take a black box view of the system.
2. Accurate counting requires certified FP specialists.
3. The user-defined function types may not be wholly appropriate for the current technology.
4. The classification of the user function types into simple, average, and complex appears to be oversimplified.
5. The choice of weights was determined by debate and trial.
6. The restriction to 14 processing complexity factors is not going to be satisfactory all time. What if a new complexity factor is to be factored in?
7. The calculation logic is more subjective and may vary from person to person.
8. There are about 20 variations of FP logics available in the market.

10.4 EXTENDED FUNCTION POINT METRICS

There are lot of metrics (refer Figure 10.5) which are called extended FP metrics which are the modified versions of FPs (e.g., include use case points (UCPs), object points, feature points, and story points).

10.4.1 Use Case Points

Use case points (UCPs) allow the estimation of an application's size and effort from its use cases. UCPs are based on the number of actors, scenarios, and various technical and environmental factors in the use case diagram. The UCP's estimation method was introduced by Gustav Karner and can be implemented using a spreadsheet.

The UCP equation is based on four variables:

- Technical complexity factor (TCF)
- Environment complexity factor (ECF)
- Unadjusted use case points (UUCP)
- Productivity factor (PF)

UCP = TCP × ECF × UUCP × PF

The UCP's method has produced estimates close to actual effort in several projects. This indicates that the UCP's method may support expert knowledge when a use case model for the project is available. Some tailoring to the company may be useful to obtain maximum benefits from the method.

10.4.2 Object Points

Object points (alternatively named application points) are an alternative function-related measure to FPs when 4Gls or similar languages are used for development.

The number of object points in a program is a weighted estimate of

- The number of separate screens that are displayed;
- The number of reports that are produced by the system;
- The number of program modules that must be developed to supplement the database code.

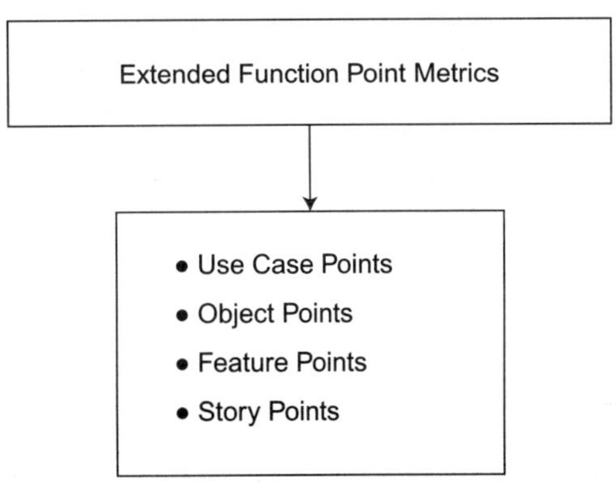

Figure 10.5 Extended Function Point Metrics Types

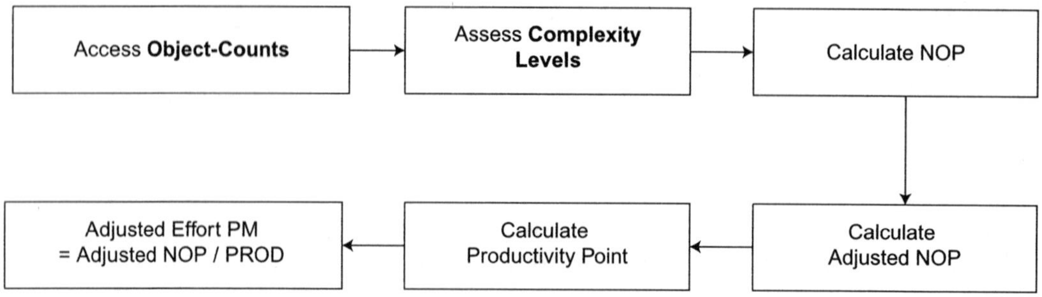

Figure 10.6 Object Point Estimation Procedure

Object Point Estimation Procedure:

Figure 10.6 depicts the object point estimation procedures.

1. Assess **object-counts** in the system: number of screens reports and 3GL.
2. Assess the complexity level for each object (use table): simple, medium, and difficult.
3. Calculate new object points (NOP) the **object-point count** of the system: add all weights for all object instances.
4. Estimate the percentage of reuse and compute the adjusted NOP "to be developed."
5. Determine the productivity rate PROD (use metrics table).
6. Compute the adjusted effort PM (person-month) = adjusted NOP/PROD

Object points are easier to estimate from a specification than FPs as they are simply concerned with screens, reports, and programming language modules. They can therefore be estimated at a fairly early point in the development process. At that stage, it is very difficult to estimate the number of LOC in a system.

Example:
Table 10.6 indicates the results of assessment of a software system.

Table 10.6 Complexity Table

	Complexity		
	Simple	**Meidum**	**Difficult**
Screen	2	0	1
Report	1	2	2
Language	2	1	2

Twenty percent of the objects could be supplied from previously developed components. Lets compute the estimated effort "PMs" needed to develop the system.

Object counts:

Table 10.7 NOP – Object Count

	NOP			
	Simple	Medium	Difficult	Total
Screen	2*1 = 2	0*2 = 0	1*3 = 3	5
Report	1*3 = 3	2*5 = 10	2*8 = 16	29
Language	2*5 = 10	1*8 = 8	2*10 = 20	38
			Total	72

NOP is calculated (refer Table 10.7) by the sum of the individual complexity factors of each of the screen, report, and language.

Adjusted NOP:

= NOP × (1 – % reuse/100)
= 72 × (1 – 20/100)
= 72 × (0.8)
= 58
For high productivity (metric table): PROD = 25 OP/P–M
Estimated effort PM = Adjusted NOP/PROD = 58/25 = 2.32 PMs.

10.4.3 Feature Point Estimation

The feature point measure accommodates the applications in which the algorithmic complexity is high. For more complex systems, the feature point count is 20–35% higher than the count determined using FPs alone. Algorithm is extra measurement added in feature point estimation compared with FP estimation. An algorithm is defined as a bounded computational problem that is included within a specific computer program. The feature point metric was so named because telecommunications software engineers used the term "feature" for major functions being developed for switching systems. (The author, Capers Jones, had worked on telecommunications systems).

Only single weight value is used for each measurement as shown in Table 10.8.

Table 10.8 Feature Point Estimation – Component versus Factor

Feature Point Estimation	
Component	Feature Point Factor
User Input	4
User Output	5
User Inqueries	4
Files	7
External Interfaces	7
Algorithms	3

The overall feature point is calculated using the feature point factor along with the adjustment factor (as per FP).

10.4.4 Story Point Sizing

A story point is actually a measure of complexity, and this is used in relative estimation techniques of agile projects to size its story. Story is in the form of a card called as story card in which the requirement is written in the form of a story. Story point is not a direct measure of the estimates (similar to FP) and is a relative measurement.

If we have two user stories with story point 1 and 4, it means that the second story is four times complex than the first user story. User story with story point 3 is three times complex than user story with point 1.

But we need to first baseline a story, which all in the team can relate to for sizing other stories.

Take an example: a team has three user stories to estimate:

1. A login screen is to be developed
2. A screen for entering customer data is required.
3. A mailing module will send periodic mails to the customers.

All the team members are very clear about what they need to do in the customer data entry screen (second story). So they took it as the baseline and assigned it the story point of 6 (any arbitrary number). Then when they started estimating the login screen (first story), they found that the login screen validations and functionalities are simpler than the customer data entry screen (second story), and thus they assigned it a number 2 (relative to the customer data entry screen story point). This means the team agrees that the customer data screen (second story) is three times more complex than the login screen (first story). And so, on this way, all the user stories are estimated relative to the baselined story point.

So, we measure complexity using story point, but in order to calculate the effort we need consider the person who will implement the story along with the complexity factor. Remember that for every team, story size could mean different things depending on what baseline they chose. If two teams are given exactly the same set of stories, one can say their total story point estimate is 41 and the other can say 14. It depends on what numbers they chose. That means the story point of one project is not comparable with the story point of another project.

10.4.4.1 Story points measurement

Agile estimation uses nonlinear scale for story points. As we have discussed, story points are a relative number of complexities. Some people use the numbers 1 to 10. Some people use the numbers 10 to 100. We need not only assign numbers to story point. Some innovative people assign T-shirt sizes to story points, say S, M, L, XL, XXL, XXL, etc. Some people use Fibonacci series numbers to story points (0, 1, 1, 2, 3, 5, 8, 13, 21 etc). Some people use a variety of animal names for user stories (cat, dog, lion, and elephant) to indicate dog is bigger than cat, lion is bigger than dog, and elephant is the biggest.

10.4.4.2 Planning poker

Planning poker provides an excellent way of estimation and is the most widely used estimation technique of agile projects. It is simple, makes fun, and results in reliable estimates. Table 10.9 indicates the story point estimated by different estimators at Round 1 and Round 2.

Table 10.9 Planning Poker Steps

Estimator	Round 1	Round 2
Anand	2	5
Balai	1	5
Shrikrishna	4	5
Manas	10	6

Rules for planning poker: Every team member (estimators) is given a card (which has numbers). The client reads the story which needs to be sized, with explanations required if any. All the team members (estimators) choose a card but did not show it to others. Then, the client asks the estimators to show the card and everybody shows the card at a time. Customer goes through the story points chosen by different estimators for the same story, and the disagreement in story point is resolved in the following ways:

- Reaching consensus with discussion
- Go with majority
- Go with high estimates
- Go with average after few rounds
- Three point estimates

A veteran team of expert estimators performing this task will reach consensus very quickly.

From Table 10.9, if we want to go with majority, then we can select 5. If we want to go with high estimates (safety side), we can select 6. Sometimes we can go with averaging all the estimates.

We can also choose three point estimations (PERT estimation) for resolving disagreements.

Choose the highest estimation (pessimistic) and choose the lowest estimation (optimistic).

Calculate the average of the remaining (most likely). Use PERT formula to calculate the estimation.

PERT estimation = (optimistic + 4 × most likely + pessimistic)/6

10.4.4.3 Velocity

Velocity is the sum of story points delivered by a team per cycle of the iteration (sprint). Sprint is usually time boxed. So we can say, velocity is the story points delivered for a period of time; it indirectly indicates the amount of work delivered by the team over a period of time. Period of time is usually 1–4 weeks, which is of normal sprint duration. Figure 10.7 depicts the relationship between velocity and various sprints.

Velocity actually changes with every iteration, and the team needs to recalculate its velocity at the end of each iteration in order to have a realistic estimation.

By comparing the velocity over a set of iterations (refer Figure 10.8), we can find out whether the team is getting faster or slower, and the customer expects the velocity to get improved over a period of time. Velocity is directly affected by the number of resources working on sprint.

Customer always expects the velocity to increase over a period of time but sudden increase in velocity is also a concern as it may be related to problem in the estimation (high estimation).

The velocity of two teams is not comparable as the estimation logic differs between teams (story point 1 in one team may be different in another team).Velocity is also proportional to the team composition; Experienced team member does more work in a given span of time and thereby velocity

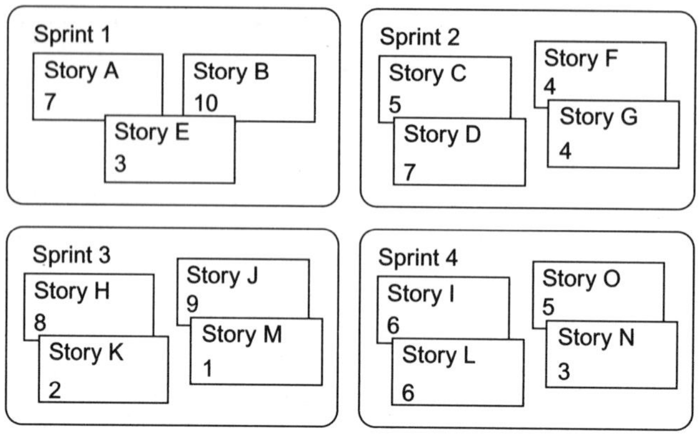

Figure 10.7 Velocity versus Sprints

Sprint	Velocity
Sprint 1	20
Sprint 2	30
Sprint 3	28
Sprint 4	32
Sprint 5	33
Sprint 6	35

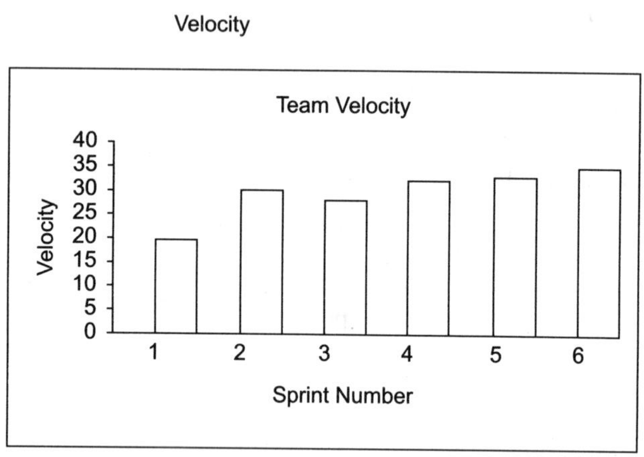

Figure 10.8 Velocity versus Sprint

increases. Lesser experienced team member does less work comparatively in the same span of time and thereby velocity decreases;. Velocity is expected to increase with team's tenure because the team gets mature and expected to execute more story points. Velocity is not a measure of productivity. We should not include bugs and rejected stories while calculating the velocity. Knowing and understanding the team's velocity helps to make commitments upfront and also with confidence. It also helps to select the story points that fit into the iteration. Customer also needs to help the team by doing proper prioritization of the story points.

10.5 OBJECT-ORIENTED METRICS

As the object-oriented (OO) paradigm began to spread throughout the software community during C++ and Java usages, people felt the need for the metrics based on objects and its characteristics rather than following traditional techniques.

Some of the specialized OO metrics constructs (factors) include:

1. Number of classes in the overall program
2. Weighted methods per class
3. Number of children per class
4. Depth of inheritance tree
5. Types of inheritance used in the overall program
6. Coupling between objects in the program
7. Types of methods used within the class
8. Number of variables used in the program
9. Number of similar variables used in the program
10. Duplication of class structures
11. Operating complexity
12. Attributes complexity
13. Reuse metrics like reusable class, reusable objects, etc.

10.5.1 Specialized OO Metrics

Some of the specialized OO metrics (refer Figure 10.9) include:

1. Chen metrics
2. Morris metrics:
3. MOOSE (metrics for OO system environments or metrics for OO software engineering). It is also called as "Chidamber and Kemerer – USA" metrics. It is also called as CK metrics.
4. MOOD (metrics for OO design). It is also called as "Abrieu – Portugal" metrics/AP metrics.
5. EMOOSE

10.5.1.1 Chen metrics

It uses (refer Table 10.10) the coupling, cohesion, and complexity metrics of objects.

Coupling: Degree of dependence among components. High coupling makes modifying parts of the system difficult, for example, modifying a component affects all the components to which the component is connected.

Cohesion: The degree to which all elements of a component are directed toward a single task and all elements directed toward that task are contained in a single component.

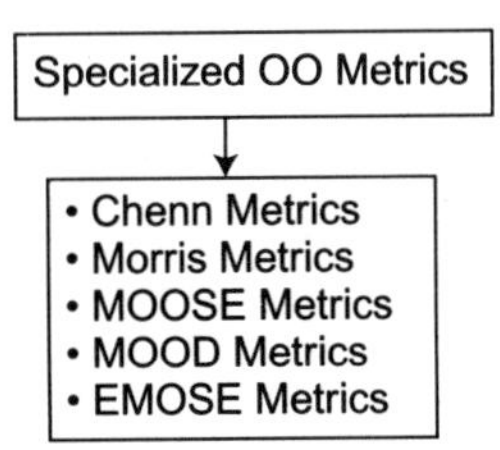

Figure 10.9 Specialized Object-Oriented Metrics Types

Table 10.10 Chen Metrics

Chen Metrics		
Coupling	**Cohesion**	**Complexity**
Class Coupling	Cohesion	Attribute Complexity
Opearing Coupling		Operating Complexity

It uses class coupling metrics (CCM) and operating coupling metrics (OCM). It uses cohesion metrics (CM). It uses attribute complexity metrics (ACM), operating complexity metrics (OXM). Reuse metrics is a Boolean metrics, with value of 0 or 1 indicating whether reusable objects are available or not available.

10.5.1.2 Morris metrics

Morris defined the complexity of the OO system in the form of the depth of the tree using subnodes. More subnodes indicate the system is more complex.

10.5.1.3 MOOSE metrics/CK metric suite

It consists of six metrics (refer Table 10.11).

1. Weighted methods per class (WMC):
2. Response for class (RFC)
3. Number of children for class (NOC)
4. Depth of inheritance tree (DIT):
5. Coupling between objects (CBO)
6. Lack of cohesion in methods (LCOM)

Table 10.11 Moose Metrics/CK Metrics

Moose Metrics/CK Metrics		
Class	**Coupling**	**Cohension**
Weighted methods per class	Coupling between Objects	Lack of Cohesion in Methods
Responce for Class		
Number of children for class		
Depth of Inheritance Tree		

WMC: This measures the complexity of the methods in a class. Complexity is determined based on the time to take to complete (write) the method and the technical difficulties involved in writing the method. A relative value is used to figure out the complexity of the methods so that all the methods inside the class are comparable. A high value of WMC indicates the class is more complex.

RFC: This measures the set of methods executed in response to the class execution and the number of messages received by the class in response to the class execution by the object of the class. A high value of RFC indicates the class is more complex and the testing efforts also increase.

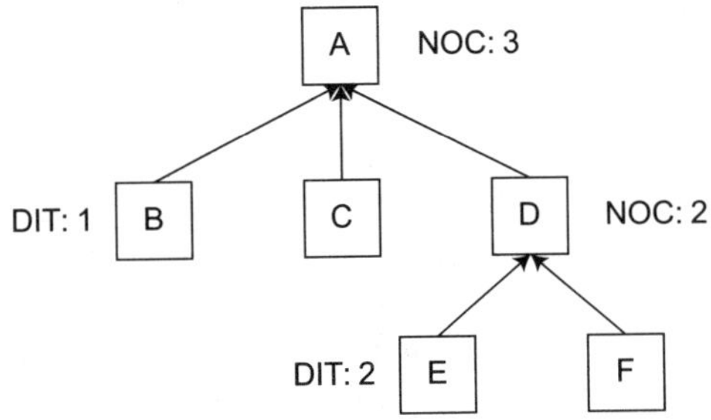

Figure 10.10 Number of Children for class - Depth of Inheritance Tree

NOC: This measures the number of subclasses (number of children) for a class (refer Figure 10.10) and also deals with method inheritance. Inheritance is a form of reuse, and if this number is greater it indicates greater potential for reuse. Higher number of NOC indicates that reuse also increases and it also indicates that testing efforts will increase.

DIT: This measure the length of the maximum path from root to the end node of the Tree (Refer Figure 10.10). It represents the complexity. Higher value of DIT (Depth of Inheritance Tree) indicates that more classes, methods are inherited which can also be considered as an indication of complexity.Higher DIT values may also indicate that many classes and methods are reused and hence more inheritence.

CBO: This measures the number of classes to which the specific class is coupled (linked to). Higher value indicates it as less attractive for reusing and also more sensitive to change as changing one class will affect the other coupled classes. When CBO increases, the reusability of the class decreases, and it also complicates the modifications. We need to keep CBO value of class as low as possible.

LCOM: This measures the number of disjoints method pairs minus the number of similar method pairs used. If LCOM increases, the coupling between methods increases and so the complexity.

10.5.1.4 Metrics for Object-Oriented Design Metrics

MOOD refers to a structural model of the OO paradigm (refer Table 10.12) using OO techniques like encapsulation, inheritance, polymorphism, and message passing. It used two main features of a class namely methods and attributes. Methods are the functions that are used to modify the status of the objects. Attributes are the status and characteristics of the objects.

Table 10.12 MOOD Metrics

MOOD Metrics			
Encapsulation	**Inheritance**	**Polymorphism**	**Message Passing**
Method Hiding	Method Inheritance	Polymorphism Factor	Message Coupling Factor
Attribute Hiding	Attribute inheritance		

Encapsulation metrics: Method hiding factor (MHF), attribute hiding factor (AHF). Inheritance Metrics: method inheritance factor (MIF), attribute inheritance factor (AIF). Polymorphism metrics: Polymorphism factor (PF). Message passing metrics: Coupling factor (CF).

MHF: It is defined as the ratio of the sum of the invisibilities of all methods defined in all classes to the total number of methods defined in the system under consideration.

AHF: It is defined as the ratio of the sum of the invisibilities of all attributes defined in all classes to the total number of attributes defined in the system under consideration.

MIF: It is defined as the ratio of the sum of the inherited methods in all classes of the system under consideration to the total number of available methods for all classes.

AIF: It is defined as the ratio of the sum of the inherited attributes in all classes of the system under consideration to the total number of available attributes for all classes.

PF: It is defined as the ratio of the actual number of possible different polymorphic situation for class to the maximum number of possible distinct polymorphic situations for class.

CF: It is defined as the ratio of the maximum possible number of couplings in the system to the actual number of couplings not imputable to inheritance.

10.5.1.5 Extended Metrics for Object-Oriented Software Engineering Metrics

Message and data coupling and data abstraction is considered here in this metrics which is not part of the original MOOSE metrics. In addition to the six metrics defined in MOOSE, the following five metrics are also used in the extended model bringing the total count of metrics to 11 – refer Table 10.13.

Table 10.13 EMOOSE Metrics

E-Moose Metrics		
Class	**Coupling**	**Cohension**
Weighted methods per Class	Coupling between Objects	Lack of Chohension in Methods
Response for Class	Message Pass Coupling	
Number of children for Class	Data Abstraction Coupling	Size 1 and size 2
Depth of Inheritance Tree		
Number of methods in class		

MMessage Pass Coupling (MPC): It means the number of messages that goes out of a particular Class during its operation.

Data Abstraction Coupling (DAC):- It is used to count the number of classes which are aggregated to the current class and involved in the current class data abstraction.

Number of methods (NOM): It is used to count the number of operations that are local to the class, i.e., only those class operations which can give the number of methods to measure it.

Size 1: It is used to find the number of LOC.

Size 2: It is used to count the number of local attributes and the number of operation defined in the class.

10.5.2 Advantages of OO Metrics

The main strengths of OO metrics are:

1. The OO metrics uses various OO terms which are understandable easily by the OO community.

2. The OO metrics distinguishes easy project versus complex projects.
3. The OO metrics are easily comparable across projects.
4. The OO metrics are easily related to the structure of the program (which is not possible with other metrics)

10.5.3 Disadvantages of OO Metrics

The main drawbacks of OO metrics are:

1. The OO metrics are not applicable for testing or maintenance and is applicable only for the development project.
2. The OO metrics are not supported by various estimating tools available in the market.
3. The OO metrics are unrelated to all other known software metrics and so converting OO metrics to FP or LOC is difficult.
4. The OO metrics do not deal with full life-cycle issues.

10.6 DEMARCO'S SYSTEM BANG

DeMarco suggested another measure of system size similar to FP and is called as System BANG. System specification document is divided into a number of functional primitives that are described as a trivial piece too small to justify further positioning. Values of functional primitives are further adjusted based on Halstead's volume/vocabulary relationship. Each functional primitive is given an empirical complexity correction factor depending on the class of primitive function. DeMarco defined 16 classes of primitives. Each weighted functional primitive is multiplied by its complexity correction factor, and the resulting functional primitive values are summed to give total System BANG called as function BANG. DeMarco also suggest the users to define our own classes and complexity factor.

System BANG based on data objects: If the system is having significant database, then BANG of the system can be calculated from the objects in the database (refer Figure 10.11). Data Object is calculated for each of the System Object and then corrected/adjsuted based on the situation. Corrected

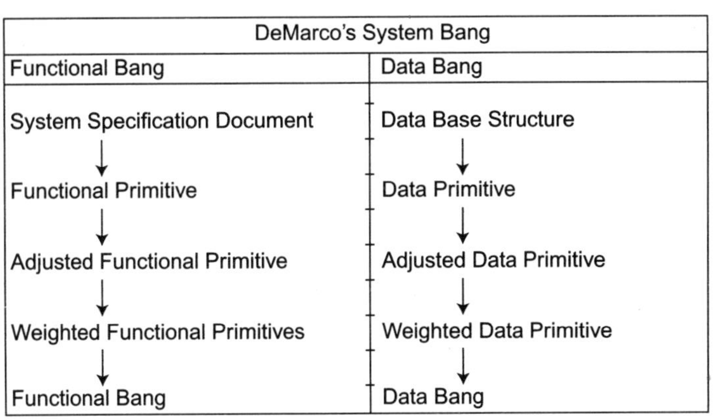

Figure 10.11 DeMarco's System BANG

objects are summed up to calculate Data Bang. For systems that are both data strong and function strong, two sets of BANG metrics are used. The two predictors (function BANG and data BANG) should not be combined.

System BANG is very easy to use when it is automated otherwise, it is very subjective in nature.

Discussion Questions

1. Compare and contrast LOC with FP estimation
2. Compare UCP and object point

Summary

- This chapter explains the concepts of LOC and FP estimation.
- LOC specifically include all lines containing program headers, declarations, and executable and non-executable codes in a software program. Since it is easy to calculate, easy to measure, and easy to report, even junior people can use LOC for estimation purpose. "Functionality of the Code" is not taken into consideration for the calculation of LOC.
- FPA is a method of quantifying the size and complexity of a software system in terms of the functions that the system delivers to the user. FPA is independent of the computer language, development methodology, technology, or capability of the project team used to develop the application.
- An object point (alternatively named application points) is an alternative function-related measure to FPs when 4GIs or similar languages are used for development.
- A story point is actually a measure of complexity, and this is used in relative estimation techniques of agile projects to size its story.
- Velocity is the sum of story points delivered by a team per cycle of the iteration (sprint).
- This chapter also discussed the following specialized OO metrics in detail: Chen metrics, Morris metrics, MOOSE metrics, MOOD metrics, and EMOOSE metrics. This chapter also discusses the Demarco's System BANG.

Answers to Exercise Questions

Exercise 10.1

PIMS is a basic project invoice management system that is planned to serve a business employing 5000 people.

Component analysis:

	Number of Components		
Components Vs Complexity	**Simple**	**Average**	**Complex**
External Input (EI)	2	0	1
External Output (EO)	1	2	2
External Query (EQ)	2	1	2
Internal Logical files (ILF)	2	1	0
External interface Files (EIF)	0	1	1

Calculate the FP of the system using the same complexity factor defined above for the components considering the value adjusted factor as 1.3.
FP calculation:

Software System Components	Complexity level									Total UFP
	Simple			Average			Complex			
	Count	Weight Factor	Points	Count	Weight Points	Points	Count	Weight Factor	Points	
	A	B	C= AxB	D	E	F= DxE	G	H	I= GxH	
External Input (EI)	2	3	6	---	4	---	1	6	6	12
External Output (EO)	1	4	4	2	5	10	2	7	14	28
External Query (EQ)	2	3	6	1	4	4	2	6	12	22
Internal Logical files (ILF)	2	7	14	1	10	10	-	15	-	24
External interface Files (EIF)	---	5	---	1	7	7	1	10	10	17
Total UFP										103

FP = 103 × 1.3 = 133.9

Model Questions
PART A (Objective type)

1. LOC specifically include all lines containing program headers, declarations, and executable and non-executable codes in a software program.

   A. True B. False

Answer: A

2. SLOC stands for:

   A. Structured LOC B. SLOC C. Size LOC D. Stable LOC

Answer: B

3. All of the following are types of SLOC, except:

   A. PSLOC B. LLOC C. CLOC D. Used SLOC

Answer: D

4. Count of lines in the text of the physical source code including comment lines, declarations, and blank lines is called as:

   A. PLOC B. LLOC C. CLOC D. RLOC

Answer: A

5. Count of lines of the only executable "statements" is called as:

   A. PLOC B. LLOC C. CLOC D. Reused SLOC

Answer: B

6. Count of lines consisting of only the comments in the source code is called as:

   A. Code SLOC B. Count SLOC C. CLOC D. Name SLOC

Answer: C

7. All of the following are the advantages of the LOC measure, except:

   A. Skilled coders can develop the same code with less lines

   B. Complex formulas are not used

   C. Repeatability is possible

   D. Measurement is easily automatable

Answer: A

8. LOC does not consider the functionality of the code.

   A. True B. False

Answer: A

9. This measures software size by quantifying the functionality provided to the user based solely on logical design and functional specifications.

   A. LOC B. Function point C. Object point D. Story point

Answer: B

10. FPA is independent of the computer language, development methodology, technology, or capability of the project team used to develop the application.

A. True B. False

Answer: A

11. Which of the following is not an objective of FP counting?

A. Measure functionality that the user requests and receives.

B. Simple enough to minimize the overhead of the measurement process

C. A consistent measure among various projects and organizations

D. Compute TDI for the project.

Answer: D

12. Data functions is a combination of

A. ILFs and EIFs B. EIs and EOs

C. ILFs and ELFs D. External inquiries and internal inquiries

Answer: A

13. A user identifiable group of logically related data or control information maintained within the boundary of the application is called as

A. ELF B. ILF C. Boundary data D. Boundary control information

Answer: B

14. User identifiable group of logically related data or control information referenced by the application, but maintained within the boundary of another application is called as

A. ELF B. ILF C. Boundary data D. Boundary control information

Answer: A

15. Unique user recognizable field from a business perspective which participates in a transaction or is stored on a logical data file is called as

A. RET B. DEA C. DET D. LDF

Answer: C

16. User recognizable subgroup of data elements within an ILF or EIF is called as

A. RET B. DEA C. DET D. LDF

Answer: A

17. EIs, EOs, or external inquiries are called as

A. Data functions B. Transactional functions

C. External functions D. Control functions

Answer: B

18. Which of the following is not an example of EI?

A. Data input screen B. Another application

C. Reports creation D. Business data

Answer: C

19. Elementary process that sends data or control information outside the application's boundary is called as EO.

A. True B. False

Answer: A

20. An elementary process that sends data or control information outside the application boundary is called as

A. EQ B. External files C. Internal inquiry D. External control

Answer: A

21. Which of the following is not true?

A. EQ is sent outside the application boundary

B. EQ is an input process that does not update ILF

C. Output side does not contain derived data

D. EQ is a data or control information that comes from outside the application's boundary

Answer: D

22. How many VAFs are available in FPA?

A. 4 B. 12 C. 14 D. 24

Answer: C

23. The correct formula for VAF is

A. VAF = (TDI × 0.02) + 0.65 B. VAF = (TDI × 0.10) + 0.65

C. VAF = (TDI × 0.01) + 0.45 D. VAF = (TDI × 0.01) + 0.65

Answer: D

24. Which of the following is not part of development FP component?

A. Application functionality B. Conversion functionality

C. Application VAF D. Conversional functionality adjustment factor

Answer: D

25. Which of the following is the formula for development FP?

A. DFP = (UFP + CFP) × VAF B. DFP = (UFP × VAF) + CFP

C. DFP = (UFP/VAF)+ CFP D. DFP = (UFP – CFP) × VAF

Answer: A

26. Which of the following is not the use of FPs?

A. It is used to measure productivity. B. Maintenance measurement

C. Financial measurement D. Operational measurement

Answer: D

27. This measures the total number of functions requested by end user expressed in terms of FPs.

A. FP B. Functional requirement size C. Reliability D. Maintainability

Answer: B

28. What is the formula for maintainability in terms of FPs?

A. Maintainability = Maintenance cost/application FPs

B. Maintainability = Application FPs/maintenance cost

C. Maintainability = Maintenance cost × application FPs

D. Maintainability = Maintenance cost + application FPs

Answer: A

29. What is the formula for reliability in terms of FPs?

A. Reliability = Number of production failures × total application FPs

B. Reliability = Number of production failures/total application FPs

C. Reliability = Number of production failures + total application FPs

D. Reliability = Total application FPs × number of production success

Answer: B

30. It measures the number of FTE resources required to support an application.

A. Assignment scope B. Rate of growth

C. Backfire value D. Support scope

Answer: A

31. It measures the growth of an application's functionality over the specific period of time

A. Functional scope B. Rate of growth C. Backfire value D. Support scope

Answer: B

32. What is the formula for rate of growth with respect to FPs?

A. Current number of FPs/original number of FP

B. Original number of FPs/current number of FP

C. Current number of FPs – original number of FP

D. Current number of FPs + original number of FP

Answer: A

33. It is the number of LOC factored by a language complexity multiplier to derive the number of FPs.

A. Functional scope B. Rate of growth

C. Backfire value D. Stability ratio

Answer: C

34. It is used to monitor how effectively an application or enhancement has met the expectations of the user (based on the number of changes that were required during the first 60–90 days of production).

A. Functional scope B. Rate of growth C. Backfire value D. Stability ratio

Answer: D

35. The formula for stability ratio:

A. Number of application FPs/number of changes

B. Number of changes/number of application FPs

C. Current number of FPs/original number of FP

D. Number of production failures/total application FPs

Answer: B

36. Which of the following is not a benefit of FPA?

A. Improves the understanding of business functions

B. Improves traceability of requirements through implementation

C. Improves the allocation of resources and reduces overtime

D. The calculation of function counts tends to take a black box view of the system.

Answer: D

37. Which of the following is not an example of extended FPs?

A. Line of points B. UCPs C. Object points D. Feature points

Answer: A

38. Which of the following allow the estimation of an application's size and effort from its use cases?

A. Line of points B. UCPs C. Object points D. Feature points

Answer: B

39. What the formula for UCP?

A. UCP = TCP × ECF × UUCP × PF

B. UCP = TCP + ECF + UUCP + PF

C. UCP = (TCP/ECF) × UUCP × PF

D. UCP = UUCP × PF

Answer: A

40. This measures and accommodates applications in which the algorithmic complexity is high.

A. Line of points B. UCPs C. Object points D. Feature points

Answer: D

41. It is actually a measure of complexity, and this is used in relative estimation techniques of agile projects.

A. Line of points B. UCPs C. Story points D. Feature points

Answer: C

42. Sum of story points delivered by a team per cycle of the iteration (sprint) is called as:

A. Total story points B. Velocity C. Delivery points D. Sprint points

Answer: B

43. Velocity actually changes with every iteration, and the team needs to recalculate its velocity at the end of each iteration.

A. True B. False

Answer: A

44. All of the following are examples of specialized OO metrics, except:

A. MOOSE metrics B. EMOOSE metrics C. MORRIS metrics D. EMORRIS metrics

Answer: D

45. CCM is used in:

A. Chen metrics B. Morris metrics C. MOOD metrics D. MOOSE metrics

Answer: A

46. Degree of dependence among components is called as

A. Coupling B. Cohesion

C. Degree of dependence D. Intracomponent dependency

Answer: A

47. A high value of WMC indicates the class is more complex.

A. True B. False

Answer: A

48. A high value of RFC indicates the class is more complex and the testing efforts also increase.

A. True B. False

Answer: A

49. Higher number of NOC indicates that reuse also increases and it also indicates that testing efforts will increase.

A. True B. False

Answer: A

50. This measures the length of the maximum path from root to the end of node of the tree:

A. CBO B. NOC C. DIT D. RFC

Answer: C

51. Increase in this Morris metrics indicates the decrease in reusability.

A. CBO B. NOC C. DIT D. LCOM

Answer: A

52. Increase in this Morris metrics indicates the increase in coupling and complexity.

A. CBO B. NOC C. DIT D. LCOM

Answer: D

53. Structural model of the OO paradigm is called as

A. MOOD B. MOOSE C. MORRIS D. CHEN

Answer: A

54. Total number of EMOOSE metrics is

A. 21 B. 11 C. 12 D. 5

Answer: B

PART B (Answer in one or two lines)

1. Write notes on LOC.
2. What are all the types of SLOC measures?
3. What is physical SLOC?
4. What is LLOC?
5. What is CLOC?
6. What is RLOC?
7. Write any three advantages of the LOC measure.
8. List down any three drawbacks of the LOC measure.
9. Write notes on FP count.
10. What is FPA?
11. What are all the objectives of FP counting?
12. List down three stages of FP calculation steps.
13. List down the various elements used in FPA.
14. What is data function and transactional function in FP?
15. Write notes on data functions.
16. Write notes on DET and RET related to FPs.
17. Write notes on transactional functions of FP.
18. What is EO related of FPA?
19. What is EQ related to FP?
20. What is VAF in FPA?
21. What is FP count? Give an example for its calculation.
22. Write notes on development project FP calculation.
23. What are all the uses of FPs?
24. Write notes on delivered functionality and development functionality.
25. What is functional requirement size?
26. How FP is used in financial measurement of projects?
27. What is maintainability and reliability with respect to FPs?
28. What is assignment scope with respect to FPs?
29. Write notes on "rate of growth" with respect to FPs.
30. What is backfire value and stability ratio with respect to FPs?
31. Write any three benefits of FPA?

32. Write any three drawbacks of FPA?
33. Write notes on extended FP metrics.
34. What is UCPs?
35. What are all the variables involved in UCP equation?
36. What is object points?
37. What is feature point estimation?
38. What is story point sizing?
39. Define Velocity.
40. Write notes on velocity versus sprints
41. What is OO metrics?
42. List down the various types of specialized OO metrics.
43. Write notes on Chen metrics.
44. What is coupling and cohesion?
45. Write the names of six Morris metrics.
46. Write notes on WMC Morris metrics.
47. Write notes on RFC Morris metrics.
48. Write notes on NOC Morris metrics.
49. Write notes on DIT Morris metrics.
50. Writes notes on CBO Morris metrics.
51. Write notes on LCOM Morris metrics.
52. Write notes on MOOD metrics.
53. What are all the MOOD metrics related to encapsulation?
54. What is MHF of mood metrics?
55. What is AHF of mood metrics?
56. What is MIF of mood metrics?
57. What is AIF of mood metrics?
58. What is PF of mood metrics?
59. What is DF of mood metrics?
60. What is EMOOSE metrics?
61. What are all the advantages of OO metrics?
62. What are all the disadvantages of OO metrics?
63. Write short notes on DeMarco's System BANG based on data objects.

PART C (Descriptive type)

1. Define four types of SLOC measure and explain it with an example.
2. Discuss the advantages of the LOC measure.
3. What are all the drawbacks of the LOC measure?
4. Compare and contrast LOC with FP?
5. List down three FP's estimation calculation steps and discuss the same in detail.
6. Explain data functions of FP in detail with examples.
7. Define transactional functions of FP in detail with examples.
8. Explain various VAFs of FP.
9. Discuss the uses of FPs in detail.
10. What are all the benefits of FPA?
11. What are all the drawbacks of FPA?
12. Discuss object point in detail.
13. Discuss the various extended FP metrics in detail.
14. Discuss story point sizing in detail with example.
15. What is planning poker? Discuss in detail.
16. What is OO metrics? List down specialized OO metrics factors?
17. What is Morris metrics? Discuss in detail.
18. Write notes on MOOSE metrics/CK metrics.
19. Discuss MOOD metrics in detail.
20. What are all the strengths and drawbacks of OO metrics?
21. Discuss various specialized OO metrics constructs (factors).
22. Discuss EMOOSE metrics in detail.
23. Write notes on velocity in detail.
24. Discuss Demarco's System BANG in detail.

Section 5:
Software Metrics and Estimation

11

Software Estimation Tools, Techniques and Models

CHAPTER COVERAGE

1. *Introduction*
2. *Definition of Estimation*
3. *Importance of Accurate Estimation*
4. *Efforts and Duration*
5. *Estimation Process*
6. *Basic Estimation Principles*
7. *Estimation Techniques*
8. *Estimating Styles*
9. *Precision versus Accuracy*
10. *Tools for Analyzing Metrics and Estimations*
11. *Project Cost Estimation*
12. *Earned Value Management*
13. *Other Concepts in Costing*

11.1 INTRODUCTION

Various types of estimations techniques are available for software engineers and project managers, which help them to do the software estimation precisely and accurately. Some of the estimation techniques are expert judgment, top down estimation, bottom-up estimation, analogous estimation, and parametric estimation. Various types of models are available for the estimations which can be directly used while estimating the software. In particular, cost estimation models are of great help for the estimators and are being used predominantly. Metrics are of no use if they are not analyzed correctly and hence, we need to understand various tools that are helpful in analysis of estimation.

11.2 DEFINITION OF ESTIMATION

To form an approximate notion of the amount, number, magnitude or position of anything, without actual enumeration or measurement.

– Oxford English Dictionary

To complete any activity in a planned manner the estimation is very important. For example, to arrive for an interview at a particular time, first estimate how long it will take to travel so as to plan the starting time accordingly. But this will be the case of estimate by guess and for a multi-million dollar software project to be executed in a planned manner, the estimate should be more accurate and thus needs to follow some scientific methodologies.

11.3 IMPORTANCE OF ACCURATE ESTIMATION

1. Inaccurate estimate may result in inefficient usage of resources,
2. Inaccurate estimate may result incorrect decision,
3. Inaccurate estimate may result in cost overrun, schedule overrun,
4. Inaccurate estimate may result in customer dissatisfaction, and
5. Inaccurate estimate may result in loss of faith and in turn loss of business from the customer.

Discussion Questions

Discuss the importance of accurate estimation with examples for the above points.

11.4 EFFORTS AND DURATION

In estimation process the difference between the efforts and duration should be very clear. Effort is the exact amount of work required for completing particular task. Duration is defined as the time elapsed between start and end of the particular task.

Example: For writing a particular piece of code, it requires 2 resources working for 10 h then overall estimation is 20 h but it will take 3 days to complete the task, which is the duration of the task.

Discrete Effort (DE): The concept of DE applies directly to the specific work efforts that can be directly traced and identified as having a direct tie to ultimate completion of the project-related work which is directly measurable.

Apportioned Effort (AE): The concept of AE applies not directly to the specific work efforts, but related to some other tasks apportioned here. For example, project management efforts for finishing a task.

Level of Effort (LOE): In project management, LOE is a support-type project activity that must be done to support other work activities or the entire project effort.

11.5 ESTIMATION PROCESS

It is the process (Figure 11.1) of calculating/forecasting/approximating the effort, time, and cost of completing project deliverables. Customer expectation along with various constraints and assumptions are also taken into consideration during the estimation process.

The task of balancing the stakeholder expectations and at the same time operating within the boundary of the project (constraints, assumptions) is crucial for the estimation process. Constraints limit various options available. For example, the customer wants to finish the project on a particular date is a constraint and the estimation is based on that. Number of resources is a constraint in the project because the project needs to finish only with the available resources. Assumptions are certain statements or actions or events which are considered to be true or false in deriving the estimate. An estimate is always a qualified guess based on assumptions. All estimation has its associated assumptions and it needs to be specified so that the basis of estimate is known to all the stakeholders of the project and can be validated. Lot of assumptions is made about the experience and skill set of the resources during the estimation process. It is assumed that all the resources are uniformly skilled; the customer will give the sign off on time. If the assumption goes wrong it creates adverse effect on the estimation. The estimation is right only when the assumption is right.

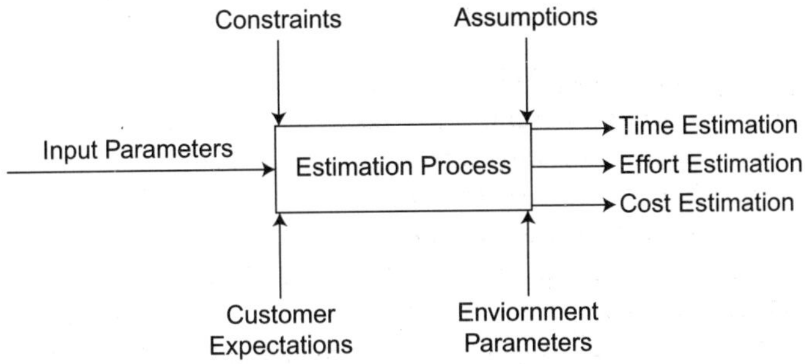

Figure 11.1 Estimation Process

Customer expectations are also to be considered while estimating the project. Customer expectations also keep on changing. Customer expectations are related to time, schedule, effort, and quality parameters of the project. Environment parameters include various environment-related factors that can affect the project which includes status of the project, risks involved in the estimation and the project, cost involved in the estimation, time involved in the estimation, difficulty of the estimation process, expertise availability for the estimation, etc.

11.5.1 Basic Steps in Software Estimation Process

Basic steps in software estimation process are described in Figure 11.2.

Identify the Project Objectives: The estimation process should be in line with the objective of the project. If the estimation is not in line, the measuring and estimating may be something which is of no use to the project. In particular, the objectives which are related to the context and requirements for the project are crucial to identifying during the estimation.

Identify the Objectives of the Estimation: It states what to achieve by estimation. Estimation objectives are identified based on project objectives, business objective, and technical team feedback

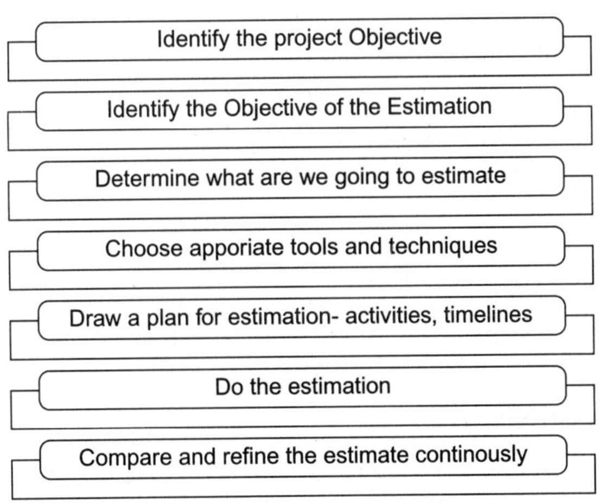

Figure 11.2 Estimation Process Steps

mechanism. During the measurement process, the whole team should be focused on the right estimation objectives.

Determine Parameters and Tools: What needs to be measured is the important parameter of the estimation process. Will the height, weight, cost, and duration be measured? The parameter identification helps to choose the appropriate tools for the estimation. For example, the tools and techniques of estimating the cost are different from the schedule.

Draw Out a Plan for the Estimation: Planning helps to ensure all the available information is available before starting the estimation. Draw out a schedule indicating the various activities of the estimation process along with appropriate timeline of the estimation. This helps to monitor and control the estimation process. Resources involved in the estimation process are also listed and mapped against the tasks for better tracking. There is no right or wrong plan, whatever works is fine.

Doing the Estimation: Estimation is calculating to derive the value as per the plan. Here finding a value (number) that is close enough to the right value (number) and in other words estimations are always approximation.

Refine the Estimation: Continuous refinement of the value and the estimation process makes the success of the estimation. The value (estimation) is continuously refined as more information about the risks, resources, and contexts are known in clear at later point of time and even the estimation process is refined based on the continuous feedback and experience. Some uncontrollable events/situations may dictate a re-estimation of the cost and schedule.

11.6 BASIC ESTIMATION PRINCIPLES

Following are the basic estimation principles that can be followed with any estimation.

1. Use more than one technique to derive the estimate,
2. Use more than one method of estimation,
3. It is better to obtain at least two estimates using each method,
4. Involve the people who will be doing the actual work,
5. Get the commitment from the team who will be doing the work,
6. Get the feedback from the project sponsor,
7. Ensure the estimation are reviewed independently,
8. Add contingencies based on the risks level,
9. Ensure the assumptions are clearly documented, and
10. Refine the estimate as more information is known.

Discussion Questions

Discuss the importance of basic estimation principles with examples for each points described above.

11.7 ESTIMATION TECHNIQUES

Estimations techniques are of great help for the estimators and can be used across various situations. The appropriate technique needs to be found according to the environment factors. Various known estimations techniques are expert judgments, top down estimation, bottom-up estimation, analogous estimation, and parametric estimation.

11.7.1 Expert Judgment

One or more experts who are good in a particular field of domain/technology/process use their experience to predict the estimation (cost, schedule, etc.). The discussion continues until consensus is reached. The estimation is accurate if the expert has direct experience on the system and the metrics under study. Finding experts are difficult.

Advantages:

1. It is useful in the absence of quantified data,
2. It can factor in impacts of new technology in the market,
3. It can factor in the experience of the past project which is impossible to quantify and measure otherwise, and
4. It can factor in realistic assumptions and constraints based on the past project data.

Disadvantages:

1. Estimate is only as good as expert's opinion,
2. It is hard to express the opinion of the expert,
3. It is hard to justify the accuracy of the output,
4. Different experts differ in their opinion, and
5. It is hard to document the factors used by the experts.

11.7.2 Brainstorming

In brainstorming session, the facilitator should guide the entire session and encourage active participation from all involved. Participants from different backgrounds and various departments across the organization need to be involved so that they can bring fresh ideas (estimations) that can inspire. It is important that the purpose of the meeting be explained clearly well in advance to the participants, and it is helpful if they are prepared when they arrive at the meeting. Brainstorming usually is effective with groups of 8–12 and also should be performed in a relaxed environment.

Advantages:

1. It considers the opinion of the entire team,
2. Quick and easy technique, and
3. Fresh ideas and large set of ideas possible.

Disadvantages:

1. If the facilitator is not strong enough the technique fails,
2. Positive bias and negative bias surfaces,
3. Opinions of the members are not always useful, and
4. Effective only with groups of 8–12.

11.7.3 Delphi Technique

The Delphi method relies on a panel of independent experts and is a way to reach consensus among experts on the estimation. After each round, the facilitator provides an anonymous summary of the experts' forecasts of estimates (figures) from the previous round as well as the reasons they provided for their judgments without telling which expert contributed. Experts are encouraged to revise their earlier estimations and resubmit the answers based on the summary results from previous round. During this process the group will converge toward the estimation and finally, the process is stopped after a pre-defined stop criterion such as number of rounds, stability of results, etc. The mean or median scores of the final rounds determine the final result.

POINTS TO PONDER

Delphi method is expert technique and anonymous. The experts may not know the details of other experts involed in the process.

Advantages:

1. Independent experts do the estimation,
2. There is no biasing as anonymous technique followed,
3. Experts are given opportunity to correct and revise their figures based on others figures and justification,
4. Final outcome is more accurate, and
5. Final outcome is accepted by all.

Disadvantages:

1. Time consuming (as it goes for more rounds of discussion),
2. The result is as good as the experts chosen for the purpose,
3. Identifying experts takes time,
4. Determining the number of experts to be involved in critical for the success,
5. Facilitator needs to be strong and not biased, and
6. Facilitator needs to spend lot of time collating the details.

11.7.4 Bottom-up Estimation

In this technique the cost of individual work items are estimated and then summarized rolling-up to get the overall project total. It is more accurate than top down approach. Accuracy of bottom-up estimating is driven by the size and accuracy of the estimations of the individual work items. The disadvantage of this type of estimate is the cost of detailed estimating and the time to produce the estimate is considerably high, as there are lot of data calculations involved in this type of estimation.

POINTS TO PONDER

Bottom up estimation is more accurate and detail than any other method but it depends on accurate data of the project under study.

Advantages:

1. More detailed as all individual work items being considered,
2. More accurate than top down approach, and
3. More details about individual work items come up during the process.

Disadvantages:

1. More time consuming,
2. System level activities not considered,
3. Cost of detailed estimating is very high,
4. Not possible to do in the beginning of the project, and
5. Accuracy is driven by the accuracy of the individual estimations.

11.7.5 Top Down Estimation

It is also called as macro model as the estimation happens at macro (higher) levels. In this technique the individual work items are not considered for the estimation. The estimation is based on the external factors, and it is partitioned into individual work items (low-level components).

Advantages:

1. Requires only minimal detail,
2. System level (higher level) activities considered, and
3. It is fast and easy.

Disadvantages:

1. Low-level components and activities not considered,
2. Usually not in detail, and
3. No justification or logic for estimation (it is just distribution technique of available numeric).

11.7.6 Analogous Estimation

Here the estimations happen by comparing the project with a similar kind of project (application/domain). Analogous means comparison. This technique is used only when limited amount of information is available for the current project under study. This will be accurate only if the similar project data are available and it is difficult if the similar kind of projects are not available and also if the data of the similar project(s) are not available. Analogous estimation is considered as top down approach and is not accurate as other estimation techniques.

Advantages:

1. Easy to implement,
2. Cost involved for the estimation is less,
3. Similar projects taken into consideration, and
4. Individual tasks need not be identified.

Disadvantages:

1. Project components and activities not considered,
2. Difficult to estimate for projects with uncertainty,
3. Depends entirely on the comparative project,
4. Not possible if data not available for similar projects, and
5. Not possible to apply for new kind of projects.

11.7.7 Parametric Estimation

It is a more accurate estimation technique compared to other available techniques and uses some formula (statistical relationships) connecting various variables (parameters) of the project for deriving the estimation. Because various parameters are used to derive the estimation, it is called as parametric estimation. For example, one similar module in a previous project cost 600 $ per module and this new project has 10 similar module and so it will cost around 6000 $.

Advantages:

1. More accurate than analogous estimation,
2. Individual work items and risks of the projects are considered,
3. Micro and macro parameters of the projects are considered, and
4. Tries to connect various parameters of the project.

Disadvantages:

1. Not possible if data not available for the project under consideration.

11.7.8 Pricing to Win

Here the estimations happen not for the system or any of its parameters, but for the prediction of customer expectation price. Particularly this happens in cost estimation. The deal is won if the estimate is correct. This technique (approach) seems to be unethical.

Advantages:

1. It meets the customer expectation,
2. It gets the blessings of the customer, and
3. Probability of winning the deal is high using this estimation.

Disadvantages:

1. The characteristics of the project is not considered,
2. This may yield worst impact on all parameters of the project,
3. Project profitability may be impacted because of this technique (when the price is too low), and
4. This technique seems to be unethical (How to know the customer price in ethical way?).

11.7.9 Vendor Bid Analysis

Analysis what the project should cost based on the responsive bids from the qualified vendors who submitted their quotes or bids for this project (This technique is used by the customers). When multiple vendors are involved for each deliverables, the price of individual deliverables are calculated to derive a cost that supports the final total project cost.

Advantages:

1. It is the cheapest method for the customer – free of cost,
2. Varieties of estimation techniques can be applied here, and
3. Customer can understand the estimation process of vendors.

Disadvantages:

1. It solely depends on the vendors and they may bias the estimation,
2. It is applicable and effective only when multiple vendors are involved, and
3. Vendors may skew the estimation depending on the demand and the market conditions.

11.7.10 Parkinson Law

Parkinson law states that work expands to fill the time available. If there are three resources and the software to be delivered in 10 months then the efforts required to do the software = 3*10 = 30 person month.

Advantages:

1. Easy and quick estimation,
2. All the resources are being utilized in the estimation.

Disadvantages:

1. It is applicable only for smaller companies,
2. The estimation may not be accurate as it does not consider project parameters, and
3. This technique considers all the resources of same experience and skill level.

11.7.11 Three Point Estimation

Project managers know this technique through program, evaluation, and review technique (PERT). This technique believes there is very small probability that a project will be completed on a given date estimated in the beginning of the project.

The project manager estimates three types of estimations namely best, worse, and most likely duration for finishing an activity.

O = the best-case estimate
M = the most likely estimate
P = the worst-case estimate
Expected value = $(P + 4M + O)/6$
Standard Deviation $SD = (P - O)/6$

Discussion Questions

Calculate Expected Time

Optimistic time = 15 minutes
Mostly likely time = 30 minutes
Pessimistic time = 60 minutes

11.8 ESTIMATING STYLES

1. Subjective estimate – based on personal experience,
2. Statistical estimate – based on comprehensive historical data,

3. Comparative estimate – based on similar projects, and
4. Empirical estimate – based on real data of the project.

Subjective estimate style is based purely on personal experience. Expert judgment is the best example of subjective estimation style. Subject estimation can be improved using paired comparison method.

Statistical estimation style is completely based on a comprehensive historical data. If the historic data is wrong, the estimation yields wrong results. Even if the historic data are right, proper interpretation of the data is required for better estimation.

Comparative estimation is based on similar kind of projects. If the similar project has no data, wrong data, then it affects the result.

Empirical estimation is based on the real data of the current project, but the proper empirical estimation can be done only at the end of the project because the correct information will be known only at the end and hence empirical data cannot be used in the beginning of the project.

11.9 PRECISION VERSUS ACCURACY

Precision means the values of repeated measurements and accuracy means the measure value is very close to true (actual) value. Precise measurements need not be accurate.

Here is an example. A project manager forecasts the cost variance at the end of the project between 40 and 60% based on the data available today. The actual cost variance at the end of the project turns out to be 53%. In this case the forecast was accurate but not very precise. Another project manager forecast cost variance at the end of the project as 51.47%. It turns out to be 62% and this forecast was precise, but completely inaccurate. A very accurate measurement is not necessarily means precise. The project management team needs to determine the level of accuracy and precision.

Discussion Questions

How to determine the level of accuracy and precision for projects? Will this priority changes over the time with the life cycle of the project? What is the role of availability of data in calculating precision and accuracy?

11.10 TOOLS FOR ANALYZING METRICS AND ESTIMATIONS

Metrics are of no use if they are not analyzed properly. Ishikawa's 7 "old" tools can be used for this purpose.

- Checklist,
- Pareto diagram,
- Histogram,
- Scatter diagram,
- Run chart,
- Control chart, and
- Cause-and-effect diagram.

11.10.1 Checklists

A checklist is an instruction sheet for an inspector to use for verification purpose. The checklists are generic in nature and more tailored checklist can be used (if necessary) to meet the needs of a particular project, program, or activity. When a checklist is created, it indirectly tells certain defined activities that are planned to be done. Checklist will be used to verify whether all the activities are done as per the customized checklist. Checklist can be used to analyze the metrics.

11.10.2 Pareto Diagram (Pareto Chart)

Pareto developed the concept of 80–20 rule, 80% of the problem are due to 20% of the causes. Pareto chart is a histogram ordered by frequency of occurrence and is used by the Project team to find out the causes creating the greatest number of defects. The problems in a process are arranged in the order of importance using factors, such as cost, time delay, or some other parameter.

Steps for Pareto diagram:

1. Determine the classification of defect you will use in the graph (e.g., number of defects).
2. Decide on a time period to be covered on the graph.
3. Total the frequency of occurrence for each category for the period and each total will be shown by the length of the bar.

In Figure 11.3 "Cause A" alone is responsible for about 50% of the problem with more than 15 defects. Most of the problem will get solved if steps are taken to remove the defective item A.

11.10.3 Histogram

It is a graphical representation (Figure 11.4) of the frequency distribution of the variable under consideration, and the values of the variables are grouped into intervals and shown on the horizontal axis and the frequency of occurrence of values in various intervals is shown in the vertical axis.

If any unusual events affect the process during the time period of the histogram, analysis of the histogram shape probably cannot be generalized to all time periods. First the meaning of histogram's shape needs to be analyzed.

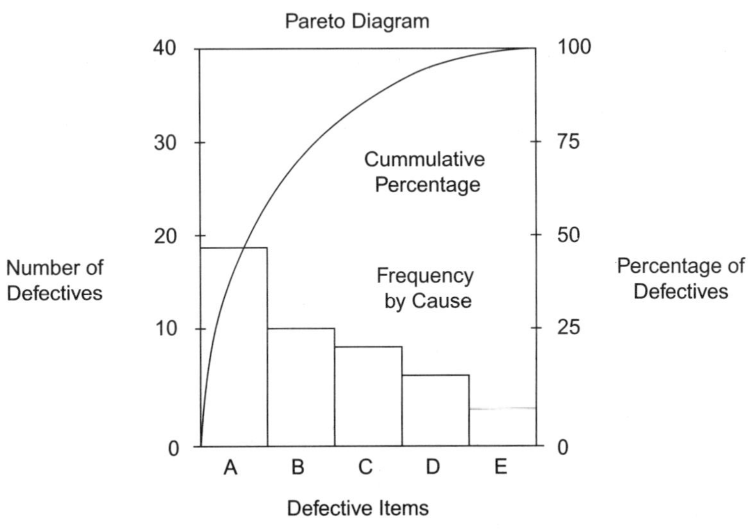

Figure 11.3 Pareto Diagram

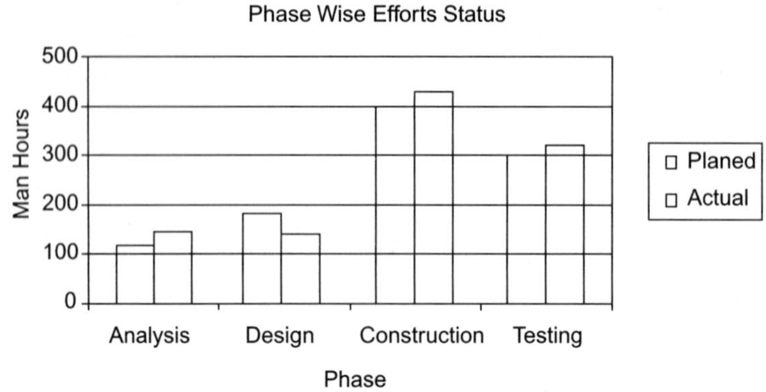

Figure 11.4 Histogram

11.10.4 Scatter Diagram

A scatter diagram (scatter graph – Figure 11.5) is used to analyze the relationship between two variables.

Y-axis has the variable to be predicted.

X-axis has the variable to make the prediction.

Correlation is the indicative measure of the relationship between two sets of numbers or variables (here the variables are plotted at *X*- and *Y*-axes).

Correlated variables form a line or curve kind of structure while plotted in a graph.

11.10.5 Run Chart

A run chart (Figure 11.6) also called as a run-sequence plot is a graph that displays observed data in a time sequence. Trend analysis is performed on a run chart to forecast future outcomes based on the historical data.

1. Technical performance – How many defects were identified and how many defects were closed out of it?
2. Cost and schedule performance – How many activities per period were completed within SLA defined?

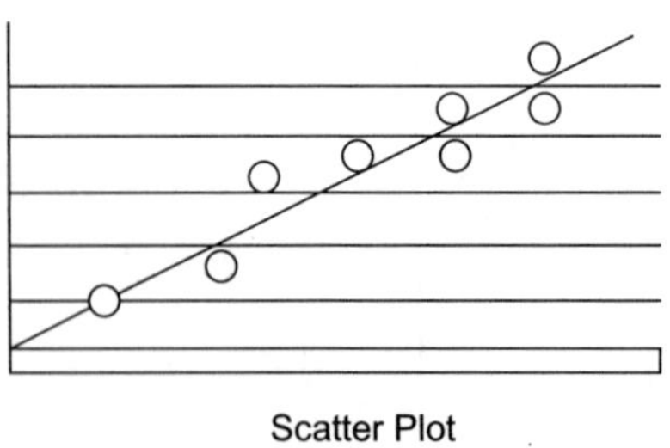

Figure 11.5 Scatter Plot

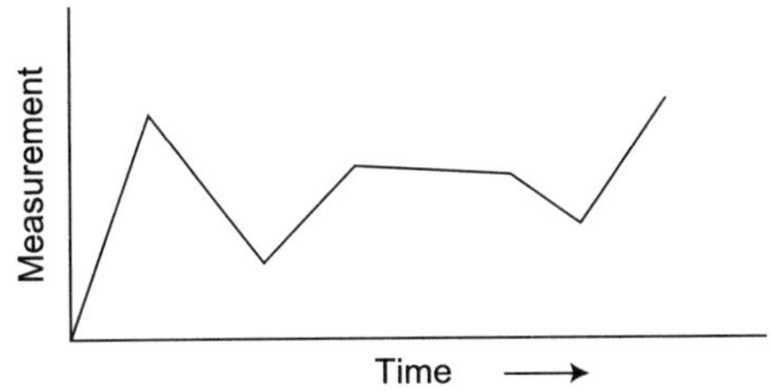

Figure 11.6 Run Chart

11.10.6 Control Charts

It (refer Figure 11.7) is used to assess whether the process is "in control" and also to determine whether the observed variations in a process are due to normal process variations or due to any other problems. Control charts help do corrections to the process before producing bad output.

> **POINTS TO PONDER**
>
> Run of seven continuous points toward upper or lower control limit in a particular direction may indicate that process is out of control. This called as rule of seven. Variations may be caused by diffrence in machines, workers overtime for which causes are well known and no need for further investigations and this is called Assignable Causes

There are two types of control charts namely variable control charts and attribute control charts.

Variable control charts deals with items that can be measured like height, cost, schedule, etc. X bar chart, R chart, and MA chart are examples of variable control charts.

Attribute control charts are used to test the attributes of a product to find out whether product is going out of control. P chart, *C* chart, and U chart are examples of attribute control charts.

1. Choose the control chart fitting into your data.
2. Determine the appropriate time period required for collecting the data and plotting the data collected.

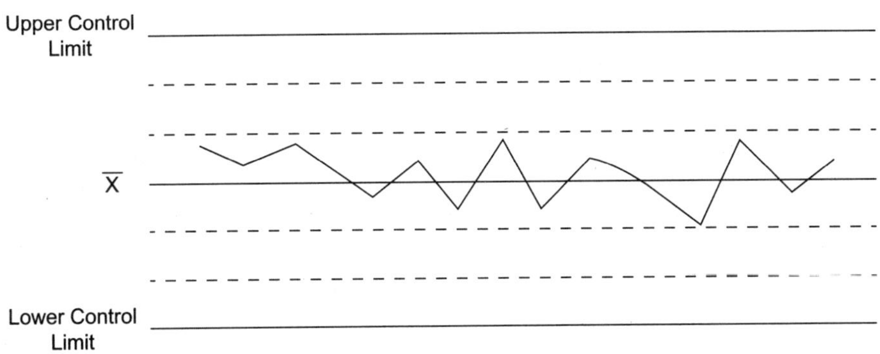

Figure 11.7 Control Chart

3. Collect the actual data construct your chart and analyze the data.
4. Look for "out-of-control signals" on the control chart just drawn and investigate the cause. Document the entire process.

Center line is mean
UCL = 3* Standard Deviation above mean
LCL = 3* Standard Deviation below mean
Tolerances – The result is acceptable if it falls with the range specified by the tolerance.
Control limits – The process is said to be in control if the result falls within the control limits.
Out of Control – Process is out of control when one of the following condition are met

- At least one point outside the control limits,
- Seven points in a row above the average value (even within limit), and
- Lot of points in a row near the control limits (this indicates a problem).

11.10.7 Cause and Effect Diagrams

It is also known as the fishbone diagram or Ishikawa diagram (Figure 11.8) developed by Kaoru Ishikawa. It is useful in determining the root cause problems. This can be used to analyze the problem related to metrics. It helps us to analyze all the possible causes associated with the problem under study.

A possible root cause can be uncovered using Why–Why and How–How diagrams as shown in Figures 11.9 and 11.10, respectively.

Causes in a cause and effect diagram are frequently arranged into five major categories such as manpower, methods, materials, measurement, and machinery. More classifications can be added as per the situation and need.

11.11 PROJECT COST ESTIMATION

Definition of Cost: Cost is a resource sacrificed, foregone, or consumed to achieve a specific objective or something given up in exchange for something in return. In the context of project management, resources are spent in exchange for profits. Costs associated with a project are the costs of

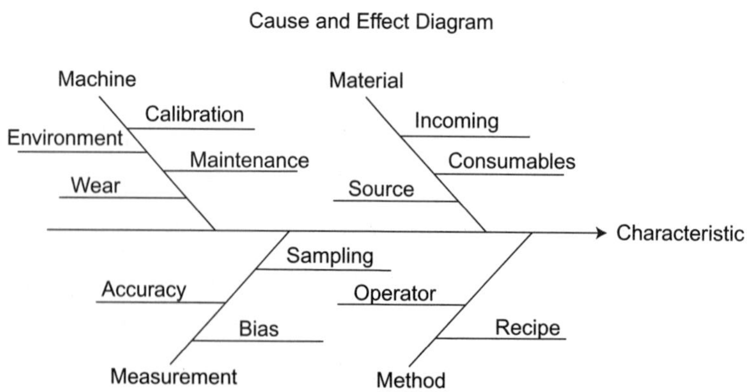

Figure 11.8 Cause and Effect Diagram

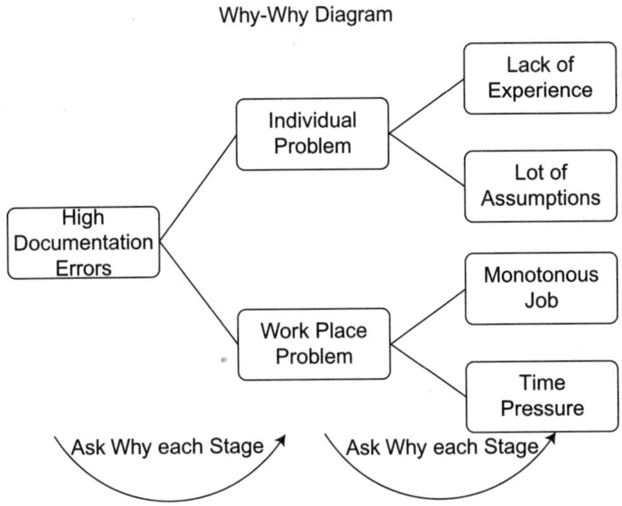

Figure 11.9 Why–Why Diagram

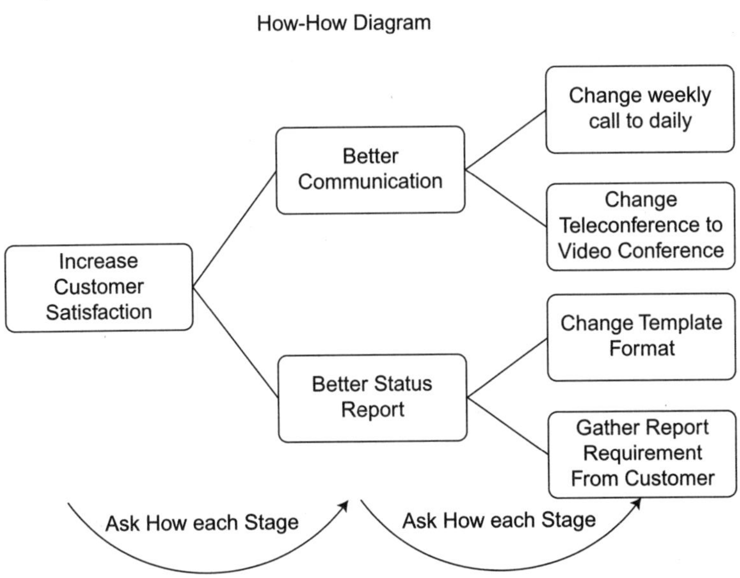

Figure 11.10 How–How Diagram

equipment, material, and human resources required to complete all the activities of a project. Project cost is usually measured in monetary units. Accurate project cost estimation is difficult because of the uncertainties inherent in project execution, particularly so in the case of complex projects. However, if project costs are effectively managed, predicted, accounted for, and controlled, the gap between planned costs and actual costs could be kept to a minimum or, sometimes, even zero.

The ability of stakeholders to influence project cost is greatest in the early stages of project execution. On projects of narrow scope, cost estimating and cost budgeting are so tightly linked that project managers look at them as a single process.

Discussion Questions

1. Why a project manager needs to know about costing?
2. What is halo effect?
3. What cost management tool is used in the projects?
4. How will you determine the cost of the whole project?

11.11.1 Types of Costs

Variables Costs: Costs that change with the number of units produced, such as costs of material and wages.
Fixed Costs: Costs that do not change as number of units' changes, such as rentals, machine costs, etc.
Direct Costs: Costs which are directly connected and accountable to the work on the project, such as project travel costs, salaries, and project-related software.
Indirect Costs: Costs incurred for the benefit of more than one project is accountable in each and every project, such as fringe benefits.
Opportunity Cost: The cost of selecting and investing in a particular project and therefore, not getting the potential benefits of other projects which were not selected.
Design-to-Cost: It is a process where cost goals of each activity are also considered in design along with usual technical performance.

Cost management consists of three processes.

1. Estimate costs,
2. Determine budget, and
3. Control cost.

To control the flow of expenses, cost management process needs to be implemented.

11.11.2 Estimate Cost

It is the process of developing an approximation for the cost of the resources necessary to complete the activities of the project.

Cost estimation is done throughout the life cycle of the project from the beginning to the end, and should be based on a work breakdown structure to improve accuracy. If the cost estimates is too high and need to be decreased, the project manager can look for the options of using reusable components, cutting scope (work) of the project, outsourcing the entire project, sub contracting part of the project or use cheaper resources and at the same time closely monitoring the impact of changes on the project schedule. Cost estimating also includes identifying and considering cost alternatives for managing risks.

Distinction between cost estimating and pricing:

- Cost estimating: Assessing how much the organization will spend to provide the product or service.
- Pricing: How much the organization (executing vendor) will invoice (charge) for the product or service to the customer.

11.11.2.1 Pricing Factors

There is no simple relationship between the development cost and the price charged to the customer. Broader organizational, economic, political, and business considerations influence the price charged and Table 11.1 explains few of the possible factors that determine the pricing.

Table 11.1 Pricing Factors

Factor	Description
Requirement Complexity	Organization runs thru the requirements and if the complexity is low and requirement is clear then ussually quote lower price.
Risks Involved (Uncertainly)	Organization runs thru the requirements and if there are high risks involved in the project then qoute higher price to adjust the risks.
Contractual Terms	If the Customer is letting the code developed to be used with other customer then less price may be charged.
Financial position of the Organization	Organization in financial crisis may qoute lower price to win the contract
Market Position	Organization who wants to enter new market quote lesser price to capture the market

Reserve analysis – Contingency reserve at the discretion of project manager to deal with anticipated but not certain events to manage risks associated with the project. Proper reserve analysis will also increase the chance of project success and proper estimation of costs.

Cost of quality – Quality level determines the cost associated with the activities. To set higher quality levels, the cost of the activities will be more and for lesser quality levels the cost estimation will be lower. It includes cost such as reviews, audits, inspections, quality control, etc.

11.11.2.2 Types of Cost Estimates

Order of Magnitude Estimate: It is also called as ball park estimate. It is based on high-level objectives and the variations are high meaning accuracy is low (refer Table 11.2).

The Budget Estimate: It is more accurate compared with order of magnitude estimation. It should be formulated early in the project's planning stage; the budget estimate is most often based on analogous estimating considering budget lessons learned from a similar project and applying them to the current project (refer Table 11.2).

The Definitive Estimate: It uses bottom-up technique and is the most accurate of the estimate types, but takes the most time to create as there are lots of calculations and data collections involved and this is done using WBS of the project (refer Table 11.2).

Table 11.2 Types of Cost Estimates

Type of Estimate	When Done	Why Done	How Accurate
Rough Order of Magnitude (ROM)	Very early in the project life cycle, often 3–5 years before project completion	Provides estimate of cost for selection decisions	–25% to +75%
Budgetary	Early, 1–2 years out	Puts dollars in the budgets plans	–10% to +25%
Definitive	Later in the project, less than 1 year out	Provides details for purchases, estimates actual costs	–5% to +10%

11.11.2.3 Problems in Estimating Accurate Costs

- Developing an estimate for large project is a complex task.
- Lots of training and standards required.
- People usually have underestimation bias or over estimation bias.

Exercise 11.1: Choose the tool to use (d) in the below scenario.

You got a new project in new domain and you called raja who already worked in that domain and asked his input to estimate the total cost for your project.	Analogous Estimation	Parametric Estimation
You estimate the cost for each and every activity and rolls up to estimate for the whole project cost estimation.	Top down Approach	Bottom-up Approach
You have historical information about similar kind of projects and adjusting the same as per the attributes of the existing project to arrive the cost estimation.	Analogous Estimation	Parametric Estimation
You have the estimation for the overall project as a whole and you are distributing it to the individual activities.	Top down Approach	Bottom-up Approach

11.11.2.4 Cost Estimation Models

Cost estimation models are mathematical algorithms that help the software engineer and the project manager to estimate the cost in more accurate and sophisticated manner. Nowadays computerized software, which is built as per the models, helps for the estimation along with spread sheets based models. Input parameters of the model include the attributes of the product and project under study. Outputs of the models are usually the resource requirements of efforts, cost, and time.

Constructive Cost Model (COCOMO) model is the famous model of cost estimation and other models are Putnam's software life-cycle model (SLIM), parametric review of information for costing and evaluation – software (PRICE-S), and software evaluation and estimation of resources – software estimating model (SEER–SEM).

In almost all the models, cost is estimated as a mathematical function of product, project, and process attributes whose values are estimated by project managers. They are called as algorithmic (parametric) models.

Effort = A ′ Size^B ′ M

A is a constant and organization-dependent.

B is a size factor in the complexity based on size.

M is a multiplier representing attributes of product, process, and people.

Most models are basically similar in nature but with different values for A, B, and M. Accuracy of these kind of model can be improved by calibrating (modifying) the model to the specific environment.

Putnam's Software Life-cycle Model (SLIM)

It was created by Sr. Lawrence Putnam in late 1970 based on the analysis of the life cycle and is based on Rayleigh distribution which describes the time and effort required to finish a software project of specified size. It is intended mainly for large projects and has only few parameters as input.

$$\text{Effort} = \left[\frac{\text{Size}}{\text{Productivity.Time}^{4/3}}\right]^3 .B$$

Effort is the total effort of the project denoted in person-years.

Size is the product size (usually ESLOC – Effective source line of code).

B is a scaling function and is based on size.

Productivity is the product productivity (it is the ability of the organization to create software of a given size at a particular defect rate).

Time is the total schedule (duration) of the project in years.

Plotting effort as a function of time yields the time–effort curve.

The points along the curve indicate the estimated total effort to complete the project at a particular time. One of the distinguishing features of the Putnam model is that total effort decreases as the time to complete the project is extended.

Three tools derived based on **Software Life-cycle** model are

1. SLIM-Estimate
2. SLIM-Control
3. SLIM-Metrics

Advantages of **Software Life-cycle** model

1. Simple and repeatable estimations,
2. Only few parameters, and
3. Easy to refine and customize formulas.

Disadvantages of **Software Life-cycle** model

1. Unable to deal with exceptional conditions,
2. Experience not quantified.

Constructive Cost Model

COCOMO is a mathematical empirical model and was developed at TRW, a US defense contractor (Boehm) in 1981 based on a cost database from 63 different historical software projects. It is well documented and is not tied to any specific software vendor.

It exists in three different varieties namely basic, intermediate, and advanced model.

1. Basic – Gives single "ball-park" estimate based on product attributes.
2. Intermediate – Modifies the basic estimate (which was based only on the product) attributes using project and process attributes.
3. Advanced – Estimates project phases and its parts separately.

Basic Constructive Cost Model

It gives single "ball-park" estimate based on product attributes

$$PM = C \times KDSI^{S} \times M$$

1. PM (effort is measured in person–months)
2. C is a complexity factor (2.4/3.0/3.6)
3. KDSI is a product metric (kilo delivered source instructions)
4. Exponent S is close to 1 (1.05/1.12/1.20), and
5. M is a multiplier based on process, product, and development attributes (~ 1)

Project Complexity	Efforts Required	Development Time
Simple	$2.4(KDSI)^{1.05}$	$2.5(Efforts)^{0.38}$
Medium	$3.0(KDSI)^{1.12}$	$2.5(Efforts)^{0.35}$
Embeded	$3.6(KDSI)^{1.20}$	$2.5(Efforts)^{0.32}$

People required = Efforts required / Development time

Simple projects are said to be executed in organic mode. Moderate projects are said to be executed in semi-detached mode and highly complex projects are said to be executed in embedded mode.

Intermediate Constructive Cost Model

Intermediate COCOMO model takes into consideration

1. Product attributes (3 sub attributes),
2. Hardware attributes (4 sub attributes),
3. Personnel attribute (5 sub attributes), and
4. Project attributes (3 sub attributes).

In total 15 attributes were considered in intermediate COCOMO model (Table 11.3).

Table 11.3 Intermediate Constructive Cost Model Attributes

Product Attributes	Hardware Attributes	Personal Attributes	Project Attributes
1. Reliability	1. Run time Performance	1. Analyst capability	1. Use software tools
2. Size	2. Memory Constraints	2. Engineering Capability	2. Application of software engineering methods
3. Complexity	3. Volatility of the virtual machine	3. Applications experince	3. Requires development schedule
	4. Required turn about time	4. Virtual machine experince	
		5. Programming language experience	

Effort adjustment factor (EAF) which varies for the attributes and have typical values range from 0.9 (minimum) to 1.4 (maximum) (refer Table 11.4).

Table 11.4 Effort Adjustment Factor with Cost Drivers

Cost Drives	Ratings (EAF)					
	Very Low	Low	Nominal	High	Very High	Extra Hight
Product attributes						
Required software reliability	0.75	0.83	1	1.15	1.4	
Size of application database		0.94	1	1.08	1.16	
Complexity of the product	0.7	0.85	1	1.15	1.3	1.65
Hardware attributes						
Run - time performance constraints			1	1.11	1.3	1.66
Memory Constraints			1	1.06	1.21	1.56
Volatility of the virtual machine machine		0.87	1	1.15	1.3	
Requires turnabout time		0.87	1	1.07	1.15	
Personnel attributes						
Analyst capability	1.46	1.19	1	0.86	0.71	
Applications experince	1.29	1.13	1	0.91	0.82	
software engineer capability	1.42	1.17	1	0.86	0.7	
Virtual machine experince	1.21	1.1	1	0.9		
Programming language Experince	1.14	1.07	1	0.95		
Project attributes						
Application of engineeering methods	1.24	1.1	1	0.91	0.82	
Use software tools	1.24	1.1	1	0.91	0.83	
Required development schedule	1.23	1.08	1	1.04	1.1	

The below table helps to calculate the efforts required using the intermediate model.

Project Complexity	Efforts Reguired
Simple	$EAF*3.2\,(KLOC)^{1.05}$
Medium	$EAF*3.0\,(KLOC)^{1.12}$
Embeded	$EAF*3.8\,(KLOC)^{1.20}$

Detailed Constructive Cost

The detailed model considers all the parameters of intermediate model and it estimates the project phases (refer Figure 11.11 for phases) and its parts separately.

The effort is calculated as a function of program size.

Constructive Cost Model II

COCOMO II is the successor of COCOMO 81 and is better suited for estimating modern software development projects and got published in the year 1995. It addresses the issue on non-sequential and rapid development process models along with reuse driven and object-oriented approaches.

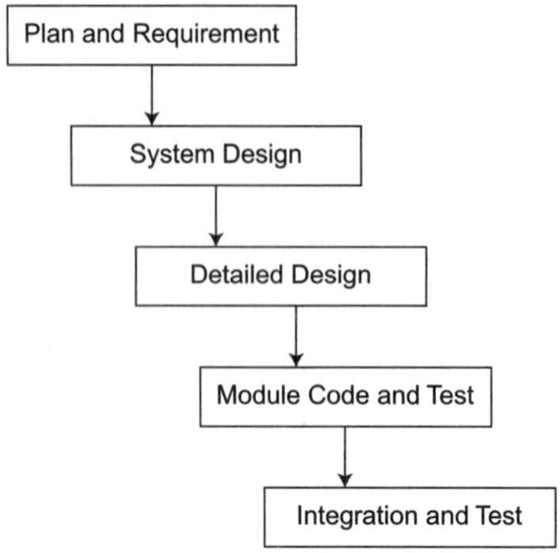

Figure 11.11 Detailed Constructive Cost Steps

It has three sub models namely

- Early prototyping level,
- Early design, and
- Post-architecture.

In the early prototyping model the estimates are based on object points. In the Early design model the estimates are based on Function points.

In the post-architecture model the estimates are based on SLOC

11.11.3 Determine Budget

It is the process of allocating the overall cost estimate of the project to individual activities or work packages to establish a cost baseline for measuring project performance of individual activities and in turn for the overall project. A cost baseline should not be changed without proper approval process for change and these changes are usually approved in the integrated changed control process.

We usually add some extra dollar which is not really needed for that purpose and needed for some other purpose and is called padding and is not an ethical project management practice. For example, getting cost approval for training and utilize it for procuring software and vice versa.

Determine budget process using the following techniques

Cost aggregation – Aggregate costs of individual work packages of WBS and this cost estimates are then aggregated for higher component level of WBS (control account) and ultimately for the entire project.

Reserve analysis – It can reserve both the contingency reserve and management reserve of the project. Contingency reserves are allowances for unplanned but potentially required changes that can result from realized risk. Management reserve is a separately planned quantity used to allow for future situations, which are impossible to predict and they are intended to reduce the risk of missing cost or schedule objectives.

Funding limit reconciliation – The expenditure of funds should be reconciled with any funding limits on the commitment of funds for the project and large variations in the periodic expenditure of funds are usually undesirable for organizational operations. The expenditure of funds is reconciled with the funding limits set by the customer or performing organization on the disbursement of funds for that particular project.

Cost baseline – Freezing the costs estimation will be used to measure and monitor the cost performance of the project.

Project Funding Requirements – It is derived and directly based on the cost baseline and can be established to exceed, usually by a fixed margin, to allow for either early progress or cost overruns, which is inevitable. Funding usually occurs in incremental amounts and is not usually continuous. The total funds required are those included in the cost baseline plus the management contingency reserve defined for that project.

Exercise 11.2: What tool is used to build the budget?

Petrol price got suddenly increased 10% and your project has lot of travels and so you reserve 500 $ aside to deal with the petrol hike.	Reserve Analysis	Cost Aggregation
Anand helps Balaji to add up all the estimations to control accounts to find out how much it will cost more than the previous account.	Cost Aggregation	Funding limit Reconciliation
Once the budget is done, you are looking over again to make sure we can afford everything on time.	Cost Aggregation	Funding limit Reconciliation

11.11.4 Control Cost

- Influence the factors that create changes to the cost baseline,
- Manage the actual changes when and as they occur,
- Detect variances from the plan,
- Ensure all appropriate changes are recorded,
- Prevent inappropriate or unauthorized changes,
- Inform the appropriate stakeholders about the changes,
- Analyze positive and negative variances, and
- Find how variances affect other control processes.

Tools and Techniques of Control Cost

Forecasting

Learning Curve: As time moves on the total costs will increase but the cost per unit will drop because repetition increases efficiency of the work involved in producing the output.

$Y_x = Kx^{\log_2 b}$

Where

K is the number of direct work hours to produce the first unit

Y_x is the number of direct work hours to produce the xth unit

X is the number of unit produced

B is the learning percentage.

Law of Diminishing Returns: Just by adding more resources the project cannot finish early, addition of more resources may increase overall output in the beginning, but will eventually decrease individual productivity. Adding thrice as many people to the same task may not cause the task to be finished thrice as fast.

11.12 EARNED VALUE MANAGEMENT

It is a method of measuring project performance and any professional project manager should know how to calculate this for the project to have better control on the project. It is calculated by comparing planned amount of work with that actual work accomplished, which helps to determine if cost and schedule performance are going as per the plan. Project cost and schedule performance measurements should be managed as an integrated elements and earned value management is really helpful for that integration.

Table 11.5 shows various terms used in earned value and its explanations. It is the most famous method of performance measurement and used by most professional project managers across the globe. It combines cost and schedule performance in one report and helps the project manager to control the entire project.

Table 11.5 EV Explanations Table

EV Terms		
Data Element	**Term**	**Definition**
Scheduled Work	Planned Value (PV)	Budgeted Cost of Work Schedule (BCWS)
Work Accomplished	Earned Value (EV)	Budgeted Cost of Work Perdormance (BCWP)
Actual Cost of Work Accomplished	Actual Costs (AC)	Actual Cost of Work Performed (ACWP)
Authorized Work	Budget at Completion	
Forecasted Cost	Estimate at Completion	
Work Variance	Schedule Variance	
Cost Variance	Cost Variance	
Completion Variance	Variance at Completion	

The difference between earned value and planned value is schedule variance (SV = EV – PV).
The difference between earned value and actual cost is cost variance (CV = EV – AC).
The ratio of earned value to planned value (PV) is schedule performance index (SPI = EV/PV).
The ratio of earned value to actual cost is your cost performance index (CPI = EV/AC).

Estimate to Complete (ETC): It is the expected additional cost needed to complete the project from the point of calculation. ETC is obtained by doing adjustments with the original cost estimate based on project performance (ETC = EAC – AC).

Estimate at Completion (EAC): It is the expected total cost of the project at the end of the project (when the defined scope of work has been completed).

There are five different formulas to calculate EAC.

1. An easy way of calculating EAC is budget-at-completion divided by the cost performance index (EAC = BAC/CPI).
2. EAC can also be computed as BAC/(CPI*SPI), which would reflect the compound impact of schedule and cost issues on the project.
3. If you have grounds for believing that all the past problems and issues will get corrected. EAC = Actual cumulative cost + ETC.
4. EAC = AC + (BAC – EV) (When AC = EV then EAC = BAC or EAC = BAC\CPI more accurately)
5. EAC = AC + (BAC – EV)/CPI

Variance at Completion (VAC): It is the difference between budget at complete BAC and estimate at completion EAC.

VAC = BAC – EAC

To Complete Performance Index (TCPI)

TCPI = Work Remaining/Cost Remaining

Work remaining is calculated using the formula BAC – EV. As already mentioned EV is the actual work completed and BAC is the planned at the end of the project. Cost remaining is calculated using the formula EAC – AC. AC is the actual cost spent and EAC is the estimated cost at the end of the project.

TCPI = (BAC – EV)/(EAC – AC)

Example 1:

PV	EV	AC		
$1	$1	$1	On schedule	On Cost
$2	$2	$1	On Schedule	Under Cost
$1	$1	$2	On schedule	Over cost
$1	$2	$2	Ahead of Schedule	On cost
$1	$2	$3	Ahead of Schedule	Over cost
$1	$2	$1	Ahead of Schedule	Under cost
$3	$2	$1	Behind Schedule	Under cost
$2	$1	$3	Behind Schedule	Over Cost
$2	$1	$1	Behind Schedule	On Cost

Example 2:
BAC = $ 40k
EV = $ 20k
PV = $ 28k
AC = $ 26k

- % of work scheduled — PV/BAC = $28K / $40K = 70 %
- % of budget spent — AC/BAC = $26K / $40K = 65 %

- % of work accomplished — EV/BAC = \$20K / \$40K = 50 %
- Cost variance — EV – AC = \$20K – \$26K = -\$ 6K
- Schedule variance — EV – PV = \$20K – \$28K = -\$ 8K

IF	AC > EV	AC = EV	AC < EV
THEN	CV < 0	CV = 0	CV > 0
	CPI < 1	CPI = 1	CPI > 1
The project is	Over budget	On budget	Under budget

IF	PV > EV	PV = EV	PV < EV
THEN	SV < 0	SV = 0	SV > 0
	SPI < 1	SPI = 1	SPI > 1
The project is	Behind schedule	On schedule	Ahead of schedule

Exercise 8.3: EV Calculation exercise

If EV = 94000 \$ and SPI = 0.87 what is planned value?

If PV = 257000\$ BAC = 330000\$ what is scheduled % complete?

11.13 OTHER CONCEPTS IN COSTING

Depreciation is the decrease in value (of an asset) over a period of time.

- Straight line method (asset depreciates the same amount every year).
- Double declining balance (in the first year there is a higher deduction in the value of the asset - twice the amount of straight line).
- Sum of year digit method (Say the life of an object is six years. The total of one to six is twenty one (6 + 5 + 3 + 2 + 1). In first year 6/21 is deduce from the cost, in second year 5/21, and so on).

Measuring Progress of Individual Tasks

Assuming the duration of a task is 10 days. The work is planned to start January 1st and gets over by 10th.

Based on 5th January calculate the percentage of calculation with reference to the following table.

Measuring rule for progress of individual tasks			
Rule	**Task begins**	**Task completed**	**Progressed (%)**
50/50	Y	N	50
50/50	Y	Y	100

20/80	Y	N	20
20/80	Y	Y	100
0/100	Y	N	0
0/100	Y	Y	100

Work Performance Measurement

Calculated CV, SV, CPI, and SPI are examples of work performance measurement.

Budget Forecasts

Calculated EAC value or bottom-up EAC value represents the budget forecasts and is communicated to all stakeholders.

Discussion Questions

1. How is historical information useful for the cost management process?
2. What are all the difficulties faced for calculating the cost of a particular tasks?

Summary

- Importance of accurate estimation:
  1. Inaccurate estimate may result in inefficient usage of resources,
  2. Inaccurate estimate may result incorrect decision,
  3. Inaccurate estimate may result in cost overrun and schedule overrun,
  4. Inaccurate estimate may result in customer dissatisfaction, and
  5. Inaccurate estimate may result in loss of faith and in turn loss of business from the customer.
- **(DE):** The concept of DE applies directly to the specific work efforts that can be directly traced and identified as having a direct tie to ultimate completion of the project-related work which is directly measurable.
- **(AE):** The concept of AE applies not directly to the specific work efforts, but related to some other tasks apportioned here. For example, project management efforts for finishing a task.
- **(LOE):** In project management, LOE is a support-type project activity that must be done to support other work activities or the entire project effort.
- Basic Estimation Principles
  1. Use more than one technique to derive the estimate,
  2. Use more than one method of estimation,
  3. It is better to obtain at least two estimates using each method,
  4. Involve the people who will be doing the actual work, and
  5. Get the commitment from the team who will be doing the work.

- **Expert Judgment:** One or more experts who are good in a particular field of domain/technology/process use their experience to predict the estimation (cost, schedule, etc.).
- **A brainstorming:** The facilitator guide the entire session and encourage active participation from all involved. Participants from different background and various departments across the organization need to involve so that they can bring fresh ideas (estimations) that can inspire.
- **The Delphi method** is a way to reach consensus among experts on the estimation.
- **Bottom-up estimation:** In this technique the cost of individual work items are estimated and then summarized rolling-up to get the overall project total. It is more accurate than top down approach.
- **Top down estimation:** It is also called as macro model as the estimation happens at macro (higher) levels. In this technique the individual work items are not considered for the estimation.
- **Analogous estimation:** Here the estimations happen by comparing the project with a similar kind of project (application/domain). Analogous means comparison.
- **Parametric estimation:** It is an accurate estimation technique out of all the available techniques and uses some formula (statistical relationships) connecting various variables (parameters) of the project for deriving the estimation.
- **Pricing to win:** Here the estimations happen not for the system or any of its parameters, but for the prediction of customer expectation price.
- **Vendor bid analysis:** Analysis what the project should cost based on the responsive bids from the qualified vendors who submitted their quotes or bids for this project (This technique is used by the customer).
- **Parkinson Law:** Work expands automatically to fill the time available.
- **Three point estimation:** Project managers know this technique through program, evaluation, and review technique PERT.This technique believes there is very small probability that a project will be completed on a given date estimated in the beginning of the project.
- Estimating Styles:
  1. Subjective estimate – based on personal experience,
  2. Statistical estimate – based on comprehensive historical data,
  3. Comparative estimate – based on similar projects, and
  4. Empirical estimate – based on real data of the project.
- **Precision versus accuracy:** Precision means the values of repeated measurements and accuracy means the measure value is very close to true (actual) value. Precise measurements need not be accurate.
- Metrics are of no use if they are not analyzed properly. Ishikawa's 7 "old" tools can be used for this purpose.
  - Checklist,
  - Pareto diagram,
  - Histogram

  - Scatter diagram,
  - Run chart,
  - Control chart, and
  - Cause-and-effect diagram.

- **Checklists:** A checklist is an instruction sheet for an inspector to use for verification purpose.
- **Pareto diagram (Pareto chart):** Pareto developed the concept of 80–20 rule, 80% of the problem are due to 20% of the causes.
- **Histogram:** It is a graphical representation of the frequency distribution of the variable under consideration, and the values of the variables are grouped into intervals and shown on the horizontal axis and the frequency of occurrence of values in various intervals is shown in the vertical axis.
- **A scatter diagram** (scatter graph) is used to analyze the relationship between two variables.
- **A run chart:** It is also called as a run-sequence plot is a graph that displays observed data in a time sequence. Trend analysis is performed on a run chart to forecast future outcomes based on the historical data.
- **Control charts:** It is used to assess whether the process is "in control" also to determine whether the observed variations in a process are due to normal process variations or due to the process getting out of control.
- **Cause and effect diagrams:** It is also known as the fishbone diagram or Ishikawa diagram developed by Kaoru Ishikawa. It is useful in determining the root cause problems. This can be used to analyze the problem related to metrics.
- **Constructive cost model:** Constructive Cost Model (COCOMO) is a mathematical empirical model and was developed at TRW, a US defence contractor (Boehm) in 1981 based on a cost database from 63 different historical software projects. It exists in three different varieties namely basic, intermediate, and advanced model.
  1. Basic – Gives single "ball-park" estimate based on product attributes.
  2. Intermediate – Modifies the basic estimate (which was based only on the product) attributes using project and process attributes.
  3. Advanced – Estimates project phases and its parts separately.
- **Learning curve:** As time moves on the total costs will increase but the cost per unit will drop because repetition increases efficiency of the work involved in producing the output.
- **Earned value management:** It is a method of measuring project performance. It is calculated by comparing planned amount of work with actually accomplishment.
- If cost management process is not followed, then there is a higher possibility of projects using more or less money than allocated, and it would be difficult to get control on the profitability of the project. Poor cost management will also affect funding of future projects. The work breakdown structure is the basis of the cost estimate and drawing correct WBS is the first success factor for better cost management. Cost

estimation is done throughout the life cycle of the project. Cost control is easily possible through proper usage of the earned value reporting system, which makes it possible to measure performance to schedule and performance to budget in the same system using simple formulas. Project expenditures are less in the beginning and the end. The expenditure is more in the middle phase of the project.

- **Actual cost (AC):** AC is the total cost incurred in accomplishing work during a given time period. It is also being referred as actual cost of work performed (ACWP).
- **Budgeted cost of work performed (BCWP):** This is called EV and this is the cumulative sum of the approved cost estimates for activities completed during a given period (usually project-to-date).
- **Budgeted cost of work scheduled (BCWS):** The sum of the approved cost estimates for activities scheduled to be performed during a given period as per the plan.
- **Chart of accounts:** Numbering system used to monitor project costs by category (for example, wage cost, material cost) and the project chart of accounts is based on the corporate chart of accounts of the main performing organization.
- **Code of accounts:** Numbering system used to uniquely identify each element of the WBS. Mostly it is numeric system for easy identification of the levels.
- **Contingency reserve:** Time to manage future situations ("known unknowns"), intended to reduce the impact of missing cost or schedule objectives and is included in the project's cost and schedule baselines.
- **Cost budgeting:** Process of allocating the cost estimates to each individual project components.
- **Cost estimating:** Cost estimation of the resources needed to complete project activities defined.
- **Cost performance index (CPI):** The ratio of budgeted costs to actual costs (BCWP/ACWP) and CPI is often used to predict the magnitude of a possible cost overrun.
- **Cost of quality:** Cost to keep the quality to a particular level defined which includes review cost.
- **Cost variance (CV):** Difference between the estimated cost of an activity and the actual cost of that activity.
- **Earned value:** It is the method of measuring project performance by comparing the amount of work planned with that of actual accomplishment.
- **Estimate at completion (EAC):** The expected total cost at the end of the project and EAC = Actual-to-date + ETC.
- **Estimate to complete (ETC):** The expected cost needed to complete an activity, a group of activities, or the project and this is also known as forecast final cost.
- **Fixed costs:** Costs that are fined and do not change based on the number of units and is nonrecurring.
- **Management reserve:** To manage future situations which are impossible to predict ("unknown unknowns"). It is used to reduce the risk of missing cost or schedule objectives and use of this requires a change to the project's cost baseline.

- **Parametric estimating:** It is purely based on statistical relationship between historical data and other variables to calculate an estimate.
- **Payback period:** The number of time periods at which cumulative revenues exceed cumulative costs and, therefore, the project has turned a profit.
- **Planned value (PV):** PV is the budgeted cost for the work scheduled to complete an activity and is also referred as BCWS.
- **Schedule performance index (SPI):** It is the ratio of work performed to work scheduled.
- **Schedule variance (SV):** It is the difference between the scheduled completion of an activity and the actual completion of that activity.
- **Value analysis:** Careful analysis of a design or item to identify all the functions and the cost of each item to reduce cost associated with it. It decides whether the function is necessary and also possibility of providing the same at a lower cost without degrading performance or quality.

Answers to Exercise Questions

Exercise 11.1 Answers: Choose the tool to use(d) in the below scenario.

You got a new project in new domain and you called Raja who already worked in that domain and asked his input to estimate the total cost for your project.	**Analogous Estimation**	Parametric Estimation
You estimate the cost for each and every activity and rolls up to estimate for the whole project cost estimation.	Top down Approach	**Bottom-up Approach**
You have historical information about similar kind of projects and adjusting the same as per the attributes of the existing project to arrive the cost estimation.	Analogous Estimation	**Parametric Estimation**
You have the estimation for the overall project as a whole and you are distributing it to the individual activities.	**Top down Approach**	Bottom-up Approach

Exercise 11.2: Answer

Petrol price got suddenly increased 10% and your project has lot of travels and so you reserve 500 $ aside to deal with the petrol hike.	**Reserve Analysis**	Cost Aggregation
Anand helps Balaji to add up all the estimations to control accounts to find out how much it will cost more than the previous account.	**Cost Aggregation**	Funding Limit Reconciliation
Once the budget is done, you are looking over again to make sure we can afford everything on time.	Cost Aggregation	**Funding Limit Reconciliation**

Exercise 11.3: EV calculation exercise

SPI = EV/PV So PV = EV/SPI = 94,000/0.87 = 108,046$

PV= BAC * Schedule % Completion
Scheduled % Completion = PV/BAC
= 257,000/330,000 = 77%

Model Questions
PART A (Objective type)

1. Exact amount of work required for completing particular task is called as

   A. Effort B. Duration C. Time D. Completion time

Answer : A

2. The time elapsed between start and end of the particular task is called as

   A. Effort B. Duration C. Time D. Completion time

Answer: B

3. For writing a particular piece of code, if 2 resources worked for 10 h and took 3 days to complete the tasks. What are the overall estimation and the duration of the tasks?

   A. 20 h, 3 days B. 3 days, 20 h
   C. 6 h, 30 days D. 2 hours, 30 h

Answer: A

4. The specific efforts that can be directly traced and identified as having direct tie to ultimate completion of project-related work is called as

   A. Discrete effort B. Apportioned effort C. Level of effort D. Direct effort

Answer: A

5. This effort applies not directly to the specific work efforts but related to some other tasks.

   A. Discrete effort B. Apportioned effort C. Level of effort D. Direct effort

Answer : B

6. This effort is a support-type project activity that must be done to support other work activities or the entire project effort.

   A. Discrete effort B. Apportioned effort C. Level of effort D. Direct effort

Answer : C

7. Which of the following is not an estimation technique?

   A. Expert judgments B. Top down estimation
   C. Analogous estimation D. Horizontal estimation

Answer: D

8. One or more experts who are good in a particular field of domain/technology/process use their experience to predict the estimation (cost, schedule, etc.). It is called as

A. Expert judgments
B. Top down estimation
C. Analogous estimation
D. Brainstorming technique

Answer : A

9. In this type of estimation technique everybody participates to get more ideas

A. Expert judgments
B. Top down estimation
C. Analogous estimation
D. Brainstorming technique

Answer : D

10. Panel of independent experts are used in this technique and also being used anonymously.

A. Bottom-up estimation
B. Top down estimation
C. Delphi technique
D. Brainstorming technique

Answer : C

11. In this technique the cost of individual work items are estimated and then summarized.

A. Bottom-up estimation
B. Top down estimation
C. Delphi technique
D. Brainstorming technique

Answer : A

12. This technique is also called as macro model technique.

A. Bottom-up estimation
B. Top down estimation
C. Analogous estimation technique
D. Parametric estimation

Answer : B

13. In this technique the estimations happen by comparing the project with a similar kind of project.

A. Bottom-up estimation
B. Top down estimation
C. Analogous estimation technique
D. Parametric estimation

Answer : C

14. This technique is an accurate estimation technique out of all the available techniques and uses some formula

A. Pricing to win technique
B. Top down estimation
C. Analogous estimation technique
D. Parametric estimation

Answer : D

15. In this technique the estimations happen not for the system or any of its parameters but for the prediction of customer expectation price

A. Pricing to win technique
B. Vendor bid analysis
C. Analogous estimation technique
D. Parametric estimation

Answer : A

16. In this technique the estimation is based on qualified outside organizations.

A. Pricing to win technique
B. Vendor bid analysis
C. Analogous estimation technique
D. Parametric estimation

Answer : B

17. Work expands to fill the time available is called as Parkinson law

A. True
B. False

Answer : A

18. Formula for calculating expected value as per PERT estimation is

A. Expected value = (P + 4M + O) * 6
B. Expected value = (P – 4M + O) / 6
C. Expected value = (P + 4M + O) / 6
D. Expected value = (P – 4M – O) * 6

Answer: C

19. Formula for calculating Standard Deviation as per PERT estimation is

A. Standard Deviation SD = (P * O)/6
B. Standard Deviation SD = (P + O)*6
C. Standard Deviation SD = (P + O)/6
D. Standard Deviation SD = (P – O)/6

Answer : D

20. This type of estimation is completely based on personal experience

A. Subjective estimate
B. Statistical estimate
C. Comparative estimate
D. Empirical estimate

Answer : A

21. This type of estimation is completely based real data of the project

A. Subjective estimate
B. Statistical estimate
C. Comparative estimate
D. Empirical estimate

Answer : D

22. Expert judgment is the best example of

A. Subjective estimate
B. Statistical estimate
C. Comparative estimate
D. Empirical estimate

Answer : A

23. This kind of estimation is based on similar kind of projects.

A. Subjective estimate
B. Statistical estimate
C. Comparative estimate
D. Empirical estimate

Answer : C

24. Values of repeated measurements is called as

A. Accuracy
B. Precision
C. Metrics
D. Comparative estimate

Answer : B

25. This means that the measure value is very close to true value.

A. Accuracy B. Precision C. Metrics D. Comparative estimate

Answer : A

26. Which of the following is not a tool of Inshikawa 7 old tools?

A. Check list B. Histogram C. Pareto chart D. Flow chart

Answer : D

27. An Instruction sheet for an inspector to use for verification purpose is called as

A. Check list B. Pareto chart C. Histogram D. Run chart

Answer : A

28. 80–20 rule based chart is called as

A. Check list B. Pareto chart C. Histogram chart D. Run chart

Answer : B

29. It is a graphical representation of the frequency distribution of the variable under consideration and the values of the variables

A. Check list B. Pareto chart C. Histogram chart D. Run chart

Answer : C

30. It is a graph that displays observed data in a time sequence.

A. Control chart B. Pareto chart C. Histogram chart D. Run chart

Answer : D

31. Two types of control charts are

A. Variable control charts and attribute control charts

B. Data control charts and information control charts

C. Process control charts and product control charts

D. Cause control charts and problem control charts

Answer : A

32. Which of the following is not a condition of a process said to be out of control in a control chart?

A. At least one point outside the control limits,

B. Points moving frequently moving up and down but within the limits,

C. Seven points in a row above the average value (even within limit), and

D. Lot of points in a row near the control limits (this indicates a problem).

Answer : B

33. Cost that change with the number of units produced is called as

A. Variable cost B. Indirect cost C. Opportunity cost D. Unit cost

Answer : A

34. Cost that does not change with the number of units produced is called as

A. Variable cost B. Indirect cost C. Fixed cost D. Unit cost

Answer: C

35. The cost of selecting and investing in a particular project and therefore, not getting the potential benefits of other projects which were not selected is called as

A. Variable cost B. Indirect cost C. Fixed cost D. Opportunity cost

Answer : D

36. COCOMO model stands for

A. Cost of component model
B. Code cost model
C. Constructive cost model
D. Constructive code-based model

Answer : C

37. What is SEER–SEM model?

A. Software evaluation and estimation of resources – software estimating model (SEER–SEM).
B. Software execution and estimation of resources – software estimating model (SEER–SEM).
C. Software evaluation and estimation of resources – software execution model (SEER–SEM).
D. Software evaluation and estimation of resources – software estimating model (SEER–SEM).

Answer : A

38. What is the disadvantage of SLIM model?

A. Simple and repeatable estimations
B. Experience not quantified
C. Only few parameters
D. Easy to refine and customize formulas

Answer : B

39. Which of the following is not a variety of COCOMO model?

A. Basic model B. Intermediate model C. Advanced model D. Complex model

Answer : D

40. Just by adding more resources the project cannot finish early, addition of more resources may increase overall output in the beginning, but will eventually decrease individual productivity.

A. True
B. False

Answer : A

41. Formula for variance at completion (VAC) as per EV technique is

A. VAC = BAC * EAC
B. VAC = BAC + EAC
C. VAC = BAC – EAC
D. VAC = BAC / EAC

Answer : C

42. Formula for TCPI as per EV technique is

A. TCPI = Work Remaining / Cost Remaining
B. TCPI = Work Remaining – Cost Remaining
C. TCPI = Work Remaining * Cost Remaining
D. TCPI = Work Remaining + Cost Remaining

Answer : A

PART B (Answer in one or two lines)

1. What is the definition of estimation?
2. List down any three importance of accurate estimation in a software project.
3. Define efforts and duration.
4. Give example for the difference between efforts and duration in a software project.
5. Define discrete effort (DE).
6. Define apportioned effort (AE).
7. Define level of effort (LOE)
8. What are estimation techniques?
9. List down various software estimation techniques you are aware of.
10. What is expert judgment technique?
11. What is brainstorming technique?
12. Write notes on Delphi technique.
13. Write notes on bottom-up estimation technique.
14. Write notes on top down estimation technique.
15. Write notes on analogous estimation technique.
16. Write notes on parametric estimation.
17. Write notes on pricing to win technique of estimation.
18. Write notes on vendor bid analysis technique of estimation.
19. What is Parkinson law?
20. What is three point estimation technique? What is the formula used in three point estimation technique?
21. What are the different estimating styles you are aware of?
22. What is Subjective estimation style?
23. What is statistical estimation style?
24. What is comparative estimation style?
25. What is Empirical estimation style?
26. Define precision and accuracy.
27. Discuss various tools for analyzing metrics and estimations.
28. Write notes on Check list.
29. Write notes on Pareto diagram (Pareto chart).
30. What is histogram?
31. Write notes on run chart.

32. What is Control Chart?
33. Write notes on two types of control charts?
34. What is the condition of a process to be out of control in control charts?
35. Write notes on cause and effect diagrams.
36. Write notes on cost of a project.
37. What is variable cost and fixed cost?
38. What are direct cost and indirect cost?
39. What is opportunity cost?
40. Write notes on cost estimation process.
41. Differentiate cost estimating and pricing.
42. What are all the problems in estimating accurate costs?
43. What are all the types of cost estimates?
44. Write notes on cost estimation models.
45. Give examples for cost estimation models?
46. List down any three advantages of SLIM model.
47. List down the disadvantages of SLIM model.
48. What is COCOMO model?
49. What are all the flavors of COCOMO model?
50. Write notes on detailed COCOMO model.
51. What is COCOMO II model?
52. Write notes on cost aggregation.
53. What is reserve analysis?
54. What is funding limit reconciliation?
55. Write notes on learning curve.
56. Write notes on law of diminishing returns.
57. Write notes on earned value management.
58. What is EAC in EV technique?
59. What is VAC in EV technique?
60. What is to complete performance index (TCPI) in EV technique?

PART C (Descriptive type)

1. Discuss estimation process in detail.
2. Discuss the basic steps in software estimation process in detail.
3. List down various estimation principles which helps for the estimations.
4. What is expert judgment technique of estimation? List down its advantages and disadvantages.
5. What is brainstorming technique of software estimation? List down its advantages and disadvantages.
6. What is Delphi technique? List down its advantages and disadvantages.
7. What is bottom-up estimation technique? List down its advantages and disadvantages.
8. What is top down estimation technique? List down its advantages and disadvantages.
9. What is Analogous Estimation Technique? List down its advantages and disadvantages.
10. What is parametric estimation technique? List down its advantages and disadvantages.
11. What is pricing to win techniques of estimation? List down its advantages and disadvantages.
12. What is vendor bid analysis? List down its advantages and disadvantages.
13. What is Parkinson law of estimation? List down its advantages and disadvantages.
14. What are all the types of estimating styles? Discuss in detail.
15. Discuss the checklists and Pareto diagram in detail.
16. What is histogram? Explain with example.
17. What is scatter diagram? Explain with example.
18. What is run chart ? Explain it with example.
19. What is control chart? Explain in detail.
20. What is project cost? Discuss different types of costs?
21. Discuss three project cost management process in detail.
22. Discuss Putnam's software life-cycle model (SLIM) in detail.
23. What is basic COCOMO model? Explain in detail.
24. Discuss intermediate COCOMO model in detail.
25. Write notes on COCOMO II model.
26. What is earned value management? Discuss the variables related to schedule and cost in EV technique?
27. What is depreciation? What are all the types of Depreciation?
28. What are all the different types of cost estimates?

Section 6:
Software Configuration

12

Software Configuration Management

CHAPTER COVERAGE

1. *Introduction*
2. *Basic Concepts of Configuration Management*
3. *Software Configuration Management Process*
4. *Configuration Identification*
5. *Configuration Control*
6. *Configuration Status Accounting*
7. *Configuration Authentication*
8. *Tools Used in Software Configuration Management*
9. *SCM and SEI Capability Maturity Model*
10. *Configuration Management Activities*
11. *Software Configuration Management Plan (SCMP)*

12.1 INTRODUCTION

Configuration management (CM) is a discipline of controlling the evolution of complex systems; software configuration management (SCM) is a specialization under this discipline in computer programs and associated documents.

SCM is the overall management of a software design project, as it evolves into a software product or system. This includes technical aspects of the project, all levels of communications, organizations, and the control of modifications and changes to the project plan by the programmers during the development phase. SCM is also called as Software Control Management.

12.2 BASIC CONCEPTS OF CONFIGURATION MANAGEMENT

The important terms that need to be understood before delving into the Configuration Management are:

- Configuration Item
- Change Request
- Versions and Configurations
- Promotion
- Release
- Repository
- Workspace

A piece of software or work product which is subject to change is a configuration item.

A version identifies the state of a particular configuration item or a configuration at a well-defined point in time.

A promotion is a version of a configuration item/CM aggregate that is available to other developers in a project.

A release is a version that is available to the user or the client.

A repository stores various releases of a CM item/aggregate; it is a library of promotions.

12.3 SOFTWARE CONFIGURATION MANAGEMENT PROCESS

The traditional SCM identifies four procedures that must be defined for each software project to ensure that a good SCM process (refer Figure 12.1) is implemented, which are as follows:

- Configuration Identification
- Configuration Control
- Configuration Status Accounting
- Configuration Authentication

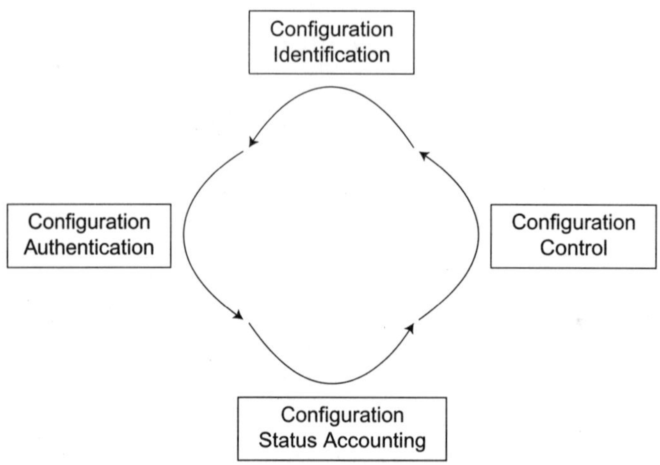

Figure 12.1 Configuration Management Cycle

12.4 CONFIGURATION IDENTIFICATION

Any software is usually made up of several programs. Each program, their related documentation and data are called as a "configurable item" (CI). The number of CIs in any software project and grouping of artifacts that make up a CI are decided according to the requirement of the project. The end product is made up of a bunch of CIs.

The status of the CIs at a given point in time is called as a baseline. The baseline serves as a reference point in a software development life cycle. Each new baseline is the sum total of an older baseline plus a series of approved changes made on the CI.

A baseline is considered to have following attributes:

1. Functionally complete: A baseline exhibits a defined functionality. Features and functions of a baseline are documented and available for reference. Thus, the capabilities of the software at a particular baseline are well-known.

2. Known Quality: The quality of a baseline is well-defined; i.e. all known bugs are documented and the software undergoes a complete set of tests before being defined as the baseline.
3. Immutable and completely recreatable: A baseline, once-defined, cannot be changed. The list of the CIs and their versions are set in stone. Also, all the CIs are controlled under version so that the baseline can be recreated at any point in time.

12.5 CONFIGURATION CONTROL

Configuration control is the process of deciding, coordinating the approved changes for the proposed CIs, and implementing the changes on an appropriate baseline.

It is important to know that configuration control addresses the process only after changes are approved. Evaluating and approving the changes to software are considered under the purview of an entirely different process called change control.

12.6 CONFIGURATION STATUS ACCOUNTING

Configuration status accounting is the bookkeeping process of each release. This procedure involves tracking of the components of each version of software and the changes that lead to this version.

Configuration status accounting keeps a record of all the changes made to the previous baseline to reach the new baseline.

12.7 CONFIGURATION AUTHENTICATION

Configuration authentication (CA) is the process of assuring that all the planned and approved changes have been incorporated in new baseline. This process involves verifying the completeness of the functional aspects of the software and also the delivery in terms of the right programs, documentation, and data being delivered. The CA is an audit performed on the delivery before it is released.

12.8 TOOLS USED IN SOFTWARE CONFIGURATION MANAGEMENT

Free software tools that help in SCM are

1. Concurrent Versions System (CVS)
2. Revision Control System (RCS)
3. Source Code Control System (SCCS)

Concurrent Versions System

Concurrent Versions System (CVS) is a version control system. It is used to record the history of the source files. For example, bugs, sometimes, creep in when software is modified, and they are not detected until a long time after modifications have been made. Using CVS, old versions can be easily retrieved to see exactly which change caused the bug; this can sometimes be a big help.

Revision Control System (RCS)

In order to change a configuration item, the developer has to lock that item first, and prevent other developers from changing the item at the same time.

The developer specifies a label for each configuration item. Using this label, developers can check out consistent set of versions.

Source Code Control System

The source code control system (SCCS) is a complete set of commands that allow specified users to control and track changes made to an SCCS file. SCCS files allow several versions of the same file to exist simultaneously, which is helpful when developing a project requiring many versions of large files.

Examples of Source Code Control Systems

1. Rational Clear Case
2. PVCS
3. Microsoft Visual Source Safe

12.9 SCM AND SEI CAPABILITY MATURITY MODEL

The Capability Maturity Model defined by the Software Engineering Institute (SEI) describes principles and practices to achieve a certain level of software process maturity. The model is intended to help software organizations to improve the maturity of their software processes in terms of an evolutionary path from *ad hoc*, chaotic processes to mature, disciplined software processes. The CMM also helps organizations to improve their software processes for building better software faster cost-effectively.

Associated with each level from level two onwards are key areas which an organization is required to focus on to move on to the next level. Such focus areas are called as Key Process Areas (KPA) in CMM parlance.

12.10 CONFIGURATION MANAGEMENT ACTIVITIES

- Configuration item/CM aggregate identification
- Promotion management
- Release management
- Branch management
- Variant Management
- Change Management

12.11 SOFTWARE CONFIGURATION MANAGEMENT PLAN (SCMP)

A SCMP documents the way the configuration management will be implemented and followed in an organization. Before the teams can actually follow the CM steps, it is important that they prepare the plan highlighting the areas like, the items to be put under CM, the tool to be used for it, the persons who will be handling the different roles of CM, the audits to be performed etc. This plan should be developed early in the lifecycle of the project to control the changes from the early stage. A SCMP should contain the key sections described in the following sections:

12.11.1 Purpose

This is a generic section which explains the purpose of Configuration management and why it is important. The purpose of Software Configuration Management (SCM) is to establish and control the integrity of work products using:

- Configuration Identification
- Configuration Control
- Configuration Status Accounting
- Configuration Audit

These steps are briefly explained in this section.

12.11.2 Objectives

What we are planning to convey though this plan is described in this section. For example:

This SCM Plan defines the configuration management policies and procedures to be followed for this project. In this plan we will first address activities that are platform independent. As the project advances through the lifecycle stages, this plan will be expanded to reflect platform specific activities.

12.11.3 Software Configuration Management Resources

This section identifies different roles at individual as well as group level that will participate in the SCM process. It also describes the relationships between individuals and groups. The key points documented in this sub-section are:

SCM related Roles and Responsibilities of Project Manager, Configuration Management Manager, Configuration Control Bard etc. are mentioned here. Let us look into few sample roles and responsibilities of these resources.

Project Manager (PM)

- Frame the overall project schedule for SCM related activities along with Configuration Management Manager (CMM)
- Ensure team members have enough training and knowledge about SCM concepts and techniques and that those are applied to project activities
- Make sure that the SCM standards and procedures set by the CMM, the Configuration Control Board (CCB), and any other affected groups as outlined in this plan are followed by the team

Configuration Management Manager (CMM)

This is the most important role in terms of SCM. This person is responsible to create and/or update the SCM Plan with assistance from the Project Manager as well as communicating the contents of the plan to the project team.

- Identify the Configuration Items (CIs)
- Create and maintain the SCM Plan, standards, and procedures
- Communicate the new as well as updated SCM Plan, standards, and procedures to all stakeholders

- Make sure that all project team members are aware of the SCM process through training on their roles
- Create SCM products (baselines, application environments) and get those authorized by the CCB
- Process and track change requests
- Ensure that configuration item change requests and problem reports for all CIs follow the steps like initiation, recording, review, approval, and tracking according to the SCM Plan
- Make sure the Functional and Physical Configuration Audits are performed

Configuration Control Board (CCB)

- Monitor the changes/updates to project requirements
- Approve the identified list of CIs and the baseline of the same
- Review and approve changes to the baselines
- Review, discuss, prioritize and approve the change requests

12.11.4 Software Configuration Management Tasks

This section contains the detailed steps for completing the Configuration Management tasks:

- Identification of Configuration Items and Baseline

  The project team along with the CMM should identify the items that they need to monitor and update under the configuration management framework. These items are properly labelled and a baseline version is created which acts as the foundation of the CM system. At this step the CIs are grouped, categorized and labelled in a logical fashion so that it is easy to refer to any of the items at a later point of time. This is also called CI Register. The Table 12.1 shows the sample CI register:

Table 12.1 Sample CI Register

Configuration Items	Item Code	Responsible for Placing Item Under Control	When Item is Put Under Control
Project Plan	PPM-0003	Project Manager	Initiation & Planning Stage End
Requirements Specification	RES-0402	Business Owner	Requirements Stage End
Requirements Traceability Matrix	RES-0403	Project Manager/DTMB Analyst	Requirements Stage End
Test Plan	TST-0601	Business Owner/Test Manager	System Design Stage End
Test Type Approach (1...n)	TST-0603	Business Owner/Test Manager	System Design Stage End
Design Document	DES-0204	Project Manager/DTMB Analyst	System Design Stage End
Test Case Document	TST-0606	Project Manager/DTMB Analyst	Coding End
Etc...			

- Version control (control changes before and after release to customer)

  Each work product under CM may undergo changes due to many reasons like multiple people working on the same item; the users initiated a change, the review comments to be incorporated etc. so, it is important that the Cm system engages a version control system to maintain and track the different versions of the work products which allows to refer to any previous version incase needed. The hierarchical approach and proper labelling done in the previous step ensures success of this step.
- Change control

  The tasks involved in this step are like checking out the existing work product from the system, making changes to it, synchronize the versions, branching of the versions in case multiple people are working on the same item, merging multiple versions, approving the changes and then checking in the changed version into the repository. So, the change control process takes help of the version control task.
- Configuration auditing

  Periodic audit or authentication ensures that changes made properly and processes are followed. Configuration audits focus on identifying the robustness of the CM process and whether for each item the CM processes are followed properly. The attributes of the CI's should reflect the correct status and the changes to pass the audit process.
- Reporting

  This is also a periodic task where each stakeholder is apprised of the updates and changes to the configuration database, problems found, steps taken to arrest future problems and other configuration audit findings.

12.11.5 Change Requests and Approvals

SCM Plan documents the procedures for initiating change requests, enforcing the flow of the change process, prioritizing the changes, capturing CCB decisions, and reporting the process information.

Some of the tools used for controlling change request work flow are:

- Remedy flow and procedures
- Rational software
- Serena Team Track
- Microsoft Excel
- Microsoft Word

12.11.6 Change Control Process

Controlling the changes to the configuration items is one of the main tasks of a CM system. This section highlights how the CCB should control changes that impact schedule, function, and the configuration of the system as a whole.

12.11.7 Management of Release Documentation

Releasing the correct version of the document and software to the stakeholders is key to the success of any project. The CM system ensures that when the CIs are released to external stakeholders a consistent process is followed. Following are the documents that are normally required for the release to production:

- Installation Plan (including a rollback plan)
- Release notes
- Updated user documentation
- Training materials

12.11.8 Configuration Control Tools and Techniques

This section focuses on the tools and techniques that will be employed for implementing the SCM processes. The purpose of these tools may be to manage access to the repositories, to process change requests and to report status of CIs.

The basic set of tools includes:

- Database management systems
- Report generators
- Tools for maintaining separate dynamic and controlled repositories
- File system with the capability to manage the check in and check out of units, for controlling compilations, and capturing the resulting products

Some examples of specific tools are:

- Infrastructure Configuration Management Build Application
- Remedy
- Issue Tracker
- Oracle Repository
- Serena Version Manager

Summary

Configuration management is very crucial for evolving software systems. Change in many large software systems is inevitable. Careful planning is required considering aspects like the components that are likely to be changed, any other subsystems that may have to be changed for the modification of the given system, analysis of cost etc. CM makes sure that these changes do not cause undesired impact on the other subsystems.

- Basic Configuration management activities are
  Configuration Identification
  Configuration Control
  Configuration Status Accounting
  Configuration Authentication

- Few common version management tools are
  Concurrent Versions System (CVS)
  Revision Control System (RCS)
  Source Code Control System (SCCS)

- Software Configuration Management Plan includes

  Purpose

  Objectives

  Software Configuration Management Resources

  Software Configuration Management Tasks

  Change Requests and Approvals

  Change Control Process

  Management of Release Documentation

  Configuration Control Tools and Techniques

Model Questions

PART A (Objective type)

1. SCM stands for:

   A. Software Configuration Management B. Software Control Management

   C. Software Change Management D. Software Code Management

Answer: A

2. A piece of software work product which is subject to change is called as

   A. Change Item B. Change Request C. Work Item D. Configuration Item

Answer: D

3. The process of deciding, coordinating the approved changes for the proposed CIs, and implementing the changes on an appropriate baseline is called as

   A. Change Control B. Change Request C. Work Item D. Configuration Control

Answer: D

PART B (Answer in one or two lines)

1. What are the SCM tools you are aware of?
2. What are the traditional SCM process steps?
3. What is configuration control?

PART C (Descriptive type)

1. With a suitable example, explain the change control process in detail.
2. With a suitable example, explain SCR Life Cycle in detail.
3. Explain in detail about SCM process.
4. Describe in detail configuration audit and its types.

Section 7:
Software Project Management

13

Project Management Introduction

CHAPTER COVERAGE

1. *Introduction*
2. *Process*
3. *Project*
4. *Environmental Factors that Mandate Projects in Organizations*
5. *Project Management*
6. *Program Management*
7. *Portfolio Management*
8. *Project Management Office*
9. *Project Planning and Monitoring*
10. *Project Scope Management*
11. *Project Quality Management*

13.1 INTRODUCTION

Organizations aspire not only to complete projects successfully but also to execute them professionally to stay ahead in the competition; and this objective assumes more significance at times of economic recession. The only way to effectively execute the projects and realize the desired outcome of a project is strict project management. In spite of appropriate technical setup and robust architecture of the product, the project fails because of the weak project management. Primary objective of the project management framework is completing the project within the triple constraint of Time, Cost, and Scope maintaining the desired quality.

13.2 PROCESS

A *process* is a set of interrelated activities performed to create prespecified products, services, or results.

Suppose you plan to go to your bank to withdraw money. What steps would you follow?

1. Check whether the bank is working on the day
2. Go to the bank
3. Get a service ticket for your service
4. Fill in a form, if any
5. Wait for your turn
6. Get serviced

These activities constitute a process—a set of interrelated activities performed to achieve a prespecified service, here, the withdrawal of money from a bank. Figure 13.1 is a process diagram that illustrates the process flow involved in this process.

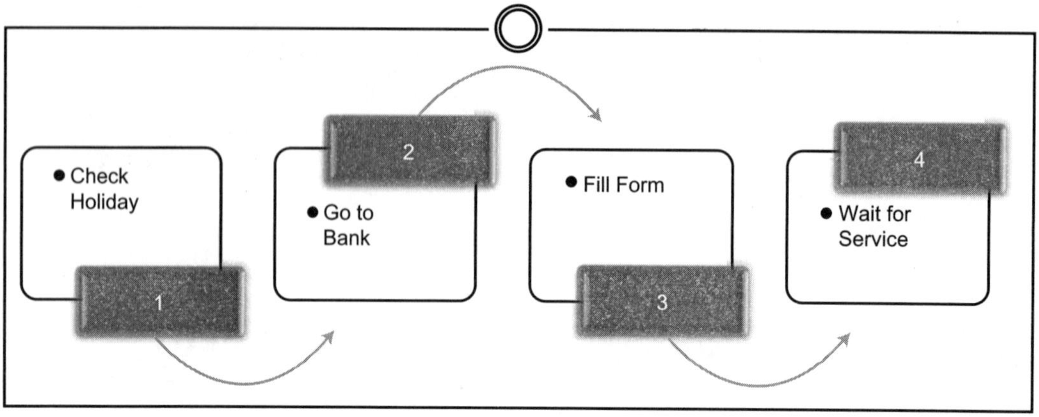

Figure 13.1 Process Flow Diagram for Withdrawing Money from a Bank

A typical process has 3 components, namely, input, tools and techniques and output. Input comprises of the things that are necessary to run the Process. Input is transformed to the Output by the Process using the specified Tools and Techniques.

Let us look into the example given in Figure 13.1:

Check Holiday is the name of the Process. What are the primary inputs required here?

1. Calendar to check for the usual holidays
2. Newspaper to check for unusual holidays
3. Steps indicating how to browse through the calendar (Plan)

What is the primary output required here?

1. Knowledge of the holiday flag
2. Knowledge of the calendar used.
3. Technique of browsing the calendar.

Sometimes, we may need inputs for a process that may not be directly related to the output but they may be necessary for the execution of the process. For example, let us take the "Go to Bank" process. It requires an input such as Scooter/Car, which may not be directly related to the process of receiving a banking service. However, we may reach the bank earlier if we use the car instead of the scooter. The point to be noted here is that while some inputs may be directly related to the output, a few others that are not directly related to the output may be required for the execution of the process. We shall discuss this later at an appropriate place in the book.

Let us consider another example: Suppose that making a Dosa (an Indian dish) is the process. If we call five different people (chefs) and give them the same ingredients and tools required to make the dosa, will the output be th e same? The size and taste of the dosa is bound to vary. Why is it so? This is not only because of the difference in skills possessed by the chefs but also due to the techniques they have learnt over a period.

Thus, we need to understand and learn the techniques of a process in order to produce a better output.

13.3 PROJECT

Before discussing what a *project* is, let us consider an example: the construction of the Big Temple at Thanjavur, Tamil Nadu. In his 19th regnal year (AD 1009 to AD 1010), Rajaraja Chola ordered the construction of the temple. The following are some details of the Big Temple:

1. The temple lies within a spacious inner *prakara* 240.9 m long (east–west) and 122 m wide (north–south).
2. It has its *gopura* on its eastern side.
3. There are three other ordinary entrances, one each on each lateral side and the third on the rear.
4. A double-storied *malika* with *parivaralaya*s surrounds the *prakara*.
5. The *gopura* does not cast a shadow outside itself.

From a project management perspective, the following points are of note:

1. There was a start date for constructing this temple and an end date, that is, an inauguration date.
2. The task was unique.
3. The temple was constructed at a previously unused site (see "Progressive Elaboration: Integrating the Unique and the Temporary").
4. To haul the *vimana* (*gopura*) to the top, a slope-like structure was constructed to the top from Vallam (15 km from Thanjavur).

Although no written records exist on how this project was managed, it is likely that many unique and best practices and methods (*processes*) were followed, all some 2,000 years back.

However, such is the sophistication of modern project management techniques, completing a project of this magnitude and complexity today would not pose as much difficulty as it would have in the times of Rajaraja Chola.

Other examples of projects are:

1. Construction of a house
2. Construction of a bridge
3. Election campaigning

So what is the common binding factor in these examples that define the term "Project"?

13.3.1 Definition

The PMI defines a project as a temporary endeavor undertaken to create a unique product, service, or result.

We also need to keep in mind that a project is progressively elaborated. Hence, the outcome of a project is called as Product. There are three key words that define the term "Project". They are

1. Temporary
2. Unique
3. Progressive Elaboration.

We shall examine each of these terms in detail in the subsequent sections.

13.3.2 The Temporary Nature of a Project

Every project should have specific start and end dates. *Temporary* does not imply *short in duration.* But it does mean that a project should have a planned end date. Some projects last years; some run for more than 10 years. The principle is that, when managing a project, you should always have planned start and end dates.

Project activities are intentionally woven together with the purpose of accomplishing a specific objective, and the project ceases to be in operation when its objectives have been achieved. A project can have more than one objective; for example, the Alpine House project (see table below) has two objectives: reduce costs by 75% and reduce manual errors in the existing process by 95%. Moreover, a project team, which is formed to manage a project, is generally released upon the completion of the project. Thus, you may say that the team itself is temporary and only lasts the duration of the project.

Example Project Objectives

Project Name	Project Type	Estimated Start	Estimated Finish
ABC Corporation	Business continuity planning	January 4, 2010	March 4, 2010
Adventure Works	Business process re-engineering	January 20, 2010	February 21, 2010
Alpine House	Cost reduction and error reduction	February 6, 2010	April 16, 2010

The business opportunity or market window that mandates a project is often of a temporary nature. Owing to this reason, we cannot continue with a project indefinitely. The temporary nature of the market window requires that we complete a project per plan and move the product to the market within the time frame the market window provides us. Assume, for example, that we started a project in 1993 in FoxPro with a planned duration of 10 years. In 2003, the project would be of no use as customers may no more require a product in FoxPro; instead they may need the same product in Java or another technology. This time-bound nature of project management makes it challenging.

13.3.3 The Unique Nature of a Project

A project involves work that has not been attempted before and is therefore unique. However, *unique* does not mean that a project is completely so. We may use reusable components of past projects or existing systems to simplify our efforts. Suppose we develop a banking software that requires coding for 10 components. This requirement does not mean that we need to write the code (develop) for all 10 components of the software. We can reuse five existing components from our previous projects, and write the remaining five components afresh. But, as you may note, the combination is unique (see Figure 13.2).

Because of the unique nature of projects, there may be uncertainty about achievement of their goals, that is, realization of intended products, services, or results. A project manager *manages this*

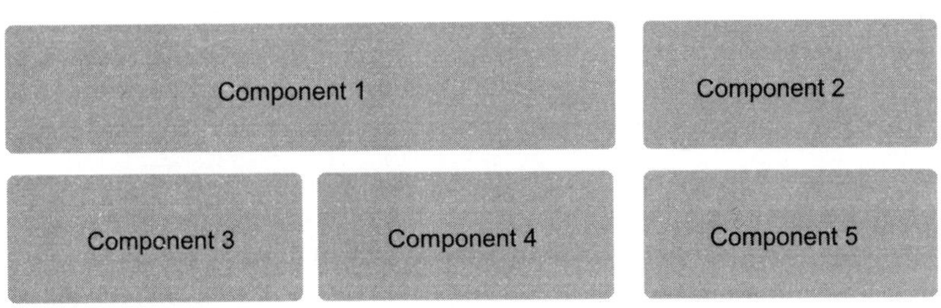

Figure 13.2 New and Existing Components of a Project

uncertainty. In fact, project managers can be called *uncertainty managers*, because they generally manage uncertainties. If we are able to anticipate the uncertainty to an extent, we stand a better chance of managing it effectively.

13.3.4 Outcome of a Project

The outcome of a project may be:

1. A product (e.g., a banking software).
2. A capability to perform a service (e.g., election campaigning for an upcoming election).
3. A result, such as an outcome or a document (e.g., a requirement analysis document).

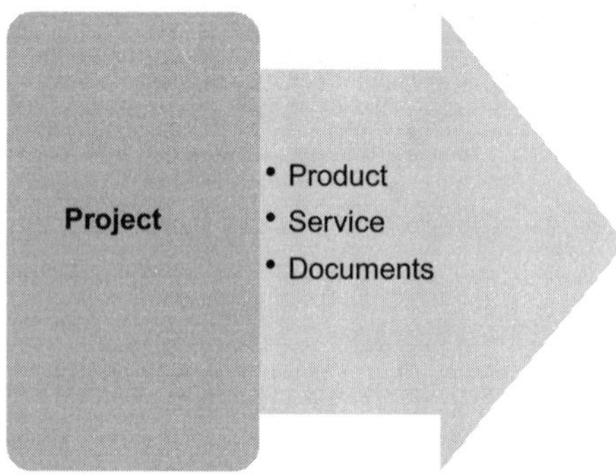

13.3.5 Progressive Elaboration: Integrating the Unique and the Temporary

Sometimes, product characteristics are progressively elaborated. *Progressive elaboration* is the characteristic of a project that integrates the concepts of the unique and the temporary: Start with nothing and slowly move forward to create valuable results.

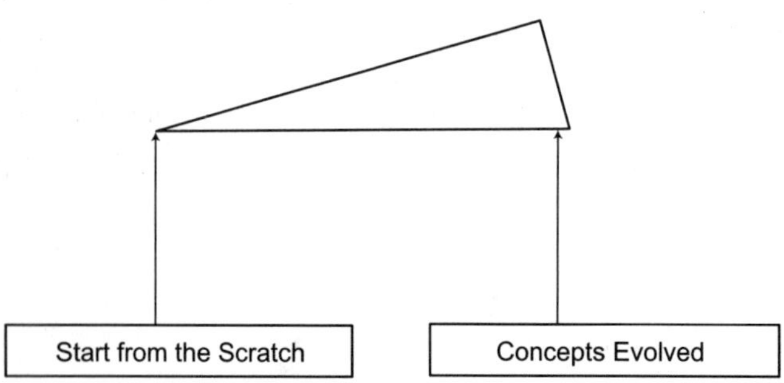

Progressive elaboration refers to developing in steps with continuous improvement. Goals and objectives that we set in the beginning are slowly elaborated and made clearer and more detailed as the project progresses. Progressive elaboration allows a project management team to manage at a greater level of detail as the project moves along. Basically, it is the process of identifying the characteristics of a project.

The project plan is continuously modified and refined as more sets of information becomes available to the project using the progressive elaboration technique. As a result, the modified project plan becomes more accurate and complete. This technique of progressive elaboration is widely used in the project planning stage. Real use of progressive elaboration leads to the Agile principles of project management.

Rolling wave planning is a form of progressive elaboration technique. Let us see what is a rolling wave. If you go to the sea shore and observe the waves (snapshot), at a particular point of time, one wave will just be starting, another would be in the process of ascending, a third would have already reached its crest. There would also be a wave that is in the process of descending and another that would have completely subsided (the last stage). Likewise, in a project, we need to plan the activities in such a way that immediate activities are planned in detail while activities scheduled for a far-away period (say, next year) would be charted at a macro level. Planning of all other activities that fall between these timelines would be at an intermediate level, that is, between micro and macro levels. This is called rolling wave planning in project management. It is a step-by-step planning where higher details of the activities are specified for the immediate future.

For example, if we are planning to visit Thanjavur (South India) in the upcoming summer, the first thing we do is to book the flight and hotel considering the start and end date of our tour plan. But the local trips within Thanjavur will be planned in detail once we reach the town. This is called as rolling wave planning.

13.3.6 Projects versus Operations

The following table presents the salient differences between a project and an operation.

Projects	Operations
Projects are temporary and unique.	Operations are ongoing and repetitive.
The purpose of a project is only to attain its objectives; the project is terminated once objectives have been achieved.	The main objective of operations is to sustain the business.

Characteristics common to both projects and operations are as follows:

1. Both are performed by people.
2. Both are planned, executed, and controlled.
3. Both have limited resources.

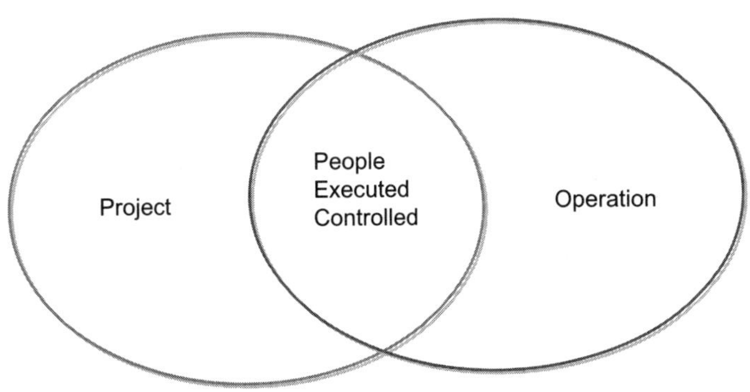

However, the implementation of projects intersects with that of operations at various points during a product's life cycle, for example, at the closeout phase of the project (see "Project Management"), when developing a new product, and at the end of the product's life cycle.

Project interacts with operation at various stages of its life cycle. It cannot run in isolation. For example:

1. Team members entering is an operation
2. Project manager raising the invoice and billing is an operation
3. Project manager approving the leaves of the team members is an operation

In these examples, projects cannot run without the operations. Thus, projects interact with operations during their execution.

What happens to the product after the execution of the project? The product will be deployed in the production environment and used by the end-user. This is an operation.

During the production support, if the customers (end-users) want an enhancement (additional functionality), the concerned enhancement alone will be considered as a separate project.

Exercise 1.1 Classify below activities as "Project" or "Operation".

1. Construction of a bridge
2. Production activities
3. Establishment of new business processes
4. Manufacturing activities
5. Accounting activities

POINTS TO PONDER

There will be a few questions in the exam asking you to differentiate projects and operations; so understand both concepts clearly.

13.3.7 Projects and Strategic Planning

Projects are often used to achieve an organization's strategic plan. In such projects, the project team is either formed out of employees of the organization or contracted.

Exercise 1.2 Write down some reasons for an organization to initiate a project.

____

____

____

____

____

From a strategic perspective, projects are initiated for the following reasons: market demand, organizational needs, customer requests, technological advances, and legal requirements. The following table amplifies this point.

13.4 ENVIRONMENTAL FACTORS THAT MANDATE PROJECTS IN ORGANIZATIONS

Market demand	A bank initiates a project to offer customers an option to transfer money to other accounts over the Internet, following an increase in the use of the Internet for such intrabank and interbank transactions.
Business needs	A company initiates a new project to design a portal for business-to-business transactions as the current manual process of transaction is slow.
Customer requests	A bank initiates a project to develop a loan automation system to automate verification and sanction, as the existing manual system generated customer dissatisfaction. Customer feedback required a new system to reduce processing time and errors.
Technological advances	Whenever a new technology comes to market, every company manufactures a proof of concept (POC) product in the new technology to showcase its ability in the new technology; for example, when Java was introduced in late 1990s, many companies initiated POC projects in Java technology to showcase their ability in the new technology and generate new business.
Legal requirements	New income tax laws might require modifications or new programming to the existing income tax system.

Exercise 1.3 List down the activities of a project manager in your organization.

Let us first compare and analyze the Project Management, Program Management and Portfolio Management, and also try to understand how these are related to each other.

13.5 PROJECT MANAGEMENT

Although many may believe that project management is nothing more than paper work, it is, in reality, a complex activity, which is both an art and a science. Project management involves application of knowledge, skills, tools, and techniques to control project activities so as to meet project requirements; thus, it converts the abstract into the concrete or an organization's vision to reality.

The project management life cycle has five distinct phases (Figure 13.3):

1. Initiation
2. Planning
3. Execution
4. Control
5. Closure

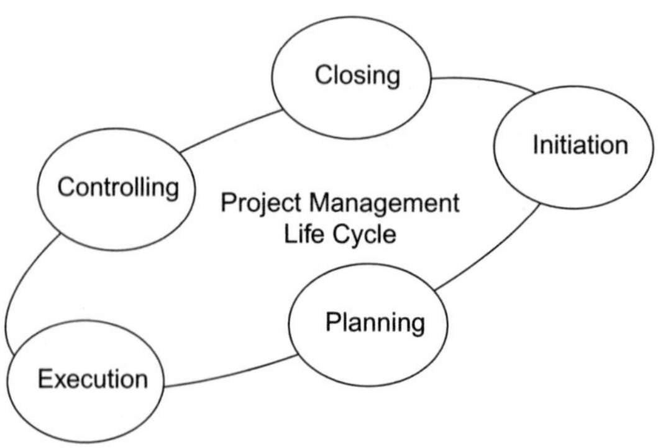

Figure 13.3 Project Management Life Cycle

Figure 13.4 shows the examples of pharma and construction project lifecycles. Based on the domain and technology, the lifecycle model differ, but it is always performed within the five stages mentioned before.

As it is known that the spectrum of project management is quite big, it is divided into following 10 knowledge areas to give each of these areas equal importance. For managing a software project effectively, we need to focus on all these knowledge areas (Figure 13.5):

1. Project scope management
2. Project time management
3. Project quality management
4. Project communication management
5. Project risk management
6. Project cost management
7. Project human resource management
8. Project integration management
9. Project procurement management
10. Project stakeholder management

Figure 13.4 Examples of Project Management Life Cycle

Figure 13.5 Knowledge Areas of Project Management

13.6 PROGRAM MANAGEMENT

A program is a group of projects managed in a coordinated way to obtain benefits and control that would not have been achieved had the projects been managed separately. Program management focuses on project interdependencies and help determine the optimal approach for managing them effectively. An example of a program would be a new communication satellite system program, which comprises the related projects for designing the satellite, constructing and integrating the individual systems, and launching the satellite. Figures 13.6 and 13.7 show the structure of a program and general reporting line of a program manager.

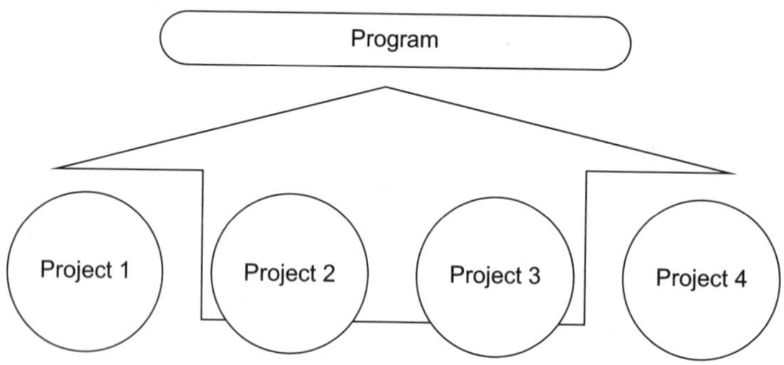

Figure 13.6 Structure of a Program

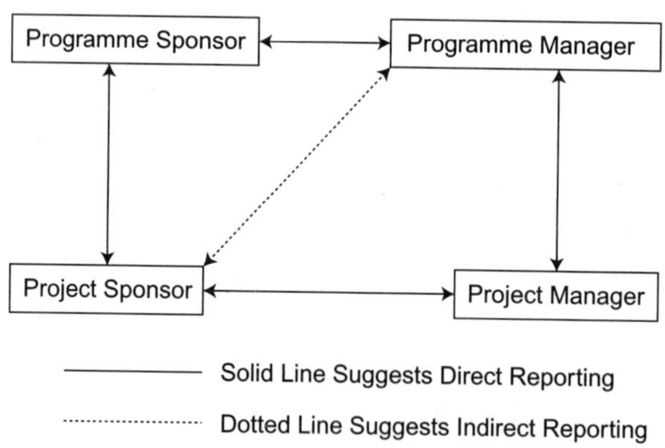

Figure 13.7 Reporting Line of a Program Manager

13.7 PORTFOLIO MANAGEMENT

By portfolio, we refer to a collection of projects or programs that have been grouped together to facilitate the effective management to meet strategic business objectives. Portfolio management refers to the selection process based on the need, profitability, and affordability of the proposed projects. The projects or programs that belong to a portfolio may not necessarily be interdependent or directly

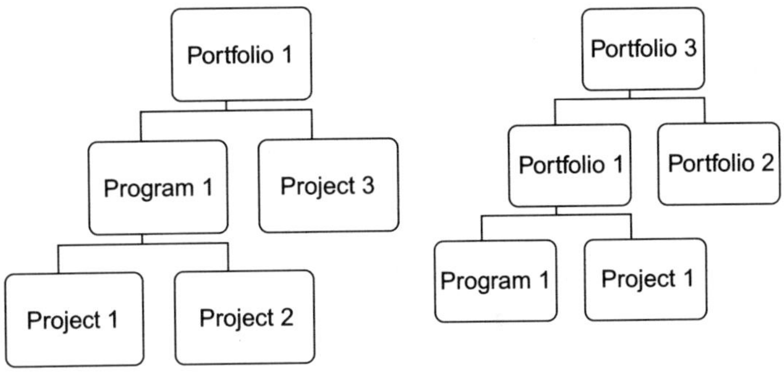

Figure 13.8 Sample Structures of a Portfolio

related. Portfolio management also refers to the centralized management of one or more portfolios, as detailed in the following section.

Portfolio comprises a collection of subportfolios, programs, and operations grouped together in order to meet strategic business objectives of the organization. Programs which are grouped within a portfolio may comprise their own subprograms, projects, or other work to support the corresponding portfolio. Individual projects that are either within or outside the program are still considered to be part of a portfolio (Figure 13.8).

13.8 PROJECT MANAGEMENT OFFICE

The primary function of a project management office (PMO) is to support project managers in a variety of ways with the final goal of making the project management more effective and successful. More informally, "PMO means vastly different things to different people with only this as their common thread: Something that's going to fix our project management mess" (PM Network, February 2001). The PMO manages methodologies, standards, overall risks/opportunities, and interdependencies among projects at the enterprise level; it also manages the project team and organizes the common services of projects. Moreover, it can operate in following areas:

1. Project support
2. Project management process/methodology
3. Reference or 'go to' persons for project managers
4. Internal consulting and mentoring
5. Project management software tools
6. Portfolio management

Different organizations indicate their PMOs using different terms: project police, project support group, or project consulting. Types of PMO and their roles are as follows:

1. **Supportive PMO:** Supportive PMO provides templates, best practices and lessons learnt from other projects to the project team. The degree of control is low.
2. **Controlling PMO:** Controlling PMO provides support and ensures compliance by adopting project management frameworks or methodologies. The degree of control is moderate in this model.

3. **Directive PMO:** Directive PMO directly manages and controls the projects. The degree of control is high in this model.
4. **Project Governance PMO:** This is a comprehensive and consistent method of controlling the project, thereby ensuring its success by defining and documenting reliable, repeatable project practices. It actually defines responsibility and accountability for the success of a project.

13.9 PROJECT PLANNING AND MONITORING

Time, Resource and Cost need to be estimated and budgeted first for executing a project. Once the project starts, the actual time, resource and cost estimates need to be monitored closely against the plan and necessary corrective action needs to be initiated in case there is any deviation. This is the main principle of project planning and monitoring. Under Section 13.5, 10 subprocesses of software project management have been listed. These subprocesses help in the proper planning and monitoring of the project.

In this chapter, a few subprocesses of the project management methodologies have been discussed. Bigger subprocesses are discussed in detail in separate chapters. Project Scope Management and Project Quality Management have been discussed in the subsequent sections of this chapter. Project risk management is discussed in Chapter 14, Communication and human resource management are discussed in Chapter 15, Time and Cost management is covered in Chapter 16, and Stakeholder management in Chapter 17.

13.10 PROJECT SCOPE MANAGEMENT

Project scope management involves the processes required to identify and ensure that a project includes all the work and only the work required for successful project completion. It is primarily concerned with identification and control of the work, that is, what is and what is not a part of project requirements. Project failure is most often related to incorrect understanding of project requirements and lack of control on the already agreed upon project scope.

13.10.1 Types of Scopes

In the context of project management, there are two types of scopes, product scope and project scope.

Product scope: It refers to unalterable features and functions that are to be included in a product or service; for example, a particular characteristic of a product, such as Internet Explorer browser compatible or Netscape Navigator browser compatible.

Project scope: It refers to the work that must be done to deliver a product with specified features and functions; for example, all tasks involved in an office construction project.

Consider a scenario: It is 7AM on a Sunday morning and you just wake up from bed. You want to prepare bread sandwich for the breakfast. Now, let us look at that extent of work (scope) that we need to do in order to prepare the sandwich:

1. Take out the bread from refrigerator
2. Put those in toaster
3. Prepare the filling
4. Keep out the plates, etc.

Are all the above activities required to prepare the bread sandwich? Yes. However, while some of these steps (scope) are directly related to what type of bread sandwich (product) you are going to prepare, a few other steps not directly related to the activity are also required to prepare the sandwich. This is the difference between product scope and project scope. In general, technical analyst takes care of the product scope and the project manager takes care of project scope. (Of course, the project manager is responsible for the whole project.) Product scope is validated against the project requirements and project scope is validated against the project management plan.

Product Scope	Project Scope
Features and functions characterize a product or service	Work that must be done to deliver a product
Required processes, tools, and techniques vary by application area	Required processes, tools, and techniques are similar across application areas
Defined in a project life cycle	Defined in a project management life cycle
Completion of product scope is validated by measurement against product requirements	Completion of project scope is validated by measurement against project management plan

13.10.2 Work Breakdown Structure

Work breakdown structure (WBS) is developed by breaking down the project work into manageable pieces while highlighting the deliverables originating from the work involved. Establishing an effective WBS involves a process called decomposition, which is a process of subdividing major project deliverables into smaller, more manageable components until deliverables are defined in sufficient detail to support project activities.

WBS (refer Figures 13.9 and 13.10) identifies and serves as a blueprint for all tasks and deliverables mandatory in a project. It follows that if a piece of work or task has not been included in the WBS, it is not part of the project. The WBS also serves as a reference point for all stakeholders as a list of tasks and deliverables entailed in a project. In practice, the WBS manifests as a visual representation of the hierarchy of the project and the work specified in the project scope statement.

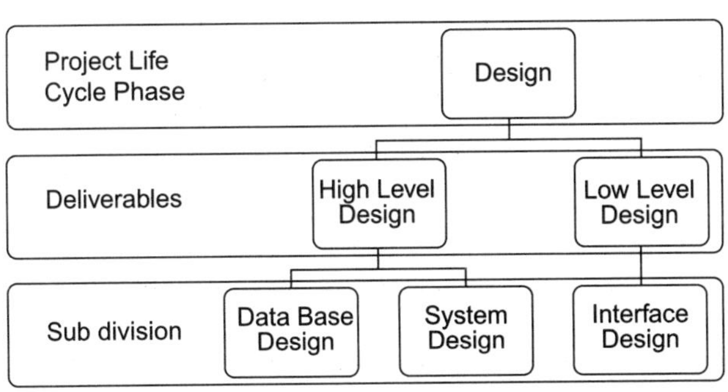

Figure 13.9 Type 1 WBS

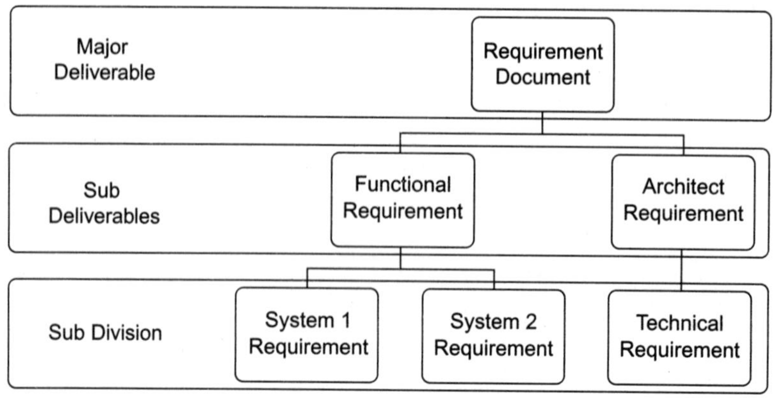

Figure 13.10 Type 2 WBS

Alternative Forms of WBS

In a complex project which has many uncertainties yet to be resolved, decomposition may not be possible for all the deliverables to be made. In such projects, the project management team generally defers the WBS process until deliverables are clarified to enable their breakdown into manageable pieces. This technique of deferring the WBS process is referred to as rolling wave planning.

A common error in the management of complex projects is to attempt to establish a complete WBS at "one go," which is not possible and also not necessary. Elaboration of tasks and deliverables may be completed in short-term, that is in 1 month. Further elaboration may be made as details emerge and requirements become clearer.

A WBS can also be generated as follows:

1. With the phases of a project life cycle at the first level of decomposition and the product and project deliverables at the second level of decomposition
2. A WBS can be established using major project deliverables at the first level of decomposition
3. A WBS can be established using subprojects developed by a third-party organization

Salient advantages of creating a WBS for a project are as follows:

1. Components of a WBS assist stakeholders in readily viewing the deliverables of the project.
2. The process of establishing the WBS for a project often leads to important updates to the scope statement.
3. As a WBS subdivides major project deliverables into manageable components, it serves to improve the quality of cost, time, and resource estimates.
4. A WBS provides a baseline for assigning responsibilities.
5. A WBS is often used to crosscheck with the client about team's understanding of the project scope.
6. A WBS helps understand the project team about fitting of the work packages in the overall project management plan.
7. A WBS indicates the project team about the impact of their work on the project as a whole.

8. A WBS helps prevent change.
9. A WBS provides a basis for estimating resources, cost, and time, and proof of need for resources, cost, and time required.

Once the scope of the project is base lined, it is very important to control the scope throughout the project. Therefore, it is important to track, monitor, manage, and document the change in a robust system for project success. The objective of controlling the scope is effective change management; that is, to ensure that scope creep is prevented or minimized. All changes to project scope occur only through an authorized change process.

Control Scope process controls changes to project scope by

- Influencing the factors that create scope changes and ensure the changes are beneficial
- Determining whether a scope change has occurred
- Managing the changes when they occur

13.11 PROJECT QUALITY MANAGEMENT

Quality means different things to different people. A customer can define quality as "Fitness for Use" and a vendor defines it as "meeting the requirements." Quality management is generally defined as the processes necessary to ensure that the project satisfies the needs for which it was undertaken.

Quality management addresses both the management of the project and the product of the project, and it actually improves project management as well as the quality of the product.

13.11.1 Quality versus Grade

According to Project Management Body of Knowledge Guide, quality is "the degree to which a set of inherent characteristics fulfil requirements", whereas grade is a category assigned to products or services that are intended for identical or similar functional applications but possess different technical characteristics.

For example, coins made of 22 carat gold, 20 carat gold, and 18 carat gold are gold products of stated differing grades. A fitness-for-intended-use comparison of 22 and 18 carat gold would not be valid. A fitness-for-intended-use comparison is valid, however, between two 5 g coins of 22 carat gold bought from two vendors, and quality of the two coins can be compared with proper judgment.

Discussion Questions

1. What are the quality characteristics that need to be looked into while buying a kilogram of bread from market?
2. If there is a tradeoff between quality and grade, how the customer should be convinced (customer usually demands higher quality and higher grade at the same time)?

13.11.2 Importance of Quality

Juran defined quality as "fitness for use," and Deming defined 14 steps to total quality management; he also advocated the Plan-Do-Check-Act cycle as the basis for quality improvement, Philip Crosby popularized the concept of the cost of poor quality; he also advocated prevention over inspection and "zero defects." Crosby believed that quality is "conformance to requirements."

Modern quality management method such as TQM complements project management and both recognize the importance of following features:

- **Customer satisfaction:** Understand, manage, and influence the needs of the customer so that customer expectations are met or exceeded always.
- **Prevention over inspection:** The cost of avoiding mistakes is always lower than the cost of correcting them.
- **Management responsibility:** Although success requires participation of all members, it is the responsibility of the management to provide resources and supports needed.
- **Continuous improvement:** Plan-Do-Check-Act cycle, defined by Shewhart and modified by Deming, is a useful tool for continuous improvement and can be used in any process.

Discussion Question

1. Do you know the quality policy of your organization? What is the importance of quality policy?

13.11.3 Quality Policy

The quality policy of an organization generally defines the primary goal and vision of the organization and outlines the latter's plan to achieve its goals.

According to the "Project Management Body of Knowledge," a quality policy is defined as the "overall intentions and direction of an organization with regard to quality as formally expressed by the top management."

If the organization lacks a formal quality policy, or if the project involves multiple performing organizations, the project management team needs to define a quality policy for the project.

The design and structure of the quality management system of an organization are built upon and derived from the organization's quality policy. The project management team is responsible for ensuring that all project stakeholders are aware of the applicable quality policy and their contribution to achieve it. This is to ensure that the contributions of all the project stakeholders are aligned with quality policy.

13.11.4 Costs of Quality

Costs of quality (COQ), in the context of project management, refer to the total cost incurred by the organization in its attempt to produce deliverables conforming to requirements in a project. Each task in a project is associated with its own cost, that is, cost of conformance and non-conformance, and establishing an appropriate balance, which is the responsibility of the project team, is mandatory.

COQ include prevention costs and appraisal costs; failure costs are costs of poor quality. The costs of not meeting quality requirements are always considered before establishing the outgoing quality level of a particular parameter, because planning for and achieving a much higher quality level than that required may add to COQ without a trade-off in returns.

In general, COQ are discussed under two heads and four subheads:

- Costs of conformance, namely,
  - Prevention costs
  - Appraisal costs

- Costs of non-conformance
  - Internal failure costs
  - External failure costs

Costs of conformance: Costs of conformance refer to the accumulation of costs related to the work performed to conform to the quality aspects in the project. There are two types of costs of conformance, prevention costs and appraisal costs. Prevention costs are the costs related to the factors that are used to prevent errors in the product/service; and appraisal costs are the costs related to the factors that are used to appraise the quality standards of the product/service. Activities related to prevention costs are planning, vendor surveys, requirement and design reviews, code reviews, and schemes to promote good services or products. Activities related to appraisal costs are inspections, reviews, and laboratory tests.

Costs of non-conformance: Costs of non-conformance refer to the accumulation of costs related to the work, which are related to overcome the defects, called non-conformance, already produced in the project. There are two types of costs of non-conformance, such as internal failure costs and external failure costs. Internal failure costs: For example, costs associated with scrap/rework, repair, downtime, defect evaluation, and corrective measures. External failure costs: For example, costs associated with rejects, returns, complaints, and customer inspections.

13.11.5 Control Charts

The control chart, also known as the Shewhart chart or process-behavior chart, is a tool used to determine whether a process is in statistical control or not. If it is not in statistical control, needless to say, it should be brought into control. Control charts are often used as part of quality control processes, feedback from which can be used for planning. Therefore, a control chart may be considered as a planning tool.

13.11.6 Performance Metrics

A metric is a verifiable measure stated in quantitative or qualitative terms that translates customer needs into performance measures; for example, defect frequency, failure rate, availability, reliability, and test coverage.

13.11.7 Quality Assurance

Quality assurance refers the process of auditing and analyzing the established quality requirements and process results to ensure that appropriate and valid quality standards and operational definitions are in place. This also validates the systematic and planned activities implemented to provide confidence to all stakeholders (particularly, the customers, shareholders, and the organization's management) that all processes established for successful project execution are in place and comply with applicable quality standards. Continuous improvement activities form part of quality assurance initiatives.

13.11.8 Quality Audits

A quality audit is the task of systematic examination of the effectiveness of a quality system carried out by a quality auditor or an audit team, and is the key engine of a quality system. It is generally a scheduled task. Results of quality audits, along with quality control reports, form the basis of measuring the functioning of a quality assurance system.

13.11.9 Statistical Sampling

This is the term used to infer that within a given confidence level, a randomly selected sample of items from a population will reflect the same characteristics that occur in the population. This will reduce the overall quality control costs and is used mostly in the electrical or manufacturing field for quality control.

Let us suppose that we want to test a process (manufacturing process), which produces car wheels. We cannot test all the wheels, as we know testing involves subjecting wheel under extreme conditions. Hence, we select wheels randomly from the whole set of wheels, which will reflect the same characteristics of the whole population (all wheels produced).

Summary

- *Enterprise environmental factors*: These are factors that surround (the environment) or influence the success of the project.
- *Process*: This is a set of interrelated activities performed to create pre-specified products, services or results.
- *Project*: The PMI defines a project as a temporary endeavor undertaken to create a unique product, service, or result.
- *Progressive elaboration*: It is the characteristic of a project that integrates the unique and temporary concepts; it starts with nothing and slowly moves forward to create valuable results.
- *Program*: It is a group of projects managed in a coordinated way for benefits and control that would not have been obtained had the projects been managed separately.
- *Portfolio*: By portfolio, we refer to a collection of projects or programs that have been grouped together to facilitate effective management to meet strategic business objectives.
- *Product scope*: It is the inalterable features and functionalities of a product or service.
- *Project scope*: It is the work that must be performed to deliver a product or service with specified features and functions.
- *Scope*: All processes, products, and services a project involves and intends to accomplish better control.
- *Work breakdown structure (WBS)*: It refers to the deliverables-oriented grouping of project elements that organize and define the total scope of the project. The output of a process is decomposing major project deliverables into smaller, more manageable components to provide the WBS dictionary. A component of detailed project scope definition is used to verify that the deliverables being produced and accepted are included in the approved project scope.
- *Control charts*: This is a graphic display of the results over time and against established control limits, which is used if the process is in control or in need of adjustment.
- *Costs of quality*: It is the cost incurred to ensure quality, which includes quality planning, quality control, quality assurance and rework.
- *Quality assurance (QA)*: It is the process of evaluating overall project performance to provide confidence that the project satisfies the relevant quality standards, which usually happens in regular intervals.

- *Quality control (QC)*: This is the process of monitoring particular project results to determine if they comply with the quality standards and identifying ways to eliminate the causes related to the problems.
- *Quality policy*: This involves the overall quality intentions and direction of quality, as formally expressed by the top management.

Model Questions
PART A (Objective type)

1. A project is a temporary endeavor undertaken to create a unique product or service. Here, temporary means

   A. The project has a short duration

   B. It has a beginning but no definite end

   C. It has a definite beginning and an end

   D. It creates a temporary product or service

Answer: C

2. Six project managers were discussing products and projects. Which of the following is not true?

   A. A project can result in a product that can be a component of another product

   B. A project can result in a product that can be an end product in itself

   C. A project can result in an outcome or a document

   D. A project always involves many people

Answer: D

3. Which of the following is not a project?

   A. Changing the structure of an organization

   B. Constructing a building

   C. Implementing a new business process

   D. Manufacturing operations

Answer: D

4. Two program managers discuss the relationship between projects and programs. Which of the following is not true?

   A. A project may or may not be part of a program

   B. A program will always have projects

   C. Programs will include elements of related work outside the scope of discrete projects in the program

   D. Programs will not have elements of related work outside the scope of discrete projects in the program

Answer: D

5. A pharmaceutical drug manufacturer authorizes a project to establish safety guidelines for handling its toxic chemicals. This may be an example of project initiation driven by a

A. Market demand B. Business need C. Technological advance D. Legal requirement

Answer: D

6. Projects are authorized typically as a result of one or more of the following strategic considerations, except

   A. Market demand B. Business need C. Utilizing free resources D. Customer request

Answer: C

7. A program manager is in discussion with senior managers about the structure of a proposed PMO. Which of the following is true regarding the structure of the proposed PMO?

   A. The structure of the PMO depends on the PMO head

   B. The structure of the PMO depends on the projects it is likely to handle

   C. The structure of the PMO depends on the needs of the organization

   D. The structure of the PMO depends on the stakeholders of the PMO

Answer: C

8. The outcome of a project is generally called a

   A. Deliverable B. Project C. Process D. Product

Answer: D

9. A portfolio manager tells another that he has two programs in his portfolio, but they are not related. Is it possible and true?

   A. True B. False

Answer: A

10. Which of the following is a subprocess of costs of conformance?

    A. Prevention costs B. Internal failure costs

    C. External failure costs D. Total cost

Answer: A

PART B (Answer in one or two lines)

1. Define the term "Process" with an example.
2. Define the term "Project" with examples of project.
3. What are the subprocesses under project management?
4. Define program management.
5. Define portfolio management.
6. Define project scope management.
7. What is product scope?
8. Define Quality and Grade.
9. What is the importance of WBS?

10. What is Quality Policy?
11. Describe Cost of Quality.
12. What is costs of non-conformance.
13. What is control chart?
14. Define quality assurance.
15. Define statistical sampling.

PART C (Descriptive type)

1. Discuss the environmental factors that mandate a project in detail with examples.
2. What is a program? Discuss in detail.
3. What is project management office? Discuss various types of PMO in detail.
4. What are different types of scopes? Explain with examples.
5. Discuss WBS in detail.
6. Discuss quality versus grade.
7. Discuss the cost of quality in detail with its various types.
8. Define quality and its importance.

Section 7:
Software Project Management

14

Risk Analysis and Management

CHAPTER COVERAGE

1. *Introduction*
2. *Software Risk*
3. *Types of Risk*
4. *Plan Risk Management*

14.1 INTRODUCTION

There is an element of risk in every activity or enterprise, but effective risk management techniques can mitigate the harmful effects of risks coming to fruition. The American Express Bank, for example, obviously succeeded in managing risk effectively and professionally, because their centers in New York were back in operation just one day after the 9/11 attacks. Project managers, too, are required to plan for and manage risks, because cost overruns, loss of stakeholder confidence, or even outright project failure can result if any or all threats associated with project risks do materialize.

An important responsibility of a project manager and the project management team is to identify all project risks, analyze and rank them in importance, and set processes and systems in place to possibly avert identified threats. Risks are events or consequences that have been estimated to have a nonzero probability of occurring during execution of a project and that are always measured by their impacts on the project. Generally, risks entail losses or benefits, contrary to an opinion that risks always represent only threats to project success. Therefore, project risk management techniques aim to increase the probability and impact of positive events and decrease the probability and impact of negative events on a project.

A high-level pictorial representation of the different phases of risk management is shown in Figure 14.1.

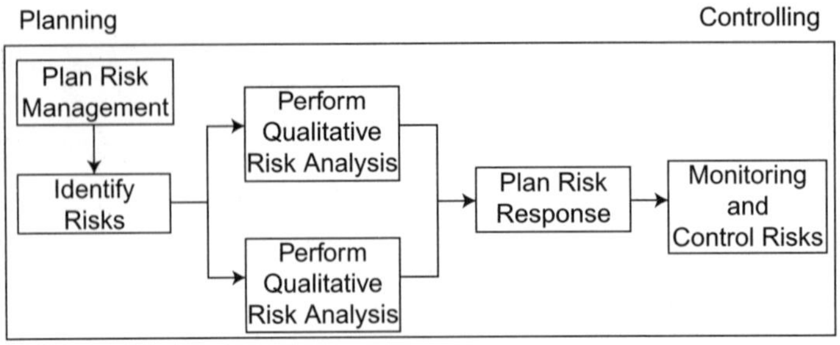

Figure 14.1 Risk Management Process

14.2 SOFTWARE RISK

The definition of risk is "A probability or threat of loss or any negative consequence which is caused by external or internal events and that may be avoided through preemptive action." This means there are two characteristics of the risk:

Uncertainty: The risk event may happen or may not happen. There is degree of uncertainty attached to event.

Loss: If the risk event occurs, there will be certain losses incurred.

14.3 TYPES OF RISK

In software projects, there are different types of risks as below:

Project risk: The project risks impact the project schedule, which in turn increases the cost of the project. There may be various reasons behind the project risks such as budget issue, resource issue, requirement issue, and customer issue, which can impact a software project.

Technical risk: The impact of technical risk is mainly on the quality and timeline of the project. There may be potential issue in the design, implementation, interface, maintenance, and unknown technology of the software, which leads to delay and quality risk in the project.

Business risk: Every project has some business goals to fulfill. But if the business alignment of the project or the software to be built is lost, then either it loses the focus of the senior management or the project may be scrapped.

The following are two important concepts related to risk management:

High-risk area: The intensity of a risk varies over a project's life cycle. Risk is usually high in the conceptual and developmental phases of a project and decreases over the project's life cycle with gradual completion of project work. Alternatively, the cost at stake is low in the early phases of the life cycle and increases as work is accomplished. The area of overlap is known as the high-risk area. Risk is very high in the beginning because of uncertainties in the project. The cost at stake is low in the beginning because we would have just started spending our money. But as we move ahead with the project, uncertainties will go down because the project scope becomes cleaner.

But the costs at stake slowly move up as the project progresses. Both these (cost at stake and risk) meet at a point forming an area called high-risk area that needs to be monitored cautiously.

Stakeholder tolerance: Different stakeholders, depending on the criticality of perceived benefits or losses, accept varying degrees of risk in a project. For example, cost variance and scope variance are acceptable up to a certain limit, beyond which it will go out of control. This is called stakeholder tolerance level.

14.4 PLAN RISK MANAGEMENT

Careful and explicit risk management planning enhances the probability of success of the risk management process. Project scope statement acts as a primary input as the entire project revolves around executing the scope of the project successfully. In addition, cost management plan and schedule management plan also act as input for this process, as risk management depends on these plans. The process of how a project manager manages the risk depends on how he manages the schedule and cost of the project (see Figure 14.2).

Arranging the risk planning meeting is the first step for planning the risk management. This meeting should involve the project manager, project team leaders, key stakeholders, and others who may be deemed authorities on providing inputs to risk management. In these meetings, risk management responsibilities are assigned. Cost elements and schedule activities of managing risks are also assigned to the project budget and project schedule, respectively.

Risk management plans of similar past projects may serve as inputs to preparing the risk management plan for a current project.

Risk categories and a risk breakdown structure (RBDS) are parts of the risk management plan which is the primary output of the planning the risk management. Risk categories help in the systematic identification of risks and contribute to the effectiveness and quality of the identify risk process. Risk categories are simply lists of common areas or sources of risk; typically, project management offices have standard lists of risk categories that all projects can use to identify risks easily.

POINTS TO PONDER

The contents of a typical risk management plan:

- Methodology to manage risks
- Roles and responsibilities for each actions
- Budget
- Frequency of occurrence of the meeting
- Risk categories
- Definitions of risk probability and impact
- Probability and impact matrix
- Scoring and interpretation
- Reporting formats

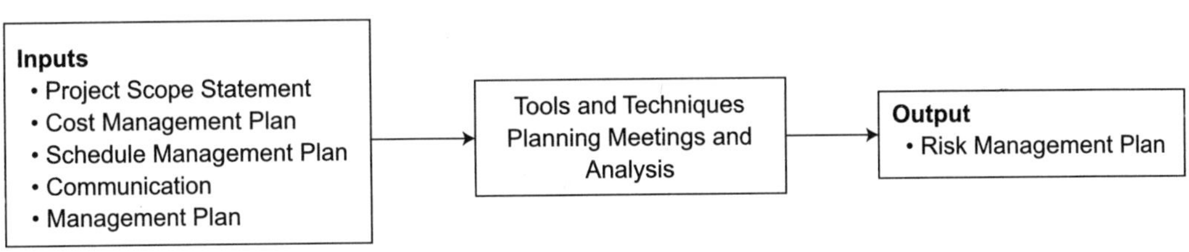

Figure 14.2 Plan Risk Management Process

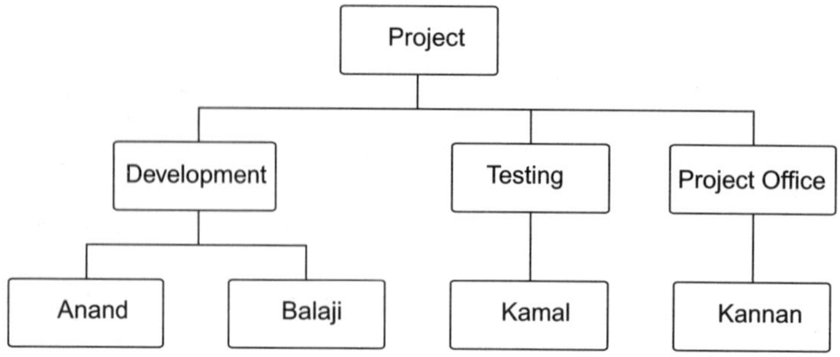

Figure 14.3 Risk Breakdown Structure

A typical RBDS (Figure 14.3) lists the categories and subcategories within which risks for a project may arise.

External categories: Government regulations, markets, customers, suppliers

Project management: Initiation, planning, controlling, closing

Organization: resources, funding, prioritization

14.4.1 Identify Risk

The identify risk process (Figure 14.4) involves determination of risks that are likely to affect a project and documentation of the characteristics of each risk. Both the positive effects (opportunities or rewards) and negative effects (threats) of risks are documented. The project team, subject matter experts, stakeholders, and other project managers are involved in the identification of risks. The identify risks process is iterative because the identification occurs over the entire life cycle of the project from beginning of the project till the end, continuously. Because project managers are often called uncertainty managers, it would be fair to call them risk managers as well.

In addition to the formal already-identified project risks, there also exist risks that may evolve over the course of project execution. A risk trigger is a symptom of and an indirect manifestation of a risk event; however, risk triggers may prove to be false alarms as well: their identification does not indicate the certainty of a risk developing. An example of a risk trigger is poor team morale. Risk triggers – if identified on time – serve project managers helpful warning signs of an emerging risk.

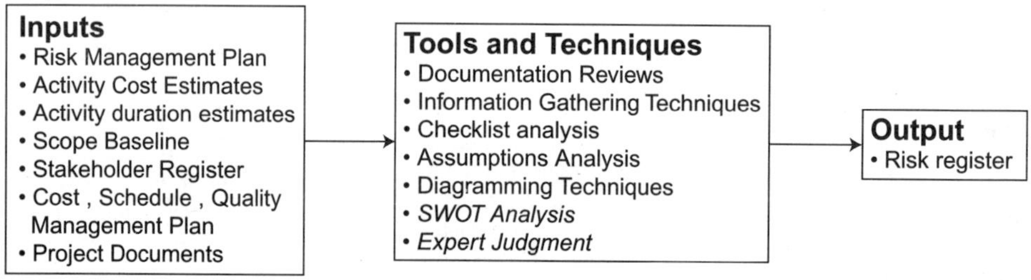

Figure 14.4 Identify Risks Process

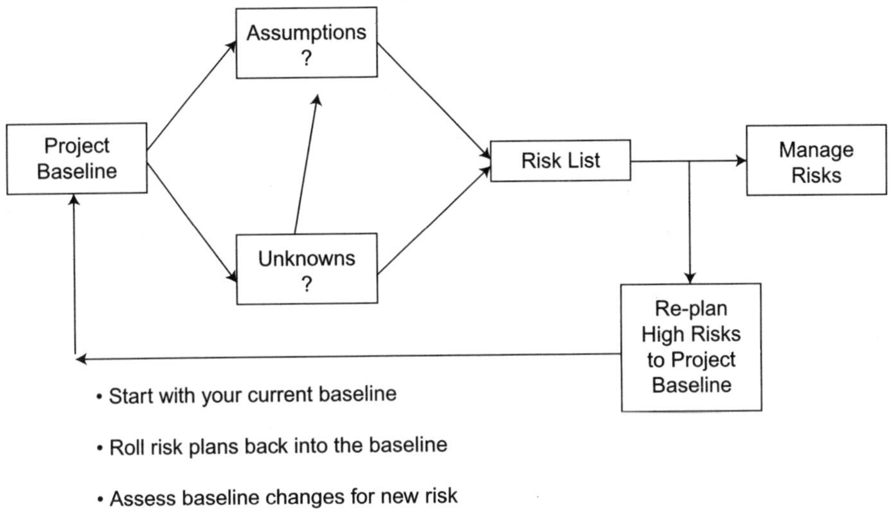

Figure 14.5 Projects Baseline versus Risk List

Few ways to identify risks are documentation reviews, brainstorming and information gathering techniques, Delphi technique, checklist analysis, diagramming techniques, assumption analysis, SWOT analysis, and expert judgment.

A structured documentation review comprises a review of all project materials, particularly project baseline documents (Figure 14.5). Use of this tool includes review of all project plans, assumptions, lessons learned, and risk management plans from previous similar projects, and contractual obligations, if any, for the project. The quality of past risk management plans, agreement if any between those plans, requirements and assumptions of those projects, agreement if any between those plans, and the actual execution of those projects can be useful sources of indicators of risks in the current project.

POINTS TO PONDER

There are many ways to identify risks: documentation reviews, brainstorming and information gathering techniques, Delphi technique, checklist analysis, diagramming techniques, assumption analysis, SWOT analysis, and expert judgment.

14.4.1.1 Information-Gathering Techniques

Brainstorming The main goal of brainstorming, a popular and widely used information-gathering technique, in risk identification is to obtain the material required to generate a comprehensive list of risks as envisioned by all project stakeholders. An important feature of brainstorming meetings is that they use participants of widely differing functional backgrounds, which enhances the likelihood fresh ideas and innovations being generated.

Delphi technique The Delphi technique (Figure 14.6) is a systematic, interactive forecasting method used for risk identification, and it uses a panel of independent experts. It is also used to help the

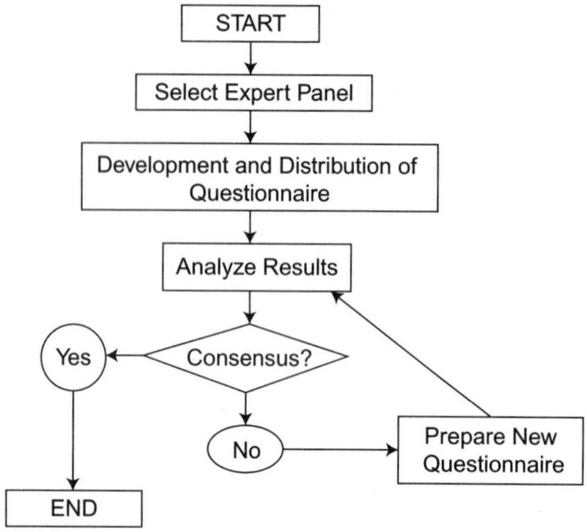

Figure 14.6 DELPHI Technique–Risk Identification

participating experts reach a consensus. Experts answer questionnaires in two or more rounds. After each round, the session facilitator provides a summary of the forecasts of each expert, one by one, without indicating the identity of the expert.

The summary also includes the reasons the experts provided for judgments made. After summaries of all experts' views have been thus presented, experts are encouraged to revise their forecasts—on the basis of the summaries presented—and resubmit them. On the completion of this process, the expert group converges on the correct answer. The process is stopped after a predefined stop criterion, such as the number of rounds or stability of results. The mean or median scores of the final rounds determine the decision adopted by the expert group. The main advantage of this technique is that it reduces bias in and eliminates subjective influences from the decision-making process. However, the success of the technique hinges on the analytical skill and subject matter expertise of the facilitator.

POINTS TO PONDER

Following are the key characteristics of the Delphi method:

1. Anonymity of the expert participants
2. Opportunity for experts to review their inputs
3. Structured information flow

Checklist analysis Risk identification checklists can be prepared on the basis of historical information available and similar past projects. The lowest level of RBDS can also be used as risk checklist.

Diagramming techniques There are different diagramming techniques such as cause-and-effect diagrams and system or process flowcharts that show how various components of a project are interrelated, and this link identification serves as a basis for risk identification. Influence diagrams, pictorial representations of a problem showing causal influences, and time ordering events may also be used as diagramming tools to identify risks.

An influence diagram, also referred to as a decision network, is a graphical and mathematical representation of a decision. It helps to take a decision, and the decision is fully based on the influence of various factors associated with the decision. Risks associated with various factors are the sources of risks for the entire decision-making process. For example, assume that you are the project manager of a construction project and you want to plan your vacation based on the weather forecast which is not conducive for the work. Figure 14.7 shows two functional arcs ending in satisfaction, one conditional arc ending in weather forecast and one informational arc ending in vacation activity. The informational arc ending in vacation activity indicates that the project manager will only know weather forecast, not weather condition, when making a choice. In other words, actual weather will be known after a choice has been made. It also indicates that vacation activity is independent of weather condition, given weather forecast is known from it. Both weather forecasts and actual weather are the sources of risks.

SWOT analysis SWOT analysis is an instrument used in strategic planning. Factors internal to an organization can be classified as strengths (S) or weaknesses (W) and those external to the organization can be classified as opportunities (O) or threats (T). The following list defines the four components of a SWOT analysis (refer Figure 14.8).

Strengths: Positive tangible and positive intangible attributes internal to an organization that are within the organization's control.

Weakness: Negative attributes that are within an organization's control representing areas for organizational improvement.

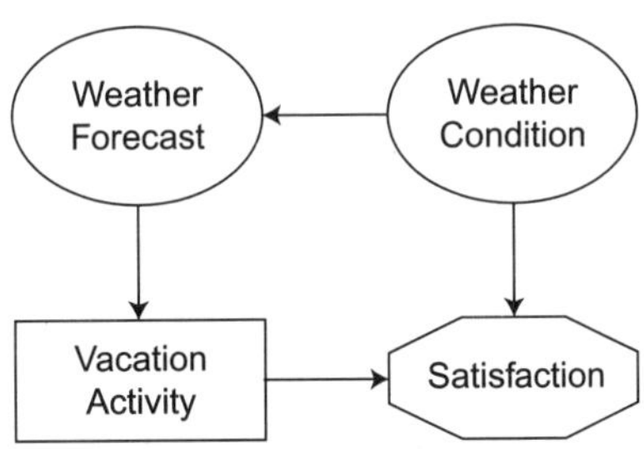

Figure 14.7 Influence Diagram

Figure 14.8 SWOT Analysis

Opportunities: Attractive factors external to the organization.

Threats: External risk factors beyond the organization's control; the organization may yet benefit from threats by having contingency plans to effectively address these threats.

POINTS TO PONDER

Following are the key characteristics of the Delphi method:

SWOT analysis do's and don'ts

- Be realistic on all the factors
- Be specific with the factors and area of comparison
- Compare factors only with core mission
- Keep analysis short and simple
- Avoid complexity

The risk register is the primary output of the identify risk process. The register is used updating risk information, because risk identification is an ongoing process. It lists identified risks, potential responses of the risks identified, root causes of identified risks, and updated risk categories.

The risk register is an important project document and is often referred to as a risk tracker sheet.

14.4.2 Risk Analysis

Risk analysis is the next important step where the probability and impact of the risks are identified. We know that risks are uncertain events. So, the plan to deal with the risks should be based on the probability of the risks as well as the loss or damage that the risk can cause. There are two ways to formally conduct the risk analysis.

14.4.2.1 Qualitative Risk Analysis Techniques

Qualitative risk analysis process (Figure 14.9) is one of assessment and evaluation of the impacts of and likelihoods of realization related to identified risks. Qualitative risk analysis is a subjective analysis of identified risks. Here, subjective refers to the classification of risks as high-impact, medium-impact, and low-impact risks. Establishing normative standards to classify identified risks reduces the element of personal bias in the classification process. Performing qualitative risk analysis process is

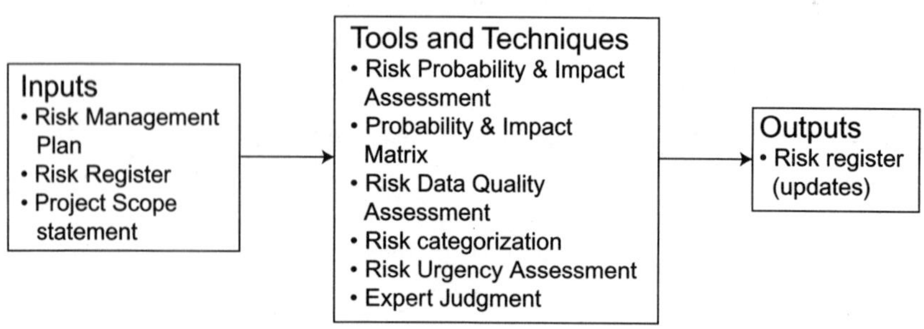

Figure 14.9 Qualitative Risk Analyses

a quick and cost-effective means of establishing priorities. The outputs of this process, however, are revised during project execution.

Qualitative risk analysis is followed by quantitative risk analysis. First, the risk needs to be qualified as high, medium, or low. Only then can we quantify the risks stating how much high or how much low.

Risk probability is defined as the chance level of risks occurring in a project, whereas risk consequences refer to the impact on projects if identified risks do materialize. Both these important factors are identified and documented in the risk management plan. The levels of risk probability and impact are assessed, measured, and analyzed in project team meetings, attended by subject matter experts as well.

Probability and impact matrix A probability and impact matrix is used to assign risk ratings, namely, low, medium, or high (Figure 14.10), to risks on the basis of a combination of (1) the probability of occurrence of that risk and (2) its impact of the risk event occurring on project objectives. Risk response action depends on the classification of the risk (Figure 14.11). Risks with high probability and high impact require further analysis, including quantification and timely management. Risks with lower probability and impact may not require action but would typically be monitored.

Ordinal scale is a ranked-order scale, such as very low, medium low, low, moderate, high, and very high. Cardinal scale values are usually linear (0.1/0.3/0.5/0.7/0.9) or nonlinear (0.05/0.1/0.2/0.4/0.8/).

Impack Scale

Consequence	Health and safety
High	> 10 Server Failure at a time
Moderate	6 to 10 server Failure at a time
Low	1 to 5 Server Failure at a time

Probability Scale

Likelihood Class	Likelihood of Occurrence (events/year)
Low	<0.01% chance of occurrence
Medium	0.01-10% chance of occurence
High	>10% chance of occurrence

Figure 14.10 Impact and Probability Scale Examples

PROBABILITY AND IMPACT MATRIX				
Probability	High			Immediate Attention
	Medium			
	Low			
		Low	Medium	High
		Impact		

Figure 14.11 Probability and Impact Matrix

Ordinal scale is an example of Likert scale (i.e., risk effects on a scale from 1 to 5). A rating of 5 would be considered to be high riskier than a rating of 1, but we cannot say that it is five times riskier than the 1. Cardinal scales have an absolute value in them and we can make quantitative comparisons between results.

Risk data quality assessment Risk data quality assessment is a technique used to evaluate the degree to which project data are useful. Needless to say, accurate data are necessary for accurate qualitative risk analyses. The technique (Figure 14.12) involves the following steps:

- Identify the extent of understanding of a risk
- Check the data available on the risk
- Check the reliability of data
- Collection of more reliable data

Risk urgency assessment Risk urgency assessment is based on the indicators of risk—such as time available to create a risk response, symptoms and warning signs, and the risk ratings (Figure 14.13).

Time-based action: A positive opportunity may be temporarily available. Only a time-bound risk response action can eliminate the risk and enable availing of the rewards offered by the opportunity.

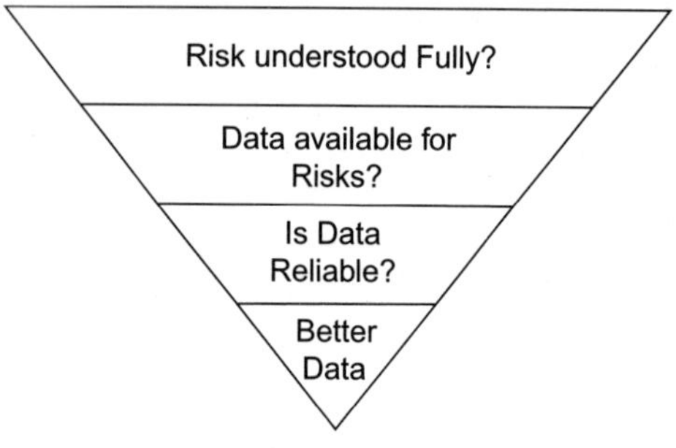

Figure 14.12 Risk Data Quality Assessment

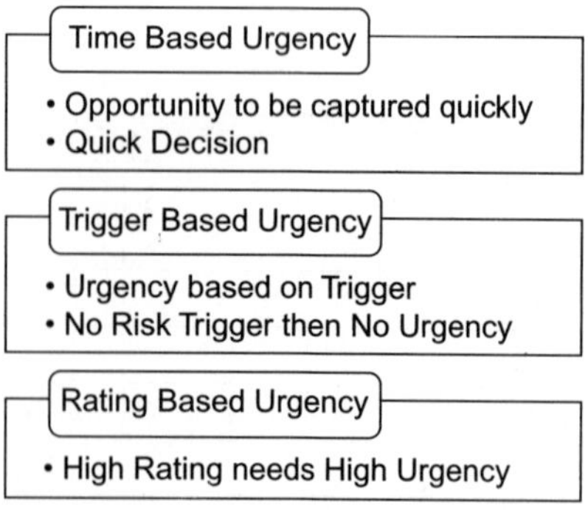

Figure 14.13 Risk Urgency Assessment

Symptoms and warning signs of risk: Such signs may allow for only a short response window, sometimes just a few hours before an indented risk event occurs. Such signs are also referred to as risk triggers.

Risk ratings: High-risk ratings are typically assigned to risk events carrying high impact and high probability of occurrence. Such risks obviously require continuous monitoring.

Risk categorization Risks in projects can be categorized on the basis of source of risks or area of the project affected. For example, risks can be categorized as operational risks, financial risks, risks related with project schedule, risks related with environment, risks related with change, risks related with resources, risks related with timeline, etc.

Operational risk: Risks due to operational factors such as loss due to improper process implementation.

Example: Lack of proper training for resources.

Schedule risk: Risks related to delay in the project schedule. Schedule risks directly affect the project and may lead to project failure.

Apart from the above-mentioned risk, there is one more category of risk associated with project management. This risk is related to attributes like project planning, project organization, and frequent requirement changes.

The above categorization helps to analyze the risks in a better way. Special treatments can be given to special categories of risks. For example, for all financial-related risks, we can assign a risk owner who is good in financial management.

The main outputs of the perform qualitative risk analysis process are updates to the risk register generated in the identify risks process. Significant risks have a description of the basis for the assessed probabilities and impacts.

Updates to the risk register may include:

1. Relative rankings of risks
2. Causes of risks
3. Risks requiring response in near term
4. List of risks for further analysis
5. Watch list of low priority
6. Any trends in analysis results

14.4.2.2 Quantitative Risk Analysis Techniques

Quantitative risk analysis process (Figure 14.14) is a process, as the term suggests, of quantifying the probability and consequences of risks taken. The process is used to quantify risk exposure

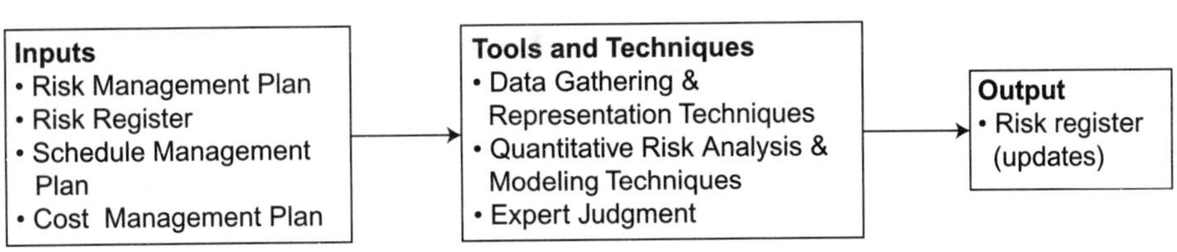

Figure 14.14 Quantitative Risk Analysis

for a project and determine achievable and realistic costs, schedules, or scope targets to manage identified risks.

Project stakeholders and subject matter experts quantify the probability and consequences of risks on various parameters such as cost, schedule, and scope. For example, a cost expert can quantify the risks related to costs in a better way. The quantification of risks is based on the determination of its impact, which depends on the accuracy of data in hand. The type of data to be gathered in turn depends on the type of probability distributions that will be used for quantitative analysis. In general, process variations tend to follow a binomial, normal, or Poisson distribution, and therefore, while quantifying risks, only use of the applicable probability distribution function would lead to a more reliable analysis.

Probability distributions A probability distribution is continuous if its cumulative distribution function is continuous and is equivalent to saying that for random variables X, P $[X = a] = 0$ for all real numbers a, that is, the probability that X attains the value a is 0, for any number a. Here X is called a continuous random variable. Continuous probability distributions represent uncertainties in values, such as durations of schedule activities and costs of project-related components. Process measurements follow discrete probability distributions when they are restricted to being within a predefined list of possible values, and the list either has a finite number of members or is at most countable. It can be used to represent uncertain project events, such as the outcome of a test or a possible scenario in a decision tree.

Decision trees A decision tree is a tool used in risk analysis and is used to investigate the risks associated with several possible courses of action. In a typical decision tree, a chance node is represented by a circle and a decision node represented by a square. In decision tree analysis, the process of risk analysis starts from the right of the tree diagram and works toward the left, that is, from the future toward the past. Future decisions are made, and they are rolled back to become part of the earlier decisions. For example, a future decision can be selection of Project A, selection of Project B, success of Project A after selection, failure of Project A after selection, success of Project B after selection, and failure of Project B after selection.

Uniform distributions are used only if there is no obvious value that is more likely than any other between specified high and low bounds, as in the early concept stage of design.

Quantitative risk analysis and modeling techniques For quantifying risks, we need the list of risks identified in the risk register along with the tolerance limits of the stakeholders, approximate cost estimation of the risks, and resources required. Once these lists are available, we can start performing quantitative risk analysis using sensitivity analysis, expected monetary value analysis, and simulation.

Sensitivity Analysis Sensitivity analysis is used to determine risks that have potentially the greatest impact on project outcome. The technique is used to examine the extent to which uncertainty associated with each project element affects the overall project objective, while assuming that the uncertainty associated with all other project elements is zero. Sensitivity analyses often involve the use of tornado diagrams (refer Figure 14.15), also called tornado plots or tornado charts, which are used to examine the relative importance of process variables.

Expected Monitory Value (EMV) is a technique in which a calculation is made to determine the average of all potential outcomes of an event when the future includes a number of scenarios that may or may not happen. The expected monetary value analysis, referred to as EMV, can be conducted at

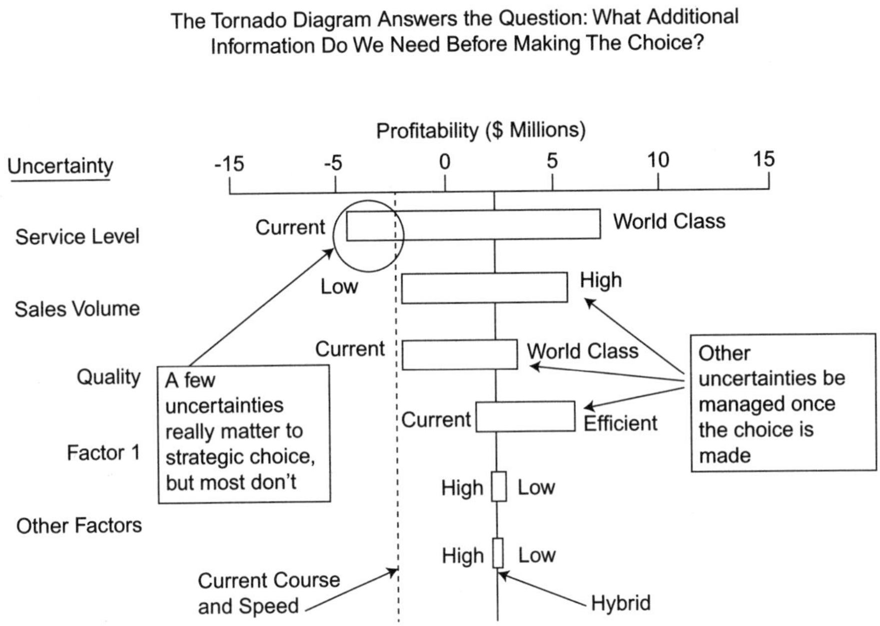

Figure 14.15 Tornado Diagram

any point in the life cycle of a project but should be done as early as possible to get the better results out of it. Risks with higher EMV need to be addressed as a priority.

Expected monetary value is given by

Expected monetary value = Probability × cost

Using this technique, project managers summarize the expected values to total project risks. Three probability values are used to calculate EMVs (not to be confused with those used in PERT calculations).

The expected value thus estimated serves as a guideline for total costs entailed to eliminate identified project risks. For example:

If a project has a 55% chance of a US $100,000 profit and a 40% chance of a US $300,000 loss, the EMV of the project is calculated as:

EMV = profit of (0.55 × 100,000) + loss of (0.40 × 300,000)
= profit of (55,000) + loss of (120,000)
= loss of 65,000 $

Modeling and Simulation Simulation techniques are widely used to generate models that analyze the behavior or performance of a system and quantify the effects of identified risks on that system. Project execution is simulated many times to obtain a statistical distribution of calculated results. The Monte Carlo analysis is a good example of simulation techniques. The Monte Carlo analysis represents a class of iterative, computational techniques that produce results to quantify the risks associated with simulated schedules and alternative plans, paths through network diagrams, and strategies for successful project outcome. The analysis results in a probability distribution, which may be inputs for further analyses.

The following content of risk register is updated as part of quantitative risk analysis.

- The probabilistic analysis of the project is updated.
- The probability of achieving time and cost objectives is updated.
- The prioritized list of quantified risks is updated.
- Trends in quantitative risk analysis results are updated.

14.4.3 Risk Mitigation Planning

Risk mitigation planning is the process to identify ways to enhance opportunities and reduce threats to project objectives and determine the action plan to implement those (Figure 14.16). Risk response planning is based on the severity of the identified risk and estimated cost-effectiveness in overcoming the challenge. Response plans should be time bound, realistic within the project context, and agreed upon by all parties involved. A risk owner is assigned who takes ownership of the risk. The risk owner has the responsibility of analyzing and controlling the project risks. A risk owner is identified based on the skill set and experience level. For example, for all project management-related risks, the project manager can be an owner and for all technical-related risks, the team leader or architect can be the owner.

Risk responses may include:

- the action plans to eliminate the threats before they happen.
- the action plans to decrease the probability and/or impact of threats.
- the action plans to increase the probability and/or impact of opportunities.
- contingency plans.
- fallback plans if contingency measures taken prove to be ineffective.

14.4.3.1 Strategies to Counter Negative Risks (Threats)

Negative risks are threats to the project and should be either avoided or the impact is minimized to reduce the damage to the project as much as possible. Below are the strategies that are followed for this.

Avoidance: This strategy attempts to eliminate a specific threat by eliminating its cause. For example, scope creep, which occurs when project scope is not frozen, may be eliminated by freezing project scope at an appropriate point in time.

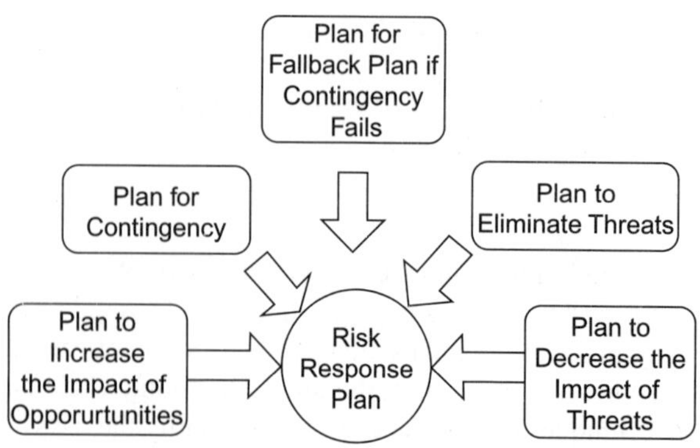

Figure 14.16 Risk Response Plan Objectives

Transference: This strategy aims at use of contracting, insurance warranties, guarantees, and outsourcing of work, all which transfer risk from the performing organization to a third party.

Mitigation: This strategy attempts to decrease the probability of occurrence of a risk, reduce the risk-event value, or both, thereby reducing the cost of managing that particular risk.

14.4.3.2 Strategies to Exploit Opportunities (Positive Risks)

On the other hand, there are positive risks which are actually the opportunities for the project to achieve more than planned. These risks should be handled in a timely manner as otherwise the opportunity for reaping benefits from these can be missed. Below are the strategies that are followed for positive risks:

- *Exploit:* This strategy attempts to ensure that the opportunity event occurs. For example, the most talented resource in a project team may be assigned to a demanding task to reduce project duration.
- *Share:* This strategy aims at allocating a part of the ownership of an opportunity to a third party to ensure that the opportunity event occurs, while decreasing the cost associated with a risk event occurring. Joint venture enterprises are an example of risk sharing.
- *Enhance:* This strategy increases the positive impact of an opportunity. For example, more buffer resources are allotted to an activity to ensure early completion.

14.4.3.3 Strategies for Both Threats and Opportunities

Acceptance is a type of strategy applicable for both the threats and opportunities. This strategy accepts the risk and develops a contingency plan, should the risk event occur. For example, in a cost plus contract, the buyer takes more risks and in a fixed bid project the seller takes more risks. The risks related with the contract are accepted, and a contingency plan is developed to tackle it.

Contingency reserve: This strategy aims at generating a contingency reserve to tackle unknown risks and accepted known risks. The quantum of the contingency reserve, which may be in the form of additional time for the project, additional resources, and/or additional billing to the customer, is based on the expected impact of the risk.

Management reserve: This strategy generates a separately planned quantity to be used to manage future uncertain scenarios that are impossible to predict—unknown unknowns. Use of management reserve requires a change to the project's cost and schedule baselines, whereas a contingency reserve is not required to be reflected in cost and schedule baselines.

The main outputs of the plan risk response process are updates to the risk register and include residual risks and contingency plans:

Residual risks: These are risks that remain after a risk response plan has been determined and put in place. Residual risks are documented and continually monitored.

Contingency plans: These are plans describing the specific actions that will be taken if identified opportunities or threat occur.

14.4.3.4 Proactive Risk Response Strategies

Identifying and mitigating the risk well ahead of their occurrence ensures the effective and well-controlled project execution. The processes that help in proactive risk identification and mitigation are as follows:

Project risk response audits: Risk auditors examine the effectiveness of established risk response plans with respect to risk avoidance, risk transfer, and risk mitigation. Checks are made on whether the organization has adopted appropriate and relevant techniques to assess the severity of the risks and whether a combination of qualitative and quantitative techniques has been used in assessment of risks. The effectiveness of risks owner is also audited.

Periodic project risk reviews: Established risk response plans are periodically reviewed for their implementation and for their continued relevance and effectiveness. If changes are deemed to be required, risk plans are appropriately updated. Risk reviews also check whether appropriate procedures are being followed.

Technical performance measurement: This tool is used to compare technical accomplishments during project execution to the project plan's schedule of technical achievements. Appropriate action is taken wherever deviations are found high.

Additional risk response planning: This technique is used to address risks not identified—not documented in the risk register—that may have emerged over project execution. Additional planning—and allocation of resources—may also be required if the impact of identified risks proves to be greater than anticipated.

Work-around: These are unplanned responses to unanticipated risk events.

Status meetings: These are meetings that are usually convened when the deviation from established risk response plans is high and this can also be convened at regular frequency to check the status.

Reserve analysis: Reserve analysis is a technique that is used to identify the quantum of reserve resources that require to be set aside for project contingencies. The magnitude of this quantum depends on the complexity of the project. Reserves may be reallocated if expected threat events do not occur or if expected opportunities do occur. Additional response planning technique is used to address the risks not identified, while reserve analysis is for the identified risks.

Summary

Risks can be effectively managed by following predefined steps. The following lists salient features of risk management:

- A project risk is a potential source of deviation from the project plan and can have a negative or positive impact on the project.
- Project risks that represent threats are classified as negative; project risks that represent opportunities are classified positive.
- Risks should be identified in all phases of the project life cycle; risk identification is an iterative process. Established risk response plans require continual review
- Work-around is unplanned response to unanticipated risk events.

Case Study

A risk register is the place where the details of the project's risks and their status are maintained. Note that this is a live document, which means the information maintained in this document are to be kept updated regularly. This document gives visibility to all the stakeholders about the nature and criticality of the risks present in the project along with the plan to mitigate those.

Sample risk register

Risk ID	Date Raised	Risk Title	Risk Description	Impact Description	Probability	Impact	Overall Risk Rating	Action Plan	Action Plan Responsibility Owner	Expected Closure Date	Status
1	1-Jan-13	FSD Sign Off	Frequent requirement changes might come after FSD sign-off	May result in effort and schedule escalation. Too many changes will threaten go live date.	Medium	Medium	Medium	1. Change management process to be leveraged to treat any change to the signed-Off FSD as a CR. 2. All CRs will go through the estimation and prioritization process. 3. Only approved CRs will be passed on for development.	Steve	1-Mar-2013	Open

Model Questions
PART A (Objective type)

1. Project risk management is defined as

A. The process of defining how to conduct risk management activities for a project.

B. The process of prioritizing risks for further analysis or action by assessing and combining their probability of occurrence and impact.

C. The process of developing options and actions to enhance opportunities and to reduce threats to protect objectives.

D. The process of conducting risk management planning, identification, analysis, response planning and monitoring, and controlling a project.

Answer: D

2. The process of numerically analyzing the effect of identified risk on overall project objectives is called

A. Plan risk responses
B. Perform quantitative risk analysis
C. Perform qualitative risk analysis
D. Plan risk management

Answer: B

3. The process of evaluating the risk process effectiveness throughout the project is called

A. Plan risk responses
B. Perform quantitative risk analysis
C. Perform qualitative risk analysis
D. Monitor and control risk

Answer: D

4. The process of developing options and actions to enhance opportunities and to reduce threats to project objectives refers to the

A. Perform quantitative risk analysis
B. Perform qualitative risk analysis
C. Plan risk responses
D. Monitor and control risk

Answer: C

5. Risk experts participate in this technique anonymously.

A. Brainstorming
B. Delphi technique
C. Checklist analysis
D. Root cause analysis

Answer: B

6. Shutting a project down on account of high risks is which types of risk response plan?

A. Transfer
B. Avoid
C. Accept (evade)
D. Mitigate

Answer: B

7. Outsourcing is a part of which risk response plan?

A. Transfer
B. Avoid
C. Accept (evade)
D. Mitigate

Answer: A

8. All of the following are examples of positive risks except.

A. Exploit
B. Share
C. Accept
D. Mitigate

Answer: D

9. Monitor and control risks can involve all of the following except

A. Choosing alternative strategies
B. Executing a fallback plan
C. Taking correction action
D. Analyzing the risk

Answer: D

10. How often should identification of risk take place?

A. Only when the project manager is free
B. One per phase is enough as the project is big
C. Throughout the project
D. One in the planning phase

Answer: C

PART B (Answer in one or two lines)

1. Define risk.
2. Name three types of risks.
3. Define high-risk area.
4. Write notes on stakeholder tolerance.
5. What is risk management plan? What are all its contents?
6. Write notes on risk breakdown structure.
7. Write notes on risk register.
8. What is probability impact matrix?
9. Write notes on risk urgency assessment.

10. Write notes on risk data quality assessment.
11. Write notes on decision tree.

PART C (Descriptive type)

1. Discuss the three types of risks in detail.
2. Explain plan risk management process in detail.
3. Explain the process of risk identification in detail.
4. Discuss SWOT analysis in detail
5. How Delphi technique is used to identify risks?
6. Write notes on influence diagram.
7. Explain qualitative risk analysis process in detail.
8. Explain the process of quantitative risk analysis.
9. What is sensitivity analysis? Explain Tornado diagram in detail with example.
10. Discuss the strategies to handle negative and positive risks.

Section 7:
Software Project Management

15

Communication and Team Management

CHAPTER COVERAGE

1. *Introduction*
2. *Dimensions of Communication*
3. *Forms of Communication*
4. *Process of Communication*
5. *Handling Communication in a Software Project*
6. *Project Performance Reports*
7. *Managing the Project Team*

15.1 INTRODUCTION

Communication management refers to the process of timely and appropriate development, collection, dissemination, storage, and disposition of project-related information. Generally, more than 90% of a project manager's time goes for communication. Project managers generate a communication management plan, prepare reports based on it, ask and discuss with stakeholders about their needs, identify what communication processes they need, and frequently revisit communication needs of stakeholders at team meetings to avoid communication-related problems.

On a high level, processes involved in the effective communication management are as follows:

1. Plan Communications: This process determines the information needs of project stakeholders and establishes a communications system.
2. Manage Communications: This is a process of implementing the communication management plan and responding to unexpected requests for information.
3. Control Communications: This is a process of collecting and presenting performance information to stakeholders on how resources are being used to achieve project objectives and to take appropriate actions to control it.

15.2 DIMENSIONS OF COMMUNICATION

Project managers are always at the center of communications; and the key to success in their role is to understand various ways to interact with different stakeholders and also with others inside

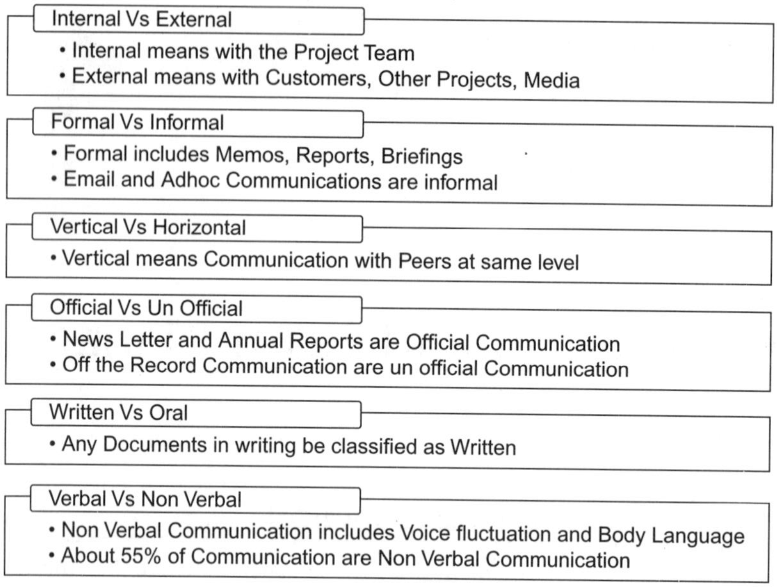

Figure 15.1 Dimensions of Communication

and outside an organization. There are different dimensions of communications, such as internal versus external, formal versus informal, vertical versus horizontal, official versus unofficial, written versus oral, verbal versus non-verbal. Choosing a particular dimension depends on the situation, context in which the communication evolves and also the purpose of the communication. About 55% of communications are non-verbal communications. Figure 15.1 represents various dimensions of communications along with the purpose of each dimension.

15.3 FORMS OF COMMUNICATION

The term "forms of communication" refers to the physical medium through which communication is made. In organizational contexts, such media may be formal or informal, oral or written. The choice of the form of communication to be used to make a communication varies over situations, priorities, and organizational cultures. Table 15.1 summarizes different forms of communication that exist in an organization.

Table 15.1 Forms of Communication in Organizations

Form of Communication	Characteristic	Examples
Written formal	Precise; transmitted through the medium of correspondence	Project charter, scope statement, project plan, WBS, project status, contract-related communication
Written informal		E-mails, notes, memos, letters

Oral formal	High degree of flexibility; use the medium of personal contact, group meetings, or telephone	Presentations, speeches
Oral informal		Conversations with team members Project meetings Break room or war room conversations
Non-verbal communication	About 55% of total communication	Facial expressions, hand movements, tone of voice while speaking

15.4 PROCESS OF COMMUNICATION

The actual process of communication involves three components:

- Sending the communication
- Receiving the communication and
- Eliciting feedback on the communication made.

A fourth component could be understanding the possible organizational barriers for effective communication. Organizations address these barriers to communicate, establish formal procedures for communication, and thereby facilitate the aforementioned three components.

Sending messages: There are four elements involved in sending a message: (1) formulate the message of communication; (2) consider possible barriers to the communication that is going to be made; (3) encode the message, and (4) clearly communicate (send) the message.

Formulating the message to be communicated is an art. First, the sender needs to be clear about what he communicates, and why he communicates; the message should not give dubious meaning and it should be clear and accurate. The format of the message also varies depending on the type of message (formal vs. informal); choosing appropriate format is also important for communication. The sender should also consider different barriers to communicate such as

1. Lack of clear communication channels, that is, using e-mail, where the server is not working properly.
2. Garrulous and voluble communication: The message should not be communicated to others rapidly without determining the understanding level of others.
3. Physical distance: People sitting in different physical working areas separated from each other should also be considered.
4. Jargons used in technical communication: Using technical jargons should be avoided when communicating with different groups. For example, RAM means both Random Access Memory and Responsibility Assignment Matrix.
5. Distracting environmental factors: Background noise in working environments is a good example.

Figure 15.2 shows various components of the communication skill a project manager needs to possess for building and managing the team effectively.

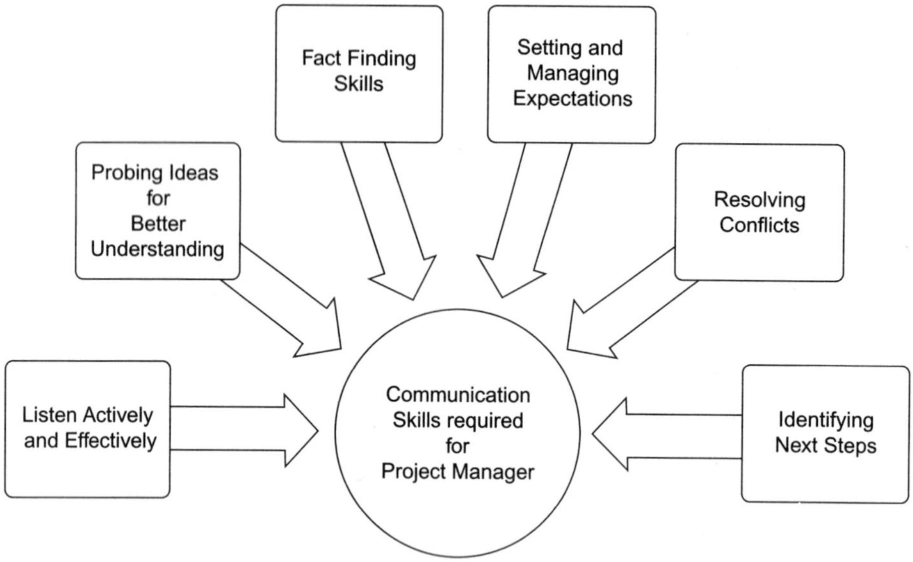

Figure 15.2 Communication Skills of a PM

15.4.1 Encoding the Message

Converting the message which is not feasible enough to communicate directly is referred to as "Encoding." For example, our voice message should be converted to digital signal before transmitting it through media.

Receiving messages: Recipients receive the message, but the latter is generally affected by external barriers and the recipient's own internal barriers, if any. Possible internal barriers are the recipient's experience level, understanding of the message, and attitude toward the subject matter of the communication made or the sender. Recipients decode the message contained in the communication received through imagination. Human mind always links the message with the already known information in order to understand the message clearly. For example, "sky blue" color is more understandable instead of light blue color.

Feedback: After a communication has been made, the senders generally confirm on the receipt of the message contained in the communication. This process of eliciting feedback may entail the sender asking the receiver questions, such as, "Do you understand what I say?"

15.5 HANDLING COMMUNICATION IN A SOFTWARE PROJECT

Communication is said to be effective when information has been provided in the right format, at the right point in time, and with the right impact on both the sender and receiver.

Here, "right impact" means that the purpose of passing the message should be achieved. For example, if you send a message stating a proposed delay in a project along with the reasons for the delay, the client, on receiving the message, should accept the delay and the reasons you describe. Efficient information, on the other hand, refers only to the process of providing the required information when needed. Figure 15.3 shows various communication-related processes.

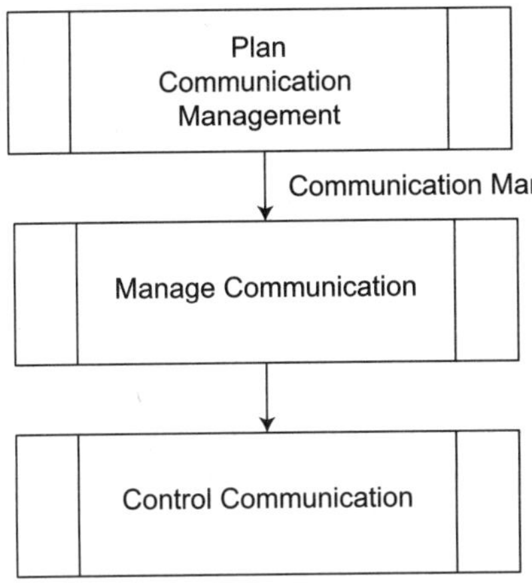

Figure 15.3 Communication Management Flow

$$\text{Number of communication channels} = N(N-1)/2$$

where N refers to the number of team members. Therefore, if there are six resources in a project team, there would be 15 communication channels among them.

POINTS TO PONDER

As the number of members in the team increases, the number of communication channels also increases. This brings a lot of complexity in the team management; thus, for bigger teams, the effective communication planning is the primary task of the leads.

15.5.1 Communication Technologies

Communication technologies are used to transfer information back and forth among project elements. Communications can take place in many ways: face to face, via fax, via e-mail, over phone, or by net meetings, video conferences, etc. The choice of technology to be used is based on following factors:

- Urgency of the need of information
- Availability of the technologies
- Expected staff of the project
- Duration of the project using the technology
- Project environment, where communication technologies are applied

15.5.2 Communication Methods

There are three types of communication methods: push communication, pull communication, and interactive communication.

Push communication: In this type, a communication is sent (pushed) to the receiver without confirmation or certification whether it has reached the intended recipient (e.g., letters, e-mails, faxes).

Table 15.2 Information Gathering and Retrieval Systems

Technique	Examples
Information gathering and retrieval systems	Manual filing systems, electronic text databases, project management software, systems that allow access to technical documentation such as engineering drawings
Information distribution methods	Project meetings, hard copy document distribution, shared access to networked electronic databases, faxes, e-mails, voice mails, and video conferencing sessions

Pull communication: In this type, recipients access the communication (pull) at their discretion. Pull communication methods are employed when large volumes of information need to be transferred (e.g., intranet).

Interactive communication: In this type, both the push and pull methods are used (e.g., phone, video conferencing).

Effective distribution of information includes a number of techniques such as choosing appropriate sender–receiver models, correct choice of communication media, writing style of the message, presentation methods, and facilitation. Information Gathering, retrievel and distrubtion system are depicted in Table 15.2 which can be used as reference model of communication.

- Sender–receiver models: An appropriate sender–receiver model is based on aspects such as whether it is a one-to-one communication or one-to-many communication, a push communication (e-mail) or a pull communication (records retrieval).
- Choice of media: Choosing the right media to convey information makes the process effective. For example, some types of information can be passed through e-mail, while others may be best disclosed face to face.
- Writing style of the message: Key elements that make an e-mail (or any other message) effective are choosing an appropriate and meaningful "subject line," use of proper salutation in the message, correct sentence structure, and appropriate use of active and passive voice.
- Meeting management techniques: Agenda, conflicts
- Presentation styles: Body language
- Facilitation techniques: Building consensus

Although several techniques exist for managing communication, team meetings continue to be the most preferred option. Following may be used as guidelines for conducting effective team meetings:

- Set and enforce strict time lines for meetings
- Meet team members regularly but not frequently, as it may distract them from their work
- Involve team members to generate agenda for the meeting
- Ensure that only point on the agenda is discussed
- Distribute the agenda beforehand to members
- Revisit the minutes of previous meetings and address pending action items, if any
- Let team members know what is expected out of them in advance
- Invite only those team members who are required for the meeting
- Set and enforce ground rules for discussions in meetings
- Document and communicate minutes of all meetings

15.6 PROJECT PERFORMANCE REPORTS

15.6.1 Types of Performance Reports

Project performance is measured against the performance measurement baselines defined in the project management plan.

Different types of performance reports are as follows:

- Status report: This report presents the current status of a project.
- Forecasting report: This report presents an estimate of future project status.
- Trend report: This report presents an analysis of project results over time to check whether performance has improved or deteriorated.
- Variance report: This report presents a comparison of actual results and baseline targets.

Performance reports generally provide information on scope, schedule, cost, quality, and possibly risks and lessons learned. They represent a basis for corrective actions and mid-course corrections, if any.

Common Formats for Performance Reports: Different formats are available to represent performance reports, such as bar charts, S-curves, histogram, tables, variance analysis report, and earned value analysis.

Bar Charts: A bar chart is a chart with rectangular bars with its length proportional to the values represented on the *X*-axis. These bars can also be plotted horizontally with the values represented on the *Y*-axis.

A project manager with effective team communication skills would

- be an effective communicator of project information
- avoid communication blockers wherever possible
- use a single office if possible for all project team members
- make meetings effective by preparing agendas and follow-ups

Following tools are widely used *forecasting methods*, which help prepare performance reports:

Time–series methods: These techniques are used to make forecasts on the basis of patterns in past data available. Time is set as an independent variable to forecast demand. Measurements are taken at successive points or over successive periods; for example, every hour, day, week, month, or year, or at any other regular (or irregular) interval.

Judgmental methods: Intuitive judgments are based on opinions and subjective estimates. Forecast by analogy, composite forecasts, Delphi method, and scenario building (analyzing possible future events based on different possible outcomes) are examples of the judgmental method.

Causal/econometric methods: Such techniques use the assumption that the underlying factors that influence the forecast variable may be identified with confidence. For example, use of many trainees in a project as key resources would lead to more escalations in the project; if causes are understood clearly, projections of the influencing variables may be forecast. Auto Regressive Moving Average Model (ARMA), regression analysis, and non-linear regression are examples of causal econometric methods.

POINTS TO PONDER

Forecasting methods include time–series methods, causal econometric methods, and judgmental methods.

15.6.2 Performance Communication Channels

These channels are used to analyze and exchange the information about progress and performance of the project. The project manager generally uses a push communication technique.

Reporting Systems

For a project manager, standard tools are helpful to capture, store, and distribute the needed information to stakeholders for reporting the performance and progress of the project.

Expert Judgment

In this, the expertise gained from similar projects worked on earlier is used to manage and control communication/process of communication management. Do's and Don'ts are implemented based on the expertise gained from previous projects.

Meetings

In order to control the communication and also to make the control realistic and accepted by the entire team, it is better to conduct team meetings. This meeting should also be attended by other stakeholders, such as project sponsors, and others who have a stake in the project. The project manager can also conduct this meeting with selected team members to control the communication, and the project manager has to ensure through the selected few that communication is happening according to the Communication Management Plan.

15.7 MANAGING THE PROJECT TEAM

Managing the project team is crucial for successful delivery of any project. Over the life cycle of a project, project managers are likely to be required to motivate the project team in times of temporary reverses, help resolve conflicts that may arise among stakeholders, or address team retention, labor relations, and performance appraisals. Therefore, project managers are expected to be effective leaders, communicators, negotiators, and problem solvers, capable of influencing stakeholders, behaviors and activities that would result in overall project success. Project human resource management, thus, comprises a set of processes required to make effective use of the people involved in a project, that is, sponsors, customers, project team members, and subcontractors.

Following points elaborate the important factors that project managers need to address as part of team management:

- Selection of appropriate techniques for better personal and organizational relationships.
- Choice of techniques that are appropriate for the current needs of the project: project human resource requirements may change over the course of project execution, the number of project stakeholders may change as the project moves from one phase to another, and their impacts may change over time.
- Awareness of the administrative human resource requirements of the performing organization to ensure compliance. The project manager ensures team awareness.
- Actions undertaken to influence project team members toward professional and ethical behaviors.

15.7.1 Organizational Theories

Organizational theories explain difference in the behavior of groups or individuals in an organization and are derived from organizational structures and procedures that took shape during the Industrial Revolution in England and Europe. These theories provide information regarding the way people function and organizations behave. Project managers apply these theories to identify strengths and weaknesses of teams, and to reduce the time and costs of projects. They represent one of the bases for generating an effective human resources plan. Three such theories are as follows:

McGregor's Theory of X and Y

This theory postulates that there are two types of employees. Theory X employees, who avoid work, do not take responsibility, and generally dislike work, are to be watched, cannot be trusted, and need to be micromanaged. Theory Y employees, who are motivated, take responsibility, and like work, are to be provided challenging assignments and encouraged to work independently.

Z Theory

According to the Z theory, workers need to be involved in the decision-making process; this makes them more responsible and accountable for their decisions.

Maslow's Hierarchy of Needs

This well-known organizational theory postulates that there exists a hierarchy of human needs. People seek higher level needs only when their lower level needs have been satisfied. The hierarchy of these needs, from the highest to lowest, is as follows:

- Self-actualization needs—seek knowledge, maximize potential
- Esteem needs—respect for others, self-respect, freedom, recognition
- Social needs—community and social anxieties
- Safety needs—job security, financial security
- Physiological needs—basic needs such as water, shelter, and food

POINTS TO PONDER

The popular organizational theories are McGregor's theory of X and Y, Maslow's Hierarchy of Needs and Z Theory, which are useful in understanding the employee behavior and effective team management.

15.7.2 Five Phases of Team Building

Five team-building phases defined in PMBOK® (Project Management Body of Knowledge) are forming, storming, norming, performing, and adjourning.

1. **Forming:** In this phase, team members are introduced to each other, with which they begin to know each other. This phase is characterized by politeness and formality in the relationships between team members.
2. **Storming:** The team starts to move from "as is" to "to be." Some team members may be in conflict with others in a clash for control or in a clash of individual identities or cultures; hence the

term storming. During the storming phase, team members tend to disagree with each other. The team's leadership or the management, however, tries to overcome their differences, and ensures they are resolved.

3. **Norming:** Following the "storm phase," team members reach a consensus on the "to be" process and learn to work together. However, when issues or concerns surface, the team may return to the storming phase. Also, when a new member joins the team, the phases of norming and storming would be reenacted for the entire team. It is in this phase that unique, team-specific norms assume shape and get entrenched with all team members; hence the term norming.
4. **Performing:** Once important team members have resolved their differences and have established strong work relationships, the team is said to be ready for high performance. Once in the performing phase, the team seldom falls back into the storming phase. In this phase, a team is characterized by high levels of initiative.
5. **Adjourning:** In this phase, the team shares its improved processes with other teams. Many relationships formed within a team continue for a long even after the team disbands following project completion.

15.7.3 Conflict Management

Conflict is inevitable in organizations, and is actually the difference of opinion between people. Evading conflict can result in consequences that could be more negative or destructive than dealing with the conflict itself. Innovative ideas emerge when there is difference of opinion. The starting point for any healthy discussion is difference of opinion and hence, conflict is inevitable.

Project managers should address conflicts early and usually engage the conflicting parties in private using a direct, collaborative approach. They consider conflict as a team issue and, during the process of conflict resolution, project managers should focus (1) on the present and not the past and (2) on the issue involved in the conflict and not the individuals involved.

Commonly used conflict resolution techniques are as follows:

Problem solving: This technique confronts the problem head on using research and objective analysis as its tools. It is widely considered as the preferred approach and aims at a healthy win–win solution to the problem.

Compromise: This technique tries to find a solution that conflicting parties find moderately satisfying and entails both parties giving up a part of their demands. This approach generally leads to lose–lose solution and is primarily used to avoid building of conflict levels.

Forcing: In this approach, the conflicting party with less power is simply asked to accept the other more powerful side's demands, leading to a win–lose solution. As this approach seriously damages relationships, it is adopted by project managers only rarely or when the gravity of the crisis calls for it.

Smoothing: Project managers use this approach to emphasize the areas of agreement and aim to ignore areas of disagreement between conflicting parties. Obviously, this approach leads only to a temporary solution.

Collaborating: This technique incorporates multiple view points and insights from differing perspectives, leading to consensus and commitment. This approach may lead to a win–win solution.

Withdrawing: Project managers use this approach when they believe that it is better that conflicting parties avoid each other. This technique generally does not solve a problem but may introduce a "cooling" period.

Summary

Communication management refers to the process of timely and appropriate development, collection, dissemination, storage, and disposition of project-related information. Generally, more than 90% of a project manager's time goes for communication.

On a high level, processes involved in the effective communication management are as follows:

1. Plan Communications: This process determines the information needs of project stakeholders and establishes a communications system.

2. Manage Communications: This is a process of implementing the communication management plan and responding to unexpected requests for information.

3. Control Communications: This is a process of collecting and presenting performance information to stakeholders on how resources are being used to achieve project objectives and to take appropriate actions to control it.

There are different dimensions of communications, such as internal versus external, formal versus informal, vertical versus horizontal, official versus unofficial, written versus oral, verbal versus non-verbal. Choosing a particular dimension depends on the situation, context in which the communication evolves and also the purpose of the communication.

The actual process of communication involves three components:

- Sending the communication
- Receiving the communication and
- Eliciting feedback on the communication made.

Communication technologies are used to transfer information back and forth among project elements. Communications can take place in many ways: face to face, via fax, via e-mail, over phone, or by net meetings, video conferences, etc.

Different types of performance reports are as follows:

- Status report: This report presents the current status of a project.
- Forecasting report: This report presents an estimate of future project status.
- Trend report: This report presents an analysis of project results over time to check whether performance has improved or deteriorated.
- Variance report: This report presents a comparison of actual results and baseline targets.

Organizational theories explain difference in the behavior of groups and individuals in an organization and are derived from organizational structures and procedures that took shape during the Industrial Revolution in England and Europe.

Maslow's Hierarchy of Needs

This well-known organizational theory postulates that there exists a hierarchy of human needs. People seek higher level needs only when their lower level needs have been satisfied. The hierarchy of these needs, from the highest to lowest, is as follows:

- Self-actualization needs—seek knowledge, maximize potential

- Esteem needs—respect for others, self-respect, freedom, recognition
- Social needs—community and social anxieties
- Safety needs—job security, financial security
- Physiological needs—basic needs such as water, shelter, and food

Five team-building phases defined in the PMBOK are forming, storming, norming, performing, and adjourning.

Conflict is inevitable in organizations and is actually the difference of opinion between people.

Memos, e-mails are examples of non-formal communication; reports, metrics are example of formal communication. Approximately 70–90% of project manager's time goes only for communicating. Project manager spends ~50% of his time in meetings.

Formula for calculating the number of communication channels is $N^*(N-1)/2$, where N is the number of people involved.

Model Questions
PART A (Objective type)

1. How much percentage of time spent by project manager for Communication?

   A. 62% B. 70% C. 82% D. 90%

Answer: D

2. The project status report is an example of which form of communication?

   A. Formal written communication B. Informal written communication

   C. Informal verbal communication D. Informal verbal communication

Answer: A

3. Effective communication means that the information is provided in right ----- at right---- and with the right-----

   A. Format, Time, Impact B. Meaning, Quality, Analysis

   C. Format, Time, Language D. Meaning, time, Impact

Answer: A

4. A project team is having 11 stakeholders. How may communication channels it has?

   A. 11 B. 10 C. 55 D. 66

Answer: C

5. Which of the following is not an example of causal/Econometric method?

   A. ARMA B. Regression analysis

   C. Non-Linear regression D. Forecast by analogy

Answer: D

6. Forecast by analogy is an example of judgmental method. Which of the following is not an example of judgmental method?

   A. Composite Forecasts B. Delphi method

   C. Scenario Building D. ARMA

Answer: D

7. Communication barriers lead to –

   A. Increase in Cost
   B. Increased Stress
   C. Increased Conflict
   D. Low output

Answer: C

8. The following are the different dimensions of communication except

   A. formal and informal
   B. internal and external
   C. written and oral
   D. Head and tail

Answer: D

9. All of the following are input of Report performance process except

   A. Budget Forecasts
   B. Work Performance Information
   C. Work Performance measurements
   D. Variance Analysis

Answer: D

10. Phone calls, Video conferencing are examples of

   A. Push Communication
   B. Pull Communication
   C. Interactive Communication
   D. Ping Communication

Answer: C

PART B (Answer in one or two lines)

1. What is project communication management? Write notes on three major processes of project management.
2. What are judgmental methods in project communication?
3. What is a causal econometric method in project communication?
4. Describe in short managing project team.
5. What is conflict? Give two examples for conflict.
6. What is the formula for calculating the number of communication channels?
7. If there are 10 team members in a project, what is the number of communication channels?

PART C (Descriptive type)

1. Describe in detail various dimensions of communication.
2. Explain in detail the different forms of communication.
3. Explain the process of communication using three components associated with it.
4. What are the different barriers of communications?
5. Explain in detail various communication skills required for a project manager.
6. Describe the role of communication technologies in project communication.
7. What are the guidelines for conducting effective team meetings?

8. Explain in detail various types of performance report.
9. Explain McGregor's theory of X, Y, and Z.
10. Explain Maslow's hierarchy of needs.
11. Explain various phases of team building in detail.
12. Discuss various conflict resolution techniques in detail.

Section 7:
Software Project Management

16

Project Time and Cost Management

CHAPTER COVERAGE

1. *Introduction*
2. *Time Management*
3. *Cost Management*

16.1 INTRODUCTION

The backbone of project management is the ability to plan the project activities, resources, and cost accurately, and then control the schedule and the cost to meet the specified time and cost goals. Project time management includes the processes required to manage timely completion of the project, whereas the cost management deals with managing the completion within budget.

16.2 TIME MANAGEMENT

The sequence of activities that need to happen for creating and maintaining a proper project schedule are as follows:

1. Define activities: The process of defining the work (activities) that must be performed to meet project objectives.
2. Sequence activities: The process of identifying and documenting the interaction and logical relationships between activities.
3. Estimate activity resources: The process of determining resources (e.g., equipment and materials) that are required, quantities of each resource that is planned to be used, and the availability of each resource to perform project activities.
4. Estimate activity duration: The process of using information on project scope and resources and developing durations for input to schedules.
5. Develop schedule: The process of determining the start, intermediate milestones, and end dates of project activities.

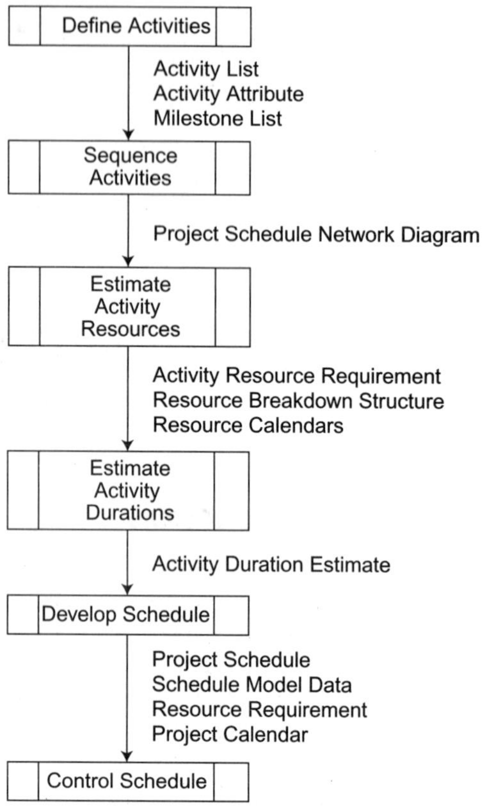

Figure 16.1 Time Management Flow

6. Control schedule: The process of monitoring the status of the project to update project progress and to manage changes to the accepted schedule.

Figure 16.1 shows the sequence of activities and the artifacts that get created in each stage. Each of these activities for time management is discussed in this chapter.

16.2.1 Define Activities

Because every project has definite start and end dates, a project schedule becomes the basic building block for definition of the entire project. Refer to Figure 16.2 for the steps involved in the define activities. The first step in the define activities process is the estimation of realistic start and end dates for each of the activities in a project, of course, is definition of the activities themselves. The lowest tier of a project's work breakdown structure (WBS) is called a work package. Decomposition of work packages leads to activities (see Figure 16.3). Activities provide a basis for estimating, scheduling, executing, monitoring, and controlling project work. The output of the define activities process is an activity list—a list of all activities to be performed as part of a project. Project assumptions and constraints, identified and documented in the project's scope statement, also serve as inputs to the process of defining activities.

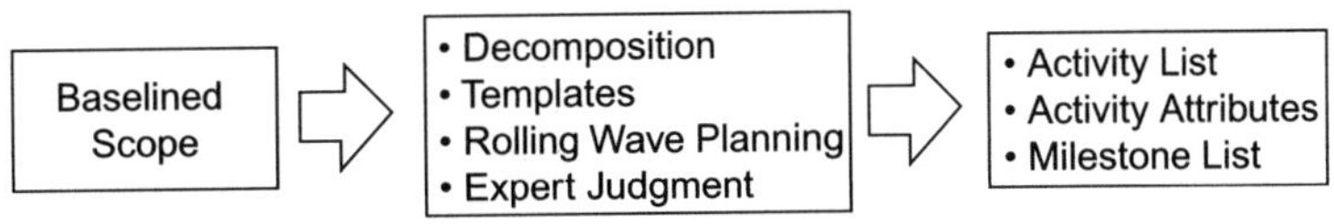

Figure 16.2 Define Activities

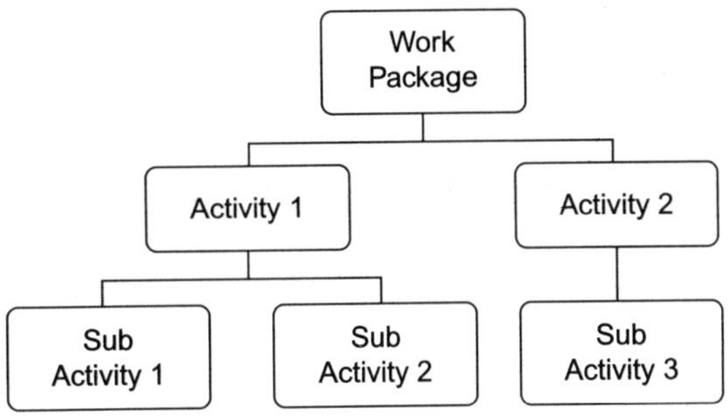

Figure 16.3 Work Packages to Activities

Required quality levels—both stated and implied—serve as project constraints and have a substantial effect on activity definition; rigorous quality standards would obviously entail more project activities.

Enterprise environmental factors and organizational process assets are also used as inputs to the define activities process. Organization process assets give the activity-related policies and procedures of a project; it also helps to define activities using historical information and lessons learnt. Enterprise environmental factors, such as infrastructure and project management software help to define the activities of the project.

16.2.1.1 Decomposition

Decomposition is the first step in the define activities process because the work packages of the WBS, which lists only deliverables-oriented components, must be broken down into the actual tasks or activities required to realize the deliverables (see Figure 16.4). The subdivision of work packages into smaller and manageable components of activities is often performed by the project team members responsible for that work package. The correct level of decomposition helps for accurate schedule estimates and timely completion of project. Correct level of decomposition means decomposing the project to such a level where all efforts of planning, executing, monitoring, and controlling are in a state that can be readily addressed and managed. Excessive decomposition leads to more work without much value added and also leads to inefficient use of resources and decreased work efficiency.

16.2.1.2 The Activity List

The primary output of the decomposition process is the activity list. An activity list is a comprehensive list of all scheduled activities required on the project. It includes the activity identifier and scope of work description for each activity in sufficient detail. An activity identifier is a unique number that identifies a particular activity. It helps to distinguish an activity from others that are similar in

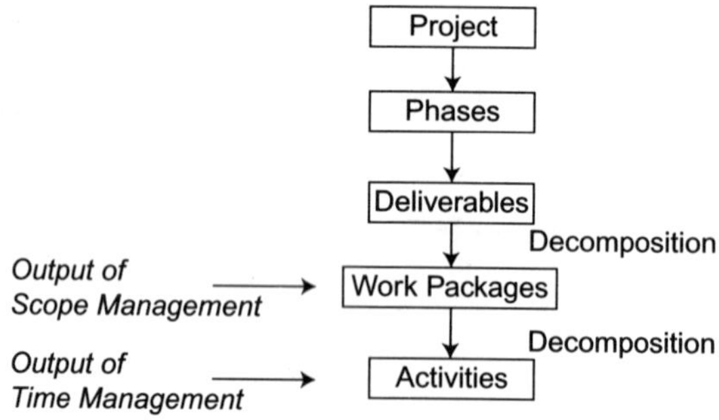

Figure 16.4 Decomposition

nature/name. These activity identifiers are unique across the entire project schedule network diagram (PSND).

16.2.1.3 Activity Attributes

Activity attributes represent the inherent properties of a particular activity. A WBS Id, an activity Id, a predecessor activity, a successor activity, leads, lags, constraints, and assumptions are attributes associated with an activity. Some activities may require a disproportionately high level of effort, whereas some others may not. The duration of some activities may be controlled by the level of effort input, whereas in some other activities, such a control over duration may be not possible. These considerations require to be factored in determining activity duration estimations of that particular activity (see later in this chapter). A related concept addresses the effort required to complete an activity. There are three types of effort namely, level of effort (LOE), apportioned effort (AE), and discrete effort (DE).

16.2.1.4 Level of Effort (LOE)

LOE refers to work of a supportive nature that does not directly add to execution of activities and does not require a definite product outcome. However, it is mandatory, as support for other work activities or the entire project effort, and consists of short amounts of work that must be repeated periodically.

Examples of such an activity are project budget accounting or oiling of machinery in manufacturing.

LOE is usually applicable for both a start—start (SS) and a finish—finish successor. It is sometimes referred to as a hammock activity or relationship and is used to define the amount of work performance within a period of time, and is measured in man days or man hours per day/week/month.

16.2.1.5 Apportioned Effort (AE)

AE is the effort that is directly related to some other measured effort and is related and proportional to measured effort in other work packages. For example, efforts of the quality assurance division may be considered (apportioned) as depending on performance of the project team as a whole.

16.2.1.6 Discrete Effort (DE)

These kinds of efforts can be directly traced against each deliverables. It is easily measurable. This is just opposite to AE.

16.2.1.7 Milestone Lists

The milestone list (generally coupled with a milestone chart) is used to provide a series of indicators regarding project progress to date and achievements or goals yet to be reached. In Figure 16.5, Tollgate 1 indicates that it will deliver System Requirement Specification document at the end of its phase. Assuming that a project consists of only four milestones of equal efforts and duration, it can be said that 50% of the project is complete as Tollgate 2 is crossed.

16.2.1.8 Templates

Templates from other projects can be used to create activity lists and also to define activity attributes. Templates can be used to define typical milestones as well. Historical data is very useful not only to stop reinventing the wheel, but also to reduce the efforts involved in defining an activity. In a typical project, the PMO provides the templates that can be used in the project. However, it is the project manager's responsibility to customize this template for its purpose.

16.2.2 Sequencing the Activities

Having defined all activities entailed by the project and generated the activity list the project team, now needs to arrange these activities in a logical sequence, from start to end. In other words, all subsequent processes that require as inputs the outputs of preceding processes need to be identified. The project team is therefore required to identify the logical relationships—and preferred relationships—between all activities. The project team accomplishes this task by identifying project dependencies. Therefore, the sequence activities process is one of documenting and identifying such relationships among all project activities. See Figure 16.6 for the steps involved in sequencing the activities.

A project is a series of activities performed in a logical order. The ordering of the activities largely depends on the inter-dependencies between the activities. In Table 16.1 different types of dependencies that can be present in a project are described.

Mile Stone	Deliverables
Tollgate 1	SRS document
Tollgate 2	Design Document
Tollgate 3	Tested Code
Tollgate 4	Deployed Code and Client Acceptance after testing

Figure 16.5 Milestone List

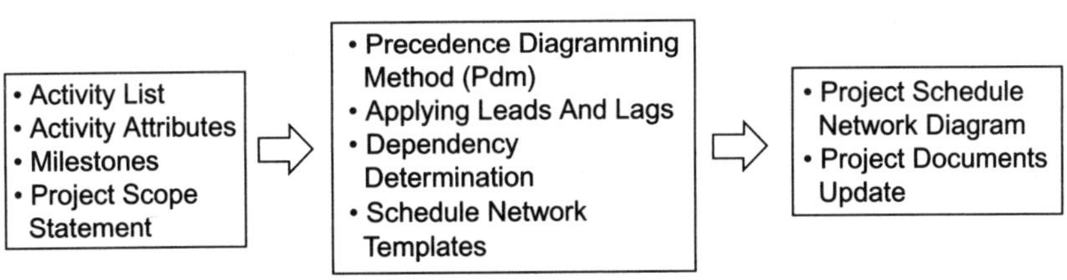

Figure 16.6 Sequence Activities

Table 16.1 Different Types of Project Dependencies

Dependency Types	Nature	Organizational Control	Example
Mandatory dependencies	Dependencies that are inherent in the nature of the work involved; also called "hard" dependencies	It is generally difficult to alter this dependency	In a building project, construction of walls of a house must necessarily precede construction of ceiling
Discretionary dependencies	Usually defined by the project management team or organization	Is generally within organizational control, but may limit later scheduling options and hence must be set with caution; flexible	Best practices of an organization
External dependencies	Involves a relationship between project activities and non-project activities	Organization may not hold as much control over these discrepancies compared with the above two	Organizational dependency on a country's economy, environmental factors, and external interfaces

16.2.2.1 The Precedence Diagramming Method

The precedence diagramming method (PDM) is widely used and available in most of the project management scheduling software available today. The PDM employs a diagram that arranges all activities of a project with the relationships and dependencies among them.

Example of PDM

Activity	Prior Activity
A	None
B	A

Also, the PDM is a technique used in the critical path method (CPM) used to construct a PSND (Refer Section 16.2.2.4). The PDM is not a diagram showing project schedule; rather, it is a technique used before the project schedule is defined. A PDM typically uses boxes to indicate project activities and arrows to connect them. The PDM usually has an activity number to identify each activity, a short description of the activity, and indications for early start, early finish, late start, late finish, and duration of the activities. An activity might have one, two, or more predecessors and one, two, or more successors.

Relationships between activities shown on a PDM can be of four types. These four types may be referred to as the logical relationships in a PDM.

16.2.2.2 Logical Relationships

A total of four logical relationships are possible between any two activities, because an activity can have start or finish relationship with another (see Figure 16.7).

A finish–start relationship between two tasks A and B

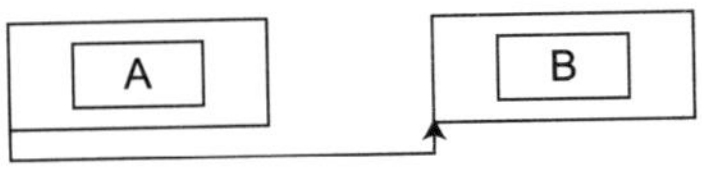

A start–start relationship between two tasks A and B

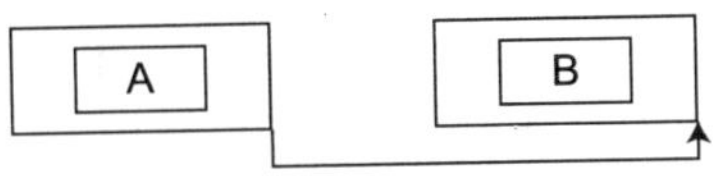

A finish–finish relationship between two tasks A and B

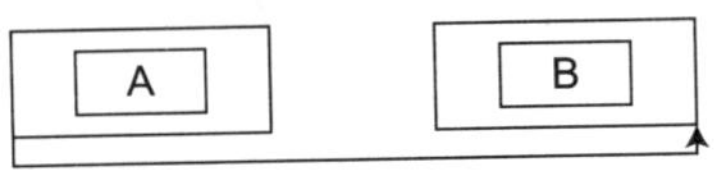

A start–finish relationship between two tasks A and B

Figure 16.7 Types of Relationship between Tasks

Finish—Start relationship: Here, the initiation of a successor activity depends upon the completion of a predecessor activity. Many project activities bear this relationship with others. For example, the user acceptance test (UAT) cannot be started until final deployment in production is completed. Deployment needs to be complete for UAT to start.

Start—Start relationship: Here, the initiation of a successor activity depends upon the initiation of a predecessor activity (Figure 16.7). Therefore, a subsequent task can start even before a preceding task has been completed; only the latter should have started and—as would be the case – partially completed. In other words, two tasks related by a start—start relationship may be performed in tandem. For example, code review can be started only after the code is written.

Finish—Finish relationship: Here, the completion of a successor activity depends upon the completion of a predecessor activity. For example, a project manager cannot close a project until customer signoff has been completed.

Start—Finish relationship: Here, the completion of a successor activity requires the start of a predecessor activity. Such a relationship is unusual but is often found in activities involved in just-in-time management processes. When people work in shifts, the beginning of one shift indicates the end of another shift. The project manager of this project can use this type of relationship.

16.2.2.3 Leads and Lags

Leads and lags refer to buffers introduced between tasks for better control of activities. A lag directs a delay in a successor activity. If a delay of x days is required between the finish of one task and the start of another, a finish—start dependency may be established with a specification lag time of x days.

Alternatively, a lead may also be established between two tasks; when a lead has been established, the two tasks involved may overlap: a successor task may start after a predecessor task has started.

For example, a technical writing team can begin on the editing of the draft of a document 10 days after it begins writing: The two tasks—writing and editing—bear a start—start relationship with each other with a 10-day lag.

> **POINTS TO PONDER**
>
> A lead time tends to accelerate a successor activity. A lag time directs a delay in a successor activity.

16.2.2.4 Project Schedule Network Diagram (PSND)

The PSND is a schematic display of project's activities and dependencies, showing the flow of project work, which is then used to develop the project schedule. A sub-network is simply a section of the overall PSND. PSNDs are an output of the sequence activities process and an input to the develop schedule process. PSNDs are generally activities on the node (AON) and use all four types of dependencies between activities (i.e., finish—start, finish—finish, start—start, and start–finish). Following are the advantages of generating PSNDs:

- PSNDs show interdependencies of all activities (a decomposition of WBS).
- They depict project work flow showing clearly the activities that need to be performed in the required sequence.
- They compress the schedule in planning and throughout the life of a project.
- If used for schedule control and reporting, they show project progress.
- They help justify the project manager's estimate for the duration of a project.

16.2.3 Estimating the Activity Resources

This is the process for determining the following factors:

1. the resources (including equipment and materials) that are required,
2. the quantities of each resource that will be used, and
3. the point in time (in the future) when each identified resource will be available to perform assigned project activities.

Refer Figure 16.8 for the steps involved in this estimation.

16.2.3.1 Resource Calendars

In the context of project management, calendars are of two types—project calendars and resource calendars. Project calendars are related to all the resources involved in the project, whereas resource

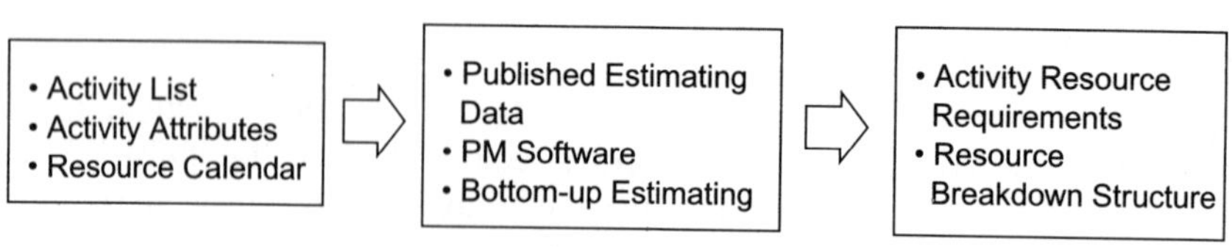

Figure 16.8 Estimate Activity Resources

calendars refer to particular resources or groups of resources and their availability. Resource calendars are used to ensure that work is scheduled only when resources are available for work. The working time settings in the resource calendar need to match those in the project calendar. Moreover, the resource calendar can be customized to show individual schedule information, such as vacations and leaves of absence. If work time settings of resources involve part-time or the night shift, a separate base calendar for each shift may be set up and applied. Also, project managers can use resource calendars to accommodate exceptions to working times of individual resources.

16.2.3.2 Bottom-Up Estimating

The bottom-up estimating technique is just the opposite of the top—down estimating. The technique is used to estimate every activity or work item individually and sum that estimate to determine a final estimate. Bottom-up estimations, although accurate, are time consuming and are used only when definitive, detailed estimates are required.

16.2.3.3 Published Estimating Data

Production rate and unit cost of the resources can be arrived at from published data based on historical information gathered from different companies. This data is useful for determining the resources of an activity. It can be used as base data to arrive at accurate estimation of resources.

16.2.3.4 Activity Resource Requirements

The activity resource requirements technique is used to identify the type and quantity of resources required for each activity in a work package. These requirements then can be aggregated to determine the estimated resources for each work package. The level of detail varies by application area.

16.2.3.5 Resource Breakdown Structure

A resource breakdown structure (RBS) is a hierarchal structure of human resources, organized by function. For example, the top level of an RBS could be the business unit to which a resource belongs; the second-to-lowest level would be a team manager to whom that resource reports, the final level being the resource itself. In the following table, the resource at Level 3, the assistant vice president of operations, could be provided access to all resources through Levels 4 through 7 (see Figure 16.9).

16.2.4 Estimating the Activity Duration

This process is for taking information on project scope and resources and then developing durations for input to schedules. Activity duration refers to the number of work periods needed to complete the activities listed in the activity list. The accuracy of estimates can be improved by considering the amount of risk in the original estimate. As more realistic risks are identified, the estimates become more accurate and realistic (see Figure 16.10).

The estimate activity duration process requires that the

- amount of work effort required to complete the schedule activity is estimated,
- assumed quantity of resource to complete the schedule activity is estimated, and
- work periods required to complete the scheduled activity is calculated.

Level	Resource
Level 1	[Organization name]
Level 2	Senior vice president
Level 3	Assistant Vice president
Level 4	Project manager
Level 5	Team manager
Level 6	Resource A
Level 7	Resource B

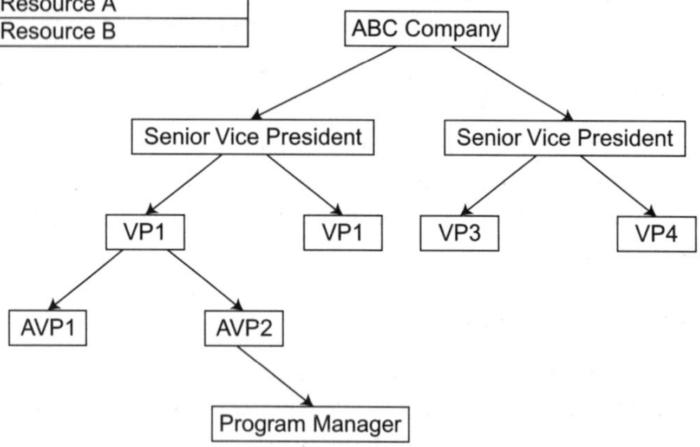

Figure 16.9 Resource Breakdown Structure

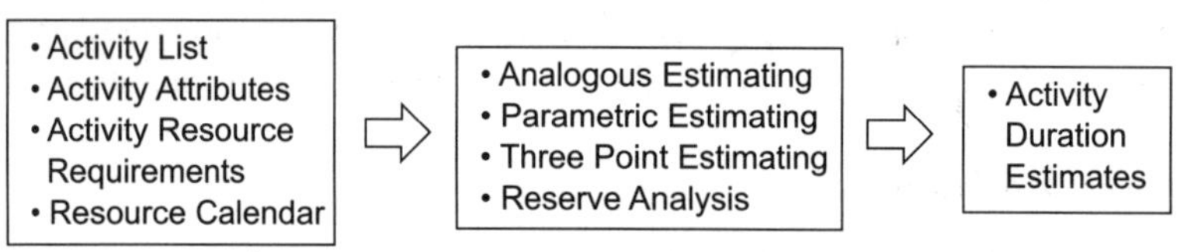

Figure 16.10 Estimate Activity Duration

Estimating activity duration accurately is of high importance for the success of a project. Inaccurate estimates lead to cost and schedule overruns. Moreover, activity duration should allow for leakage time or hidden time and intervening breaks. For example, if an activity takes 1½ days to complete and starts on a Friday morning, Saturday and Sunday being holidays, the activity duration should be calculated considering the two intervening holidays: the activity should be scheduled as complete only on the following Monday afternoon, the elapsed time being 3½ days. In activity duration calculation, the duration of a work package is equal to the amount of time required to do the work, divided by the number of people working:

Duration = Work / Unit

The remainder of the section addresses the main inputs to the estimation of activity duration.

16.2.4.1 Analogous Estimating

Experience, that is, expert judgment, and the use of historical data serve as important inputs to the activity duration estimation process, markedly improving accuracy of estimates. Use of these inputs is referred to as analogous estimating.

16.2.4.2 Parametric Estimating

When accurate information on an activity is not available, project managers use regression analysis and learning curve methods for duration estimation. In regression analysis, two variables are plotted on a graph and their relationship is derived using mathematical modeling. The regression equation deals with the following variables:

$$Y = f(X, \beta)$$

Where β is a constant, a scalar or a vector of length k
X is the independent variable
Y is the dependent variable.

The learning curve method assumes that a resource consumes progressively less time in carrying out a task, that is, all other work factors being the same, a resource always consumes less time compared with the duration consumed previously to complete a similar activity.

16.2.4.3 Heuristics

Heuristics refers to the "rule of thumb" estimate, based on knowledge of duration actually consumed after working on large number of similar activities.

16.2.4.4 Three Point Estimation—PERT

The three point estimation technique is better known as PERT (program, evaluation, and review technique). This technique assumes that there is very small probability that a project will be completed on a given date estimated at the beginning of the project. The project manager makes three types of estimations, namely, best, worse, and most likely, for completing an activity.

Expected value = $(P + 4M + O)/6$
SD = $P—O/6$
Where O is the best-case estimate
M is the most likely estimate
P is the worst-case estimate
SD is the standard deviation.

16.2.4.5 Graphical Evaluation and Review Technique (GERT)

The graphical evaluation and review technique (GERT) is a combination of network logic and activity duration estimates and usually allows looping. Consider an activity "A" which is executed five times continuously. It cannot be represented using the normal diagramming technique. GERT needs to be used to represent it. Any graphical method can be used to represent the looping.

16.2.4.6 Reserve Analysis

Reserve analysis addresses buffer in the calculation of duration estimation. Contingency reserve or buffer is generally factored in as a percentage of the overall activity duration estimation. The buffer, often set at 10% of the estimated overall activity duration, is used to manage unknown future project risks.

In case of more risks in the activity, reserve can be zero. To reduce risks, more reserve is added. However, it is better for the reserve to be always at an optimum level (neither too high nor too low). There can be some minor setbacks for the activity duration because it depends on various factors such as:

1. Resource attrition,
2. Resource at activity taking leave, and
3. External factors such as strike, etc.

We may accommodate the above factors by doing reserve analysis.

16.2.4.7 The Role of a Project Manager in Estimation

Many of the estimates discussed so far are made not by the project manager, but team members or resources who are assigned to actually carry out the activities. The project manager, however, provides team members with sufficient information for them to accurately estimate the duration of activities, after communicating to them the criticality of the accuracy of their estimates. The project manager also performs a sanity check of the estimates received, in addition to formulating a contingency management plan. As in all other processes, the project manager documents the assumptions made during estimating for later review.

16.2.5 Developing the Schedule

The next task is to determine the start and end dates of project activities. Refer to Figure 16.11 for the steps involved in this process.

16.2.5.1 Schedule Network Analysis

Schedule network analysis is a technique that generates the project schedule using the PSND. It employs various techniques, such as CPM and what —if analysis. It also uses resource leveling techniques to compress the schedule by identifying path convergence and path divergence.

16.2.5.2 Definition of Float/Slack

Total float/slack: This is the time for which completion of an activity can be delayed without delaying the project end date or an intermediary milestone.

Free float/slack: This is the time for which completion of an activity can be delayed without delaying the early start date of its successor activities.

Project float/slack: This is the time for which completion of a project work can be delayed without delaying the externally imposed project completion date (imposed by the customer).

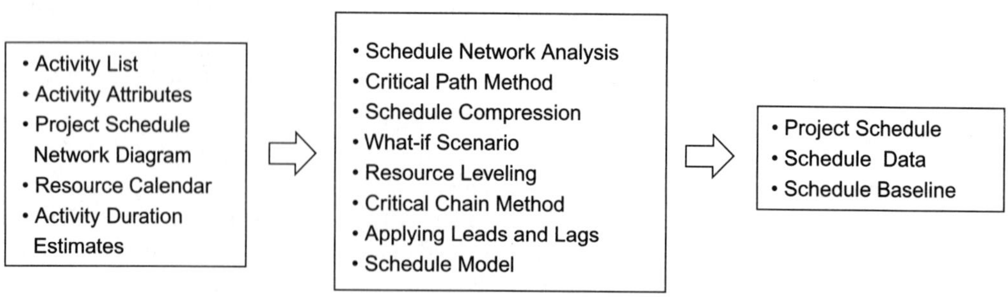

Figure 16.11 Develop Schedule

16.2.5.3 Critical Path Method (CPM)

CPM is a method of using network analysis techniques to identify those tasks that are on the critical path, that is, where any delay in the completion of these tasks will lengthen the project timescale, unless action is taken. Critical path is the longest path which is the shortest duration for completion of a project. There can be more than one critical path, which increases the risks. A critical path can change.

The network diagram does not change when the end date changes. The project manager should investigate options, such as fast tracking and crashing the schedule to meet the new date and then, with approved changes, change the network diagram accordingly.

When a project has a negative float, the project manager should consider compressing the schedule.

For all activities in critical path, the float will be zero. Figure 16.12 shows calculation of critical path for a process.

16.2.5.4 What—If Scenario Analysis

What—If Scenario Analysis (WISA) is one powerful tool that can analyze various What–If scenarios to determine the schedule of the project.

The schedule of a project depends on various parameters including but not limited to

1. Resource utilization
2. Cost factors
3. Dependencies of activities
4. Risk parameters
5. Unknown external factors, such as strike, storming, etc.

WISA estimates the effect that potential events may have on the project schedule.

16.2.5.5 Path Convergence

The merging of different network paths into the same node in a PSND is called path convergence. It is usually characterized by a schedule activity with more than one predecessor activity. The merging of different network diagrams into a single node is also called as path convergence.

Critical Path

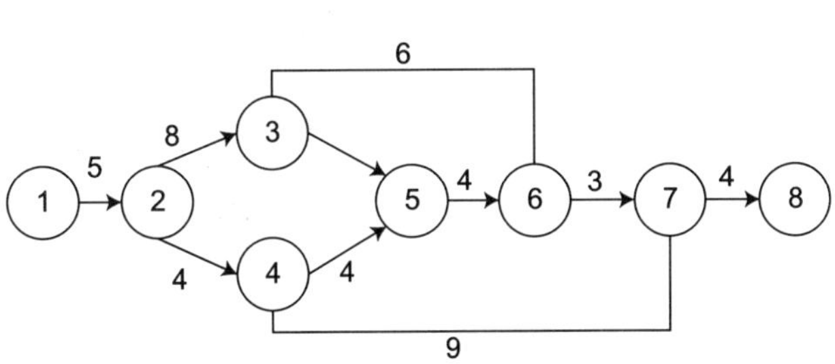

Critical path is 5 + 8 + 10 + 4 + 3 + 4 = 34 days.
Critical path = Longest path, float zero for all activities

Figure 16.12 Critical Path Calculations

16.2.5.6 Path Divergence

This is the opposite of path convergence. Branching of different paths from a single path (or) node is called path divergence. For example, when a software project is done after requirement analysis, design can be done in parallel for different modules.

See Figure 16.13 for the example on path convergence and path divergence.

The most common representation of the project schedule is through a Gantt chart. The types of Gantt charts mostly used are

Bar chart—Displays activity start and end dates, as well as expected durations.

Milestone chart—Displays scheduled start or completion of major deliverables.

Combination chart—Displays events and activities as a function of time.

Figure 16.14 shows the example of a bar type Gantt chart.

16.2.5.7 Schedule Optimization

Schedule optimization is mandated when execution of a project as per schedule has been affected because of internal or external factors, upon which the project manager is required to optimize the schedule. The following is a list of tools a project manager commonly uses to optimize a project schedule.

Crashing: Here, total project duration is decreased, with minimal compromises on original objectives. Extra resources are usually added to decrease the project duration. Consequently, the cost of the project increases due to the crashing technique.

Fast tracking: Here, activities are processed in parallel instead of being processed in sequence as per the project schedule. The risks associated with the project increase by doing things in parallel. Activities in critical path that are to be done in parallel are first identified to reduce overall project duration. In this technique, the duration of critical activities is shortened or working hours increased.

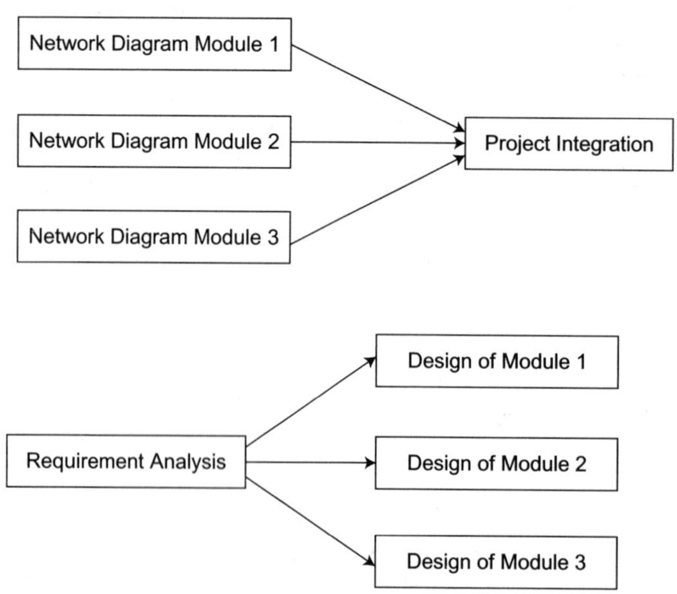

Figure 16.13 Path Convergence and Path Divergence

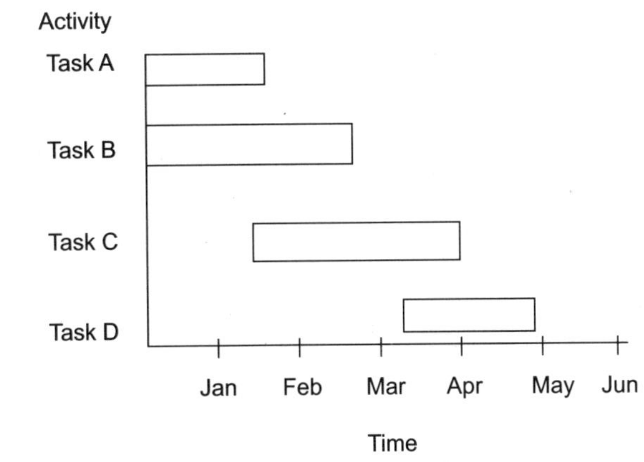

Figure 16.14 Gantt Chart Example

Resource leveling: Resource leveling is the reapportioning of available resources to avoid over-allocation or under-allocation and ensure that activities are performed with maximum efficiency.

Here, peak overloads are reduced by redistributing allocations to activities with float. This optimization technique can increase activity duration.

Figures 16.15 and 16.16 illustrate this tool. Application of resource leveling can result in the same tasks (say, Tasks A, B, and C) being completed in five days with only six resources, whereas without resource leveling tool applied, the tasks may have used eight resources.

The following is a list of key factors of resource leveling:

- *Rule of thumb:* Allocate scarce resources to critical path activities first.
- *Increased project duration*: Often results in a project duration that is longer than the preliminary schedule.
- *Reallocation:* Resource reallocation and adjustments are used to bring the schedule back or as close as possible to the originally intended duration.
- *Reverse resource allocation:* Resource is scheduled in reverse from the project ending date.
- *Critical chain:* A technique that modifies the project schedule to account for and accommodate limited resources.

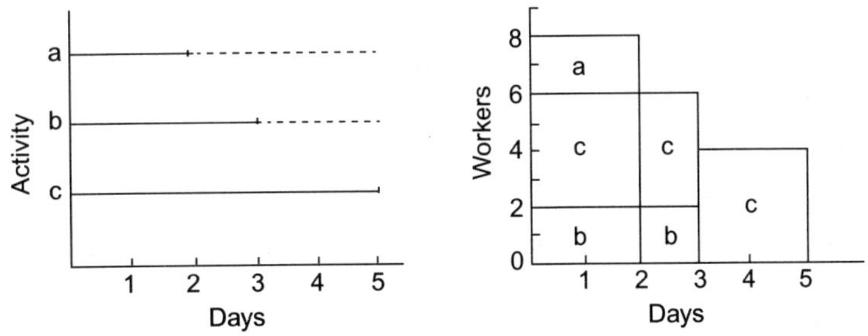

Figure 16.15 Before Resource Leveling

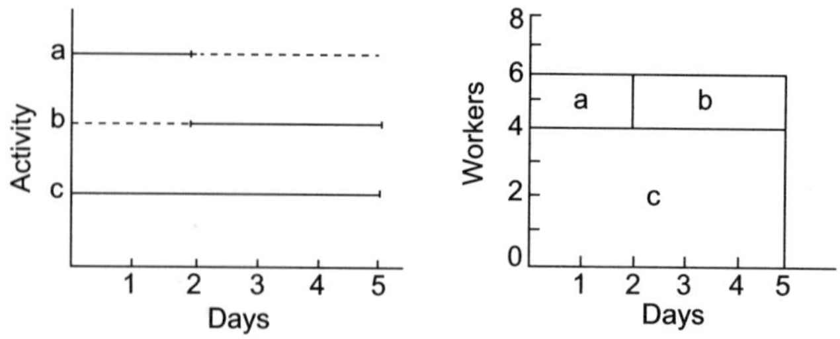

Figure 16.16 After Resource Leveling

16.2.5.8 Critical Chain Method

This technique modifies the project schedule to account for limited resources, mixes deterministic and probabilistic approaches, and puts more emphasis on the resources. When resources are always available in unlimited quantities, then a project's critical chain is identical to its critical path. This technique involves adding duration buffers, which are not actual activities. Following are steps used to calculate earliest and latest times using this technique.

Steps for calculating earliest time (TE):

1. For the start node TE = 0.
2. Begin from the start node and move toward end node in all paths. Add duration with previous node's TE to arrive the TE for the new node.
3. If more than one value comes for a particular node, insert the maximum value in that node.

Steps for calculating latest time (TL):

1. For the end node TL = TE
2. Begin from the end node and move backward toward start node in all paths. Subtract duration with previous node's TL to arrive the TL for the new node.
3. If more than one value comes for a particular node, insert the minimum value in that node.

16.2.6 Controlling the Schedule

For controlling the schedule the main steps that need to be considered are

- Measuring the current status of the project schedule.
- Influencing the factors that cause schedule changes, ensuring that these are agreed upon.
- Determining the reason for the deviation, if any.
- Managing the changes when they happen.

The schedule control process is used to monitor the status of project execution, to update on project progress, and to manage changes to the schedule baseline, if required. The following are important metric and tools concerning schedule control (see Figure 16.17).

Project schedule: The approved project schedule is called the schedule baseline; it provides the basis for measuring and reporting schedule performance.

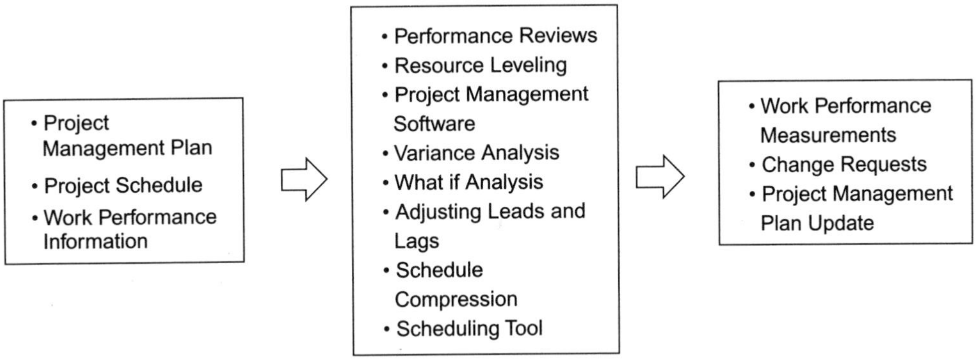

Figure 16.17 Control Schedule

Work performance information: This information updates the project manager on schedule performance, such as which planned dates have been met and which have not.

Performance reviews (earned value): This process involves assessment of schedule variations to determine whether they require corrective actions.

Progress reporting: The progress reporting and current schedule status include information, such as actual start and end dates and the remaining durations for unfinished schedule activities.

PM software: This schedule control tool is used for tracking planned dates against actual dates and forecasting.

Variance analysis: This tool compares target dates with the actual/forecast start and end dates to analyze variance.

Work performance measurements: This tool is used to calculate schedule variance (SV) and schedule performance index (SPI) values for WBS components, in particular the work packages and control accounts, and document and communicate the same to stakeholders.

POINTS TO PONDER

Tips for effective project time management

- Estimation based on a WBS will improve accuracy.
- Activity duration should be estimated by the resource actually performing the activity.
- Use of historical information improves accuracy of estimates.
- A schedule baseline should be maintained and not changed except for approved project changes.
- Estimates are more accurate if smaller-sized work components are estimated. Bottom-up estimation is most accurate type of estimation.
- Corrective and preventive actions should be recommended when schedule problems occur.
- Continuous monitoring of schedules helps in anticipating deviations.
- Plans should be revised during completion of the work.

16.3 COST MANAGEMENT

Cost is a resource sacrificed, foregone, or consumed to achieve a specific objective or something given up in exchange for something in return. In the context of project management, resources are spent in exchange for profits. Project cost is usually measured in monetary units. Calculation of project cost considers the requirements of all project stakeholders, who need project cost—related information in different ways at different points in time.

Costs associated with a project are the costs of equipment, material, and human resources required to complete all the activities of a project. Accurate project cost estimation is difficult because of the uncertainties inherent in project execution, particularly so in the case of complex projects. However, if project costs are effectively managed, predicted, accounted for, and controlled, the gap between planned costs and actual costs could be kept to a minimum or, sometimes, even made zero. The foundation of a good project cost estimate is an accurately developed WBS. The ability of stakeholders to influence project cost is greatest in the early stages of project execution, which is why early scope definition is critical: Overall project cost can be fixed on the basis of a clearly defined scope.

See Figure 16.18 for the project cost management flow.

Estimate costs is the process of developing an approximation (or estimate) for the cost of the resources required to complete the project activities. Cost estimation is based on the activity time duration and activity resources. Remember that cost estimating and pricing are not the same. Cost estimating is about "assessing how much it will cost the organization to provide the product or service," whereas pricing is "assessing how much the organization will charge for the product or service".

The budget is arrived at using cost aggregation for which the activity costs are rolled up to the work package level which is then rolled up to the control account level, which is then rolled up to arrive at the project cost. The budget is arrived at using the cost estimates and the project schedule. The budget provides the information of how much the project is estimated to cost both from a total and a periodic perspective. This information creates the cost performance baseline which is then used as critical parameter in performing earned value analysis and other cost management variance analysis techniques.

The major task of control cost is to monitor and control the outflow of project fund against the actual work accomplished. Effective cost control can only be achieved by managing the approved

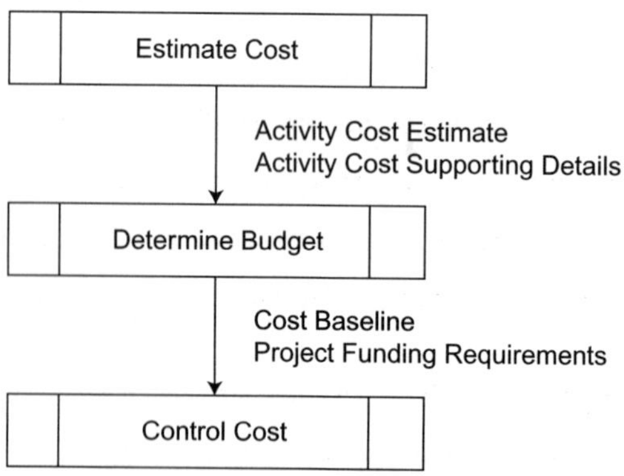

Figure 16.18 Cost Management Flow

cost performance baseline and the baseline changes. Control costs involves the activities, such as influencing the factors which change the approved cost baseline, tracking and closure of the change requests, managing the actual changes, ensuring that the outflow do not cross the funding, monitoring the cost performance baseline, updating the stakeholders on the approved changes and the cost involved, and finally maintaining the cost overruns within acceptable limits.

The following are the categories of costs incurred during project execution.

Variables costs: Costs that change with the number of units produced, that is, costs of material, wages.

Fixed costs: Costs that do not change as number of units changes, that is, rentals, machine costs, and so forth.

Direct costs: Costs that are directly connected and accountable to the work on the project, that is, project travel costs, salaries, project-related software.

Indirect costs: Costs that are incurred during the execution and benefit of more than one project; such costs are billable under each project.

Opportunity cost: The cost of selecting and investing in a particular project and thereby forgoing the potential benefits of other projects that were not selected.

16.3.1 Cost Estimation Process

Cost estimation (Figure 16.19) is done throughout the life cycle of the project and is based on the project's WBS to improve accuracy. Whenever cost-related issues or problems occur, corrective and preventive actions are implemented.

16.3.1.1 Analogous Estimating

Analogous estimating is used to estimate total project cost when detailed information is limited or no data are available about the project. This process uses the actual cost of previously completed similar projects to predict the cost; hence, the estimates are based on historical information. Analogous estimating is a form of expert judgment, as current project requirements are estimated without access to real-time data. It uses a top—down approach, and time required for estimation is less compared with that in bottom-up estimation.

The main advantages of analogous estimating are as follows:

1. speed of estimation is high,
2. cost involved in the process of estimations is less, and
3. individual tasks do not require to be identified.

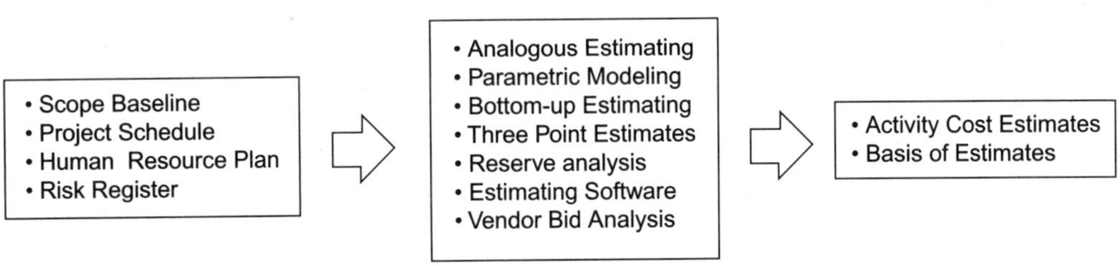

Figure 16.19 Estimate Costs

The main disadvantages of analogous estimating are as follows:

1. accuracy of the estimation is low as the latter is largely based on previous projects' process parameters, which may not be valid for the current project,
2. applicability for use in complex projects with high uncertainty is low, primarily because uncertainties vary across projects and their quantification is difficult, and
3. risk management politicking is present, as the cost associated with the risk management largely depends on the politicking involved in the project.

POINTS TO PONDER

Difference between cost estimating and pricing may be seen by the following definitions:

Cost estimating refers to assessing how much the organization will spend to provide the product or service.

Pricing refers to assessing how much the organization will invoice for the product or service.

Generally, the difference between the cost estimate and the cost price of the product or service yields the profit margin of the performing organization.

16.3.1.2 Parametric Estimating

Parametric estimating uses a mathematical model with project characteristics (or parameters) as inputs to predict costs. The input parameters can vary based on the type of work completed. The following may be seen as a rudimentary example: Assume that a module in a previous project cost 600 USD.

If the current project carries 10 similar modules, its cost would be 6000 USD. Parametric estimating often follows an analogous estimation.

16.3.1.3 Bottom-Up Estimating

In bottom-up estimating, the cost of each individual work item in the WBS is calculated; the individual costs are then summed to arrive at the total project cost. Bottom-up estimating is performed with the project team, and, although, this method yields accurate results, the cost of and time involved in performing such a detailed estimate is high.

16.3.1.4 Vendor Bid Analysis

In vendor bid analysis, an analysis of what the project should cost is made on the basis of responsive bids from qualified vendors who submitted their quotes or bids for the project concerned. When multiple vendors are involved for each deliverable, the price of an individual deliverable is calculated to derive a cost that supports the final total project cost.

16.3.1.5 Reserve Analysis

A contingency reserve is generally included in project cost. This reserve lies at the discretion of project manager, to deal with anticipated but not certain events emerging out risks associated with the project. The objective of building a reserve component into the estimated cost is to ensure that project objectives are met without cost overruns.

16.3.1.6 Cost of Quality

The desired quality level of the product or service determines the cost associated with project execution. If the final product or service requires higher quality levels, obviously the cost of project execution and deliverables would be higher. Costs of quality typically include costs of reviews, audits, inspections, and other such quality control systems and procedures.

16.3.1.7 Types of Cost Estimates

Order of Magnitude Estimate: An order of magnitude estimate is also called a ballpark estimate. It is based on high-level objectives and provides a bird's-eye view of project deliverables.

Budget Estimate: A budget estimate is more accurate than an order of magnitude estimate. It should be formulated early in the project's planning stage; the budget estimate is most often based on analogous estimating, considering budget lessons learned from a similar project and applying them to the current project.

Definitive Estimate: A definitive estimate uses the bottom-up technique and is the most accurate of all estimate types. However, it consumes considerable resources and the most time because of the many calculations and data collections involved. The definitive estimate uses the WBS of the project.

Types of Estimate	When Done	Why Done	How Accurate (%)
Rough order of magnitude (ROM)	Very early in the project life cycle, often 3–5 years before project completion	Provides estimate of cost for selection decisions	–25 to +75
Budgetary	Early, 1–2 years out	Puts dollars in the budget plans	–10 to +25
Definitive	Later in the project, less than 1 year out	Provides details for purchases, estimates actual costs	–5 to +10

POINTS TO PONDER

Understand the types of estimates and the accuracy of each type. You should be able to differentiate between types of estimates on the basis of accuracy and range of each estimate type.

16.3.1.8 Activity Cost Estimate

An activity cost estimate is the quantitative assessment of the probable costs required to complete each activity in a project. Cost is calculated for all the types of activities. Cost management plan is not an output of the estimate cost process; rather, it is an input of the estimate cost process. The cost management plan describes how cost variances will be managed, and it is a subsidiary element of the overall project plan, which in turn is the output of the develop project management plan process. This also acts an input for the estimate cost process.

16.3.1.9 Basis of Costs

It contains the logic behind the estimation of costs, with details that include the assumptions, and constraints considered for the estimation. There are different types of techniques for estimating the cost, such as analogous estimation, parametric estimation, top-down approach, bottom-up approach, and also different types of cost estimates, such as order of magnitude, budgetary, and definitive estimates. Different approaches for different types of activities are followed by considering various assumptions; these need to be detailed in the basis of estimation.

16.3.2 Creating the Budget

After the cost of each activity is estimated, the budget for the project needs to be drawn. A budget gives the idea of the resource expenditure to be planned for the project (see Figure 16.20). Few methods used to calculate the project budget are as follows:

16.3.2.1 Cost Aggregation

Cost aggregation refers to the aggregate costs of individual work packages of the WBS. These cost estimates are then aggregated for higher component levels of the WBS (control account) and ultimately for the entire project.

16.3.2.2 Reserve Analysis

Reserve analysis, discussed under the estimate cost process, can establish a contingency reserve and a management reserve of the project. Contingency reserves are allowances for unplanned but potentially required changes that can result from realized risk. Management reserve is a separately planned allowance retained to allow for use in future situations that are impossible to predict. It is intended to reduce the risk of failing to meet cost or schedule objectives.

16.3.2.3 Funding Limit Reconciliation

The use of funds should be reconciled with any funding limits on the commitment of funds for the project. Large variations in the periodic expenditure of funds are usually undesirable for organizational operations. The use of funds is reconciled with the funding limits set by the customer or performing organization on the disbursement of funds for that particular project. Reconciliation will necessitate adjustments of the scheduling to smooth or regulate those expenditures, which is accomplished by placing deadlines and schedule milestones for work packages.

16.3.2.4 Expert Judgment

Even at home, it is often seen that the expert (usually the housewife) can do better budgeting than the person who is earning the money. In project management, the experience of experts is vital to estimate accurate time and cost estimates for the project. Hence, budgeting the activities of the project

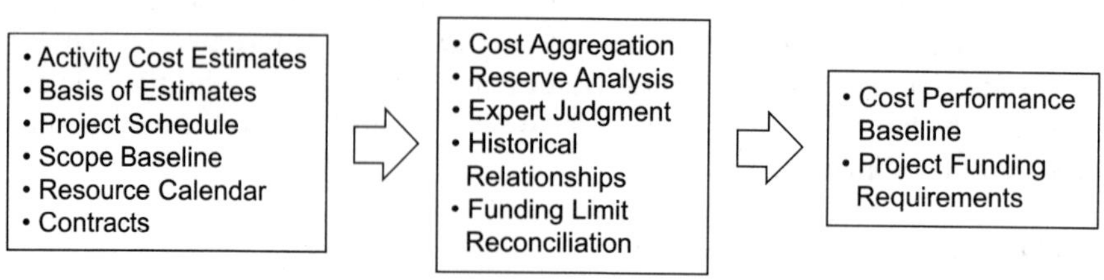

Figure 16.20 Determine Budget

based on the skill level of those who have worked on previous similar activities is considered as expert judgment.

16.3.2.5 Historical Relationships

This is also referred to as parametric estimating and is based on historical data. For example, if the project is for constructing a bridge of length 10 Km, and a previous similar project (near the current project location) found the construction costs of that particular bridge were $150,000 per kilometre, then the cost of the current project (constructing a new bridge) could be calculated based upon its length.

16.3.2.6 Cost Baseline

The cost baseline refers to the freezing of the costs estimates and is used to measure and monitor the cost performance of the project. The cost baseline is also called as spend plan or an "S-curve" because of the typical shape (refer Figure 6.19).

The cost baseline is a critical project parameter and is not changed without a proper approval process authorizing change. These changes are usually documented and approved via the integrated change control process. As may be seen, the main difference between cost estimates and cost budgets is that the former shows costs to be incurred by category, whereas the latter shows costs to be incurred over time.

16.3.2.7 Project Funding Requirements

Project funding requirements are derived and directly based on the cost baseline and can be established to exceed the baseline, usually by a fixed margin, to allow for either early progress or cost overruns.

Funding usually occurs in incremental amounts and is not usually continuous. The total funds required are those included in the cost baseline plus the management contingency reserve defined for that project.

16.3.2.8 S-Curve

A simple technique for tracking project costs is to develop a periodical cumulative budget spend plan and then track actual costs against that plan. The rate of expenditure at the beginning of the project is usually slow. Maximum cost will occur during the execution phase (middle) of a project when the spending rate is high. As the project comes to an end, the end-stage rates are low and hence, the slope of the curve is shallow, resulting in the curve's "S" shape. The slope of the graph (Figure 16.21) indicates

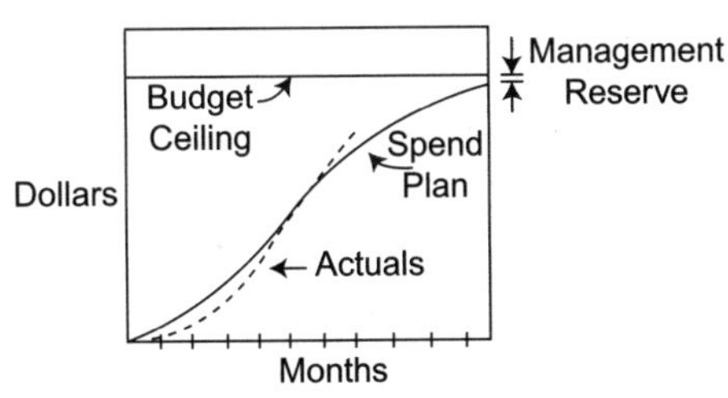

Figure 16.21 S-Curve

the project expenditure rate, sometimes called the "burn rate." By plotting actual costs against the budget planned, one can identify the differences between actual spending and the estimated plan.

POINTS TO PONDER

Understand the S-curve and the various parameters associated with it, such as actual, spend plan, management reserve, budget ceiling, with time on the x-axis and cost on the y-axis.

16.3.3 Controlling the Cost

The primary objectives of this process are to

- Influence the factors that create changes to the cost baseline.
- Manage the actual changes when and as they occur.
- Detect variances from the plan.
- Ensure that all appropriate changes are recorded.
- Prevent inappropriate or unauthorized changes.
- Inform the appropriate stakeholders about the changes.
- Analyze positive and negative variances.
- Find how variances affect other control processes.

See Figure 16.22 for the steps involved in controlling the cost.

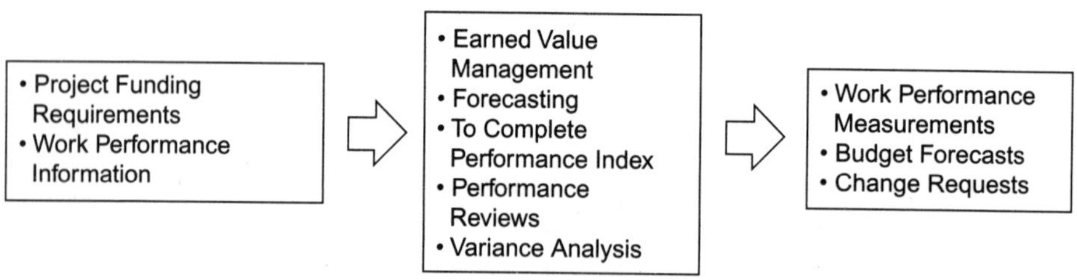

Figure 16.22 Control Costs

Learning curve: This term refers to the decrease in time taken to perform a task because of the increase in efficiency in performing the task that results solely out of repeatedly performing the task. Therefore, with passage of time, although total costs typically increase, the cost per unit drops. This pattern of cost reduction is given by

$$Yx = (Kx)\log 2\ b$$

where K is the number of direct work hours required to produce the xth unit, x the number of direct work hours to produce the xth unit, x the number of units produced, and b the learning percentage.

Law of diminishing returns: This law indicates that merely adding more resources to a project's execution by itself would not facilitate its early completion. Addition of more resources may increase overall output in the beginning, but will eventually decrease individual productivity. For example, adding thrice as many people to the same task may not cause the task to be finished thrice as fast.

16.3.3.1 Earned Value

The earned value method measures project performance against a plan to identify variances. It may also be used to identify future variances and determine final cost at project completion. The term earned value refers to the actual work completed and the allotted budgeted cost for that portion of work. For example, if 20% of work on a project with a budget of 10,000 USD (for 20% of work) has been found completed on a given date, the earned value for the performing organization on the date when 20% of the work is completed would be 10,000 USD. Project managers apply the earned value method to have better control over project execution. Earned value is calculated by comparing the planned amount of work with that actually accomplished, to determine if cost incurred and adherence to schedules and quality standards are per baseline projections. Project cost and schedule performance measurements should be managed as integrated elements. Earned value management facilitates such integration.

The earned value method is favored across the globe and widely used by project managers in project performance measurement. It integrates cost and schedule performance into a single report and helps the project manager to control the entire project.

Planned Value: It is defined as budgeted cost of work scheduled.

Earned Value: It is defined as budgeted cost of work performed.

For example, consider a project with a total budget of 10,000 USD. The total project timeline is 10 months. Assume 10% of the work will be finished every month. Total project budget (10,000 USD) is uniformly distributed across the months. Now, at the end of the first month, the planned value is 1000 USD where 10% of the work is expected to be completed. At the end of the second month, the planned value is 2000 USD where 20% of the work is expected to be completed, and so on. At the end of the tenth month, the planned value is 10,000 USD where 100% of the work is expected to be completed.

Calculation:

Now, consider the end of the third month. When the actual cost incurred is calculated, the amount is 4000 USD (AC). When the percentage of work completed is calculated, it is 20% only. However, 30% (as planned) is supposed to be completed.

So, at the end of the third month, planned value is 3000 USD (because 30% was planned to be completed) and earned value (EV) is 2000 USD (because only 20% is completed and the budgeted cost of 20% is 2000 USD).

The following formulas illustrate the important parameters used in the earned value method:

1. Schedule variance (SV) is the difference between earned value (EV) and planned value (PV): $SV = EV - PV$.
2. Cost variance (CV) is the difference between earned value and actual cost (AC): $CV = EV - AC$.
3. Schedule performance index (SPI) is the ratio of earned value to planned value: $SPI = EV/PV$.
4. Cost performance index (CPI) is the ratio of earned value to actual cost: $CPI = EV/AC$.

Summary

Time management of a project produces the schedule baseline. From WBS, in particular from the work packages, individual activities to be scheduled and activity durations for the schedule are determined. The activities are sequenced in a logical order called a network diagram using the PDM method. Fast tracking and crashing are two techniques for optimizing schedules. Buffering is a technique for adjusting the schedules for accommodating future risks. All activities on critical paths are called critical activities. Slack or float is the time for which a task can be delayed without delaying successor activities.

- **Activity:** Work performed during the course of a project (normally it has duration, cost, and resource requirements).
- **Critical path:** Longest path, float less than or equal to specified value mostly zero. This series of activities determines the earliest completion of the project and is usually defined as those activities with float less than or equal to a specified value (usually zero).
- **Float:** The overall amount of time that an activity may be delayed from its early start without delaying the project finish date (it is also called slack, total float, and path float).
- **Lag:** Modification of a logical relationship which directs a delay in the successor task and they are basically inserted waiting times in between tasks.
- **Lead:** A modification of a logical relationship where the successor task can be started earlier than planned. For example, in a FS relationship with a 6 day lead, the successor can start 6 days prior to the completion of the predecessor.
- **Milestone:** A significant event in the project, usually completion of a major deliverable, which determines the signal to go ahead to the next phase or project.
- **Precedence diagram method (PDM):** It is the network diagramming technique where activities are represented by nodes. Activities are linked by precedence relationships to show the logical sequence in which the activities are to be performed.
- **Resource leveling:** Form of network analysis in which start and finish dates are driven by resource management concerns. Resource leveling refers to keeping the resources same across the duration of the project thereby avoid resource overloading.

Project cost management is a vital component of successful project management. Generally the ultimate objective of project execution is profit; failure to manage costs effectively results in failure to achieve this fundamental project objective. Also, evidence of poor cost management affects funding for future projects. The WBS is the basis of an accurate cost estimate. Therefore, arriving at a robust WBS is the first step toward successful cost management. Cost estimation, as with several other components of project management, is performed throughout the life cycle of the project. In this regard, the earned value reporting system, which measures performance to schedule and performance to budget in the same system using simple formulas, is an effective tool available to project managers. Project expenditures are less both in the beginning and toward the closing stages of a project's execution. Expenditure is more in the middle phase of the project.

- **Cost budgeting:** Allocating cost estimates to individual project components for better control over the entire project.
- **Cost variance (CV):** Difference between the estimated cost of an activity and the actual cost of that activity.
- **Schedule variance (SV):** The difference between the scheduled completion of an activity and the actual completion of that activity.
- **Earned value:** The method of measuring project performance by comparing the amount of work planned with that of actual accomplished work.

Model Questions
PART A (Objective type)

1. Fast-tracking is also known as

A. Overtime B. Resource leveling

C. Crashing D. Concurrent engineering

Answer: D

2. Which of the following relationship represents concurrency between two activities?

A. Start-to-start B. Finish-to-start

C. Start-to-finish D. Finish-to-finish

Answer: A

3. Fast tracking usually adds more

A. Cost B. Risk

C. Time D. Scope

Answer: B

4. Project budget accounting is an example for

A. LOE B. Activity attributes

C. Apportioned effort D. Discrete effort

Answer: A

5. This kind of dependency is difficult to change

A. Mandatory dependencies B. Discretionary dependencies

C. External dependencies D. Nothing is difficult to change

Answer: A

6. This kind of dependency is inherent in the nature of the work

A. Mandatory dependencies B. Discretionary dependencies

C. External dependencies D. Team dependencies

Answer: A

7. Between any two activities how many logical relationships are possible?

A. 2 B. 4

C. 3 D. 6

Answer: B

8. Which structure is a hierarchal structure of human resources organized by function?

A. RBS B.WBS

C.OBS D.EBS

Answer: A

9. Lag allows the following type of relationship

   A. Finish – Start B. Start – Start

   C. Finish – Finish D. Start – Finish

Answer: A

10. Two lines in S-curve is made up of

    A. Income vs expenditures B. Cost baseline vs expenditures

    C. Cost vs time D. Cost estimate vs cost budget

Answer: B

11. Which of the following estimates would closely estimate the actual cost of a project?

    A. Order-of-magnitude B. Budget

    C. Definitive D. Initial

Answer: C

PART B (Answer in one or two lines)

1. Define level of effort (LOE).
2. Define apportioned effort (AE).
3. Define discrete effort (DE).
4. What is milestone list?
5. Define lead and lag. Give an example for it.
6. What is resource breakdown structure? Give example.
7. What is heuristics?
8. What is parametric estimation? Give example.
9. What is analogous estimation? Give example.
10. What is GERT?
11. What are path convergence and path divergence?
12. What are fast tracking and crashing?
13. What is the use of S-curve?
14. Define earned value.
15. Define SV and CV.

PART C (Descriptive type)

1. Discuss various project time management process in detail.
2. Discuss three different types of project dependencies in detail with examples.

3. Discuss four different types of relationships possible between any two activities with examples for each.
4. Discuss crashing, fast tracking, resource leveling with examples.
5. Discuss control schedule process in detail.
6. Describe the difference methods for cost etimation.
7. Describe different types of cost estimates with relative comparison.
8. Describe different methods used for creating project budget.

Section 7:
Software Project Management

17

Project Stakeholder Management

CHAPTER COVERAGE

1. *Introduction*
2. *Stakeholders and their Characteristics*
3. *Identifying the Stakeholders*
4. *Managing the Stakeholder Engagement*
5. *Procurement Process and Suppliers*

17.1 INTRODUCTION

Every project involves multiple individuals or groups who directly or indirectly get impacted by the project. So, keeping all of them informed about the project status, regularly communicating with them, dealing with their conflicting interest require considerable effort and planning. In this chapter, we will discuss the process of correctly identifying the parties involved in a project and handling them effectively. We will also discuss few terms related to the procurement process in an organization, as the suppliers are one of the important stakeholders we deal with.

17.2 STAKEHOLDERS AND THEIR CHARACTERISTICS

Stakeholders are team members or entities who are actively involved in project execution or whose interests may be positively or negatively affected by project outcomes. Their salient characteristics are as follows:

- Stakeholder interests may be either positively or negatively impacted by the project.
- Alternatively, stakeholders may influence project execution and project results.
- It is important for project planners to identify all the stakeholders and their requirements. Sometimes, individual stakeholder requirements may be implicit and not explicitly stated. For instance, in one of the requirements gathering workshops, a customer said that he wanted a "world class system." When he was probed further, it was understood that he wanted a system with background in golden color and transaction response time of 5 s.

- Stakeholders may have conflicting interests and objectives (managing stakeholders may not be so easy).
- Involving stakeholders in the initiation phase group improves the probability of a positive outcome for the project.
- In general, differences among stakeholders must be resolved in favor of the customer or end user.

POINTS TO PONDER

Stakeholders can be positively or even negatively influenced by the project.

17.3 IDENTIFYING THE STAKEHOLDERS

There are no hard-and-fast rules to be applied in stakeholder identification. Rules for judging stakeholder involvement are always situation-specific; rules that work in one situation may not work in another. The best way to identify stakeholders is by asking the right questions. Following questions are guidelines (a preliminary road map) and by no means exhaustive:

1. Who are the team members, entities, or organizations likely to be affected or to benefit from the intended project outcome?
2. Who would be assigned responsibility for the tasks entailed by the project?
3. Who is likely to move for or against the intended objective of the project?
4. Who can make improvements to the tasks entailed by the project? (Who can do it the better way?)
5. Who can contribute to the financial and technical resources required by the project?

Answers to these questions, which would vary across organizations, would likely yield a list of stakeholders. Procurement documents are the main inputs of this process along with the project charter.

Procurement documentation helps identify stakeholders referred to in the contract and procurement documents.

Three main steps in identifying the correct stakeholders are as follows (Figure 17.1):

Step 1: Identify all potential stakeholders and relevant information

Step 2: Identify the potential impact or support each stakeholder could generate and use a power/interest grid to classify them

Step 3: Assess how the stakeholders are likely to react or respond in various situations to help plan influencing them to enhance support or mitigate negative impacts

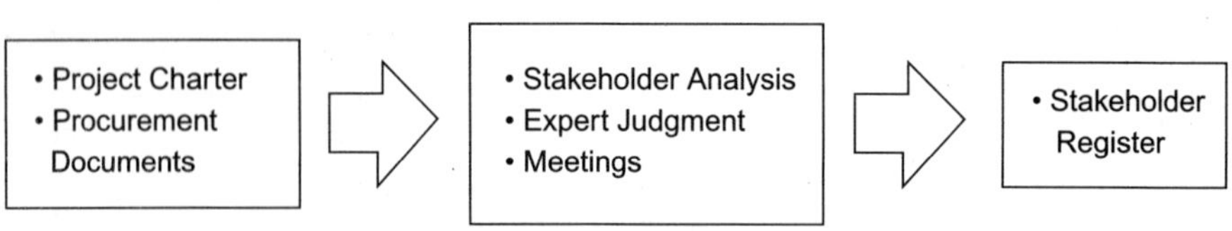

Figure 17.1 Steps Involved to Identify Stakeholders

Step 1

Project managers use group dynamic techniques, whereby key project team members are asked to identify all possible stakeholders of the project. The Crawford slip is another popular technique used for this purpose, which can be used to rapidly collate ideas from a large group of people.

Crawford is actually one of the original forms of brain-writing. The sponsor who pays money for the project is a key stakeholder. Individuals who sign on the project deliverables (usually customers) are stakeholders. The organization that executes this project is also a stakeholder, as it stands to benefit through project execution. The organization that buys the outcome of the project is also a stakeholder because its members are benefitted. The organization that provides resources for executing the project is a stakeholder. Project managers, team members, and functional managers are also stakeholders. You can identify new stakeholders by asking the existing stakeholders.

Step 2

Stakeholder register

The stakeholder register carries following elements:

1. Identification of elements of stakeholder
2. Influencing the stage of the stakeholder
3. Classification of stakeholder

Table 17.1 represents the contents of stakeholder register. It usually contains name, designation, influence stage, and classification. Depending on their skill, stakeholders involve in the appropriate life cycle of the project and this is called influence stage. For example, stakeholders if highly proficient in designing involve only in the designing stage of the project.

In Table 17.1, R. Ramya seems to have high proficiency in design, so she is being involved only in the designing stage of the project. There are people who continuously involve throughout the life cycle of the project. In this table, Pavan Kumar, the application manager, involves continuously throughout the life cycle of the project because of the nature of the work he handles. Stakeholder classification such as "supporter," "neutral," and "resistor" depends on the nature of the stakeholders. If they are negatively impacted by the outcome of the project, they are classified as "supporters." They are classified as "neutral" if they are neither "supporters" nor "resistors."

Table 17.1 A Stakeholder Register Template

Name	Designation	Influence Stage	Classification
Pavan Kumar	Application Manager	All	Supporter
Siva Ranjani	Technical Consultant	Design, Coding	Neutral
R. Ramya	Architect	Design	Rigistor
Shri Krishna	Business Manager	All	Neutral

Step 3

Stakeholder management is a difficult task requiring the formulation of a comprehensive stakeholder management strategy. Stakeholder analysis involves following steps:

- Identify all potential project stakeholders and relevant information, such as their roles, departments, interests, knowledge, expectations, and influence levels.

- Analyze the potential impact or support from each stakeholder, and classify them to define an approach strategy. In large stakeholder communities, it is important to prioritize the stakeholders to ensure the efficient use of efforts to communicate and manage their expectations.
- Assess the likely response or reaction of key stakeholders in various situations in order to plan to influence them to enhance their support and mitigate potential negative impacts.

A stakeholder analysis matrix is a tool used to represent a project's stakeholder management strategy.

Following would be contents of a stakeholder analysis matrix:

1. Stakeholder name
2. Stakeholder impact level
3. Stakeholder interest level
4. Strategies for gaining support from this stakeholder

A typical stakeholder analysis matrix may be obtained by adding a column to the stakeholder register template (see Table 17.2) titled "Strategies for Gaining Support." This strategy is based on the classification of the customer defined in Step 2 along with the influencing stage of the customer defined in Step 3.

Stakeholder Classification Model

Table 17.2 shows three stakeholder classification models based on the power and the interest, influence, and impact grids.

Model 1: Classifies the stakeholders based on Power and Interest

Model 2: Classifies the stakeholders based on Power and Influence

Model 3: Classifies the stakeholders based on Power and Impact

Table 17.2 Stakeholder Classification Model

	Power (level of authority)	Interest (level of concern)	Influence (level of involvement)	Impact (effect of involvement)
Power		MODEL 1	MODEL 2	MODEL 3
Interest	MODEL 1			
Influence	MODEL 2			
Impact	MODEL 3			

Power indicates the level of authority of a person; Interest indicates the level of concern a person has on the project; Influence indicates the level of involvement shown on the project; Impact is the effect due to the level of involvement.

Another popular stakeholder classification model is "Salience Model" (Figure 17.2), which is based on the power, urgency, and legitimacy grids. Power indicates the level of authority of a person; Urgency indicates the need for immediate action; and Legitimacy indicates whether the involvement is appropriate or not. A grid (Venn diagram) is drawn based on the above three factors to find out the type of stakeholder.

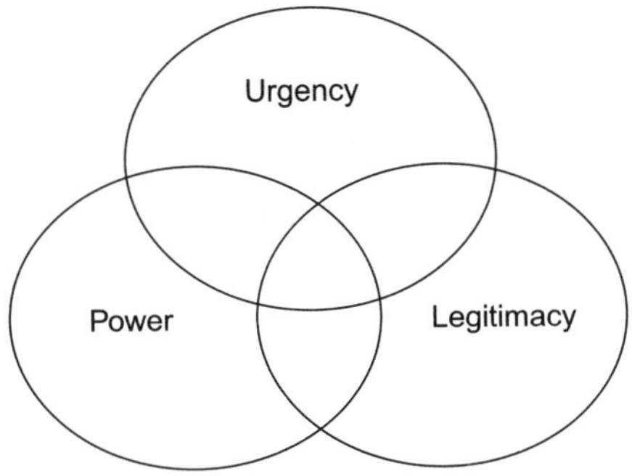

Figure 17.2 Salience Model of Stakeholder Classification

17.4 MANAGING THE STAKEHOLDER ENGAGEMENT

Project managers need to engage stakeholders throughout the life cycle of a project in order to utilize them better for the success of the project. Most of the time, bringing in the right people solves most of the problems. While we engage stakeholders, we may come across a few issues that need to be managed with our communication skills, management skills, and interpersonal skills. Issues can be managed with proper planning by creating an issue log that helps compile, analyze, and manage the issues.

Project communication with stakeholders is an important part of any project. A project manager needs to establish the lines of communication with all stakeholders and also develop a way to keep them involved and aware of the project's progress and status. Stakeholder management plan defines an approach to communications and a mechanism to provide project data to stakeholders. The stakeholder management plan can be formal or informal, highly detailed or broadly framed, based on the needs of the project. In addition to the data gathered in the stakeholder register, the stakeholder management plan often provides:

- Desired and current engagement levels of key stakeholders
- Scope and impact of change to stakeholders
- Identified interrelationships and potential overlap between stakeholders
- Stakeholder communication requirements for the current project phase
- Information to be distributed to stakeholders, including language, format, content, and level of detail
- Reason for the distribution of that information and the expected impact to stakeholder engagement
- Time frame and frequency of the distribution of required information to stakeholders
- Method for updating and refining the stakeholder management plan as the project progresses and develops

It may be necessary to develop different strategies for different groups identified during the Collect Requirement process. Some possible methods of communication are:

- Progress reports
- Meetings and briefings

- User groups (email groups)
- Access to documentation (requirements)

Meetings

To resolve an issue in a way that is realistic and accepted by the stakeholder, it is better to conduct team meetings while addressing issues. This meeting should also be attended by other stakeholders such as project sponsors and others who are responsible to contrive a solution to the problem at hand. The project manager can also conduct this meeting with selected team members who have good knowledge of the matter of contention.

Reporting Systems

Reporting Systems are standard tools that help capture, store, and distribute the information needed to manage and control stakeholders, thereby helping to resolve open issues. These systems also help managers to report the performance and progress of a project on resolving the issues.

POINTS TO PONDER

One of the main tasks of a project manager is to keep all the stakeholders informed about the project progress. The reporting system helps in achieving this.

17.5 PROCUREMENT PROCESS AND SUPPLIERS

Every organization gets involved in the procurement activities in which the suppliers are an important stakeholder. An organization may not be able to fulfill all the requirements to run a project and need to buy or outsource few items. Before engaging in a procurement process, it is important to manage the process effectively.

The procurement management plan (a component of the project management plan) describes how a project team acquires goods and services from outside the performing organization. It describes the processes of managing the procurement from developing procurement documents through contract closure. The procurement management plan may guide on:

- What is the type of contract to be used?
- Is there any risk management issue?
- Is there any need for independent estimates as one of the evaluation criteria?
- Whether the performing organization has a prescribed procurement, contracting, or purchasing department.
- Is there any need for standardized procurement documents?
- How to manage multiple suppliers?
- How to coordinate procurement with other project aspects, such as scheduling and performance reporting?
- Are there any constraints and assumptions that could affect planned procurements?
- How to handle the make or buy decisions and linking them with Estimate Activity Resources and Develop Schedule processes?

Source selection criteria are included as a part of the procurement documents. A few possible source selection criteria are as follows.

Understanding the need: How well does the seller's proposal address the procurement statement of work?

Overall or life cycle cost: Will the selected seller produce the lowest total cost of ownership (purchase cost plus operating cost)?

Technical capability: Does the seller have, or can the seller be reasonably expected to acquire, the technical skills and knowledge needed?

Risk: Identify the risks based on the statement of work. Identify the risks associated with the selected seller and also plan on how does the seller mitigate those risks.

Management approach: Does the seller have, or can the seller be reasonably expected to develop, management processes and procedures to ensure a successful project?

Technical approach: Do the seller's proposed technical methodologies, techniques, solutions, and services meet the procurement document requirements, or are they likely to provide more or less than the expected results?

Warranty: What does the seller propose to warrant the final product, and through what time period?

Financial capacity: Does the seller have, or can the seller reasonably be expected to obtain, the necessary financial resources?

Production capacity and interest: Does the seller have the capacity and interest to meet potential future requirements?

Business size and type: Does the seller's enterprise meet a specific category of business such as small business (disadvantaged, specific programs, etc.) as defined by the organization or established by government agency and set forth as a condition of the agreement award?

Past performance of sellers: What has been the past experience with selected sellers?

References: Can the seller provide references from prior customers verifying the seller's work experience and compliance with contractual requirements?

Intellectual property rights: Does the seller assert intellectual property rights in the work processes or services they will use or in the products they will produce for the project?

Proprietary rights: Does the seller assert proprietary rights in the work processes or services they will use or in the products they will produce for the project?

For understanding the procurement handling process, it is important to understand the following terms:

Contract: A contract is a formal legally binding agreement between two or more parties, individuals, businesses, organizations, or government agencies, through which the contracted parties exchange goods or services of value to each other. Contracts also specify restrictions on certain actions of the contracted parties during the tenure of the contract. Salient features of a contract are as follows.

- A contract may be written, in formal or informal terms, or it may be entirely verbal, although the former is generally preferred. The terms of a contract (e.g., who, what, where, when, how, and which of the agreement) define the binding promises of each party to the contract.
- A contract clearly states the acceptance criteria of the contracted product or service. A contract is generally deemed fulfilled only if all terms of the contract have been fulfilled.
- Solutions for resolving differences that may arise during the period of a contract are also documented in the contract. The terms of a contract clearly define the actions—or

inactions—of the contracted parties that constitute a breach of the contract, as well as force majeure conditions.

- A contract may be used as a risk management tool, because it transfers the risk from the buyer to the seller. Organizations typically handle contracts either through a centralized contracting office, which handles all project-related contracts of the organization, or through decentralized contract administrators, one of whom is assigned for each project executed by the organization.
- The terms of a contract should meet applicable legal requirements governing contracts to establish the validity of the contract.
- In a contract, a seller may be referred to as a contractor, a subcontractor, a vendor, a service provider, or a supplier.
- In a contract, a buyer may be referred to as a client, a customer, a prime contractor, a contractor, an acquiring organization, a governmental agency, a service requestor, or a purchaser.
- Depending upon the area of application, a contract is sometimes called an agreement, an understanding, a subcontract, or a purchase order.
- The roles of a buyer and a seller are predetermined when teaming agreement document is present. A teaming agreement is an understanding between different business entities to come together as a team in order to perform the activities of a particular project.
- If a buyer wants a seller to begin a high-priority, business-critical project immediately, then the seller needs "letter of intent" or "letter of contract" from the buyer to start work immediately.

Contract Types

As discussed before, a contract is a formal legally binding agreement between two or more parties, individuals, businesses, organizations, or government agencies, through which the contracted parties exchange goods or services of value to each other. There are different types of contracts based on the pricing models agreed upon between two parties, namely, the buyer and the seller. Each contract type has its own pros and cons. The project manager needs to choose the appropriate contract type based on different parameters such as scope of the project and risk level of buyers and sellers.

Fixed price (lump sum): This type of contract involves a fixed total price for the product the seller has been contracted to provide. Fixed-price contracts are often made in projects with well-defined scope and there is no ambiguity regarding requirements. The buyer and the seller know clearly what he is selling and there is no confusion between the buyer and the seller. Fixed Price-Economic Price Adjustment is a fixed-price contract which takes into consideration inflation changes, especially when the project duration is high.

Cost reimbursable: This category of contract involves reimbursement to the seller the actual costs incurred by the seller, plus a fee typically representing the seller's profit. There are three types of cost-reimbursable contracts:

Cost plus fee (CPF) or cost plus percentage of cost (CPPC): In this type, the seller is reimbursed the allowable costs for performing the contracted work and paid a fee, which represents the profit for the seller, calculated as an agreed-upon percentage of the costs incurred.

Cost plus fixed fee (CPFF): In this type, the seller is reimbursed the allowable costs for performing the contract work and paid a fixed fee that is calculated as a percentage of the estimated project costs. This fixed fee represents the profit for the seller. It does not vary with variation in actual costs incurred by the seller; but, of course, it changes if the project's scope changes.

Cost plus incentive fee (CPIF): In this type, the seller is reimbursed the allowable costs for performing the contract work and receives a predetermined fee, an incentive bonus, on achieving the predefined performance objective levels set in the contract. If the actual costs prove to be less than the estimated costs, both the buyer and the seller benefit from the cost savings based on a pre-negotiated sharing formula defined in the contract. Alternatively, there may be penalties imposed on the seller if the cost or time exceeds the units stipulated in the contract. An 80/20 split over/under target is used in the CPIF type of contract. For example, for every dollar over target cost, the contractor loses fee until minimum fee is reached. For every dollar under target cost, contractor gets additional fee until maximum fee is reached. Actually, CPIF converts to CPFF at minimum or maximum fee values.

Time and material (T&M): Here, a hybrid contractual arrangement is agreed upon that contains the aspects of both cost-reimbursable and fixed-price arrangements. The seller receives payment per unit of time spent on work activities irrespective of whether work is accomplished or not. Because this contract type presents no incentives to sellers to minimize costs or maximize efficiency, buyers generally insert a not-to-exceed total with respect to payments due to sellers.

Tables 17.3 summarizes three types of contracts discussed along with its advantages and disadvantages; Table 17.4 presents features of the contracts discussed that would help project managers make good choices while handling contracts.

Table 17.3 Advantages and Disadvantages of Different Contract Types

Contract Type	Advantages	Disadvantages
Fixed price	Less work to manage Seller has incentive to control costs Cost is predictable for buyer	Seller may charge extra for changed orders Seller may seek shortcuts to complete the project work Buyer is required to define scope extensively to avoid ambiguity or misinterpretation Proves to be more expensive compared to other contract types, as the seller adds the risk component to price quoted
Cost reimbursable	Costs lesser compared to cost of fixed-price contracts Buyer may not spend resources to extensively define the scope	Requires buyer to periodically audit the seller Seller has only a moderate incentive to meet the project scope requirements Total cost for the buyer is unknown
Time and materials	Simplest of all contracts in form May be used for staff augmentation of labor	Costs are incurred by the buyer on the basis of units of time, for example, hourly, daily Seller has no incentive to control costs Appropriate only for small volumes to be contracted

Table 17.4 Salient Attributes of Different Contract Types

Contract Type	Contract Scope Definition	Risk	Payment
Fixed price	Well-defined	Seller assumes risk	Fixed total
Cost reimbursable	Not well-defined	Buyer assumes risk	Per actual cost plus fee
Time and materials	Not well-defined	Buyer assumes risk	Per unit of time seller spends on work activities

Make or Buy Analysis

The make or buy analysis is used to determine whether a particular product can be produced cost-effectively by the performing organization or must be procured from outside the performing organization. The analysis considers

- The indirect and direct costs of in-house manufacture
- Any extra capacity or resources that may be available within the performing organization during the course of project execution
- Possible use of proprietary or business critical activity of the performing organization that may represent its core business or core competency

As mentioned earlier, the decision to make or buy is the fundamental objective of procurement management, which is mandated by a simple rule: the option that entails lesser cost while ensuring compliance to project scope requirements is taken. Although cost is the main criterion to decide the procurement, other factors such as competency level, skill sets, capacity level, and intellectual properties involved in the product are also to be considered.

For example, if the organization feels that it has the desired competency level, it can make the product by itself rather than outsource it. If the performing organization feels that a third-party organization has better competency suitable for the product, then it can outsource the product instead of manufacturing the product in-house. The same is applicable for skill sets required for developing the product.

If the organization does not have the capacity to produce the required product, then it has to go for outsourcing. Tailoring shops outsource to smaller shops during heavy demand periods such as Diwali. Demand level is also to be considered when taking a make or buy decision. If the organization does not have the required capacity, then it needs to consider the cost of adding the required capacity before opting to outsource its business.

The organization should also consider the Intellectual Property (IP) rights associated with the product.

While outsourcing, the organization needs to ensure that the product IP rights of the organization are not violated. If the product is very innovative, then it is better not to go for outsourcing.

POINTS TO PONDER

Project managers use a make or buy analysis estimate procurement requirements. If the project manager has to decide on whether to make or buy a software product, which forms part of a parent project, consider following options:

- The cost of procurement amounts to US$60,000 and that of integration with the parent project to US$2000.
- The cost of in-house development amounts to US$64,000 (the cost of seven team members paid US$3000 a month working for 3 months, as well as overhead costs of US$1000 over the 3-month period).

  Obviously, procurement would save the project manager US$2000.

  However, real-life procurement decisions are seldom this simple.

Contract Statement of Work

A contract statement of work (SOW) is a document in which the seller describes the work to be completed and/or the product to be delivered. The description is insufficient detail to enable prospective sellers to determine whether they are capable of effectively handling the contracted work. Issue of the procurement SOW is an important outcome of the Plan Procurements process, following which the buyer issues a request for quotations (RFQ). Interested sellers would return the RFQ with their proposals. The SOW document may not be complete in the beginning. It is further defined in the project scope statement in the initiating process group and planning process group.

Request for Quotation

RFQ are generally used when the decision to select sellers is expected to be based largely on quotation submitted. This is used for projects, usually of low-dollar value and when the vendor's other related information such as their competency level and unique capabilities are known in advance.

Request for Proposal

Requests for proposal (RFP) are generally used when the decision to select sellers is expected to be based largely on prospective sellers' technical skills or unique capabilities. When an organization is submitting the proposal, it should include its unique capabilities such as organization strength, competency level, number of projects executed similar to the proposed project, and other appropriate data such as customer feedback. It takes more time for writing RFP compared to RFQ.

Request for Information

Requests for information (RFI) are generally used when the decision to select sellers is expected to be based largely on the information provided.

A procurement agreement includes terms and conditions, and may incorporate other items that the buyer specifies regarding what the seller is to perform or provide. It is the project management team's responsibility to make sure that all agreements meet the needs of the project while adhering to the organizational procurement policies.

Components in an agreement document may include

- Statement of work or deliverables
- Schedule baseline
- Performance reporting
- Period of performance
- Roles and responsibilities
- Seller's place of performance
- Pricing rationale and payment terms (frequency or milestones for the payments, late payment fees, reasons for non-payment. As a response to inaccurate invoices, the buyer cannot stop all payments. They can, however, stop payments on disputed amounts)
- Place of delivery
- Inspection and acceptance criteria
- Product support
- Limitation of liability
- Fees and retainer (whether an amount of money, usually 5% or 10%, will be withheld from each payment. This money is paid when all the final work is completed and helps ensure completion)
- Penalties/incentives (Will the seller receive any benefit for aligning with the buyer's objectives of time, cost, quality, risk and performance?)
- Insurance and performance bonds
- Subordinate subcontractor approvals

- Change request handling
- Termination clause and dispute resolution mechanisms
- Force majeure (a situation that can be considered an act of God, such as fire or freak electrical storm, which is an allowable excuse for either party not meeting contract requirements. If a force majeure occurs, it is considered to be no one's fault. It is usually resolved providing the seller with an extension of time on the project)
- Waiver clauses
- Warranties (promises of quality for the goods or services that are delivered under the contract, usually restricted to a certain time period)
- Intellectual property [ownership of the intellectual property (patents, trademarks, copyrights, processes, source code, books) used in connection with or developed as part of the contract. This may also include warranties of the right to use certain intellectual property in the performance of the contract]
- Material breach (if there is a breach i.e., so large that it may not be possible to complete the work under the contract).

The buyer and the seller both require the procurement contract for similar purposes. Each of them ensures that both the parties meet their contractual obligations and that their own legal rights are protected. The legal nature of the contractual relationship makes it imperative that the project management team knows the legal implications of actions taken when controlling any procurement.

Summary

- Stakeholders are those team members or entities who are actively involved in project execution or whose interests may be positively or negatively affected by project outcomes.
- Once the stakeholders are identified, their details are maintained in a stakeholder register. Stakeholder register usually contains name, designation, influence stage, and classification.
- A contract is a formal legally binding agreement between two or more parties, individuals, businesses, organizations, or government agencies, through which the contracted parties exchange goods or services of value to each other.
- The make or buy analysis is used to determine whether a particular product can be produced cost-effectively by the performing organization or must be procured from outside the performing organization.

Model Questions
PART A (Objective type)

1. The main output of the identify stakeholders process is

   A. Risk register B. Stakeholder plan

   C. Stakeholder register D. Stakeholder management strategy

Answer: C

2. If stakeholder is having additional information needs, which of the following documents will be updated?

   A. Stakeholder register
   B. Risk register
   C. Stakeholder management strategy
   D. Issue log

Answer: C

3. All of the following are content of stakeholder register except

   A. Assessment information
   B. Identification information
   C. Stakeholder classification
   D. Urgency of the need of information

Answer: D

4. Following are the contents of stakeholder management strategy except

   A. Key stakeholders who can significantly impact the project
   B. Level of participation in the project desired for each identified stakeholder
   C. Stakeholder groups and their management
   D. Urgency of the need of information of stakeholders

Answer: D

5. Who is responsible for stakeholder expectation management?

   A. Project leader
   B. Customer
   C. Project manager
   D. Project sponsor

Answer: C

6. Which of the following is the common way to represent stakeholder management strategy?

   A. Stakeholder register
   B. Risk register
   C. Stakeholder analysis matrix
   D. Stakeholder impact matrix

Answer: C

7. Your manager asked you to find an approach to increase the support and minimize negative impacts of stakeholders throughout the entire project life cycle. What did he ask you to create?

   A. Risk register
   B. Stakeholder plan
   C. Stakeholder register
   D. Stakeholder management strategy

Answer: D

PART B (Answer in one or two lines)

1. What do you mean by "Stakeholder" of the project?
2. List the three-step process to identify stakeholders.
3. List the contents of stakeholder analysis matrix.
4. What do you mean by power and urgency of stakeholders?
5. How is communication management related to the project stakeholder management?
6. List different types of contracts.

PART C (Descriptive type)

1. Discuss various project stakeholder management processes in detail.
2. Discuss the steps of identifying the stakeholders of a project.
3. Discuss different stakeholder classification models in detail.
4. Discuss in detail the management of the stakeholder engagement process.
5. Discuss identifying stakeholder process in detail.
6. Describe in detail different contract types with relative advantages and disadvantages of each type.
7. Describe in detail the make or buy analysis process.

Section 7:
Software Project Management

18

Computer-Aided Software Engineering

CHAPTER COVERAGE

1. *Introduction*
2. *Case Tool*
3. *Case-Building Blocks*
4. *Components of Case Tools*
5. *Quality of Case Tools*
6. *Productivity of Case Tools*
7. *Functions of a Case Tool*
8. *List of White Box Testing Commercial Tools and their Purpose*
9. *Workbenches*

18.1 INTRODUCTION

Computer-Aided Software Engineering (CASE) refers to the use of software tools to assist the development and maintenance of software.

18.2 CASE TOOL

Tools that assist the development of a software are known as CASE Tools. The aim of CASE is to develop a language for describing the overall system to generate all the required programs. It is a computer-based product that supports the software engineering activities within a software development process. The CASE tools provide automated methods for designing and documenting traditional structured programming techniques, and they also include all the phases of software engineering, such as analysis, design and programming. They can automate management activities, can manage work products, and can assist engineers with analysis, design, coding, and testing work. Software engineering is hard work and tools that reduce the effort required to produce a work product or accomplish a milestone have substantial benefits.

The CASE tools assist a software engineer in producing high-quality work products, and can provide improved insight into the software product to make decisions required to improve software quality. They also complement solid software engineering practices. A good software process framework must be established and software quality must be emphasized before tools can be used effectively.

For example, data dictionaries and repository aid in the analysis and design phases.

1. A dictionary contains names and descriptions of data items, processes, etc.
2. A repository contains this dictionary information and complete coded representation of plans, models, and designs, with tools for cross-checking, correlation analysis, and validation.

18.3 CASE-BUILDING BLOCKS

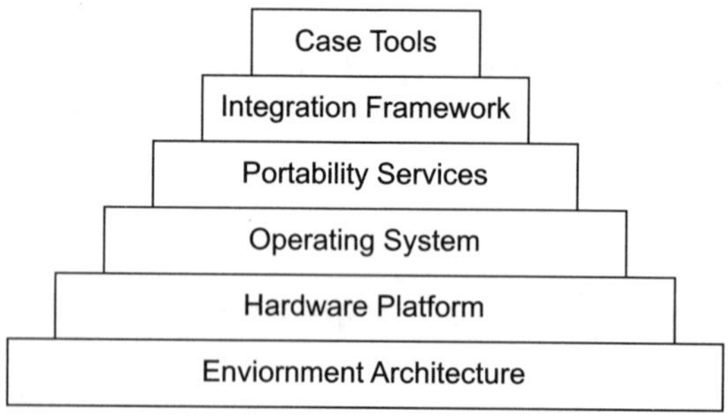

Some of the typical CASE tools are:

- Code generation tools
- UML editors and similar kind of tools
- Refactoring tools
- QVT or Model transformation tools
- Configuration management tools, including revision control

18.4 COMPONENTS OF CASE TOOLS

The CASE tools are used in all the phases of software development life cycle, and also in project identification and selection, project initiation and planning, and design phases, and in the implementation and maintenance phases.

Components of CASE Tools are categorized into three types:

- **Upper CASE Tool:** This is a CASE software tool with a bottom up approach that starts from implementation phase of the Software Development Life Cycle.
- **Lower CASE Tool:** This is a CASE tool that directly supports the implementation and database schema generation, program generation, implementation, integration, and maintenance.
- **ICASE:** ICASE stands for Integration case tool, which integrates both the upper and lower case, and both the database and implementation at the same time. Numerous automated tools are available to create diagrams, forms, and documentation by automated system development environment. It provides analysis, reporting, and code generation facilities and seamlessly shares and integrates data between tools.

Types of CASE tools are as follows:

1. **Diagramming tools:** Enable system process, data, and control structures to be represented graphically.
2. **Computer display and report generators:** Helps to draw prototype which depicts look and feel of systems, which makes easier for system analysts to identify data requirements and relationship.
3. **Analysis tools:** Automatically check for importance, inconsistent, or incorrect specifications in diagrams, forms, and reports.
4. **Central repository:** Enables the integrated storage of specifications, diagrams, reports, and project management information.
5. **Documentation generators:** Produce technical and user documentation in standard formats.
6. **Code generators:** Enable automatic generation of program and database definition code directly from design documents, diagrams, forms, and reports.

18.5 QUALITY OF CASE TOOLS

Reasons for using CASE may be very straight forward and practical, such as easier to use and makes life better. Quality of case tools directly depends on how they have improved the quality of software development. Case tool has improved software development in the following aspects:

- Simplifies program maintenance
- Promotes reusability of modules and documentation
- Improves software portability across environments
- Improves the quality of the system developed
- Increases the speed with which systems are designed and developed
- Eases and improves the testing process through the use of automated checking
- Improves the integration of development activities via common methodologies
- Improves the quality and completeness to documentation
- Helps standardize the development process
- Improves the management of the project

18.6 PRODUCTIVITY OF CASE TOOLS

Productivity is said to be the state or quality of producing something. Therefore, productivity of CASE can be achievements gained or effectiveness of using the CASE technology. Productivity has helped in the development of software in following ways:

- Provides new systems with shorter development time
- Improves the productivity of the systems development process
- Improves the quality of the systems development process
- Improves worker skills
- Improves portability of new systems
- Improves the management of the systems development process

18.7 FUNCTIONS OF A CASE TOOL

1. **Analysis:** CASE analysis tools automatically check for incomplete, inconsistent, or incorrect specifications in diagrams, forms, and reports.
2. **Design:** Blueprint of the system is created by designing the technical architecture (choosing among the architectural designs of telecommunications, hardware, and software that best suit the organization's system and future needs) and also by designing the systems model (graphically creating a model from graphical user interface, screen design, and databases to place objects on screen).
3. **Code generation:** CASE tool has code generators which enable the automatic generation of program and database definition code directly from the documents, diagrams, forms, and reports.
4. **Documentation:** The CASE tool has documentation generators to produce technical and user documentation in standard forms. Each phase of the SDLC produces documentation. Types of documentation that flow from one face to the next vary depending upon the organization, methodologies employed, and type of system being built.

Discussion Questions

1. Which tools do you like to use to track the requirements?
2. Which tools do you need to manage the state of all digital information in a project? Which tools do you like the best?
3. What kind of tools is important to you for monitoring a product during maintenance?

Types of tools are:

Business process engineering tools
Project planning tools
Project management tools
Metrics management tools
System software tools
Database management tools
Analysis and design tools
Prototyping tools
Web development tools
Static analysis tools
Test management tools
Re-engineering tools
Process modeling and management tool
Risk analysis tools
Requirement tracing tools
Documentation tools
Quality assurance tools
Software configuration management tools
Interface design and development tools
Programming tools
Integration and testing tools
Dynamic analysis tools
Client/server testing tools

Business process engineering tools: The primary objective of tools is to represent business data objects, their relationships, and flow of these data objects among different business areas inside an organization.

Process modeling and management tools: Process modeling tools are also called process technology tools, and these are used to represent the key elements of a process so that it can be better understood. They provide links to process descriptions that help those involved in the process to understand the work tasks that are required to be performed.

Project planning tools: Software project effort and cost estimation and project scheduling are the two categories in project planning.

Project scheduling tools enable the manager to define all project tasks, create a task network, represent task interdependencies, and model the amount of parallelism possible for the project.

Risk analysis tools: Identifying potential risks and developing a plan to mitigate, monitor, and manage them are of paramount importance in large projects. Risk analysis tools enable a project manager to build a risk table by providing detailed guidance in the identification and analysis of risks.

Project management tools: The project schedule and project plan must be tracked and monitored continuously. In addition, a manager should use tools to collect metrics that ultimately provide an indication of software product quality. Tools in the category are often extensions to project planning tools.

Requirements tracing tools: The requirements tracing tools follow a systematic approach to isolate requirements, beginning with the customer request for proposal or specification. It combines human interactive text evaluation with a database management system that stores and categorizes each system requirement that is "parsed" from the original RFP or specification.

Metrics and management tools: Software metrics improve a manager's ability to control and coordinate the software engineering process and a practitioner's ability to improve the quality of the software that is produced. Recently developed metrics or measurement tools focus on process and product characteristics. Management-oriented tools capture project-specific metrics that provide an overall indication of productivity or quality. Technically-oriented tools determine technical metrics that provide greater insight into the quality of design or code.

Documentation tools: Document production and desktop publishing tools support nearly every aspect of software engineering. Most of the software development organizations spend a substantial amount of time developing documents, and in many cases, the documentation process itself is quite inefficient. It is not unusual for a software development organization to spend as much as 20% or 30% of all software development effort on documentation.

System software tools: CASE is a workstation technology. Therefore, the CASE environment must accommodate high-quality network system software, object management services, distributed component support, electronic mail, bulletin boards, and other communication capabilities.

Quality assurance tools: The majority of CASE tools that claim to focus on quality assurance are actually metrics tools that audit source code to determine compliance with language standards. Other tools extract technical metrics in an effort to project the quality of the software that is being built.

Database management tools: Database management software serves as a foundation to establish a CASE database (repository), which is called project database. Emphasizing on configuration objects, database management tools for CASE are evolving from relational database management systems to object-oriented database management systems.

Software configuration management tools: Identification, version control, change control, auditing, and status accounting are the phases in Software Configuration Management. The CASE database provides a mechanism for identifying each configuration item and relating it to other items; the change control process can be implemented with the aid of specialized tools; easy access to individual configuration items facilitates the auditing process and CASE communication tools can greatly improve status accounting.

Analysis and design tools: Analysis and design tools enable a software engineer to create models of the system needs to be built. The models represent data, function, and behavior, and characterizations of data, architectural, component-level, and interface design. Consistency and validity checking on the models, analysis and design tools provide a software engineer with some degree of insight into the analysis representation and help eliminate errors before they propagate into the design, or worse, into implementation itself.

PRO/SIM tools: PRO/SIM (prototyping and simulation) tools provide the software engineer with the ability to predict the behavior of a real-time system before it is built. In addition, these tools enable the software engineer to develop mock-ups of the real-time system, allowing the customer to gain insight into the function, operation, and response prior to actual implementation.

Interface design and development tools: Interface design and development tools are actually a tool kit of software components such as menus, buttons, window structures, icons, scrolling mechanisms, and device drivers. However, these tool kits are being replaced by interface prototyping tools that enable rapid onscreen creation of sophisticated user interfaces that conform to the interfacing standard that has been adopted for the software.

Prototyping tools: Screen painters enable a software engineer to define screen layout rapidly for interactive applications. More sophisticated CASE prototyping tools enable to create a data design, coupled with both screen and report layouts.

Programming tools: The programming tools encompass the compilers, editors, and debuggers that support the most conventional programming languages. In addition, object-oriented programming environments, fourth-generation languages, graphical programming environments, application generators, and database query languages are also considered within category.

Web development tools: Activities associated with web engineering are supported by a variety of tools for WebApp development. These include tools that assist in the generation of text, graphics, forms, scripts, applets, and other elements of a web page.

Integration and testing tools: In their directory of software testing tools, Software Quality Engineering defines following testing tools categories:

- Data acquisition: tools that acquire data to be used during testing
- Static measurement: tools that analyze the source code without executing test cases
- Dynamic measurement: tools that analyze the source code during execution
- Simulation: tools that simulate function of hardware or other externals.
- Test management: tools that assist in planning, development, and control of testing.
- Cross-functional tools: tools that cross the bounds of the preceding categories.

It should be noted that many testing tools have features that span two or more of the categories.

Static analysis tools: Specialized testing languages enable a software engineer to write detailed test specifications that describe each test case and the logistics for its execution. Requirements-based testing tools isolate specific user requirements and suggest test cases that exercise the requirements. Static testing tools assist the software engineer in deriving test cases. Three types of static testing tools are used in the industry: code-based testing tools, specialized testing languages, and requirements-based testing tools. Code-based testing tools accept source code as input and perform a number of analyses that result in the generation of test cases.

Dynamic analysis tools: Dynamic testing tools interact with an executing program, check path coverage, test assertions about the value of specific variables, and otherwise increment the execution flow of the program. Dynamic tools can be either intrusive or non-intrusive. An intrusive tool changes the software to be tested by inserting probes that perform the activities just mentioned. Non-intrusive testing tools use a separate hardware processor that runs in parallel with the processor containing the program that is being tested.

Test management tools: Test management tools are used to control and coordinate software testing for each of the major testing steps. Tools manage and perform comparisons that ascertain differences between actual and expected output, and conduct batch testing of programs with interactive human/computer interfaces. In addition to the functions noted, many test management tools also serve as generic test drivers. A test driver reads one or more test cases from a testing file, formats the test data to conform to the needs of the software under test, and then invokes the software to be tested.

Client/server testing tools: The client/server environment demands special testing tools that exercise the graphical user interface and the network communications requirements for client and server.

Reengineering tools: Tools for legacy software address a set of maintenance activities that absorb a significant percentage of all software-related effort.

18.8 LIST OF WHITE BOX TESTING COMMERCIAL TOOLS AND THEIR PURPOSE

Name of the Tool	Function of Tool
Jtest	Jtest is an automatic static analysis and unit testing tool for Java development. It reduces time spent chasing and fixing bugs by automatically generating unit test cases.
PMD	PMD scans Java source code and checks for potential problems such as empty try/catch/finally/switch blocks, unused local variables, parameters and private methods, empty if/while statements.
QAC	These tools detect stylistic issues, dataflow problems, platform, and compiler portability metric.
Coverage Validator	This tool is used in unit testing; it checks that all possible code paths have been executed.
FindBugs	FindBugs is a static analysis tool to find bugs in Java programs.
Jlint	It is a tool for finding Java coding errors, especially deadlock detection.
FitNesse	This is an acceptance testing tool. It compares customers' expectations to actual results.
QA-J	This is a Java code analysis tool used to identify uninitialized and unused variables, call trees.
TBevolve	This is a tool for identifying major changes in source code and their impact on testing.
Jtest	Finds runtime bugs in Java code, e.g., illegal memory references, memory leeks, uninitialized pointers.
Jprobe	This tool provides information about diagnostics on memory usage.

CodePro Analytix	This is a Java source code analysis tool and analyzes code metrics, code coverage.
Clover	This is a Java test coverage analyzer. It identifies the bugs and improves the quality of program.
Html Unit	This is a Java unit testing framework for testing a web-based application.
Cobertura	This is a Java code coverage tool. It can be used to identify parts of Java program lacking test coverage.
Jcover	This is a Java test coverage tool. It is used for statement and branch testing.

Existing CASE tools can be classified along four different dimensions:

1. Life-cycle support
2. Integration dimension
3. Construction dimension
4. Knowledge-based CASE dimension

Need of Configuration Management Features Case Tools

- Versioning
- Dependency tracking and change management
- Requirements tracing
- Configuration management
- Audit trails

Discussion Questions

1. How do you find an error in a large file with code that you cannot step through?
2. How do you create technical documentation for your products?

18.9 WORKBENCHES

Workbenches integrate several CASE tools into one application to support specific software process activities. Hence, they achieve:

- A homogeneous and consistent interface (presentation integration)
- Easy invocation of tools and tool chains (control integration)

CASE workbenches can be further classified into eight classes:

1. Business planning and modeling
2. Analysis and design
3. User–interface development
4. Programming
5. Verification and validation

6. Maintenance and reverse engineering
7. Configuration management
8. Project management

Environments

An environment is a collection of CASE tools and workbenches that support the software process. The CASE environments are classified based on the focus/basis of integration.

1. Toolkits environments
2. Language-centered environments
3. Integrated environments
4. Fourth-generation environments
5. Process-centered environments

Toolkits Environment

Toolkits are loosely integrated collection of products that are easily extended by aggregating different tools and workbenches. Typically, the support provided by a toolkit is limited to programming, configuration management, and project management. And, the toolkit itself is an environment extended from basic sets of operating system tools; for example, the Unix Programmer's Work Bench and the VMS VAX Set. Loose integration of toolkits requires user to activate tools by explicit invocation or simple control mechanisms. Resulting files are unstructured and could be in different format; therefore, the access of file from different tools may require explicit file format conversion. However, as the only constraint for adding a new component is formats of the files, toolkits can be easily and incrementally extended.

Language-Centered Environment

The environment itself is written in the programming language for which it was developed, thus enabling users to reuse, customize and extend the environment. Integration of code in different languages is a major issue for language-centered environments, and lack of process and data integration is also a problem. Strengths of these environments include good level of presentation and control integration.

Integrated Environment

These environments achieve presentation integration by providing uniform, consistent, and coherent tool and workbench interfaces. Data integration is achieved through repository concept; they have a specialized database to manage all the information produced and accessed in the environment. Examples of integrated environment are ICL CADES system, IBM AD/Cycle, and DEC Cohesion.

Fourth-Generation Environment

Fourth-generation environments were the first integrated environments. They are sets of tools and workbenches that support the development of a specific class of program, electronic data processing and business-oriented applications. In general, they include programming tools, simple configuration management tools, document handling facilities, and, sometimes, a code generator to produce code in lower-level languages such as Informix 4GL and Focus.

Process-centered Environment

Environments in this category focus on process integration with other integration dimensions as starting points. A process-centered environment operates by interpreting a process model created by specialized tools. They usually consist of tools handling two functions:

- Process model execution
- Process model production

Applications

All aspects of the software development life cycle can be supported by software tools; so, the use of tools across the spectrum can, arguably, be described as CASE, such as from project management software through tools for business and functional analysis, system design, code storage, compilers, translation tools, test software. However, tools concerned with analysis and design, and with using design information to create parts (or all) of the software product are most frequently considered as CASE tools. CASE applied, for instance, to a database software product might normally involve:

- Modeling business/real-world processes and data flow
- Development of data models in the form of entity–relationship diagrams

Summary

CASE introduces the automated tools to support the systems development process. This chapter defines CASE, CASE tool, components of CASE tool that include upper CASE, lower CASE and Integrated CASE, each covering different stages of the SDLC. The types of CASE tools and existing tools, list of white box testing commercial tools and purpose of these are discussed.

Model Questions
PART A (Objective type)

1. Which of the following is not a component of CASE tool categorization?

   A. Upper CASE tool B. Lower CASE tool C. ICase tool D. Center CASE tool

Answer: D

2. ICASE stands for ____

   A. Integration CASE tool B. Integer CASE tool
   C. Inverter CASE tool D. Inertia CASE tool

Answer: A

3. Which of the following tools provides the software engineer with the ability to predict the behavior of a real-time system before it is built?

   A. PRO/SIM tools B. Prototyping tools
   C. Database management tools D. Analysis and design tools

Answer: A

4. Which of the following is not a type of static testing tool?

A. Code-based testing tools
B. Specialized testing languages
C. Requirements-based testing tools
D. Analysis and design tools

Answer: D

5. Which of the following integrates several CASE tools into one application to support specific software process activities?

A. Integrated Benches
B. Work Benches
C. Single CAE
D. Process Tools

Answer: B

PART B (Answer in one or two lines)

1. Give few examples for CASE tools.
2. List three components of CASE tools.
3. Write short notes on ICASE.
4. List various CASE Environment classifications?
5. List process-centered CASE Environment classification?

PART C (Descriptive type)

1. Explain in detail various types of CASE tools.
2. How does CASE tool help improve the quality of Software Development?
3. How does CASE tool improve productivity?
4. Explain in detail the functions of a CASE tool?
5. Explain in detail static analysis tools, dynamic analysis tools and test management tools related to CASE?
6. Discuss any five white box testing commercial tools and their purpose in detail.
7. Discuss tool kits and language-centered CASE tool environment.

Section 8:
Software Testing

19

Introduction to Software Testing

CHAPTER COVERAGE

1. *Introduction*
2. *Psychology of Testing*
3. *Software Testing Scope*
4. *Software Testing Objectives*
5. *Strategic Approach to Software Testing*
6. *Types of Software Testing*

19.1 INTRODUCTION

One may wonder if testing is really required if all the development was done as per the specification, and also if the developers do a good job then where and what is the necessity for software testing. True these are valid arguments for a perfect world but reality is far from it. In fact testing evolved as a separate entity much later in the history of software development. Testing was part and parcel of development up to the 1970s and no separate testing teams were involved till then.

Software systems were typically built with multiple evolving requirements and stake holder expectations. Because software is an evolving product, there is typically nothing called as complete requirements or requirements freeze. Requirements keep coming and it is up to the project team and stake holders to decide and plan.

Because of human inability to perform and communicate with perfection, software development is accompanied by a quality assurance activity.

– Deutsche (1996)

Moreover software is not something physical like a car or a computer or a manufactured object; it is difficult to be perceived completely physically. Some screens may be seen, some transactions also happening, yet the software cannot behold in its entirety and evaluate all the possible conditions that could happen. Considering these facts it is imperative that software testing must be done using some specific methodologies and techniques.

19.2 PSYCHOLOGY OF TESTING

Over the years as software testing has evolved from being synonymous with debugging to a separate independent competency aimed at improving the overall quality of the product.

Figure 19.1 shows how the thought process developed from a testing perspective.

In the very beginning (Rudimentary Level-Phase 0), the aim is to get a bug-free product without any coding errors. Testing is like debugging so it is not really testing yet. A bug-free code does not mean that the software product will meet the expected requirements.

The next level (**Basic Level-Phase 1**) is to show that the software works. This is similar to the development team goal, but testing is clearly different from debugging. But the problem with this is that no software can work under all conditions because this means that all the conditions have been tested. In a given time, only a subset of conditions can be tested due to the infinite possibilities. For example, a simple positive integer user input field can take values ranging from zero to infinity. The software may have been passed by over thousand test cases but all it takes is only one test case to prove that it is not working.

The next level of thinking (**Intermediate Level-Phase 2**) is to find areas where the software does not work. This is completely opposite to the way of thinking earlier which was along with the developers' line of thinking. There is an analogy which Boris Beizer gives here to bring out the difference in thinking, such as the difference between book keepers and auditors. The job of the book keeper is to present the accounts in the best possible way, but the auditors' job is to prove that in spite of the appearance of balance there has been embezzlement. This type of thinking leads to strong, revealing test cases.

The **Advanced level—Phase 3** of thinking evolved based on the level of confidence the tester develops on the software he is testing. Testing cannot be done forever either positive or negative cases, a logical end needs to be met and the product should be released once there is a desired level of confidence in the product. This confidence would come if harsh or difficult test cases are consistently passed by the software.

Finally, the **Optimized Level—Phase 4** of thinking is based on a strong expertise in the areas to be tested and identification of what can be tested or not. If the product is testable, then the labor for testing is reduced and also testable code will have fewer bugs than code that is hard to test. At this level the testing is optimized and it is most focused and precise. The tester has the expertise to identify the key problem areas and the skill to design test cases to capture them. This comes with the

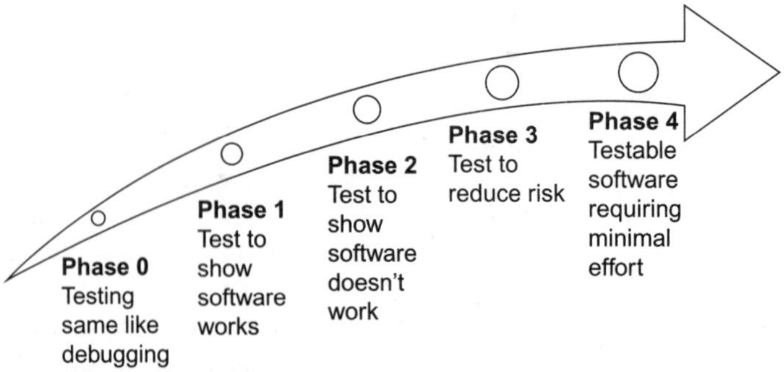

Figure 19.1 Testing Evolution Process

comprehensive knowledge of the multiple testing techniques and their practical applications. This book will provide the necessary details of the various testing techniques as we progress.

19.3 SOFTWARE TESTING SCOPE

Typically software testing scope is based on the functionality and purpose of the programs/software, that is, whether the programs are used for data processing applications (application software) or the programs are used to run the computer system itself (system software). These can be broadly classified into two main areas namely, applications software testing and systems software testing (refer Figure 19.2).

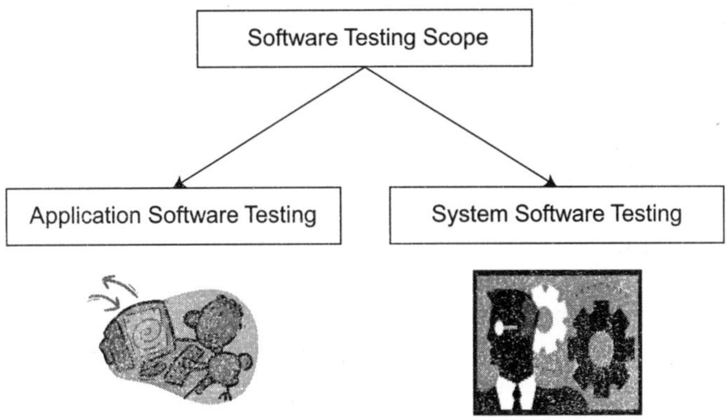

Figure 19.2 Software Testing Scope

Application software testing is testing the common applications which is seen every day and mostly used for data processing, such as banking system, insurance, payroll, inventory management system, hospital management systems, and also mobile applications.

Systems software testing is done on the programs written for running the computer/system itself which facilitate, enhance, and control various programs, such as the operating system, complier, and interpreter.

19.4 SOFTWARE TESTING OBJECTIVES

The first objective of software testing is to prevent bugs from getting into the system. This type of testing is commonly called as verification testing. This is the most effective way of minimizing the defects in software.

The other obvious objective of testing is to find and arrest bugs. The basis of finding the bugs depends on the following:

1. Whether the software product meets the specifications.
2. Whether the software product is fit for the purpose it was designed. This is more from an end user and usability perspective.
3. Whether there are faults which would cause failure during the operations of the software under various loads, user inputs, and conditions.

19.4.1 Verification Testing

Typically a tester may be asked to prepare a set of test cases or execute and may not be familiar or experienced with the verification techniques. This type of testing is a static manual process.

Static testing is done without accessing the actual application. Just as the name verification testing is done by using review based techniques (refer Figure 19.3).

The fundamental theme of verification testing is—Is right product being built?

POINTS TO PONDER

Verification Testing is to prevent bugs and Validation Testing is for acceptance of product. Verification happens internally and validation is mostly done by the Customer.

Following techniques helps for verification:

Reviews: It is a formal process in which the peers or stakeholders examine a piece of work to ensure correctness. It could be a specifications document or a technical design or a piece of code, and the purpose is to uncover errors, ambiguity, or lack of expected standards.

Walkthroughs: It is a formal process where the person responsible for a specific unit of work formally presents his work to a group of reviewers. The work has to be circulated to the group prior to the discussion giving ample time for the reviewers to examine, write comments, or prepare questions for the walkthrough meeting. The presenter will go through the document line by line during the walkthrough explaining what has been done and why.

Inspections: It is the most formal type of review. Each and every participant has to go through training to participate in the inspections. In the reviews and walkthroughs the presenter is the original owner of the materials presented, but in inspection the presenter has to learn from the owner along with his interpretations and then present it to other participants who are called as inspectors. There could be roles like moderators and recorders also assigned to the participants. Inspections have been found to be very effective in uncovering bugs for any software delivery specifically with respect to the design documents and the code.

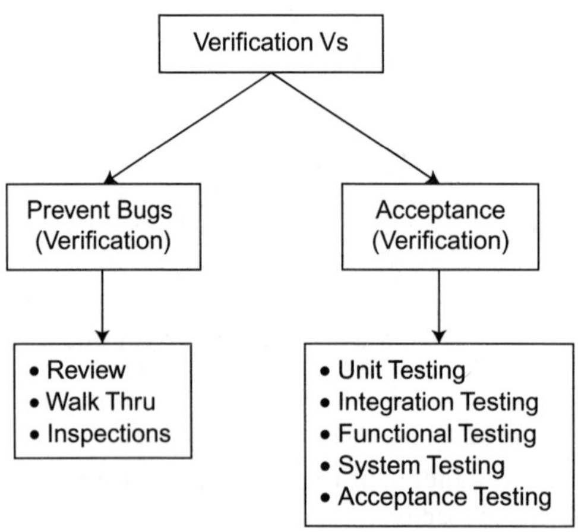

Figure 19.3 Verification and Validation

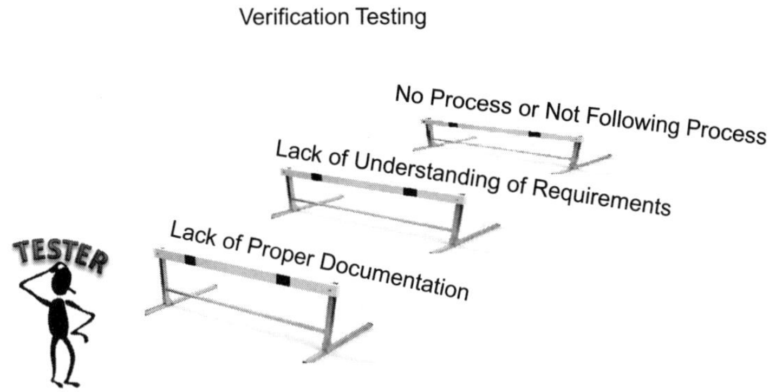

Figure 19.4 Verification–Impacting Issues

19.4.1.1 Impacting Issues of Verification Testing

Lack of proper documentation, lack of understanding requirements, not following process are the impacting issues of verification (refer Figure 19.4). How to know that a right product is being built if the required documents are not available or there is no clarity on requirements?

19.4.2 Validation Testing

The testing activities that are done to evaluate the software in the executable mode can be called as validation testing.

The previous verifications activities performed during the requirements, development, and coding stages help in minimizing the bugs coming down to the validation phase. Bugs that are discovered during the validation phase are expensive to fix, than the bugs identified in the verification phase.

This is the reason for early involvement of testers in the software development cycle. A requirement that is corrected in the initial requirement phase itself is a lot cheaper than when it is corrected after it has become a program (coded).

The common tests, such as unit, system, integration, and acceptance are performed to ensure that the software works as expected in the executable mode.

Some of the issues that a tester might face during validation (refer Figure 19.5) are

Lack of Time: Testing generally takes a hit when development schedules are extended. When this happens all the planned test cases may not be executed and number of bugs captured would also be impacted. The tester must ensure to get enough time to test.

In case the tester does not have enough time, he should prioritize and execute the test cases for critical functionalities then proceed further with the other test cases. The risks associated by not being able to execute all the test cases should be communicated to the stake holders.

Software Crashes: The software may not be in a testable stable state and as a result even some basic test conditions could bring the system down and halt testing completely. These types of delays take away valuable testing team from testers because the application is not available.

Missing Critical Defects: This is related to two problems commonly faced by tester due to lack of time and time lost due to system crash. Tester may be too occupied with these fundamental issues of having the system up and working normally that he may not be able to focus on the critical functionality testing.

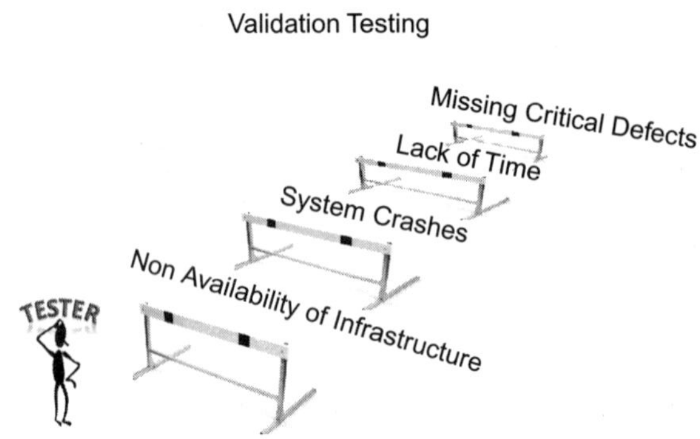

Figure 19.5 Validation Impacting Issues

Validation Testing Basic Phases

Figure 19.6 shows the various phases of development and the corresponding testing phases that could be planned in parallel.

Unit Testing: The smallest testable units of software which could be individual programs or modules are tested during the unit testing phase. This is usually done by the developer, the tester can verify with the developer if this has been done and study the unit test cases and reports. Generally, the tester is not expected to do unit testing if black box testing is only in scope. But if the tester is expected to do white box testing then tester needs to apply the various white box testing techniques covered in the following chapter and unit test the code.

Integration Testing: After the individual modules have been tested the next step is to ensure the interactions with in the software modules. This type of testing is called as integration testing; typically bugs could be found at the interfaces and the communication points between the modules.

Functional Testing: This is done to verify the end-to-end functionalities of the modules. This ensures whether the business requirements of the application have been satisfied. The tester prepares and executes the test cases based on the understanding of the business, the business requirements, and the knowledge gained through the interaction with the business SME.

Typically testing of applications would involve only functional testing and then directly into acceptance testing without much of system testing. System testing is more rigorously done for software products.

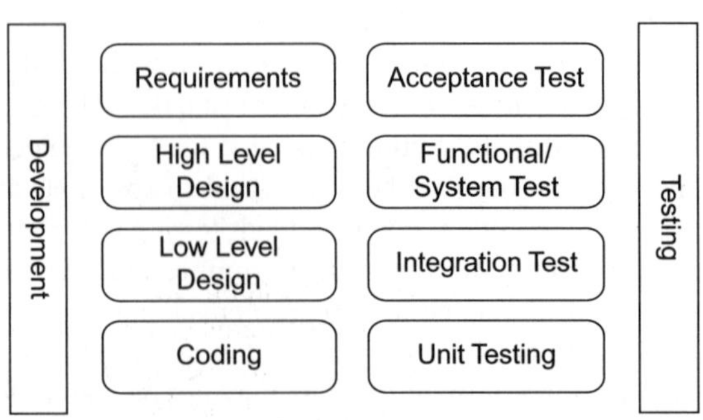

Figure 19.6 Validation Testing Phases

System Testing: This is a more comprehensive test where all the components of the system—software, hardware, external interfaces are all tested as per the specifications. This is done to ensure the delivery of a complete and fully integrated software product.

Acceptance Testing: This is the final phase of testing where the customer will execute a set of test cases to evaluate and accept the product. Here testing is not that elaborate and if a new product is getting released, the acceptance test cases would be defined as a part of the requirements phase and executed during the final phase of testing to confirm acceptance of the product.

The final code would be delivered only during the end of the project. But depending on the developmental model workable units of code can be obtained in phases in an iterative manner. Based on the delivery schedule the tester can plan the respective test case preparation and execution.

POINTS TO PONDER

The smallest testable units of software which could be individual program or modules are tested during the unit testing phase. After the individual modules have been tested the next step is to ensure that the interactions with in the software modules. This type of testing is called as Integration testing, typically bugs could be found at the interfaces and the communication points between the modules.

Even if something works fine, testing needs to be done to confirm that it does what was expected under the given conditions.

When the actual application or part of it is not yet available for testing, which would be the case in the initial stages of development, the tester would need to use the techniques of static testing, namely specifications walkthrough, pretending like the customer and visualizing the end product of the specifications, desk checking with developers, researching on the usability standards and guidelines, and study and review of a similar software that has been developed.

The most important activity for a tester is to understand the requirement specifications. The requirement specifications must typically answer the following questions in no uncertain terms and without any ambiguity. The tester will need to work with various teams to get a better picture of the requirements.

1. What is required to be tested?
2. Why do we need to test it?
3. What are the dependencies?
4. What is the available time for testing?
5. Who are the stake holders and their roles?
6. What are the expectations of the stakeholders including the end users?
7. What are the testing tools available?
8. What is the size of the development team and the development delivery schedule?
9. What are the organizations standards for testing?
10. What are the details of the development, test, and end-user environments'?

19.5 STRATEGIC APPROACH TO SOFTWARE TESTING

Test strategy is a high-level plan based on the understanding of multiple factors involved in a software development. The six key influencing factors have been defined in Figure 19.7. Based on these factors the tester should evolve a strategy which will address the product requirements after analyzing

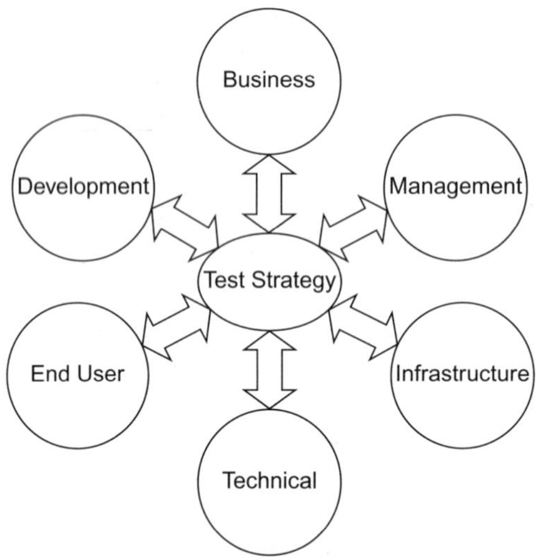

Figure 19.7 Test Strategy Areas

the risks and the testability of the requirements. The test strategy would be the base on which the test plan, test execution, and reporting would be defined.

The test strategy should be defined based on the areas mentioned in Figure 19.7 namely

- Management
  - How critical is the software application under study? What are the management expectations in terms of reporting and quality? Any existing standards for testing in the organization?
- End user
  - Who will be the end user? Will there be multi country release across geography?
- Development Methodology
  - What is the software development methodology followed in the application under study? What is the development project plan? What is the size of the team?
- Infrastructure
  - What are the hardware and software facilities available? What are the limitations of the various environments?
- Technical
  - What are the possibilities for test automation? What will be the ROI for automation? What are the performance requirements?
- Business
  - What are the key business functionalities? How are the current activities done without the new software or updates? How does business expect the new software or updates to help them?

Tester is an organic integrator of all the components of the software development. But this is something that is unwritten for most software projects, where testing is an isolated activity. The tester needs to move toward this broader goal for which the necessary adjustments have been made based on the project conditions.

19.6 TYPES OF SOFTWARE TESTING

This is an introduction to various testing types commonly practiced in the industry. The basic categories of testing namely, white and black box testing (refer Figure 19.8) are discussed along with the specific techniques for applying them.

19.6.1 Introduction to White Box Testing

Structural or white box testing is based on knowledge of internal structure and logic of programs, the coverage of specifications is validated in the code.

The synonyms for white box testing are as follows:

- Glass box testing
- Structural testing
- Clear box testing
- Open box testing
- Logical testing
- Crystal box testing
- Basis path testing

White box testing can be quite complex depending upon the application. A small application that performs a few simple operations could be white box tested quickly in minutes, while larger programming applications take days, weeks, and even longer.

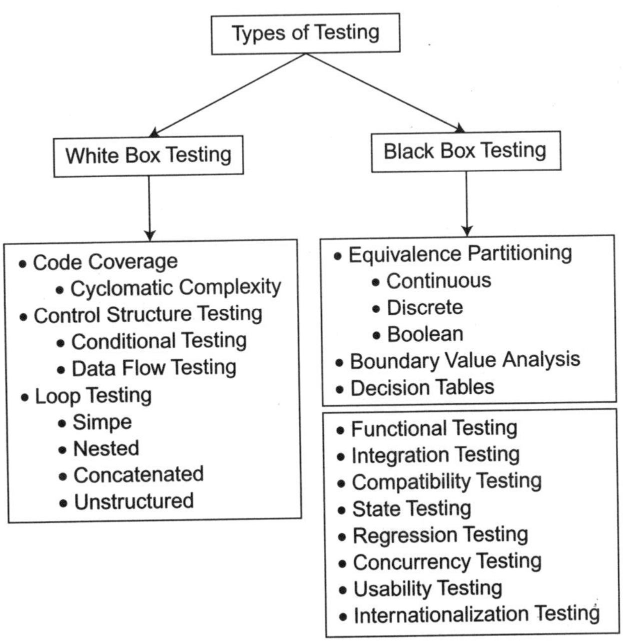

Figure 19.8 Types of Testing

White box testing ensures that all independent paths within a module have been exercised at least once. Typically the software program should have a flow for normal execution and when exceptions are encountered it should throw up meaningful error messages and exit gracefully. No unhandled exceptions should be present under any circumstances. The database interactions during the program flow should also be verified, such as when trying to update a table is not found or a field is not present in the table or if there is no space in the database to create new records.

All the logical conditions should be exercised, for example, there may be multiple statements validating "N" number of conditions as mentioned below:

```
IF THEN …
..
ELSE IF…
..
ELSE IF…
..
ELSE
..
END
```

One area of possible error is the program may never pass through the last ELSE statement under normal operations and it is possible that this could have been dropped out of the developers' radar.

19.6.1.1 Guidelines for White Box Testing

The software application should be first represented as a pseudo-code/flowchart. Assume that the application program or module is converted into a flow chart.

This flowchart should have the technical details of the main function, calling functions, input/output parameters, internal/external interfaces, and database interactions.

This flowchart should then be converted into a flow graph to determine the McCabes cyclomatic complexity number which is derived based on number of paths and nodes. McCabe's complexity is discussed in detail in the sections below. Once the complexity is defined then test cases are written for each path and branch with following criteria

- Exercise all logical decisions based on their true and false values.
- Execute all loops within operational limits.
- Exercise internal data structures to confirm validity.

White Box Testing Techniques

The following are some of the common white box testing techniques.

- Code coverage
- Control structure testing
- Loop testing

Code coverage

Each segment of code control structure is executed at least once in code coverage. Each branch in the software code is taken in each possible direction at least once.

For multiple conditions not only each direction must be tested, but also each possible combination of conditions, which is usually done by using a "truth table". Each independent path through the code is taken in a pre-determined order. All possible paths through the code are defined and covered.

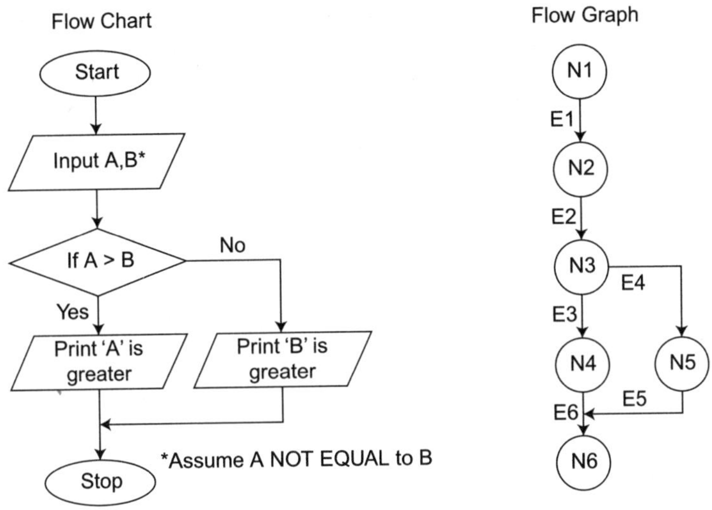

Figure 19.9 Cyclomatic Complexity

Cyclomatic complexity

It is a quantitative measure of the logical complexity of a program. It defines the number for independent paths in the basis set of a program (refer Figure 19.9). It provides us an upper bound for the number of tests that must be conducted to ensure that all statements have been executed at least once. Independent path is any path through the program that introduces at least one new set of processing statements or a new condition.

McCabe cyclomatic complexity is mathematically defined as

$M = L—N + 2P$

Where

L = the number of links in the graph

N = no. of nodes in the graph

P = number of disconnected parts in the graph (such as calling program and sub-routine).

McCabe Number = No. of Edge—No. of Nodes + 2 No. of Paths

McCabe Number = 6 — 6 + 2 = 2

This implies only 2 individual paths to be tested.

Control Structure Testing

Control structure testing involves condition testing and data flow testing.

- **Condition testing** is a test case design method that exercises the logical conditions contained in a program module. The value of a variable would determine the flow of the application which can easily be understood with an example as in the case of Boolean operators, such as TRUE or FALSE. If TRUE then the application traverses along a specific path, if FALSE it will traverse along another path. Similarly the value of an integer variable like the age can make the application behave in a certain manner. For example, if age is 18 or above certain rules may be triggered and if age is less than 18 certain other conditions may be triggered.
- **Data flow testing:** Generally all applications have variables defined and used according to their specific requirements. When a variable is defined in a program, it is actually allocated a

certain portion of the memory so that values could be assigned and reassigned to this memory location during the course of a program execution. Data flow testing is analyzing the location and variables assigned or changed or impacted during the execution of a program. The typical errors which could be found by this method are like references may be made to variables which do not exist or the variables may have unexpected values. There are typically two types of data testing namely, define/use where the variables definition and usage is analyzed through the course of program execution and program slicing where the programs are sliced to chunks of executable components to observe the impact of changes to a specific variable within these components.

Loop testing: Validity of loop constructs in a program (code) is exclusively focused here.
Type of loops

- Simple
- Nested
- Concatenated
- Unstructured

Simple Loop: Simple loops (refer Figure 19.10) are single loops that can be covered by two cases either by looping and non-looping. In loops the bugs are typically found around the minimum iteration and maximum iteration values. The minimum number of iterations is generally zero, but it need not be so always.
The minimum conditions to test the simple loop are

- Skip the loop entirely,
- One pass through the loop,
- Two passes through the loop to check any initialization errors, and
- (N–1), N, and (N+1) passes through the loop.

Nested Loops: Nested loops (refer Figure 19.11) are two or more loops where at least one of the loops logically begins and ends within another loop. In the example given below Loop 1 begins and ends within Loop 2.

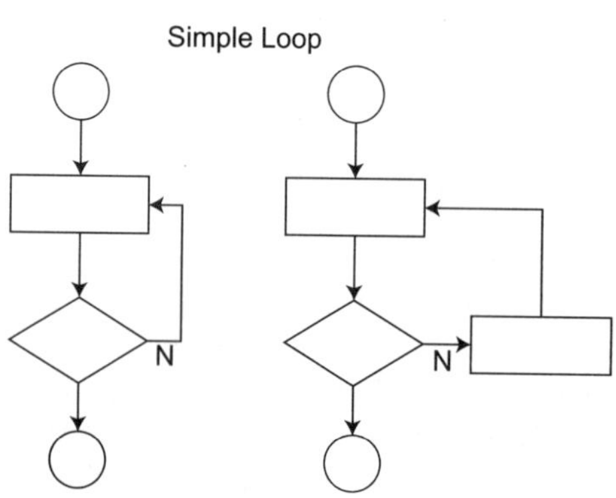

Figure 19.10 Simple Loop Structure

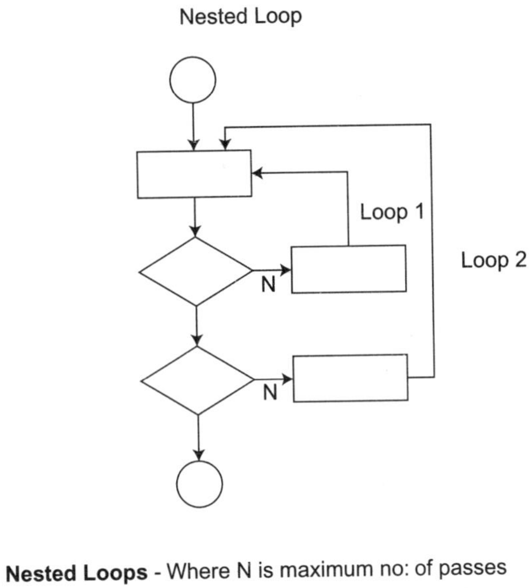

Figure 19.11 Nested Loop Structure

The basic test for simple loops should be completed for each individual loop. The additional tests for nested loop are as follows:

- Start with the innermost loop and set all other loops to minimum value.
- Test the boundaries of the inner loop minimum value −1, minimum value +1, minimum value, maximum +1 and maximum −1. The outer loop should be at minimum value.
- Work outwards keeping inner loops to typical values.
- Repeat the step with minimum value −1, minimum value +1, minimum value, maximum +1 and maximum −1 for all the nested loops simultaneously.

Concatenated Loops: Concatenated loops (refer Figure 19.12) fall somewhere in between the simple and nested loops from a testing perspective. When tested along a path if it is possible to enter one loop after exiting from another loop then the two loops are concatenated.

The iteration values in one loop is directly or indirectly dependent on the iteration values of the other loop. If the iteration values are not related then even if the loops are in the same path they are not conctenated loops.

19.6.1.2 White Box Testing Tools

The following are some of the tools that are available for white box testing.

1. Purify by rational software corporation

- Run-time error and memory-leak detection,
- C/C++, FORTRAN, and Java, and
- UNIX, NT, and W2K.

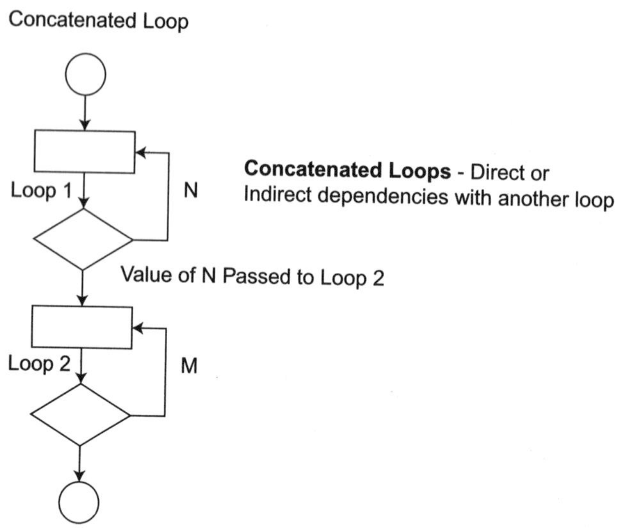

Figure 19.12 Concatenated Loop Structure

2. Insure++ by parasoft corporation
   - Run-time error and memory-leak detection,
   - Add-on module TCA measures code coverage,
   - C/C++, and
   - UNIX, NT, and W2K.
3. Quantify by rational software corporation
   - Performance profiling,
   - C/C++, Java, and VB, and
   - UNIX, NT, and W2K.
4. Expeditor by onerealm Inc
   - Source code scanner for I18N errors,
   - C/C++, Java, and HTML, and
   - UNIX, NT, and W2K.

19.6.2 Black Box Testing

Synonyms—specification testing, conformance testing, and requirements testing.
Black box testing (refer Figure 19.13) involves testing the application like an external or end user by validating the outputs received from the application based on certain inputs given to it. The internal technical mechanisms, such as the programs and the code infrastructure of the application are not considered in this type of testing. The tester has no access to the source code, nor is expected to be knowledgeable of the programming language and code structure behind the application.

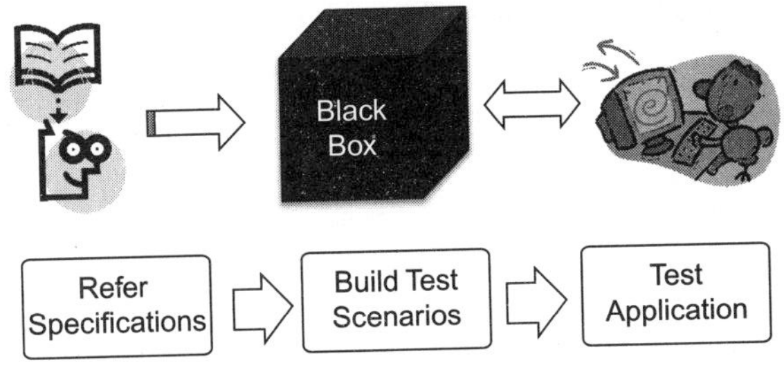

Figure 19.13 Black Box Testing Mechanism

The application is a "black box" to the tester who is aware of only the functionality to be tested, the required inputs, and the corresponding expected outputs, but nothing about the internal workings. This type of testing requires good knowledge of the business requirements of the application. For example, if it is a mobile application then the tester needs to have a good understanding of the internet world and also good analytical skills to see through the requirements to identify problem areas. The tester has to understand the requirements to an extent to be able to fill the gap for any missed specifications on both the sides, either the business or the end user. All the information or requirements related to the assignment may not be directly available; the tester should work closely with the stakeholders to get the necessary information.

Figure 19.14 shows a sample software application with approximately 25 screens, each screen having four menus, each menu having three options, and an average of 15 fields per screen. If number of test cases is calculated it would need to execute to completely test this application in a mind boggling 450,000 test cases. Even if it takes 1 min to execute a test case it will take 312.5 days working 24*7 to complete testing the entire set.

The challenge for the tester is mainly two-fold as follows:

1. Reduce the number of test cases to manageable limits,
2. Ensure that the identified subset of test cases gives sufficient coverage and

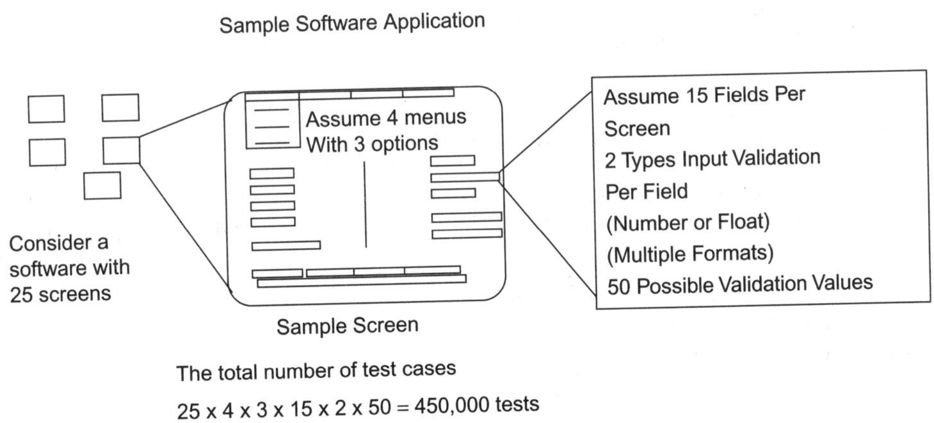

Figure 19.14 Complete Testing Example

The common black box testing techniques which are used to address these challenges are

1. Equivalence partitioning,
2. Boundary value analysis, and
3. Decision tables.

19.6.2.1 Equivalence Partitioning

Equivalence partitioning: One of the key challenges of a tester is reducing almost infinite set of possible test cases into an effective smaller set of test cases. Equivalence partitioning is a technique used to reduce the number of test cases to a manageable size level while still maintaining reasonable test coverage. In this testing approach the input or output space is partitioned into equivalence classes. An equivalence class is defined in such a way that a member of an equivalence class represents all other members of the class. This provides a way of selecting the most relevant test cases and eliminating the ones that do not have much value. For example, to verify if a given input field accepts integer values of length up to five then range of values would extend from zero to 10,000 in both positive and negative directions, which would be highly laborious to test for each and every value. Instead by applying equivalence partitioning, four classes could be here—positive integer, negative integer, zero, and fractions (for negative scenario). Just four test values representing the 4 equivalence classes would give us the required test coverage.

Types of Equivalence Partitions

Continuous: The test data are a measured value and it can take any value within a given range. For example, temperature in a city, the height of person.

Discrete: The test data are a specific value or set which can be defined or counted. For example, no. of contacts in a mobile phone, no. of states in a country.

Boolean: The test data can have only two possible values. For example, TRUE or FALSE, Yes or No, On or Off.

Type	Description	Positive Test Scenario	Negative Test Scenario
Continuous	Age of insured (0–100)	Test scenario for range 0–100	Test scenario outside the range 0–100
Discrete	The insurance policy is valid in all states in India except Goa or Diu or Daman	Test scenario confirming the policy validity for the given set of states in India	Test scenario to check policy validity in Goa, Daman and Diu
Boolean	Existing customer	Test scenario with "Yes"	Test scenario with "No"

Guidelines for Equivalence Partitions

The complete input domain data should be divided into relevant equivalence data classes by

1. Dividing the data into two or more groups based on one of the following classes.
    - Ranges (Continuous),
    - Number values (Discreet), and
    - Sets (Boolean, Continuous, Discreet).
2. Writing test cases for each VALID input.
3. Writing at least one test case for each INVALID input.

19.6.2.2 Boundary Value Analysis

This technique is a logical next step after identifying the equivalence classes; here the test cases are defined at the boundaries of equivalence classes rather than at the middle of the input data domain because the probability of finding errors is more at the boundaries.

Create test cases for each boundary value by choosing one point on the boundary, one point just below the boundary, and one point just above the boundary. "Below" and "above" are relative terms and depend on the data value's units. This ensures testing the application at the border of its planned operational limits.

Consider the example of a continuous data class such as age of the insured person which is defined as between 1 and 100.

Now two equivalence classes can be identified for testing this.

1. All ages between 1 and 100
2. All ages below 1 and above 100

The corresponding boundary values that could be tested for the above classes are

1. 0,1, and 2—lower boundary
2. 99,100, and 101 – upper boundary

The test cases with the above six data set could be used to test the application. For the values 0 and 101 the application must not accept the values, all other values 1, 2, 99, and 100 should be acceptable. Most bugs can be identified by creating two equivalence classes as above one with the data which is expected to work and the other with the data which is not expected to work.

Guidelines for Boundary Value Analysis

1. If input is a range between values A and B, test cases should be designed with values A and B and just above and just below A and B values.
2. If input specifies a number of values, test cases should be designed to exercise min, max, and just above and below min and max values.
3. Apply the same above two for output conditions.
4. Design test cases to exercise data structures at its boundaries.

Input Data Fields Testing Checklist

Generally applications have user interface through which the user inputs values which are processed by the application and corresponding outputs are generated. The input fields could be numeric, alphabets, text, or special characters. Each of the input fields could be tested for these inputs.

- Enter a valid value within the boundary limits,
- Enter the value zero,
- Press Enter do not type anything,
- Certain fields may have defaults, if so clear the defaults,
- Enter upper bound (UB) value for no. of characters/digits,
- Enter UB + 1,
- Enter UB – 1,
- Enter lower bound (LB) value for no. of characters/digits,

- Enter LB + 1,
- Enter LB – 1,
- Enter negative values,
- Type special characters, such as / : ;
- Check with wrong data types, such as number for character,
- Enter UPPER CASE letters,
- Enter LOWER CASE letters,
- Enter an expression,
- Enter special ASCII values, such as 255 (End of File),
- Leading space or zeros,
- Reserved words of the programming language,
- Any operating system filename reserved characters, such as . ,\, *
- Check with function keys, ALT, CTL, Shift, or other similar combinations,
- Simulate time outs by waiting on the field without entering,
- Move to another application and get back, and
- Overwrite the entered values verify mouse and keyboard activities.

19.6.2.3 Decision Tables

Decision tables document complex business rules that a system must implement. Here the focus is on validating business rules, conditions, constraints, and corresponding responses and actions of a software component.

Basic approach

- Identify and list all possible "conditions" (inputs) and all possible "actions" (outputs).
- Define test case to cover each case.

The general format of a decision table is given in Table 19.1.

Table 19.1 Decision Table Format

	Rules			
Conditions	Rule 1	Rule 2	....	Rule p
Condition 1				
...				
Condition m				
Actions				
Action 1				
...				
Action n				

Consider an example of an auto insurance company which gives discounts to drivers who are married and/or student. Let us begin with the conditions.

The following decision table has two conditions, each one of which takes on the values Yes or No.

- A decision table with two binary conditions.
- The possible combinations are {Yes, Yes}, {Yes, No}, {No, Yes}, and {No, No}. Each rule represents one of these combinations.

The decision tables which use binary conditions, such as here TRUE/FALSE are known as limited entry decision tables (Table 19.2). The decision tables which use multiple conditions are known as extended entry decision tables.

Table 19.2 Decision Tree—Binary Table-Limited Entry Decision Tables

Condition	Rule 1	Rule 2	Rule 3	Rule 4
Married	Yes	No	Yes	No
Student	No	Yes	Yes	No
Actions				
Discount%	20	30	40	0

Guidelines for Creating Decision Tables

- Prepare a list of all the conditions to be tested.
- Calculate the approximate number of rules to be tested which is 2^n, where "n" is the number of conditions. If number of conditions is 2 as in the example the number of rules is $2^2 = 4$.
- Define all the combinations in the table.
- Verify if there are any redundancies in the rules or inconsistencies in the combinations.
- Fill the actions for all the combinations.

The three main functional testing methods (equivalence partitions, boundary value, and decision tables) complement each other to give a more effective testing outcome which would not be possible with just one or two of the methods. The decision table testing and boundary value analysis have evolved from equivalence class testing. Here the input and outputs are grouped together into equivalence classes and the logical dependencies of the rules are tested.

Black Box Testing tries to find errors in the following categories

- Incorrect or missing functions,
- Interface errors,
- Errors in data structures,
- Errors in external database access,
- Behavioral or performance errors, and
- Initialization and termination errors.

Types of Black Box Testing

The following testing types can be categorized under black box testing.

- Functional testing,
- Integration testing,
- Compatibility testing,
- State testing,
- Regression testing,

- Concurrency testing,
- Usability testing, and
- Internationalization testing.

19.6.2.4 Functional Testing

The objective of functional testing is to make sure that the software application meets the intended requirements, the requirements may be defined in specifications document which is typically the document shared with development team for building the software or in some cases the document may not be available, which means the testing team would have to create one. Functional testing can be done both manually and also by using automated tools.

The testing team understands the application by studying the requirements document. The testing team will have to work with multiple stakeholders to ensure that they have the required information to create a test plan and design the test cases. The testing team prepares test cases, which will ensure coverage of the functionality of the system. These test cases are reviewed for coverage, correctness, and efficiency. The test cases are then executed and the defects are recorded. The defects are reported to the development team for fixing. The testing cycle is normally iterative and continues for an agreed number of iterations or until the defects have reduced to an acceptable level.

Testing Type	Pre-requisites	Expected Deliverables
Functional	• Requirements specifications • Access to application during test execution • Automation tool if applicable	• Functional test plan • Manual test cases • Automation test cases • Defect report

19.6.2.5 Integration Testing

Generally software applications consist of multiple software modules; these modules which might be coded by different programmers may or may not be within the same hardware or software platforms. In integration testing the focus is on checking data communication among these modules.

Integration testing is also known as "string testing" or "thread testing." The objective of integration testing is to verify different working components of the system perform as expected when assembled.

Testing Type	Pre-requisites	Expected Deliverables
Integration	• Technical architecture document detailing the interfaces • Unit testing completed for the modules	• Integration test plan • Manual test cases • Defect report

19.6.2.6 Compatibility Testing

Compatibility helps to determine if a product will function correctly with other hardware / software in the intended environment.

Software testing requires functional validation across a wide variety of hardware platforms, operating systems, databases, browsers, servers, and various networks. Failure to test these can introduce expensive bugs.

Investing in compatibility testing early helps reduce tech support costs at later stage.

Testing Type	Pre-requisites	Expected Deliverables
Compatibility testing	• Understanding of the multiple platforms where the software will be used • Availability of the required hardware for testing	• Compatibility test plan • Manual test cases • Defect report

19.6.2.7 State Testing

The current condition of a software application is called as a state. The application goes through various states during the course of its usage. The verification of the programs logical flow through the various states is known as state testing. Because the state of an application is constantly changing and the application is expected to be tested with relevant inputs for each specific state. This can be understood more clearly with examples, such as software games or drawing applications.

Consider the example of a simple SUDOKU application on your mobile (refer Figure 19.15).

The initial state of the application would be something like a set of squares partially filled. The final state of the application would be with all the empty squares filled with relevant values. Each time the user makes an entry the state of the application changes, certain validations takes place and user is informed if the action is correct. The user is also able to toggle back and forth between the various states starting from the initial state to the final state through the "N" number of states in between (refer Figure 19.16).

Testing Type	Pre-requisites	Expected Deliverables
State testing	• Understanding of the various application states • Conditions which trigger movement from one state to another	• State test plan • Manual test cases • Defect report

19.6.2.8 Regression Testing

Regression testing involves reuse of the existing test cases to retest the application after any change has been made. This is done to ensure that the new changes made to the software do not affect any of the existing functionality.

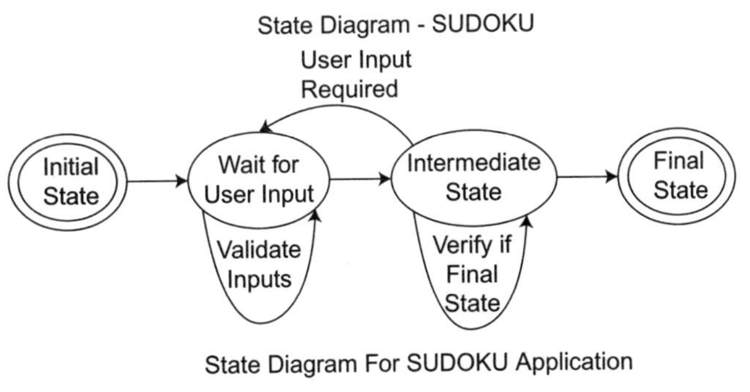

Figure 19.15 State Diagram—SUDOKU

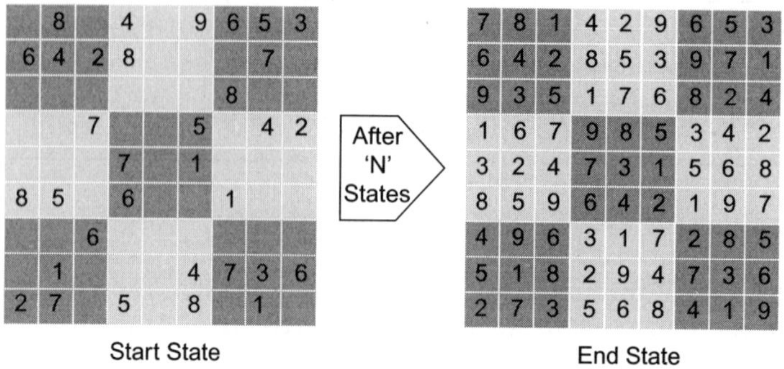

Figure 19.16 State Diagram—SUDOKU—Start and End States

Regression testing is typically done after bug fixes, new enhancements, and modification of code due to change in requirements and performance issue fixes.

Depending on the time constraints or requirements, the tester may execute the complete set of test cases or only a partial set of test cases. The test cases to be executed for regression testing can be identified using the following guidelines.

- Test cases which verify critical business functionalities. The tester needs to identify these test cases and prioritize them.
- Test cases which frequently fail or have a high probability of failing based on past experience.
- Integration test cases.
- A sample of previously successfully run sample test cases.
- A sample of previously failed test cases.

After multiple regression runs, the regression test suite could get fairly large and the tester might find it difficult to execute the entire set due to time constraints. Minimizing the regression test suite without compromising on the coverage is a difficult task. This problem is addressed to some extent by prioritizing the test cases and executing the most critical ones first during the given time. This would ensure that at least the most critical part of the application has been tested.

If the application is fairly stabilized then automation of the regression test suite can be considered. There are tools, such as Quick Test Pro (QTP), Selenium, Rational Functional Tester (RFT) which can be used for regression automation. The decision to automate should be based on the frequency of regression and a favorable return on investment (ROI) on automation. There may be no point in automation if the regression suite is run just once in a year for only 2 week period. We can complete this type of testing manually itself unless there are some strong reasons like lack of availability of manual testers for 2 week period for a very niche and critical application which require special testing skills not easily available.

Testing Type	Pre-requisites	Expected Deliverables
Regression testing	• Availability of existing set of test cases • Prioritizing of the test cases based on criticality • Detailed understanding of what has changed in the application and why	• Regression test plan • Automation feasibility report • Manual test cases • Defect report

19.6.2.9 Concurrency Testing

Concurrency testing is used to done to identify race conditions in an application which may occur when two or more users perform exactly the same transaction at the same instant of time. This results in the two or more threads competing for the same application resources, such as database, memory, printer, communication mechanism, or other hardware. These are often difficult to find and hard to simulate.

Manual concurrency testing can be performed by making two or more users perform the exact same operation at the same instant time. However, this does not ensure or guarantee that the users will execute the same operation at the same time. The test may need to be conducted several times for an issue to be identified.

These are some of the steps for manual concurrency test

1. Login two or more users on the system using different machines.
2. Execute the same transaction at the same time for both users.
3. Validate the transaction and analyze the result.

Some of the common transaction that could be done are sharing the same printer and trying to print a document at exactly same time. Interrupting the system with multiple mouse clicks or pressing keys at random when the software is the middle of another transaction or changing states.

Testing Type	Pre-requisites	Expected Deliverables
Concurrency testing	• Technical architecture of the system with its interfaces • Determine the possible concurrency scenarios • Identify necessary hardware and users	• Concurrency test plan • Automation plan (if applicable) • Defect report

19.6.2.10 Usability Testing

For any application the comfort of the end user is a very important requirement. The more the ease with which the users can learn and use the application the better it is. In usability testing the tester looks out for various aspects of usability, such as efficiency, intuitiveness, aesthetics, and ergonomics. Usability testing has to be preferably done early in the lifecycle so that user interface and workflow changes do not cause substantial rework later.

Testers first get familiarized with the domain and application functionality. They identify the different roles, corresponding workflows, and tasks performed by the end users. Each tester performs the identified tasks to evaluate the application for usability by identifying violations of usability standards, inconsistencies, and overall look and feel. Then finally recommendations are made to rectify issues.

Testing Type	Pre-requisites	Expected Deliverables
Usability testing	• End-user requirements • Use cases • User interface details • Screen prototypes • Detailed screen flows • User manual	• Usability test plan • Usability test cases • Test results • Recommendations

19.6.2.11 Internationalization Testing

This is an extension of the usability testing to ensure that the application could be used in multiple countries with different languages and culture.

This includes testing for globalization as well as localization. Testing for globalization which ensures the application can be used across multiple countries and languages. This precedes the testing for localization which is more focused on testing the usage for a specific area or country. In general, the user interface should able handle the specific linguistic and cultural expectation of the users in different countries. Language experts could be used for checking the user messages and verifying the contextual layout of the application for appropriateness. Identify and verify features of the product which may be useful in some countries and may not be relevant to others. If the features are not required verify if they are disabled. Data storage and data retrieval from multilingual application should be tested because the Unicode formats for storage and retrieval may be different.

Testing Type	Pre-requisites	Expected Deliverables
Internationalization testing	• User requirements for globalization • User requirements for localization • Design document for internationalization	• Test plan • Test cases • Test results • Recommendations

Case Study

Take an example of testing a mobile application which will help in compressing and decompressing files, such as .zip, RAR, TAR, and .gzip.

This is a very useful application in mobile phones for reading and archiving documents.

Below are some of the activities that would be done to test the application. Identify the testing type they would be fall in most appropriately (Answers in Brackets)

1. User able to download the application (functional),
2. Check the time it took to download the application (functional),
3. INSTALL the application on the mobile (functional),
4. Extract all the data from a compressed file (functional),
5. Verify if the files extracted are functional as expected—audio, video, and data (functional),
6. Apply any restrictions for download depending on country or age (functional),
7. Check how easy it was to use the application (usability),
8. Check the impact on the memory usage on your mobile (white box),
9. Check if there are any vulnerabilities for hacking and security threats (white box),
10. Check the CPU usage on your mobile for the application in various states (state testing).

11. Analyze the impact of the application when the mobile receives a call (concurrency),
12. Analyze the impact of the application on the battery (functional),
13. Check the functionalities of free and cost downloads (functional),
14. Check the complete billing flow if the download has a cost (functional),
15. Check all the above functionality of the application with different mobile brands. (compatibility),
16. Verify the application across multiple operating, such as Android, OS- X, and Windows (compatibility),
17. Check if any additional info id displayed, such as advertisements, other downloads, etc. (functional),
18. Check how clean is the UNINSTALL (functional),
19. Check if the application connects to the internet and transmits any information (white box),
20. Check impact of any upgrades or patches to the application (functional), and
21. Check the usability of application in various countries (internationalization).

Summary

- *Application software testing* is testing the common applications which is seen every day and mostly used for data processing, such as banking system, insurance, payroll, inventory management system, hospital management systems, and also mobile applications.
- *Systems software testing* is done on the programs written for running the computer/system itself which facilitate, enhance, and control various programs, such as the operating system, complier, and interpreter.
- The *basic approaches to testing* are namely, verification and validation. The different phases of testing, such as unit, integration, system, and acceptance testing were also introduced. The evolution of testing and the current expectation from tester were also studied.
- *Verification testing* is done by using review based techniques. The fundamental theme of verification testing is—Is right product being built?
- The testing activities that are done to evaluate the software in the executable mode can be called as *validation testing*.
- *Test strategy* is a high-level plan based on the understanding of multiple factors involved in a software development.
- The two fundamental testing approaches, *white box and black box testing* were discussed and the various testing techniques under each of them were studied.
- *Structural or white box testing* is based on knowledge of internal structure and logic of programs, the coverage of specifications is validated in the code.
- *Black box testing* involves testing the application like an external or end user by validating the outputs received from the application based on certain inputs given to it.

- The testing requirements are typically for black box testing unless specifically stated otherwise. The different types of black box testing were studied with the general approach, pre-requisites and the delivery expectations for functional, compatibility, integration, regression, concurrency, state, usability, and internationalization testing.

Model Questions
PART A (Objective type)

1. What is the primary objective of verification testing?

   A. Prevent bugs in the product B. Identify bugs in the product
   C. Customer satisfaction D. Creating quality product

Answer: A

2. Which of the following is not a technique of verification testing?

   A. Reviews B. Walkthroughs C. Inspections D. Audit

Answer: D

3. It is a formal process in which the peers or stakeholders examine a piece of work to ensure correctness.

   A. Reviews B. Walkthroughs C. Inspections D. Audit

Answer: A

4. It is a formal process where the person responsible for a specific unit of work formally presents his work to a group of reviewers.

   A. Reviews B. Walkthroughs
   C. Inspections D. Audit

Answer : B

5. It is a formal process in which the presenter has to learn from the owner along with his interpretations and then present it to other participants

   A. Reviews B. Walkthroughs C. Inspections D. Audit

Answer: C

6. Bugs that are discovered during the validation phase are expensive to fix than the bugs identified in the verification phase.

   A. True B. False

Answer : A

7. The smallest testable part of software which could be individual programs or modules are tested during this type of testing

   A. Unit testing B. Integration testing
   C. System testing D. Acceptance testing

Answer : A

8. This type of testing is to ensure that the interactions with in the software modules are intact.

A. Unit testing | B. Integration testing
C. System testing | D. Acceptance testing

Answer : B

9. This type of testing is more comprehensive to test the components, such as hardware, software, and external interfaces.

A. Unit testing | B. Integration testing
C. System testing | D. Acceptance testing

Answer : C

10. This is the final phase of testing where the customer himself will execute a set of test cases to evaluate and accept the product.

A. Unit testing | B. Integration testing
C. System testing | D. Acceptance testing

Answer : D

11. Which of the following is not the name of white box testing?

A. Glass box testing | B. Structural testing
C. Clear box testing | D. Conformance testing

Answer : D

12. Which of the following is not a type of white box testing?

A. Code coverage testing | B. Boundary value analysis
C. Control structure testing | D. Loop testing

Answer : B

13. Each segment of the code control structure is executed at least once in

A. Code coverage testing | B. Boundary value analysis
C. Control structure testing | D. Loop testing

Answer : A

14. Number of independent paths in the basis set of a program is called as

A. Equivalence partitions | B. Boundary value analysis
C. Cyclomatic complexity | D. Flow of the program

Answer : C

15. Which of the following is not a type of equivalence partition?

A. Continuous | B. Discrete
C. Boolean | D. String

Answer : D

16. This technique is a logical next step after identifying the equivalence classes

A. Equivalence partitions
B. Boundary value analysis
C. Cyclomatic complexity
D. Flow of the program

Answer : B

17. This type of testing make sure that the software application meets the intended requirements

A. Functional testing
B. Compatibility testing
C. State testing
D. Regression testing

Answer: A

18. This type of testing helps to determine if a product will function correctly with other hardware / software in the intended environment.

A. Functional testing
B. Compatibility testing
C. State testing
D. Regression testing

Answer : B

19. This type of testing helps to determine the current condition of a software application.

A. Functional testing
B. Compatibility testing
C. State testing
D. Regression testing

Answer: C

20. This type of testing involves reuse of the existing test cases to retest the application after any change has been made

A. Functional testing
B. Concurrency testing
C. Usability testing
D. Regression testing

Answer: D

21. This type of testing is used to identify race conditions in an application which may occur when two or more users perform exactly the same transaction at the same instant of time.

A. Functional testing
B. Concurrency testing
C. Usability testing
D. Regression testing

Answer: B

22. This type of testing takes care of the comfort of the end user

A. Functional testing
B. Concurrency testing
C. Usability testing
D. Regression testing

Answer : C

PART B (Answer in one or two lines)

1. Write the objectives of doing software testing.
2. Write notes on verification testing.
3. What are all the three techniques used for software verification?

4. How reviews are useful for verification?
5. How walkthroughs are useful for verification?
6. Write notes on inspections.
7. What is validation testing?
8. What are all the issues of validation testing?
9. Write notes on unit testing.
10. Write notes on integration testing.
11. Write notes on system testing.
12. Write notes on acceptance testing.
13. What is white box testing?
14. Write few other names of white box testing?
15. What are all the types of white box testing?
16. Write notes on code coverage testing.
17. Write notes on cyclomatic complexity.
18. What is black box testing?
19. What are all the types of equivalence partitions?
20. What is boundary value analysis?
21. What is functional testing?
22. What is compatibility testing?
23. What is state testing?
24. What is Regression testing?
25. What is concurrency testing ?
26. What is usability testing?

PART C (Descriptive type)

1. Why do we need to test software? Why do we need special methodologies for software testing?
2. What are the two main objectives of software testing? Describe in detail.
3. Explain software testing scope in detail.
4. How has the role of a tester evolved over past few decades?
5. What is verification testing? What are the methods of verification testing and discuss those in detail?
6. What is validation testing? What are the different ways of validation testing and discuss those in detail?
7. Discuss validation testing phases in detail.

8. What is a test strategy? Describe the various components that need be considered for creating a test strategy?
9. Discuss White Box Testing in detail.
10. What are all the guidelines for doing white box testing?
11. Discuss various white box techniques in detail.
12. Explain cyclomatic complexity in detail.
13. Explain simple and nested loop testing in detail.
14. Discuss concatenated loop in detail.
15. Write notes on various white box testing tools.
16. Discuss the black box testing, explain with an example.
17. What are equivalence partitions and what are all the types of it?
18. What are the guidelines for defining equivalence partitions?
19. What is boundary value analysis? How is it different from equivalence Partitioning?
20. What are the guidelines for applying Boundary Value Analysis?
21. What is a decision tree? How can you use this technique for testing? Explain with an example.
22. List down the guidelines for creating decision table.
23. Discuss functional testing in detail.
24. Discuss Integration Testing in detail.
25. Discuss concurrency testing in detail.
26. Discuss usability testing in detail.
27. Discuss internationalization testing in detail.

Section 8:
Software Testing

20

Software Testing Plan and Test Case Preparation

CHAPTER COVERAGE

1. *Introduction*
2. *Test Plan*
3. *Introduction to Test Case*

20.1 INTRODUCTION

After understanding the different types of testing in the previous Chapter 19, it is now time to deep dive into the two main artifacts for testing—test plan and test cases. Based on these two the test execution takes place. The quality of the testing performed largely depends on how well these two artifacts are created.

20.2 TEST PLAN

The test plan is the next step after preparing a test strategy. The overall approach for preparing test strategy based on the various key factors in a software project was discussed in Chapter 19. The test strategy though at a high level can be used as a starting point for building a detailed test plan. The outputs of the test strategy will be used as the inputs for preparing the test plan. The test plan will detail the implementation of the various test processes and tools to achieve the objectives of testing for the given application.

20.2.1 Key Components for a Test Plan

The key factors (refer Figure 20.1) that need to be considered in detail for the test plan are

1. The important functionalities that the product should have to ensure its success.
2. The different testing techniques and tools that could be leveraged for testing the various product functionalities.
3. The various risk factors which need to be considered and their impact to the product.

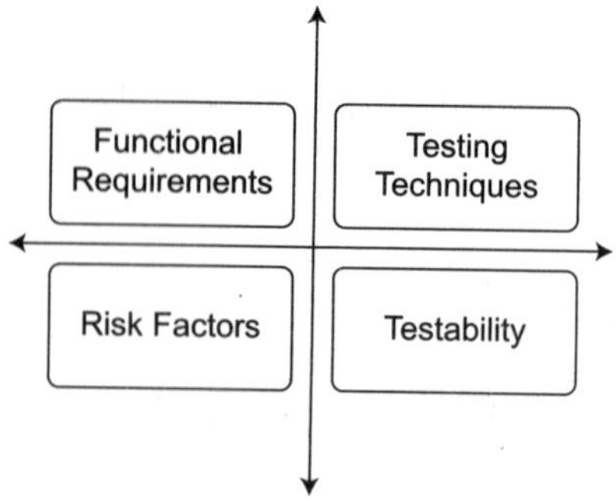

Figure 20.1 Key Components /Factors of a Test Plan

4. The testability of the product and areas of the product which may not be testable.

Look at the above points in detail.

20.2.1.1 Identify Key Functionalities

The specifications could be a starting point for this. Unless the functionalities in the application and the expectations from the stakeholders are known, it will be difficult to prioritize them based on their importance. The critical and most important functionalities should be given more time for understanding and testing effort. Because testing is an expensive activity, only activities which would minimize the risks that would matter for the final product are focused upon and comprehensively tested.

After going through the specifications the tester should define the scope of testing. At this point the tester may not know the exact priority for testing though through his experience he may be able to logically create the list of functionalities to be tested. This list of functionalities could be discussed with the key stakeholders, such as the business Subject Matter Expert and the management to understand further in terms of why the product or application is important to them and what are the key pain points or problems they are trying to solve using the product. Based on the inputs from these discussions and the tester's experience, the key list of functionalities should be defined.

20.2.1.2 Testing Techniques and Tools

After determining what needs to be tested, the next logical step would be to identify the necessary testing techniques and tools that would be feasible to use for testing the given product.

The testing techniques (refer Figure 20.2) can be broadly classified into six main categories and the testing should be ideally diversified among all these categories. This is done to increase the probability of capturing bugs. For example, by using diversified techniques the bugs which were missed by a particular technique could be captured by another technique.

i. **Tester focused:** This testing is based on who is doing the testing. Based on the complexity and the requirements of the product there could be multiple types of testers each with different type of skills and objectives of testing. Some of the common types of testers are
   a. End user: This user belongs to the final audience who would be using the product. This could happen at any stage of the development cycle based on the overall plan and availability of the end users. The tester will do the necessary analysis by working together with the end user.

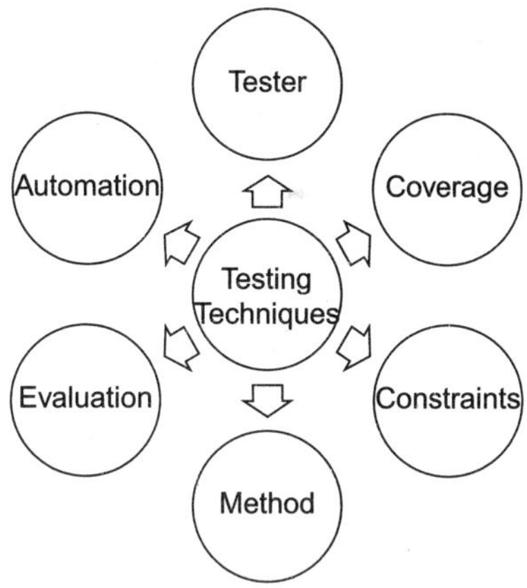

Figure 20.2 Testing Techniques—Focus Areas

b. Alpha tester: Alpha testing is done in-house by the testing team and other relevant stakeholders or interested personnel internal to the organization.

c. Beta tester: Beta testing is done by end users who are not part of the product organization, but are part of the group or the target audience of the product.

d. Business expert tester: The product is tested by an expert who knows the business requirement and the problems which the product was expected to address.

ii. **Test Coverage Focused:** One of the main challenges for a tester is how much and how effectively he can test in a given time. The test coverage part is how much of product functionality will be tested. It is not practical to test all the functionality yet the tester has to evaluate the product. This is done by applying some techniques as given below.

a. Functional testing: Each function is tested one by one in a sequential manner till there is enough confidence that the functions work. The testers can apply both black box and white box testing techniques based on the state of the product and the requirements. White box testing at a functional level is more like unit testing. Basis path testing can be done to verify the internal path of the program; this could help in minimizing the bugs in the longer paths which could be traversed during the program execution because the longer paths are typically a combination of the various sub paths. Statement coverage and branch coverage techniques could be applied, if every line of code is tested then the statement coverage is 100%. Similarly if every branch of code is tested, that is from one program to another, then the branch coverage becomes 100%.

b. Configuration testing**:** A product which passes successfully with 100% statement and branch coverage could possibly fail when tested on a different configuration. This could be seen with mobile applications or printers. Suppose there are approximately 100 mobile phones available in the market and a new android application could work with 10 mobile phones but could fail on the next different mobile phone. The coverage achieved here is about 10% in these cases special tests to increase the coverage or minimize the risk would be required. All the 100 mobiles may not be tested but the tests may be optimized for maximum coverage using techniques, such as Pair-Wise testing.

c. Specifications and requirements testing: These types of testing will fall under the category of verification testing. Each and every documented specification of the product, such as manuals, marketing, or advertisement material and other technical operations instructions are analyzed and verified for accuracy. Similarly the requirements documents are verified with the corresponding programs to ensure that each and every requirement is satisfied.

iii. **Constraints Based Testing:** The software applications fundamentally do the following: accept inputs, perform some computations, store the data or information, and produce an output as required. There are limitations on how much the software can handle these parameters. For example, there are restrictions on how many values an input field can handle, if a program can handle only 16 digits of data then the program must indicate the problem when a user tries to input a value greater than 16 and also gracefully exit when such an input is given. Similarly, there are restrictions on the data storage and retrieval also which should be handled by the programs. Data may be successfully handled by the programs, but output may not be processed like data may not be displayed on the screen or printer may fail to print the output.

iv. **Testing Method Based:** There are multiple methods of testing applicable at various phases of the testing cycle which the tester may choose to use. Some of the methods are given below

a. Smoke testing: This testing is done to verify if any changes to an existing application has impacted some of the basic functionalities which were working fine earlier. This is done after regression testing has been completed which is more rigorous test where the areas of potential impact due to changes in the application are thoroughly tested.

b. Exploratory testing: New test cases are created and tested as the knowledge of the application increases during the course of testing. The tester is not stuck with any set of test cases but constantly evolves new test cases to challenge the product. Guerrilla testing is a form of exploratory testing but it is done by a senior experienced resource and is time-boxed, this resource would test a critical part of the application with powerful test techniques.

c. Performance testing: The products go through multiple releases, it is important to check the performance for each and every release based on the benchmarks set by previous releases or based on the specific requirements given by the user. Load and stress testing is also some of the common tests which could reveal the functionality of the product under high utilization or when there is resource crunch. Endurance testing could also be done to verify the performance of the product when run for long hours, weeks, or days, this could unearth some memory leak and out of memory errors.

v. **Test Evaluation Criteria:** This is based on how the tester would judge whether the given test case passed or failed. Some of the techniques are

a. Using the data from manual calculations and comparing with the data returned through the application.

b. The test results of previous regression tests could be compared with the current test results.

c. Verification based on a valid set of test data which could be from a production environment. This is another commonly used method of creating test data where the entire or a part of the database from the production environment is copied to the test environment.

d. Heuristic approach based on the available information, past experience of testing similar products, and the intuitive knowledge gained after working for some time on the product.

vi. **Test Automation:** Test automation is a very important area in contemporary software testing. Although it could have been easily classified as one of the testing methods, it really requires more detailed study and analysis because it is something that is given in testing these days hence it has been listed out separately. Moreover as we move toward agile methodologies it becomes important to have test cases automated as one progresses with testing. The test cases that were executed successfully on given day would be expected to be automated for the next day because in agile methodologies, such as extreme programming there would be having daily builds. This would help the tester to ensure nothing has regressed as he focuses on manual testing of the new functionalities. Even otherwise in any case valuable time could be saved for the tester through automation and the time saved could be utilized for more creative or exploratory type of testing which would increase the quality of the overall product.

During the test planning stage it needs to be understood whether automation could give substantial benefits for the cost it would take. All the test cases cannot be automated so the scope for automation should be defined. The feasibility and cost should provide an acceptable return on investment (ROI) to the customer.

20.2.1.3 Risk Factors Approach

Risk is an event which has a probability of occurring and which could impact the quality or cost of the product.

Risks can be identified by having "brainstorming" sessions (Figure 20.3) with people who have the experience on the application, knowledge of the business requirements, and past experience working in a similar application or technology. The Synergy of this group is the key success factor for this analysis. The group members challenge each other and evolve a realistic set of risks applicable to the given requirements.

The other approach is more generic where the common list of risk for any software application as given in Figure 20.4, is studied with the key objective to identify applicable risks specific to the

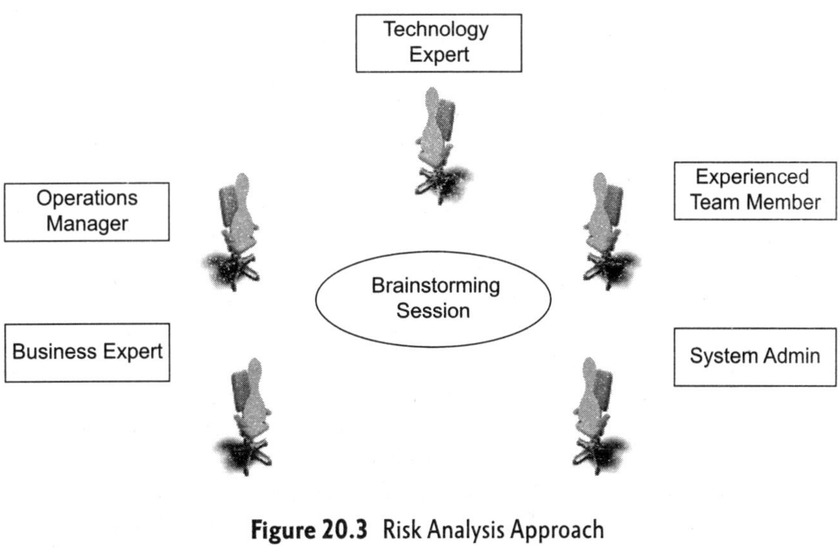

Figure 20.3 Risk Analysis Approach

Figure 20.4 Potential Risk Areas

current software product. This method requires lesser skill and may be less comprehensive. Here the list of risks provides the necessary starting point for analysis.

Some of the common areas of risk for any automated application (refer Figure 20.4).

Security: The system resources, their users and access privileges should be defined. Typically a system would have multiple users with different privileges. A user may be able to view the data but may not be able to update or delete it. Similarly there may be a user who may be able to update information but may not be able to delete. Based on the requirements a definite mapping of system resources, users and privileges must be created and tested.

The internet has opened the business systems to the entire world which includes a large number of users and also hackers with the intent of getting at critical data. This area of testing is a specialized one which is done with sophisticated tools and techniques. This needs to be implemented and tested for any internet-based applications.

Audit Trails: When a transaction is executed in an application, it transitions from one state to another. This is because the set of information representing the application in its current state is changed due to the addition or modification of one or more attributes during a transaction. In case the application has encountered a problem with a particular transaction and needs to rollback to a previous state, options for recovery should be available. An audit trail of all the changes made to a system may be required for critical systems. There may be regulatory compliances which require sufficient supporting evidences for transactions.

Processing Continuity: Impact due to the failure of the application processes should be understood. If the application becomes unavailable for some time then what would be the impact. There could be a threat to life or substantial financial loss when certain applications are down even for a second. Based on the requirements appropriate precautions need to be built in to the application and tested, to ensure that they will be able to provide service without any breaks 24 * 7 all days of the week. Some applications may not be having critical requirements and the risk is low for these obviously and it will not be a major issue if such an application for some time. But again it should be understood clearly how long can the application be down without having a major impact, it could be 30 s, 1 min, 1 h, 2 h, or even more depending on the application.

Interfaces: A system will have multiple interfaces interacting with multiple external systems. Each interface point will have its own format for input/output which would be unique for that interface. Generally a lot of issues could be seen around the interfaces starting with the interface itself not being available because these are independent entities outside the scope of the development of the current project.

The system is required to send or receive input from an external system but that external system may not be ready. This scenario could be handled by creating a stub which will behave like an interface in a very basic form so that the programs to the external interface could be developed and tested. Again the stub is not the real thing it is only a temporary mechanism, there could be a lot of whole new problems when the actual interface get ready and these may not be known clearly in the initial stages.

Performance: The user expectation of response time for the application performance must be defined and evaluated. The application may be able to do the required processing but if the user has to wait very long to get a result, it could be very frustrating. Everyone would have faced this while login to order something on the web and the website just hangs without any response, one may not know whether the amount transferred was done or not, in some cases the amount may be debited but it may not give the credit for the product ordered. Similarly the application could be fine but the network could be slow. In these cases the transaction get closed or reversed on failure within a given period of time should be ensured.

Usability: This is done to ensure that the users of the application are comfortable in using it. It starts with the look and feel of the application. In the era of multi-country releases appropriate attention needs to be given to the locale, cultural, and business standards. There is a separate topic of testing commonly known as localization and internationalization which provide the necessary details of the techniques. For example, extensive use of colors, such as bright RED may be totally acceptable in China but it may be a no in the US. The application may fail its test on its first look itself depending on the country it is released. The skill level of the user must be known so that appropriate training and workshops could be planned to familiarize the user with the application. It is commonly known that application which are difficult to use or having features which are complex to use are not used often. Simple easy to use applications which are functional are used more. The application must be easy to navigate and it should be natural and intuitive.

Portability: The application should be able to work on multiple hardware, OS, and browsers. Today web applications are accessed from different parts of the world with different hardware (SUN or IBM or Solaris or Intel), different OS (MAC, Windows, UNIX or LINUX), browsers (IE, Firefox, Opera). Depending on the usage across the various environments appropriate risks must be evaluated.

20.2.1.4 Testability of Features

The testability of the features of the product should be analyzed. This is very important area of software testing which helps to uncover the defects which are very difficult to detect. It is also an important component of the test plan which facilitates the creation of better quality software.

Let us look at the fundamental difference between testing and testability. Let us look at the fundamental difference between testing and testability. Testing enables us to identify defects in the system. Testability we understand the possibility to test areas of the system where the potential of defects could be high.

The software testability should be considered during the design phase. The product that is developed should be made testable to the maximum extent possible. There should be significant control to the user during the various stages of product usage to understand and analyze the internal workings of the product. The user must be able to know the state of a transaction as it is, where it is in the database, how the current state is different than the state before the transaction. The more the controllability on the product, the greater would be the ability to test and also automate the process of testing.

If black box testing methods cannot be used for testing an application due to lack of testability, such as non-availability of GUI then appropriate white box testing techniques should be planned. Similarly it would be impossible to test a real time bank caller system with thousands of users calling with wide range of requests. The closest that could be done to test these types of systems is through simulators which can mimic the scenario to a large extent. Again all these should be understood in the initial design stages itself so that appropriate effort and costs can be planned for any special testing requirements.

1. **Sample Test Plan Structure:** Introduction
   1.1 Background
   1.2 References
   1.3 Development Methodology
   1.4 Change Control Procedure
   1.5 Test Assumptions
2. Scope
   2.1 Technical Overview of the Application
   2.2 Technical components or architecture diagram
   2.3 Business Overview of the application
   2.4 Business or Data Model Diagram
   2.5 External Interfaces
   2.6 Testability
   2.7 Out of Scope
3. Test Strategy
   3.1 Features to be tested
   3.2 Types of testing
   3.3 Testing Approach
4. Release
   4.1 Activity Guidelines
   4.2 Defect Tracker Setup
   4.3 Test case pass/fail criteria
   4.4 Test suspension criteria
   4.5 Test resumption requirements
   4.6 UAT Release criteria
5. Critical Dates

20.3 INTRODUCTION TO TEST CASE

Test cases are the most important deliverable in a testing project. This is because it is the quality of the test cases that help to improve the overall quality of the software. Effective test cases will challenge the best of programmers, whereas ineffective test cases will let the simplest of defects pass through to production resulting in great loss or embarrassment for the product owner. The primary objective of testing is to ensure the usability of the software product for the purpose it was intended at a reasonable cost. Test case writing is almost like an art, they are no specific methods for any given requirement and the methods used for a particular requirement may not be useful in another. A tester should equip with multiple skills to identify the "bugs that matter" and which can provide real value to the clients. The objective of this chapter is to provide some tried and tested guidelines to writing test cases.

20.3.1 What is Test Case?

A tester works on the software product with the purpose of validating its functioning with respect to its intended specifications defined explicitly in the software requirements specifications (SRS) document or in the use cases, and also the implied requirements which are necessary for the acceptance of the product, though not clearly mentioned or documented.

To achieve these objectives the tester must challenge the product with probing questions which could expose or uncover areas on the software product that behave in a manner which is not expected or not acceptable to the users. Each set of these series of logical steps exercised on the application is called as a test case.

For the validation of the results the tester has to provide details of the "expected result" of executing the steps in a test case and also capture the "actual result" when executing the tests. Test cases are written to ensure optimum coverage of the software requirements under multiple environments and data inputs.

The following are some of the fields in a test case document

1. Test Case Id—A unique sequential number to identify each test case.
2. Short Description—A brief description of the functionality tested in a few words.
3. Description—A more detailed description of the functionality in a few sentences.
4. Pre-requisites—The data that would be required to set up or the environment should be available.
5. Test Steps—A set of logical steps to test a particular functionality of the application. The test steps could be written for positive as well as negative tests.
6. Test Data—The data that are required to test the particular flow.
7. Status—The pass/fail of the test case execution.
8. Remarks—Any comments or information which the tester would like to share for future reference.

Below sample test case document is typically used in a testing assignment.

SN	SRS Ref No.	Test Case	Test Case ID	Test Condition	Expected Results	Actual Result	Status	Remarks
1	1.1, 1.2	Anonymous User	1-TC-1	Anonymous user tries to click on links provided on Login Page	User is able to access the login page containing text and links			
	1.1, 1.2	Anonymous Users	1-TC-2	Anonymous user tries to login with some username, password	Access to product is granted only with an "Authorizied Client" username and password			

	1.1, 1.2	Client User	1-TC-3	Client user tries to click on links provided on Login Page	User is able to access the login page containing text and links			
2	1.1, 1.2, 1.3	Client User	1-TC-4	Client user enters Approved username and Password	Upon enterning an approved username and password the user wil be granted access to the product. The user will be redirected to home page screen.			
	1.1, 1.2	Client User	1-TC-5	Clent user logs on to the website and click on the Home page Link.	Clicking on Homepage link wil redirect user loged on client Homepage			
	1.1, 1.2	Client User	1-TC-6	After login into the application, from any screen, user clicks on Home From global header	User will be redirected to Client Homepage			

20.3.2 Approach to Writing Test Cases

To write test cases one has to have good knowledge of the functionality of the product. The information provided by the client may not be complete because of multiple reasons like assumptions, which are not clearly specified or it may be something very simple from the client perspective hence may not be mentioned. It is also impossible for a tester to know all the domain functionality in and out because testing projects are temporary and moves from one assignment to another. Even if the tester specializes in the same domain, for example, banking, it will have different varieties in different banks. The tester should be prepared with the basic knowledge of the product and at least understand it at a high level before starting any testing.

The tester should understand the technology in which the software has been developed. By understanding technology it only means the implications of the technology or how it is practically used. If the application has been developed in Java, it is not required that the tester should have a very good programming knowledge of Java. It only means he should at least have an understanding of some of the common best practices in Java, what is the database and how is the data access happening. Whether any specific framework has been used what are the pros and cons of that framework. The tester should ask for the technical architecture diagram and the diagrams for the data model of the product for his study if not already provided by the client.

20.3.3 Different Types of Test Cases

Figure 20.5 describes sample software testing process.

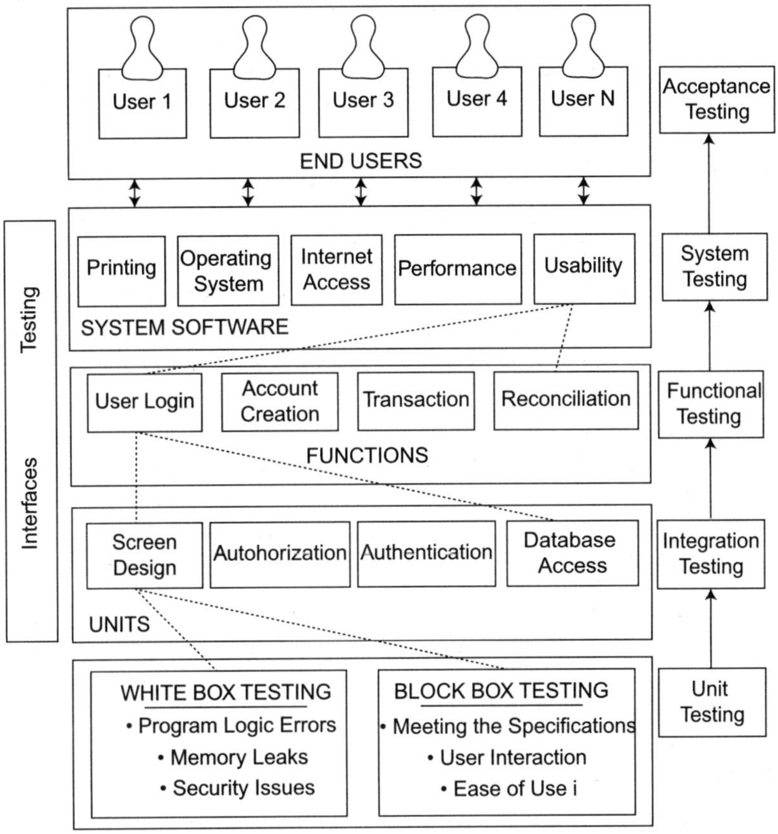

Figure 20.5 Software Testing Process

20.3.3.1 Unit Test Cases

Unit test cases are typically written at a modular or unit level. Generally a program will have multiple sub-programs, sub-routines, and procedures. Instead of testing the program as a whole, the logical smaller units which are the building blocks of the program are tested.

In this type of testing there are three main advantages

1. The smaller units are easy to manage and help in focusing on specific areas of the program at a time.
2. It is easier to pin-point and fixing a bug at a particular unit rather than on a program as a whole.
3. Multiple units can be tested in parallel so it is easier to divide the work among a group of testers.

For designing unit test cases we would need the specifications of the module or unit to be tested and its source code.

Unit testing is typically done by the developers who wrote the program. It is primarily oriented toward white box testing because the objective is to find errors in the program logic.

Progress from testing the program logic to validating the programs performance with respect to the specifications means moving toward black box testing methods where the program is evaluated through user interaction only. We login as a user and access the program through the front-end screens or any user interface provided and evaluate, we do not look at the source code at this point of time.

20.3.3.2 Integration Test Cases

There are multiple points of interactions both internally and externally for a system. In a software system the following are some of the integration points

- Unit-to-unit or module-to-module: Interaction across smallest logical units in a program.
- Function-to-function: A set of logical units form a function. User login is a function which would comprise the following units or modules: user I/o or screen, database access, authorization, and security.
- Component-to-component: A set of functions form a component. A printer is system component which would have multiple functions, such as requests handling, spooling, paper loading, ink monitoring, print formatting, paper jam recovery, and wireless printing.
- External Systems: These systems are very common in today's applications, such as a web services call, external news feeds, and validation of inputs with an external database.

The integration test cases are very important for an application; this is because the probability to find bugs is relatively high at the integration points. The boundary area between two interacting entities is a grey area and they could be written or owned by totally different groups or person with limited communication with each other.

20.3.3.3 Functional Test Cases

The purpose of functional test cases is to ensure that the software product meets the specifications both implicitly and explicitly. The following are some of the ways of writing functional test cases.

1. **Software Requirements Specifications (SRS):** The tester can use the SRS document as the basis for writing the test cases. The tester should study the details thoroughly, discuss with the business and other stakeholders to ensure he understands their pain points. If there is an area, such as a program or concept which is not clear or if it is confusing, then it could be an area where errors could be found because the developer might also have had a similar problem and could have proceeded with some assumptions which may not be exactly correct.
2. **Use Cases:** A use case diagram represents the user interactions with the system. It is a methodology used in system analysis for representing complex systems in simplified flows. It defines the various paths that could be traversed by the system for any given requirement and the interactions which trigger the system flow along a specific path. The paths can be called as the test scenarios in purely testing terms. The use cases define the various events in the system, the triggers behind the events, and the sequence of operations.
3. **Past Experience:** There could be relevant experience of working in similar technology or domain. The tester could leverage his experience to come up with a list of test cases which could apply to the current requirements.
4. **Inference:** Competing or related products could be studied to get feel of what the client is actually expecting. In some cases the tester may be expected to test an upgrade of an existing

product, in this requirement the tester has the option of looking at the previous version of the product. The other areas of inference could be based on

a. The formal/informal communication the tester has had with the business and stakeholders, such as emails, chats, and walkthroughs.
b. Any written material available on the domain, such as a magazine article which talks about a statutory requirement by the government impacting the clients business or a reference book on a domain, such as insurance.

20.3.3.4 System Test Cases

System testing is one of the least understood areas of software testing; one of the main reasons is that it is often confused with functional testing. In system testing evaluation is needed if the objectives of the software product have been achieved, whereas in functional testing evaluation is needed if the software product conforms to the specifications.

It would be impossible to do any system test if the objectives of the software product are not defined. Also system test using the SRS document will not be possible because it would be the same as a functional test.

Thc uscr manual is a document which would be used for system testing. The tester should use the programs, the program objectives, and the user manual to design and build system test cases. System testing is an area of testing which is most complex and requires creativity from the tester because there are no specific test design methodologies for system test cases. The following categories of test cases could be applied for system testing based on the applicability for a given product. These categories of testing have already been covered in Chapter 19 in detail.

- System objectives versus user manual documentation,
- Programs versus system objectives,
- Performance testing (load, stress, database),
- Security testing,
- Configuration testing,
- Conversion testing,
- Usability testing,
- Installation testing,
- Disaster recovery testing,
- Maintainability testing, and
- Operations testing.

The system testing resources are the key to the success of this very form of testing which requires multiple skills and innovative thinking.

System testing should not be done by the following resources

- The development team who built the system because there will be some psychological association with the system. Development team would like to pass the system test as smoothly as possible and may not be motivated to demonstrate that the system testing objectives have not been satisfied.
- The way a programmer thinks is different from the way an end user would think. Programmers will not know the end user environment and will intuitively understand things, such as screen

navigation which the end user may not be comfortable with. Thus, programmers should not be doing the system test because it would require a complete understanding of the end-user environment and the practical usage of the program on a day-to-day basis.

Now the question is who can do system testing. The importance of the end user in system is already known because he is the one who is actually going to use the system. Hence, there could be one or two end-user resources. The end users may not have the technical expertise to perform all the tests listed above in system testing; a specialist team of experts who do only system testing is needed. Last but not the least an original software designer is required who performs the preliminary work to understand the system and define the objectives. There may appear to be a slight contradiction to the earlier statement that the development team members should not be a part of the system team when the designers who are part of the overall development are included. But here it is an exception because the system analysts who designed the programs are at the very beginning of the development life cycle and by the time the design is converted into programs it would have gone through many hands and iterations that there will not be any psychological association for the system analyst with the program; hence, there will not be any bias during system testing. So to summarize the system testing team should consist of

- One or two end users,
- System testing experts, and
- Original system designer.

The other option for system testing is to completely outsource it to another vendor who specializes in system testing.

20.3.3.5 Acceptance Test Case

This is the last phase of testing which means it is last opportunity for the customer to evaluate whether to go live or not with the software. This is usually done by the customer himself with the end users to ensure that the software meets the original business requirements.

One of the key practices to successful acceptance testing is keeping the end user in all communications during the development and testing phases. In this way when any functionality is being developed, if there is any ambiguity or misunderstanding of the requirement, the end user might be able to point out during an early stage itself rather than at the end of the project when it might prove to be too expensive.

20.3.4 Test Case Design Techniques

Test cases are designed with the intent of finding an error when executed on an application under test (AUT). If the test case does not find an error it is not considered as a good test case. In other words a good test case is one which has a high probability of finding an error.

The testing of functionality and verifying if it meets the requirements is the secondary aspect. Test cases should be traceable to the requirements. Due to limitations of time, exhaustive testing of any application is not possible which means testing has be to planned carefully to produce results. Pareto principle needs to be understood which means 80% of the defects are in 20% of the components. This means that for the tester to be successful tester needs to identify the areas of potential failure and keep working on them systematically applying the various testing techniques.

The test case design techniques have already been defined in the earlier chapters. Their usage in a unit or module testing with an example is as follows:

There is a module called **"INCENTIVE"** to be tested for a retail chain store.

An incentive of Rs.10,000 is to be given to all employees who are NOT managers and whose salary is less than Rs.125,000 per annum if their branch has made a sale of over Rs.500,000 in that festival season. If the employee is manager or if the employee salary is greater than or equal to 125,000 then an incentive of Rs.5000 should be paid. If the branch's sale is less than 500,000 then no incentive will be paid for any employee.

Employee

Name	Designation	Branch	Salary (in Rs.)
Ram	Manager	B1	150,000
Shyam	Worker	B1	100,000
Krishna	Worker	B1	125,000
Tony	Worker	B2	110,000
Guhaa	Worker	B2	130,000
Ramani	Manager	B2	200,000

Branch

Branch_Name	Sales (in Rs.)
B1	510,000
B2	490,000

If the source code is analyzed, the following decision points would be obvious for the given requirement. There could be other decision points pertaining to the actual programming language or logic with respect to the error codes or exceptions which would also need to be validated. The areas specific to the functionality are as follows:

File layouts:

Employee:

```
R EMPREC
   EMPCOD        5
   EMPNAM       40
   EMPDSG        1
   EMPBRN        3
   EMPSAL        6 0
K EMPCOD
```

Branch:

```
R BRNREC
   BRNCOD        3
   BRNNAM       40
   BRNSAL        9 0
K BRNCOD
```

Code segment:

```
FEMPPF    IF   E             K         DISK
FBRNPF    IF   E             K         DISK
I                "BRANCH NOT FOUND"     C             NOBRN
C                        READ EMPREC                       90
C            *IN90       DOWEQ*OFF
C            EMPBRN      CHAINBRNPF                    80
C            *IN80       IFEQ *ON
C            NOBRN       DSPLY
C                        ELSE
C            BRNSAL      IFLT 500000
C                        Z-ADD0         EMPBON 50
C                        ELSE
C            EMPSAL      IFGE 125000
C            EMPDSG      OREQ "M"
C                        Z-ADD5000      EMPBON  50
C                        ELSE
C            EMPDSG      IFNE "M"
C            EMPSAL      ANDLT125000
C            BRNSAL      ANDGT500000
C                        Z-ADD10000     EMPBON  50
C                        ENDIF
C                        ENDIF
C                        ENDIF
C            EMPNAM      DSPLY
C            EMPBON      DSPLY
C                        ENDIF
C                        READ EMPREC                       90
C                        ENDDO
C                        SETON                       LR
C                        SETON                       RT
```

The code listed above can easily found the decision or the code coverage statements in the program.

1. BRNSAL IFLT 500000
2. EMPSAL IFGE 125000

3. EMPDSG OREQ "M"
4. EMPDSG IFNE "M"
5. EMPSAL ANDLT125000
6. BRNSAL ANDGT500000

Some initial verification is done by the program to check if there are any available employees and branches.

- If the total no. of employees is greater than equal to 0
- If the total no. of branches is greater than equal to 0

Then the following conditions which come under the category of "code coverage" testing should be validated.

1. If the sales of a branch is less than to 500,000,
2. If the employee salary greater than or equal 125,000,
3. Or if employee is a manager,
4. If employee is not a manager,
5. AND if employee salary is less than 125,000, and
6. AND If the branch sales is greater than 500,000.

Decision	Positive Scenario	Negative Scenario
1	At least one branch has sales less than 500K	One or more branches have sales greater than 500K
2.	There is at least one employee with salary greater than 125K	One or more employees are having a salary less than 125K
3.	At least one employee is a manager	One or more employees is not a manager
4.	One of the employees is eligible for the full incentive	None of the employees are eligible for full incentive
5.	There is at least one employee in a branch for full incentive	The branch is eligible none of the employees are eligible for full incentive
6.	One of the branches is eligible for incentive	At least one branch is not eligible for incentive

The first level of testing is done by white box testing techniques. Then gradually apply black box testing techniques, such as equivalence partitioning, boundary value analysis, cause effect graphing for specific inputs to the application.

20.3.5 Test Case Generation and Tools Support

Manual test case generation process is already discussed. Now the automation test case generation tools available of the shelf or these can be created for specific purposes or for data generation requirements using Java or Perl. The automated test case generation process is done for generating test cases around the decision points in a program. These test cases help in creating a preliminary set of test cases covering the application.

Summary

Being a tester one of the challenges is writing a test plan. This is because there are multiple stakeholders, such as developers, client manager, business SME all of whom need to be considered for getting an understanding of the important areas to be tested. If tester just looks at the requirements documents or development plan and starts working on a test plan it is sure to fail. Most of the information may not be present in the requirements or communicated (written) appropriately in the requirements document. The tester has to come up with a focused approach which will mitigate the software application risks within the given period of testing. This chapter highlighted the various components of the test plan and a general approach for creating a test plan assimilating the various testing techniques. The basic definition of a test case and the practices that must be followed for optimal results for writing test cases are also discussed. The various types of test cases for unit, integration, functional, system, and acceptance testing were discussed and the various activities that would be done during these phases. The usage of white box testing techniques in the beginning for a sample program and also progress to more specific black box testing was also highlighted. An example was taken for INCENTIVE calculation to show how testing can be applied and how test cases can be written.

Sample Filled in Test Plan

Revision History

Date (MM/DD/YY)	Reason for change(s)	Author(s)
	First Draft	

LIST OF STAKEHOLDERS

Role	Name	Phone	Email
Project Manager			
Test Manager			
Production Support			
Business SME			
Developer			
Developer			
Data Base Administrator			
Tester Lead			
Testers			
Client Senior Management			
Project Sponsor			
Product Support Team			

Client Signoff

Name	Date	Phase	Signature
		Test Design	

1 INTRODUCTION

The objective of this document is to provide a comprehensive test plan that will verify the functionality of the "test case generator" for BPM applications. The product has to be user friendly and provide the necessary support to the testers to perform quick and accurate testing. The time consumed by the testers is expected to be reduced for executing the pure "vanilla" test cases. Thus, allowing more time for more creative, exploratory, and also complex scenario testing. The following are some of the key areas of focus for the test plan.

- Roles and responsibilities
- Scope
- Risks and contingencies
- Testing approach
- Entry exit criteria
- Hardware environment
- Test plan and schedule
- Estimation and cost

1.1 Background

This product has been created to automate the generation of test cases for applications developed using BPM tools, such as Pega and IBM-BPM. There are no backward compatibility requirements because it is a new product

1.2 References

List of books which have been used as a reference:
Software Testing Techniques–Boris Beizer
Lessons Learned in Software Testing–Kaner, Bach, Pettichord
Managing the testing Process–Rex Black
The Art of Software Testing–Myers
Effective Methods of Software Testing–William E Perry

1.3 Development Methodology

The product is developed using agile based scrum methodology. Testing will be involved from the initial stages of product development.

1.4 Change Control

The agile mode of development is more flexible to change in requirements. The requirement though is fixed for a given sprint; if any changes are required it goes through a formal process of review and approval through the change control board. The changes are taken up as requirement in one of the future releases or sprints.

1.5 Test Assumptions

It is required to list the assumptions based on which the test plan is prepared. This helps to keep everyone in sync on the basis of the test plan.

Assumptions	Impact
The testing environments will be available when required to support the various test phases and testing types. All the necessary connectivity, software, and hardware will be available.	Non-availability of test environment will result in schedule slippage. Lesser number test may be executed in the available time which could affect quality.
The business users will be available during SIT and UAT to test the product.	This could impact the schedule and delay in the product release.
Based on the testing requirements resources will be allocated to test teams from project team. Testing will have top priority for resources during key test phases as outlined in the test plan.	Testing quality will be impacted if appropriate testing resources are not available. The schedule could also be impacted resulting in delays.
The defect turnaround should be quick during sprints. The team member to whom the defect has been allocated will be responsible for closure of defect.	This would impact the schedule, quality, and test coverage.
Requirements will be frozen before each sprint, any new requirement will be considered for next sprint.	The quality, schedule, and delivery of the product will be highly impacted.

2 SCOPE

2.1 Technical Overview of the Application

The product is a web-based application built using Java for the front end and Oracle as the back-end database. There is a future scope of expanding this product to the cloud. Appropriate design consideration should be taken for this planned expansion at a later date. The application is expected to work with the common browsers such as MS-Internet Explorer, Mozilla-Firefox, and Google-Chrome.

2.2 Technical Components or Architectural Diagram

The diagram below shows the high-level architecture of the system. This provides a pictorial representation of the system in a simple manner. It shows the Java controller, the oracle database, and the end-user interaction. The primary area of testing is typically from a client perspective which is black box testing; testing does not involve testing the Java code or Oracle procedure unless specifically stated then in that case it becomes white box testing.

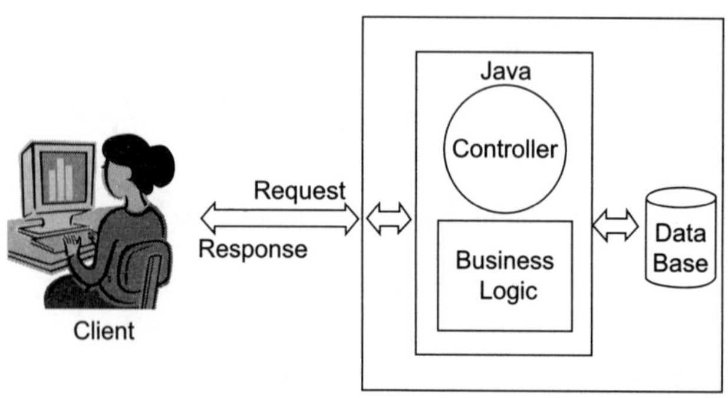

Technical Architecture Overview

2.3 Business Overview of the Application

The product addresses the test data requirements for any testing requirement. The business user can define the data requirements using the tool and generate any number of test data with the required integrity. The business logic of the application can also be captured using the tool. The data requirements captured once can be used for multiple iterations or releases. New set of data can be generated at the click of button for each release. The business logic captured during the testing process can be used for training new resources freeing the valuable Business SME time for other activities.

2.4 Business / Data Model Diagram

The business model diagram would give an understanding of the various entities, attributes, and their relationships. There is a four step process of creating the business model diagrams namely, identification of entities, identification of attributes, identification of relationships, and identification of keys. This should be available with the development team or could be constructed with discussions with the business SME.

The database model will give the actual representation of the application data in the database. The database model will show the various tables, columns along with the relationships. This information will be required to query the database for testing.

2.5 External Interfaces

The data generated by the tool could be imported/exported to/from excel or quality center. These are the two main external interfaces of the tool. The format for the input and output parameters along with the respective data should be tested.

2.6 Testability

Testability is expected to be high for the product with appropriate considerations for controllability during the product design stage. The tester will have access to the database to execute queries for verification. The product will also generate audit logs, where all the steps taken during processing for a transaction can be tracked. The tester will also be able to archive and review previous versions of the logs. The business layer and the presentation layer are also separated.

2.7 Out of Scope

1. The product need not be tested for the cloud.
2. The maximum volume of data that could be created is 1 million records. The product need not be tested beyond 1 million.
3. Unit testing will be done by development team.

3 TEST STRATEGY

3.1 Features to be Tested

Below is a list of features that will be tested. The tester can add an additional column for the requirements that are being added in each sprint for tracking purposes. Based on the discussions with the business and other stakeholders a table of features is created. This is at a high level and covers the overall scope of testing. The details will be gradually worked out and every feature/requirement below should be converted into a set of functional requirements.

Feature	Name	Description
R001	Business flow of the application	Creation, modification, deletion of accounts, projects, data requirements, data scenarios, and data screens.
R002	Generate test data	Static data sets, such as name, address, phone numbers, credit card numbers, etc. Dynamic data sets based on special requirements, such as registration no. of a car, SSN, transaction numbers, etc. Dependent data sets based on already created data for data integrity.
R003	Master data sets	Create a same database itself based on the defined tables, attributes, and relationships.
R004	Export data	The test cases and corresponding data created should be exported to EXCEL and quality center.
R005	Test case repository	The test cases and the data requirements should be mapped. After defining the test case once should be able to utilize the data generated for multiple iterations.

3.2 Types of Testing

There are multiple testing types which could be applicable to minimize the overall risk of the product. The table below suggests some of the common testing types which should be considered and factored into the test plan if required.

Types of Testing	Risk Level
Performance Testing Basic performance testing criteria to be ensured. Comprehensive performance testing by separate team	Low
GUI Standards: High standards expected for GUI because it is a product which needs to be user friendly and comfortable to the end user	Critical
Portability : This testing is used to warrant that the application will run on multiple platforms	Med
Localization: Localization testing is done to guarantee that the application will work properly in different languages and locales. To be released in English language only for US	Low
Stress Testing: This will be done by a separate performance testing team	Low
Conversion Testing: This being a new application built from scratch; there will be no data conversion from legacy systems	Not Applicable
Parallel Testing: There is no existing system to test the application and compare with the current application	Not Applicable
Regression of unchanged functionality: Because it is a new product regression will be required from Sprint 2 only. Sprint 1 will not have any regression because all the functionality will be new and being tested for the first time	Low
Automated Testing: Automation is more cost effective when started in a stable application. If Sprint 1 is stable, automation can begin in Sprint 2 after identification of the relevant functionalities that can be automated	Med

Installation Testing: This is an important area of testing for the test data generation tool which will be installed in multiple environments and by multiple ways either through internet download or shipping the CDs	High
End to End / Interface Testing: The communication between the various interacting modules should be tested. Also the products external interfaces should be tested with multiple inputs and outputs as applicable	High
Usability: Usability of the product is a very important area, the comfort of the user in the screen navigation, the level of intuitive controls, the visual appearance of the screens, and the productivity improvement from an end-user perspective should be verified	Critical
User's Guide / Training Guides: This testing is done to ensure that the user would be comfortable with the training guide and the contents of the guide are accurate	Med
Guerrilla Testing: Guerrilla testing is typically done by an expert tester, the overall objective is given to the tester not the exact steps. The tester will come up with his own unstructured tests to break the software	Low
Security Testing: The access and authorizations for usage of the various features in the product should be verified. Security risks related to the exposure of the product to the internet should also be addressed and tested	High
Network Testing: This can be done as a part of the performance testing effort. The purpose is to understand that the performance of the product due to network latency	Med
Hardware Testing: This testing is not in scope all the required hardware is expected to be available and functional	Not Applicable
Multiple instances of application: Test like if the same user logs in different machines or multiple users logging from different instances in the same machine	Med
Temporal Testing: This type of testing will not be applicable here because it is test data generation product for a given set of requirements	NA
Disaster Recovery (Backup / Restore): In the event of a system crash, how soon can the system be restored. Verify availability of the backups, frequency of backups, and restore procedures	High
Input and Boundary Tests: Verify the field inputs and perform boundary value analysis with appropriate data for each field	Med
Out of Memory Tests: Large volumes of data should be generated any memory leaks could possibly crash the system or slow down the process. Also check with developers on their efforts to identify and fix memory leaks	Critical

3.3 Testing Approach

The testing team will begin designing their detailed test plans and test cases for a sprint while the development team is designing and coding. The team will use a defect tracker to enter the test cases and track the defects.

The builds will be delivered to system test via visual source safe drops coordinated by the development team. Each sprint will be duration of 1 week, there will be daily builds with logical units of work completed every day. The development team will deploy the builds in the test environment. The build notes will be shared with the testing team which will specify what are the functionalities completed in the each new build and any changes to the product since the previous build.

When a build is delivered the testing team will run a series of scripts to see if the basic functionalities or the previously working key functionalities are still in order. This is necessary to confirm if the build is acceptable for testing and also known as "smoke testing". The smoke testing scripts are manual but can be automated once the system is more stable. In case of critical errors during the smoke test the build will not be accepted by the testing team and will be returned to the development team. There will be no further testing till the smoke testing is successfully completed.

When the build is accepted the manual test cases are executed based on agreed upon priority after discussions with the business and management. Defect triage meetings will be held after each sprint on a weekly basis to understand the defects in more details and confirm if it is a defect. The defect triage team consists of tester, developer, and project or client manager.

Defect trackers are used to enter the defects, monitor them and finally close the defects. There are quite a few defect trackers available in the market some of them are free. Because there are multiple stakeholders in the project the defect tracker helps to sync up everyone on the status of the defect. The defects typically have the following status—new, open, assigned, fixed, and closed.

4 RELEASE

4.1 Activity Guidelines

Below are the activities for each phase of the project.

Phase	Typical Activities	Responsibility
Sprint 0	Project initiation. This includes finding a test lead for the project and setting up a project in defect tracker	Test Manager
Sprint 0	Kick off meeting. This is done to familiarize the client manager with the test methodology and test deliverables, set expectations, and identify next steps	Test Manager
Sprint 0	Functional requirement scrubbing. Attend meetings to create functional specifications. Offer suggestions if anything is not testable or poorly designed	Test Lead
Sprint 0	Create initial draft of the test plan The functionality of the product would be broken down at high level for further exploration as we progress. This plan would be reviewed with the stakeholders The test plan is an evolving document hence any changes or new requirements will be accommodated in the upcoming sprints The test activities for any given sprint should be signed off by the stakeholders after formal review	Test Lead/Test Manager
Sprint 1-N	For each sprint detailed test cases are prepared and reviewed. The test cases are stored in the defect tracking tool. Each test case includes the steps necessary to perform the test, the expected results, and any data needed to perform the test	Tester, guided by the Test Lead
Sprint 1-N	Project and test plan traceability. Review the test plan to ensure all points of the functional specification are accounted for. Likewise, ensure that the test cases have traceability with the test plan and functional spec. Finally, that the project plan has traceability with the test plan	Test Lead

Sprint 1-N	Triage meetings will be held for each sprint or on daily basis to clarify bugs and accept fixes. This meeting should be attended by someone from the testing team, development team, and the overall project manager	Test Lead
Weekly	Weekly updates on the project and the changes in the project plan should be shared with all stakeholders. The percentage of work planned and completed	Test Lead
Weekly	Weekly status report. The project manager will specify who is to receive the weekly status report. This report will identify the percentage of completed tasks that should be due by that week, the tasks to be worked on in the next week, metrics indicating the testing statistics (once testing begins), budgeting information, and any issues or risks that need to be addressed	Test Lead
Interfaces and end-to-end testing	The inputs and outputs of the interfaces will be thoroughly tested and documented. Also the end-to-end testing of the entire application will be carried out. The various end-to-end flows which could be traversed by the end user would be tested	Test Lead
End Game	Post mortem analysis. This is done to analyze how well our testing process worked	Test Lead, Development Team, User Team

4.2 Defect Tracker Setup

The test lead will create a project in the defect tracker so that bugs can be tracked. The defects will have the following status: Open, Assigned, Fixed, Closed, and On-Hold. Once the defect is identified by the tester it will be logged into the defect tracker in "Open" status. When the defect will be assigned to a developer it will be changed to "Assigned" status. The developer after fixing the defect will change the status to "Fixed". The tester will test the "Fixed" defect and if the defect has been rectified he will change the status to "Closed".

In case of any doubts or discrepancies in any feature which are on discussion or which are deferred for a later build then the status of the defect would be on "On-Hold".

4.3 Test Case Pass/Fail Criteria

The two basic components of a test case are the feature to be tested and the expected output when the test case is executed in the system.

Fail Criteria:

If the output of the test case execution does not match the expectation as defined in the expected output then the test case is marked as failed. The actual output is documented and in case of a failure it is called as a defect, it is tracked separately till closure through a defect tracker or similar process.

The defects which are not clear or ambiguous are discussed in the defect triage meeting. It may not be a defect, just a misinterpretation of the expected output or lack of clear documentation.

If there are dependencies between test cases , the dependent test cases wil be tested only if the current test case is passed.

If the current test case itself fails then the dependency cases will not be tested and it may even be marked as failed to enable us to test the dependency cases at later point of time.

Pass Criteria:

All the test cases will pass with no unexpected results.

All the test cases will complete within an acceptable time limit based on the bench marks for performance required by the business.

4.4 Test Suspension Criteria

The testing activities could be suspended either fully or partially under any of the conditions mentioned below.

- There are missing files in the new build,
- There are problems in installing the latest build or a package,
- There are configuration issues with the new build like some of the earlier corrected defects are reappearing,
- An important feature which is critical to test other parts of the system is defective,
- The build does not have the expected changes for the sprint,
- An excessive amount of bugs are found during any sprints,
- A major problem or system crash which prevents any further testing,
- Earlier problems or defects not fixed as required by development team, and
- A newer version of the software is about to be released hence, there would be no point in continuing with the testing.

4.5 Test Resumption Requirements

The following are some of the requirements to resume testing after it had been suspended

- The earlier problems which were responsible for stopping the testing have been rectified.
- The previous versions of the code should have been completely cleaned up.
- The new build must be reinstalled without any issues.
- A complete list of the new modules, changes to existing modules, and fixes with description are provided to the testing team.

4.6 UAT Release Criteria

The UAT is the final stage of testing which is done by the business or the actual end users of the system. This is an important phase of testing which could decide whether the application can move into the production or not. Even if all the features are technically available but the end users are not comfortable with the system then it could raise major problems. It is advisable to keep the UAT team also in the loop for all major communications and testing results of previous builds so that they are not surprised by anything and they would have an opportunity to clarify any issue at an earlier stage itself.

- There are no high severity defects.
- The integration and end-to-end testing have successfully passed.
- The final regression testing has to be completed with no major defects.

5 CRITICAL DATES

Task	Begin	End
Test Data Generator	February 01, 2013	April 30, 2013
Test Planning	February 15, 2013	March, 31 2013

Resource Set up	March 01, 2013	March 08, 2013
Sprint 0	March 01, 2013	March 08, 2013
Sprint 1	March 12, 2013	March 16, 2013
Sprint 2	March 19, 2013	March 23, 2013
Sprint 3	March 26, 2013	March 30, 2013
Sprint 4	April 02, 2013	April 06, 2013
Interfaces / End-to-End Testing	April 09, 2013	April 13, 2013
End Game Testing	April 16, 2013	April 30, 2013

Model Questions
PART A (Objective type)

1. White box testing at a functional level is more, such as unit testing.

A. True B. False

Answer: A

2. This testing is done to verify if any changes to an existing application has impacted some of the basic functionalities which were working fine earlier.

A. Smoke testing B. Exploratory testing

C. Performance testing D. Unit testing

Answer: A

3. Guerrilla testing is a form of

A. Smoke testing B. Exploratory testing

C. Performance testing D. Unit testing

Answer: B

4. Testing the application on multiple hardware, OS, and browsers is called as

A. Portability testing B. Software testing

C. Browser testing D. Operating system testing

Answer: A

PART B (Answer in one or two lines)

1. What are the four key components of a test plan?
2. What are the six testing techniques for a test plan?
3. What are the two methods of identifying risks?
4. Define testability and how it impacts the test plan?

5. What is the role of an alpha tester?
6. Explain how we factor interfaces in test plan
7. Explain how we factor usability in test plan
8. List at least four typical risk areas in an application.
9. What is regression testing? How can it be speeded up?
10. Explain how we factor portability in test plan
11. Give an example of "constraints based" testing.
12. What are the three test coverage techniques? How do they differ?
13. What are the three test methods you are aware of?
14. What should be the objective when writing a test case?
15. What is a test case?
16. What are the different types of test cases?
17. What is acceptance testing?
18. Write notes on test automation
19. How is a test case different from a use case?

PART C (Descriptive type)

1. Describe different testing techniques in detail.
2. What are the contents of a typical test plan? List and explain the information to be provided in the contents.
3. Discuss risk factored approach of testing in detail along with various risk factors.
4. What are all the contents of a test case document?
5. Write essay on system test case document and system testing in detail.
6. Write essay on unit test cases and unit testing in detail.

Section 8:
Software Testing

21

Test Automation

CHAPTER COVERAGE

1. *Introduction*
2. *Expectations from Test Automation*
3. *Limitations of Automation*
4. *Automation Strategy*
5. *Automation Frameworks*
6. *Automation Metrics*

21.1 INTRODUCTION

Test Automation is one of the sought after areas in software testing. In the current world, where there is a great necessity to do things faster, it is an expected and also a good practice for a tester to understand automation. All applications under test may not be automated from testing perspective, the automation may not be feasible in some cases, but the tester must analyze and confirm. This chapter highlights some of the key principles of test automation and a tester's approach to it. Many enthusiastic clients buy these automation tools, but later find that the tools are not effective for them or find that the automatic scripts need more maintenance than initially planned. As a result, a lot of tools are kept idle because clients may not have enough budget or the application feasibility to effectively use the tool.

The role of test automation specialist is to understand the clients' application, check the feasibility and scope of automation, based on the analysis whether automation can provide some quantifiable return on investment (ROI) and quality improvement, and then use appropriate tools to prepare the automation scripts such as QTP, Win Runner, report automation test results and maintain the scripts for each release.

21.2 EXPECTATIONS FROM TEST AUTOMATION

Generally, automation process (Figure 21.1) is expected to help in reducing the testing time and at the same time improve the quality of the application. Test Automation helps in following ways:

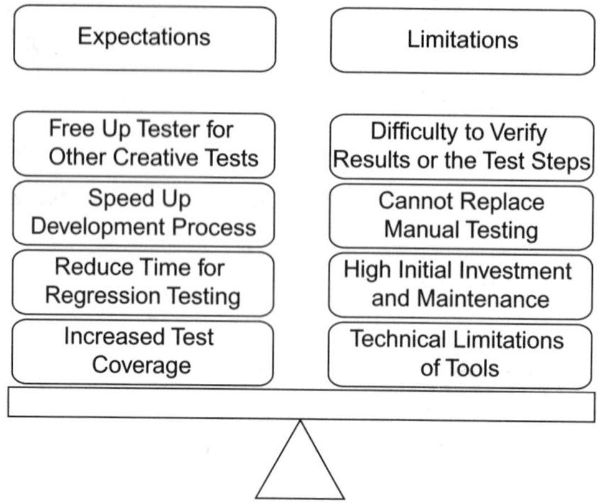

Figure 21.1 Expectations versus Limitations

1. **Increase Test Coverage**

   The manual tester would generate test data for a few critical scenarios and execute the test. Using test automation, he runs the same test with almost unlimited set of data with different combinations. He sets up about a million data sets, runs them overnight and checks the results the next morning. This type of comprehensive testing would not be possible manually. Hence, it can be said that the test coverage has increased; in other words, the data combinations have increased and have minimized the risk of a defect occurring at these data points.

2. **Reduce Time for Execution of Regression Tests**

   Regression testing is done for every release with new updates to verify if the already existing functionalities before this release are working properly. Generally, a standard set of test cases identified by the stakeholders are available, which would be executed for regression. It will be a subset of the entire test bed. As these test cases need to be executed for every release, they are automated depending upon the frequency of the releases and the effort it takes to manually execute them. If the releases are frequent and manual regression execution take a week, it makes sense to automate. This regression automation is one of the most common areas of test automation.

3. **Reduce Repetitive Manual Tests, Freeing Time for More Testing**

   Automation of test scripts involves more effort initially when the test scripts are being prepared. But once a set of scripts is working, then a lot of time is saved during the test executions. This extra time which the testing team gets could be used for more intelligent or creative tests or for testing areas of the application which could not be automated.

4. **Speedup the Development Process**

   Automation can also be considered as a tool for speeding up the development process. One way of looking at it is, if unit test cases are automated, then the developer will save time in manually executing the scripts; unit tests could be executed quickly whenever required and defects could be detected much early in the software life cycle. It is known that the cost of defects increases if they are detected at a later stage. This results in better quality software to the testing team.

Automation of smoke tests helps the development team know if something is wrong with the build immediately after the deployment, as smoke tests are a set of preliminary tests which determine whether the application is suitable for testing. If smoke test fails, the developers can then quickly check the build, correct the issue, and then redeploy. This saves a lot of time if issues such as these are found by the development team rather than the testing team.

Other way to look at automation is purely from a testing perspective, especially when methodologies such as Agile are used when the gap between the development and testing team is minimal. When the actual development team is working on the software for next release, the test automation team would be simultaneously developing the scripts for automating the previous release.

Assume there is an agile project in which builds are happening on a weekly basis. If the testing of all the builds including the previous week's build is automated, then the testing team would focus on only the manual testing of the current week's build.

21.3 LIMITATIONS OF AUTOMATION

Automation cannot Replace Manual Testing: They can aid manual testing in regression testing process. The number of bugs found by automated regression test suits on an average is about 15% based on informal surveys. But if the regression test suits are used during the development itself, then the probability of finding bugs is higher.

Difficult to know the Coding: It is difficult to know or verify what has been coded and what the automation tests are doing. It is not sure if the automation code has been developed according to the requirements. As errors are made in the development projects, the assumptions of the automation scripter may not be correct.

Difficult to Verify the Results: The status provided by the automation test reports after test execution may not be correct. The test results could have been set to "Pass" unless some inevitable failure incidents such as system crash happen. There may be bugs in the automation scripts which may fail to report a failure.

Lack of Human Insight: The automation scripts will "Pass" a test case as long as the expected results match the specifications in the script. There could be obvious failures, which could be easily captured by human intelligence, such as a disabled button or misspelled texts that have been missed by the automated script.

Technical Limitations: A few tool limitations which could impact are as follows:

- Some tools may not be able to identify all the GUI objects; hence, automation would not be possible when those objects are involved.
- There could be multiple steps for complex scenarios which are unrelated to each other and an element of intelligence would be required for proceeding with the next step. In such cases, it would be difficult to automate.
- GUI testing such as look and feel, accessibility, and color will not be possible.

Script Maintenance: Building an automation test suite is just enough for the upcoming releases. There will be some changes in each release, which would require changes to the existing automation scripts. A simple change in the user interface can cause a major portion of the automation scripts to fail. Maintenance is another area which needs to be considered from the cost and effort perspective.

High Initial Investment: The customers think sometimes that if an automation tool is given to the tester, he can just go ahead and automate the testing with the record and play back facility. On practical application, we can find that the record and play back options have a lot of issues such as even a small change in the field position will cause the script to fail.

Test automation is definitely a development project by itself. The management must be fully aware of this. Specialists with technical skills are required for deciding the test automation approach, framework design, and script creation.

There are two schools of thought when it comes to expectation from automation: One school of thought is purely based on the ROI where the client has invested some money and he would like to know when he would start getting returns out of it. This depends on the frequency of the releases and the amount of usage of the automation scripts.

The formula for manual or test automation is

Manual/Automation Effort = Test Preparation Time + n * (Test Execution Time)
Where n is the number of executions.

The other school of thought (Hoffman 1999) does not approve the ROI method because it is considered as flawed. Manual and automation tests are not comparable, as they do not provide the same kind of information. It does not make sense to compare the automated execution of test cases 100 times with manual execution 100 times, as who would execute the same tests manually for 100 times? Yes, we do save time by automation, but only if we have to run all the scripts manually.

21.4 AUTOMATION STRATEGY

Figure 21.2 represents the automation strategy that is generally being followed in any software projects.

1. **Feasibility**

   Automation is an expensive activity; proper analysis is required to determine if automation would be beneficial to the client. If we find that automation is not beneficial, then we should recommend the client accordingly so that there is no unnecessary wastage of resources and failed expectations.

   Feasibility analysis phases can be divided into five parts:

   i. **Business Need Analysis**

   The first step is to understand if there is a justifiable need for automation of regression test suits and if there are any parts of the application which could be tested better if automated.

   Let us consider the regression testing; in order to successfully automate, following points need to be considered:

   1. A stable application for at least the business scenarios identified for automation. These business scenarios should not be changed in the next release or should not change frequently. In case this requirement is constantly changing, then it is a high risk and the automation team needs to be communicated appropriately so that they will plan accordingly.
   2. Prioritize the scenarios based on the criticality. Scenarios with higher priority will be taken up for automation first; the other scenarios will be taken up afterwards in sequential order.

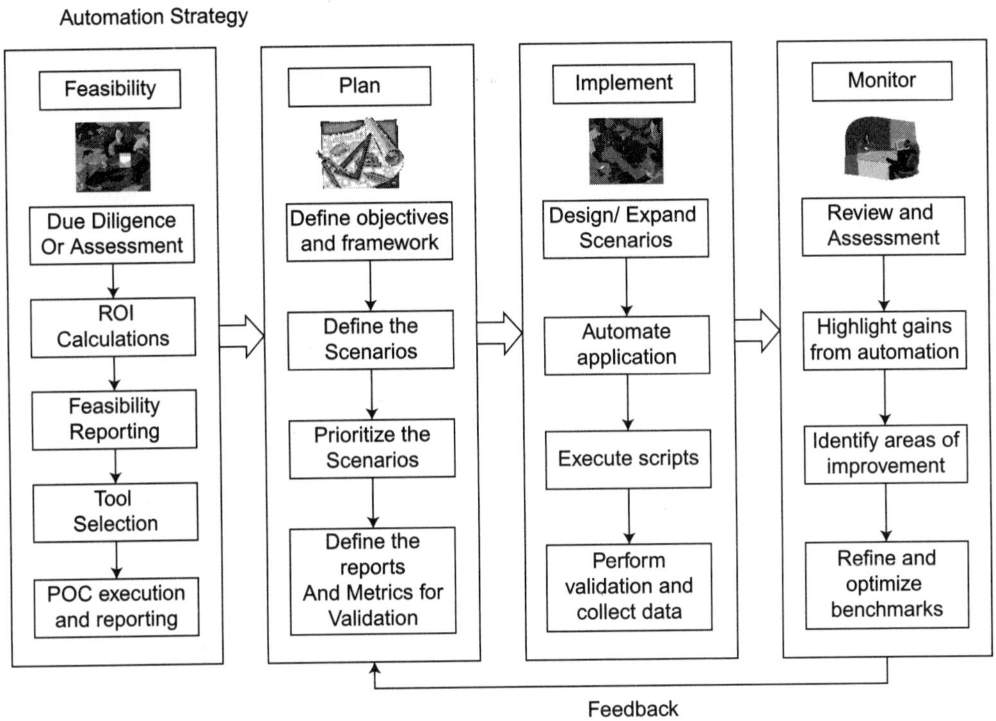

Figure 21.2 Automation Strategy

3. Availability of complete manual test cases for the business scenarios along with the data sets and the status of last execution. The test cases will be reviewed for completeness and automation; if there are any gaps, then they should be addressed. Either if there are unaddressed gaps or if the scenario cannot be automated, then the scenario should not be considered for automation.

   The above steps detail the identification of scenarios for regression automation. Other areas which could be considered for automation are as follows (excluding performance testing-related areas, as it is a separate area):

   a. **Configuration Testing:** Present-day applications need to run on multiple platforms. The same set of test cases which were executed successfully on one platform could fail in another platform, unless it has been addressed during the development. It would be laborious to execute the same set of test cases in multiple platforms, hence automation could be considered.

   b. **Race Conditions:** These happen when multiple threads of an application start contending for the same resource; the resource could be memory, printer, or database, etc. These are hard to simulate manually because there should be simultaneous requests from multiple users. By using automation, we can easily simulate these conditions so that we get an opportunity to address it before it is discovered in production when hundreds of users are using the application.

c. **Combinatorial Testing:** This involves creating multiple complex test scenarios and large number of data sets in millions which test the interactions of several interfaces and application features. These kinds of tests would be manually impossible to create; automation would be the only option.

ii. **ROI Calculations**

One of the ways for calculating the ROI is described in Figure 21.3. This method could be used for giving an approximate projection to the client as to when the automation efforts will earn the amount spent, which is called as the "Break-Even point".

Manual Testing			Automated Scripts testing		
Average test case preparation time	Mp	10 hrs	Average test case preparation time	Mp	10hrs
			Average coding script	Ap	6 hrs
			Acerage automated prep/script	Mp + Ap	16 hrs
Estimated number of test cases	n	25	Estimated number of test cases	n	25
Total maual preparation time	n(MP)	250 hrs	Total automated preparation time	n(Mp + Ap)	400 hrs
Average execution time/case	Me	3.2hrs	Average execution time/script	Ae	.3 hrs
Total manual execution time	n(Me)	80hrs	Total automated execution time	n(Ae)	7.5 hrs

Break-Even Point →

Break Even Analysis: [Automated Prep + Execution]/[Manual prep + Execution]

For R Test Executions: [n(Mp + Ap) + Rn(Ae)] / [n(Mp) + Rn(Me)]

One Test Execution	:[400 + 1(7.5)] / [250 + 1(80)] = 407.5 / 330	123%
Two Test Executions	:[400 + 2(7.5)] / [250 + 2(80)] = 415 / 410	101%
Three Test Executions	:[400 + 3(7.5)] / [250 + 3(80)] = 422.5 / 490	86%
Five Test Executions	:[400 + 5(7.5)] / [250 + 5(80)] = 437.5 / 650	67%
Ten Test Executions	:[400 + 10(7.5)] / [250 + 10(80)] = 475 / 1050	45%

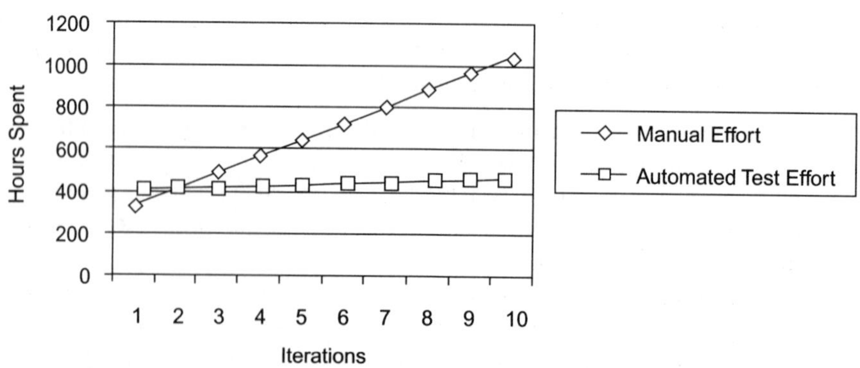

Figure 21.3 Break Even Chart

Sample ROI Calculation

iii. **Feasibility Reporting**

A report with details of the functionalities to be automated is provided along with pros and cons. Along with the regression functionalities, other areas of automation such as race conditions, portability, combinatorial testing will also be considered. The ROI calculations will be shared as shown above with the client. This would help the client to understand the automation effort and scope so that he can decide to go ahead with it or not.

iv. **Tool Selection**

Multiple tools are available in the market for automation. There are open source tools such as Selenium, Watir, and FIT. Other tools off the shelf such as QTP, RFT, and Test Partner are also available. Detailed information about the functionality of the tools is available in the web. So, based on the specific requirements and tool capabilities, an appropriate tool can be selected. Today, a large portion of the market is with QTP, but other open source tools such as Watir or Selenium are also being used. Key features that a tool must have are (we could have a checklist of these for evaluation):

- Coding language support such as Java, C++, C
- Easy implementation of standard automation frameworks
- External file support, error handlers, and checkpoints
- Bulk execution of multiple scripts at a time
- Facility to store and retrieve test results
- Auto execution without manual intervention
- Must fit into the clients hardware environment
- Cost should be acceptable

v. **Proof of Concept**

A proof of concept is done for a sample scenario. The scenario must be fairly complex to get a good understanding of the test environment, the tool, and the requirements. Once the scenario is identified, it is then taken up for automation with the recommended tool. This helps understand if the selected tool is able to identify the GUI objects or not, and the approximate cost of automation could also be determined. The other benefit is that it helps evaluate the technical competencies of the automation resources and ascertain whether they will be able to handle the complete automation project.

If one tool does not meet the requirements, then other viable options could be considered. Most of the application objects and common features in the product should be tested as part of the scenario. The evaluation version of the tools is sufficient for a POC, which would be free usually.

This is the most important phase in terms of understanding what automation can do and how the client will be benefitted out of it. The automation tester may be new or an existing member of the project team, but he needs to get clarity on some of the key questions listed below. If the right questions are not asked and not understood in this phase, then it will be very difficult to come back at a later stage for corrections, as it would be too expensive then or the project would be over by then.

- Why do you want to automate, what can be done better or faster? What are the areas or functionalities to be automated?
- How will automation help the client in terms of time to deliver and quality?
- What is the test environment—hardware and software?
- Any preferences from client or has already bought some automation tool?
- What is the development status of the application to be automated?
- Do we have a stable version of the application for analysis?
- Any previous experiences with automation and the lessons learned?
- What would be a good end-to-end test scenario for a POC?
- What are the interfaces to the application and the possibility of calling these interfaces through the automation tool?
- How will the test data be prepared for feeding the automation scripts in POC and also later?

2. **Plan**

   This stage starts once the POC has been successfully completed and POC results are encouraging enough to start automation of other functionalities. In other words, the feasibility analysis results show that there could be significant gain to the client through automation. The expectations of the client and the possible outcomes of automation are defined as the basic objectives. Then, all other functionalities to be automated are specified and prioritized. The automation framework is defined and additional technical skills for scripting and resources are identified. The test data requirements for the automation script should be defined and the process for generation of test data is initiated.

3. **Implement**

   This phase requires more technical expertise and project management skills unlike the previous phase, where it was more of analytical, such as defining the requirements and setting the expectations. This phase requires more technical expertise. The functionalities identified for automation are scripted, tested and executed just like a new application development project. The automations results are reported to the stakeholders and the metrics required for the validation are also captured.

4. **Monitor**

   This is the final phase where the impact of automation is evaluated based on the reports and metrics that could be captured on implementation. Based on these outputs, the plan should be updated for optimum performance, or necessary corrective action should be taken in areas of improvement.

21.5 AUTOMATION FRAMEWORKS

What is an automation framework?

Whenever automation implementation is discussed, the first thing to consider is the kind of automation framework that will be used. Let us try to understand what we mean by framework and the basic building blocks of an automation framework.

In terms of software applications, an automation framework could be defined as a reusable design structure with formally defined components to support code libraries, drivers, and environment configurations, test data, and test scripts.

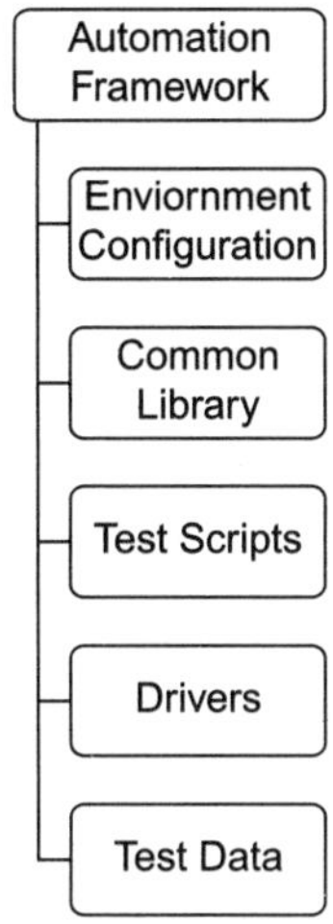

Figure 21.4 Basic Automation Framework Components

In simple terms, the framework is like a folder where we have a hierarchy of structure that encapsulates multiple shared components. Figure 21.4 shows a basic automation framework with the components in a hierarchical manner. There could be many more components added to this list as we move towards more evolved frameworks.

Basic Automation Framework Components

Let us discus the basic automation framework components in detail:

Environment Configuration: All the files related to the environment are stored as variables, special parameters, and other settings. If the test environment changes, we need to add only a file with the respective details to this folder and the existing test scripts could be run in the new environment.

Common Library: This consists of routines and functions which could be accessed by any automation script prepared by the tester. For example, if the test script encounters a "Radio Button" or "List of Values" on the screen, then corresponding functions in the library could be called and the necessary actions are coded.

Test Scripts: The actual automation scripts written by the testers are stored in this folder. This is extremely useful while verifying the scripts written for a given project or for handing over the scripts to a maintenance team after completion.

Drivers: They are the heart of the automation framework, just like an operating system is the heart of a computer. The drivers integrate all the individual components or resources of the framework present in multiple locations and present them as unified whole when the automation scripts are executed.

Test Data: The automation scripts need to be backed up by relevant test data during execution. The data which the user would enter in a particular scenario should be passed to the automation scripts during execution. Creation and maintenance of test data are a major challenge in most of the applications; in fact, this test data creation alone is treated as a separate project in some applications and separate teams are used for just creating the test data.

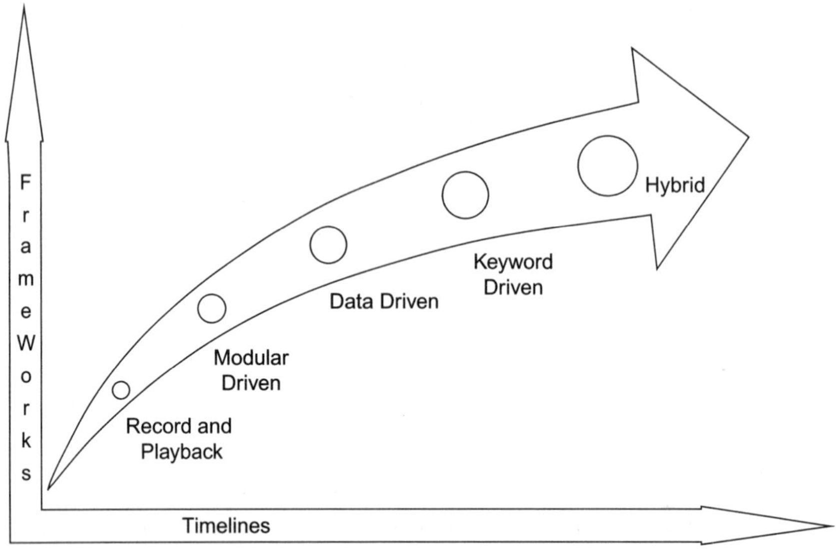

Figure 21.5 Evolution of Automation Frameworks

Evolution of Automation Frameworks

Evolution of automation framework can be explained in five different phases (Figure 21.5).

1. **Record and Playback**

   During the initial years of automation, the "Record and Playback" mechanism was used extensively. Whatever the tester does on the screen while executing a test case was recorded and then played back whenever testing of the same scenario was required. Although it sounds good, the problem with this approach is that all the data are hard coded and the automated tests were always executed with the same data. Even a small change such as changing the size of a button or adding a field in one of the screens affects all the test cases which traverse that screen.

   The maintenance effort of these scripts is so high that for every release, the automation testers struggle to get the existing scripts and the new scripts working. This makes a lot of automation suites useless because they are NOT available when required. On the positive side, in order to address the above problems with record and play back, the automation framework starts evolving.

2. **Modular-Driven**

   Modules are reusable, small independent units of code. Let us consider a simple example such as login, which is common to most applications. The login module will be called whenever the user wants to login. In a modular drive framework, the user credentials of a particular user are hardcoded in the login module. So, if another user wants to login, then the login module had to be copied and the user credentials are modified for the new user. Although there was an element of reusability, it was limited and the maintenance cost of the scripts was also very high.

3. **Data-Driven**

   Data-driven frameworks have evolved to clearly separate the test scripts and the data. This allowed the usage of multiple combinations of input data on a common test script. Now, if we consider the same login example as above, in this case, the login module would have the script and data separately so that the same script can be reused with multiple data sets. A data set is generally a row in a table; in this case, the data set would have two columns, namely login and password, and the number of rows depends on the number of users to be evaluated. The data could also be stored in an Excel and called during test execution through the script. This framework requires no programming skills from a tester perspective, as the automation experts would be creating all the data-driven test procedures; and the job of the tester is to only create the appropriate test data.

Disadvantages with this process are it requires highly skilled automation programmers, and multiple data files need to be maintained for each test case.

4. **Keyword Driven**

Keyword-driven framework can be considered as an extension of the data-driven approach because it requires the creation of keywords in addition to the data tables as in data-driven approach. These keywords and data tables are not dependent on the automation tool. There is a controller code behind each and every keyword, which determines the steps to be executed when a particular keyword is called. The test scripts are written through step tables in which the keyword name, the screen component, the action to be performed and the test data are mentioned. Let us look at our "Login" example again through this framework.

Keywords	Functionality
InitApp	Initialize or start the application
ChkLogin	Check if login is successful
EditTBox	Enter Text into the EditTbox
Button	Click on a button

Keyword and Functionality Map

In order to create a test script, the users define the keywords in the step table in the logical order of execution. For example, for the login functionality, the step table would be as below:

Steps	Keyword	Screen Component*	Action	Test Data
Step1	InitApp			
Step2	EditTbox	User Name	Enter Data	User1
Step3	EditTbox	Password	Enter Data	Pass123
Step4	Button	Login	Click	SingleLeftClick
Step5	ChkLogin			

Step Table for Login

*Note: The screen components are the ones that you see on the application screen for login; here it is the username, password and the Login button.

Advantages

- The maintenance cost decreases as test cases are written in the form of a step table.
- Minimum technical skills are required for writing the automation scripts, and some training manual testers will be able to prepare the automation scripts.

Disadvantages

- Logical conditions and loops are not supported. New test cases on different Excel are required to handle logical flow changes and data changes. This requires use of a large number of excels, which could lead to maintenance issues.
- High cost for building the initial framework and needs skilled resources.
- The users need to be trained, hence training cost is involved.
- Dynamic objects may not be supported or support is limited.

5. **Hybrid Framework**

   The hybrid frame work is a combination of the data-driven and the keyword frameworks. The main difference from a normal keyword-driven framework is that the data files are stored separately for each step table and they are linked with the step table during run time. Owing to this, the duplication of test cases for variations in test data can be avoided.

   Other advantages and disadvantages are same as a keyword-driven framework.

21.6 AUTOMATION METRICS

A metric is a standard of measurement. It is a measure which gives us insight into the past or present performance; it also predicts future performance based on the trend.

We had briefly studied about capturing the requirements for a metric, and implementing them so that we can understand the progress, effectiveness, and the quality of the automation project.

We will look at some key metrics for coverage, progress, and quality.

Percentage Automatable (PA): This provides the percentage of the application that has been automated.

$$PA = (ATC/TC)*100$$

Where PA is percentage automatable; ATC is the total number of test cases automatable and TC is the total number of all test cases

Automation Test Coverage (ATC): This metric gives a measure of extent of the total application testing that has been automated.

$$ATC = (AC/C)*100$$

Where AC is automation coverage in terms of KLOC/FP and C is the total coverage in terms of KLOC/FP.

Automation Progress (AP): The ideal number for AP is 100%. This provides the percentage of test cases automated out of possible test cases.

$$AP = (AA/ATC)*100$$

Where AA is the total number of test cases automated and ATC is the total number of test cases selected for automation.

Defect Leakage Rate (DLR): This is defined as the total number of defects leak into production versus the number of defects found during regression testing.

$$DLR = NDD/ (NDR + NDD)$$

Where *NDD* is the number of defects found after delivery and *NDR* is the number of defects found in regression.

Defect Removal Efficiency (DRE): This is defined as the number of defects found by test automation during regression versus the total defects found in the application.

$$DRE = NDR/\ (NDR + NDD)$$

Where *NDD* is the number of defects found after delivery and *NDR* is total number of defects found in regression.

These metrics mentioned above are specific to automation. There are other common metrics for testing as whole, which will be discussed in the next chapter.

When you can measure what you are speaking about, and can express it in numbers, you know something about it; but when you cannot measure it, when you cannot express it in numbers, your knowledge is of a meagre and unsatisfactory kind.

—Lord Kelvin, a physicist

Summary

- This chapter is an introduction to the basics of automation testing. The expectations from test automation and the limitations of test automation are discussed in detail.
- The four phases of the test automation strategy are discussed with detailed analysis of the feasibility phase, where the "go or no go" decision for an automation project would be taken.
- The ROI calculations were discussed and a simple example of when a break-even would happen is illustrated.
- Phases of the automation strategy are Plan, Implement, and Monitor, and we have discussed kind of skills required at each phase.
- We have discussed the meaning of a framework and the components associated; the importance of having a framework and how different frameworks such as modular, data-driven, keyword-driven and hybrid evolved with their advantages and disadvantages.
- Finally, we have discussed some of the key metrics that could be captured for an automation project in terms of coverage, progress, and quality.

Model Questions
PART A (Objective type)

1. Which of the following is true with respect to Automation?

   A. All the applications under test may not be automated

   B. All the applications may be automated

   C. All the applications must be automated

   D. All the applications cannot be automated

Answer: A

2. Which of the following is incorrect regarding expectations of automation?
   A. Increase test coverage
   B. Reduce repetitive automation tests, freeing time for more testing
   C. Speed up the development process
   D. Reduce time for execution of regression tests

Answer: B

3. Which of the following is a true limitation of Automation?
   A. Automation can replace manual testing
   B. Lack of human insight
   C. Easy to know what has been coded
   D. Easy to verify the results

Answer: B

4. The phases of Automation strategy are Feasibility, Plan, Implement and _______?
   A. Test B. Check C. Verify D. Monitor

Answer: D

5. Which types of testing can be automated in addition to Regression testing?
   A. Configuration testing, trace conditions, combinatorial testing
   B. Configuration testing, race conditions, combinatorial testing
   C. Configuration testing, race conditions, combinatorial testing
   D. Confederation testing, race conditions, combinatorial testing

Answer: C

6. Which of the following is not a component of test automation framework?
   A. Test Results B. Test Data C. Test Scripts D. Drivers

Answer: A

7. Hybrid framework is a combination of which of the following frameworks?
   A. Keyword-driven, Record and Playback
   B. Data-driven, Keyword-driven
   C. Data-driven, Modular
   D. Modular, Record and Playback

Answer: B

8. Which of the following is not an automation metrics?
   A. Automation Test Coverage
   B. Defect Leakage Rate
   C. Defect Leakage Efficiency
   D. Defect Removal Efficiency

Answer: C

PART B (Answer in one or two lines)

1. List any two expectations from automation testing.
2. List any two limitations of automation testing.
3. Name four areas where automation testing could be applied.
4. What is the formula for ROI analysis?
5. What is break-even point? Why is it important?
6. What are the Automation Test Strategy Phases?
7. During which phase of automation do you report metrics?
8. Which phase of test automation requires maximum technical skills?
9. Why do we need an automation framework?
10. What are the components of an automation framework?
11. Describe one coverage and one quality metric.

PART C (Descriptive type)

1. One of your company's clients is interested in test automation and they have requested you for a feasibility analysis and an automation strategy. The client tried automation earlier and also brought a tool from Compuware, but was not successful; they also say that they have automation scripts, they are outdated. How would you prepare a preliminary report for the client?
2. Explain the keyword-driven framework with a login example. What are the advantages and disadvantages of keyword-driven framework? How is a Hybrid framework different from the keyword-driven framework?

Section 9:
Software Maintenance

22

Software Maintenance

CHAPTER COVERAGE

1. *Introduction*
2. *Maintenance Activities*
3. *Maintenance Process*
4. *Maintenance Cost*
5. *Software Evolution*
6. *Reverse Engineering*
7. *Re-engineering*
8. *Re-structuring*
9. *Maintenance Strategies*
10. *Maintenance Mind Set*
11. *Service Perspective to Software Maintenance*
12. *Gap Model - Service*
13. *Software Maintenance Tools*
14. *Issues in Software Maintenance*
15. *Difference between Software Maintenance and Support*
16. *Common Metrics in Software Maintenance and Support*

22.1 INTRODUCTION

Software maintenance is one of the core aspects of software engineering. System gets deployed into the production environment after the system development. The process of modifying the production system after the delivery to correct the faults, for improving performance, and for adapting to the changing environment is called as software maintenance.

Software evolution and maintenance was first addressed by Lehman in 1969. Key findings of his research (Lehman 97) called as Lehman law states that maintenance decisions depend on what happens to systems (and software) over time. According to him, the software systems continuously evolve over a period of time with more complexity.

The difference between the development and maintenance which will help us to understand the maintenance-related activities in detail is listed in Table 22.1.

22.1.1 Development vs. Maintenance

Table 22.1 Difference between Development and Maintenance

Development	Maintenance
Application is not into the production environment	Application is already into the production environment
End user is not using the system	End user started using the system
It is not driven by the end users. It is driven by the project team	It is completely driven by the end users

(continued)

Table 22.1 (Continued)

Opportunity for innovation is more	Opportunity for innovation is less
Time frame to fix bugs are well framed	Time frames to fix bugs are not well framed and it varies depending on the nature of the bugs
Team has freedom to decide what is necessary for the situation	Team may not have such freedom and constraint by the production system and end-user preference
Defects have no immediate effect on the production system	Defects may disrupt production system if not addressed properly
Developing a new system from the scratch is something unique	Maintenance activities are mostly repetitive in nature

22.2 MAINTENANCE ACTIVITIES

There are four types of maintenance activities namely

1. Adaptive maintenance
2. Corrective maintenance
3. Perfective maintenance
4. Preventive maintenance

All these four activities in are explained in detail in the following sections.

22.2.1 Adaptive Maintenance

Adjusting the system adaptively based on the environment changes is called as adaptive maintenance. The system has no faults (errors) on its own, but needs adapting (changing) as per the environment changes. For example, healthcare-related systems need to be updated during protocol changes by Health Insurance Portability and Accountability Act (HIPAA). Adjusting the system parameters as per the new hardware changes/OS changes is also an example of adaptive maintenance. Mostly in adaptive maintenance, there will not be a change in functionality. Adaptive maintenance cost can be minimized by isolating system dependencies features. Figure 22.1 shows a website got upgraded once the newer version of the internet explorer browser was released. A maintenance program undertaken to make the website compatible with the new version of the software is an example of adaptive maintenance.

22.2.2 Corrective Maintenance

It is the process of identifying, isolating, and repairing the faults (errors) that are discovered in the system so that the system can be restored and operational. Corrective maintenance includes repair or replacement of equipment. This activity may be the result of a regular inspection, which identifies the failure (errors) in time and leads to corrective maintenance. Corrective maintenance happens after the fault.

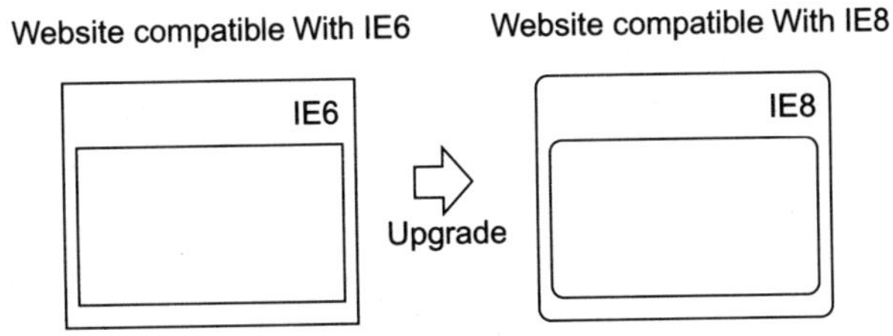

Figure 22.1 Example of Adaptive Maintenance

Types of corrective maintenance

1. "Immediate corrective maintenance" (actual work starts immediately after failure and is critical in nature) and
2. "Deferred corrective maintenance" (in which work is delayed in conformance to stakeholders).

Faults (errors) can be user based, coding (software) based, or hardware based. The following life cycle is being followed for corrective maintenance.

1. Notify help desk,
2. Diagnose the error,
3. Fix the error,
4. Test the error,
5. Plan the release (installation),
6. Release, and
7. Post-release activities.

22.2.3 Perfective Maintenance

It is the system upgrade kind of work which makes the system work more efficiently. About 50% of the maintenance is perfective maintenance. Upgrading hardware, software, and band widths are examples of perfective maintenance. Perfective maintenance happens due to adapting changes and due to user requirements.
Examples:

1. Providing short cut commands for the system,
2. Performance tuning—to increase the speed of the server,
3. Applications consolidations—for easy management, and
4. Automatic help to users to choose data.

The older version of the key boards did not have the multimedia keys (Figure 22.2). But with the popularization of multimedia applications, it became necessary to provide the users some short-cut keys for accessing the multimedia functionalities directly from the keyboard. This is an example of the predictive maintenance from the keyboard manufacturing companies.

Adaptive and perfective maintenance alone contributes 75% of the maintenance work as per a survey.

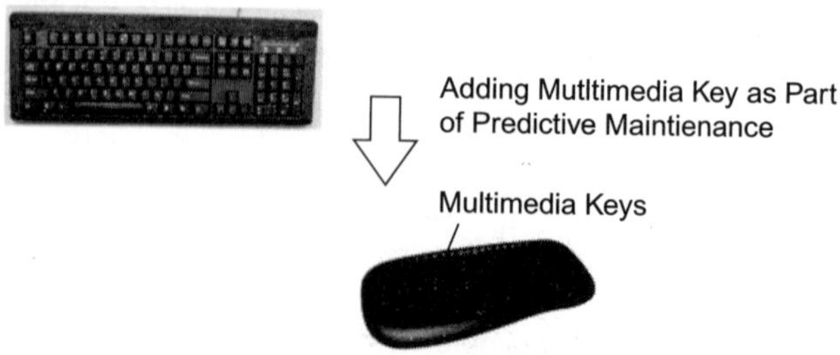

Figure 22.2 Example of Perfective Maintenance

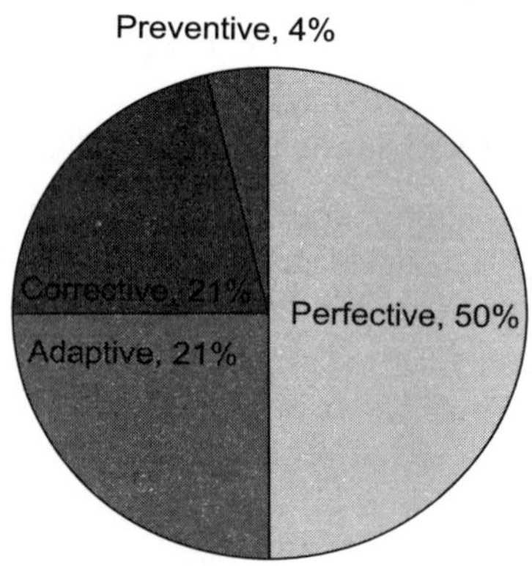

Figure 22.3 Maintenance-type Ratios Chart

22.2.4 Preventive Maintenance

Activities that are aimed at increasing the maintainability are called as preventive maintenance. Preventive maintenance activities avoid system outages and errors. In automobile the car's engine oil gets changed every 5000 km to prevent errors and is an example of preventive maintenance. Documenting the existing system is the best example for preventive maintenance. Identifying system component that may fail depending on the trend is an example of preventive maintenance. Continuously monitoring the size of the database as the system grows to prevent sizing-related errors are examples of preventive maintenance.

Refer Figure 22.3 for maintenance-type ratios. It clearly indicates perfective maintenance is more than any type and it contributes 50%. Only 4% of maintenance types are preventive maintenance.

22.3 MAINTENANCE PROCESS

Maintenance process (refer Figure 22.4) depends on the software being maintained and it varies considerably across software. But still the common maintenance activities can be listed down that are executed across all the software maintenance.

Here are those activities in detail.

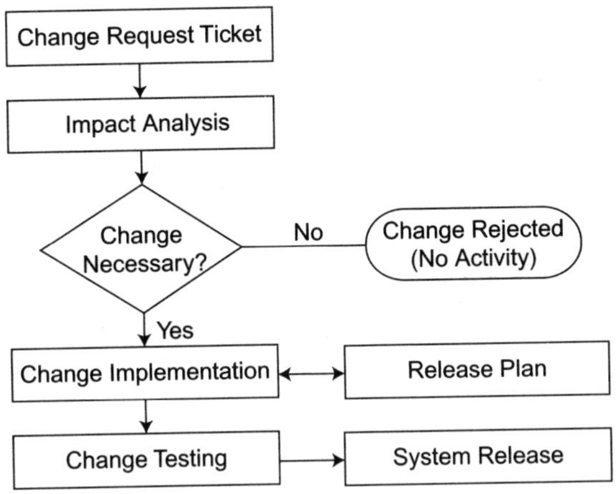

Figure 22.4 Maintenance Process

Change request are the part and parcel of all the software maintenance process. Change request are usually raised by the end users requesting for a change in the system that are being used by them. Sometime the change requests are raised by the management.

Once the change request is received it should be analyzed (impact analysis). The purpose of the analysis is to find out whether the change is necessary. Unnecessary changes need to be avoided at this stage itself. Once it is decided that the changes are going to be implemented, next the impact of that particular change request on any other part of the system needs to be found out. Change in one component may impact other components; careful analysis of those dependent components and its impact is needed.

Change implementation will happen after the impact analysis is consistent with the release plan. Change implementation strategy should be in sync with the release plan strategy. Delay in the implementation part of the change will affect the release plan.

System release will happen once the change is implemented and thoroughly tested.

In practice some change requests are implemented urgently and directly into the production environment due to business emergencies (or change in production environment) which needs to be avoided as it caters to lot of risks to the environment and the product.

22.4 MAINTENANCE COST

Maintenance cost is usually higher than the overall development cost of the software and sometime it is as high as 100 times the development cost. Old aging software can have high support cost than the latest technology software, as getting the specialized technical resources is difficult for the old technology-based software. Furthermore, the maintenance activities also tend to corrupt the software structure further increasing the software maintenance cost.

There are various factors that determine the maintenance cost of the software, such as

1. Complexity of the system: When the complexity of the system to be maintained increases the maintenance cost also increases.

2. Volume of work involved: Sometimes the complexity may be less but the quantum of work involved in the maintenance activities may be high and hence the cost of maintenance also will be high.
3. Aging of the software: As the software age increases, the structure is degraded and hence it is harder to maintain and thereby increasing the overall maintenance cost of those systems.
4. Soft skills: Maintenance cost also involves various types of skills required to maintain the software. It not only depends on the quantity of the skills required, but also on the experience level of the people required to support the system.
5. Contractual responsibility: The maintenance cost also depends on the contractual responsibility of the vendor. If there is no incentive the vendor may not be interested for quick changes in the system.

22.5 SOFTWARE EVOLUTION

Software evolution and maintenance was first addressed by Lehman in 1969. Key findings of his research (Lehman 97) called as Lehman law states that maintenance decisions depend on what happens to systems (and software) over time. According to him, the software systems continuously evolve over a period of time with more complexity.

It is impossible for anybody to create a system of any size which does not need to be changed. Any system after putting into use—new requirements will keep on emerging; the existing requirements will keep on changing or evolving. These software evolutions are mainly due to changes in the business environment and technological environment. Sometimes part of the software may have to be modified to correct the errors and bugs in the system or to improve the performance which are related to the non-functional characteristics. Software systems always evolve in response to demand for change.

22.5.1 Laws of Software Evolution

Laws of software evolution which force the maintenance to occur, for example, two laws of software evolution are 1. law of increasing complexity and 2. law of continuing change.

Law of increasing complexity: As the system evolves over a period of time the complexity of the system also increases. This will also increase the overall maintenance cost.

Law of continuing change: A system that is being used goes for continual change, until it is judged more cost effective to restructure the entire system or replace it by a completely new version.

22.6 REVERSE ENGINEERING

Reverse engineering (refer Figure 22.5) concepts is helpful for maintaining the software.

Engineering process helps to build the system based on the system requirements and the system design. Reverse engineering is analyzing the software system to identify and understand the overall system components, design, and the requirement flow of the system. It helps to understand the relationships between various components.

Reverse engineering concept helps to reconstruct the lost blue print of the system. It is the design recovery process.

In many legacy systems, the system documents, design documents, etc. are not available. There is only the software source code as the reliable information to understand the overall system. Reverse

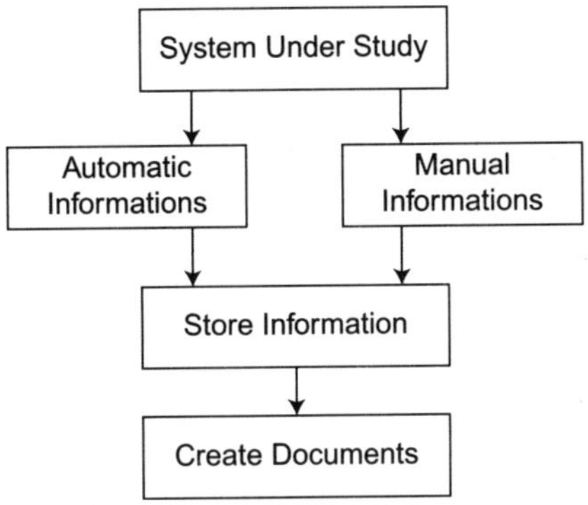

Figure 22.5 Reverse Engineering Process

engineering helps to reconstruct the requirements, design, test case, and user documentation in consistent with the source code of the system.

Design recovery after re-engineering result at higher level of abstraction and re-documentation result is at the same level of abstraction.

In the reverse engineering process all the information about the system is generated (automatic generation and manual generation) and stored in a database before producing the documents. Reverse engineering is a three-step process namely

1. Generation of information,
2. Storage of information, and
3. Creation of documents.

Reverse engineering is often the initial activity in a re-engineering project. Below sections discusses what is re-engineering in the subsequent.

22.7 RE-ENGINEERING

Re-engineering (refer Figure 22.6) involves putting efforts to make the system easier to maintain. In this process the source code is getting changed for easy maintenance and functionality of the system also gets changed during the process. Code cleaning happens over here along with the enhancement of the system.

Re-engineering may also lead to re-writing the software in entirely new programming language.

Re-engineering may lead to re-documentation of the system. Re-engineering reduces the risks of the overall maintenance of the system. The cost of re-engineering is usually lesser than the cost of developing the new software.

22.7.1 Re-engineering Process

First step (in re-engineering) is to understand the overall system. Do reverse engineering which helps to understand various components. Re-structure the system in a logical fashion. Modularize the program and data to improve the functionality to complete the re-engineering process. Refer Figure 22.7 to understand re-engineering process.

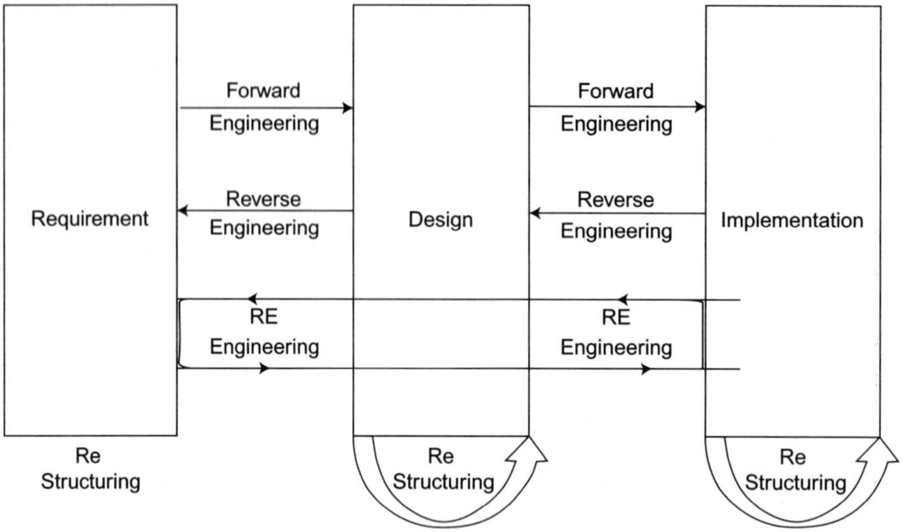

Figure 22.6 Forward, Reverse, Re-engineering, Re-structuring

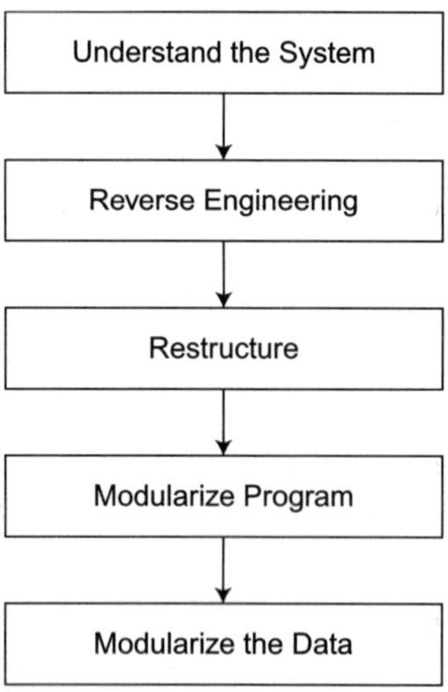

Figure 22.7 Re-engineering Process

22.7.2 When to Re-engineer?

Re-engineering should happen in the following condition.

1. When the system changes are mostly confined to part of the system then re-engineer that part,
2. When hardware or software of the system becomes obsolete, and
3. When tools to support re-structuring are available.

22.7.3 Advantages of Re-engineering

1. It reduces the risks: There may be high risks if we try developing new software; risks may be related to staffing problems, design problems, and specifications problems.
2. It reduces the cost: The cost of re-engineering is usually lesser than the cost of developing new software.

22.8 RE-STRUCTURING

Re-structuring is similar to re-engineering. Here the transformation of a system from one representation to another happens at the same level of abstraction. Functionality of the system does not change. Only code cleaning happens. Revamping of the screens of the software can happen. Migration from one version of the software to another version of the software is the best example of re-structuring.

22.9 MAINTENANCE STRATEGIES

There are two types of maintenance strategies

1. Systematic strategy and
2. As-needed strategy.

In the systematic strategy everything happens in a systematic and planned manner. The maintenance team understands the overall system under maintenance. A systematic top-down study of the system happens. There is clear cut documentation for the entire flow of the system. The team has better insight of the components and its causal relationship between them.

In the as-needed strategy of maintenance, team does not maintain any documentation of the system. Team directly touches the code and hypothesis is formulated based on the local information available about the system. A more technically equipped team is needed here than the systematic strategy.

22.10 MAINTENANCE MIND SET

Maintenance programmers directly read the code rather than studying the documentation.

Maintenance programmers spend lot of time reading the code than the time taken to fix or change the code.

Maintenance programmers always follow step-by-step approach rather than a big bang approach of fixing the problem. They do small code change and test it completely before proceeding to the next code change.

Maintenance programmers always follow stereotypical action, meaning they just concentrate whether the code works or not rather than studying the set of code copied from other source.

Maintenance programmers do not change the code unless they are 100% sure on it.

22.11 SERVICE PERSPECTIVE TO SOFTWARE MAINTENANCE

There are lot of difference (refer Table 22.2) between a product and service. Still software maintenance can be attributed to service part also. Before getting into the service perspective of software maintenance, below are the difference between the product and service.

Table 22.2 Difference between Product and Service

Product	Service
1. Product is tangible	1. Services are intangible
2. Product is perishable	2. Services are not perishable
3. Produced and consumed at later point of time	3. Produced and consumed at the same time
4. Product articulation is easy	4. Service articulation is difficult
5. Centralization and mass production is possible	5. Centralization and mass production is difficult

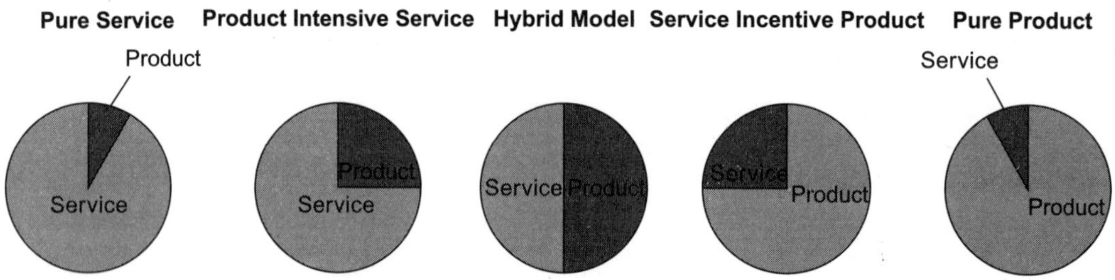

Figure 22.8 Pure Service to Pure Product

Maintenance often is seen as providing service to end users as opposed to delivering a product. Maintenance quality needs to be judged as different from the development. Service capacity, service efficiency, and service responsiveness are considered important factors in maintenance.

Information technology infrastructure library (ITIL) is being followed as default practices in software maintenance. ITIL is a set of practices for information technology service management (ITSM) that focuses on aligning IT services with business needs of the organization.

ITIL describes processes, procedures, tasks, and checklists for establishing integration with the organization's vision, strategy, value, and maintaining a minimum level of competency.

Maintenance always has some percentage of service associated with it. The percentage will vary from situation to situation (refer Figure 22.8).

A hybrid model of maintenance has exactly 50% product and 50% service.

In service intensive product, the service percentage is more than 25%.

In productive intensive service, the product percentage is more than 25%.

22.12 GAP MODEL - SERVICE

Gap model (Figure 22.9) is used to illustrate the difference between expected service and the service delivery.

Gap 1 is the difference between the expected service perceived by the service provider and the expected service by the customer. This reveals that the service provider focuses on something which is not relevant to the customer. To bridge the gap, the service provider needs to clearly document and translate the customer service expectations into a service agreement.

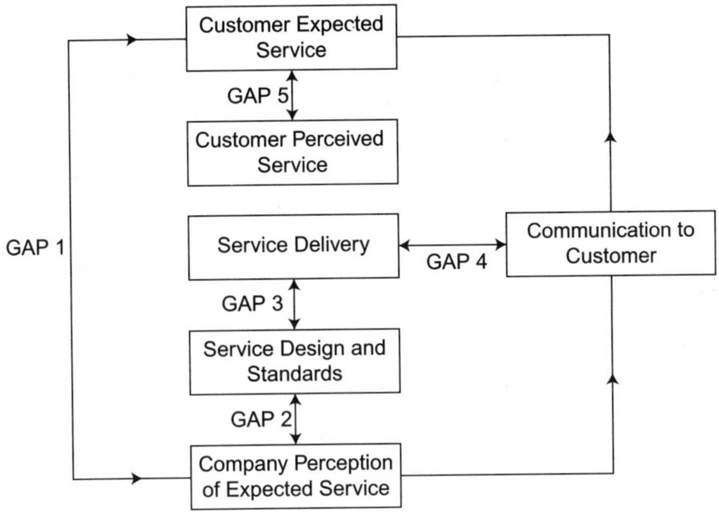

Figure 22.9 Service GAP Model

Gap 2 is the difference between the written service specification and the expected service perceived by the service provider. Customer expects immediate quick response or work around when a production server goes down, but service provider will start doing the analysis as per the service specification agreed.

Gap 3 is the difference between the written specification and the actual service delivery. This may be due to human resource efficiency, balancing demand and supply, customer not doing his role, and customers not following rules written.

Gap 4 is the difference between the actual delivery and communication about the service. Ineffective horizontal communication is the best example for Gap 4. Here the service provider will simply send an email to the customer mentioning all the solved problems and services restored, but the customer will still be facing the problem. This is mainly due to the communication gap. It can be addressed having a common bug tracking tool.

Gap 5 is the difference between the customer perceived service and the actual expectation of the customer. Most of the projects fail due to this reason.

22.13 SOFTWARE MAINTENANCE TOOLS

There are lot of software tools available in the market that can be used by the software maintenance team for different purpose.

Tools to maintain version history and document repository: Tools, such as Visual Source Safe (VSS) and Open Source Tool (CVS) are used to maintain the versions of various documents and software. This software has features, such as check in and checkout which ensures only one person is changing the code which ensures consistency.

Tools for bug tracking: Tools, such as Bug Zilla and Mantis are used to track and report errors. These tools also help to do easy root-cause analysis and aging of various bugs reported. Service level tracking and reporting is easy with these tools.

Tools to manage issues: Tools, such as Trac is used for issue tracking. It also has features, such as wiki and integration to subversion. This also helps to do easy milestone tracking.

Static behavior analysis tools: There are tools available to do static behavior analysis of various software; they can also be used to do the forward and backward engineering. This helps to understand the coding without actually executing the code. Static code analyzer tool varies with the programming language as the structure of the program changes. It also helps to understand the security vulnerable if any in the code.

Dynamic behavior analysis tools: There are tools available to understand the various flows within the system by executing the code. Dynamic code analyzer executes all the possible flow within the system and thereby helps the programmer to understand the system easily.

22.14 ISSUES IN SOFTWARE MAINTENANCE

1. Alignment with end user priorities during maintenance,
2. Staffing people with system experience,
3. Estimating the cost of maintenance,
4. Measuring the maintenance (maintain ability),
5. Testing the system,
6. Understanding the system,
7. Unstructured code, and
8. Insufficient documentation.

First three items are management issues and last five items are technical issues.

During the maintenance process, each and every end user may expect the team to solve their problems on priority basis. When the number of problems (issues) is more, alignment with the end user priorities is very difficult. End user priorities are mostly based on business priorities and not based on technical feasibilities and possibilities.

Staffing suitable people with system experience under maintenance is always a difficult task. Understanding the system which is already there in the production is difficult and retaining the experienced resources is still difficult.

Estimating the cost of maintenance is difficult not only at the customer side, but also at the performing organization side (vendor side). The basic parameters based on which the estimating the maintenance cost keep on changing. The ball park estimate says that cost of maintenance is 50% of the full life cycle cost of development. This does not consider the complexity of the system and hence may not hold good for all the system.

Defining measurable metrics for maintenance is always difficult in particular for a new system. Main objective in maintenance is to fix the defects as soon as possible and also with excellent quality for higher customer satisfaction. Usually when the defects are fixed quickly, it may lead to quality-related issues which may also lead to customer dissatisfaction and hence defining measurable metrics is difficult.

Defects need to be fixed as well as tested quickly. Testing only the modified code may not be a problem, but testing the inter dependencies of the code change is difficult due to lack of time. This is actually a big issue in maintenance.

Understanding the system fully and then start fixing the defects is difficult as most of the system have unstructured code and inefficient documentation. In most of the cases, the system is divided into modules and a set of specific people gets assigned to those modules. Coordinating changes across modules and understanding the same is difficult.

Other issues in software maintenance are quality of the original application under maintenance, quality of the documentation of the existing system, lack of time for updating the documentation, bad maintenance management and lack of model for maintenance, different programming styles of the people, and people not showing interest in the maintenance as not much of learning after a time.

22.15 DIFFERENCE BETWEEN SOFTWARE MAINTENANCE AND SUPPORT

Maintenance comes in the form of change request (which is also being raised in the form of ticket). Maintenance part is directly linked to changes in application.

As already discussed there are four types of maintenance activities namely

1. Adaptive maintenance,
2. Corrective maintenance,
3. Perfective maintenance, and
4. Preventive maintenance.

Adaptive maintenance: The system has no faults (errors) on its own but adapting (changing) as per the environment changes.

Corrective maintenance: It is the process of identifying, isolating, and repairing the faults (errors) that are discovered in the system so that the system can be restored and operational.

Perfective maintenance: It is the system upgrade kind of work which makes the system to work more efficiently.

Preventive maintenance: These kinds of activities avoid system outages and avoid errors.

Support usually follows ITIL framework (incident management, problem management, SLA management, etc.). Support part is directly linked to serving (supporting) the customer to do their jobs. There are three levels of support namely Level 1, 2, and 3.

Level 1 support will act as interface point to the customer (end users) and is called as service desk. Service desk need not have any technical capability to solve customer problems, but will understand their pain points and record it. Service desk people talk in the language of the customer. Few tickets will get closed at this level itself (if the pain area is known and the solution or the reason is known to the service desk). If the ticket is not solved at this level, it will get passed to Level 2, but still service desk will track the ticket until closure.

Level 2 support will do quick fix (minor enhancements, changes) with the application directly at production environment. If not able to solve at this level, it will get passed to Level 3.

Level 3 will focus on corrective modifications and changes and will plan for the releases.

22.16 COMMON METRICS IN SOFTWARE MAINTENANCE AND SUPPORT

1. **Client satisfaction index (CSI):** It is also called as customer satisfaction index. What the customer feels about the quality of the service in the main index. Customer satisfaction index helps to channelize the overall maintenance efforts toward the customer critical activities. It also helps to understand service rating against other service providers. Usually CSI is obtained from the customer in the form of a survey, at least once in a quarter. Various components (parameters) of CSI are 1. Product-related feedback (rating), 2. service-related feedback (rating), 3. sales-related feedback (rating), 4. quality-related feedback (rating), 5. feedback against other providers, etc. Depending on the environment these parameters can be customized. These parameters are measure in the scale of 1–5.

2. Acknowledgment SLA Percentage for closed tickets—The formula for calculating Acknowledgment SLA Percentage for closed tickets is number of tickets acknowledged with in target time / total ticket closed * 100. This is usually calculated for tickets of a particular period (1 month duration usually).

   Example 1: ABC project closed 400 tickets last month and out of this 380 tickets were acknowledged within target acknowledgment limit. Find out Acknowledgment SLA Percentage for closed tickets.

   Acknowledgment SLA Percentage = Number of tickets acknowledged with in target time / total ticket closed * 100

   Acknowledgment SLA Percentage = (380 / 400) * 100 = 95%

   Example 2: Green way project's ticket acknowledgment distribution is given below. SLA for acknowledgment of any ticket is less than or equal to 20 min. Calculate Acknowledgment SLA Percentage for closed tickets.

S. No	Acknowledgment Time	Total Tickets
1	1-5 min	15
2	6-10 min	150
3	11-20 min	180
5	21-55 min	55

   Acknowledgment SLA Percentage = Number of tickets acknowledged with in target time / total ticket closed * 100

   Acknowledgment SLA Percentage = ((15 + 150 + 180) / 400) * 100 = (345/400)* 100 = 86.25%

3. Acknowledgment SLA Percentage for open tickets—The formula for calculating Acknowledgment SLA Percentage for open tickets is number of tickets acknowledged with in target time for open tickets / total ticket open * 100 . This is usually calculated for tickets of a particular period (1 month duration usually).

   Example 1: Number of open tickets in ABC project is 134 out of which 120 tickets were acknowledged within the set acknowledgment limit. Calculate Acknowledgment SLA Percentage for open tickets.

   Acknowledgment SLA Percentage for open tickets is number of tickets acknowledged with in target time for open tickets / total ticket open * 100.

   Acknowledgment SLA Percentage = (120 / 134) * 100 = 89.55%

   Example 2: Green way project's ticket acknowledgment distribution is given below. SLA for acknowledgment of any ticket is less than or equal to 20 min. Calculate Acknowledgment SLA Percentage for open tickets.

S. No	Acknowledgment Time	Total Tickets	Closed Tickets
1	1-5 min	15	10
2	6-10 min	150	125
3	11-20 min	180	180
5	21-55 min	55	45

First calculate the number of open tickets in each stage.

S. No	Acknowledgment Time	Open Tickets
1	1–5 min	5
2	6–10 min	25
3	11–20 min	0
5	21–55 min	10

Total number of open tickets = 40

Total number of open tickets within acknowledgment limit = 30

Acknowledgment SLA Percentage for open tickets is number of tickets acknowledged with in target time for open tickets / total ticket open * 100.

Acknowledgment SLA Percentage for open defects = (30/ 40) * 100 = 75%

4. Resolution SLA Percentage for closed tickets—The formula for calculating Resolution SLA Percentage for closed tickets is number of tickets resolved within target time / total ticket closed * 100. This is usually calculated for tickets of a particular period (1 month duration usually).

Example 1: Following table represent SLA agreement for ABC project.

	Service Level Agreement				
	Categogory	Overall	Response	Resolution	Avalibility
Service Level Class	Platinum	Sev1	25 min	3 h	99. 50%
		Sev2	25 min	5 h	
		Sev3	45 min	10 h	
		Sev4	1h 45 min	80 h	
	Gold	Sev1	25 min	3 h	97. 00%
		Sev2	40 min	5 h	
		Sev3	1.2 min	10 h	
		Sev4	1 h 45 min	80 h	
	Silver	Sev1	35 min	5 h	96. 00%
		Sev2	1.2 h	6 h	
		Sev3	2.2 h	25 h	
		Sev4	3.2 h	90 h	
	Bronze	Sev1	1.2 h	5 h	95. 00%
		Sev2	2.2 h	6 h	
		Sev3	2.2 h	25 h	
		Sev4	4 h	90 h	

Following table indicates the resolution trend for a particular period for Platinum Sev1 Category of tickets. Calculate Resolution SLA Percentage for closed tickets for Platinum Sev 1 Category.

S. No	Resolution Time (in minutes) (Sev 1 Platinum	Total Tickets Closed for the period
1	1 to 30	15
2	31 to 60	120
3	61 to 180	160
4	181 to 300	55

Resolution SLA Percentage for closed tickets is number of tickets resolved within target time / total ticket closed * 100.

Resolution SLA Percentage for closed tickets = (15 + 120 + 160)/ (15 + 120 + 160 + 45) = (295/350)*100 = 84.2%

5. Ticket back log percentage: The formula for calculating ticket backlog percentage for a particular period is [(Number of tickets carry forwarded from previous periods + Number of new tickets received in the reporting period – Number of tickets closed during the reporting period)/ (Number of tickets carry forwarded from previous periods + Number of new tickets received in the reporting period)] * 100.
6. Backlog Management Index (BMI): (Number of tickets closed during the period / Number of tickets arrived during the period)*100
7. Percentage of improvement in Mean Time to Resolve (MTTR): Formula for calculating percentage of improvement in Mean Time to Resolve is ((Baseline MTTR – Current MTTR)/ Baseline MTTR) for the reporting period*100. Baseline MTTR is the average MTTR for previous periods (usually over 6 month's period).
8. Ticket productivity: Formula for calculating ticket productivity is (actual effort of closed tickets / Number of closed tickets) for the reporting period.
9. Load factor of maintenance team: Actual effort spent on maintenance activities / Overall available effort of the team.
10. Cost of Poor Quality (COPQ): Formula for calculating COPQ is given as (effort expended on rework /actual effort) for the reporting period*100.
11. Cost of Quality (COQ): Formula for calculating COQ is given as (Effort spent on appraisal cost + Effort spent on prevention cost + Effort spent on failure cost) / (Effort spent on prevention cost + Effort spent on appraisal cost + Effort spent on failure cost + Effort spent on production cost) * 100.
12. Defect density by effort: Formula for calculating defect density by effort is ((Number of pre-shipment defects + Number of post-shipment defects + Number of post-production defects) / (Overall actual effort)) for the reporting period.
13. Defect removal efficiency percentage: Formula for calculating defect removal efficiency percentage is pre-shipment defects / (Pre-shipment + Post-shipment defects + Post-production defects) * 100.

Example: Below table represents the distribution of defects. Calculate defect removal efficiency percentage.

S. No	Defect Type	Number of Defects
1	Pre shipment Defects	10
2	Post shipment Defects	11
3	Post production Defects	6
4	Total	27

Defect removal efficiency percentage = Pre-shipment defects / (Pre-shipment + Post-shipment defects + Post-production defects) * 100 = (10/27) * 100 = 37%

Summary

Software maintenance is the core aspects of software engineering. After the system development, the system gets deployed into the production environment. The process of modifying the production system after the delivery to correct the faults, improving performance, and adapting to the changing environment is called as software maintenance.

There are four types of maintenance activities namely adaptive maintenance, corrective maintenance, perfective maintenance, and preventive maintenance.

1. Adaptive maintenance: Adjusting the system adaptively based on the environment changes is called as adaptive maintenance. The system has no faults (errors) on its own, but adapting (changing) as per the environment changes.
2. Corrective maintenance: It is the process of identifying, isolating, and repairing the faults (errors) that are discovered in the system so that the system can be restored and operational. Corrective maintenance includes repair or replacement of equipment.
3. Perfective maintenance: It is the system upgrade kind of work which makes the system to work more efficiently. About 50% of the maintenance is perfective maintenance. Upgrading hardware, software, and band widths are examples of perfective maintenance.
4. Preventive maintenance: Activities that are aimed at increasing the maintainability is called as preventive maintenance. Preventive maintenance activities avoid system outages and errors.

- Maintenance process

  Maintenance process depends on the software being maintained and it varies considerably across software. But still the common maintenance activities that are executed across all the software maintenance cannot be listed down.

- Maintenance cost

  Maintenance cost is usually higher than the overall development cost of the software and sometime it is 100 times of the development cost. Old aging software can have high support cost than the latest technology software, as getting the specialized technical resources is difficult for the old technology-based software. Furthermore, the maintenance activities also tend to corrupt the software structure further increasing the software maintenance cost.

- Laws of software evolution

  The laws of software evolution which force the maintenance to occur, for example, two laws of software evolution are 1. law of increasing complexity and 2. law of continuing change.
- Reverse engineering is analyzing the software system to identify and understand the overall system components, design, and the requirement flow of the system. It helps to understand the relationships between various components.
- Re-engineering involves putting efforts to make the system easier to maintain. In this process the source code is getting changed for easy maintenance and functionality of the system also gets changed during the process. Code cleaning happens over here along with the enhancement of the system.
- Re-structuring is similar to re-engineering. Here the transformation of a system from one representation to another happens at the same level of abstraction. Functionality of the system does not change. Only code cleaning happens.
- Maintenance strategies: There are two types of maintenance strategies
  1. Systematic strategy and
  2. As-needed strategy.
- There are lot of difference between a product and service—software maintenance can be attributed to service part also.

Model Questions
PART A (Objective type)

1. All of the following are types of maintenance activities, except

A. Adaptive maintenance B. Corrective maintenance

C. Perfective maintenance D. Proactive maintenance.

Answer: D

2. Opportunity for innovation is less in maintenance projects.

A. True B. False

Answer: A

3. Maintenance activities are not repetitive in nature.

A. False B. True

Answer: A

4. Adjusting the system based on environment changes is called as

A. Adaptive maintenance B. Corrective maintenance

C. Perfective maintenance D. Preventive maintenance

Answer: A

5. Which type of maintenance is the process of identifying, isolating and repairing the faults (errors) that are discovered in the system so that the system can be restored and operational?

A. Adaptive maintenance B. Corrective maintenance
C. Perfective maintenance D. Preventive maintenance

Answer: B

6. Which type of maintenance happens after the fault?
A. Adaptive maintenance B. Corrective maintenance
C. Perfective maintenance D. Preventive maintenance

Answer: B

7. Two types of corrective maintenance are immediate corrective maintenance and deferred corrective maintenance.
A. True B. False

Answer: A

8. Which of the following is not a phase of corrective maintenance?
A. Notify help desk B. Diagnose the error
C. Fix the error D. Automatic help to users to choose data

Answer: D

9. It is the system upgrade kind of work which makes the system to work more efficiently.
A. Adaptive maintenance B. Corrective maintenance
C. Perfective maintenance D. Preventive maintenance

Answer: C

10. All of the following are examples of perfective maintenance, except
A. Documenting the existing system,
B. Performance tuning—to increase the speed of the server,
C. Applications consolidations—for easy management, and
D. Automatic help to users to choose data.

Answer: A

11. Activities that are aimed at increasing the maintainability are called as
A. Adaptive maintenance B. Corrective maintenance
C. Perfective maintenance D. Preventive maintenance

Answer: D

12. Documenting the existing system is the best example of
A. Adaptive maintenance B. Corrective maintenance
C. Perfective maintenance D. Preventive maintenance

Answer: D

13. Complexity of a system is directly proportional to the maintenance cost of the system.
A. True B. False

Answer: A

14. Volume of a system is directly proportional to the maintenance cost of the system.

A. True B. False

Answer: A

15. Aging of a system is not related to the maintenance cost of the system.

A. True B. False

Answer: B

16. Contractual responsibility of a system is not related to the maintenance cost of the system.

A. True B. False

Answer: B

17. It is impossible for anybody to create a system of any size which does not need to be changed.

A. True B. False

Answer: A

18. Two laws of software evolution are law of decreasing complexity and law of continuing change.

A. True B. False

Answer: B

19. As the system evolves over a period of time the complexity of the system decreases.

A. True B. False

Answer: B

20. This is analyzing the software system to identify and understand the overall system components, design, and the requirement flow of the system.

A. Reverse engineering B. Re-engineering C. Structuring D. Restructuring

Answer: A

21. Which of the following is not a step of reverse engineering process

A. Generation of information B. Storage of information

C. Creation of documents D. Creation of information

Answer: D

22. In this process the source code is getting changed for easy maintenance and functionality of the system also gets changed during the process

A. Reverse engineering B. Re-engineering

C. Structuring D. Restructuring

Answer: B

23. All of the following are about re-engineering except

A. It may lead to re-writing the software

B. It may lead to re-documentation of the system

C. It reduces the risks of the overall maintenance of the system

D. The cost of re-engineering is higher than the cost of developing new software

Answer: D

24. First step in re-engineering is to understand the overall system

A. True B. False

Answer: A

25. Which of the following is false about re-engineering?

A. It reduces the cost

B. It increases the risk

C. It may lead to re-writing the software

D. It may lead to re-documentation of the system.

Answer: B

26. Restructuring is similar to

A. Reverse engineering B. Re-engineering C. Structuring D. Re-structuring

Answer: B

27. Migration from one version of the software to another version of the software is the best example of

A. Reverse engineering B. Re-engineering C. Structuring D. Re-structuring

Answer: D

28. Here the transformation of a system from one representation to another happens at the same level of abstraction.

A. Reverse Engineering B. Re-engineering C. Structuring D. Restructuring

Answer: D

29. Which of the following is the difference between the expected service perceived by the service provider and the expected service by the customer.

A. Gap 1 B. Gap 2 C. Gap 3 D. Gap 4

Answer: A

30. Which of the following is the difference between the written service specification and the expected service perceived by the service provider?

A. Gap 1 B. Gap 2 C. Gap 3 D. Gap 4

Answer: B

31. Which of the following is the difference between the written specification and the actual service delivery?

A. Gap 1 B. Gap 2 C. Gap 3 D. Gap 4

Answer: C

32. Which of the following is the difference between the actual delivery and communication about the service

A. Gap 1 B. Gap 2 C. Gap 3 D. Gap 4

Answer: D

33. Ineffective horizontal communication is the best example for

A. Gap 1 B. Gap 2 C. Gap 3 D. Gap 4

Answer: D

34. Which of the following is the difference between the customer perceived service and the actual expectation of the customer?

A. Gap 2 B. Gap 3 C. Gap 4 D. Gap 5

Answer: D

PART B (Answer in one or two lines)

1. Opportunity for innovation is less in maintenance projects. Explain and write notes on this.
2. Maintenance activities are mostly repetitive in nature. Explain and write notes on this.
3. List down four types of maintenance activities.
4. Write notes on adaptive maintenance
5. Write notes on corrective maintenance.
6. What are all the types of corrective maintenance?
7. List down the life cycle activities of corrective maintenance.
8. What is perfective maintenance?
9. Give examples for perfective maintenance.
10. What is preventive maintenance?
11. Give examples for preventive maintenance?
12. Write notes on maintenance cost of a software?
13. How complexity of a system is related to maintenance cost of the system?
14. How volume of a system is related to maintenance cost of the system?
15. How aging of a system is related to maintenance cost of the system?
16. How soft skills are related to maintenance cost of the system?
17. How contractual responsibility is related to maintenance cost of the system?
18. Write notes on software evolution.
19. What are all the laws of software evolution?
20. Write notes on law of increasing complexity of software evolution?
21. Write notes on law of continuing change of software evolution?
22. Write notes on reverse engineering of a system?
23. What are all the steps of reverse engineering process of a system?
24. Write notes on re-engineering process of a system?
25. What are all the steps involved in re-engineering of a system?
26. When to re-engineer a system?
27. List down any two advantages of re-engineering?
28. What is re-structuring?
29. What are all the two types of maintenance strategies?

30. Write notes on systematic strategy of maintenance?
31. Write notes on as-needed strategy of maintenance?
32. Write notes Gap 1 service model of maintenance?
33. Write notes Gap 2 service model of maintenance?
34. Write notes Gap 3 service model of maintenance?
35. Write notes Gap 4 service model of maintenance?
36. Write notes Gap 5 service model of maintenance?
37. List down any fours issues of software maintenance

PART C (Descriptive type)

1. Differentiate software development and maintenance.
2. Write notes on adaptive maintenance with examples.
3. Write notes on corrective and perfective maintenance with examples.
4. Write notes on preventive maintenance with examples.
5. Discuss maintenance process in detail.
6. What is maintenance cost? Discuss factors which determine maintenance cost.
7. Write notes on 1. law of increasing complexity and 2. law of continuing change.
8. What is reverse engineering. Discuss it in detail.
9. Differentiate forward engineering, reverse engineering, and re-engineering, restructuring in detail through a diagram.
10. Discuss re-engineering process in detail.
11. Discuss two maintenance strategies in detail.
12. Write notes on maintenance mind set.
13. List down the difference between product and service.
14. Product cannot exist without service—describe in detail.
15. What is service gap model? Discuss in detail.
16. Discuss various software maintenance tools and its usage.
17. List down and discuss issues in software maintenance.
18. List down and discuss any five metrics used in Software maintenance and support.
19. Green way project's ticket acknowledgment distribution is given below. SLA for acknowledgment of any ticket is less than or equal to 20 min. Calculate Acknowledgment SLA Percentage for closed tickets.
20. Green way project's ticket acknowledgment distribution is given below. SLA for acknowledgment of any ticket is less than or equal to 20 min. Calculate Acknowledgment SLA Percentage for open tickets.
21. Following table indicates the resolution trend for a particular period for Platinum Sev1 category of tickets. Calculate Resolution SLA Percentage for closed tickets for Platinum Sev 1 category.

Section 10:
Web Engineering

23

Web Engineering

CHAPTER COVERAGE

1. *Introduction*
2. *Introduction to Web*
3. *General Web Characteristics*
4. *Web Applications Categories*
5. *How Web Application Work?*
6. *Advantages of Web Applications*
7. *Drawbacks of Web Applications*
8. *Web Engineering*

23.1 INTRODUCTION

Web (World Wide Web) is not only the way to browse today, but many large, sophisticated, and mission critical applications are built on web platform now-a-days. As you can understand, few characteristics of the web applications are very unique over the traditional applications such as usability, performance, security, and scalability. But yet many web applications are developed in an ad hoc fashion still now. The web engineering section of the software engineering deals with the systematic, disciplined, and quantifiable approach toward the web development.

23.2 INTRODUCTION TO WEB

Literal meaning of web is "a network of Thread constructed by Spider." In software engineering, the term web (World Wide Web) is a collection of computers connected by a network (Figure 23.1). Web is an indispensable and an evolving and transformative technology. It helps virtually in every aspect of modern living. It changes the way of doing things and the way to acquire and disseminate information.

Web helps us to place any information and documents in web in electronic formats and retrieve the same from web at later point of time from any part of the world. Known electronic formats in which we can store information are text file, graphics file, sound files, and movie files. Web also helps to access other people's information from web, thereby enhancing our knowledge. Web has search facility to search and retrieve only the required information from web. Web not only helps to store and retrieve the

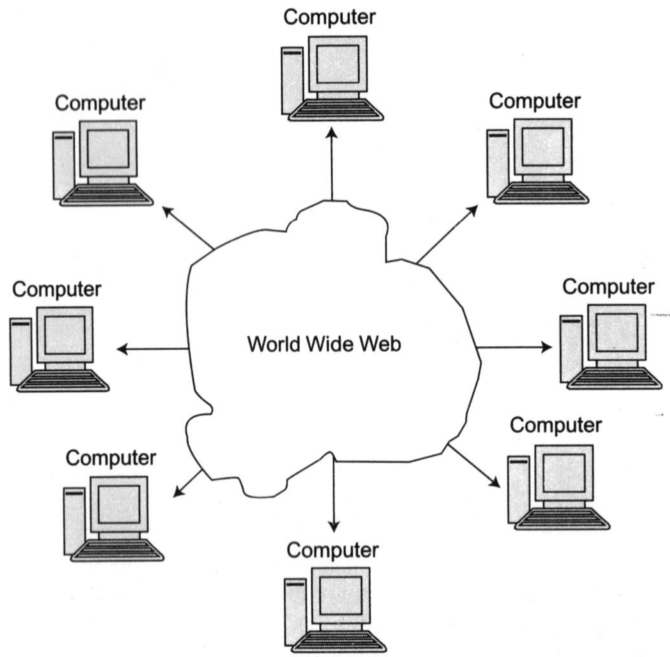

Figure 23.1 World Wide Web

information but also helps to place the whole application (web-based application) in the web which caters the users accessing the application through web. Web also has authorization concepts wherein only authorized user can access those information.

23.3 GENERAL WEB CHARACTERISTICS

Client server is the basic concept under which World Wide Web system acts. Client machine or client is the computer that uses the applications of the web and retrieves and uses data (Figure 23.2). Client machine has a software called as web browser(s) for this purpose. A web browser software which runs on a client machine helps to access the World Wide Web.

Popular web browsers are:

1. Microsoft Internet explorer
2. Google chrome web browser

Server machine or server is the computer in which the actual application and information are stored. Server also has web application that communicates with the client browsers. Information can also be stored in the server using database (Figure 23.3).

Note: A single client can access the information resided in multiple servers through web applications. A client can also act as a server for some other application and vice versa. (A Server can also act as a client for some other application).

Examples of web applications include: (web application can be accessed using www)

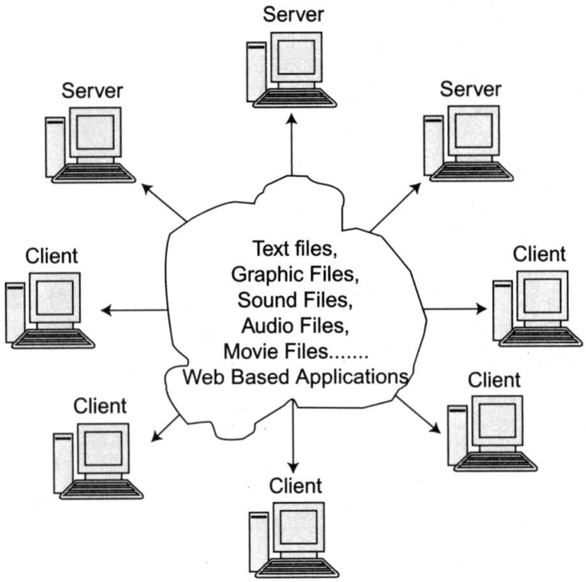

Figure 23.2 World Wide Web Characteristics

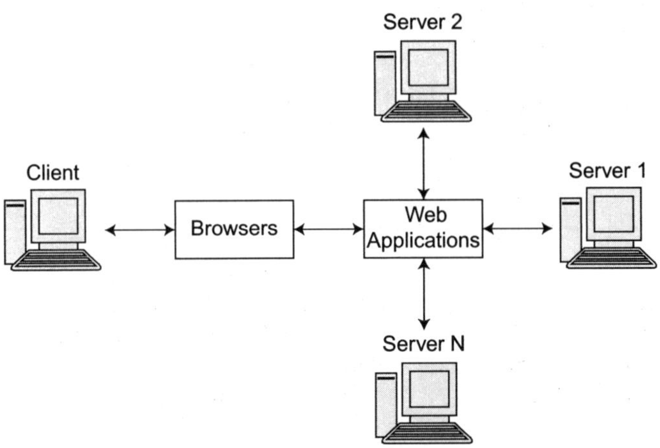

Figure 23.3 Web Browsers and Web Applications

1. www.thehindu.com, www.indiatimes.com (for latest news)
2. www.amazon.com, www.flipkart.com (for electronic shopping)
3. www.india.gov.in (Indian government portal)
4. www.Naukri.com (job portal)
5. www.Irctc.co.in (for travel—Indian railway)

23.4 WEB APPLICATIONS CATEGORIES

Web applications are categorized into three based on where it runs:

1. Client-side web applications
2. Server-side web applications
3. Middleware web applications

Client-side web applications:

This web application runs at the client side in browser. Resources (pages) are loaded at the client side. Client side applications are coded using technologies such as HTML, CSS, and JAVA Scripts.

Server-side web applications:

This web application runs at the server only. Server-side applications are coded using technologies such as JAVA, ASP, and PHP.

Middleware web applications:

This web application acts in between the client and server. Technologies include enterprise Java Beans, Java Servlet, etc.

Web applications can also be categorized based on its usage:

1. Online news provider (www.indiatimes.com)
2. Online web e-mail provider (www.webmail.com)
3. Document-sharing web sites (downloadable documents) (www.4shared.com)
4. Online chat sites (www.yahoo.com)
5. Blog-based sites (www.wordpress.com)
6. Social networking sites (www.Facebook.com, www.twitter.com, etc.)
7. Online Search Engines—to find and download documents
8. Portals (for specific purpose)

23.5 HOW WEB APPLICATION WORK?

Web application has three layers namely presentation layer, application layer (logical layer) and data layer (Storage layer). Presentation layer consists of a basic browser which runs HTML kind of pages. Application layer does basic calculation and business logic, and it is also called as logical layer. Data layer consists of database and other storage devices. Database software is used to access the database (Figure 23.4).

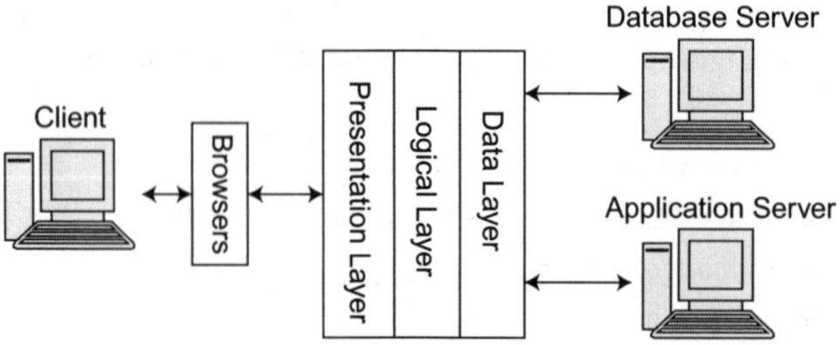

Figure 23.4 Layers of Web Application

23.6 ADVANTAGES OF WEB APPLICATIONS

1. Application can be accessed from anywhere in the world from any machine.
2. Only browser is needed at the client side to connect with the web application. No other special software is required at the client side.
3. Operation system (Windows, Linux, and Mac) at the client side is not a bottleneck to access the application. Any operating system will run the application.
4. Database and objects are running at the server end, and so load at the client side is always low.
5. Upgrading the web application is easy as it required the application to be updated only at a single place (server side). In a stand-alone system, the application will be running at different machines, and upgrading is a tedious task.

23.7 DRAWBACKS OF WEB APPLICATIONS

- Security is the main drawback of any web application. Without proper security, the web applications are prone to get hacked easily by hackers: We can practice ethical hacking, thereby finding all the possibilities of hacking the developed web application and addressing it through counter mechanism. We need to ensure all the security engineering aspects are taken care of even from the beginning stage of the web development, thereby ensuring the development of a secured web application.
- Data theft is possible easily in web application: We can ensure security engineering aspects are taken care of even from the beginning stage of the development, thereby avoiding data theft. We can also ensure proper backup mechanism of the data such as cold backup and hot backup systems to reduce the impact of the theft. We can also use data-masking mechanism to avoid data theft.
- Application also can be copied (duplicated) easily in the web: We need to follow the engineering principles and best practices to avoid this. Security engineering is a specialized field of engineering that focuses on the security aspects of a system. It ensures the security of the system is taken care in the entire life cycle of the system including requirements and design of the system.

23.8 WEB ENGINEERING

> **Web Engineering** - *is the application of systematic, disciplined, and quantifiable approches to the design, production, deploymemt, operation, maintenance and evolution of Web - based software products.*
>
> — Gaedke, 2000

Web engineering is also defined as the process of creating high-quality web-based applications.

Web engineering in addition to software engineering also consists of the following engineering aspects related to the development of web-based application (Figure 23.5).

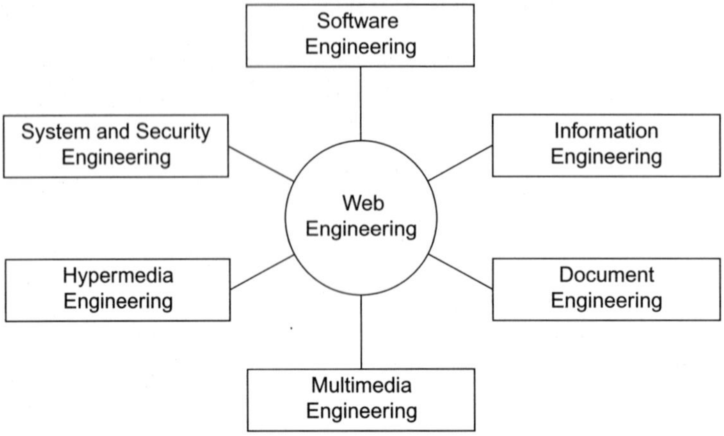

Figure 23.5 Web Engineering

- Information engineering: Information engineering can be defined as an approach of designing and developing information systems. It can also be defined as the generation, distribution, interpretation and use of information in systems. It also takes care of the availability of the information, accessibility of the information, security of the information, and authenticity of the information.
- Document engineering: Document engineering can be defined as an approach of designing and developing document-based system which helps to get ideas from various information and systems. This is the next level of information engineering. In addition to the attributes of information engineering, the documentation engineering takes care of the look and feel of the documents, performance (time to create and retrieve the documents), and concurrency of the documents.
- Multimedia engineering: Multimedia engineering can be defined as an approach of designing and developing a system based on multimedia concepts such as animations, voice, and audio. It can be defined as the generation, distribution, and interpretation and use of multimedia concepts in a system.
- Hypermedia engineering: Hypermedia is a term which describes the form and structure of online information connecting electronic data. It is mainly used for interactive information. It analyzes the purpose for which a web site or CDROM is created and thereby defines a process of creating it.
- System engineering: System engineering is an interdisciplinary field of engineering that focuses on integrating all the aspects of a system such as project management, control engineering, and industrial engineering including human resource interaction of the system.
- Security engineering: Security engineering is a specialized field of engineering that focuses on the security aspects of a system. It ensures the security of the system is taken care in the entire life cycle of the system including requirements and design of the system. Security engineering also takes care of passing the message in a secured way between systems by various mechanisms such as cryptography and ethical hacking.

23.8.1 Goals of Web Engineering

Following are the goals of web engineering:

1. Develop high-quality web application as per the requirement
2. Develop effective and efficient web application
3. Continuously adapt to the requirement and environment change
4. Use web engineering process model
5. Continuously follow security and administrative regulations

23.8.2 Web Engineering versus Software Engineering

Table 23.1 differentiates software engineering and web engineering.

Table 23.1 Software Engineering versus Web Engineering

	Software Engineering	Web Engineering
User base	Small	Large
User Requirements	Specific	Changes fast
Cost of Development	Varies	Usually Low
Infrastructuew Cose	High	Comparatively Low
Release Cycle	Longer	Shorter
Security	Not so Important	Highly important
Architecture Complexity	Low	High

23.8.3 Attributes of Web Engineering

Attributes of web engineering can be easily derived from the web engineering and its associated aspects (related engineering fields). Web engineering attributes are the combination of associated aspects.

Attributes of information engineering:

1. Security of information
2. Availability of information
3. Accessibility of information
4. Authenticity of information

Attributes of document engineering:

In addition to the attributes of information engineering, the documentation engineering has the following attributes:

1. Type of documents
2. Concurrency
3. Performance (time to create)
4. Look and feel of the document

Attributes of multimedia engineering:

In addition to the attributes of document engineering, the multimedia engineering has the following attributes:

1. Loading and refreshment time
2. Sensitive contents (age restrictions)

Attributes of hypermedia engineering:

In addition to the attributes of multimedia engineering, the hypermedia engineering has the following attributes:

1. Compatibility (browser compatibility)
2. CPU utilization at customer side
3. CPU utilization at server side

Attributes of system and security engineering:

1. Server size
2. System network type
3. System (server and client) distribution
4. Server load
5. Authority level
6. Authenticity level

23.8.4 Principles of Web Design

Usability: Usability is the degree of user interface design consideration, which takes care of making the system effective and efficient and satisfying the users by taking into account the human psychology and physiology of the users. Any user interface has four elements, namely users, tasks, contents, and environment. All these factors need to be analyzed. Refer three golden rules of Mandel which we discussed in Chapter 7. In addition to Mandel's rule, the following principles can also be followed:

1. Target for simple model always.
2. Similar components (elements) can be placed at same place (together) in a page.
3. Proper and uniform distribution of heavy and light elements within a page is necessary.
4. More emphasis can be given to important components (elements) in a page.
5. Consistencies need to be maintained between pages (colors, menus, etc.).

23.8.5 Web Engineering Process

We already discussed the difference between software engineering and web engineering, and it indicates separate process required for web engineering catering its unique need. The web engineering process must also be agile (incremental and iterative) as user's requirements evolve over time (user base is usually huge for web-based applications) and changes occur frequently.

When it comes to web engineering, each phase needs to be iterative and incremental in nature. (Figure 23.6).

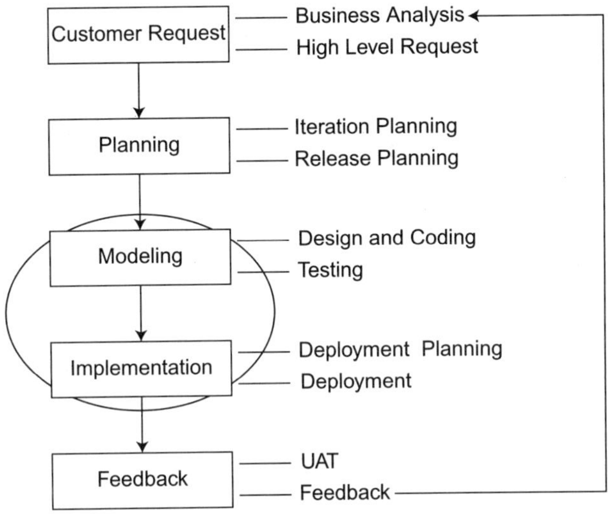

Figure 23.6 Web Engineering Process

Customer request phase

Customer request phase is the first phase of web software development in which the customer and the business analysts (usually developer) interact with each other and document the necessities of the outcome of the web application.

Business need: Business need of the web site (web application) is being discussed here. Business outcome is defined in the form of business statements or vision statements.

Requirement collection: Customers would state their requirements (business statements, vision statements)—how and what the web application should perform. The requirements may also include the appearances (interface requirements), the functionalities (functional requirements) and the web application output expectations (non-functional requirements).

The steps in this phase include:

- Feasibility study if required
- Eliciting requirements at high level
- Requirement analysis
- Specify and validate requirements

Some of the factors to be considered in this phase include:

1. Degree to which the organization's success is directly dependent on the success of the web application
2. Relationship between business need and requirements
3. Technical feasibility of the web application to be developed
4. Number of users of the web application. This is a critical parameter while designing the web page.

5. Number of stakeholders (analysis can help to identify conflicting requirements coming from different sources)
6. Size of the web engineering team
7. Degree to which members of the WebE team have worked together before (analysis can help develop a common understanding of the project)

Output of this phase: Business case document, requirement specification document, and feasibility study output

Planning phase

Planning phase is the second phase of web development in which the feasibility study outcome and requirement specifications are analyzed and a decision is taken to move forward or not.

Iteration planning and release planning: Planning phase sets the stage for both iteration planning and release planning. The entire set of requirements are divided into release buckets (release backlog) based on the release cycle. A release will have its own release backlog. Now release backlog are further subdivided into iteration backlog based on the iteration cycle. A release will have multiple iterations. Iterations are time-boxed and ranges from 1 to 4 weeks and follow a strict schedule.

Team will start coding the web application by going through iteration by iteration. Iterations are the heartbeat of an agile project. It is inside the iteration that the actual work is achieved. Iteration plan consists of iteration backlog (requirements of the iteration), assumptions, risks, actions, dependencies, and communication. The team will determine what features can be accommodated in the current iterative cycle (can also be called as sprint). It also orders (priorities) the features of the current immediate iterative cycle. Iterations follow a consistent, unchanging schedule in which each activity is time-boxed:

- Demonstrate previous iteration (up to an hour)
- Hold retrospective on previous iteration (1 h)
- Plan iteration (half an hour to 4 h)
- Commit to delivering stories (15 min)
- Develop stories (remainder of iteration)
- Prepare release (1 h)

This helps the team keep focused on the main activities and avoid spending time on the low-priority tasks. Modeling and implementations are execution part of the iteration planning.

Output of this phase: Iteration backlog (iteration requirements) and release backlog (release requirements).

Modeling and implementation phase

"Modeling and implementations" phases together form the execution part of the iteration planning. In modeling phase designing, coding and testing of the iteration-related tasks happens. This is called as modeling phase as the entire application is getting refined and changed multiple times until it is getting implemented. During the feedback stage, the customer accepts part of the web application (iteration outcome) after demo.

We keep the basic design framework and keeps on adding and refining the design framework when we move iteration to iteration. Modeling includes interface design and architectural design.

Design of the web application depends on the complexity level of the web site, the graphical interfaces required, and simplicity needed in usage of the end users.

Design of the web application should be:

1. Precise and specific
2. Conform to budget and requirements
3. A direct solution to the problem

Coding and testing: The coding is defined as the phase where the document format is transformed into lines of codes in web programming language (HTML, ASP, JAVA, etc.). Writing standardized coding for software not only helps to maintain it properly once it is built but also helps to enhance the code easily at later point of time; it also helps to identify and fix the bugs quickly and easily, and so writing the proper working code alone is not enough and focus should be on writing a standard code. After the coding phase is completed, the lines of code have to be tested for ensuring its right functionality in the platform. Testing is carried out by a separate team of experts (software testers) specialized in generating sample cases and subjecting the product to various tests. Only after the product has been proved to be reliable over the tests, it enters into the implementation phase.

Following aspects are tested typically for a web application:

- Testing web application at different operating systems
- Testing web application at different browsers (or other interface devices such as set-top boxes, personal digital assistants (PDAs), and mobile phones)
- Testing web application at different hardware platforms
- Communications protocols checking
- "Backroom" applications checking

In implementation phase, the deployment planning and deployment happens which will make the web application ready for demo, feedback, and customer acceptance.

Feedback phase

In feedback phase, the user acceptance testing happens for the particular iteration. Any further refinement and changes are carried out in the next iteration which make the web site (web application) getting evolved over a period of time. Feedback phase is vital for the web site development as it is used to implement the changes at the next upcoming iterations. Normally, the iteration demo marks the end of the iteration followed by the team retrospective. Key elements of the retrospective meeting are:

- Process improvements are made at the end of every iteration—ensures that the project team is always in self-improving mode.
- The retrospective is a collaborative process between all members of the team.
- All team members identify what went well and what can be improved.
- The actions and lessons learnt are prioritized based on the team direction
- Team works out a solution to most prominent problems—helps to build the team ownership and self management.
- Helps the team formation and bonding as the areas of conflict can be identified and dealt with.

23.8.6 Web Engineering Best Practices

- Understand the business need of the web application
- Always follow iterative and incremental steps for web engineering

- Use as many re-usable components as possible
- Give more importance to security (encryption, firewalls, etc.)
- Always concentrate on consistency and quality
- Always follow Internet standards
- Use good web programming tools
- Prepare a project schedule and continuously update it

23.8.7 Web Metrics

1. *Web traffic*: How many users are using the web site on average per day?
2. *Popularity of web application (web pages)*: This is the comparative rating of web traffic in comparison to similar kind of web applications.
3. User accessibility of the web application.
4. *Loading time of the web application*: How much time it takes the application to display on the client browser?
5. *Business realization percentage*: Any web application starts with a business case and how much of the business objective got realized because of the web application.

Summary

- Web-based information system (WIS) development process is different and unique.
- Web engineering is multi-disciplinary; no single discipline (such as software engineering) can provide complete theory basis, body of knowledge and practices to guide WIS development.
- Issues of evolution and lifecycle management when compared to more "traditional" applications.
- WIS and applications are pervasive and non-trivial. The prospect of web as a platform will continue to grow and it is worth being treated specifically.
- Literal meaning of web is "a network of thread constructed by spider". In software engineering, the term web is a collection of computers connected by a network.
- Client server is the basic concept under which World Wide Web system acts. Client machine or client is the computer that uses the applications of the web and retrieves and uses the data. Client machine has a software called as web browser(s) for this purpose.
- Server machine or server is the computer in which the actual application and information are stored. Server also has a web application that communicates with the client browsers. Information can also be stored in the server using database.
- Web applications are categorized into three based on where it runs:
  1. Client-side web applications
  2. Server-side web applications
  3. Middleware web applications
- Web applications can also be categorized based on its usage.

- Advantages of web applications:
  1. Application can be accessed from anywhere in the world from any machine.
  2. Only browser is needed at the client side to connect with the web application. No other special software is required at the client side.
  3. Operation system (Windows, Linux, and Mac) at the client side is not a bottleneck to access the application. Any operating system will run the application.
- Web engineering is also defined as the process of creating high-quality web-based applications.
- Following are the goals of web engineering:
  1. Develop high-quality web application as per the requirement
  2. Develop an effective and efficient web application
  3. Continuously adapt to the requirement and environment change
  4. Use web engineering process model
- Web engineering phases:
  1. Customer request phase
  2. Planning phase
  3. Modeling phase
  4. Implementation phase
  5. Feedback phase

Model Questions
PART A (Objective type)

1. Which of the following is not a category of web applications based on distribution models?

   A. Client-side web application B. Server-side web application

   C. Middleware web application D. Online web application

Answer: D

2. Which of the following is not a category of web application based on its usage?

   A. Online news provider B. Middleware application

   C. Online e-mail provider D. Document-sharing web sites

Answer: B

3. Which of the following is not an advantage of web applications?

   A. Application can be accessed from anywhere in the world from any machine.

   B. No other special software required at client side except browser

   C. Any operating system will run the application.

   D. Application also can be copied (duplicated) easily in the web.

Answer: D

4. Which of the following is not a goal of web engineering?
   A. Develop high-quality web application as per the requirement
   B. Develop a cheaper web application to satisfy the customer
   C. Continuously adapt to the requirement and environment change
   D. Develop effective and efficient web application

Answer: B

5. Which of the following is not a web engineering best practice?
   A. Understand the business need of the web application
   B. Always follow iterative and incremental steps for web engineering
   C. Use as many re-usable components as possible
   D. Using software code from other web sites for easy reference

Answer: D

PART B (Answer in one or two lines)

1. Write notes on client server concept.
2. Write the names of web browsers you are aware of.
3. Define web engineering.
4. What are all the categories of web applications based on distribution models?
5. What are all the categories of web applications based on its usages?
6. List down any three advantages of web applications
7. List down three drawbacks of web applications.
8. List down any three goals of web engineering.
9. Define usability.
10. List down any three web engineering best practices.
11. List down any three web-related metrics.

PART C (Descriptive type)

1. Draw the layers of web application in a diagram.
2. Discuss the general web characteristics.
3. What are all the advantages of web applications?
4. List down three drawbacks of web application. Suggest how we can overcome it.
5. Discuss engineering practices related to web engineering.
6. Compare software engineering with web engineering.
7. List down the attributes of web engineering.

8. Discuss the principles of web design.
9. Discuss the customer request phase of web engineering process in detail.
10. Discuss the planning phase of web engineering process in detail.
11. Discus web engineering process in detail.
12. List down any five web engineering best practice.
13. Discuss web engineering metrics you are aware of.

Section 11:
Emerging Trends in Software Engineering

24

Emerging Trends in Software Engineering

CHAPTER COVERAGE

1. *Introduction*
2. *Web 2.0*
3. *Rapid Delivery*
4. *Open Source Software Development*
5. *Security Engineering*
6. *Service-Oriented Software Engineering*
7. *Web Service*
8. *Software as a Service*
9. *Service-Oriented Architecture*
10. *Cloud Computing*
11. *Aspect-Oriented Software Development (AOSD)*
12. *Test-Driven Development (TDD)*
13. *Social Computing*

24.1 INTRODUCTION

Software engineering field is evolving constantly as well as rapidly; so adapting to new changes is imperative for success of this field. Unlike other fields, software engineering undergoes several changes with the invention of new technology and innovation awareness. Various factors determine the trend in software engineering field, such as

1. Technology
2. Business environment
3. Economy situation
4. Innovation
5. Increase in business complexity
6. Competitive world

In this chapter, let us look at some of the emerging trends in software engineering.

24.2 WEB 2.0

Web 1.0 is considered as web pages created with static pages (HTML) and is completely content-driven; and user of the website has no role to play other than just reading the website and it is just one-way communication. Web 2.0 is (Figure 24.1) considered as a collaborative technology, which is more than the static web pages in which users take part collaboratively and contribute to the content; websites are created using dynamic web pages. Users can also edit and update the already existing website content.

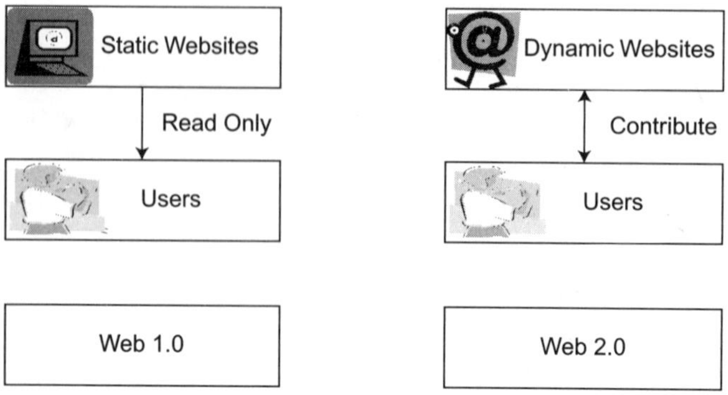

Figure 24.1 Representation of Web 2.0

Web 2.0 uses social media for interactions. Blogging is the best example for Web 2.0 principle; Gmail, Google maps, wikies, and Flickr are a few examples of Web 2.0.

Web 2.0 websites include following features and techniques, which are referred as SLATES (Figure 24.2) by Andrew McAfee (Source: http://en.wikipedia.org/wiki/Web_2.0).

Search: Obtaining information through keyword search.

Links: Connects information together into a meaningful information ecosystem using the model of the Web, and provides low-barrier social tools.

Authoring: The ability to create and update the content leads to the collaborative work of many rather than just a few web authors. In wikis, users may extend, undo, and redo each other's work. In blogs, posts and comments of individuals build up over time.

Tags: Tags categorization of content by users adding "tags"—short, usually one-word descriptions—to facilitate searching, without depending on pre-made categories. Collection of tags created by many users within a single system is referred as "folksonomies" (i.e., folk taxonomies).

Figure 24.2 SLATES–Web 2.0

Extensions: Software that makes the Web an application platform as well as a document server, which include softwares such as Adobe Reader, Adobe Flash player, Microsoft Silverlight, ActiveX, Oracle Java, QuickTime, and Windows Media.

Signals: The use of syndication technology such as RSS- Rich Site Summary to notify users of content changes.

These days, web 3.0 is talked about; the machines (computers) generate the data and their associated new information on their own based on the need. In Web 3.0, computers start interacting with humans. Now the trend is moving from Web 2.0 to Web 3.0

24.3 RAPID DELIVERY

Software engineering principles (life cycles) are being followed in parallel rather than in sequence, as the customer wants to see the outcome quickly. Agile software development is the best example for rapid delivery. As we have already discussed in the previous chapter, agile is iterative and incremental (Figure 24.3) way of developing software.

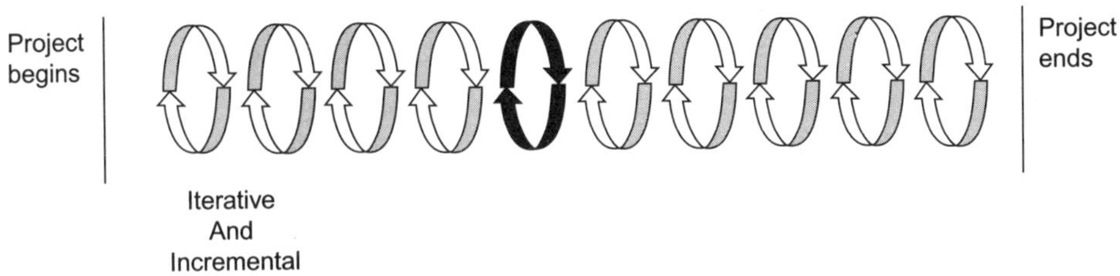

Figure 24.3 Iterative and Incremental Delivery

A time box (usually 2–4 weeks of time frame) is fixed and whatever possible during this boxing period will be delivered as a workable incremental software product to the customer. Changes in the interim product as well as addition will be carried out in the subsequent iteration and this repeats until all the requirements are fulfilled. This takes the software to the customer quickly and thereby customer gets early value from the product.

Examples for Rapid Delivery include:

1. SCRUM Methodology
2. XP Methodology
3. Dynamic Software Development Methodology (DSDM)
4. KANBAN Methodology

24.4 OPEN SOURCE SOFTWARE DEVELOPMENT

As the name suggests, open source not only gives the executable code to the users but also the source code to the users (Free license), which has a lot of advantages (Figure 24.4). The users can customize the code further based on his needs. He can also contribute his changed code to others (Open). This way of development of code is cost-effective and also ensures that software is being used as an

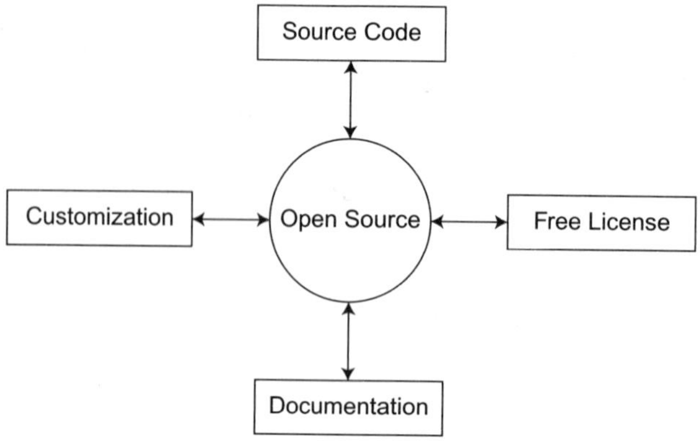

Figure 24.4 Open Source Software Development

enabler for life and business rather than controlling the life of the people in the name of warranty, support, and maintenance. Documentation of the entire source code is also available free of cost.

A few examples of Open Source software products are as follows:

1. Eclipse—Integrated Development Environment
2. Mozilla Firefox—Famous Web browser
3. Word press—Web publishing platform (website creation)
4. PHP—Scripting language of Web
5. Linux—famous Operating system (like UNIX)

24.5 SECURITY ENGINEERING

Security engineering is a specialized field of engineering that focuses on the security aspects of the software system. Security is given high priority during the requirement analysis and designing stage of the system itself so that we ensure nobody else hacks (intrude) into the system and modifies the code maliciously. It also aims to prevent misuse of data in the system. Owing to technological advances, the software system becomes complex and we need to give a lot of attention to security aspects of the system. Common coding errors lead to security vulnerability and developers need to follow security-related best practices while writing the code. Default deny and Default permit are two fundamental principles (Figure 24.5) of security engineering aspects.

Default deny indicates that the call to the source code is denied except special permission calls. In other way, special permitted code can only be called from outside and all others are denied. Default permit is dangerous, which is opposite to Default deny. In default permit mode, everything is default permitted, which is a big security threat to the code.

While gathering the functionality requirements, we also need to gather the security requirement of the system. For example, security needs to be given a lot of attention while developing core banking applications dealing with sensitive data. Data hiding and information hiding principles need to be worked on. Common software programming errors lead to security lapses.

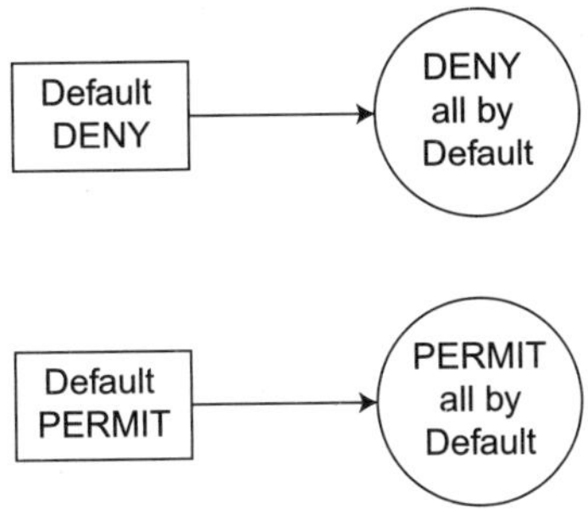

Figure 24.5 Default Deny and Default Permit

24.6 SERVICE-ORIENTED SOFTWARE ENGINEERING

Service-oriented software engineering (SOSE) is the development of software system using reusable components and services from other providers (Figure 24.6). Parts of these systems are called as components, but it differs from component-based software engineering, as the service outcome of those components are focused on and it has the ability to locate the services at run time.

SOSE acts as a middle layer between the business and system developers (IT). Business users will only look into the services rather than the implementation of those services in the system, and IT provider will take care of it. Iterative development is mostly suitable in this case.

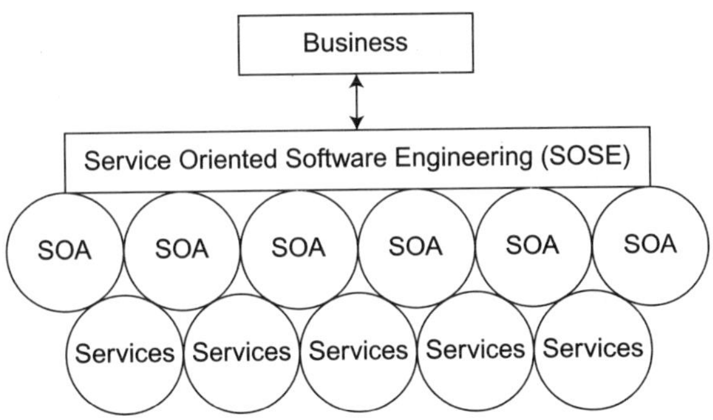

Figure 24.6 Service-oriented Software Engineering (SOSE)

24.7 WEB SERVICE

Web Service concepts are famous because of SOSE (Figure 24.7). Services usually do not have interfaces and are independent of each other. Services depend solely on the input messages that are being passed on to it, which are usually in the XML format. Web Service Description Language (WSDL), which is also XML based, is used to describe the services provided, Format of the service, accessibility of the service. It provides Introduction, Interface, Implementation related to the service, and helps locate the services.

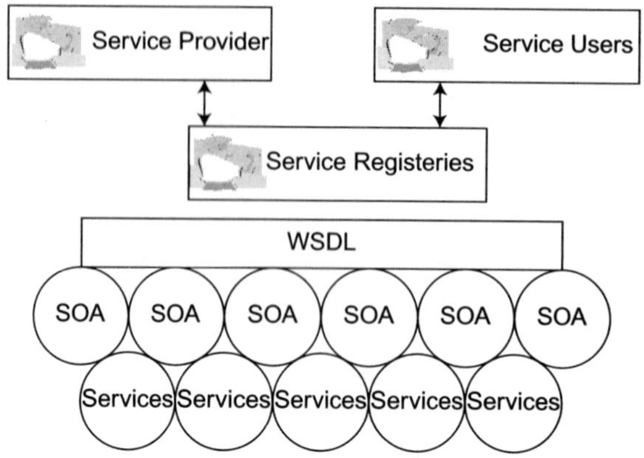

Figure 24.7 Web Services

There are three types of Players in any service-oriented interaction: service providers (who provide the service), service users (who actually use the services provided) and service registries (who act as intermediary between service provider and service users). Service providers register their service in service registries. Service users will search the service registries for suitable service and if found, use those service according to the terms and conditions.

24.8 SOFTWARE AS A SERVICE

Software as a Service (SAAS) is a model of software delivery (Figure 24.8), where the software company (Software Provider) provides maintenance, daily technical operation, and support for the software provided to their client (Source: Wikipedia).

SAAS may use Service-oriented architecture (SOA). Salesforce.com, who is a CRM service provider, is the best example of SAAS.

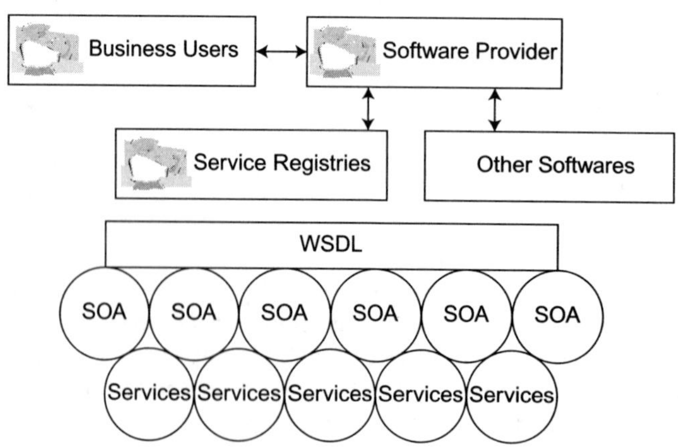

Figure 24.8 Software as a Service (SAAS)

Key characteristics of SAAS are as follows:

1. Software is available through internet
2. Services charged on pay per user basis
3. Activities are managed at central location
4. Upgradation of services happens to all at the same time
5. Installation not required and free maintenance
6. No upfront licensing and usage-based cost

Disadvantages of SAAS are as follows:

1. It fully depends on broadband connection
2. Customization is little
3. Not feasible for high volume of data
4. Security is still an issue.

24.9 SERVICE-ORIENTED ARCHITECTURE

SOA does not provide full business as service, instead a small process (part of the overall service). It is a manufacturing hub, where it allows applications to exchange data with one another. SOA offers services to other applications, but does not provide services to the end users; Whereas SAAS offers services directly to the end users. SOA is an architectural style of building SAAS. Only industry-proven technology is used in building SOA, which helps communicate with another application easily. Services are cataloged and are also discoverable. SOA may service SAAS.

24.10 CLOUD COMPUTING

IT infrastructure as a service is called as cloud computing (Figure 24.9). Cloud application may be delivered using SAAS. In cloud computing, infrastructure itself is programmable (customizable). Dynamic scalability is easily achieved in cloud computing. Basic components of client computing

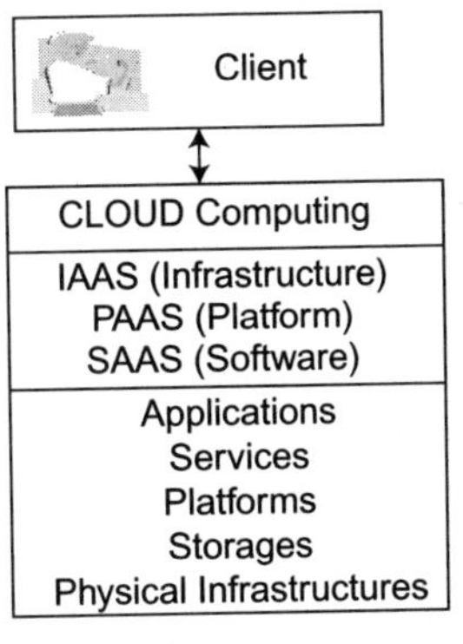

Figure 24.9 Cloud Computing

are (1) clients; (2) services; (3) application; (4) platform (internet infrastructure); (5) storage; and (6) physical infrastructure.

IT infrastructure as a service (IAAS), IT platform as a service (PAAS) and IT SAAS form the architecture of cloud computing (Cloud computing Layers). SAAS is accessed by end users; PAAS is accessed by developers; and IAAS is accessed by infrastructure engineers.

24.11 ASPECT-ORIENTED SOFTWARE DEVELOPMENT (AOSD)

Aspect means concerns. Concerns of the system are separately addressed as an Object (in addition to functional Objects) and are being addressed throughout the software life cycle. The entire system is modularized into Objects based on functionality, and a special object called as Aspect is also created, which represents the aspects of the entire system (in turn the aspects of the objects). It addresses each concern separately so that overall concerns of the system are being addressed. When all the concerns are addressed, the system is developed automatically.

24.12 TEST-DRIVEN DEVELOPMENT (TDD)

In this concept, a testing code is written separately in order to test a software Code (Figure 24.10). The testing code is written even before the actual code is written. But when the testing code is compiled, it fails (Test Fail) as the calling code (actual code) is not available.

Now, the developer writes the basic skeleton of the code (Write Code) and then compiles the testing Code, which will now get compiled. But when it is invoked, it will not give out the correct result, as the actual code is not written completely. Now, the actual code is strengthened (Refactor Coding) for actual implementation. Now, when we invoke the testing code, it will not only run but also gives the results correctly. Testing reusability is the main advantage of TDD, and it also ensures that all the code snippets are thoroughly tested before the delivery.

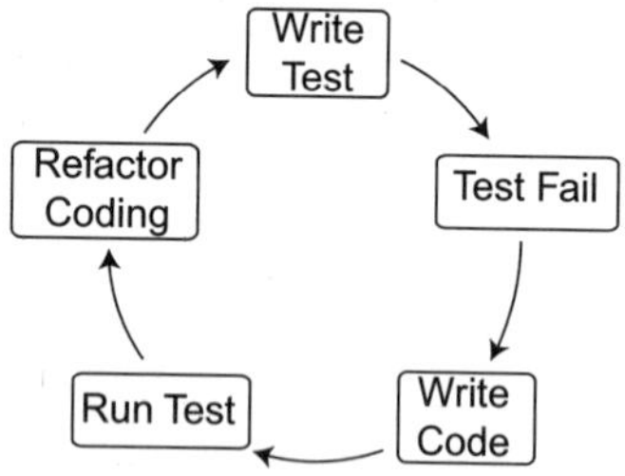

Figure 24.10 Test-driven Development (TDD).

24.13 SOCIAL COMPUTING

Social computing means using the social software to connect with society. There are two main components of social computing: (1) Contents and (2) Connections. Contents are getting shared through (by) Connections, for example, Blog, Face book, Twitter, LinkedIn, wikis, instant messaging (Skype, Google talk), etc. Online identity is the identity of a person in social media (it refers to the profile of the users). It is also possible to use pseudo names here. Social computing is usually used for marketing, branding, collaboration, and communication purposes.

Summary

- Web 2.0 is considered as a collaborative technology, which is more than the static web pages where users take part collaboratively and contribute to the content; websites are created using dynamic web pages.
- Rapid Delivery: Software engineering principles (life cycles) are being followed in parallel rather than in sequence, as the customer wants to see the outcome quickly. Agile software development is the best example for Rapid delivery.
- Open Source Software Development: As the name suggests, Open source not only gives the executable code to the users but also the source code to the users (Free license), which has a lot of advantages.
- Security engineering is a specialized field of engineering that focuses on the security aspects of the software system. Security is given high priority during the requirement analysis and designing the stage of the system itself, so that we ensure nobody else hacks (intrude) into the system and modifies the code maliciously.
- Service-oriented Software Engineering (SOSE) is the development of software system using reusable components and services provided by other providers.
- Web Service concepts are famous because of SOSE. Services usually do not have interfaces and are independent of each other; and depend solely on the input messages that are being passed on to it, which are usually in the form of XML.
- Software as a Service (SAAS) is a model of Software delivery, where the software company (Software Provider) provides maintenance, daily technical operation and support for the software provided to their client (Source: Wikipedia).
- IT infrastructure as a service is called as cloud computing. Cloud application may be delivered using SAAS. In Cloud computing, infrastructure itself is programmable (Customizable). Dynamic scalability is easily achieved in Cloud computing.
- Aspect-Oriented Software Development (AOSD): Aspect means concerns. Concerns of the system are separately addressed as an Object (in addition to functional Objects) and are being addressed throughout the software life cycle.
- Test-Driven Development (TDD): In this concept, a testing code is written separately in order to test a software code. The testing code is written even before the actual code is written.
- Social Computing: It means using the social software to connect with society. There are two main components of social computing: (1) Contents and (2) Connections. Contents are getting shared through (by) Connections.

Model Questions
PART A (Objective type)

1. Which of the following is not an example of Rapid Delivery?

   A. SCRUM Methodology B. XP Methodology

   C. DSDM (Dynamic Software Development Methodology) D. Iterative

Answer: D

2. Which of the following is a model of Software delivery, where the software company (Software Provider) provides maintenance, daily technical operation, and support for the software provided to their client?

A. SOSE B. Software as a Service (SAAS)

C. Platform as a Service (PAAS) D. Open Source

Answer: B

3. Which of the following is not an example of Cloud Computing?

A. SOSE B. Software as a Service (SAAS)

C. Platform as a Service (PAAS) D. Infrastructure as a Service (IAAS)

Answer: A

4. What is the correct sequence of activities in TDD?

A. Write code, Write Test, Test fail, Run Test, Refactor Code

B. Write Test, Test fail, Refactor Code, Write code, Run Test

C. Write Test, Test fail, Write code, Run Test, Refactor Code

D. Test fail, Write code, Write Test, Run Test, Refactor Code

Answer: C

PART B (Answer in one or two lines)

1. Write notes on following:
   - Web 2.0
   - Rapid Delivery
   - Open Source Software
   - Security Engineering
   - SOSE
   - SAAS
   - SOA
   - Web Services
   - Cloud Computing
   - AOSD
   - TDD
   - Social Computing

25

Introduction to Agile Software Development

CHAPTER COVERAGE

1. *Introduction*
2. *What is Agile?*
3. *Various Characteristics of Agile Projects*
4. *Agile manifesto*
5. *Generic Agile Project Life Cycle*
6. *Agile-related Concepts*
7. *Epics, Features, User Stories*
8. *Communication in Agile Projects*
9. *Different Agile Methodologies*

25.1 INTRODUCTION

Agile is a topic of growing importance in software industry that helps the organization to be more flexible to change and to deliver workable software in a shorter span of time benefiting both the customer and the executing organization. It has been a subject of long debate since the time the concept of agile methodology arrived whether agile is a better methodology than the traditional waterfall. Understanding the difference in philosophy of the traditional project execution model versus Agile is very important before exploring different agile methodologies. This chapter discusses the definition of agile, agile manifesto values and principles, names of different agile methodologies, and terminologies related to agile methodology.

25.2 WHAT IS AGILE?

Agile frame work tries to address the limitations of traditional methodologies.

Limitation of traditional project execution methodologies

1. Modern projects are constrained by lot of uncertainties more on what is expected/What is anticipated in the beginning of the project.
2. Although there is as process to handle difficult situation, people should be empowered to execute it.
3. It is difficult to change the plan once it is base lined. Customer needs to follow a change control system. Customer happens to pay even for genuine change.

4. End users see the end product only at the end of the project.
5. There is a huge gap between the expectations of the customer and the end users of the product and because of which most of the IT projects face problem in user acceptance testing phase.
6. Project is often isolated from the business changing scenario. Once initiated the changes are often very difficult to be inserted by the customer however genuine case it may be.
7. Most of the projects are scrapped due to change in technologies and business conditions during the execution of the project.
8. Traditional project management tries to define the timeline and cost based on the scope of the project. But as the project progresses, the scope is getting changed but the timeline is not revised which leads to team frustration.
9. Often the customer is ending up paying more than what was estimated for the project in the beginning.
10. As team is not empowered to take decisions, the execution part is entirely different from the planning (mostly owned by the project manager). Most of the time, the execution is not happening as per the initial plan.
11. Customer only sees the interim deliverables during the various phases of the project, which may not reflect the actual final product.

How agile methodologies overcome the limitations of traditional project execution?

1. Agile project involves the end user throughout the life cycle of the project to avoid conflicts at a later stage.
2. Agile project produces incremental product at the end of every phase of the project (the concept of phase getting changed).
3. Agile project delivers important features first.
4. Customers are given flexibility to add/modify/delete the requirement until the team actually starts working on it. Customers are also given options to prioritize the requirements.
5. Agile project engages all the stakeholders (usually in traditional project management only the team is involved and engaged).
6. Agile project gets the commitment from the team (in traditional project management, only the tasks are allocated to the team without getting their commitment).
7. Agile project does planning at multiple levels of the projects (in traditional project management, only high-level planning is done and once it is fixed execution starts. There are no plans at execution levels.).
8. Agile project encourages proactive risk identification.
9. Agile project allows open and transparent project management
10. Agile project continuously improves product, process, and people (in traditional project management more concentration is on process.).

Agility: Agility is the ability to both create and respond to change in a turbulent business environment and depends on the common sense. Common sense of the team is the primary driving factor of agile.

Agile: Definition of agile: Scott Ambler definition of agile "Agile is an iterative and incremental (evolutionary) approach to software development which is performed in a highly collaborative manner with 'just enough' ceremony that produces high-quality software which meets the changing needs of its stakeholders." Iterative means "Re Do or Repeat." Incremental means "add on to."

Agile is a philosophy that uses organizational models based on people, collaboration, and shared values (Source: PMI Agile Specification). From these definitions of agile, it is clear that agile is both iterative and incremental way of developing software which delivers continuous value to the customer. Agile inherits the advantages of both iterative and incremental software development methodologies. Incremental and iterative development gives us the opportunities not only to improve the development process, but also to adjust the requirements to the continuous changing world. At the end of each iterative cycle output is incremental working product rather than interim deliverable. The traditional project tries to give more interim deliverables (documents) before releasing the final product. But agile project tries to give incremental product itself at every stage of the project rather than giving an interim deliverable in the form of documents.

Agile project actually considers every project as business rather than seeing it as an individual project. Agile project tries to understand business problem at every stage of the execution, whereas traditional project considers this at the beginning of the project only and tries to freeze the plan and execute that plan in a single stretch. Agile projects are being executed closer to the business and interacts with business often and involves end user every iterations thereby it actually feels and understand business pain. Agile project does not kill business people with plan. Agile project management actually tries to do inward orientation as well as outside orientation at the same time, whereas the traditional project management does only inward orientation and it does not do outward orientation.

25.3 VARIOUS CHARACTERISTICS OF AGILE PROJECTS

Adaptability in Agile Projects: In traditional projects (all at once development), the adaptability is only in the beginning of the project and it goes down drastically once the project starts. There is no adaptability in the traditional projects once the execution of the project starts. In agile project, because it follows an iterative development approach, the adaptability is maintained throughout the life cycle of the project and is depicted in the below picture. Agile is adaptable every iteration (Refer Figure 25.1).

Visibility in Agile Projects: In traditional projects (all at once development), the visibility of the product is high only at the end of the project, as the product is given to the customer only at the last phase of the project. There is no visibility in the traditional projects until the end of the execution of the project. In agile project, because it follows an iterative development approach, the visibility is maintained throughout the life cycle of the project and is depicted in Figure 25.2. Visibility is maintained throughout the project and the customer knows what he wants and what is happening.

Value in Agile Projects: In traditional projects (all at once development), the value is delivered to the customers and end users only at the end, so the value map increases only at the end. In agile

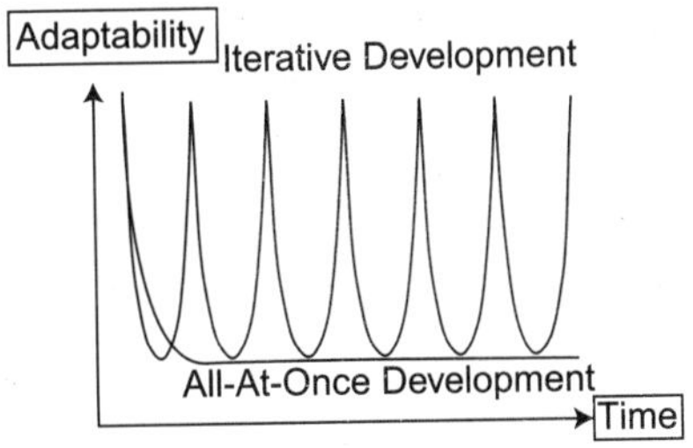

Figure 25.1 Adaptability in Agile Projects

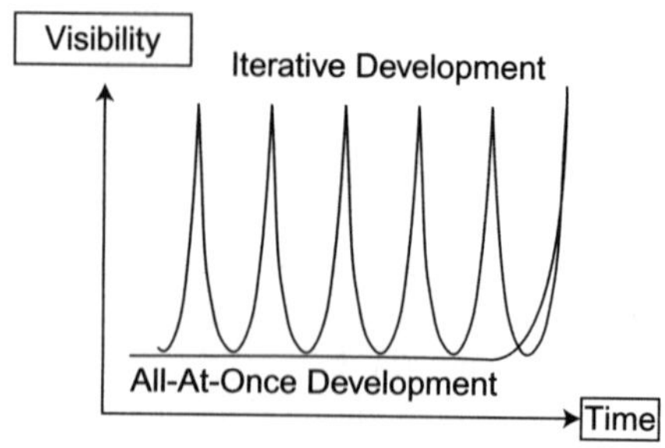

Figure 25.2 Visibility in Agile Projects

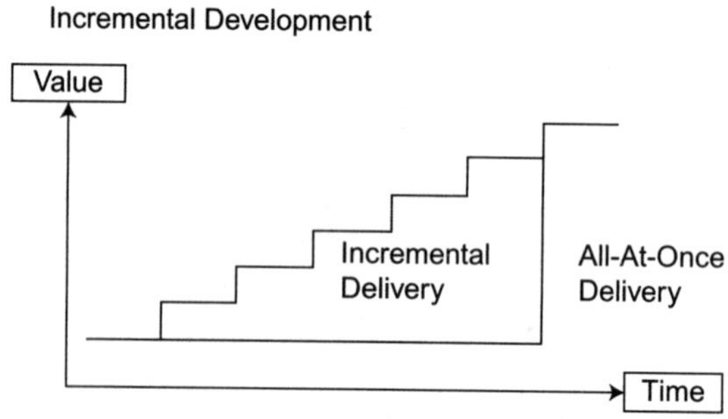

Figure 25.3 Value in Agile Projects

project, due to its incremental nature, the value is also delivery incremental in steps as shown in the Figure 25.3. Customer gets early value in the agile project than in traditional projects.

Risks in Agile Projects: In traditional projects (all at once development), the risks level gets lowered only at the end after the product is delivered to the customer. In agile project, the risks gets decreased every iteration as highly risky items are executed in the first few iterations (Refer Figure 25.4). Fail early is the principle of agile.

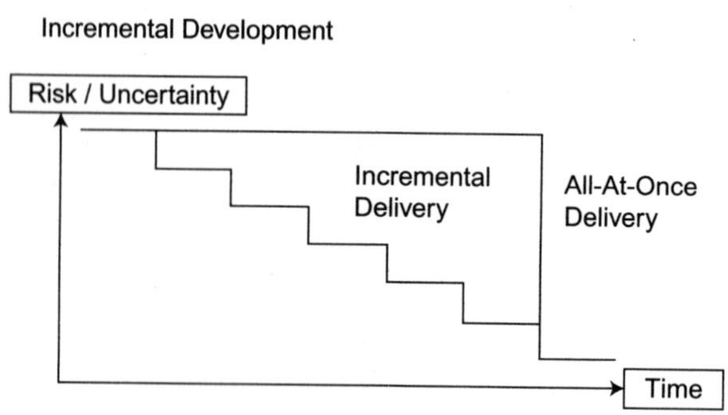

Figure 25.4 Risks in Agile Projects

25.4 AGILE MANIFESTO

Different people called their methodology as agile but there were no generic definition and guideline for agile. To derive an understanding and listing down the common aspects across all the agile methodology, 17 prominent figures who are regarded as catalysts of agile methodologies and are representatives from extreme programming, SCRUM, DSDM, adaptive software development, crystal, feature-driven development, pragmatic programming, and others sympathetic to the need for an alternative to documentation driven, heavy weight software development processes convened in a place in 2001 at the Snowbird ski resort in Utah, and they coined the terms "Agile Software Development" and "Agile methods" and they also created the agile manifesto. Agile manifesto talks about 4 values and 12 principles applicable for agile projects.

A public declaration of the agile philosophy and principles created in February 2001 (Source: http://agilemanifesto.org/principles.html).

Four values of agile as per agile manifesto are shown in Figure 25.5.

Below each manifesto items are discussed clearly (Refer Figure 25.5).

Individuals and interactions over processes and tools: Agile focuses on empowered and self-organized team which gives more importance to interactions. Daily planning is based on this value, which helps to overcome the impediments faced by the team members in frequent manner. Frequent interactions also help to get the team commitment and get more focus on the tasks on the hand. Team helps each other because of this. This does not mean that process and tools were not required for the execution of agile projects, it means that more importance is given to individuals and interactions. Wherever possible, individual interactions need to be encouraged rather than using tools for communication.

Working software over comprehensive documentation: Documentation needs to be prepared only wherever necessary and more importance to be given to working software. Lot of people misunderstood this statement as an agile project does not require any documentation. This is not the actual meaning. Documentations, such as end user manual are very much necessary and it adds more value and it must be created. Compliance-related documents need to be prepared because it is compliant with the rules and regulations. But rather than converting the requirement into various types of documentation and converting the documentations into the final product, agile stresses the importance to covert the requirements straight into the product thereby delivering value early to the customer. Agile project gives incremental working software as deliverable rather than documentations, such as what is done with traditional project management. Measurement of the project progress not measured based on the milestone deliverables but based on the feature delivered into the system incrementally.

Customer collaboration over contract negotiation: In traditional projects everything is decided (scope, price, and time) upfront and put it in a contract before starting the project. There are lots of disadvantages because of this. Team stretch their working hours and they work day, night to meet the deadline, because of which the quality of the product may go down. Because the scope is fixed, even

Individuals and Interactions over process and tools
Working software over comprehensive documentation
Costomer collaboration over contract negotiation
Responding to change over following a plan

Figure 25.5 Manifesto for Agile Software Development

for a minor change the vendor ask for a change request and the customer gets frustrated because of this. Customer collaboration process makes the customer a part of the development process and the customer understand the pain of the team members and help to overcome the difficulties they face. Customer collaboration also happens in sharing the profit with the customer and thereby both the parties get the benefit.

Responding to change over following a plan: Agile project plan is prepared just in time. In the plan-driven development the requirements freezes upfront, but the plan can be accurate only at the end of the project. Agile manifesto does not state that plan is not required or not important, but preference is given responding to change. Agile follows a rolling wave approach thereby responding to change.

Twelve principles behind agile manifesto: Fundamental truths and shared values that drive the agile methodologies are called as agile principles. Agile principles help to manage change, manage the uncertainty, increase efficiency, reduce Cost, increase value to the stakeholders, and improve project progress predictability. Following 12 principles are derived based on four values of agile manifesto.

1. The highest priority is to satisfy the customer through early and continuous delivery of valuable software.
2. Welcome changing requirements, even late in development. Agile processes harness change for the customer's competitive advantage.
3. Deliver working software frequently, from a couple of weeks to a couple of months, with a preference to the shorter timescale.
4. Business people and developers must work together daily throughout the project.
5. Build projects around motivated individuals. Give them the environment and support they need, and trust them to get the job done.
6. The most efficient and effective method of conveying information to and within a development team is face-to-face conversation.
7. Working software is the primary measure of progress.
8. Agile processes promote sustainable development.
9. Continuous attention to technical excellence and good design enhances agility.
10. Simplicity—the art of maximizing the amount of work not done— is essential.
11. The best architectures, requirements, and designs emerge from self-organizing teams.
12. At regular intervals, the team reflects on how to become more effective, then tunes and adjusts its behavior accordingly.

Benefits of using Agile methodologies

What kind of Organization Structure best fit for Agile Project Execution?

Agile fits best with Projectized structure where the team will have more authority than other structures. Team is characterized by nimble results, adaption to change, more scope for innovation but agile also fits well with matrix kind of Organization structure which gets the benefit of both the functional and projectized structure. In matrix kind of structure, Agile works well only when the functional manager and Project manager understand each other well and tries to complement each other, if they tries to compete with each other it will be a difficult situation for executing agile Projects. Team will be more empowered when the collaboration happens. When multiple Organizations involved in the same Project then agile may not be suitable but the same project is being integrated (managed) by the customer then Agile may be possible, basically the style of project management needs to be fine tune according to the situation.

As per Dr. Dobbs Agile Community Survey (Figure 25.6), 82% of the people agreed that using agile methodologies improves productivity. Only 18% felt there is no improvement or decrease in productivity while using agile methodologies; 87% of the people felt that quality is improved while using agile methodologies; 78% of the people felt that agile project execution increases business stakeholder satisfaction levels; 72% of the people felt that cost of system development goes down while using agile methodologies.

As per Agile Consortium Survey 2007 (Figure 25.7), agile project development is 61% cheaper than traditional project execution. Agile project is 24% faster than traditional project execution methodology; 83% improvement in defects while using agile methodologies.

All these data indicate that agile project execution not only delivers value to the customers and end users, but also to the executing organizations.

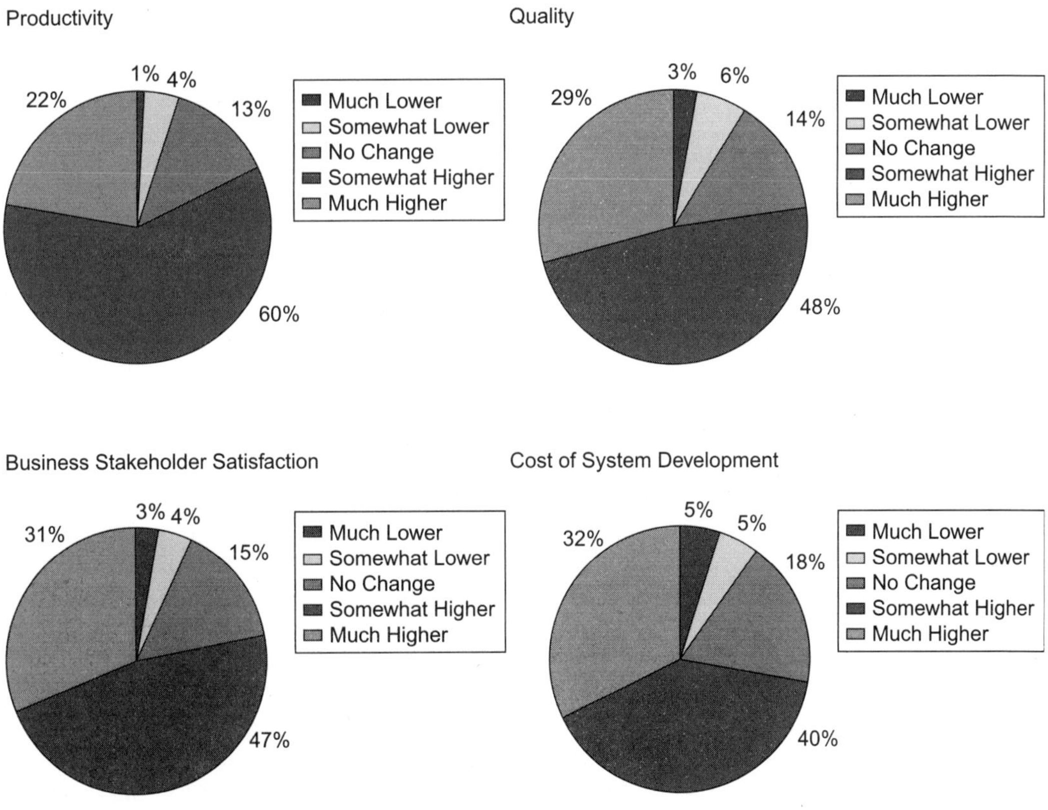

Source: Dr. Dobbs Agile Community Survey

Figure 25.6 Benefits of Agile Methodologies

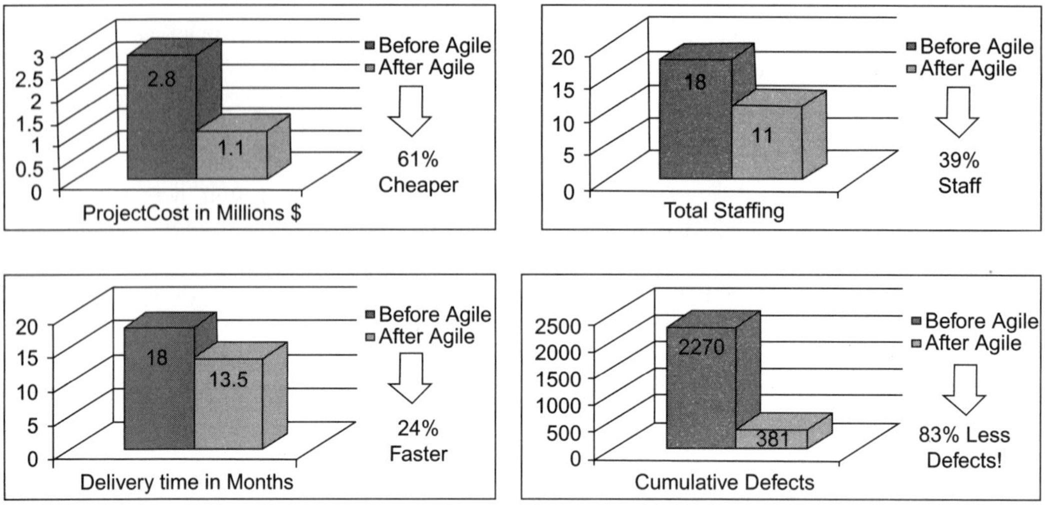

Source: Cutter Consortium Survey 2007

Figure 25.7 Benefits of Agile Projects

25.5 GENERIC AGILE PROJECT LIFE CYCLE

A simplified life cycle for this agile methodology is shown in Figure 25.8. In agile projects the customer requirements are called as backlogs. Product requirements called as product backlog is created as an outcome of product vision phase of the project.

Product visioning: This planning helps to get the commitment from all the stakeholders involved in creating the product by determining money involved in each level of the iterative cycle. Product visioning documents the vision of the product owner, which documents what to be changed or created and the overall efforts involved in creating the product, the target customers, key differentiator from the competitor. Rolling wave planning and progressive elaboration are the techniques used in creating this plan.

Release planning happens in repeated flow creating release plan which also determines the number of iterations inside each releases. Release period depends on the following factors.

Deadline from competitor supporting the contract, to meet predetermined schedule, supporting a financial deadline when there is enough value, and to test the product. Release is actually a set of iterative cycles and so a release consists of multiple related iterative cycles. Sometimes separate iterative cycle will be executed by separate team. This is particularly applicable when multiple teams are involved. A typical release happens in 2–4 months of time. Release plan is also being defined by the product owner. The delivery team and the product owner need to agree on the number of iterative cycles (sprints) in each release. Release planning usually happens in one full day. The purpose of release planning is actually to establish a sense of how big a release might be. Release plan actually determines the time plan (time box) for each release and in turn for each iterative cycle by determining the current team capacity. During release planning, the set of selected user stories are split into much smaller user stories that focus on narrower features.

Types of release plan: Two basic types of release plans that are widely used are scope-boxed release plans and time-boxed release plans. In a scope-boxed plan the work what the team will do is defined

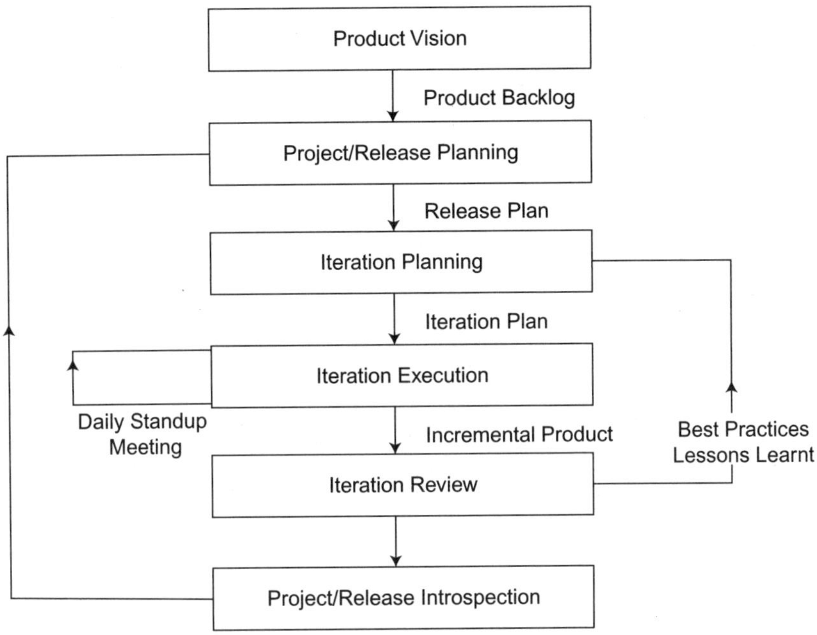

Figure 25.8 Agile Project Information Flow

in advance, but the release date (time) is uncertain. In a time-boxed plan the time and release date is defined in advance, but the specific work what people will do is uncertain and is being elaborated with time. Time-boxed plans are mostly preferred way of release planning. This will constrain the amount of work and people will automatically start doing the prioritization which is the fundamental concepts of agile.

At the beginning of each iteration, iteration planning happens followed by iteration execution, iteration demo, and iteration retrospection. In an agile project the team works in iterations to deliver the final end product.

Iteration plan consists of iteration backlog, assumptions, risks, actions, dependencies, and communication. Team will determine what features can be accommodated in the current iterative cycle (sprint). It also orders (priorities) the features of the current immediate iterative cycle. Features are decomposed into tasks (minute level). Now the team can determine the capacity of the team and the tasks on hand in the current iterative cycle (sprint) and both should be mapped.

The team is responsible to come up with the exhaustive list of tasks. The team brainstorms the tasks that they need to finish all the iteration's stories. Some tasks will be specific to a single story; others may be useful for multiple stories. Take the opportunity to brainstorm the high-level design or the ideas on how to develop the software during this session without going too much into details. This sometimes brings out the perspectives that a single developer or tester would have missed during the actual software development. Take advantage of the on-site customer's presence to ask about the detailed requirements for each story. What do the customers expect when the story is done? This will make the acceptance test criteria for the iteration and is the most important piece for getting the customer sign-off. After the brainstorming tasks, list out on a sequential manner and spread them out on the table and look at the whole picture. The team should discuss now—are these tasks enough to finish all of the stories and are there any duplicates or overlaps? If anybody is uncertain about how the plan works with the way the software is currently designed then discuss and clear out the ambiguity. Discuss and fix any problems. Finish the brainstorming before starting the estimation.

Daily stand up meeting happens every day during the iteration execution. Agile principle strongly recommends daily standup meeting as this helps in surfacing the problems early and attacking it early. Each iteration starts with planning based on user stories and closes with a demo of the interim product and a retrospective. Iteration happens multiple times within a release before moving to next release. At the end of every release, release retrospection is performed.

25.6 AGILE-RELATED CONCEPTS

Here are some of the agile-related concepts. These are predominantly used in all agile methodologies.

Iteration: The ceremony in which working software is produced in agile project is called as iteration. In agile project, working software is produced at the end of the iteration. The result of an iteration which is usually working software is being used as the starting point of the next subsequent iteration. Iteration demo to the customer happens at the end of the iteration followed by iteration retrospection, which helps to improvise the next iteration cycle execution. Iteration is usually a time-boxed event.

Adaptive planning: Adaptive planning expects to define only a high-level plan for the far-end features, but a detailed plan for the next immediate iteration. This is always a more comfortable and realistic situation to live in, right? This is also referred to as rolling wave planning as the process of planning for a project is happening in waves as the project becomes clearer and complexities unfold. Only key milestones are highlighted in the initial stages for reference.

Time boxing: It is a fixed time frame within which the team tries to achieve the planned tasks for the iteration and stops the iteration as soon as the timeline is over. Iterations follow a consistent, unchanging schedule in which each activity is executed and these events are called as time-boxed events.

- Demonstrate finished iteration outcome (up to an hour),
- Hold retrospective on previous iteration (1 h), and
- Plan iteration (half an hour to 4 h).

This helps the team keep focused on the main activities and avoid spending time on the low-priority tasks.

Minimal marketable future (MMF): MMF is the basis minimum feature of the product so that people can start using it rather than waiting for all the futures. There will be a release after minimal marketable futures gets created. It actually enables incremental delivery of the product. Multiple MMF makes the whole product. MMF has value to the end user on its own.

Agile triangle: In traditional projects, the scope is fixed; Time and Cost are the deriving factors of scope. In agile projects, time and costs and fixed through time boxing but scope is not fixed for the entire project in a single stretch. It is being developed using just in time plan for the iteration. So agile Triangle is the inverse triangle of traditional project where Time and Cost are represented at the top and scope is derived from them (which is at the lower side).

Customer involvement: Agile manifesto recommends active customer participation and involvement rather than time and effort expended on negotiating contracts. Agile software development stresses in—evolving requirements accomplished by direct user involvement in the development process, rapid iterations—small and frequent releases (Gaurav Kumar, Pradeep Kumar Bhatia, 2012). Customer involvement in the software development process is very critical to the success of the project. The agile methods state that the customer should be part of the development process from analysis and design to implementation and maintenance (Juyun Cho, 2008).

Re-factoring: Restructuring the code without changing the functionality is called as re-factoring. It helps to strengthen the code further enabling for further addition of functionalities. It helps to simplify the code. In agile projects, the same piece of code is re-factored multiple times to enable future requirement to fit in.

Servant leader: Servant-leadership represents a model of leadership in agile projects in which the leader assumes a service-orientated role as servant, serving the team. Servant leader will find the need of the team and helps the team to solve the problem. Servant leader will not give any instructions or commands to the team rather help them servicing and empowering the team.

Spike: Spike can be defined as a small learning period or technical investigation for solving a problem. Spike explores potential solutions for a difficult technical or design problem which can be used to provide a more accurate estimate. If the team does not know whether a particular design approach will work out or not, it is recommended to do spikes to find out which design approach will work out for the team. Spike solutions use controlled experiments to provide information.

Technical debt: Technical debt is the total amount of less-than-perfect design and implementation decisions in the agile project. It is a known technical problem in the code. As the technical debt decreases, velocity (number of story points completed per iteration) will start rise again. A thumb rule in agile project is to spend 10% of the iteration on technical debt.

Pair programming: Two people sit opposite to each other to code the program while the first person is actually coding the program, and other is checking the possible errors that might occur as reviewer of the code. They also exchange the seats and thereby the roles (coders, reviewers). Pair programming doubles the brainpower available during coding, and gives one person in each pair the opportunity to think about strategic, long-term issues.

25.7 EPICS, FEATURES, USER STORIES

In agile project, the requirements are maintained in the forms of epics, features, and user stories. Epics are collections of features, typically 1–3 months in duration. Features are smaller than epics, typically executed in 2–4 weeks duration. User stories are the smallest increment of value (created from feature) typically executed less than a week. A user story describes what the user does with the software and how the software responds. A user story is a functional requirement that resembles a use case and test case. In agile terminology product features are otherwise called as user stories. User stories are much smaller than the usage requirement artifacts, such as use cases or usage scenarios; user stories will be captured in the dialog format and anybody can understand it easily. Three parts (3Cs) of user stories are card, conversation, and confirmation. In agile stories are written in the form of a card (postal card size). In agile stories are written in the form of conversation and it has a format: As a [Role] I want to do [feature] so that I can do [reason/benefit]. It is actually the format of [Who] [What] [Why].

Example: As an end user I want to purchase the model question papers online so that I can avoid delay in purchase. [Why] part is optional but it is better to describe it. Confirmation is the acceptance criteria of a user story. The customer captures these criteria in acceptance tests, designed to exercise the system in enough ways to demonstrate that the feature really works.

Types of user stories: User stories are of three types namely business user story, technical user story, and bug user story. A technical story is a non-functional requirement that describes the functionality supporting the user-facing features in user stories. Technical stories are usually written by team members and are added to the product backlog. The product owner must be familiar with these stories and understand the dependencies between these and user stories in order to rank all stories for implementation.

Backlogs: In agile projects the requirements are maintained in the name of backlogs. It is actually a to-do list of the project. Backlogs contain epics, features, user stories, bugs, and errors. Iterative cycle backlog (sprint backlog) is a to-do list of that particular iterative cycle (sprint). Iterative cycle backlog is being created by the team based on the high priority list of release backlog. A release consists of multiple iterative cycles (sprints).

25.8 COMMUNICATION IN AGILE PROJECTS

Daily standup meeting (daily scrum meeting): Agile team works as per the principle of TEAM (Together Everybody Achievers More). Each agile team members tries to help other team members to finish their tasks. Team commitment is more important in agile projects. Nobody allocates tasks to the team members; the team decides what tasks need to be executed on a particular day in a ceremony called as daily standup meeting. They are short (15 min maximum) but structured meetings that aim at uncovering any impediments (backlogs) in executing the assigned tasks. Every team members gathers in a regular place and updates the team, what tasks they executed yesterday, what tasks they are going to executing today, and what are all the impediments while executing the tasks. There will not be any discussions or debate in this meeting. It is not a status report meeting, as in agile projects team does not report status to anybody but they just move the tasks board to reflect the current status of the tasks which will act as information radiators for others.

Information radiators: Agile has a practice called "informative workspace" which is similar to war room of the traditional project team, where the team is displaying the product backlogs, release backlogs, and iteration backlogs which are usually in the form of story cards or task cards on the wall. Other graphs and charts prepared by the team is also being pasted on the wall which are sometimes called "information radiators" or "Visible Big Charts." There is no hard and fast rule for the information radiators and the team displays the items, whatever they feel is useful for them and for the execution of projects.

Burn charts: Burn charts helps to track the agile projects. It helps to show case the amount of work completed, amount of work remaining, and projected completion dates. Team members are actually motivated by the amount of work remaining steadily reduced. There are three types of burn charts namely

- Burn down chart
- Burn up chart
- Combined chart

Burn charts are used for sprints as well as for releases. Burn down chart is also called as estimate to complete chart. Because it is moving downward it is called burn down chart. It actually draws the story points (measure of story) yet to be completed. While moving some story points are done and so pending story points starts to come down and hence the chart points goes down. A sprint burn down chart (or "sprint burn down graph") compares actual and expected progress, and shows whether the team is ahead or behind expectations. Expected progress line is a line drawn between total story points to be completed and zero. Burn down chart is drawn either with the story points or time estimate. It is up to the team to decide which one to choose for the project; whichever is comfortable with the team can be chosen. Team can draw the burn down graph for sprint, release, and multiple releases too. Time scale is longer for release and multiple release charts.

Burn down chart shows only how much work is pending (remains to be completed) at the end of each iteration and does not show up whether there is any change in the total story points, and it also does not show how much work actually accomplished in each iteration. Burn up chart is helpful to showcase how much work is actually completed.

Combined chart is the combination of both burn down chart and burn up chart. Both the charts are showing in the same graph.

Retrospection: Agile is not a prescriptive methodology, but rather it is a framework that should be adapted according to the given project, team, and specific circumstances. The iteration retrospective is an important mechanism that allows a team to continuously evolve and improve through the life of a project. Key elements of the retrospective meeting are

- Process improvements are made at end of every iteration—ensures that the project team is always in self-improving mode.
- The retrospective is a collaborative process between all members of the team.
- All team members identify what went well and what can be improved.
- The actions and lessons learnt are prioritized based on team direction.
- Team works out solution to most prominent problems—helps to build the team ownership and self-management.
- Helps the team formation and bonding as the areas of conflict can be identified and dealt with.

OSMOTIC communication:

- Osmotic communication means that information flows into the background hearing of members of the team, so that they pick up relevant information by osmosis. In osmotic communication, the information flow happens at the same time to all stakeholders and people pick the relevant information required, answer the relevant question for which they know the answer, and ask questions if any to clarify the doubts. This is normally accomplished by seating in the same room. Then, when one person asks a question, others in the room can either tune in or tune out, contributing to the discussion or continuing with their work. The cost associated with osmotic communication is low but it is very effective in agile project communication. The feedback rate is also very high while using osmotic communication in agile projects. It usually happens within the war room. Agile project team is self-organized and self-disciplined team and hence, this kind of communication is very effective and useful.

  Consider this example: a team member Lisa is writing an email notification module and is asking her peer how to integrate the solution with Microsoft outlook. They are working in a collocated facility in an agile project. David, another team member sitting in the same war room had worked on a similar thing in his previous project and when he overhears their conversation he walked in and provided the guidance which immediately resolved the problem Lisa was facing. Here a lot of back and forth communication channel is saved because of the osmotic communication channel available to the team. But do not assume that the osmotic communication is possible only if the team is collocated; with effective use of SharePoint, wiki, and other collaboration tools this can easily be achieved for the distributed team as well.

25.9 DIFFERENT AGILE METHODOLOGIES

Frameworks and process which are based on about agile manifesto are called agile methodologies. Agile is a principle which is followed in different project execution methodologies based on the type of engagement and project dynamic. Figure 25.9 discusses the most popular agile methodologies and will also discuss the situations where each of these is most relevant.

Following are the examples of agile methodologies:

1. Scrum methodology
2. Extreme programming (XP)
3. Dynamic system development method (DSDM)
4. Agile unified process (AUP)
5. Feature-driven development (FDD)
6. Lean software development
7. Crystal methods

25.9.1 Scrum Methodology

Scrum uses standard project management concepts but with different terminology and best practices. Scrum is the most widely used methodology framework of agile (Refer Figure 25.10). The term scrum is related to the Rugby sports. Chicken and pigs are the characters in scrum. Pigs are involved and committed to the project, whereas chickens are involved but not committed to the project and can be considered as outsiders. Some of the scrum best practices are short fixed iterative cycle, adjustable scope, customer satisfaction through quick turnaround time, responding to change quickly, and customer collaboration throughout the project. Scrum concepts have vision, product backlog, release backlog, and sprint backlog. Product backlog is the highest level of the requirement. Release backlog is prepared from the product backlog. Sprint backlog is prepared from the release backlog.

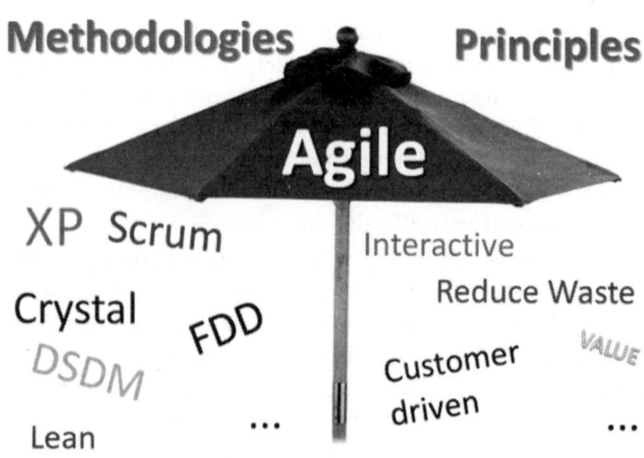

Figure 25.9 Agile project Methodologies vs. Principles

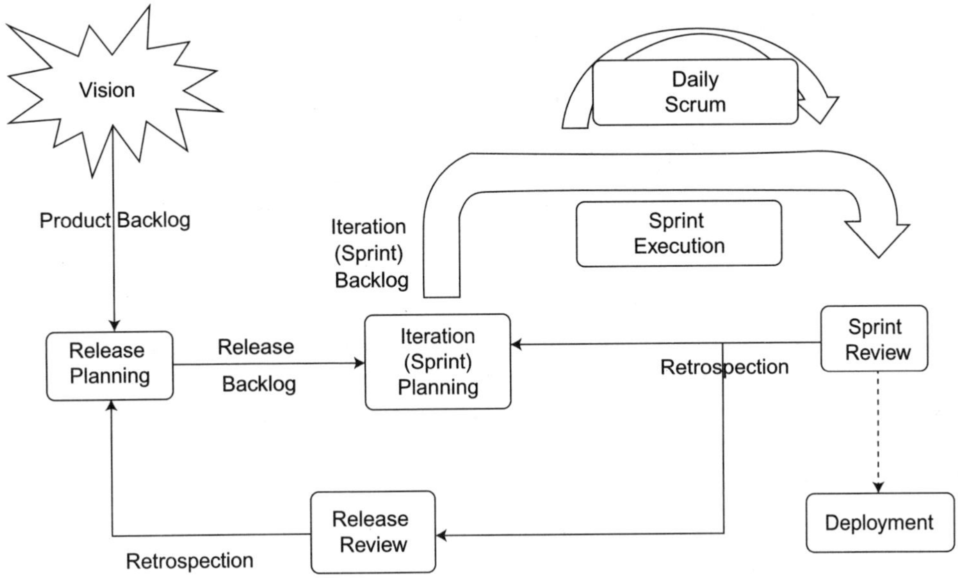

Figure 25.10 Agile Scrum Methodology Flow

The scrum project execution is explained as follows:

Step 1: Collect the product features(product backlog),
Step 2: Get the product features (backlog) in order,
Step 3: Plan the number of releases,
Step 4: Plan the number of iterative cycle in each release,
Step 5: Iterative cycle (sprint) planning: clarify the requirements,
Step 6: Iterative cycle (sprint) planning: estimate individual tasks,
Step 7: Create work environment for executing the iteration,
Step 8: Execute the iterative cycle (sprint),
Step 9: Conduct standup meeting to track the iterative cycle,
Step 10: Conduct iterative cycle retrospection at the end of iterative cycle,
Step 11: Go to Step 5 if there are more iterations in the release,
Step 12: Conduct release retrospection at the end of the release, and
Step 13: Go to Steps 3 and 4 if there are more releases to execute.

This methodology consists of three phases namely pregame, development phase, and post-game. Iterative cycle is called as sprint. Sprint planning is happening in pregame phase. Actual sprint execution is happening in development phase. Integration, retrospection is happening in the post-game phase.

SCRUM methodology has the following elements

- A project team called a SCRUM team,
- A product backlog is a list of all known requirements,
- A sprint backlog is a list of all known requirements which team is going to work currently (in the current sprint),

- A period of work is called as sprint (it is actually the current phase of the project) and it is time boxed usually.
- Daily standup meetings happens with the SCRUM team,
- A burn down chart, burn up chart to track progress of the sprint,
- An incremental product is delivered to the customer at the end of each sprint,
- SCRUM master is a facilitator and leader and also responsible for teaching others how to use the scrum process to deal with every new complexity encountered during a project,
- Story point is the metric used for estimation,
- Scrum product owner is a customer representative (preferably) with highest business knowledge who can prioritize the requirements based on the business value,
- Scrum master connects the team with the management and ensures that the team is able to progress smoothly throughout the iteration cycle by helping them removing the impediments, and
- Scrum team is a group of people doing the actual work for the project creating the potentially shippable product at the end of the sprint.

SCRUM methodology challenges are

- Resistance and unlearning from team members on working on scrum, especially resources who are used to waterfall methodology.
- Managing expectations from clients—the clients may assume that any requirements change at any time can be easily accommodated in scrum projects.
- Adhering to standards—expectations on detailed documentation.
- Code brittleness—in scrum, the same piece of code is re-factored multiple times after it is deployed to enable future requirements to be fitted in. This continuous re-factoring may make the code brittle and thereby impact the code quality.

25.9.2 Extreme Programming (XP)

Extreme programming is a method that is based upon agile concepts and the supporting XP principals of rapid development, flexibility, team empowerment, and customer-based quality management. The author recently came across a project where the customer was changing the requirements more often than expected (almost every day) and also the domain and technology tool used was a new one for the company. Customer changes the requirement even after the entire coding gets over, but customer wanted everything quickly. The environments outside the project were total chaos and there were total uncertainty. Author felt this project is a good example for extreme programming. Following are the characteristics of XP

- Requirements changing almost every day,
- Total chaos in the project environment,
- Customer wants everything fast,
- Handling with new domain/technology, and
- Total uncertainty in everything.

In a nutshell, high speed, high change, and high uncertainties are the characteristics of XP. Traditional project management (TPM) is actually just opposite to XP. Pair programming is related to XP where two people sitting together and writing the same code.

XP has four accelerators, four business questions, five critical success factors, and ten shared valuesunder its umbrella (Refer Figures 25.11 and 25.12).

Critical success factors are essential for success of XP—To keep in mind the five critical success factors, self–flexible–real–agile–leader should be remembered.

Business questions ensure that if addressed properly then the customer gets value. It can be remembered easily as 1. What is requested by the customer? 2. What needs to be done to get the requirements? 3. All for that work can be received? 4. Is it worth doing?

Accelerators unleash the motivation and innovation. Simple- Change- Desire-Ownership can be remembered easily.

XP emphasizes face-to-face collaboration.

XP life cycle uses INSPIRE model of execution (Refer Figure 25.13).

Extreme programming actually supports test-driven development (TDD).

Figure 25.14 lists out the difference between traditional, adaptive, and extreme framework. Extreme as the name implies indicates an extreme position of total chaos and the number of iterations is not known and even the length of the iteration also varies from one iteration to another. Scope is unknown.

25.9.3 Adaptive Project Framework (APF)

Adaptive project framework uses five phases

1. Version scope
2. Cycle plan

XP		
4 Accelerators	**4 Business Questions**	**5 Critical Success Factors**
1. Make change your friend	1. Who needs what and why?	1. Self-Mastery
2. Build on people's desire to make a difference	2. What will it take to do it?	2. Leadership by Commitment
3. Create ownership for results.	3. Can we get what it takes?	3. Flexible Project Model
4. Keep it simple	4. Is it worth it?	4. Real-Time Communication
		5. Agile Organization

Figure 25.11 XP Accelerators and CSFs

XP Values

10 Shared values	
1. Client Collaboration	6. Fast Failures
2. People First	7. Early Value
3. Clarity of Purpose	8. Visibility
4. Result Orientation	9. Quality of life
5. Honest Communication	10. Courage

Figure 25.12 XP shared Values

INSPIRE Model

Initiate

- Establish Project Time Box and Cost
- Define the Project Goal

Speculate

- Prioritize the Requirements
- Plan for later Phases

Incubate

- Assigning Resources
- Producing Deliverables

Review

- Go/No Go Decision
- Re Prioritizing the requirements

Figure 25.13 INSPIRE Model

Traditional, Adaptive, eXtreme

Traditional	Adaptive	Extreme
No Chaos	Chaos	Total Chaos
One Iteration	Known iteration	Unknown Iteration
Fixed Scope	Variable Scope	Unknown Scope
Change Intolerant	Change part of the System	Change necessary

Figure 25.14 Traditional, Adaptive, Extreme Differences

3. Cycle build
4. Client checkpoint
5. Post-version review

Version scope is similar to product vision, cycle plan is similar to sprint (iterative cycle) plan, cycle build is similar to sprint execution, client check point is similar to sprint review, and post-version review is similar to product review. Figure 25.15 lists out the various phases of adaptive project framework along with main output of the same.

25.9.4 Test-Driven Development (TDD)

TDD can be used without extreme programming also. It actually recommends writing the automated unit test first before writing the code. The test will not compile itself at the first instance, so write the basic minimal code to make it compile. Run the test and see it fails because full code was not implemented. Write the full code and make it pass. Re-factor for clarity and repeat. It actually increases

Adaptive Project Frame Work (APF)

Phases	Main Output
Version Scope	Prioritized Functionality, number of cycle
Cycle Plan	Low level WBS, Dependencies and Schedule
Cycle Build	Build Functionality
Client Check Point	Quality review of completed functionality
Post Version	Check on Business Outcome, Lessons Learnt

Figure 25.15 Adaptive Project Framework Methodologies

the speed and also improves the quality. Three A model (Arrange, Act, and Assert) is a type of TDD. Following are the steps in TDD model (Refer Figure 25.16).

- Write a single test
- Compile the test. It will not compile because the code is not written,
- Implement the just enough code to enable the test to compile,
- Run the test and see it fails because there is no content inside,
- Implement just enough code to see the test pass,
- Run the test and see it pass,
- Re-factor the code for clarity, and
- Repeat the process.

25.9.5 Feature-Driven Development (FDD)

FDD is very simple methodology (Refer Figure 25.17) and consists of only five processes namely, develop an overall model of the system, build the features list, plan by feature, design by feature, and build by feature.

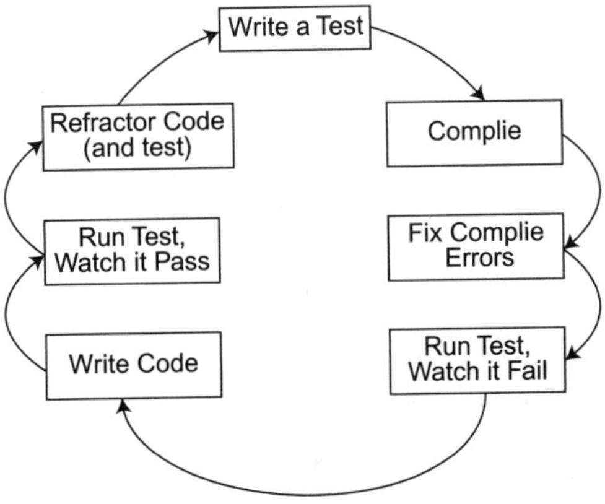

Figure 25.16 TDD Methodology Flow

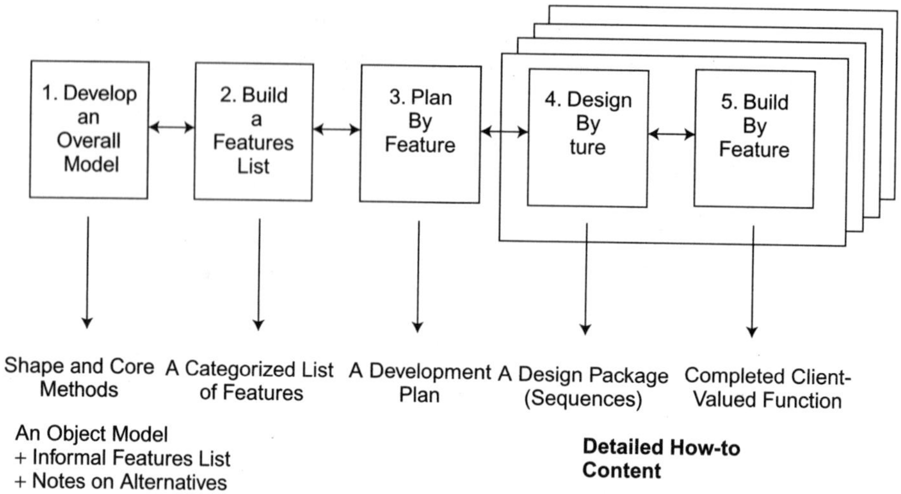

Figure 25.17 FDD Methodology Flow

The features to be built are small aspects of client valued functionality that can be expressed in the form of <action> <result> <object>. FDD refers individual code ownership and seeks to avoid re-factoring by concentrating on domain knowledge.

25.9.6 Kanban Method.

Kanban means "signs board." Kanban is similar to scrum but it limited WIP at a time. It actually uses PULL system, customer pulls out what he wants from the supplier. Supplier just supplies what the customer wants. WIP limit helps in avoiding the piling up of tasks at a particular stage.

In Figure 25.18 WIP (2) indicates that only two items will always be in WIP at any point of time indicating work in progress limit. Kanban focuses on continuous flow of work (Refer Figure 25.19) rather than wasting time on time-boxed tasks. There are two different types of Kanban namely, production Kanban and withdrawal Kanban.

Rules for using Kanban effectively are

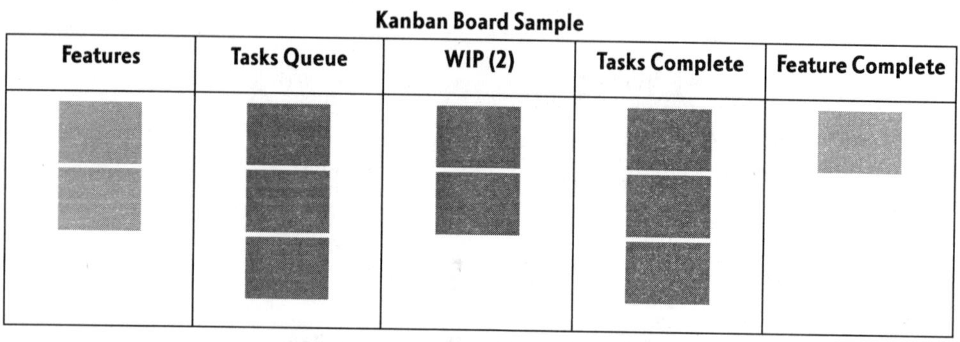

Figure 25.18 KANBAN Methodology Flow

Kanban Board Features

Time
• Release • Iterations (Sprint) • Days
Tasks
• Features • Stories • Tasks
Team
• Managers, Customers, Developers

Figure 25.19 KANBAN Board Features

- Start with a plan. The plan for every part (PFEP) is the cornerstone of the Kanban card implementation.
- Order only what you need,
- Make only what is ordered,
- Kanban is official. No items are made or moved without a Kanban, and
- Quality is no. 1. Defective parts and incorrect amount are never sent to the next process.

25.9.7 Agile Unified Process (AUP)

This is the simpler version of rational unified process (RUP). It is summarized by Scot Ambler as "serial in large, iterative in small, delivering incremental release over time." Inceptions, elaboration, construction, and transition are the four phases of AUP and are risk-driven which contains various optional artifacts.

25.9.8 Dynamic Systems Development Method (DSDM)

It combines the project management life cycle and product development life cycle. Pre-project, project life cycle, post-project are the phases of DSDM. Project life cycle phase is broken into five parts namely, feasibility, foundation, exploration, engineering, and development. Important roles of DSDM team are developer, tester, technical coordinator, ambassador user, and the visionary. Visionary is the person actually initiated the project and have idea about the whole project.

25.9.9 Crystal Methods

Color principle is used to denote the set of standards to employ. Maroon is for heavy projects followed by red, orange, yellow, and crystal clear (lightest). The above color grid is used to define the process to be employed.

25.9.10 Lean Software System

Lean 5S tool for improvement: 5S tool is a foundation tool (Refer Figure 25.20) of continuous improvement in lean. 5S are called housekeeping standards. As per the lean principle 95% of the lead time is non-value added.

Lean Tools - 5s

Sort	Sort All Tools and Materials
Straighten	Organizebased on size/Remove is not Required
Shine	Keep Work Area Clean
Standardize	Keep Lable
Susstain	Put back in place

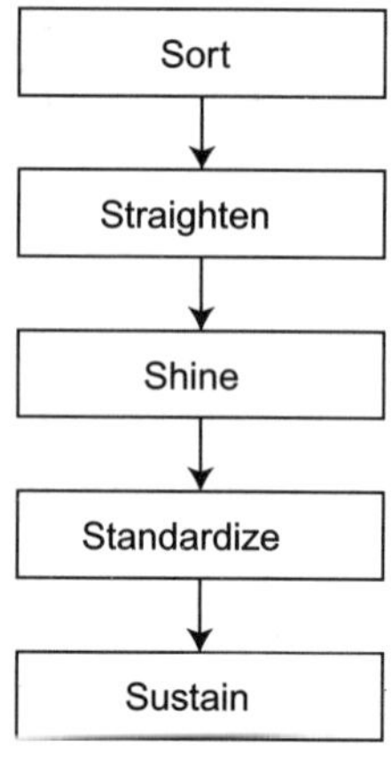

Figure 25.20 LEAN 5S Tools of Agile Methodology

Summary

- Time boxing—it is a fixed time frame within which the team tries to achieve the planned tasks for the iteration and stops the iteration as soon as the timeline is over.
- Osmotic communication means that information flows into the background hearing of members of the team, so that they pick up relevant information by osmosis. In osmotic communication, the information flow happens at the same time to all stakeholders and people pick the relevant information required, answer the relevant question for which they know the answer, and ask questions if any to clarify the doubts.
- **Minimal Marketable Future (MMF):** MMF is the basis minimum feature of the product so that people can start using it rather than waiting for all the futures. There will be a release after minimal marketable futures gets created. It actually enables incremental delivery of the product. Multiple MMF makes the whole product. MMF has value to the end user on its own.
- In agile project, the requirements are maintained in the forms of epics, features and user stories. Epics are collections of features, typically 1–3 months duration. Features are smaller than epics, typically executed in 2–4 weeks in duration. User stories are the smallest increment of value (created from feature) typically executed less than a week.
- Sprint is a time-boxed iteration cycle within which the team works with a list of requirement with an aim to produce working software at the end of the iteration.
- Scrum product owner is a customer representative (preferably) with highest business knowledge who can prioritize the requirements based on the business value.
- Scrum master connects the team with the management and ensures that the team is able to progress smoothly throughout the iteration cycle by helping them removing the impediments.
- Team is a group of people doing the actual work for the project creating the potentially shippable product at the end of the sprint.

- Unlike traditional project delivery models where the detailed plan is baselined before the start of work in the project, the approach that agile projects take is more like evolving the plan over time. Also the project monitoring and tracking approach is quite different from the traditional model as more focus is given in making the progress information available to the stakeholder and making the team self-organized so that they can correct the problems themselves. This chapter discusses the concepts of adaptive planning, progressive elaboration, user story, agile planning, time boxing, agile contracting, agile project tracking using the information radiators, such as burn up chart, burn down chart, Kanban board, the importance of retrospective, and how innovation games can improve the quality of retrospectives.
- Adaptive planning/rolling wave planning/progressive elaboration is a multi-step, intermittent process of planning which is based on the philosophy that the plan can be detailed out only as more details are revealed with time and with the changing scenario in the project.
- User story describes what the user does with the software and how the software responds. A user story is a functional requirement that resembles a use case and test case.
- Burn charts is the pictorial representation of the remaining work for an iteration or release which can be used to predict whether all the tasks can be completed for the iteration with the current pace.
- Task/Kanban board displays the status of various works over different stages. A look at the Kanban board indicates the progress and also how much work needs to be done further.
- Retrospectives–The iteration retrospective is an important mechanism that allows a team to continuously evolve and improve through the life of a project.

Model Questions
PART A (Objective type)

1. All the projects are moving from traditional project management to agile project management.

A. True B. False

Answer: B

2. All of the following are agile methods except

A. Scrum

B. Continuous integration

C. Crystal methods

D. Lean software developments

Answer: B

3. Agile project is more suitable in uncertain environment

A. True B. False

Answer: A

4. Agile manifesto talks about—values and—principles applicable for agile projects.

A. 4, 12 B. 12, 4 C. 4, 5 D. 6, 12

Answer: A

5. Daily standup meeting happens in

A. Any period as per the team wish | B. Less than 15 min
C. More than 15 min | D. More than 1 h

Answer: B

6. Choose the correct agile philosophy as per agile manifesto

A. Individuals and interactions over processes and tools
B. Working software over following a plan
C. Responding to change over comprehensive documentation
D. Stop all project work until the issues if any is resolved

Answer: A

7. All of the following are examples of agile methodology except

A. DSDM   B. TDD   C. Scrum   D. RADD

Answer: D

8. Agile is based on

A. Only iterative model
B. Only incremental model
C. Iterative and incremental model
D. Neither iterative nor incremental model

Answer: C

9. Which role is responsible for prioritizing features according to market value in scrum methodology ?

A. Scrum master | B. Product owner
C. Team | D. Agile coach

Answer: B

10. Which role shields the team from external interferences in an agile project?

A. Scrum master | B. Project leader
C. Project manager | D. Stakeholders of the project

Answer: A

11. Who is responsible for enacting agile values and practices in an agile project?

A. Scrum master | B. Project team member
C. Customer | D. End user

Answer: A

12. Which of the following is the best approach for determining the iteration (time box) length in agile projects?

A. Iterations (time boxes) should always be 4 weeks
B. The team calculates iteration (time box) length by dividing the total number of story points by the average velocity of the team

C. Ideal Iterations (time boxes) is 2 weeks

D. The team will consider the size and complexity of the project into and should agree on the length of the iteration (time box) through discussion

Answer: D

13. Which of the statements best represents the Agile's approach toward planning?

A. Everything is ad hoc, there is no scope for planning in agile

B. Planning should be done in detail at the beginning of the project and then not to be revisited

C. Planning is an iterative job and should involve the whole team

D. Planning is done by the project manager and the team members follow the plan

Answer: C

14. Why the presence of customer representative made mandatory in agile projects?

A. The customer representative is the main judge for business value

B. The project leader should build rapport with the customer representative

C. The customer representative can dictate the project plan

D. Customer representative acts as project manager controlling the project

Answer: A

15. Which statement below is true regarding an agile approach?

A. Get something as quickly as possible without thinking about quality

B. Get something simple up and running as quickly as possible

C. Get business-values delivered as quickly as possible, consistent with the right level of quality

D. Even half-done items can be delivered and approved

Answer: C

16. What is a Kanban?

A. A list of activities that should be banned for the team

B. The set of values defined for a project

C. A visible chart of work for the team for tracking purpose

D. A ban on team meetings

Answer: C

17. While creating the release plan for a project, the team is exploring the basic minimum features of the product so that people can start using it rather than waiting for something else. What is this set of features called?

A. Minimum marketable feature B. Product backlog

C. Sprint backlog D. Basic feature list

Answer: A

18. Which of the below is not a part of the 3Cs of user story?

A. Card B. Conversation C. Confirmation D. Collocation

Answer: D

19. In terms of size what is the ordering of the below items from biggest to smallest?

A. Epic, Theme, Story
B. Theme, Story, Epic
C. Story, Theme, Epic
D. These are not related at all

Answer: A

20. Which of the below statement best describes the benefit of WIP limit?

A. Helps in avoiding the piling up of tasks at a particular stage
B. Makes developers freely choose tasks
C. Makes the testing more robust
D. Limits the product backlog size

Answer: A

21. In a user story card where are the acceptance criteria documented?

A. At the front of the card
B. At the back of the card
C. In a separate document
D. This is not important information to capture

Answer: B

22. Agile principle strongly recommends daily standup meeting as this helps in

A. Surfacing the problems early
B. Keeping the team together
C. Making the team disciplined
D. As status meeting for the project manager

Answer: A

28. An agile team is working in a workspace where the big information radiators are kept on the walls. What is this type of workspace called?

A. Closed workspace
B. Agile workspace
C. Ideal workspace
D. Informative workspace

Answer: D

29. What is the method of addressing the issue of too many WIP items?

A. Burn down chart
B. Burn up chart
C. WIP limits in a Kanban system
D. Feature Kanban board

Answer: C

30. Following are the colors used in crystal methodology except

A. Maroon
B. Black
C. Red
D. Yellow

Answer: B

31. Following are the phases of scrum methodology

A. Pregame, development phase and post-game.
B. Pre-project, project life cycle, post-project
C. Inceptions, elaboration, construction, transition
D. Initiation, planning, execution

Answer: A

32. Following are the phases of AUP methodology

A. Pregame, development phase and post-game.

B. Pre-project, project life cycle, post-project

C. Inceptions, elaboration, construction, transition

D. Initiation, planning, execution

Answer: C

33. A list of known requirements in scrum on which team is going to work in the current iteration is called

A. Sprint backlog B. Release backlog

C. Product backlog D. Functional requirement

Answer: A

34. In scrum methodology a period of work is called as (choose the one most appropriate)

A. Time box B. Sprint

C. Iteration D. Story point

Answer: B

35. Concept of high speed, high change, high uncertainties is the characteristics of

A. Scrum B. XP

C. Crystal D. Traditional project management

Answer: B

36. Different types of Kanban are

A. Production Kanban, WIP Kanban

B. Production Kanban, deposit Kanban

C. Production Kanban, withdrawal Kanban

D. Kanban 1, Kanban 2

Answer: C

37. In FDD methodology, the features to be built are small aspects of client valued functionality and that is expressed in the form of

A. <action> <result> <object> B. <action> <object> <result>

C. <object> <result> <action> D. <object> <action> <result>

Answer: A

38. Choose the order of projects life cycle parts of DSDM

A. Foundation, Feasibility, Exploration, Engineering and development.

B. Feasibility, Foundation, Exploration, Engineering and development.

C. Feasibility, Foundation, Engineering, Exploration and development.

D. Feasibility, Foundation, Exploration, Development and Engineering.

Answer: B

39. Scot Ambler summarized AUP as

A. "serial in large, iterative in small, delivering incremental release over time."

B. "serial in small, iterative in large, delivering incremental release over time."

C. "serial in large, iterative in small, delivering documents over time."

D. "serial in large, iterative in small, delivering product at the end."

Answer: A

40. Kanban uses the following system

A. Push system　B. Pull system

C. Interactive system　D. Hub and spoke system

Answer: B

41. Choose the right order of process in FDD

A. Build the features list, develop an overall model of the system, plan by feature, design by feature, build by feature

B. Develop an overall model of the system, build the features list, plan by feature, design by feature, build by feature

C. Develop an overall model of the system, plan by feature, build the features list, design by feature, build by feature

D. Build the features list, plan by feature, design by feature, build by feature, and develop an overall model of the system

Answer: C

42. Which methodology recommends writing the automated unit test first before writing the code?

A. FDD　B. TDD　C. AUP　D. DSDM

Answer: B

43. Following is a type of TDD

A. 3 A Model　B. 3 C Model　C. 3 B Model　D. 6 P Model

Answer: A

44. 3 A model of TDD stands for

A. Act, Arrange, Assert　B. Arrange, Act, Assert

C. Assert, Act, Arrange　D. Assert, Arrange, Act

Answer: B

45. Following are the phases of adaptive project framework except:

A. Version scope　B. Cycle plan　C. Cycle build　D. Verify scope

Answer: D

46. XP uses the following model

A. INVEST model　B. SMART model　C. INSPIRE model　D. INDUCT model

Answer: C

47. INSPIRE model of XP stands for

A. Initiate, Speculate, Incubate, Review

B. Independent, Small, Initiate, Review

C. Iterative, Sprint, Integrative, Review

D. Independent, Negotiable, Small, Pair, Integrative, Relative

Answer: A

48. Prioritizing the requirement is happening in which phase of INSPIRE model

A. Initiate B. Speculate C. Incubate D. Review

Answer: B

49. Assigning resources is happening in which phase of INSPIRE model

A. Initiate B. Speculate C. Incubate D. Review

Answer: C

50. Re-prioritizing the requirement is happening in which phase of INSPIRE model

A. Initiate B. Speculate C. Incubate D. Review

Answer: D

51. The meaning of Kanban

A. Signs board B. Information board

C. Message board D. Action board

Answer: A

52. Which agile methodology is being indicated by "customer pulls out what he wants from the supplier. Supplier just supplies what the customer wants."

A. DSDM B. AUP C. Scrum D. Kanban

Answer: D

53. Lightest project in crystal is denoted by

A. Maroon B. Red C. Orange D. Crystal clear

Answer: D

PART B (Answer in one or two lines)

1. List down any three agile methodologies you are aware of.
2. What is adaptive planning?
3. What are the points discussed in daily scrum meeting.
4. Mention the four values as defined in agile manifesto.
5. What are the main elements of a user story?
6. What is the difference between a burn down and a burn up chart?

7. Write notes on time-boxing element of agile.
8. Explain AUP methodology in detail.
9. Explain DSDM methodology in detail.
10. Write notes on pair programming concept.
11. Write notes on re-factoring in agile projects.
12. Write notes on servant leadership.

PART C (Descriptive type)

1. List down various limitations of waterfall methodology.
2. Explain the difference in approach for the traditional software development and agile software development.
3. Write down the values of agile as defined in agile manifesto and explain in detail.
4. Explain how adaptability, visibility, value, and risks taken care in agile projects.
5. Explain generic agile project life cycle in detail.
6. Explain TDD in detail

26

Case Studies on Software Engineering Practices

CHAPTER COVERAGE

Case Study 1
Case Study 2
Case Study 3
Case Study 4
Case Study 5

CASE STUDY 1: SOFTWARE PROJECT MANAGEMENT LIFECYCLE - A PRODUCT DEVELOPMENT CASE STUDY

The Project at a Glance

Customer Name: BigLeap Corp.
Customer Domain: Commercial IT Products
Location / Country: USA/Japan/India
Type of Project: Product Development
Team Size: 35 (Refer Figure 26.1 for team structure)
Project Duration: 12 Months

About the Customer: (For e.g. products/services, turnover, market position, geographic locations, etc.)

The customer BigLeap Corp. has presence in the IT products space and currently they offer products for manufacturing automation. One of their products is TrueDoc which is a distributed Document management application to automate the process of publishing content to multiple websites of the client in multiple languages.

Technical Overview: (Technology used: Hardware, Operating Systems, Tools, Database, Server and Language.)

Client

- Purpose – Enter required Information
- Software – IE 5.x, Netscape
- Operating System – Windows

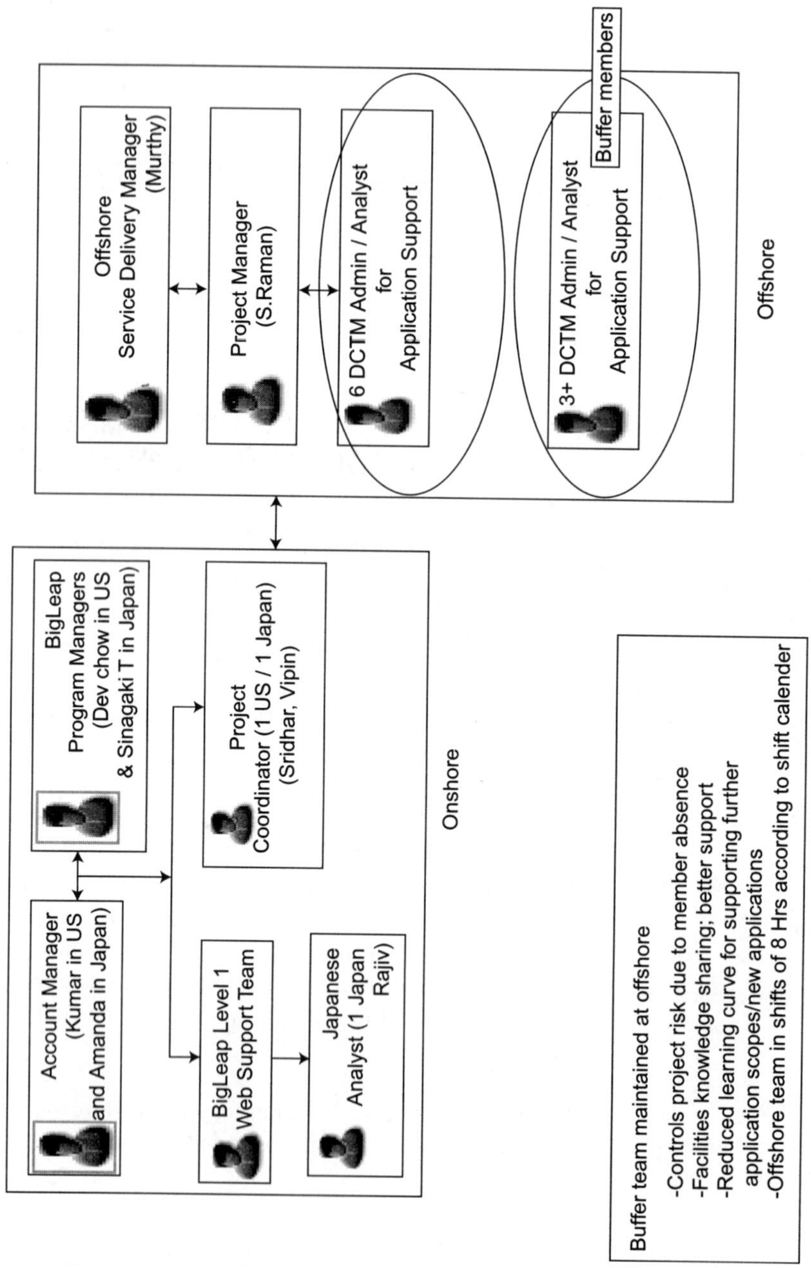

Figure 26.1 Project Team Structure

Web Server

- Purpose – Handles HTTP request
- Software –Apache
- Operating System – Windows Server

Application Server

- Purpose – Deploy application components Use container provided services for application development
- Software – WebLogic / Websphere
- Operating System – Windows Server

Database Server

- Purpose – Persist Application Data
- Software – Oracle 9i
- Operating System – Windows Server

Rule Engine

- Purpose – To execute business rules on data
- Software – JBoss Rules

Business Problem: (Customer's Business problem/Need for improvement, existing business situation, existing technology)

The product is an initiative by which the customer can help address the pain areas in the Automotive Sales and Marketing Space: End Customer Warranty and Concern Management. For top manufacturers, warranty costs 3-5 % of revenue. This is a big bite in the revenue keeping in mind the dip in sales that some of the global manufacturers are facing. Failures during the warranty phase also erode the brand value. Early Detection and Correction of problems identified through Warranty data will help reduce the defect rectification time cycle and in turn reduce warranty costs.

The development and support of this product encompasses

- A Database of reusable technical, marketing, and internal content (using Documentum/ SmartSearch)
- An External "Regionalized" Web site
- Secured Extranet(s) for partners (Sales Reps, Distributors, etc.) and large customers
- Intranets for BigLeap employees
- FAQ Database
- Global Registration System
- Web Metrics and Analytics
- BigLeap Repository

The technical architecture consists of 2 data centers.

- The primary (master) data center is located in Tokyo Japan.
- The secondary data center is located in San Jose, California, USA.

Each data center has been configured in the same manner from a hardware perspective.

The client has the stated the following project success criteria which need to be considered while planning and executing the project:

- Project customer satisfaction should be more than 4 on scale of 1–5
- Delivery of all the deliverables within time
- Should meet the service levels mentioned in RFP
- There should not be any Critical and High Open defects in the system
- Profitability should be minimum 40%

Step by Step approach to Solution: (Scope: 1) Customer's Business Applications addressed 2) the services delivered; for e.g. Development (full or partial), support, operations etc. Overview of the solution proposed to customer).

The project team started the project lifecycle with the **Initiation** phase and then went into **Planning** stage. The **Execution** and **Monitoring** process started after that.

Project Initiation

- What preparation was made for a smooth project initiation?

During this phase team defined the scope of the project (Refer Figure 26.2) and also estimated the amount of money needed to cover all costs - considering not only the ones that exist at the very beginning of the project but also the ones that appear at the later points of time. This means team ensured that the project won't fail because of lack of money at any critical juncture.

Also during this phase team calculated the risks and the probability of occurrence of those risks (Refer Figure 26.3) and ensured that they have a backup plan that we might use in case of need. Simply knowing the risks don't mean being ready for them, but a proper risk mitigation plan was important.

Project Charter - a formal document providing authority to the project manager to conduct a project within scope, quality, time and cost and resource constraints as laid down in the document. The primary outputs of this initiation phase were:

1. Project charter released
2. Risk identified
3. KickOff presentation presented

Project Planning

The planning phase is a very important part of a project. During this phase a primary objective is to identify and assign the tasks until the end of the project. These tasks will be given to team members according to skills and also preferences.

1. Software Project Plan (SPP) to be released
2. Tailoring Guidelines to be prepared
3. Business continuity planning (BCP) to be prepared

The Project Plan was communicated to the customer thru mail and team got the formal signoff. This has helped the BigLeap team and the client to understand the way they work together for this Project.

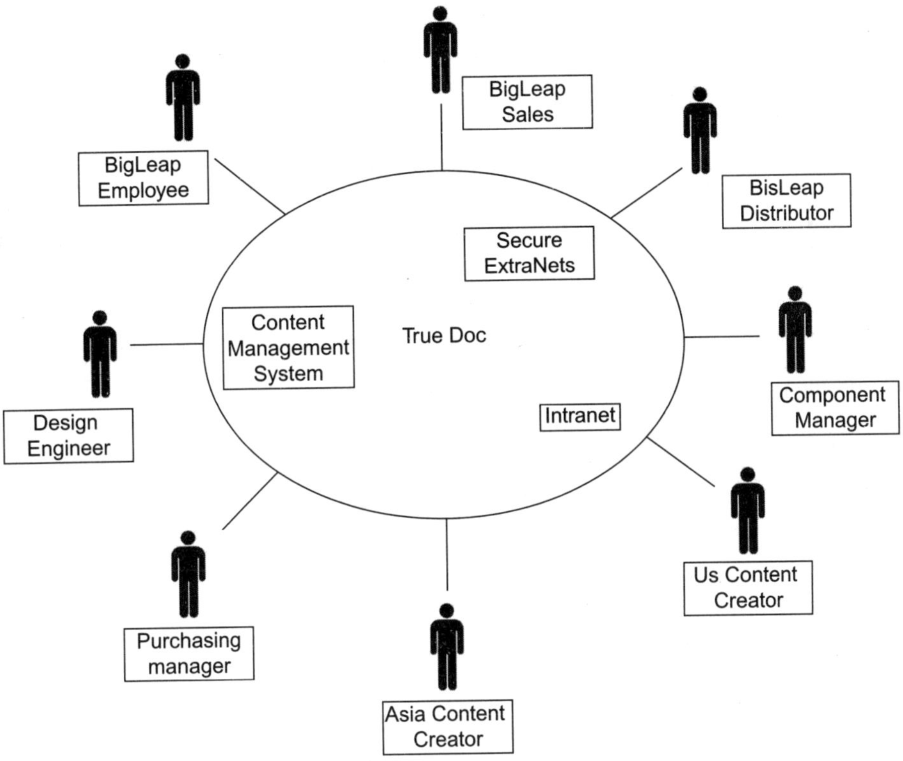

Figure 26.2 Stakeholder Distribution for BigLeap

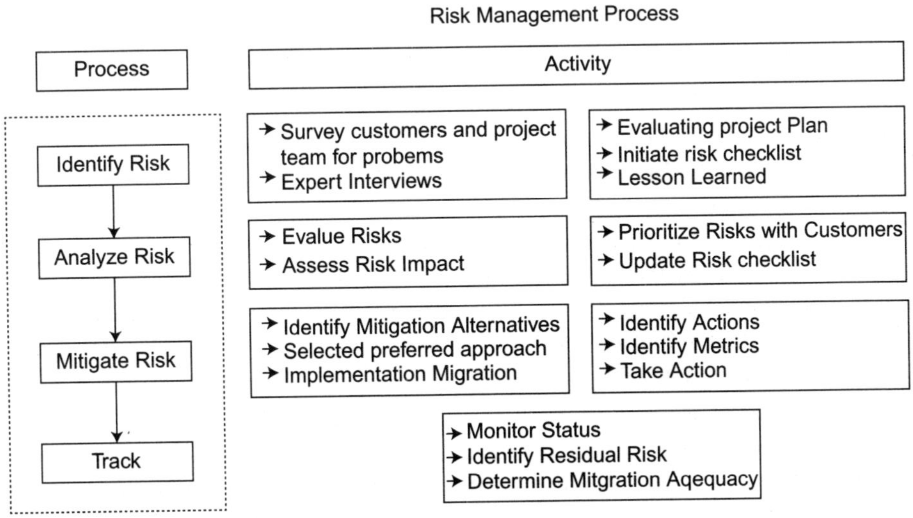

Figure 26.3 How the Project Managed the Risks

The overall Project estimation (effort, cost, and billing) was appropriate because of the involvement of the Project manager who knows the domain well at the early stage itself.

Risk Response Planning

- Developing options and determining actions to enhance opportunities and reduce threats to the project objectives.
- Inputs: Prioritized list of quantified risks, list of potential responses, risk owners and thresholds.
- Tools: Avoidance, mitigation, acceptance, transference.
- Output: Risk Response Plan + Contingency Plans/reserves required for the project

Here is the risk management process followed by the BigLeap team:

Organization structure and Resource Planning

Team requirements were identified and documented with Roles and Responsibilities which brings the input at the start of every task:

- Skills needed?
- Individuals identified?
- When are they needed?
- Where are they?
- Training needed?
- Interpersonal compatibility?

Basic Elements of the Control System

- A project plan: Scope, schedule, estimates
- A monitoring system which measures performance against plan
- A reporting system which identifies deviations from the plan
- A system which communicates deviations to the right people
- Corrective actions
- Forecasting the project outcome
- Cost: who/when/how often
  - How well were this tracked and the corrective actions taken?

  Cost control is done by the Project manager along with the help of RBU Japan Unit. Project Manager maintains a Costing Form which is getting shared with RBU Japan team and they will take appropriate action (raising the invoice) based on that.
- Schedule: who/when/how often
  - How well did this work?

  Schedule is defined and negotiated with the client for the enhancements. This is done by the Project Manager. This happens for every Request we receive. Period of Change Request depends on the End Client. At least one CR for a month. For Normal day-to-day activities the SLAs are defined clearly in the contract. If any tasks were not able to finish within SLA, after solving the ticket the team has to get the consent of the Client.

What steps were taken to bring customer involvement as per plan?

- Developed good Communication
- Ensure Timely Participation on issues
- Included the Customer on the Project Team thru the Process defined
- Developed Trust and Confidence

Detailed Process Function

- With the help of the Client, BigLeap's Business analyst identifies the requirement and functional requirement document is generated.
- Full information of functional and high level technical requirements is sent to the offshore team.
  - If the Requirement is not clear in understanding then the same shall be discussed and Offshore Project Manager and Client mutually agrees to a Negotiated Start and End dates.
  - Feedback (questions/doubts), if any, on requirements to be provided to client to be discussed if required.
- Unit and system testing is to be done based on the test criteria as defined
  - Test Cases shall be realistic considering that testing is to be done on local server or Development server.
  - Unit Test & System test will be performed only where the data is properly.
- Code review at offshore will be performed to check the quality (offshore internal process).
- Developers submit deliverables to offshore PM.
- Perform Delivery Inspection. The deliverables are checked at offshore to ensure that it meets the quality level. (To make sure that the code is error free and satisfies the Design and follows standards).
- Delivery. Offshore Project Manager sends the deliverables to the Client.
- Feedback from client is mandatory.
- Client acceptance process:
- Client on receiving the delivery informs the offshore team about its status.
- Status indicates confirmed against completed (written by offshore) if accepted by client and not completed if not accepted by client.
- Project plan indicates % completion against each delivery.
- If not accepted, a feedback with details of issues will be sent back to Offshore Project Manager along with the task and/or discussed and offshore team will rectify the task and will resend it to the client.
- Offshore team maintains all proper documentation (forms/docs/specs/ sign-off forms etc.) of all the offshore tasks.
- Documentation shall be for off shore's internal purposes only.

Did product meet customer acceptance criteria?

Customer's acceptance criteria got defined in the SOW & the deliveries has to fall within SLA.

All the deliverables were within SLA defined. The report is getting shared across all stake holders every month end.

Performance Against Budget

Number of Resource at Offshore = 6
Number of Language coordinator = 1
Number of Resource at Onsite = 2
Total Revenue for one month = $ 51100 (4100*6 + 6500 + 10000*2)

Salary cost estimated for offshore = $4 /hr
Salary cost estimated for Onsite = $31/hr
So Total Salary cost estimated offshore per month = (756*6) = $4536
So Total Salary cost estimated offshore per month=(4960*3) = $14880
Total Salary Cost = $19416

Total Revenue Estimated = $51100
Salary Cost = $19416
Communication cost(2.5%) = $1277
Work Station(263*6) = $1578
Contingency(10%) = $2254
Total Cost Estimated = $24525
Profitability Expected = 52%

Best Practices: (Any new or innovation on existing process/practice/tools designed or a new methodology/process adopted that increased the project efficiency. A 'best practice' that could be replicable across different projects in different scenarios.)

Risk Management

- Identifying relevant risks
- Deciding on the right threshold using the Risk contingency provided.

Quality Assurance

- Defects to be mapped to one root cause for effective prevention.

Communication

- Communicate effectively by all means.

Issue Management

- Identify the right issue to provide the right solution

Change Management

- Educate the customer/ team on formal change control process
- Put yourself in the customer's shoes.

Customer Involvement

- Involve the Customer throughout the project lifecycle.

Challenges Faced: (Challenges faced in project execution/program management challenges.)

1. Lack of technology
   - This was overcome using KT process within team
2. Maintaining existing code
   - Complete testing cycle not followed.
   - No formal regression techniques used.
3. Problems in new code
   - Q/A not part of code construction.
   - No source code reviews.
   - Even though organizations are CMM certified, e.g. level 4, but do not follow rudimentary coding practices.
4. Release Management is not there
   - Development & QA environment
   - Change Management Board
5. Pending Tickets – review meetings not conducted
6. Multiple channel for Prioritization to be streamlined
7. Multiple channels for reporting to be tied up
8. Complete Project Management tool for tracking is not there

Benefits to the Customer: (Immediate as well as long term benefits. Quantifiable as well as intangible benefits.)

- Reduced IT intervention due to changing Warranty Policies.
- Manual Effort needed to process claims is reduced by using a Rule Based Engine
- Completes the warranty life cycle by interacting with Finance, Parts and Dealer Management Systems
- Interfaces with limited functionality for Dealers
- Timely detection of problems by analyzing data from various sources including Customer Complaints
- Improved Project Management Framework for managing problem resolution
- Effective Knowledge Repository helps in avoiding re work while maintaining security
- The product facilitates physical parts retrieval and tracking between the dealers and the Manufacturer
- Product generates TREAD Act Reports from Warranty and Field Analysis Data
- Initiation and Management of Recalls
- An effective administration module to manage the entire product
- The product will seamlessly integrate with other Rule Engines in the marketplace.

Case Study questions

1. Discuss about the Project planning part in a development project?
2. Discuss how the financial part of the project is controlled?
3. How can we overcome the challenges described above?
4. Discuss the benefits received by the customer vis-a-vis what is planned.
5. What are the best practices we learnt from this project?
6. Discuss the benefit of the organization structure that this team has followed.

CASE STUDY 2: MAINTENANCE PROJECT CASE STUDY – LIFECYCLE AND HOW IT IS MANAGED

The Project at a Glance

Customer Name: A Large Global Bank
Customer Domain: Banking
Location / Country: Global
Type of Project: Maintenance
Team Size: 120
Project Duration: On going 3 yrs completed

About the Customer: (For e.g. products/services, turnover, market position, geographic locations, etc.)

Large Global Bank, 120 Full Time Employees supporting 100+ applications since 2010
Handling ~40,000 Incident tickets in a year with 24*7 support model through L1/L2/L3 services
Approx. $1.3 MN savings delivered through Continuous Service Improvement and Transformation programs in the last 3 years

Technical Overview: (Technology used: Hardware, Operating Systems, Tools, Database, Server and Language.)

Unix, Sun OS; Autosys, Oracle, Tibco Messaging, Tibco Hawk, HP Service Center, Java, Swing, J2EE, Struts

Business Problem: (Customer's Business problem/Need for improvement, existing business situation, existing technology)

1. Need for strategic partner providing Level 1,2 and 3 support to its client facing applications
2. Over 100 application in-scope covering functional areas:
3. Single vendor handling multiple application
4. Single view of the system for the customer is expected

Key Asks from the Customer:

1. Estimation Accuracy
2. Build SMEs Quickly

3. Quicker turnaround of Product defects
4. Proper utilization of team

Step by Step approach to Solution: (Scope: 1) Customer's Business Applications addressed 2) the services delivered; for e.g. Development (full or partial), support, operations etc. Overview of the solution proposed to customer.)

The steps followed in executing the maintenance project activities are as below

1. Preventive Maintenance: Repair of any application issues to minimize the risk of recurring problems
2. Adaptive Maintenance: Addressing application enhancement (routed to CTB Enhancements track)
3. Build and unit testing of Enhancements and defects for month on month release items
4. Provide support to SIT team and UAT
5. Provide support for Production implementation
6. Support Factory in tier II location
7. 24/7 support model
8. Complete ITIL adoption
9. Catalog based service delivery
10. Alternative pricing models

Continuous service improvement was proposed as part of the Solution

1. Transformation journey for existing customers
2. Service management integration
3. CMMi for Services

Pricing Assumptions

1. Revalidate estimation and price after 6 months, or the steady state
2. Every release work will be estimated and validated with the customers
3. Flexi team will be enabled through change order if there is additional scope to be delivered.
4. Onsite support teams will be provided with laptop and cell phones for performing on-call support as applicable.
5. The decrease in cost, year-on-year, is achieved by assuming increase in productivity and offshore leverage
6. All major enhancements will go through agreed quality gates and will have warranty of 60 days before handing over to support

Metrics used to track the project

1. Client Satisfaction Index (CSI)
2. Acknowledgement SLA Percentage for Closed Tickets

3. Resolution SLA Percentage for Closed Tickets
4. Backlog Management Index (BMI)

Governance Structure

To meet the stringent service level required by the customer, it was imperative that a strong governance structure (Refer Figure 26.4) is in place for this project. Also, because the client was initially skeptical about the offshoring of the applications, the project team had created regular connect calls with the client to make them aware of the progress and issues if any as early as possible.

Best Practices: (Any new or innovation on existing process/practice/tools designed or a new methodology/process adopted that increased the project efficiency. A 'best practice' that could be replicable across different projects in different scenarios.)

1. Metrics driven monthly reporting and updates
2. Introduce and implement application performance improvement
3. Perform Root Cause Analysis on Production Supports Incidents to suggest improvement in service levels
4. Free Code Review Tool : 70% of manual code review effort has been saved, Manual oversights during code review has been eliminated, Code quality improved
5. Automated Agent Monitoring tool used: Enhances the productivity of support team

Challenges Faced: (Challenges faced in project execution/program management challenges.)

1. Stringent Non Functional Requirements
2. Stringent SLAs

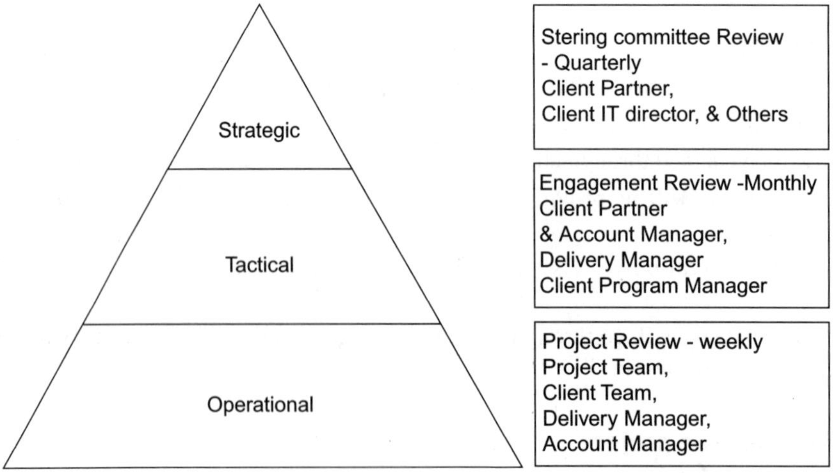

Figure 26.4 Engagement Governance Model

3. Aggressive timelines
4. Different release cycles such as quarterly, monthly, Weekly and sometime biweekly releases
5. Resource skilled with multiple technologies

Benefits to the Customer: (Immediate as well as long term benefits. Quantifiable as well as intangible benefits.)

1. Proactive initiative to automate, solve user pain-points and enable self-help
2. Advanced metrics reporting & tool based monitoring, Knowledge management
3. Managed service model
4. Improvement on application stability through continuous performance improvement initiatives & RCA for a permanent fix and lowering the ticket count
5. Productivity improvements through self-developed automated application monitoring tool
6. Significant reduction in outstanding number of incidents with lower operational costs.
7. Better Delivery Quality, Leverage Maintenance COE & QA capabilities

Case Study Questions

1. Discuss about ITIL Process and how it is useful for support and maintenance projects?
2. What is the meaning of L1, L2 and L3 support?
3. How can we overcome the challenges describes above?
4. Write notes on preventive maintenance with examples.
5. Discuss factors which determine maintenance cost
6. List down and discuss issues in Software maintenance

CASE STUDY 3: AGILE PROJECT CASE STUDY – HOW IT IS STRUCTURED AND EXECUTED

The Project at a Glance

Customer Name: Multinational Telecom
Customer Domain: Telecom
Location / Country: Multinational
Type of Project: Development
Team Size: 50
Project Duration: 3 week Sprints – 6 months

About the Customer: (For e.g. products/services, turnover, market position, geographic locations, etc.)

A big multinational telecom company having operations in 25 countries across Asia and Africa with over 250 million customers across its operations and is headquartered in Delhi, India. Company's product offerings include fixed wire line services, wireless services, Broadband services, ISP, MPLS-VPN and ISDN.

Technical Overview: (Technology used: Hardware, Operating Systems, Tools, Database, Server and Language.)

Interconnect Billing System: "Inter Trace" from Modula Suite of components
Reporting Tool: Business Objects (6.1)
RDBMS: Oracle
OS: Unix
Others (Web Portal): Java, JSP Servlets

Business Problem: (Customer's Business problem/Need for improvement, existing business situation, existing technology)

Given the multi-operator, multi-services telecom networks with operations all over the geography this customer was in need of a centralized system to process the interconnect usage Call Detail Record (CDR) and get the single view of flow of traffic. Further, the existing homegrown interconnect settlements system was not scalable to handle the large volumes interconnect CDRs and the frequently changing regulatory requirements of the Govt. Customer has floated a tender for inviting bids from System Integrators for a implementation of the mediation and CDR based Billing and Accounting System in an Application Service Provider (ASP) Bureau based model.

Customer wants to see the end product quickly. They were ready to work with the vendor team directly if required but wants to speed up the delivery. They were also having time pressure from the competitor and so wanted to reduce go to market duration.

Step by Step approach to Solution: (Scope: 1) Customer's Business Applications addressed 2) the services delivered; for e.g. Development (full or partial), support, operations etc. Overview of the solution proposed to customer.)

Agile project life cycle model - Scrum methodology was proposed for solving the business problem.

Why Agile scrum methodology was proposed and followed?

1. Customer wants to see the end product quickly
2. Time pressure from the competitor
3. To reduce go to market duration
4. To provide early value to the customer
5. Requirements were evolutionary keeping up with market demands.

Other solutions

1. Releases are time boxed
2. Three weeks iteration cycle followed.
3. Agile Center of Excellence provided training to client IT and business teams - Total of 50 people
4. Implemented an effective customized release and iteration planning.
5. Development team breaks the scope into multiple iterations and updates using Dev-track tool

6. High risk and high value items taken up in early iterations
7. Adaptive planning for each iteration focusing on top business priorities
8. Delivered a working software after every iteration
9. Demo of features/functionalities to stakeholders after every iteration

In Figure 26.5 you can see how the life cycle of the Agile project is different from a waterfall or iterative methodology based project. Lot of emphasis was given on the regular demo to the client and the continuous endeavor of the project team was to release the working software as early as possible. This benefitted the customer to a large extent as they started reaping the Return on Investment from the very early stage of the project.

Best Practices: (Any new or innovation on existing process/practice/tools designed or a new methodology/process adopted that increased the project efficiency. A 'best practice' that could be replicable across different projects in different scenarios.)

1. ASP Bureau Based Model (New Service Offering experience) followed
2. Network Roll Out & Design for data collection from approx. 700 Points of Customer (Technology)

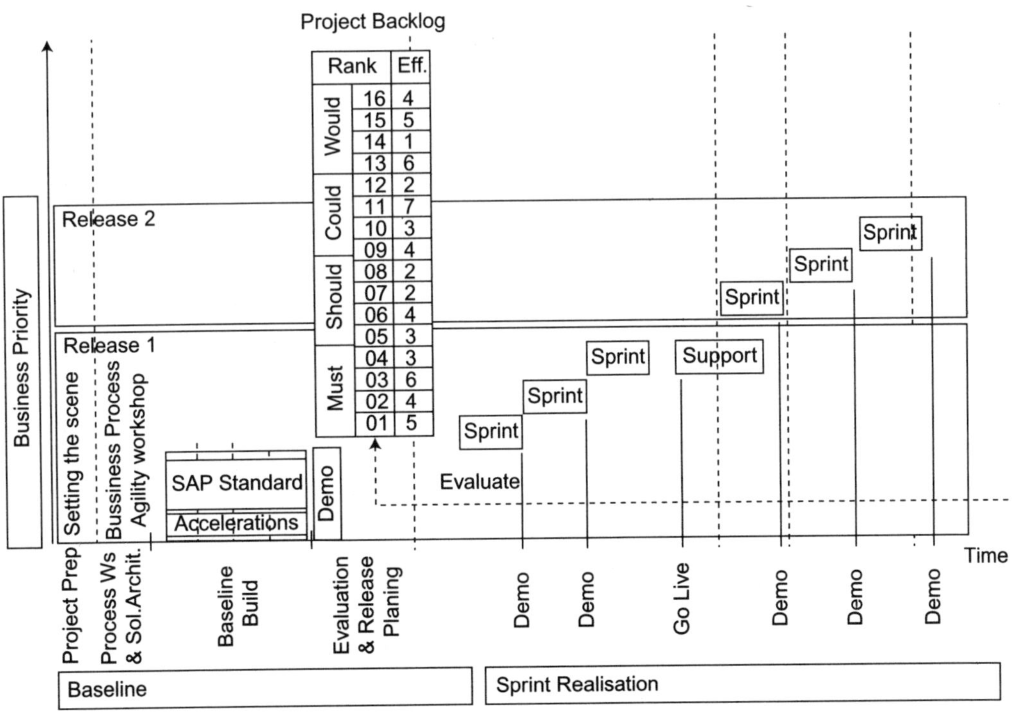

Figure 26.5 Project Structure

3. Automation of Data Reconciliation for end-end operations for an effective traceability of requirements
4. Continuous integration that helps identify problems early
5. Scrum of Scrums models to integrate multiple scrum team
6. Build, release and deployment activities done from Offshore
7. Framework and the necessary components are abstracted and refined iteratively (Code Refactoring)
8. Tool-based approach for the design and implementation processes.
9. For each Iteration, features are continuously integrated
10. Customer Subject Matter Experts co-located with the Dev team to support on clarifications

Challenges Faced: (Challenges faced in project execution/program management challenges.)

1. Program Management with Partners & Various field units of the customer was difficult
2. Aggressive implementation time frame and coordination with multiple points of contacts was difficult
3. Integration with legacy switches from 5 different technologies & other financial systems was difficult
4. Complex Interconnect scenarios and charging principles.
5. Availability of the POI PCs/Data on time during operations

Benefits to the Customer: (Immediate as well as long term benefits. Quantifiable as well as intangible benefits.)

1. Iterative, Incremental development while Architecture, Requirements and DB were still evolving facilitated early identification of issues and improvements thru feedback
2. With a working software the client could see value after every iteration

   Received early and continuous customer feedback which were translated into requirements, prioritized and taken up for Development
3. Processes followed were lightweight and value driven
4. Reduction of unplanned work
5. Framework facilitates consistency in code across modules
6. The framework is reusable by other products within the organization
7. Effective use of product knowledge to build a SME team at vendor side
8. Product went LIVE with Minimal Marketable Futures (MMFs)

Case Study questions:

1. What are all the other benefits given to the customer by following SCRUM methodology?
2. What are all the difficulties of following SCRUM Methodology?
3. Will any other agile methodology fit into this problem? If so why?

CASE STUDY 4: TESTING CASE STUDY – HOW THE TESTING METHODOLOGIES ARE USED IN A PROJECT

The Project at a Glance

Customer Name: Application Software Company
Customer Domain: Ecommerce, Mobile Applications
Location / Country: Multinational
Type of Project: Test Automation
Team Size: 4
Project Duration: 2 Months

About the Customer: (For e.g. products/services, turnover, market position, geographic locations, etc.)

A leading e-commerce solution provider that has years of experience in diverse areas to meet their clients business needs. The software solution provider develops the Online catalog for the client's products through Mobile Application, as well as Flash & HTML browser applications. The applications are supported for Android & IOS mobile phones as well.

The client is a home furnishings retailer, one of the world's largest designer and retailer of well-designed, inexpensive, and functional furniture for the home. The client is also a leading furniture company which sells flat-pack design furniture at affordable prices. They also sell accessories of bathroom and kitchen items in retails stores around the world.

Technical Overview: (Technology used: Hardware, Operating Systems, Tools, Database, Server and Language.)

Tools: Robotium, Ranorex, Selenium
Browsers: Mobile Browsers, Flash And HTML
OS: Windows, IOS, Android
Others(Web Portal): Java, JSP Servlets

Business Problem: (Customer's Business problem/Need for improvement, existing business situation, existing technology)

There were too many defects in the product that was getting in to the production system. The software provider had to ensure that relatively defect free code gets delivered every time. The testing team was small and unable to capture all the issues in the very limited time given to them for testing.

With over 500 manual test scenarios for one Mobile OS (i.e., Android, IOS) & for Flash & HTML Browser applications, the QA process for the Client's application was quickly becoming very challenging to maintain. The application was constantly growing (more features were added) and had to find a way to reduce testing times, increase the amount of test cases and improve the system quality overall without introducing more additional testing time.

Step by Step approach to Solution (Scope: 1) Customer's Business Applications addressed 2) the services delivered; for e.g. Development (full or partial), support, operations etc. Overview of the solution proposed to customer (Refer Figure 26.6).

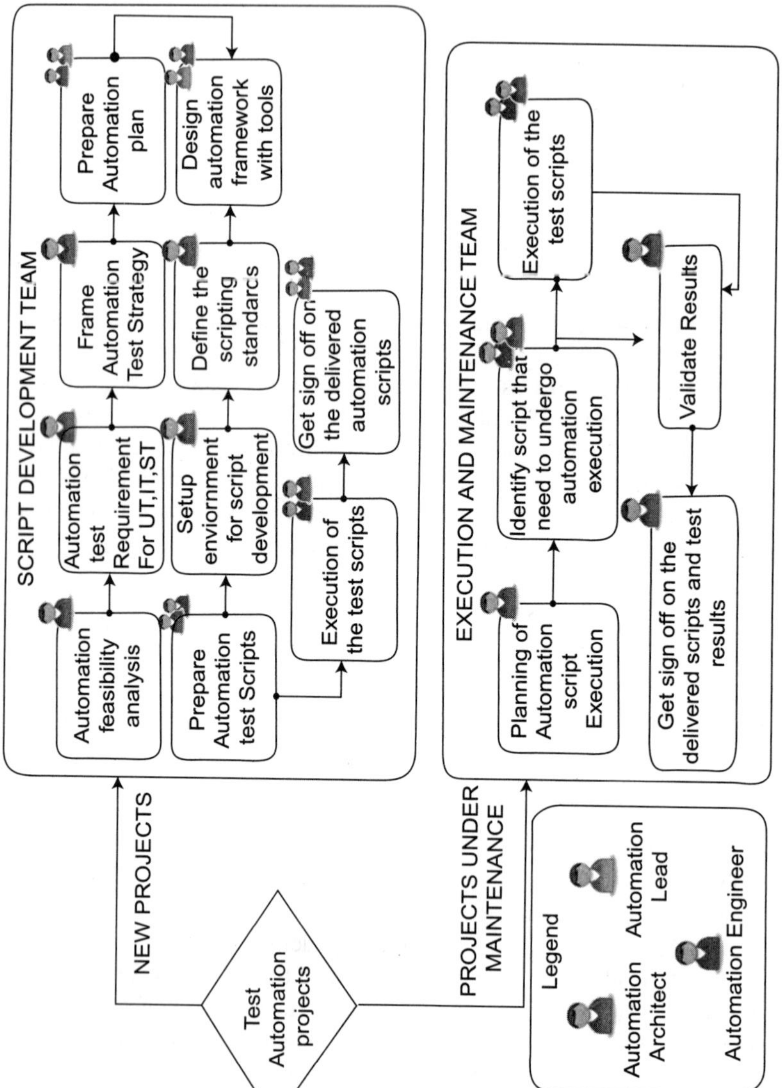

Figure 26.6 Work Flow and Team Structure

- Automation Testing needed to cover iOS, Android, HTML and Flash builds (Refer Figure 26.7)
- Build test lab with selected tools for testing almost all devises & Mobile OS
- Maintaining the testing environment to support all devices/ Mobile OS require different testing tools to support it
- Testing with Multiple devices and Mobile OS
- Multi devices connection and testing Wi-Fi/ Bluetooth combination
- Running the test on the device itself
- Controlling the test from a System / Computer
- Scripts should be reusable for testing the same device repeatedly
- Unit level testing to be done by development team, System Testing by QA team
- Screen Flow Test need to be automated

Best Practices: (Any new or innovation on existing process/practice/tools designed or a new methodology/process adopted that increased the project efficiency. A 'best practice' that could be replicable across different projects in different scenarios.)

1. Set up of process management guidelines for development and testing.
2. Ensure proper Design & Mock-up of screen documents & other supporting documents before starting the Project / New Requirements development.
3. Unit Testing to be done by Development team & need to provide the Release Notes to the QA team for each build released for testing. The QA team should NOT be doing the unit testing.
4. Test Automation to be implemented using appropriate tools wherever possible.
5. Standard template to be followed for design of the test cases. The test cases should cover the functional points, Test data, Navigations etc. in detail.
6. The Test results to be shared with Screenshot and the Test data used for testing the scenario with other detail information for both PASS & FAIL test cases.
7. Setup the Configuration Management process.

Challenges Faced: (Challenges faced in project execution/program management challenges.)

- Due to unavailability of some of the features in the application, 70% of the test scenarios in the selected 20% were obsolete.
- Individual scripts were written for the same functionality for different OS (Android & IOS).
- Objects referred in the script were changing frequently. Hence the written script would run for some time and later would fail due to unable to find the Object.
- Scripts were re- written when the Ranorex tool is upgraded from 4.1.5 to 5.0 version.
- For IOS application, deployment is working through USB & the testing needs to be done through Wi-Fi.
- Need to do the instrumentation for the Flash application before writing the script. Otherwise, Ranorex is not able to recognize the Objects.
- Due to requirement changes & Enhancements, Script design was stopped in between.

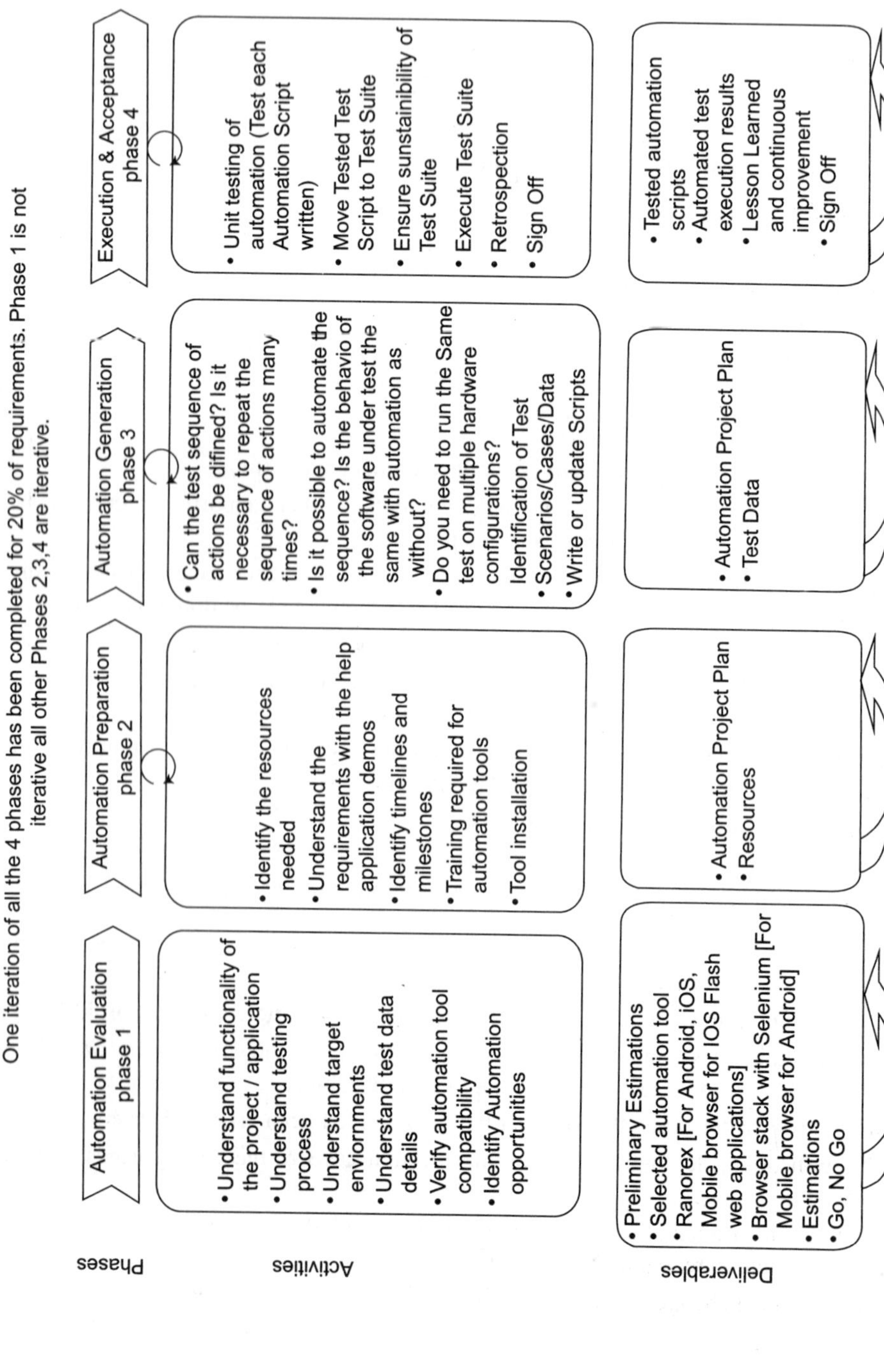

Figure 26.7 Test Automation Process

- Since the latest build was not provided in the initial stages, application was closed intermittently while doing the automation execution.
- Selenium-Browserstack base license is restricted to 8 hrs. /day. If the testing hours are more than either license need to be upgraded or the additional hours cost need to be paid.

Benefits to the Customer: (Immediate as well as long term benefits. Quantifiable as well as intangible benefits.)

- Helped the Client to reduce the test processing time by 40%, added hundreds of additional test cases without affecting schedules and keep test cycles under control.
- Provided the solution to automate the Smoke test scenarios during the 2 months period of time.
- No need to put extra effort for creating the test results & test report. Ranorex tool will provide the test results with the screenshots for each step.
- QA team can concentrate on the New / Manual test scenarios, since the automation script can be reused for different builds. It will reduce the QA team effort to test the same scenarios again and again.
- Due to Unit Test automation, more bugs can be identified at the development stage itself & the code with proper quality can be given to the QA team for testing.

Case Study questions

1. What is the business challenge addressed here by the ecommerce solution provider?
2. What are all the difficulties in implementing the test automation solution?
3. What were the benefits to the end client due to the Test Automation?
4. List at least 4 tools mentioned here for test automation along with their usage

CASE STUDY 5: SOFTWARE SDLC CASE STUDY

The Project at a Glance

Customer Name: Applied Technology
Customer Domain: Semiconductor Manufacturing
Location/Country: Bangalore, India
Type of Project: Development, Maintenance, Production Support
Technology Used: Lotus Notes 652
Team Size: Two (2)
Project Duration: Development: 3 months
Production Support: Till date

About the Customer: (For e.g. products/services, turnover, market position, geographic locations, etc.)

Applied Technology develops and manufactures the complex and rapidly changing technologies and equipment used to manufacture semiconductors–the engines that drive the Information Age.

Applied Technology' customers are located all over the world. The regions manage our customer relationships with more than 70 offices in 14 countries.

Applied Technology manufactures equipment that performs virtually all front-end semiconductor manufacturing processes, including plasma etch, dielectric chemical vapor deposition, physical vapor deposition, metal chemical vapor deposition, electrochemical plating, epitaxial deposition, ion implantation, thermal processing, chemical mechanical polishing, and metrology and inspection.

Technical Overview: (Technology used: Hardware, Operating Systems, Tools, Database, Server and Language.)

Hardware: Pentium IV Processor, 512 MB RAM.
Operating System: Windows XP
Tools and languages: IBM Lotus Domino v6.5.2, LotusScript, Formula Language and @commands.

Business Problem: (Customer's Business problem/Need for improvement, existing business situation, existing technology)

The basic need of the project is to automate the overall Engineering Change Order procedure. The functionalities involved earlier was time consuming and were not fulfilling the requirement. The basic idea was to integrate the other related process with the ECO update.

The situation required a process by which all the persons involved in an Engineering Change Order share the same platform to process a particular request. The database works in that direction. There are other related processes which were being incorporate to process an Engineering Change Request like SPS, ESW and Oracle database.

Challenges Faced: (Challenges faced in project execution/program management challenges.)

There are number of challenges which were experienced during the development phase at initial stages:

1. Due to the very demanding requirements of the customers the project team had to perform lot of analysis and research.
2. One of the main challenges was to get the automated charts and excel reports from the data listed in the Notes Database. There are various kinds of charts and reports are being generated which helps the client for their revenue tracking as well as man power incorporated, but the project team should discuss with the client which ones are necessary and focus on those only.

Benefits to the Customer: (Immediate as well as long term benefits. Quantifiable as well as intangible benefits.)

Customer got a workflow based application that was helping all the involved personnel to share a common platform and work together. The application allowed onsite and offshore individuals to work at the same time which saved lot of time.

The project created replicas of the same application across the globe so individual users had individual databases working for them. As a result, there was an application which incorporated other concerned processes and databases all together to speed up customer's individual process.

By making minor modification the application can be used for a long term with upcoming versions of Notes.

Step by Step approach to solution: (Process flow, team structure, etc.)

The SDLC process followed in this project was Waterfall model. Here are the different stages of the project (Refer Figure 26.8):

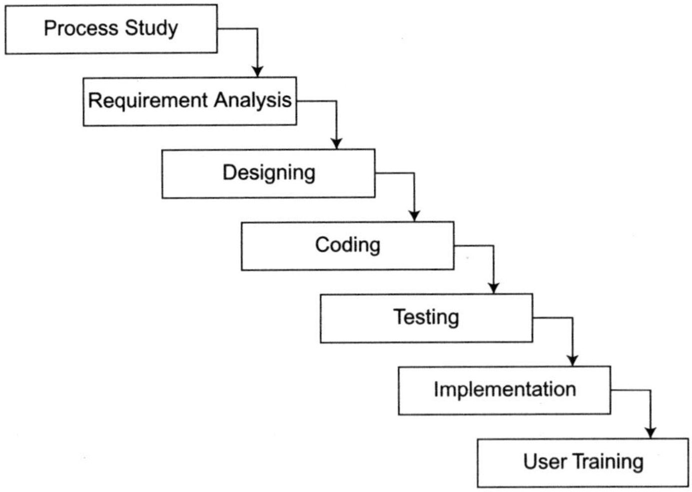

Figure 26.8 Project Lifecycle

Process Study:

To perform a process study on the Requirement and prepare user requirement document accordingly

Requirement Analysis:

To compare the new requirements with the existing ETCH ECR (Engineering Change Order Database) Design and identify and consolidate enhancement requests.

High Level Design:

To design system architecture. To discuss the architecture with Client IT team to review it based on the hardware constraints and finalizes the same.

Low Level Design:

To elaborate enhancement requests into changes needed in existing ETCH ECR Database Design. Forms, Lotus Notes and lotus notes classes to be created.

Development Schedule:

To make development plans and schedules. Discuss and finalize the same after discussions with project manager and developers.

Change Management:

Handle requirement changes, architecture and development issues that arise during the course of development. To discuss and finalize the changes and prepare change documents.

Database Administration:

To perform administrative activities including monitoring and troubleshooting Domino server for replication tasks and maintains user profiles in the application for customization.

User Training:

Prepare user training schedules and training content.

Best Practices: (Any new or innovation on existing process/practice/tools designed or a new methodology/process adopted that increased the project efficiency. A 'best practice' that could be replicable across different projects in different scenarios.)

There are number of procedures which are being used in the project like:

1. To get the employee details from the People Soft Database of Applied Technology. This is a standard practice and now being followed by some other databases as well.
2. To get the Documents from SPS and ESW databases. The SPS and ESW databases are being used in processing's of the Engineering Change Request. The procedure checks the status of SPS and ESW number inserted in the Engineering Change Request. Now a days the functionality have become a standard practices.
3. There is a unique feature in the database called New Releases. This feature notifies the entire user base about the new enhancements as well as makes them aware about the new functionalities incorporated. This feature has been highly appreciated by the client.
4. Last but not the least, Feedback process feature allows users to log any issues in the database. The issues logged in the processes are usually addressed to database manager. Developer as well as maintenance in charge personals. This feature has also been appreciated by client.

Case Study questions

1. Discuss what life cycle model was used in this project?
2. Can you name few other lifecycle models and discuss if any other model would have been useful for this project?
3. What are the different steps followed in this life cycle model?
4. Discuss the benefit of the organization structure that this team has followed.

Model Question Paper

PART A

(10 × 2 = 20)

1. What are the processes involved during the development of a software?
2. Define stakeholders.
3. What do you mean by requirement engineering?
4. Define architecture.
5. What is the need for modularity?
6. Define program management.
7. What is Quality Audit?
8. List any four advantages of WBS.
9. Define software risk.
10. What are the factors to be considered for writing test plan?

PART B (Descriptive type)

(5 × 16 = 80)

11. Explain spiral model for software engineering development.

    (or)

12. Write notes on Code Review.
13. Explain in detail about
    i) Requirements specification
    ii) User Interface Design basic concept and golden rules
14. Explain the following i) coupling ii) object oriented metrics

    (or)

15. Discuss key steps for SCM.
16. Explain different types of Requirements with example.
17. Explain waterfall model with neat diagram.
18. Explain back box testing and why it is important with an example.

    (or)

19. List and explain software re-engineering activities

Model Solved Question Paper

PART A

(10 × 2 = 20)

1. What are the processes involved during the development of a software?

Answer: Design
Analysis
Code
Testing
Maintenance

2. Define stakeholders.

Answer: People or entities (Organsiations) actively involved in the projects otherwise affected by outcome of the defined project are called as stakeholders.

3. What do you mean by requirement engineering?

Answer: Definition of requirement as is given in IEEE Std 610.12-1990: 'A condition or capability needed by a user to solve a problem or achieve an objective.' And 'A condition or capability that must be met or processed by a system or system component to satisfy a contract, standard, specification, or other formally imposed documents.'

4. Define architecture.

Answer: Software Architecture defines the logical relationship among the major structural elements of a system and also the relationship between corresponding components at high level in order to execute the functionalities of the overall system.

5. What is the need for modularity?

Answer: Possibilities of dividing a single project into smaller units which is termed as modules are called modularity of the project. It helps in designing the system in better way. Modularity ensures that each module communicates and does the specific task assigned to it. Modularity also helps in reusability and maintainability.

6. Define program management.

Answer: A program is a group of projects managed in a coordinated way to obtain benefits and control that would not have been achieved had the projects been managed separately. Program management focuses on project interdependencies and helps to determine the optimal approach for effectively managing them. An example of a program would be a new communications satellite system program which comprises the related projects for designing the satellite, constructing and integrating the individual systems, and launching the satellite.

7. What is Quality Audit?

Answer: A quality audit is the task of systematic examination of the effectiveness of a quality system carried out by a quality auditor or an audit team and is the key engine of a quality system. It is generally a scheduled task. Results of quality audits, along with quality control reports, form the basis of measuring the functioning of a quality assurance system.

8. List any four advantages of WBS.

Answer:

1. The components of a WBS assist stakeholders to readily view the deliverables of the project.
2. The process of establishing the WBS for a project often leads to important updates to the scope statement.
3. Because a WBS subdivides major project deliverables into manageable components, it serves to improve the quality of cost, time, and resources estimates.
4. A WBS provides a baseline for assigning responsibilities.

9. Define software risk.

Answer: The definition of risk is "A probability or threat of loss or any negative consequence which is caused by external or internal events and that may be avoided through preemptive action." This means there are two characteristics of the risk:

Uncertainty: the risk event may happen or may not happen. There is degree of uncertainty attached to event.

Loss: if the risk event occurs there will be certain losses incurred.

10. What are the factors to be considered for writing test plan?

Answer: The key factors that need to be considered in detail for the test plan are:

1. The important functionalities that the product should have to ensure its success.
2. The different testing techniques and tools that could be leveraged for testing the various product functionalities.
3. The various risk factors which need to be considered and their impact to the product.
4. The testability of the product and areas of the product which may not be testable.

PART B (Descriptive type)

(5 × 16 = 80)

11. Explain spiral model for software engineering development.

Answer: Spiral model is an evolutionary model proposed by Boehm that introduced the concept of risk analysis in the earlier stages of development process. Other name of Spiral model is Risk Spiral Model. This model combines the software development life cycle with Risk Management principles to control the risks at early stage of the project. Taking the importance of a risk management process and testing process into account, the spiral model defined new strategies of integrating the risk analysis at every incremental step of the lifecycle.

A spiral model encompasses the iterative steps in a spiral representation as shown in the figure. Each circle in the model denotes a succeeding level of the previous state. These are divided task regions which represents the selective process. The task regions may vary from the complexity level of different product.

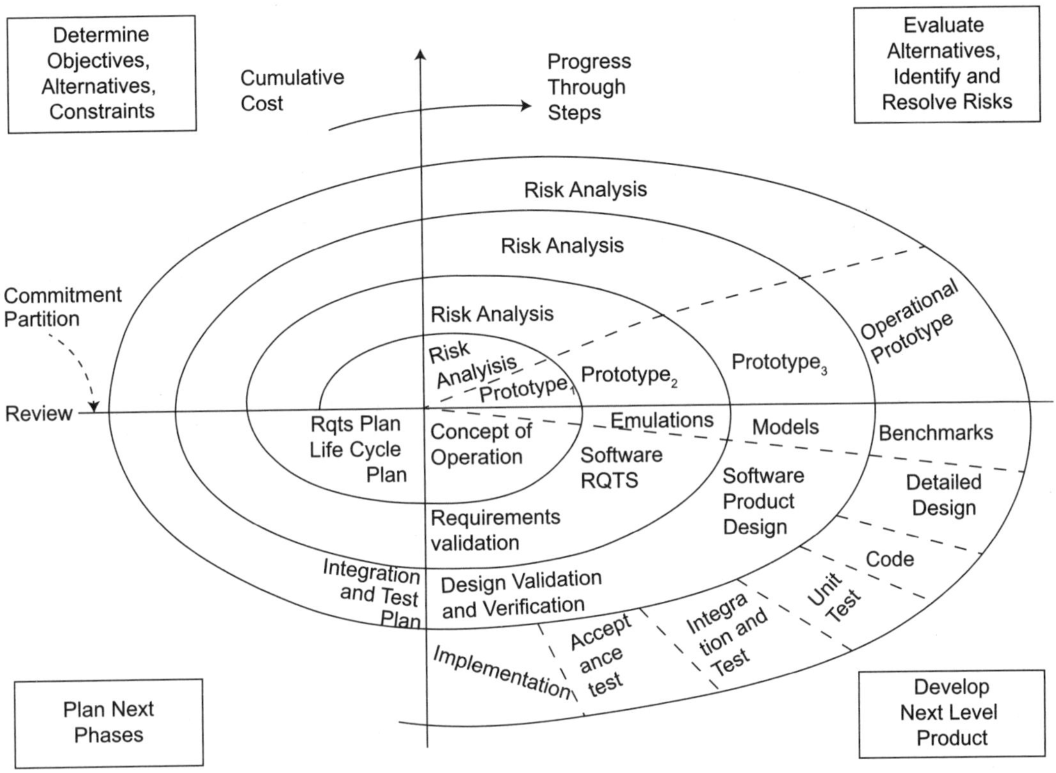

The planning part includes the tasks for designing an efficient framework as a solution to the objectives. Planning also happens in steps. Life Cycle Plan is prepared first. Development Plan is prepared in the next level; Integration Plan is prepared at the last level.

In the Risk Analysis Phase the prototype is being developed. The risk analysis would report the identification and effects of the present risks in the prototype. Assessments of risks at every rotation of the spiral evolution reduce the problems and time required for solving at the final stage. The risk analysis strategies have to be stringent enough such that even no small errors are left out. Prototyping, incremental and premature risks detection proves this method to be an efficient method over the other process models. Elimination of risks occurs in next iteration. The feedbacks from the customers are noted for updating the next prototype. The final prototype after stated suggestions is subjected to risk analysis process and is being developed.

Construction and release also happens in iterative fashion based on the base prototype developed. At every level it is also being strengthened and final level is the final code to be delivered to the Customer.

The number of iterations is determined by the team manager depending upon the rectifications made and completion of the product. The cost and schedule cannot be assumed right at the beginning phase as the prototypes are altered at every rotation. The team manager adjusts cost and time metrics after every circle.

Advantages:

- Risk reduction mechanisms are in place

- Supports iteration and reflects real-world practices
- Systematic approach

Disadvantages:
- Requires considerable expertise in risk evaluation and reduction
- Complex and relatively difficult to follow strictly
- Applicable only to large systems
- Risk assessment could cost more than development
- Need for further elaboration of spiral model steps (milestones, specifications, guidelines and checklists)

(or)

12. Write notes on Code Review.

Answer: Code review is a systematic process which is also called as peer review. This is used to find and fix the mistakes in the early phase of the coding and it helps to improve the code quality and improve the coding skills of the developers.

Code reviews happen in the form of
1. Formal Inspection
2. Light weight Code Review
3. Pair Programming
4. Automatic Code reviewing software

In the case of formal inspection, a review checklist is being used to review the code along with proper plan like scheduled time, duration of review, scope of review, coding standards etc. Multiple stakeholders take part in formal inspection process and the entire code set is being reviewed line by line. Most of the time the review happens in multiple iterations as it takes considerable time to go thru line by line. Formal inspection processes is thorough in nature and have been effective.

Lightweight walkthrough can happen at any point of time that is convenient to both the parties and no check list is being used here and the review happens on adhoc manner. It requires less overhead than the formal code review method. It is equally effective as formal review process if conducted properly. Lightweight processes are usually conducted as part of the development process.

In pair programming, the review happens simultaneously while the code is getting developed jointly as the coding the done by two programmers instead of one. Pair programming saves lot of time and reduces rework as the mistakes are identified at the early stage of coding itself.

Automatic code review software helps to the code review in more efficient manner where the code review is conducted with help of automated tools.

13. Explain in detail about

i) Requirements specification

Answer: The next step of requirement elicitation and analysis is called requirement specification where all the knowledge gathered in elicitation and analysis stage is documented in a clear, concise and unambiguous manner so that the design and development teams can use it going forward. While creating the requirement specification it is also important that the same is validated with the customers and users to demonstrate that customer's needs are really captured at this stage. Software Requirement Specification (SRS) is the outcome of this requirement specification and validation stage.

Once created Software Requirement Specification (SRS) document becomes the main source for any requirement clarification and dissemination to all stakeholders. There are several purposes that the SRS document can be used for:

- It may form the basis for the contractual agreement between the customer and the suppliers. The suppliers in an unambiguous fashion describe what will be developed as part of the project and thus any change in this agreed understanding will be re-negotiated between the customer and the suppliers.
- This is the foundation document for the test engineers to develop their strategy on how to test the proposed system fully.
- The design and development team start their work based on this document. As all the stakeholders think through what they need from the system and get it documented in the SRS, the chance of redesign or re-construction work gets minimized if the SRS is developed well.
- The resourcing, budgeting, scheduling and pricing for the project are based on the volume and complexity of the requirements captured in this document. The modern estimation techniques take direct input from the use cases and models developed in the SRS.
- A good SRS ensures that future maintainability of the project and enables the customer to switch to a different supplier during the maintenance phase of the project. The new supplier's team will use the SRS document as the primary artifact to understand the capabilities wanted by the stakeholders from the system and can validate that against the developed capabilities.

ii) User Interface Design basic concept and golden rules

User interface design creates an effective communication medium between a human (user of the system) and a computer. It proposes a set of interface design principles such that it identifies the objects and methods involved and then creates a screen layout that forms the basis for a user interface.

User Interface design focuses on three basic areas:

1. Interface between components of the system
2. Interface between the system and the humans (users)
3. Interface between the system and other system (non-humans)

According to Theo Mandel there are three "golden rules" in interface design:

1. Place the user in control.
2. Reduce the user's memory load.
3. Make the interface consistent.

14. Explain the following i) coupling ii) object oriented metrics

Answer: Coupling: Coupling is one of the characteristics considered for designing the modularity of projects. It is a measure of how tightly two entities or modules are related to each other. Coupling measures the strength of relationships between entities or modules. It is very easy to measure coupling both quantitatively and qualitatively.

There are many different ranges of coupling:

- Content coupling
- Common coupling
- Control coupling
- Stamp coupling
- Data coupling
- Uncoupled

In content coupling one component refers the content of another component and here the coupling is considered as higher. Example includes: Module 1 access the data of Module 2 and change it.

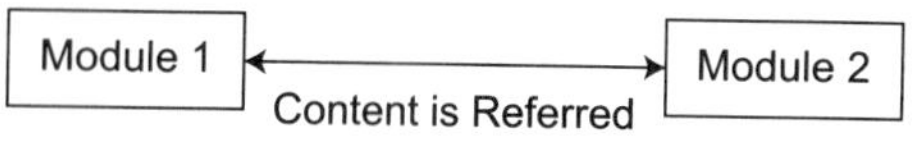

In Common coupling one or more module share the same data which is common in nature. This is an example of Bad design and is to be avoided.

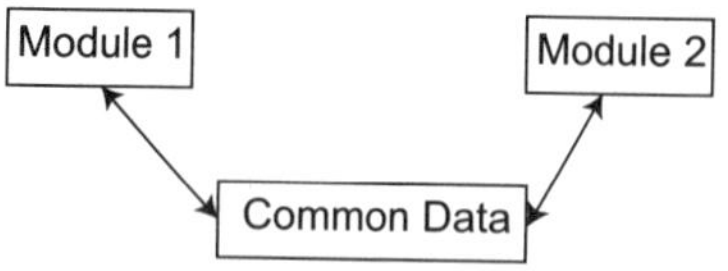

In Control coupling, a module passes its control component to another module. Depending on what control are being passed, it is considered as good or bad. Module 1 calls Module 2 and Module 2 passes the Flag that indicates a status.

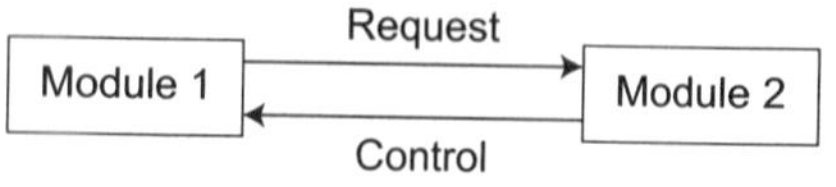

In Stamp coupling, a module passes a data structure to a module which doesn't have access to the entire data structure. It sends the data structure to another module to understand it. The module does not have power and it just acts as a stamp and so is called as stamp coupling.

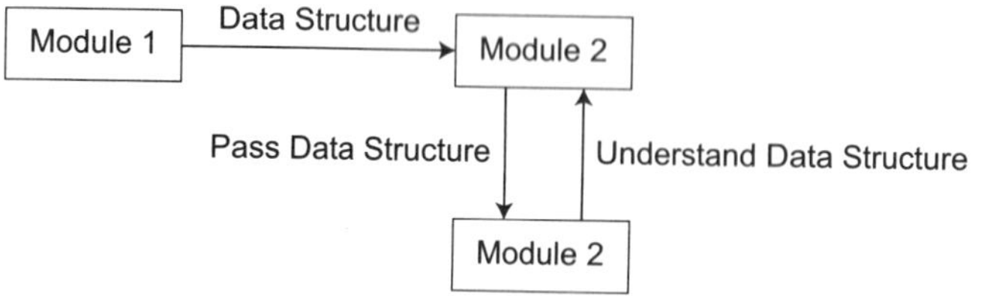

Two modules are data coupled, if there are homogenous data items or structure.

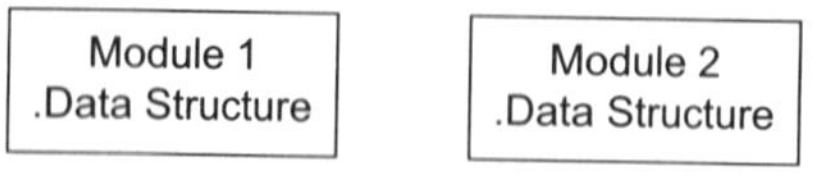

A good design should minimize coupling so that it

a) can be used independently
b) is easier to test
c) is easier to replace
d) is easier to understand

Object Oriented metrics:

As the object-oriented (OO) paradigm began to spread throughout the software community during C++ and Java usages, people felt the need for the estimation techniques based on Objects and its characteristics rather than following traditional techniques.

Some of the specialized OO metrics constructs (factors) include

1. Number of Classes in the overall program
2. Weighted methods per class

3. Number of children per Class
4. Depth of inheritance Tree
5. Types of inheritance used in the overall program
6. Coupling between Objects in the program
7. Types of methods used within the Class
8. Number of variables used in the program
9. Number of similar variables used in the program
10. Duplication of class structures
11. Operating Complexity
12. Attributes Complexity
13. Reuse metrics like reusable class, reusable Objects etc...

Some of the specialized OO metrics include:

1. Chen Metrics
2. Morris Metrics
3. MOOSE (Metrics for Object Oriented System Environments) or (Metrics for Object Oriented Software Engineering). It is also called as "Chidamber and Kemerer – USA" Metrics. It is also called as CK Metrics.
4. MOOD (Metrics for Object Oriented Design). It is also called as "Abrieu - Portugal" metrics / AP Metrics.
5. EMOOSE

Advantages of Object Oriented Metrics
The main strengths of OO metrics are:

1. The OO Metrics uses various Object Oriented terms which are understandable easily by the Object Oriented community.
2. The OO metrics distinguishes easy project Vs Complex Projects.
3. The OO metrics are easily comparable across projects.
4. The OO metrics are easily related with the structure of the program (which is not possible with other metrics)

Disadvantages of Object Oriented Metrics
The main drawbacks of OO metrics are:

1. The OO Metrics not applicable for testing or maintenance and is applicable only for the development project.
2. The OO metrics not supported by various estimating tools available in the market.
3. The OO metrics are unrelated to all other known software metrics and so converting OO Metrics to FP or LOC is difficult.
4. The OO metrics do not deal with full life-cycle issues.

(or)

15. Discuss key steps for SCM.

Answer: Software Configuration Management has four key steps that must be defined for each software project to ensure a good SCM process is implemented. These are

- Configuration Identification
- Configuration Control
- Configuration Status Accounting
- Configuration Authentication

Configuration Identification: Software is usually made up of several programs. Each program, its related documentation and data is termed as a "configurable item" (CI). The number of CI in any software project and the grouping of artifacts that make up a CI is a decision made by the project team.

Configuration Control: The process of coordinating the approved changes for the proposed CIs and implementing the changes on the appropriate baseline are called Configuration control.

Configuration Status Accounting: Configuration status accounting is the book keeping process of each release. This procedure involves tracking what is in each version of software and the changes that lead to this version. Configuration status accounting keeps a record of all the changes made to the previous baseline to reach a new baseline.

Configuration Authentication: Configuration authentication (CA) is the process of assuring that the new baseline has incorporated all the planned and approved changes. The process involves verifying that all the functional aspects of the software are complete and it also verifies whether the delivery is complete in terms of the right programs, documentation and data being delivered. The configuration authentication is an audit which is performed on the delivery before it is opened to the entire world.

16. Explain different types of Requirements with example.

Answer: Requirements can be categorized into 3 main types: Functional (User) Requirements, Non Functional (System) Requirements, Interface Specification.

Functional (User) Requirements: The set of requirements which define what the system will do or accomplish are called functional requirements. These are the requirements which determine how the software will behave to meet certain user needs. The requirements may be for performing some calculation, data manipulation, processing, logical decision making etc. which form the basis of the business rules. Functional requirements are often captured as Use Cases. Functional requirements are the main driver for the Application Architecture of the system. An example of functional requirement is – a retail shop billing software must have the functionalities of capturing commodity prices, calculate the discounts, generate the bill, print the invoice etc.

Non Functional (System) Requirements: Functional requirements are supported by Non-functional requirements. The quality attributes and the design and architecture constraints that the system must have are called the Non-functional requirements.

Some of the quality attributes of the system from end user's vie are: Performance, availability, usability and Security.

Some of the system quality attribute from developer's view are : Reusability, testability, maintainability, portability.

Non functional (system) requirements are critical in most of the software projects than the functional requirements. Non functional Requirements cater to the architectural needs of the overall system where as functional requirements caters to the design needs of the overall system.

Non functional requirements may be related to the product or organization or the external requirements of the system.

Examples for Product related non functional requirements are : Performance, availability, maintainability, portability, reliability, security, scalability, testability, usability.

Examples for Organization related non functional requirements are : Standards requirements , Implementation requirements.

Examples for External non functional requirements are : Legal Requirements , Ethical requirements.

Example of non-functional requirements are :

'The system should be available 24X7' (Availability)

"The system should save or fetch 1000 records in 1 second' etc. (Performance)

Interface Specification: Most of the software systems don't work alone and in order to work those need to interact with other systems. They interact with many other systems to receive and send data, get help in processing logic, store information in other systems and for other reasons. The interaction requirement of one system with another is defined in the Interface specification.

This helps in building different systems in such a fashion that they can seamlessly interact with each other to produce the desired outcome. In our previous example of the retail shop billing system may interact with another system - an inventory system to make sure that the warehouse keeps track of the stock of the material at hand and the protocol of how these two systems interact with each other are captured in the interface specification document.

(or)

17. Explain waterfall model with neat diagram.

Answer: Waterfall model is one of the Software Development Life Cycle (SDLC) models. This model was devised by Royce in 1970. Since then many organizations implemented this process model and till date this is one of the majorly used software development process. The software lifecycle activities like Requirements Specification (phase 1), Design (phase 2), Construction (phase 3), Integration (phase 4), Testing (phase 5) and Debugging (phase 6), Installation (phase 7) and Maintenance (phase 8) are proceeded one after the other (like a waterfall). So, at the beginning of the project the necessities and conditions are obtained from the customer as the first step. This specification and analysis is the next step which is taken up by the developer team. Then the developer team will start to design a framework for achieving the objectives. Following the efficient design, the coding begins. After this, the testing process ensures the correctness of the code. Once the system is installed and launched as the live system it enters the maintenance stage. All these stages are taking place one after the other without any overlap.

General Overview of "Waterfall Model"

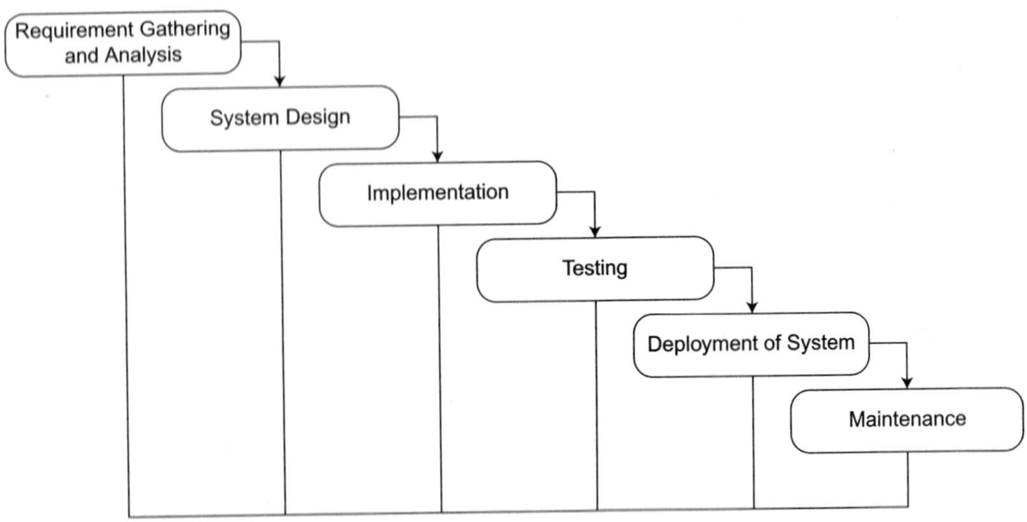

Advantages of Waterfall Model:

1. Very easy to understand
2. Easy for implementation
3. Widely used and known; hence, all stakeholders understand this
4. Identifies deliverables and milestones upfront.

Disadvantages of Waterfall Model:

1. Does not match well with reality
2. It is unrealistic to freeze the requirement upfront
3. Software is delivered only at the last phase
4. Difficult and expensive to make changes (CRs always)

18. Explain back box testing and why it is important with an example.

Answer: Black Box testing involves testing the application like an external or end-user by validating the outputs received from the application based on certain inputs given to it. The internal technical mechanisms like the programs and the code infrastructure of the application are not considered in this type of testing. The tester has no access to the source code nor is he expected to be knowledgeable of the programming language and code structure behind the application.

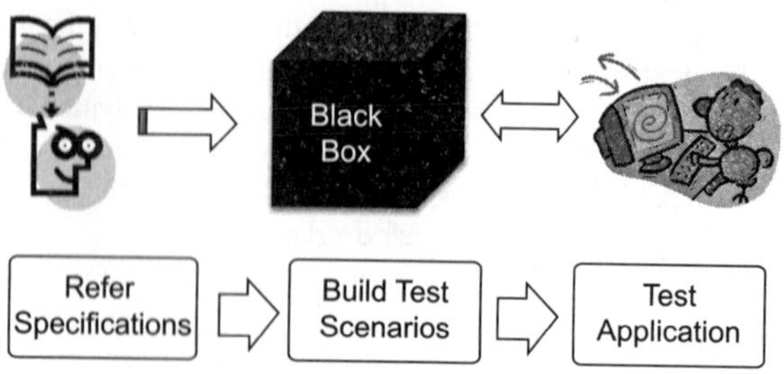

The application is a "Black Box" to the tester who is aware of only the functionality to be tested, the required inputs and the corresponding expected outputs but nothing about the internal workings. This type of testing requires good knowledge of the business requirements of the application. For example if it is a mobile application then the tester needs to have a good understanding of the internet world and also good analytical skills to see through the requirements to identify problem areas. The tester has to understand the requirements to an extent that he should be able to fill the gap for any missed specifications either from the business or from the end user. All the information or requirements related to the assignment may not be directly available; the tester should work closely with the stakeholders to get the necessary information.

The figure below shows a sample software application with about 25 screens, each screen having 4 menus, each menu having 3 options and an average of 15 fields per screen. If we calculate the number of test cases we would need to execute to completely test this application, it is a mind boggling 450,000 test cases. Even if it takes 1 minute to execute a test case it will take 312.5 days working 24*7 to complete testing the entire set.

The challenge for the tester is mainly two-fold as follows:

1. Reduce the number of test cases to manageable limits
2. Ensure that the identified subset of test cases gives sufficient coverage

Sample Software Application

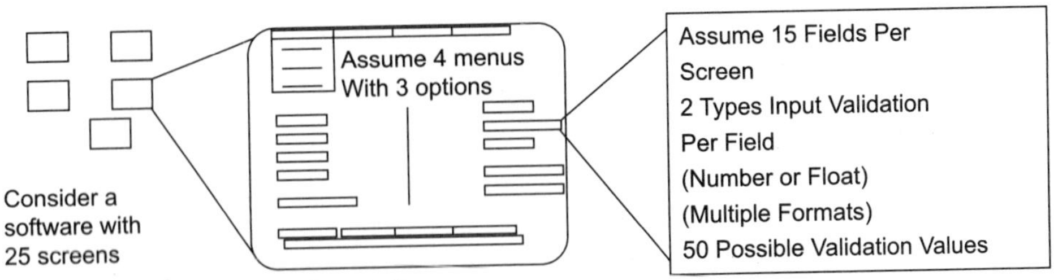

Sample Screen

The total number of test cases

25 x 4 x 3 x 15 x 2 x 50 = 450,000 tests

The common Black Box testing techniques which are used to address these challenges are:

1. Equivalence Partitioning
2. Boundary Value Analysis.
3. Decision Tables

(or)

19. List and explain software re-engineering activities

Answer: Reengineering involves putting efforts to make the system easier to maintain. In this process the source code is gets changed for easy maintenance and enhanced functionality of the system. Code cleaning can also happen at this stage along with the enhancement of the system.

The steps involved in re-engineering are:

1. Understand the overall system – this is an important step as the correctness of the re-engineering process depends largely on how well the original system is understood.
2. Do reverse engineering – this helps in identifying and understanding various components that comprise the system
3. Re structure the system in a logical fashion – at this step the original system is re-structure, either with more efficient code, latest technological superior programming language or enhanced functionalities.
4. Modularize the program and data-this step will improve the functionality to complete the reengineering process

Index

A
Abstraction, 139
Acceptance test case, 498
Activity attributes, 402
    guidelines, 508
    list, 401
    resource requirements, 407
Adaptive project framework (APF), 595
Additional risk response planning, 380
Agile, 579–601
    characteristics, 581
    communication in, 590
    introduction, 579
    manifesto, 583
    methodologies, 592
    project life cycle, 586
    related concepts, 588
    triangle, 588
Agile unified process (AUP), 599
Alpha tester, 487
Analogous estimating, 297, 408
Analysis
    content, 180
    modeling approaches, 83
    object-oriented, 102
    task, 179
    user, 178
    work, 181
Application generation, 17
Application software, 3
Application under test (AUT), 498
Apportioned effort (AE), 402
Apps Hungarian, 206
Architectural design, 114
Architectural notations, 115
Architecture
    distributed system, 118
    mapping requirements into, 116
    software, 115
Aspect-oriented software development (AOSD), 576
Assessing alternative architectural design, 118
Association notation, 158
Attribute complexity metrics (ACM), 276
Attributes, 133
Automation
    frameworks, 520
    Limitations of, 515
    metrics, 524
    strategy, 516

B
Behavioral modeling, 100
Behavioral patterns, 142
Beta tester, 487
Black box and white box metrics, 241
Black box testing, 468
Booch methodology, 155
Bottom-up approach, 120
Bottom-up estimation, 296, 407
Boundary value analysis, 471
Brainstorming technique, 55, 295, 369
Budget estimate, 307
Business expert tester, 487
Business modeling, 17
Business process engineering, 27

C
Capability maturity model integration (CMMI), 19
Cardinality, 88
Case studies on software engineering practices, 609–632
Case tools, 443
    Functions of, 446
    Productivity of, 445
    Quality of, 445
Causal/econometric methods, 391
Centralized structure, 118
Change control board, 66
Change control process, 66
Checklist analysis, 370
Chen metrics, 275
Child diagrams, 97
CK metric suite, 276
Class, 130
Class coupling metrics (CCM), 276
Client, 118
Client satisfaction index (CSI), 541
Cloud computing, 575

Code
 inspections, 218
 review, 216
 sharing, 215
Coding
 conventions, 202
 standards and guidelines, 212–213
 top-down and bottom-up, 213
Cohesion, 109
 Coincidental, 111
 Communicational, 111
 Functional, 111
 Logical, 111
 Procedural, 111
 Sequential, 111
 Temporal, 111
Cohesion metrics (CM), 276
Comments, 208
Communication
 Dimensions of, 386
 Forms of, 386
 handling, 388
 management, 385
 methods, 389
 Process of, 387
 technologies, 389
Communication and team management, 385–396
Communication gap, 50
Compatibility testing, 474
Component-based development model, 25
Composite word scheme, 205
Computer-aided design (CAD), 220
Computer-aided machine (CAM), 220
Computer-aided software engineering (CASE), 443–452
Concept of control specification (CSPEC), 99
Concurrency testing, 477
Concurrent versions system (CVS), 333
Configurable item (CI), 332
Configuration authentication (CA), 333
Configuration control tools and techniques, 338
Configuration management (CM), 331
Configuration management activities, 334
Conflict management, 394
Constructive cost model (COCOMO), 260, 309
Content analysis, 180
Control chart, 303, 359
Control flow model, 99
Control specification (CSPEC), 121
Controlling PMO, 353
Conventional analysis technique, 150
Conventional versus OO approach, 153
Cost estimation models, 308
Cost management, 416–423
Costs of conformance, 359
Costs of quality (COQ), 358
Coupling, 111
 Common, 112
 Content, 112
 Control, 112
 Data, 112
 Stamp, 112
 Uncoupled, 112
Coupling between objects (CBO), 277
Creational patterns, 142
Critical chain method, 414
Critical dates, 510
Critical path method (CPM), 411
Crystal methods, 599
Cyclomatic measure, 240

D

Data abstraction coupling (DAC), 278
Data
 design, 114
 dictionary, 91
 flow, 96
 flow diagram, 92
 flow notations, 95
 modeling, 17, 86
 source notation, 96
 store, 95
Data flow diagram (DFD), 92
Decentralized structure, 119
Decision tables, 472
Decision trees, 376
Decomposition, 401
Defect tracker setup, 509
Define activities, 400
Definitive estimate, 307
Delimiter-separated words, 205
Delphi technique, 295, 369
Demarco's system bang, 279
Demarco–yourdon symbols, 95
Dependency notation, 158
Deployment level design, 114, 122
Depth of inheritance tree (DIT), 277
Design
 Architectural, 114
 Component, 114
 Data, 114
 Deployment level, 114
 documentation, 122
 heuristics, 117
 models, 114
 patterns, 141
 process, 107
Design and architectural engineering, 107–123
Designing the user interface, 182
Diagramming techniques, 370

Diagrams
- Activity, 163
- architectural, 160, 169
- Behavioral, 160, 163
- Class, 161
- Collaboration, 166
- Implementation, 160, 169
- Object, 162
- Sequence, 164
- State chart, 168
- Structural, 160
- Use case, 166

Direct measures, 238
Directive PMO, 354
Discrete effort (DE), 402
Distributed system, 118
Distributed system architecture, 118
Domain analysis, 151
Dynamic systems development method (DSDM), 599

E

Earned value management, 248, 314
Effort adjustment factor (EAF), 310
Elicitation techniques, 51
E-moose, 278
Encapsulation, 134
Encoding the message, 388
Engineering
- Product, 31
- Requirements, 41

Entities, 94
Entity relationship diagrams, 90
Environment
- Fourth-generation, 451
- Integrated, 451
- Language-centered, 451
- Process-centered, 452
- Toolkits, 451

Equivalence partitioning, 470
Estimate cost, 306
Estimating the activity duration, 407
Evolutionary process models, 23
Expected monitory value (EMV), 376
Extended function point metrics, 269
Extended metrics, 278
External input (EI), 263
External inquiry (EQ), 263
External interface files (EIF), 263
External output (EO), 263
Extreme programming (XP), 594

F

Feasibility
- Economic, 48
- Operational, 4
- Technical, 4

Feature point estimation, 271
Feature-driven development (FDD), 597
Five phases of team building, 393
Flow-oriented modeling, 92
Forecasting methods, 391
Form study prototype, 55
Formal methods model, 26
Fourth-generation techniques (4GT), 28
FP estimation, 260
Framework activities, 18
Frameworks, 143
Function point (FP), 260
Functional
- modeling, 92
- prototype, 55
- test cases, 496
- testing, 474

Function-oriented design, 108

G

Gane–Sarson symbols, 95
Gap model – service, 538
Generalization notation, 159
Graphical evaluation and review technique (GERT), 409

H

Halstead measure, 239
Has–a relationship, 139
Health insurance portability and accountability act (HIPAA), 530
Heuristics, 409
Histogram, 301
Hoare logic of correctness, 218
Human–computer interface (HCI), 177
Hungarian notation, 206
Hybrid convention, 205
Hybrid structure, 119

I

IEEE standard SRS template, 60
Incremental development of code, 213
Incremental model, 22
Indirect measures, 238
Information hiding, 211
Inheritance, 135–137
Initial operational capability (IOC), 25
Integration test cases, 496
Integration testing, 474
Intelligent software agent, 220
Interface specification, 45
Intermediate constructive cost model, 310
Internal logical files (ILF), 263

International ergonomics association (IEA), 176
Internationalization testing, 478
Is–a relationship, 139
Iterative life cycle model, 214

J
Jacobson's model, 156
Judgmental methods, 391

K
Kanban method, 598
Kaner and bond's evaluation framework, 248
Key process areas (KPA), 334

L
Lack of cohesion in methods (LCOM), 277
Layered technology, 13
Leads and lags, 405
Lean software system, 599
Learning curve, 250
Length of the identifiers, 203
Letter case and numerals, 204
Letter-case-separated words, 205
Level of effort (LOE), 402
Life cycle architecture (LCA), 25
Life cycle objectives (LCO), 25
Linear sequential model, 12
Lines of code (LOC), 257

M
Macro development process, 155
Maintenance
  Adaptive, 530
  Corrective, 530
  cost, 533
  mind set, 537
  Perfective, 531
  Preventive, 532
  process, 532
  strategies, 537
Managing the project team, 392
Man–machine interface (MMI), 177
Many-to-many relationship (M:N), 80
Mapping requirements into architecture, 116
Maslow's hierarchy of needs, 393
McCall's quality factors, 242
McGregor's theory of x and y, 393
Measure, 31
Measurement, 31
Measurement, software, 235–240
Message pass coupling (MPC), 278
Messages, 133
Methods, 133
Metrics, 31
  Attribute complexity, 276
  Chen, 275
  Class coupling, 276
  Cohesion, 276
  Extended function point, 269
  for maintenance, 247
  for object-oriented design metrics, 277
  for testing, 246
  for the analysis model, 245
  for the design model, 245
  Kaner and Bond's evaluation framework for, 248
  MOOSE, 276
  Morris, 276
  Operating coupling, 276
  Process, 244
  Product, 242
  Productivity, 247
  Resource, 244
Metrics for object-oriented design metrics, 277
Micro development process, 156
Milestone lists, 403
Minimal marketable future (MMF), 588
Modality, 88
Modeling and simulation, 377
Modular design approach, 120
Modularity, 109, 110
MOOD, 277
MOOSE, 278
Morris metrics, 276
Multiple word identifiers, 205

N
Naming convention, 203
Nonfunctional requirements (NFRS), 44
Number of children for class (NOC), 277
Number of methods (NOM), 278

O
Object, 130
  model, 155
  points, 269
Object-oriented analysis, 102, 150
Object-oriented analysis and design (OOAD), 149–169
Object-oriented business engineering (OOBE), 156
Object-oriented concepts, 129–143
Object-oriented design, 108, 129, 152
Object-oriented metrics, 274
Observation technique, 56
OMT dynamic model, 155
OMT functional model, 155
One-to-many relationship (1:M), 80
One-to-one relationship (1:1), 80

OO design *See* object-oriented design
OOD modeling techniques, 153
Open source software development, 571
Open source tool (CVS), 539
Operating coupling metrics (OCM), 276
Organizational theories, 393

P
Parametric estimation, 298, 408
Parametric review of information for costing and evaluation – software (PRICE-S), 308
Pareto diagram (PARETO CHART), 301
Parkinson law, 299
Path convergence, 411
Path divergence, 412
People capability maturity model (PCMM), 20
Performance metrics, 359
Periodic project risk reviews, 380
Phase
    Coding and testing, 6
    Designing, 5
    Implementation, 6
    Maintenance, 7
    Requirements analysis, 5
Planning poker, 272
PM software, 415
Polymorphism, 137–139
Portfolio management, 352
Positional notation, 206
Precedence diagramming method (PDM), 404
Proactive risk response strategies, 379
Probability and impact matrix, 373
Probability distributions, 376
Procedural design, 121
Process, 94, 341
    assessments, 20
    framework, 17
    metrics, 243
    modeling, 17
    notations, 96
    pattern, 20
Process specification (PSPEC), 121
Process-behavior chart, 359
Procurement process and suppliers, 434
Product metrics, 242
Productivity metrics, 247
Program, evaluation, and review technique (PERT), 299
Program management, 352
Programming
    guidelines, 201
    practices, 202
    principles, 200
    principles and rule of thumb, 207
    productivity, 220
    structured, 210–211
    style, 215
Progressive elaboration, 346
Project, 343
    cost estimation, 304
    cost management, 416–423
    governance PMO, 354
    management, 350
    calendars, 406
    management body of knowledge, 393
    management introduction, 341–361
    management office, 353
    performance reports, 391
    planning and monitoring, 354
    quality management, 357
    risk response audits, 380
    scope management, 354
    stakeholder management, 429–440
    strategic planning, 348
Project management body of knowledge (PMBOK), 393
Project management office (PMO), 353
Proof-of-principle prototype, 55
Prototypes, 54, 64
    Form study, 55
    Functional, 55
    Proof-of-principle, 55
    Types of, 54
    Visual, 55
    Working, 55
Prototyping model, 14
Proving correctness, 218
Published estimating data, 407
Putnam's software life-cycle model (SLIM), 309

Q
Qualitative risk analysis techniques, 372
Quality
    assurance, 359
    audits, 359
    policy, 358
    importance, 357
Quantitative risk analysis and modeling techniques, 376
Quantitative risk analysis techniques, 375
Questionnaires, 55

R
Rad model, 16
Rapid prototyping (RP), 220
Real-time software design, 113
Re-engineering, 535
Refining architectural design, 118
Regression testing, 475
Relationships, 139

Requirements
analysis, 5, 57
analysis modeling, 83–102
change, 65
Conflicting, 50
elicitation, 48
engineering, 41
Functional, 43
identification, 65
Importance of, 42
management, 64
Nonfunctional, 44
Specifying, 58
status tracking, 66
traceability, 66
Types of, 43
Validating, 62
Volatile, 50
Reserve analysis, 380, 409
Resource breakdown structure (RBS), 407
Resource leveling, 413
Resource metrics, 244
Response for class (RFC), 276
Re-structuring, 537
Reverse engineering, 534
Revision control system (RCS), 333
Risk analysis and management, 365–380
Risk categories and a risk breakdown structure (RBDS), 367
Risk factors approach, 489
Risk spiral model, 23
Risk, 379
analysis, 372
business, 366
categorization, 375
data quality assessment, 374
Identify, 368
mitigation planning, 378
negative, 378
operational, 375
Positive, 379
Project, 366
Schedule, 375
Software, 366
Technical, 366
urgency assessment, 374
RTS design, 113
Rumbaugh et al.'s object modeling technique, 154
Run chart, 302

S
Scatter diagram, 302
Schedule, 410
controlling, 414
network analysis, 410
project, 414
optimization, 412
Schedule performance index (SPI), 415
Schedule variance (SV), 415
Scope of control of a module, 113
Scope of effect of a module, 113
Scrum methodology, 592
S-curve, 249
Security engineering, 572
Sensitivity analysis, 376
Server, 118
Service-oriented architecture (SOA), 574
Service-oriented software engineering (SOSE), 573
Shewhart chart, 359
Simulation techniques, 377
SLOC, 257
Comment, 257
Logical, 257
Physical, 257
Reused, 257
Social computing, 576
Software
Application-based, 9
architecture, 115
Changing nature of, 8
characteristics, 7
coding, 199–222
configuration management, 331–339
design, 107
estimation, 291–300
In-built, 8
maintenance tools, 539
measurement, 235–240
metrics, 240–249
myths, 9
process, 12
process models, 20
product, 28
risk, 366
System-based, 8
Software as a service (SAAS), 574
Software configuration management (SCM), 331–339
Software configuration management plan (SCMP), 334
Software development life cycle (SDLC), 21
Software development, phases in, 4
Software engineering
Generic view of, 10
introduction, 1
process, 27
Role of management in, 11
What is, 10
Why study, 10
Software engineering institute (SEI), 334
Software estimation tools, techniques and models, 291–321

Software evaluation and estimation of resources – software estimating model (SEER–SEM), 308
Software evolution, 534
Software life-cycle model (SLIM), 309
Software maintenance, 529–546
Software requirements specifications (SRS), 496
Software reuse, 221–222
Software test case, 492–501
Software testing, 455–480
 objectives, 457
 scope, 457
 Strategic approach to, 461
 plan, 485–492
 techniques, 486
 tools, 486–492
 Types of, 463
Source code control system (SCCS), 334
Source LOC (SLOC), 257
Specialized oo metrics, 275
Spiral model, 23
SRS document, 61
SRS template, 60
Stakeholders, 49
State testing, 475
State transition diagram (STD), 100
Statement of work (SOW), 439
Static program analysis, 217
Statistical sampling, 360
Story point sizing, 272
Story points measurement, 272
Strategies for both threats and opportunities, 379
Strategies to counter negative risk, 378
Strategies to exploit opportunities, 379
Structural patterns, 142
Structured analysis, 85
Sub rule to reduce users' memory load, 188
Sub rules of place users in control, 186
Sub rules to make the interface consistent, 193
Substitute performance measures, 238
Superclass, 131
Supportive PMO, 353
SWOT analysis, 371
Symbolic execution, 218
System architecture document (SAD), 122
System
 bang, 279
 software, 3
 test cases, 497
 hungarian, 206

T
Task analysis, 179
Technical performance measurement, 380
Test
 automation, 489, 513–525
 case, 492
 case pass/fail criteria, 509
 coverage focused, 487
 evaluation criteria, 488
 strategy, 505
Test-driven development (TDD), 576, 596
Testing
 approach, 507
 Automated, 506
 Compatibility, 474
 Concurrency, 477
 configuration, 487
 constraints based, 488
 Conversion, 506
 exploratory, 488
 Functional, 474, 487
 Guerrilla, 507
 Hardware, 507
 Input and boundary, 507
 Installation, 507
 Integration, 474
 Interface, 507
 Internationalization, 478
 method based, 488
 network, 507
 out of memory, 507
 Parallel, 506
 performance, 488, 506
 Regression, 475
 security, 507
 smoke, 488
 State, 475
 Stress, 506
 Temporal, 507
 Tester focused, 486
 Types of, 506
 Usability, 477
Three point estimation, 299, 409
Time management, 399
Time–series methods, 391
Tools
 Analysis and design, 448
 Business process engineering, 446
 Client/server testing, 449
 Database management, 447
 Documentation, 447
 Dynamic analysis, 449
 Integration and testing, 448
 Interface design and development, 448
 Metrics and management, 447
 PRO/SIM tools, 448
 Process modeling and management, 446
 Programming, 448
 project management, 447
 Project planning, 447

Prototyping, 448
Quality assurance, 447
Reengineering, 449
Requirements tracing, 447
Risk analysis, 447
Software configuration management, 447
Static analysis, 448
System software, 447
Test management, 449
Web development, 448
Tools for analyzing metrics and estimations, 300
Tools used in software configuration management, 333
Top down estimation, 297
Top-down approach, 120
Traditional project management (TPM), 594
Transaction
flow, 116
mapping, 117
flow, 116
mapping, 117
Trends in software engineering, 569–577
True performance measures, 238

U
Unified modeling language (UML), 6, 64, 122, 141 154, 157–161
architecture, 159
diagrams, 160
modeling types, 160
Unadjusted function point (UFP), 262
Unified process model (RUP), 213
Unit test cases, 495
Usability, 194
Usability testing, 477
Use case modeling, 151
Use case points (UCPS), 269
User acceptance test (UAT), 405
User analysis, 178
User interface (UI), 175
design evaluation, 185
design models, 194
elements of, 177
User interface design, 121, 175–195
evaluation, 185
Golden rules of, 185
models, 194
User profile model, 194
Uses–A relationship, 141

V
Variance analysis, 415
Velocity, 273
Vendor bid analysis, 298
Visual prototype, 55
Visual source safe (VSS), 539

W
Waterfall model, 21
Web (world wide web), 553, 569
applications, 556–557
characteristics, 554
design, principles of, 560
engineering, 553
Introduction to, 553
service, 573
Weighted methods per class (WMC), 276
What—if scenario analysis (WISA), 411
Win–win spiral model, 25
Work breakdown structure (WBS), 355
Work environment analysis, 181
Work performance information, 415
Work performance measurements, 415
Workbenches, 450
Working prototype, 55

Z
Z theory, 393